The Making of Drama
idea and performance

edited by
Norman M. Small
assisted by
Maurice L. Sutton

Polk Community College

Holbrook Press, Inc.   Boston

Library of Congress Catalog Card Number: 73-171436

ACKNOWLEDGMENTS

Oedipus the King by Sophocles, translated by Kenneth Cavander, published by Chandler Publishing Company, San Francisco. Copyright © 1961 by Chandler Publishing Company. Reprinted by permission.

Richmond Y. Hathorn, "The Existential Oedipus" is reprinted by permission of *The Classical Journal*.

David Welker, "Directing Oedipus Rex" is reprinted by permission of the author.

William Hazlitt, "On the Character Hamlet," from *Characters in Shakespeare's Plays*, is reprinted by permission of J. M. Dent & Sons Ltd.

Tyrone Guthrie, "Costuming *Hamlet*," from *A New Theatre* by Tyrone Guthrie. Copyright © 1964 by Wharton Productions, Ltd. Used with permission of McGraw-Hill Book Company.

Tartuffe by Molière, translated by James L. Rosenberg, published by Chandler Publishing Company, San Francisco. Copyright © 1962 by Chandler Publishing Company. Reprinted by permission.

"Preface to *Tartuffe*" and "Petitions to the King," translated by William F. Mitchell. Copyright © 1972 by Holbrook Press.

Robert Strane, "Notes on Transplanting a Classic" is reprinted by permission of the author.

The Servant of Two Masters by Carlo Goldoni, edited and translated by Edward J. Dent, published by Cambridge University Press, 1969, is reprinted by permission of the publishers.

From *Memoirs of Carlo Goldoni*, edited by William Drake, published by Random House, Inc., is reprinted by permission of the publishers.

Joseph Spencer Kennard, from *Goldoni and the Venice of His Time*, is reprinted by permission of Katharine Cleland Davis.

D. C. Gerould, "The Cherry Orchard as Comedy," from *The Journal of General Education* (Vol. XI, 1958), is reprinted by permission of *The Journal of General Education*.

Tyrone Guthrie, "A Director's View of *The Cherry Orchard*," from *The Cherry Orchard* by Anton Chekhov, translated by T. Guthrie and Leonid Kipnis for Minnesota Drama Editions, University of Minnesota Press, Minneapolis, © 1965 by Tyrone Guthrie. Reprinted by permission.

Maxim Gorki, "Observations on the Theatre" is reprinted by permission of Eyre & Spottiswoode Publishers.

Constantin Stanislavski, "Journey to Khitrov Market," from *My Life in Art* by Constantin Stanislavski, translated by J. J. Robbins, copyright 1924 by Little, Brown & Company, Copyright 1948 by Elizabeth Reynolds Hapgood, Copyright Renewed 1952. Reprinted with the permission of the publishers, Theatre Arts Books, New York.

Elmer Rice, *The Adding Machine*, Copyright, 1922, 1929 by Elmer Rice. Copyright, 1923, by Doubleday, Page & Company. Copyright, 1949, (in renewal), by Elmer L. Rice. Copyright, 1950, (in renewal), by Elmer L. Rice. Copyright, 1956, (in renewal), by Elmer L. Rice. Reprinted by permission of Samuel French, Inc.

Elmer Rice, "The Birth of a Play" is reprinted by permission of the Trustees of the Elmer Rice Literary Trust.

Ludwig Lewishon, "Creative Irony: Mr. Rice's *The Adding Machine*" is reprinted by permission of *The Nation*.

Barnard Hewitt, "Director's Notes on *The Adding Machine*" is reprinted by permission of the author.

Bertolt Brecht, *The Caucasian Chalk Circle*, Eric Bentley, translator, © 1961, 1963, by Eric Bentley. Prologue © 1959 by Eric Bentley. First published in *Parables for the Theatre: Two Plays by Bertolt Brecht*, University of Minnesota Press. Reprinted by permission.

Bertolt Brecht, "Theatre for Pleasure or Theatre for Instruction" and "A New Technique for Acting" are from *Brecht on Theatre* translated and edited by John Willett. This translation and notes © 1964 by John Willett. Reprinted by permission of Hill & Wang, Inc.

Maria P. Alter, "The Technique of Alienation in Bertolt Brecht's *The Caucasian Chalk Circle*," published in the *CLA Journal* (September 1964), is reprinted by permission of the *CLA Journal*.

Oh Dad, Poor Dad, Mamma's Hung You in the Closet and I'm Feelin' So Sad, by Arthur Kopit. Copyright © 1960 by Arthur L. Kopit. Reprinted by permission of Hill & Wang, Inc.

"Arthur Kopit: An Interview" is reprinted by permission from *Mademoiselle;* Copyright © 1962 by The Condé Nast Publications Inc.

Stephen H. Foreman, "*Oh Dad, Poor Dad:* Atmosphere and Fantasy" is reprinted by permission of the author.

Norman DeMarco, "Thoughts on Directing *Oh Dad, Poor Dad*" is reprinted by permission of the author.

For Rose, Linda, and Denise—
the three women of my life

Contents

It has become a cliché to say that a play is written to be seen. Nevertheless, this is an essential truth. The full realization of the meaning, message, and beauty of a drama can never be achieved until its actual performance. In this respect, then, this and other anthologies fail—fail to make drama what it ought to be—literature brought to life before an audience. Here, however, an attempt has been made to bring the reader a step closer to the ideal of actual performance by including comments from those who help bring that drama to life: the playwright, the critic, and the director. These are the people who know most about the "making of drama," and, since one of the ideas basic to this anthology is to display the practical and visual side of the theatre as well as the theoretical, comments from these three theatre practitioners should not only heighten the reader's appreciation of the literature, but also should aid him in "seeing" the drama.

The Makers Of Drama

The playwright, when his comments are available, performs an invaluable service by perhaps providing clues to the meaning of the play; indeed, those words may supply a reason for the play's existence. His comments may range from the function of drama and theatre (Gorki) to the explanation of the circumstances surrounding the actual writing or inception of the play (Molière and Rice). For us, the "why" of the play may be answered at the same time we read the thoughts and relive the labors of each playwright. In essence, one can go no further than this.

While he can only guess what the playwright already knows, the critic, nevertheless, also provides a valuable service. He may present an interpretation of the play necessary for its understanding. He may set up guidelines for the reading or evaluation of the play. He may comment on the purpose or theme of the play. He may consider the play's relationship to dramatic development, or he may criticize the play as a piece of literature. The critics included in this text have done all of these things; that is, their comments afford the reader a better chance at recognizing what a play says, as well as what a play is, and in doing so, further expand the reader's ability to "see" the drama.

Finally, the director's comments serve as a vehicle for bringing life to the play. And since a play is incomplete until staged, those comments further help lift the play from the abstract page to the spotlit stage. The relative comments on the direction of each particular play afford the reader a first-hand account of the play's staging merits and problems, as well as making it more real. The director's interpretation, his staging, and his problems make the direction as much a part of the drama as the script. Those who wonder how a particular play might be presented — as well as those who might want to present it themselves— may thus benefit from those who already have. The end result is that the reader is brought one step closer to actually sitting in the audience.

It is believed, then, that by the combination of comments by the playwright, critic and director, the reader will have not only the broadest and most definitive study of a particular play, but also the maximal opportunity for the actual visualization of the play. This is, after all, what theatre is all about.

The Kinds Of Drama

Attempts also have been made in this anthology to shift from the traditionally historical approach to drama to a more categorical method of classification, according to dramatic modes and to dramatic types.

By dramatic modes is meant a way of presentation, a style of production. For example, a play can be presented naturalistically; that is, with an almost obsessive concern for detail and the re-creation of actuality. If the play distorts or disfigures its characters or scenery, we would say it was done expressionistically. But more than this, the dramatic modes all evolved as a revolt against previous forms familiar to the stage. The realist was thoroughly dissatisfied with melodrama's portrayal of man; the naturalist belittled the realist for not going far enough in the search for truth; the expressionist criticized both as wrong approaches; and the exponents of epic theatre attacked all modes as being too much medium and not enough message. (Each of these modes, as well as the *forms* of drama mentioned below, is explained and defined preceding its representative play.)

The second approach to classification involves dramatic types, or forms of drama. These are traditional ways of classifying a *kind* of drama, and include tragedy, comedy, melodrama, farce, and theatre of the absurd. Each of the dramatic types has certain recognizable distinguishing traits. A tragedy, for example, must have as its central character a person of nobility.

Dramatic modes (styles of production) are to be distinguished as being separate from dramatic types (basic forms or genres of drama). For example, melodrama, a *type* of drama, can be presented in a realistic *mode*.

The dramatic types and modes included here should not be taken as having no exceptions. Many plays are a combination of the types of drama and may contain many shades of these forms. Plays like Oscar Wilde's *The Importance of Being Earnest* and Aristophanes' *The Frogs* have been called comedy by some, and farce by others; and playwright George Bernard Shaw's works defy classification. Even Shakespeare's *Hamlet*, included here, contains comic as well as tragic material. Still, as a jumping-off point, the categories included here allow us to proceed to a basic understanding of what drama is—and together with the comments of playwright, critic, and director—of what drama can be.

Special thanks must go to the library of Polk Community College, whose vast help was greatly disproportionate to its size, and particular thanks to Adele Oldenburg, Juanita Crawford, Janet Slaughter, and Neysa Nelms. Appreciation is extended to the Harvard Lending Library, the Theatre Collection of the New York Public Library, and to Paul Myers for certain considerations. Grateful acknowledgment is given for the assistance of Professors David Welker, Barnard Hewitt, and Norman DeMarco, and of Robert Strane and Stephen Foreman who wrote original papers for this text, and to the many educational and repertory theatres who contributed photographs for inclusion in the text.

NMS

Tragedy

Tragedy, the most exalted form of drama, deals with kings and nobles, man and god. Lecturing, teaching, questioning, pondering, tragedy requires us to turn inward and examine our motives, desires, and flaws. Tragedy encompasses the whole of mankind, and forces us to apply its teachings universally as well as personally.

We shall be concerned here with tragedy of the traditional genre, the tragedy of Sophocles and Euripides, of Shakespeare and Marlowe. Modern tragedy—from Henrik Ibsen to Arthur Miller—can be studied as a unique form of drama, distinguished by its concern for the psychological, sociological, and environmental problems of man. Some critics distinguish modern tragedy as dealing with forces outside of, rather than within, the tragic hero. Though modern tragedy is an important genre, it differs in conception and magnitude from the traditional tragedy we shall consider here.

The Subject of Tragedy

Tragedy deals with universal problems—problems that are timeless and applicable to mankind: excessive pride, curiosity, jealousy. This universality, this ability to transcend the physical representation—to involve everyone—distinguishes tragedy from lesser forms of drama. The subject of tragedy is never trivial or superficial; it is deep and lasting. It concerns itself with internal values or ideas, not external escapes and rescues.

The magnitude of tragedy precludes concern with insignificant men and mundane events. The physical story in tragedy is secondary; therefore, any catastrophe befalling the hero becomes important not as an event, but rather as a vehicle for helping the universality of the play emerge. In *Oedipus Rex*, for example, Sophocles is attempting to affirm the supremacy of the gods' will, and to portray that in tempting the fates man is doomed. The catastrophe of Oedipus' self-torture stands only secondary to this. Again in *Antigone*, Sophocles points to the sovereignty of divine or unwritten law. When there is a conflict between the laws of god and man, he is saying, divine law should and will dominate. Any suffering sustained by Creon remains subsidiary to this. The universality of *Hamlet* does not lie in the act of avenging a father's murder, but rather in the idea that we will *all* face perplexing problems and momentous decisions in our lives.

The Tragic Hero

At first reading, tragedy may seem far removed from us, with identification difficult. In dealing with kings and nobles, the spiritual and the divine, tragedy seems to remain at a distance, detached from reality. It appears grand and elevated. But in reading tragedy, two thoughts must be kept in mind. First, though they are far removed from *us*, nobles and kings were a rich part of the mythology Greeks treasured, and an actual part of the life of Elizabethans. Secondly, and more important, this *separateness* is necessary if tragedy is to achieve its goal, for "if *kings* suffer, how vulnerable are *we?*" We are the common folk, more susceptible to moral injury and prideful arrogance. Through the universality of the protagonist, we are included in the tragedy. Because so much can befall the lofty protagonist, we see that flaws can destroy or maim us, too. In sensing the universality of *Oedipus Rex*, it is not significant to question whether we will ever be confronted with marrying our mother, but rather we should examine our susceptibility to the flaw of insatiable curiosity and our tendency to disregard our personal sense of right in our obsession with a cause. *We* may never face the exact situation Creon does, but we do face conflicts between man-made and divine law.

The hero in tragedy is a man, with attendant virtues and vices, as well as a king. His being is lofty, and he has a special—often obsessive—mission, which is his flaw and which causes his downfall. For Creon (*Antigone*) the flaw is pride; for Oedipus, incessant curiosity and the questioning it brings.

In tragedy, the emphasis is on the conflict *within* the hero. There is an internal struggle, suffering, and a fall. Hamlet agonizes within to find the right course of action, and Creon does the same. If, in the interest of projecting the play's universality, it becomes necessary for the hero to die, he will die. Though his fate may seem unfairly harsh to us, the tragic hero cannot be spared. He is an exalted figure in an exalted drama, seemingly far away, yet at the same time close to us. As Henry Meyers explains: "The tragic hero has enough in common with other men to make his fate significant to them, and at the same time is unusual enough to excite and hold their interest."[1]

The Meaning in Tragedy

So far we have seen that the subject matter of tragedy is treated honestly, and the events are possible. We have learned that each tragedy has a *protagonist*, called the tragic hero, who must suffer in some way due to his flaw. This suffering and the resulting catastrophe bring forth the play's meaning, or the universality of the drama. But this "catastrophe" deserves more comment, lest it be confused with the heart-rending struggles of the hero in melodrama, for the catastrophe in tragedy, as mentioned, is secondary. It is not the catastrophic event befalling the hero that should

---

[1]Henry Alonzo Myers, *Tragedy: A View of Life* (Ithaca: Cornell University Press, 1956).

command our attention—but rather the lesson to be drawn from that catastrophe: its causes, effects, and ramifications. Whether or not the protagonist dies (Hamlet), or does not die (Creon) is not of primary concern. Oedipus lives on after discovering the circumstances surrounding his birth; for him, life is more of a punishment than death. The self-torture is his retribution, and though gruesome it may seem, it still remains subsidiary to the condition that caused it and the conclusions it forces. In tragedy, there is no attempt to spare the hero hardship, as long as that suffering, whatever it may be, transcends the play's action. For the audience, what must remain after the play's end is the *meaning for* the protagonist's suffering.

That meaning is brought about primarily by two methods, recognition and discovery (though some use these two terms synonymously). The protagonist's discovery of some external event leads to his problem, as when Hamlet discovers the ghost's identity and must then decide what to do. Creon discovers it is Antigone who buried Polynices and is faced with the problem of what action to take. Oedipus' past is unfolded to him in a gradual series of revelations, the discovery of each external event continuing to cause other problems. These discoveries make the plot interesting.

But if the unfolding of the story and the resulting catastrophes were of primary importance, the play would be melodrama, and not tragedy. More important to tragedy than those outside discoveries are the internal or self-discoveries they lead to. The external discovery serves only to compel the hero to introspect, to force him to examine his motivations and conflicts. He then *recognizes* his tragic flaw. He becomes aware of his fault. Hamlet discovers the ghost's identity, but later *recognizes* his indecision to act. He must go through agonizing self-analysis (suffering) to determine his choices, to reconcile his behavior with reality, and to act on his indecision (recognition). His death is the end result (catastrophe—we must keep in mind, though, his death is subordinate to the play's purpose). Creon learns it is Antigone who has buried her brother (discovery), but he suffers more by analyzing the surrounding circumstances and coming to the realization that he, too, is to blame for these events (recognition). This recognition, according to Goldman, "marks a change from ignorance to knowledge."[2] This self-discovery has been called "enlightenment."

The self-discovery of the protagonist is not, however, an end in itself. As Hazilitt says, "As the protagonist makes his discovery, we discover something of ourselves."[3] This reiterates what I have said before: that the tragic flaw and its discovery by the hero seems to tell us that we, too, are

[2]Mark Goldman and Isadore Trascher, *The Drama: Traditional and Modern* (Boston: Allyn and Bacon, 1968), p. 3.
[3]Theodore Hazilitt, *Orientation to the Theatre* (New York: Appleton-Century-Crofts, 1962), p. 74.

only mortals, potentially dangerous to ourselves, subject to fate, and possessing certain flaws. Like Hamlet, we must make up our minds concerning important problems and decisions. Like Creon, we discover that unwritten law sometimes is stronger than our own. *We* must come to the realization—through the hero's self-discovery—that tragedy can befall us. The questions and problems posed in tragedy are thus universal.

Tragedy and Catharsis

The last element of tragedy that deserves mention is catharsis, perhaps the most difficult and yet most distinguishing characteristic of tragedy. Although originally discussed by Aristotle in his definition of tragedy, psychology now uses this term to refer to the "alleviation of certain fears, complexes, and problems by bringing them to consciousness and giving them expression." In tragedy, the effect is very much the same. The audience is *purged* of the fear and pity it feels toward the protagonist by the discoveries, recognition, and catastrophes. This pity and fear, it must be noted, are not the sensual or superficial emotions associated with melodrama. They are, rather, pity and fear felt *for*, as well as with, a character. In watching a TV melodrama, for example, we may feel fear *along with* the hero, but rarely are we afraid *for* him. No matter how battered he becomes this week, we know he'll come back swinging (and, I might add, in perfect health) the next.

Though it is not necessary that we identify with the actual physical events on the stage, tragedy must lead us to the discovery that *we* will have to make choices, that *we* possess certain deficiencies, that *we* must examine ourselves as well. Tragedy achieves this through arousing the emotions of pity and fear. This is the spiritual cleansing, or catharsis, we must go through.

It is possible, too, as Brockett says,[4] that pity and fear are complementary. At the same time we feel fear for ourselves (in *Antigone*, for example), we feel concern for others. Thus we fear that, like Antigone, we will someday suffer death, while at the same time we feel solicitude for those who will sacrifice themselves for a higher law. While we experience fear of Creon (and others in life like him), we still feel concern for those who must make such decisions. These two emotions create a sense of concern for mankind in general, hence their universality. Because of this, it becomes possible to say that tragedy has a higher purpose, and that catharsis plays a major role in its achievement.

---

[4]Oscar Brockett, *The Theatre: An Introduction* (New York: Holt, Rinehart and Winston, 1969), p. 44.

Oedipus the King and *Hamlet* represent two very different kinds of tragedies. While the Greek playwrights did not mix comic and tragic material, Shakespeare interposed his tragedies with humor to provide comic relief. The role of the chorus varied, too, between the two types of tragedies. The Greek chorus was dominant, while the Elizabethans subordinated or eliminated altogether their chorus. Other differences that can be seen include the emergence of violence on the stage in Elizabethan tragedy (in *Oedipus the King* characters suffer offstage, in *Hamlet* onstage), and the Shakespearean disregard for the unities of *time* (the play's action must take place in a single day), *place* (the action must be confined to a single locality), and *action* (there could be but one plot), stressed by the Greeks. Still more important than these differences is the recurring thought in *all* tragedy, that the inner conflict within each hero is larger than its physical representation. There is a lesson to be drawn from this conflict, whatever the fate of the hero. According to Wright and Downs, whether it be Elizabethan or Greek tragedy, "always the force is greater than the individual, who must go down in defeat."[5] It is up to us to take from tragedy this meaning or universal message that transcends the play's action.

------

[5]E. A. Wright and C. H. Downs, *A Primer for Playgoers* (Englewood Cliffs: Prentice-Hall, 1969).

Oedipus is called on to solve the murder of Laius. Note how positioning of chorus focuses attention on Oedipus. Wayne State University. Directed and designed by Richard Spear; costumes by Robert Pusilo; lighting by Gary M. Witt.

Employment of the chorus as a powerful element in Oedipus the King. Wayne State University. Directed and designed by Richard Spear; costumes by Robert Pusilo; lighting by Gary M. Witt.

Must helpless man,
  in ignorance sedate,
Roll darkly down
  the torrent of his fate?
  Samuel Johnson

Oedipus the King

Sophocles

Oedipus the King

Translated by Kenneth Cavander

Characters   OEDIPUS, *King of Thebes*
PRIEST
CREON, *brother of* JOCASTA
CHORUS *of Theban Elders*
TEIRESIAS, *an old blind prophet*
JOCASTA, *wife of* OEDIPUS
MESSENGER
SHEPHERD
SERVANT

Scene   *Ancient Thebes*

In front of the palace of OEDIPUS *at Thebes. Near the altar stands the* PRIEST
with a large crowd of supplicants.
          (*Enter* OEDIPUS.)
OEDIPUS   My children, why do you crowd and wait at my altars?
          Olive branches . . . and wreathes of sacred flowers—
          Why do you bring these, my people of Thebes? Your streets
          Are heavy with incense, solemn with prayers for healing,
          And when I heard your voices, I would not let
          My messengers tell me what you said. I came
          To be your messenger myself, Oedipus, whose name
          Is greatest known and greatest feared.
          (*To* PRIEST) Will you tell me, then? You have dignity enough
          To speak for them all—is it fear that makes you kneel
          Before me, or do you need my help? I am ready,
          Whatever you ask will be done . . . Come, I am not cold
          Or dead to feeling—I will have pity on you.
PRIEST   King Oedipus, our master in Thebes, if you will look
          At your altars, and at the ages of those who kneel there,
          You will see children, too small to fly far from home;
          You will see old men, slow with the years they carry,
          And priests—I am a priest of Zeus; and you will see
          The finest warriors you have; the rest of your people
          Kneel, praying, in the open city, in the temples
          Of Athene, and in the shrine where we keep a flame
          Always alive and the ash whispers the future.
          Look about you. The whole city drowns

And cannot lift its hand from the storm of death
In which it sinks: the green corn withers
In the fields, cattle die in the meadows,
Our wives weep in agony, and never give birth!
Apollo brings his fire like a drover and herds us
Into death, and nature is at war with herself.
Thebes is sick, every house deserted, and the blind
Prison of the dead grows rich with mourning
And our dying cries.
Eternal powers control our lives, and we do not
Think you are their equal; yet we pray to you, as your children,
Believing that you, more than any man, may direct
Events, and come to terms with the powers beyond us.
When the savage riddle of the Sphinx enslaved
Thebes, you came to set us free. We
Were powerless, we could not tell you how to answer her.
And now they say, and it is believed, that you
Were close to God when you raised our city from the dead.
Oedipus, we pray to your power, which can overcome
Sufferings we do not understand; guard us
From this evil. In heaven and earth there must
Be some answer to our prayer, and you may know it.
You have struggled once with the powers above us and been
Victorious; we trust that strength and believe your words.
Oedipus, you are the royal glory of Thebes—
Give us life; Oedipus—think. Because
You overpowered the evil in the Sphinx
We call you savior still. Must we remember
Your reign for the greatness in which you began, and the sorrow
In which you ended? The country is sick, and you
Must heal us. You were once our luck, our fortune, the augury
Of good we looked for in the world outside. Fulfil
That augury now. You are king of Thebes, but consider:
Which is it better to rule—a kingdom? Or a desert?
What is a castle or a ship if there are
No men to give it life? Emptiness! Nothing!

OEDIPUS　My children, I know your sorrows, I know why
You have come, and what you ask of me. I see
The pain of sickness in you all, and yet in all
That sickness, who is so sick as I? Each
Of you has one sorrow, his grief is his own—
But I must feel for my country, for myself,
And for you. That is why you did not find me
Deaf or indifferent to your prayers. No,
I have spent many tears, and in my thoughts
Traveled long journeys. And then I saw
That we could be saved in one way only;
I took that way and sent Creon, my brother-

In-law, to the Oracle of Apollo; there
The god will tell him how I can save the city—
The price may be an act of sacrifice, or perhaps
A vow, a prayer, will be enough. . . . But the days
Run on and the measure of time keeps pace with them
And I begin to fear. What is he doing?
I did not think he would stay so long—he should not
Stay so long! . . . But when he comes I will do
Whatever the god commands; if I disobeyed
It would be a sin.

PRIEST   Heaven listened then;
This messenger says that Creon is returning.

OEDIPUS   My lord Apollo, let his news be the shining sun
That answers our prayers and guides us out of death!

PRIEST   I can see him now . . . the news must be good.
Look, there is a crown of bay thick with flowers
Covering his hair.

OEDIPUS   At last we shall know the truth.
If I shout, he will hear me . . . Creon!
My brother, son of Menoeceus, Lord of Thebes,
What answer does Apollo send to us? Do you bring
An answer?
            (*Enter* CREON)

CREON   Our danger is gone. This load of sorrow
Will be lifted if we follow the way
Where Apollo points.

OEDIPUS   What does this mean? I expected
Hope, or fear, but your answer gives me neither.

CREON   I am ready to tell you my message now, if you wish;
But they can hear us, and if we go inside . . .

OEDIPUS   Tell me now and let them hear! I must not think
Of myself; I grieve only when my people suffer.

CREON   Then this is what I was told at Delphi:
Our land is tainted. We carry the guilt in our midst.
A foul disease, which will not be healed unless
We drive it out and deny it life.

OEDIPUS   But how
Shall we be clean? How did this happen to us?

CREON   The crime of murder is followed by a storm.
Banish the murder and you banish the storm, kill
Again and you kill the storm.

OEDIPUS   But Apollo means
One man—who is this man?

CREON   My lord,
There was once a king of Thebes; he was our master
Before you came to rule our broken city.

OEDIPUS   I have heard of him . . . I never saw your king.

CREON   Now that he is dead your mission from the god

Is clear: take vengeance on his murderers!
OEDIPUS   But where are they now? The crime is old,
And time is stubborn with its secrets. How
Can you ask me to find these men?
CREON   The god said
You must search in Thebes; what is hunted can
Be caught, only what we ignore escapes.
OEDIPUS   Where was the murder? Was Laius killed in the city?
Or did this happen in another country?
CREON   He was traveling
To Delphi, he said. But he never returned to the palace
He left that day.
OEDIPUS   Did no one see this?
A messenger? The guard who watched his journey? You could
Have questioned them.
CREON   They were all killed, except
One. He ran home in terror, and could only
Repeat one thing.
OEDIPUS   What did he repeat?
Once we have learnt one thing, we may learn the rest.
This hope is the beginning of other hopes.
CREON   He said they met some robbers who killed the king.
He talked of an army, too strong for the servants of Laius.
OEDIPUS   Robbers would not dare to kill a king—unless
They had bribes. They must have had bribes from the city!
CREON   We suspected that, but with Laius dead
We were defenceless against our troubles.
OEDIPUS   Were
Your troubles so great that they prevented you
From knowing the truth? Your king had been murdered . . . ?
CREON   But the Sphinx
Had a riddle to which there was no answer, and we thought
Of our closest sorrows. We had no time for other
Mysteries.
OEDIPUS   But I will begin again, and make your mysteries
Plain. Apollo was right, and you were right,
To turn my thoughts to the king who died. Now
You will see the measure of my power; I come to defend you,
Avenging your country and the god Apollo.
(Aside) If I can drive out this corruption and make the city
Whole, I shall do more than save my people,
Who are my friends, but still my subjects—I shall save
Myself. For the knife that murdered Laius may yet
Drink from my heart, and the debt I pay to him
Lies to my own credit.
My children, quickly, leave this altar and take
Your branches. I will have the people of Thebes assembled
To hear that I shall do all the god commands.

And in the end we shall see my fortune smiling
From heaven, or my fall.
> (*Exit* OEDIPUS.)

PRIEST   Let us go, my sons; our king has given the order
We came to hear. May Apollo, who sent this answer
From his oracle, come to lay our sickness
To rest, and give us life.
> (*Exeunt* PRIEST, CREON, *and some of the elders.*)
> (*Enter* CHORUS.)

CHORUS   From golden Delphi Apollo replies to Thebes
And the words of heaven send a warning.
As a lyre is strung and tightened, so we
Are tightened by fear.
As a lyre trembles, so we tremble at the touch of fear.
Apollo, god of healing, god of newness,
We fear you, and the commands you send to humble us.
Do you ask a new submission? Or is your command
The same as we hear in every wind, and every season, and every year?
Only the child of golden hope, whose voice
Will never die, only the spirit of truth can tell us.
First in my prayers is the goddess Athene, the daughter of Zeus;
Second, her sister Artemis, who is queen in Thebes,
For she sits at our country's heart, pure and honored,
In a temple like the sun. And third in our prayer
Is Phoebus Apollo, whose arm reaches over all the world.
Come three times to drive our wrongs before you!
If ever in the past, when evil and blindness
Rose like a wave, when grief was burning in our city,
If ever you banished that grief,
Come now to help us.
There is no numbering our sorrows;
The whole country is sick, and mortal will and human mind
Are no weapons to defend us.
The great earth whom we call our mother
Is barren and dead; women weep in the pain of childbirth
But they fall sick and die.
Look, can you see the dying go following each other,
Gliding like gentle birds, quicker
Then the restless flash of fire that will never sleep,
The dying on their flight to the shore
Where evening sits like a goddess?
The city of the dying goes countless away
And the children of life fall to the earth,
The toys of death,
With no pity and no remembering tears.

In the rest of our city wives and mothers
Stand gray at the altars,
Which tell us of a certainty resisting the seas of doubt;

They weep, pray, plead for release
From the harsh revenge which heaven brings.
A cry for healing rises and burns above the still crowd
That mourns in the city.
Send us strength that will look kindly on us,
Golden daughter of Zeus.
Ares, the god of war, confronts us, bitter in his cruelty,
And his shout burns like fire;
But his war is fought with no armor, and Ares
Carries no shield, for he brings his conflict
Into the moment of our birth and death.
Oh, turn him flying down the winds, turn him
Back and dash him from our country
Into the wide chambers where Amphitrite sleeps,
Or to the lonely cliffs of Thrace where the seas
Allow no guests. For Ares comes to finish
The deadly work left undone by the night.
Zeus, you are the lord of lightning, lord of fire,
Destroy him with your thunder, crush our enemy!

Lord Apollo, god in the sun, we pray for your light;
Strike with your golden spears and your hands of fire,
Strike to protect us.
We pray for Artemis to bring her chaste fires,
Which we see her carry like a shining torch across
The mountains where the wolf runs.
I call you, the god with the golden crown,
Born in our country, Bacchus,
With the fire of wine in your cheek,
And the voice of wine in your shout,
Come with your pine branch burning, and your Maenads
Following the light, the fire of heaven's madness
In their eyes, come to guard us against the treacherous power
Who goes to war with justice and the harmony of heaven!
    (*Enter* OEDIPUS.)

OEDIPUS   You have told me of your need. Are you content
To hear me speak, obey my words, and work
To humor the sickness? . . . Then you will thrust away
The weight with which you struggle, and fulfil
Your need. I am a stranger to this story,
And to the crime; I have no signs to guide me,
And so if I am to trap this murderer, my hunt
Must follow every hope. I am speaking, then,
To every citizen of Thebes, and I shall not
Exempt myself, although I am a citizen only
In name, and not in blood.
Whoever knows the murderer of Laius, son
Of Labdacus, must make his knowledge mine.
It is the king's command! And if he is afraid,

Or thinks he will escape, I say to him, "Speak!
You will go into exile, but you will go unharmed—
Banishment is all you have to fear."
Or if you know the assassin comes from another
Country, you must not be silent. I shall pay
The value of your knowledge, and your reward
Will be more than gratitude.
But if I find only silence, if you are afraid
To betray a friend or reveal yourself, and lock
The truth away, listen, this is my decree:
This murderer, no matter who he is, is banished
From the country where my power and my throne
Are supreme. No one must shelter him or speak to him;
When you pray to heaven, he must not pray with you;
When you sacrifice, drive him away, do not
Give him holy water, beat him from your doors!
He carries the taint of corruption with him—for so
The god Apollo has revealed to me. . . . You see
How I serve the god and revenge the king who died!
I curse that murderer; if he is alone, I curse him!
If he shares his guilt with others, I curse him! May
His evil heart beat out its years in sorrow,
Throughout his life may he breathe the air of death!
If I give him shelter, knowing who
He is, and let him feel the warmth of my fire,
I ask this punishment for myself.
This must be done; In every word I speak
I command obedience, and so does the god Apollo,
And so does your country, which a barren sickness
And an angry heaven drag to death. But even
If it is not a god that comes to punish you
It would be shame to leave your land impure.
Your king was killed—he was a royal and noble
Man; hunt his murderer down!
I live in Laius' palace, my queen was once
The queen of Laius, and if his line had prospered
His children would have shared my love.
But now time has struck his head to earth
And in revenge I will fight for him as I
Would fight for my own father. My search will never
End until I take in chains the murderer
Of Laius, son of Labdacus. I pray heaven
That those who will not help me may watch the soil
They have ploughed crumble and turn black, let them see
Their women barren, let them be destroyed by the fury
That scourges us, but may it rage more cruelly!
And for all the Thebans who will obey me gladly
I ask the strength of justice, and the power of heaven.

So we shall live in peace; so we shall be healed.
CHORUS   Your curse menaces me, my lord, if I lie.
  I swear I did not kill him, nor can I tell
  Who did. Apollo sent the reply, and Apollo
  Should find the murderer.
OEDIPUS   Yes, we believe
  It is Apollo's task—but we cannot make
  The gods our slaves; we must act for ourselves.
CHORUS   Our next
  Hope, then, must be . . .
OEDIPUS   And every hope
  You have. When I search, nothing escapes.
CHORUS   We know a lord who sees as clearly as the lord
  Apollo—Teiresias; we could ask Teiresias, my king,
  And be given the truth.
OEDIPUS   Creon told me, and his advice
  Did not lie idle for want of action. I have sent
  Two servants. . . . It is strange they are not here.
CHORUS   And there are the old rumors—but they tell us nothing . . .
OEDIPUS   What do these rumors say? I must know
  Everything.
CHORUS   They say some travelers killed him.
OEDIPUS   I have heard that too. But the man who saw those travelers
  Was never seen himself.
CHORUS   The murderer will leave our country;
  There is a part of every man that is ruled
  By fear, and when he hears your curse . . .
OEDIPUS   A sentence
  Holds no terror for the man who is not afraid
  To kill.
CHORUS   But now he will be convicted. Look,
  They are leading your priest to you; Teiresias comes.
  When he speaks, it is the voice of heaven
  That we hear.
   (*Enter* TEIRESIAS, *guided by a boy.*)
OEDIPUS   Teiresias, all things lie
  In your power, for you have harnessed all
  Knowledge and all mysteries; you know what heaven
  Hides, and what runs in the earth below, and you
  Must know, though you cannot see, the sickness with which
  Our country struggles. Defend us, my lord, and save us—
  We shall find no other defence or safety.
  For Apollo—and yet you must have heard the message—
  Apollo, whom we asked in our doubt, promised release—
  But on one condition: that we find the murderers
  Of Laius, and banish them, or repay the murder.
  Teiresias, the singing birds will tell you of the future,
  You have many ways of knowing the truth. Do not grudge

Your knowledge, but save yourself and your city, save me,
For murder defiles us all. Think of us
As your prisoners, whose lives belong to you!
To have the power and use that power for good
Is work to bring you honor.

TEIRESIAS   When truth cannot help
The man who knows, then it brings terror. I knew
That truth, but I stifled it. I should not have come.

OEDIPUS   What is it? You come as sadly as despair.

TEIRESIAS   Send me away, I tell you! Then it will be easy
For you to play the king, and I the priest.

OEDIPUS   This is no reply. You cannot love Thebes—your own
Country, Teiresias—if you hide what the gods tell you.

TEIRESIAS   I see your words guiding you on the wrong
Path; I pray for my own escape.

OEDIPUS   Teiresias!
You do not turn away if you know the truth; we all
Come like slaves to a king with our prayers to you.

TEIRESIAS   But you come without the truth, and I can never
Reveal my own sorrows, lest they become
Yours.

OEDIPUS   You cannot? Then you know and will not tell us!
Instead, you plan treason and the city's death.

TEIRESIAS   I mean to protect us both from pain. You search
And probe, and it is all wasted. I will not tell you!

OEDIPUS   You demon! You soul of evil! You would goad
A thing of stone to fury. Will you never speak?
Can you feel, can you suffer? Answer me, and end this!

TEIRESIAS   You see wrong in my mood, you call me evil—blind
To the mood that settles in you and rages there.

OEDIPUS   Rages! Yes, that is what your words
Have done, when they shout your contempt for Thebes.

TEIRESIAS   The truth will come; my silence cannot hide it.

OEDIPUS   And what must come is what you must tell me.

TEIRESIAS   I can tell you no more, and on this answer let
Your fury caper like a beast.

OEDIPUS   It is
A fury that will never leave me. Listen, I know
What you are. I see now that you conspired to plan
This murder, and you committed it—all but the stroke
That killed him. If you had eyes, I would have said
The crime was yours alone.

TEIRESIAS   Oedipus, I warn you!
Obey your own decree and the oath you swore.
Never from this day speak to me, or to these nobles;
You are our corruption, the unholiness in our land.

OEDIPUS   How you must despise me to flaunt your scorn like this,
Thinking you will escape. How?

TEIRESIAS   I have escaped.
I carry the truth; it is my child, and guards me.
OEDIPUS   Truth! Who taught you? Heaven never taught you!
TEIRESIAS   You taught me; you forced me to the point of speech.
OEDIPUS   Repeat your words, I do not remember this speech.
TEIRESIAS   You did not understand? Or do you try to trap me?
OEDIPUS   I know nothing! Repeat your truth!
TEIRESIAS   I said, you are the murderer you are searching for.
OEDIPUS   Again you attack me, but I will not forgive you again!
TEIRESIAS   Shall I say more to make your anger sprawl?
OEDIPUS   All you have breath for—it will all be useless.
TEIRESIAS   Then . . . you live with your dearest one in burning
     Shame, and do not know it; nor can you see
     The evil that surrounds you.
OEDIPUS   Do you think
     You will always smile in freedom if you talk like this?
TEIRESIAS   If truth can give strength, I will.
OEDIPUS   It can—
     But not to you; you have no truth. Your senses
     Have died in you—ears: deaf! eyes: blind!
TEIRESIAS   Yes, be bitter, mock at me, poor Oedipus.
     Soon they will all mock as bitterly at you.
OEDIPUS   You live in perpetual night; you cannot harm
     Me, nor anyone who moves in the light.
TEIRESIAS   Your downfall
     Will come, but I will not be the cause. Apollo
     Is a great power; he watches over the end.
OEDIPUS   Did you or Creon plan this?
TEIRESIAS   Creon is not
     Your enemy; you carry your enemy with you—in your soul.
OEDIPUS   We have wealth and power, the mind reaches higher, grows,
     Breaks its own fetters, our lives are great and envied,
     And the world rewards us—with spitefulness and hate!
     Consider my power—I did not come begging, the city
     Laid its submission in my hands as a gift.
     Yet, for this power, Creon, my trusted, my first
     Friend, goes like a thief behind my back,
     Tries to exile me, and sends this wizard,
     This patcher of threadbare stories, this cunning peddler
     Of the future, with no eyes except
     For money, and certainly no eyes for mysteries.
     Tell me, tell me, when did you ever foretell the truth?
     When the Sphinx howled her mockeries and riddles
     Why could you find no answer to free the city?
     Her question was too hard for the simple man,
     The humble man; only heaven's wisdom could find
     A reply. But you found none! Neither your birds
     Above you, nor the secret voice of your inspiration

Sent you knowledge—then we saw what you were!
But I came, ignorant Oedipus, and silenced her,
And my only weapon was in my mind and my will;
I had no omens to teach me. And this is the man
You would usurp! You think, when Creon is king
You will sit close to the throne; but I think
Your plans to drive the accursed away will return
To defeat you, and to defeat their architect.
You are old, Teiresias, or else your prophetic wisdom
Would have been your death.

CHORUS   Your majesty, what he has said
And your reply—they were both born in anger.
We do not need this wildness; we ask the best
Fulfilment of Apollo's commands. This must be the search.

TEIRESIAS (*To* OEDIPUS)   You flourish your power; but you must give me the
      right
To make my reply, and that will have equal power.
I have not lived to be your servant, but Apollo's;
Nor am I found in the list of those whom Creon
Protects. You call me blind, you jeer at me—
I say your sight is not clear enough to see
Who shares your palace, nor the rooms in which you walk,
Nor the sorrow about you. Do you know who gave you birth?
You are the enemy of the dead, and of the living,
And do not know it. The curse is a two-edged sword,
From your mother, from your father; the curse will hunt you,
Like a destruction, from your country. Now
You have sight, but then you will go in blindness;
When you know the truth of your wedding night
All the world will bear your crying to rest,
Every hill a Cithaeron to echo you.
You thought that night was peace, like a gentle harbor—
But there was no harbor for that voyage, only grief.
Evil crowds upon you; you do not see
How it will level you with your children and reveal
Yourself as you truly are. Howl your abuse
At Creon and at me. . . . All men must suffer,
Oedipus, but none will find suffering more terrible
Than you.

OEDIPUS   Must I bear this? Must I be silent?
Die! Go to your death! Leave my palace now!
Get away from me!

TEIRESIAS   Yet you called me here, or I would not have come.

OEDIPUS   If I had known you would talk in the raving language
Of a madman, I would never have sent for you.

TEIRESIAS   I am no more than you see. You see a madman,
The parents who gave you life saw a prophet.

OEDIPUS   My parents? Wait! Who were my parents?

TEIRESIAS   Today will be your parent, and your murderer.

OEDIPUS   Always riddles, always lies and riddles!

TEIRESIAS   You were best at solving riddles, were you not?

OEDIPUS   When you think of my greatness, it inspires your mockery.

TEIRESIAS   That greatness has conspired to be your traitor.

OEDIPUS   I saved this country, I care for nothing else.

TEIRESIAS   Then I shall go. . . . (*To his guide*) Boy, lead me away.

OEDIPUS   Yes, lead him. . . . You come and trouble me—you are nothing
But hindrance to my plans. Go, and I shall be safe.

TEIRESIAS   I came to speak, and I shall not leave until I speak.
I need not cower at your frown, you cannot
Harm me. This man for whom you search,
Whom you threaten, and to the people call "the murderer
Of Laius," this man is here, a stranger, a foreigner;
But he will see his Theban blood, though he will not
Have any joy at the discovery.
He will be blind—though now he sees; a beggar—
Though now he is rich, and he will go feeling
Strange ground before him with a stick.
He is a father to children—then he will
Be called their brother; he is his mother's son—
Then he will be called her husband, then
He will be called his father's murderer.
Consider this when you walk between your palace walls;
If you find I have been false to you, then say
That all my prophetic wisdom is a lie.
(*Exeunt all but the* CHORUS.)

CHORUS   In the rock at Delphi there is a cave
Which is the mouth of heaven; now
The cave warns us of one man, whose hands are red
With murder, and whose actions
Break the unspoken laws that shackle us.
Time tells him now to escape,
Faster than the jostling horses of the storm,
For Apollo, the son of Zeus, leaps down on him,
Armed with lightning, dressed in fire,
And the terrible avengers follow where he goes,
The Furies who never mistake and are never cheated.
From the snow of Parnassus over Delphi the message
Gleamed and came shining to Thebes.
We must all hunt the murderer
Who hides from justice. Like a lonely bull
He crosses and crosses our country, through the harsh forests,
The hollows of the mountains, and the rocks.
Sadly trying to escape
The words that came from Delphi, the heart of the world.
But their wings are always beating in his head.

The wisdom of the priest sets fear, fear, beating in our blood;
Truth or lies, nothing comforts, nothing denies.
The world is built out of our beliefs,
And when we lose those beliefs in doubt,
Our world is destroyed, and the present and the past
Vanish into night.
We must have proof, a certainty that we can touch
And feel, before we turn against Oedipus.
The land is peopled with rumors and whispers—
They cannot make us avenge King Laius,
Whose death is guarded by such mystery.

All that men may do is watched and remembered
By Zeus, and by Apollo. But they are gods;
Can any man, even the prophet, the priest,
Can even he know more than us?
And if he can, who will be judge of him, and say he lied
Or spoke the truth.
Yet wisdom may come to us, not the wisdom that sees
How the world is ruled, but the wisdom that guides
The modest life. In this alone we may excel.
But the proof must be clear and certain,
Before I can accuse Oedipus.
Remember that the Sphinx came flying
To meet him, evil beyond our comprehension,
And we saw his wisdom then, we knew and felt
The goodness of his heart towards our country.
Thoughts cannot be guilty traitors to such a man.
         (*Enter* CREON.)

CREON   Lords of Thebes, this message has called me here
     In terror. . . . These crimes of which our king accuses me—
     No one would dare to think of them! If he
     Believes I could wrong him, or even speak of wrong,
     At such a time, when we are in such sorrow,
     Let me die! I have no wish to live out my years
     If I must live them suspected and despised.
     I will not bear this slander, which is no trifle
     To forget, but the greatest injury—the name
     Of traitor. The people will call me that, even
     You will call me that!

CHORUS   His fury mastered him;
     Perhaps he did not mean the charge.

CREON   He said
     To you all—you all heard—that the priest
     Had been told to lie, and that I had planned the answer?

CHORUS   He said that, but I know he did not mean it.

CREON   And when he

Accused me, he seemed master of his thoughts, and there was
Reason in his voice?
CHORUS   I cannot remember,
I do not observe my king so closely. . . . But here
He comes from the palace himself to meet you.
        (*Enter* OEDIPUS.)
OEDIPUS   So,
My citizen, you have come to your king? Your eyes have great
Courage—they can look on my palace out of a murderer's
Face, a robber's face! Yes, I know you;
You blaze, you thief of power . . . In heaven's name
Tell me: when you planned to kill me, did you think I had
Become a coward or a fool? Did you think I would not
Notice your treason stalking me? Or were you sure
That if I knew, I would not dare defence?
See your insane attempt! You try to capture
Power, which must be hunted with armies and gold;
But no one will follow you, no one will make
You rich!
CREON   Wait! You have accused, but you must not judge
Until you have heard my defence; I can reply.
OEDIPUS   You talk with the fangs of cleverness; but how
Can I understand? I understand only
That you are my enemy, and dangerous.
CREON   There is one thing I must say; hear it first.
OEDIPUS   One thing you must not say: "I am innocent."
CREON   You are stubborn, Oedipus, your will is too hard;
It is nothing to treasure, and you are wrong to think it is.
OEDIPUS   Treason, crimes against a brother, will not
Escape justice: you are wrong to think they will.
CREON   I do not quarrel with your talk of justice.
But tell me how I have harmed you: what is my crime?
OEDIPUS   Did you persuade me—perhaps you did not—to send for
The priest whom we used to worship for his wisdom?
CREON   And I still have faith in that advice.
OEDIPUS   How long
Is it since Laius . . .
CREON   What has Laius to do
With this? I do not see . . .
OEDIPUS   Since he was hidden
From the living sun, since he was attacked and killed?
CREON   The years are old and the time is long since then.
OEDIPUS   Was Teiresias already a priest and prophet then?
CREON   As wise as now, and no less honored and obeyed.
OEDIPUS   But at the time he did not mention me?
CREON   I did not hear him. . . .
OEDIPUS   But surely you tried to find
The murderer?

CREON   We searched, of course, we could discover
    Nothing.
OEDIPUS   If I was guilty, why did Teiresias
    Not accuse me then? He must have known, for he is wise.
CREON   I do not know. If I cannot know the truth
    I would rather be silent.
OEDIPUS   But there is one truth
    You will confess to; none knows it better . . . ?
CREON   What is that? I shall deny nothing. . . .
OEDIPUS   That only by some insidious plan of yours
    Could Teiresias ever say I murdered Laius!
CREON   If he says that, I cannot unsay it for him;
    But give me an answer in return for mine.
OEDIPUS   Question till you have no questions left;
    You cannot prove me a murderer.
CREON   Now,
    You have married my sister?
OEDIPUS   I do not deny it; the truth
    Was in your question.
CREON   You and she rule
    This country, you are equal?
OEDIPUS   If she has a wish
    I grant it all to her.
CREON   And am I not
    Considered equal to you both?
OEDIPUS   Yes, there your friendship
    Shows the face of evil it concealed.
CREON   No, reason to yourself as I have reasoned.
    First, imagine two ways of ruling, each
    Bringing equal power. With one of these fear
    Never leaves you, but with the other you sleep
    Calm in the night. Who do you think
    Would not choose the second? I feel no ambition
    To be the king, when I have the power of a king.
    For I have my place in the world, I know it, and will not
    Overreach myself. Now, you give me all
    I wish, and no fear comes with the gift;
    But if I were king myself, much more would be forced
    Upon me. Why should I love the throne better
    Than a throne's power and a throne's majesty
    Without the terrors of a throne? Now,
    I may smile to all, and all will bow to me;
    Those who need you petition me,
    For I am their hopes of success. Is this such a worthless
    Life that I should exchange it for yours? Treason
    Is for those who cannot value what they have.
    I have never had longing thoughts about your power,
    Nor would I help a man who had. Send

To Delphi, make a test of me, ask the god
Whether my message was true, and if you find
I have plotted with your priest, then you may kill me—
I will be your authority, I will assent
When you decree my death. But do not accuse me
Yet, when you know nothing. You wrong your friends
To think them enemies, as much as you do wrong
To take enemies for friends. Think, be sure!
You banish life from your body—and life you love
Most dearly—by banishing a good friend.
Time will set this knowledge safely in your heart;
Time alone shows the goodness in a man—
One day is enough to tell you all his evil.

CHORUS   My king, a cautious man would listen; beware
Of being convinced too quickly. Suddenness is not safety.

OEDIPUS   When the attack is quick and sudden, and the plot
Runs in the darkness, my thoughts must be sudden
In reply. If I wait, sitting in silence,
He will have done his work, and I lost
My chance to begin.

CREON   Your decision then! Will you
Banish me?

OEDIPUS   No, not banishment; I
Will have your life! You must teach men the rewards
That I keep for the envious and the cruel.

CREON   Will you not listen to persuasion and the truth?

OEDIPUS   You will never persuade me that you speak the truth.

CREON   No, I can see you are blind to truth.

OEDIPUS   I see
Enough to guard my life.

CREON   My life is as precious
To me.

OEDIPUS   But you are a traitor!

CREON   You know nothing!

OEDIPUS   Yet the king must rule.

CREON   Not when the king is evil.

OEDIPUS   My city! My city!

CREON   It is my city too, do not forget that!

CHORUS   Stop, my lords! Look, here is Jocasta coming to you
From the palace, at the moment when she may help you
To bring this quarrel to rest.
            (*Enter* JOCASTA.)

JOCASTA   My lords, it is pitiful to hear your senseless voices
Shouting and wrangling. Have you no shame? Our country
Is sick, and you go bustling about your private
Quarrels. My king, you must go inside, and you,
Creon, go to the palace. At this time
We have no troubles except the plague; all
Others are pretence.

CREON   My sister, your sovereign, Oedipus,
     Condemns me cruelly in his efforts to be just.
     He will banish me, or murder me; in both he does wrong.
OEDIPUS   No, I have found a traitor, my queen, who plots
     Against my life.
CREON   Never let me breathe
     In freedom again, let me die under your curse,
     If I am guilty of those crimes!
JOCASTA   Oh, Oedipus,
     Believe him. Believe him for the sake of those words
     Which heaven witnessed; you have a duty to that oath,
     And to me, and to your people.
CHORUS   Obey her, my lord, I beg you; do not be harsh,
     Be wise.
OEDIPUS   Must I be ruled by you?
CHORUS   Creon was always wise and faithful in the past; his oath was great
     And you must respect it.
OEDIPUS   You know what you are asking?
CHORUS   I know.
OEDIPUS   Tell me, what do you advise?
CHORUS   He is your friend—that is a truth
     As simple as the light of day;
     But only confused and uncertain rumors call him traitor;
     No cause to rob him of his honor.
OEDIPUS   But listen, in asking this, you ask
     For my banishment, or for my death.
CHORUS   No! By the sun who is prince of the sky!
     If that was ever my intention,
     I pray for death, without friends on earth
     Without love in heaven,
     Death in pain and misery.
     Now, now, when the decaying earth eats our lives
     Away, will you add your quarrels to all
     That we already suffer?
OEDIPUS   Let him go then; I shall die, I do not care;
     I shall be driven into banishment and disgrace.
     I do this for love and pity of you. For him, I feel none;
     Wherever he goes, he cannot escape my hatred.
CREON   For you submission is a torment—you do not hide it.
     And when you force your way against the world
     You crush us all beneath you. Such natures
     Find their own company most terrible to bear.
     It is their punishment.
OEDIPUS   Leave my sight, then! Leave me to myself!
CREON   I shall leave you. In all the time you knew me,
     You never understood me. . . . They see my innocence.
          (*Exit* CREON.)
CHORUS   My queen, take our king to the palace now.
JOCASTA   I must know what has happened.

CHORUS Doubt and suspicion. Oedipus spoke without thinking;
    He was unjust, and Creon cannot bear injustice.
JOCASTA Both were to blame?
CHORUS   Yes.
JOCASTA   What was said?
CHORUS The country is weary with sickness already;
    I am content, content to go no further
    And let the evil rest.
OEDIPUS You see what you have done, you good,
    Good adviser? My temper was a spear
    And you have turned the edge and blunted it.
CHORUS Your majesty, I have repeated many times—
    But I tell you again;
    I would have been robbed of all my senses,
    Emptied of all my reason,
    If I caused your death.
    You came like the wind we pray for in danger,
    When the storm was conquering us with sorrows,
    And carried our country into safety. Again
    You may bring a spirit to guide us.
JOCASTA But I still do not know why you were quarreling, my king,
    And I must know, for they talked of your death.
OEDIPUS   Jocasta.
    You may command me when even my people may not,
    And I let Creon go. But he had conspired
    Against me. . . .
JOCASTA   Treason! Is this true? Can you prove it?
OEDIPUS He says I am Laius' murderer.
JOCASTA   How
    Can he know? Has he always known, or has someone told him?
OEDIPUS He sent that priest Teiresias, the wicked Teiresias.
    Creon's lips do not commit themselves to words!
JOCASTA Then set all this talk aside and listen. I
    Will teach you that no priest, no holy magic
    Can know your future or your destiny. And my proof
    Is as short as the stroke of a knife. Once, an oracle
    Came to Laius —I will not say it was from
    Apollo—but from Apollo's priests. It told him
    He was destined to be murdered by the son that I
    Would bear to him. But Laius, so they say,
    Was murdered by robbers from another country at a place
    Where three roads meet. A son was born
    To us, but lived no more than three days. Yes,
    Laius pinned his ankles together and sent him
    Away to die on a distant, lonely mountain.
    Once he was there, no power could make him a murderer,
    Nor make Laius die at the hands of his son—
    And he feared that above anything in the world.

You see how you may rely upon priests and their talk
Of the future. Never notice them! When god wishes
The truth discovered, he will easily work his will.

OEDIPUS   As I listened, my queen, my thoughts went reaching out
And touched on memories that make me shudder. . . .

JOCASTA   What memories? You stare as if you were trapped.

OEDIPUS   You said—I heard you say—that Laius' blood
Was spilt at a place where three roads meet.

JOCASTA   We were all told that, and no one has denied it.

OEDIPUS   And where is the place where this happened?

JOCASTA   The country
Is called Phocis; the road splits, to Delphi
And to Daulia.

OEDIPUS   When did all this happen?

JOCASTA   The city was given the news a little before
You became king of Thebes.

OEDIPUS   God,
What do you hold prepared for me?

JOCASTA   Oedipus!
What made you frown when I talked of your becoming king?

OEDIPUS   Do not ask me yet. . . . Laius—what was he like?
His appearance, his age, describe them to me.

JOCASTA   He was tall, his hair beginning to be flecked with a down
Of white; he was built like you. . . .

OEDIPUS   Stop! You torture me!
I have hurled myself blindly against unthinking
Fury and destruction!

JOCASTA   How? I cannot bear
To watch you, my lord.

OEDIPUS   So little hope is frightening.
Listen, Teiresias the priest was not blind!
But one more answer, one more, will be better proof.

JOCASTA   I dare not answer; but if my answers help you,
Ask.

OEDIPUS   When he left Thebes, was he alone,
Or did he have a company of men at arms
So that all could recognize he was a king?

JOCASTA   No, five were all the travelers, and one
Was a herald. A single chariot carried Laius. . . .

OEDIPUS   Yes! Now I see the truth. . . . Who told you this?

JOCASTA   A servant, the only man who returned alive.

OEDIPUS   Is he still in the palace with us?

JOCASTA   No, after
He escaped, and found that you were king, and Laius
Dead, he implored me by my duty to a suppliant
To send him away. To the country, he said, herding
Sheep on the hillsides, where he could never see
The city he had left. . . . And I let him go; he was

A good servant, deserving more than this
Small favor.
OEDIPUS   He must be found at once;
Can this be done?
JOCASTA   Yes, but why do you want him?
OEDIPUS   My queen, as I look into myself I begin to fear;
I had no right to say those things, and so
I must see this man.
JOCASTA   He will come. But I
Expect to be told your sorrows, my king, when they weigh
So heavily.
OEDIPUS   And I will not refuse you, Jocasta.
I have come to face such thoughts, and who should hear
Of them before you? I walk among
Great menaces.
My father is king of Corinth—Polybus; my mother—
Merope from Doris. In Corinth I was called
Their prince, their greatest noble, until
This happened to me—it was strange, yet not
So strange as to deserve my thoughts so much.
A man, stuffed with wine at a feast, called out
To me as he drank. He said I was a son only
In the imagination of my father. Anger
And pain would not let me rest that day; the next
I went to my parents and questioned them. They answered
The drunkard harshly for his insulting story,
And for their sakes I was glad he lied. Yet I always
Felt the wound, and the story spread in whispers.
At last I went to Delphi—my parents did not know—
But Apollo thought me unworthy of an answer
To that question. Instead he foretold many trials,
Many dangers, many sorrows. I was to be
My mother's husband, I was to murder my own
Father, my children would carry the guilt and none
Would dare look on them. When I heard this
I ran from my home and afterwards knew the land
Only by the stars that stood above it.
Never must I see the shame of that evil prophecy
Acted out by me in Corinth. I traveled
Until I came to this place where you say your king
Was killed. . . . My wife, this is the truth. . . . I will tell you. . . .
My journey brought me to the meeting of three roads;
And there a herald, and an old man who rode
A chariot drawn by mares, came towards me. . . .
Jocasta, the rider was like the man you described!
He and the herald, who went in front, tried
To force me out of their path. In a rage I struck
The one who touched me, the servant at the wheel.
The old man watched me, and waited till I was passing;

Then from the chariot he aimed at the crown of my head
With the twin prongs of his goad. It was a costly
Action! Slashing with my stick I cut at him
And my blow tumbled him backwards out of the chariot—
Then I killed them all! If this man I met may be said
To resemble Laius, to be, perhaps, Laius,
I stand condemned to more sorrow than any man,
More cursed by an evil power than any man.
No one in Thebes, no stranger, may shelter me
Or speak to me; they must hunt me from their doors.
And I, it was I, who cursed myself, cursed myself!
And the dead king's pillow is fouled by the touch
Of my murdering hands. Is the evil in my soul?
Is my whole nature tainted? Must I go into exile,
Never see my people again, nor turn home
And set foot in Corinth?—for if I do, I must wed
My mother, and kill my father—Polybus, who gave me
Life and youth. Can you see this happen, and then
Deny that a cruel power has come to torture me?
No! You heavens, you pure light and holiness!
Let me die before that day, hide me before
I feel that black corruption in my soul!

CHORUS   My king, this is a frightening story. But hope,
Until you hear from the man who saw what happened.

OEDIPUS   Yes, that is all the hope I have. Oedipus
Waits for one man, and he is a shepherd.

JOCASTA   What makes you so eager for him to come?

OEDIPUS   I reason like this. We may find that his story
Matches yours. Than I shall be as free
As if this had never happened.

JOCASTA   Was there anything in what
I said that could have such power?

OEDIPUS   You said
He told you robbers murdered Laius. If he still
Says "robbers" and not "a robber," I am innocent.
One man cannot be taken for many.
But if he says a murderer, alone,
The guilt comes to rest on me.

JOCASTA   But we all
Heard him say "robbers"; that is certain. He cannot
Unsay it. I am not alone, for the whole city heard.
But even if he swerves a little from his old account,
That will not prove you Laius' murderer,
Not in truth, not in justice. For Apollo said
He was to be killed by a son that was born to me . . .
And yet my son, poor child, could not have killed him,
For he died first . . . but that shows the deceit
Of prophecies. They beckon at you, but I
Would fix my eyes ahead, and never look at them!

OEDIPUS   You are right. Nevertheless send someone
    To bring that servant; do not forget.
JOCASTA   Yes,
    I will send now. Let us go to the palace;
    I would do nothing that could harm or anger you.
        (*Exeunt all but the* CHORUS.)
CHORUS   All actions must beware of the powers beyond us, and each word
    Must speak our fear of heaven. I pray
    That I may live every hour in obedience.
    The laws that hold us in subjection
    Have always stood beyond our reach, conceived
    In the high air of heaven. Olympus
    Was their sire, and no woman on earth
    Gave them life. They are laws
    That will never be lured to sleep in the arms of oblivion,
    And in their strength heaven is great and cannot grow old.
    Yet man desires to be more than man, to rule
    His world for himself.
    This desire, blown to immensity
    On the rich empty food of its ambition,
    Out of place, out of time,
    Clambers to the crown of the rock, and stands there,
    Tottering; then comes the steepling plunge down to earth,
    To the earth where we are caged and mastered.
    But this desire may work for good
    When it fights to save a country, and I pray
    That heaven will not weaken it then.
    For then it comes like a god to be our warrior
    And we shall never turn it back.

    Justice holds the balance of all things,
    And we must fear her.
    Do not despise the frontiers in which we must live,
    Do not cross them, do not talk of them,
    But bow before the places where the gods are throned.
    Time will come with cruel vengeance on the man
    Who disobeys; that is the punishment
    For those who are proud and are more than men—
    They are humbled
    If a man grows rich in defiance of this law,
    If his actions trespass on a world that he should fear,
    If he reaches after mysteries that no man should know,
    No prayer can plead for him when the sword of heaven is raised.
    If he were to glory in success
    All worship would fall dumb.

    Delphi is the heart of the world and holds its secrets;
    The temple of Zeus, and Olympia, command our prayers;
    But we shall never believe again

Until the truth of this murder is known.
Let us be sure of our beliefs, give us proof.
Zeus, you may do your will; do not forget that you are immortal,
Your empire cannot die; hear our prayers.
For the oracle given to Laius in the years of the long past
Is dying and forgotten, wiped from the memory,
Apollo's glory turns to shadows,
And all divinity to ruin.
      (Enter JOCASTA.*)*

JOCASTA   My lords, I have been summoned by my thoughts
To the temples of the gods, and I have brought
These garlands and this incense for an offering.
Oedipus is like a lonely bird among
The terrors that flock about his mind. He forgets
His wisdom, and no longer thinks the past will guide him
When he tries to foresee the future. Instead, he is
The slave of any word that talks of fear.
I try to reach him, to make him see that there is hope,
But it is useless; I have failed. And so I turn
To you, Apollo, nearest to us in Thebes,
A suppliant with prayers and gifts. Resolve this doubt
By sending the truth. He is the guide and master
Of our ship. What shall we do when even he
Is struck into bewilderment?
      (Enter MESSENGER.*)*

MESSENGER   I do not know this country. Will you show me the palace
Of King Oedipus? I must find King Oedipus. . . .
Do you know where he is?

CHORUS   This is his palace, sir.
He is inside, and you see his queen before you.

MESSENGER   Heaven give her and all she loves riches
And happiness if she is the queen of such a king.

JOCASTA   I return you greeting. You have spoken well and deserve
Well wishing. But what do you want with Oedipus?
Or do you bring a message for us?

MESSENGER   A message
Of good, for your palace and your husband, my queen.

JOCASTA   What is it? Who sent you here?

MESSENGER   I come from Corinth.
My story may be quickly told. You will be glad, of course,
For the news is glad, and yet . . . yet you may grieve.

JOCASTA   Well, what is this story with a double meaning?

MESSENGER   The people of Corinth—it was already announced
There—will make Oedipus their king.

JOCASTA   But why?
Your king is Polybus. He is wise, revered . . .

MESSENGER   But no longer our king. Death hugs him to the earth.

JOCASTA   Is this true? Polybus is dead?

MESSENGER   By my hopes of living out my years, it is true.

JOCASTA   Servant, go, tell this to your master. Run!

   (*Exit* SERVANT.)

  Where are the prophecies of heaven now? Always
  Oedipus dreaded to kill this man, and hid
  From him. But look, Polybus has been murdered
  By the careless touch of time, and not by Oedipus.

   (*Enter* OEDIPUS.)

OEDIPUS   Dear Jocasta, dear wife, why have you called me
  Here from the palace?

JOCASTA   This man brings a message;
  Listen, and then ask yourself what comes
  Of the oracles from heaven that used to frighten us.

OEDIPUS   Who is this man? What has he to say to me?

JOCASTA   He comes from Corinth, and his message is the death
  Of Polybus. You will never see Polybus again!

OEDIPUS   You said that, stranger? Let me hear you say that plainly.

MESSENGER   Since you force me to give that part of my message first,
  I repeat, he walks among the dead.

OEDIPUS   A plot?
  Or did sickness conspire to kill him?

MESSENGER   A small
  Touch on the balance sends old lives to sleep.

OEDIPUS   So, my poor father, sickness murdered you.

MESSENGER   And many years had measured out his life.

OEDIPUS   Oh look, look, who would listen to Apollo
  Talking in his shrine at Delphi, or notice birds
  That clamor to the air? They were the signs
  That told me—and I believed—that I would kill
  My father. But now he has the grave to protect him,
  While I stand here, and I never touched a sword . . .
  Unless he died of longing to see me—
  Then perhaps he died because of me. No!
  Polybus lies in darkness, and all those prophecies
  Lie with him, chained and powerless.

JOCASTA   I told you long ago how it would happen. . . .

OEDIPUS   Yes, but I was led astray by fears.

JOCASTA   Then think no more of them; forget them all.

OEDIPUS   Not all. The marriage with my mother—I think of it.

JOCASTA   But is there anything a man need fear, if he knows
  That chance is supreme throughout the world, and he cannot
  See what is to come? Give way to the power
  Of events and live as they allow! It is best.
  Do not fear this marriage with your mother. Many
  Men have dreams, and in those dreams they wed
  Their mothers. Life is easiest, if you do not try
  To oppose these things which seem to threaten us.

OEDIPUS   You are right, and I would agree with all

You say, if my mother were not alive. And though
You are right, I must fear. She is alive.
JOCASTA   Think of your father, and his grave.
There is a light to guide you.
OEDIPUS   It does guide me!
I know he . . . But she is alive and I am afraid.
MESSENGER   You are afraid of a woman, my lord?
OEDIPUS   Yes,
Merope—Polybus was her husband.
MESSENGER   How can you be afraid of her?
OEDIPUS   A prophecy warned me
To beware of sorrow. . . .
MESSENGER   Can you speak of it, or are you
Forbidden to talk of these things to others?
OEDIPUS   No,
I am not forbidden. The Oracle at Delphi
Has told me my destiny—to be my mother's husband
And my father's murderer. And so I left
Corinth, many years ago and many
Miles behind me. The world has rewarded me richly,
And yet all those riches are less than the sight
Of a parent's face.
MESSENGER   And you went into exile because
You feared this marriage?
OEDIPUS   And to save myself from becoming
My father's murderer.
MESSENGER   Then, my king,
I ought to have freed you from that fear since I
Wished to be thought your friend.
OEDIPUS   Your reward
Will be measured by my gratitude.
MESSENGER   I had hoped for reward
When you returned as king of your palace in Corinth.
OEDIPUS   I must never go where my parents are.
MESSENGER   My son,
You do not know what you say; I see you do not.
OEDIPUS   How, sir? Tell me quickly.
MESSENGER   . . . If you live in exile
Because of Polybus and Merope.
OEDIPUS   Yes, and I live
In fear that Apollo will prove he spoke the truth.
MESSENGER   And it is from your parents that the guilt is to come?
OEDIPUS   Yes, stranger, the fear never leaves my side.
MESSENGER   You have no cause to be afraid—do you know that?
OEDIPUS   No cause? But they were my parents—that is the cause!
MESSENGER   No cause, because they were not your parents, Oedipus.
OEDIPUS   What do you mean? Polybus was not my father?
MESSENGER   As much as I, and yet no more than I am.

OEDIPUS   How could my father be no more than nothing?

MESSENGER   But Polybus did not give you life, nor did I.

OEDIPUS   Then why did he call me son?

MESSENGER   Listen, you were
     A gift that he took from my hands.

OEDIPUS   A child
     Given him by a stranger? But he loved me
     Dearly.

MESSENGER   He had no children, and so consented.

OEDIPUS   So you gave me to . . . Had you bought me for your slave?
     Where did you find me?

MESSENGER   You were lying beneath the trees
     In a glade upon Cithaeron.

OEDIPUS   What were you doing on Cithaeron?

MESSENGER   My flocks were grazing in the mountains;
     I was guarding them.

OEDIPUS   Guarding your flocks—you were
     A shepherd, a servant!

MESSENGER   It was in that service that I saved
     Your life, my child.

OEDIPUS   Why? Was I hurt or sick
     When you took me home?

MESSENGER   Your ankles will be my witness
     That you would not have lived.

OEDIPUS   Why do you talk
     Of that? The pain is forgotten!

MESSENGER   Your feet were pierced
     And clamped together. I set you free.

OEDIPUS   The child
     In the cradle had a scar—I still carry
     The shame of it.

MESSENGER   You were named in remembrance
     Of that scar.

OEDIPUS   In heaven's name, who did this?
     My mother? My father?

MESSENGER   I do not know. The man
     Who gave you to me knows more of the truth.

OEDIPUS   But you said you found me! Then it was not true . . .
     You had me from someone else?

MESSENGER   Yes, another
     Shepherd gave me the child.

OEDIPUS   Who? Can you
     Describe him?

MESSENGER   They said he was a servant of Laius.

OEDIPUS   Laius, who was once king of Thebes?

MESSENGER   Yes,
     This man was one of his shepherds.

OEDIPUS   Is he still
    Alive; could I see him?
MESSENGER   Your people here
    Will know that best.
OEDIPUS   Do any of you,
    My friends, know the shepherd he means? Has he
    Been seen in the fields, or in the palace? Tell me,
    Now! It is time these things were known!
CHORUS   I think
    He must be the man you were searching for, the one
    Who left the palace after Laius was killed.
    But Jocasta will know as well as I.
OEDIPUS   My wife, you remember the man we sent for a little
    Time ago? Is he the one this person means?
JOCASTA   Perhaps . . . But why should he . . . Think nothing of this!
    Do not idle with memories and stories. . . .
OEDIPUS   No, I have been given these signs, and I must
    Follow them, until I know who gave me birth.
JOCASTA   No! Give up this search! I am tortured and sick
    Enough. By the love of heaven, if you value life . . .
OEDIPUS   Courage! You are still a queen, though I discover
    That I am three times three generations a slave.
JOCASTA   No, listen to me, I implore you! You must stop!
OEDIPUS   I cannot listen when you tell me to ignore the truth.
JOCASTA   But I know the truth, and I only ask you to save
    Yourself.
OEDIPUS   I have always hated that way to safety!
JOCASTA   But evil lies in wait for you. . . . Oh, do not let him
    Find the truth!
OEDIPUS   Bring this shepherd to me,
    And let her gloat over the riches of her ancestry.
JOCASTA   My poor child! Those are the only words
    I shall ever have for you. . . . I can speak no others!
        (*Exit* JOCASTA.)
CHORUS   What is the torment that drives your queen so wildly
    Into the palace, Oedipus? Her silence threatens
    A storm. I fear some wrong. . . .
OEDIPUS   Let the storm
    Come if it will. I must know my birth,
    I must know it, however humble. Perhaps she,
    For she is a queen, and proud, is ashamed
    That I was born so meanly. But I consider
    Myself a child of Fortune, and while she brings me
    Gifts, I shall not lack honor. For she has given me
    Life itself; and my cousins, the months, have marked me
    Small and great as they marched by. Such
    Is my ancestry, and I shall be none other—
    And I will know my birth!

CHORUS   There are signs
    Of what is to come, and we may read them,
    Casting our thoughts into the future,
    And drawing in new knowledge.
    For we have seen how the world goes
    And we have seen the laws it obeys.
    Cithaeron, mountain of Oedipus, the moon
    Will not rise in tomorrow's evening sky
    Before our king calls you his true father,
    His only nurse and mother—and then
    You will have your greatest glory.
    You will be honored with dances and choirs
    For your gentle kindness to our king—Hail
    To the god Apollo! May he be content
    With all our words.

    Pan walks among the mountains, and one
    Of the immortal nymphs could have lain with him;
    Who was the goddess who became your mother, Oedipus?
    Or was she the wife of Apollo, for he loves
    The wild meadows and the long grass.
    Or was it the prince of Cyllene, Hermes?
    Or, Bacchus, whose palace is the mountaintop?
    Did he take you as a gift from the nymphs of Helicon,
    With whom he plays through all his immortal years?
OEDIPUS   I never knew the shepherd or encountered him,
    My people, but the man I see there must be
    The one we have been seeking. His age answers
    My riddle for me; it holds as many years
    As our messenger's. And now I see that those
    Who lead him are my servants. But you have known him
    Before, you can tell me whether I am right.
CHORUS   Yes, we recognize him—the most faithful
    Of Laius' shepherds.
OEDIPUS   And you, Corinthian,
    You must tell me first. Is this the man you mean?
MESSENGER   It is; you see him there.
            (*Enter* SHEPHERD.)
OEDIPUS   You, sir, come to me,
    Look me in the eyes, and answer all my questions!
    Did you once serve Laius?
SHEPHERD   Yes, and I was born
    In his palace; I was not brought from another country. . . .
OEDIPUS   Your life? How were you employed?
SHEPHERD   Most
    Of my life I watched his flocks.
OEDIPUS   And where
    Was their pasture? They had a favorite meadow?

SHEPHERD   Sometimes Cithaeron, sometimes the places near.
OEDIPUS   Do you recognize this man? Did you see him on Cithaeron?
SHEPHERD   Why should anyone go there? Whom do you mean?
OEDIPUS   Here! Standing beside me. Have you ever met him?
SHEPHERD   I do not think so. . . . My memory is not quick.
MESSENGER   We should not wonder at this, your majesty;
　　　　But I shall remind him of all he has forgotten.
　　　　I know that he remembers when for three
　　　　Whole years I used to meet him near Cithaeron,
　　　　Six months, from each spring to the rising of the Bear;
　　　　I had a single flock and he had two.
　　　　Then, in the winters, I would take my sheep to their pens
　　　　While he went to the fields of Laius. . . . Did this happen?
　　　　Have I told it as it happened, or have I not?
SHEPHERD   The time is long since then . . . yes, it is the truth.
MESSENGER   Good; now, tell me: you know the child you gave me . . . ?
SHEPHERD   What is happening? What do these questions mean?
MESSENGER   Here is the child, my friend, who was so little then.
SHEPHERD   Damnation seize you! Can you not keep your secret?
OEDIPUS   Wait, Shepherd. Do not find fault; as I listened
　　　　I found more fault in you than in him.
SHEPHERD   What
　　　　Have I done wrong, most mighty king?
OEDIPUS   You will not
　　　　Admit the truth about that child.
SHEPHERD   He wastes
　　　　His time. He talks, but it is all lies.
OEDIPUS   When it will please me, you will not speak; but you will
　　　　When I make you cry for mercy. . . .
SHEPHERD   No, my king,
　　　　I am an old man—do not hurt me!
OEDIPUS (To GUARDS)   Take his arms and tie them quickly!
SHEPHERD   But why,
　　　　Poor child? What more do you want to know?
OEDIPUS   You gave
　　　　The boy to this Corinthian?
SHEPHERD   Yes, I did. . . .
　　　　And I should have prayed for death that day.
OEDIPUS   Your prayer will be answered now if you lie to me!
SHEPHERD   But you will surely kill me if I tell the truth.
OEDIPUS   He will drive my patience to exhaustion!
SHEPHERD   No!
　　　　I told you now, I did give him the child.
OEDIPUS   Where did it come from? Your home? Another's?
SHEPHERD   It was not mine, it was given to me.
OEDIPUS   By someone
　　　　In the city? . . . I want to know the house!

SHEPHERD   By all that is holy,
    No more, your majesty, no more questions!
OEDIPUS   You die
    If I have to ask again!
SHEPHERD   The child was born
    In the palace of King Laius.
OEDIPUS   By one of his slaves?
    Or was it a son of his own blood?
SHEPHERD   My king,
    How shall I tell a story of such horror?
OEDIPUS   And how shall I hear it? And yet I must, must hear.
SHEPHERD   The child was called his son. But your queen in the palace
    May tell you the truth of that most surely.
OEDIPUS   Jocasta gave you the child?
SHEPHERD   Yes, my king.
OEDIPUS   Why? What were you to do?
SHEPHERD   I was to destroy him.
OEDIPUS   The poor mother asked that?
SHEPHERD   She was afraid.
    A terrible prophecy . . .
OEDIPUS   What?
SHEPHERD   There was a story
    That he would kill his parents.
OEDIPUS   Why did you give
    The child away to this stranger?
SHEPHERD   I pitied it,
    My lord, and I thought he would take it to the far land
    Where he lived. But he saved its life only for
    Great sorrows. For if you are the man he says,
    You must know your birth was watched by evil powers.
OEDIPUS   All that was foretold will be made true! Light,
    Now turn black and die; I must not look on you!
    See, this is what I am; son of parents
    I should not have known, I lived with those
    I should not have touched, and murdered those
    A man must not kill!
        (*Exit* OEDIPUS.)
CHORUS   Every man who has ever lived
    Is numbered with the dead; they fought with the world
    For happiness, yet all they won
    Was a shadow that slipped away to die.
    And you, Oedipus, are all those men. I think of the power
    Which carried you to such victories and such misery
    And I know there is no joy or triumph in the world.

    Oedipus aimed beyond the reach of man
    And fixed with his arrowing mind
    Perfection and rich happiness.

The Sphinx's talons were sharp with evil, she spoke in the mysteries
Of eternal riddles, and he came to destroy her,
To overcome death, to be a citadel
Of strength in our country.
He was called our king, and was
The greatest noble in great Thebes.
And now his story ends in agony.
Death and madness hunt him,
Destruction and sorrow haunt him.
Now his life turns and brings the reward of his greatness. . . .
Glorious Oedipus, son, and then father,
In the same chamber, in the same silent room,
Son and father in the same destruction;
Your marriage was the harvesting of wrong.
How could it hold you where your father lay,
And bear you in such silence for such an end?

Child of Laius, I wish, I wish I had never known you,
For now there is only mourning, sorrow flowing
From our lips.
And yet we must not forget the truth;
If we were given hope and life, it was your work.
            (*Enter* SERVANT.)
SERVANT   My lords of Thebes, on whom rest all the honors
Of our country, when you hear what has happened,
When you witness it, how will you bear your grief
In silence? Weep, if you have ever loved
The royal house of Thebes. For I do not think
The great streams of the Phasis or the Ister
Could ever wash these walls to purity. But all
The crimes they hide must glare out to the light,
Crimes deliberate and considered. The sorrows
We choose ourselves bring the fiercest pain!
CHORUS   We have seen great wrongs already, and they were frightening.
Do you bring new disasters?
SERVANT   I bring a message
That I may tell, and you may hear, in a few
Swift words. Jocasta is dead.
CHORUS   Then she died in grief. What caused her death?
SERVANT   It was her own will. Of that terrible act
The worst must remain untold, for I did not watch it.
Yet you will hear what happened to our poor queen
As far as memory guides me. When she went
Into the doomed hall of the palace, whirled
On the torrent of her grief, she ran straight
To her marriage chamber, both hands clutched at her hair,
Tearing like claws. Inside, she crashed shut the door
And shrieked the name Laius, Laius who died

So long ago. She talked to herself of the son
She once bore, and of Laius murdered by that son;
Of the mother who was left a widow, and became
Wife and mother again in shame and sorrow.
She wept for her marriage, in which her husband gave
To her a husband, and her children, children.
How her death followed I cannot tell you. . . .
We heard a shout, and now Oedipus blazed
And thundered through the door. I could not see
How her sorrow ended, because he was there,
Circling in great mad strides, and we watched
Him. He went round begging to each
Of us; he asked for a sword, he asked to go
To his wife who was more than a wife, to his mother in whom
His birth and his children's birth, like two harvests
From the same field, had been sown and gathered. His grief
Was a raging madness, and some power must have guided him—
It was none of us who were standing there. He gave
A cry full of fear and anguish, then, as if
A ghost was leading him, he leaped against the double
Doors of Jocasta's room. The hinges tilted
Full out of their sockets, and shattered inside
The chamber—and there we saw his wife, hanging
By her throat in the grip of a tall rope. And when
He saw her, he shrieked like a wounded beast, wrenched loose
The knot that held her, and laid her on the ground.
What followed was terrible to watch. He ripped
The gold-worked brooches from her robes—she wore them
As jewels—and raised them above his head. Then he plunged them
Deep into the sockets of his eyes, shouting
That he would never look upon the wrongs
He had committed and had suffered. Now
In his blackness he must see such shapes as he deserved
And never look on those he loved. Repeating
This like a chant, he lifted his hands and stabbed
His eyes, again and again. We saw his eyeballs
Fill with tears of blood that dyed his cheeks,
And a red stream pouring from his veins, dark
As the blood of life, thick as storming hail.
Yes, this is a storm that has broken, a storm
That holds the queen and the king in its embrace.
They were rich and fortunate, and they were so
As we should wish to be. Now, in one day,
See how we must mourn them. The blind rush
To death, the shame, all the evils that we
Have names for—they have escaped none!

CHORUS   Has our poor king found ease for his sorrow yet?

SERVANT   He shouts at us to open the doors and show

To all Thebes the murderer of his father
And his mother's . . . his words are blasphemous,
I dare not speak them. . . . He will be driven from Thebes,
Will not stay beneath this curse that he called upon
Himself. Yet he needs help and a guide. No one
Could bear that agony. . . . But he comes himself to show you;
The great doors of the palace open, and what you will see
Will turn you away in horror—yet will ask for pity.
       (*Enter* OEDIPUS.)
CHORUS   This suffering turns a face of terror to the world.
There is no story told, no knowledge born
That tells of greater sorrow.
Madness came striding upon you, Oedipus,
The black, annihilating power that broods
And waits in the hand of time. . . .
I cannot look!
We have much to ask and learn and see.
But you blind us with an icy sword of terror.
OEDIPUS   Where will you send this wreckage and despair of man?
Where will my voice be heard, like the wind drifting emptily
On the air. Oh you powers, why do you drive me on?
CHORUS   They drive you to the place of horror,
That only the blind may see,
And only the dead hear of.
OEDIPUS   Here in my cloud of darkness there is no escape,
A cloud, thick in my soul, and there it dumbly clings;
That cloud is my own spirit
That now wins its fiercest battle and turns back
To trample me. . . . The memory of evil can tear
Like goads of molten fire, and go deep,
Infinity could not be so deep.
CHORUS   More than mortal in your acts of evil.
More than mortal in your suffering, Oedipus.
OEDIPUS   You are my last friend, my only help; you have
Waited for me, and will care for the eyeless body
Of Oedipus. I know you are there . . . I know . . .
Through this darkness I can hear your voice.
CHORUS   Oedipus, all that you do
Makes us draw back in fear. How could you take
Such vivid vengeance on your eyes? What power lashed you on?
OEDIPUS   Apollo, my lords, Apollo sent this evil on me.
I was the murderer; I struck the blow. Why should I
Keep my sight? If I had eyes, what could delight them?
CHORUS   It is so; it is as you say.
OEDIPUS   No, I can look on nothing. . . .
And I can love nothing—for love has lost
Its sweetness, I can hear no voice—for words
Are sour with hate. . . . Take stones and beat me

From your country. I am the living curse, the source
Of sickness and death!
CHORUS   Your own mind, reaching after the secrets
Of the gods, condemned you to your fate.
If only you had never come to Thebes . . .
OEDIPUS   But when my feet were ground by iron teeth
That bolted me in the meadow grass,
A man set me free and ransomed me from death.
May hell curse him for that murderous kindness!
I should have died then
And never drawn this sorrow on those I love
And on myself . . .
CHORUS   Our prayers echo yours.
OEDIPUS   Nor killed my father,
Nor led my mother to the room where she gave me life.
But now the gods desert me, for I am
Born of impurity, and my blood
Mingles with those who gave me birth.
If evil can grow with time to be a giant
That masters and usurps our world,
That evil lords its way through Oedipus.
CHORUS   How can we say that you have acted wisely?
Is death not better than a life in blindness?
OEDIPUS   Do not teach me that this punishment is wrong—
I will have no advisers to tell me it is wrong!
Why choke my breath and go among the dead
If I keep my eyes? For there I know I could not
Look upon my father or my poor mother. . . .
My crimes have been too great for such a death.
Or should I love my sight because it let me
See my children? No, for then I would
Remember who their father was. My eyes
Would never let me love them, nor my city,
Nor my towers, nor the sacred images
Of gods. I was the noblest lord in Thebes,
But I have stripped myself of Thebes, and become
The owner of all miseries. For I commanded
My people to drive out the unclean thing, the man
Heaven had shown to be impure in the house
Of Laius.
I found such corruption in me—could I see
My people and not turn blind for shame? . . .
My ears are a spring, and send a river
Of sound through me; if I could have dammed that river
I would have made my poor body into a bolted prison
In which there would be neither light nor sound.
Peace can only come if we shut the mind

Away from the sorrow in the world outside.
Cithaeron, why did you let me live? Why
Did you not kill me as I lay there? I would
Have been forgotten, and never revealed the secret
Of my birth. Polybus, Corinth, the palace
They told me was my father's, you watched over
My youth, but beneath that youth's nobility lay
Corruption—you see it in my acts, in my blood!
There are three roads, a hidden valley, trees,
And a narrow place where the roads meet—they
Drink my blood, the blood I draw from my father—
Do they remember me, do they remember what I did?
Do they know what next I did? . . . The room, the marriage
Room—it was there I was given life, and now
It is there I give the same life to my children.
The blood of brothers, fathers, sons, the race
Of daughters, wives, mothers, all the blackest
Shame a man may commit. . . . But I must not name
Such ugly crimes. Oh, you heavens, take me
From the world and hide me, drown me in oceans
Where I can be seen no more! Come, do not fear
To touch a single unhappy man. Yes, a man,
No more. Be brave, for my sufferings can fall to no one
But myself to bear!

CHORUS   Oedipus, Creon came
While you were praying; he brings advice and help.
You can protect us no more, and we turn to him.

OEDIPUS   What can I say to Creon? I have given him
No cause to trust me or to listen. In all I said
Before, he has seen that I was wrong.

            (*Enter* CREON *with* ANTIGONE *and* ISMENE.)

CREON   I have not come scorning or insulting you, Oedipus,
For those wrongs. (*To servants*) Have you no shame before
Your countrymen? At least show reverence to the sun's
Flame that sends us life, and do not let
This curse lie open to disfigure heaven.
Neither earth, nor the pure falling rain, nor light
May come near it. Take him to the palace now!
When evil grows in the family, only the family
May hear of it and look without pollution.

OEDIPUS   Creon, I thought . . . but now you have struck those fears
Away—you will be a gentle king.
But I ask one thing, and I ask it to help you,
Not myself, for I am hated by powers too strong
For us.

CREON   What do you ask so eagerly?

OEDIPUS   Banish me from the country now. I must go
Where no one can see or welcome me again.

CREON   I would have done so, Oedipus, but first
    I must know from Apollo what he commands.
OEDIPUS   But we have heard all his answer—destroy the
    Parricide, the unholiness, destroy me!
CREON   So it was said. . . . And yet we are in such danger;
    It is better to hear what we must do.
OEDIPUS   Why need you
    Go to Delphi for my poor body?
CREON   Delphi will never deceive us; you know it speaks
    The truth.
OEDIPUS   But Creon, I command you! . . . I will kneel
    And pray to you . . . Bury my queen as you wish
    In her royal tomb; she is your sister
    And it is her right. But as for myself, I
    Must never think of entering my father's city
    Again, so long as its people live. Let me
    Have no home but the mountains, where the hill
    They call Cithaeron, my Cithaeron, stands.
    There my mother and my father, while
    They lived, decreed I should have my grave.
    My death will be a gift from them, for they
    Have destroyed me. . . . And yet I know that sickness
    Cannot break in and take my life, nothing
    May touch me. I am sure of this, for each moment
    Is a death, and I am kept alive only
    For the final punishment. . . . But let it go,
    Let it go, I do not care what is done with me.
    Creon, my sons will ask nothing more from you;
    They are men, wherever they go they will take what they need
    From life. But pity my two daughters, who will have
    No love. All that was owned by me, they shared,
    And when I banqueted, they were always beside me.
    You must become their father. . . . But let me touch them
    And talk to them of our sorrows. Come, my lord,
    Come, my noble kinsman, let me feel them
    In my arms and believe they are as much my own
    As when I saw . . . I cannot think. . . . Their weeping,
    Their dear voices are near. Creon has pitied me
    And given me my children. Is this true?
CREON   I sent for them; I know what joy they would give you
    And how you loved them once. Yes, it is true.
OEDIPUS   May heaven bless your life, and may the power
    Watching us, guard you more safely on the throne
    Than me. My children, where are you? Come near, come
    To my hands; they are your brother's hands and they
    Went searching out and took your father's seeing
    Eyes to darkness. I did not know my children,
    And did not ask, but now the world may see

That I gave you life from the source that gave me mine.
Why is there no light? I cannot see you! . . . And tears
Come when I think of the years you will have to live
In a cruel world. In the city they will shun you,
Fear your presence; when they feast and dance in the streets
You will not be allowed to watch, and they
Will send you weeping home. And when you come
To the years of marriage, children, who will there be
So careless of his pride as to accept the shame
That glares on my birth and on yours? "Your father
Killed his father!" "Your father gave life where he
Was given life, you are children where he was once
A child." That will be your humiliation!
And who will wed you?
No one, my daughters, there will be no one, and I see
You must pine to death in lonely childlessness.
Creon, you are their father, you alone.
For they have lost their parents. Do not let them go
Into beggary and solitude—their blood is yours.
I have nothing, but do not afflict them with
My poverty. Have pity on them. See, so young
And robbed of all except your kindliness.
Touch me once, my lord, and give your consent.
My children, I would have said much to comfort
And advise you—but how could you understand?
But pray, you must pray to live as the world allows
And find a better life than the father whom you follow.

CREON   No more now. Go inside the palace.
OEDIPUS   It is hard, but I must obey.
CREON   All things are healed
    By time.
OEDIPUS   But Creon, I demand one thing before
    I go.
CREON   What do you demand?
OEDIPUS   Banishment!
CREON   Only heaven can answer your prayer. When Apollo . . .
OEDIPUS   But Apollo can only detest me.
CREON   Then your prayer will be
    The sooner heard.
OEDIPUS   You mean what you say?
CREON   I cannot
    Promise, when I see nothing certain.
OEDIPUS   Now!
    Exile me now!
CREON   Go then, and leave your children.
OEDIPUS   You must not take them from me!
CREON   You give
    Commands as if you were king. You must remember
    Your rule is over, and it could not save your life.

CHORUS   Men of Thebes, look at the king who ruled
          Your country; there is Oedipus.
          He knew how to answer the mystery
          Of evil in the Sphinx, and was our greatest lord.
          We saw him move the world with his will, and we envied him.
          But look, the storm destroys him, the sea
          Has come to defeat him.
          Remember that death alone can end all suffering;
          Go towards death, and ask for no greater
          Happiness than a life
          In which there has been no anger and no pain.

From the Critic

For close to 2500 years critics have been interpreting the story of Oedipus the King, and twentieth century man is no exception. **Richmond Y. Hathorn** *sees the quest of Oedipus as existential, that the problem of Oedipus together with its solution are inextricably linked. Mankind and Myself are not always separate entities. The riddle that Oedipus must solve is the mystery of himself.*

The Existential Oedipus

Existentialism has suffered the fate, certainly rare among philosophies, of becoming a fashionable byword. The results of this are such as might have been expected: satire, contempt, and misunderstanding on the part of the general reader; hostile criticism and supercilious interpretation on the part of the professional thinker. Generally speaking, philosophers outside of Germany and France find it hard to take existentialism seriously, being committed to an orthodoxy of a very different kind. Nor has the school's reputation been helped by the political vagaries of some of its leading exponents, by Heidegger's flirtation with the Nazis, Sartre's recently exploded romance with Red Russia, or Simone de Beauvoir's expressions of hatred for America and all its works. In spite of all this, existentialism deserves to be taken seriously, if for no other reason than that it addresses itself to a serious task.[1]

The task of the existentialist thinker is similar to that of Socrates in the late fifth century B.C.: to bring philosophy back from a preoccupation with merely linguistic and narrowly pragmatic considerations—such a concern with ancillary studies being certain to lead to moral indifferentism—and to focus on philosophy's only proper point of concentration, a concern with ethics, thereby setting again

---

[1]Treatments of Sophoclean drama from an existentialist standpoint are nothing new; well known are Heinrich Weinstock's *Sophokles* (Wuppertal, 1948) and Karl Reinhardt's *Sophokles* (Frankfurt, 1947), both of which represent third editions. Weinstock's suggestive theory about *Oedipus Rex*, that man's limited knowledge, in contrast to the omniscience of the gods, inevitably involves every human action in guilt and evil ("Wer unwissend handelt, muss schuldig werden"), thus leading to a state of existential "Angst," which is best converted by the individual into a reverence strictly religious—this theory has been justly criticized, on the grounds that Weinstock's Original Sin (the "Allverschuldung" and "Allverantwortung" of every human being) is only glancingly treated by Sophocles, whereas Oedipus' anxieties and fears arise from quite definite occasions and are by no means identical with the "Daseinsangst" or "Weltangst" of existentialism. Reinhardt, in a discussion equally suggestive, if rather rhapsodical, develops the implications of the "Schein-Sein" antithesis in the play—an issue by no means strictly existentialist—while having much also to say about "Angst."

for the activity of human thought the only goal that can evoke in a human being a sense of personal urgency. From Socrates' time onward the ancient world never forgot that the Groves of Academe are indeed barren ground unless they bear fruit in ethics.[2] Yet in most schools of philosophy today, if the layman asks for bread he is given a calculus.

For the nineteenth century largely forgot Socrates' lesson. The abstractness of absolute idealism, the impersonality of scientism, the absence of moral challenge in bourgeois optimism stirred the bile of Kierkegaard and Nietzsche, just as the continuing ethical indifference of twentieth-century positivism provokes the reaction of Heidegger, Jaspers, Marcel, Sartre, and others. Existentialism has thus mainly arisen in protest against the excessively abstract and the excessively impersonal tendency of the mainstream of modern rationalistic thought. It may be defined, then, as including all thinking that by a method of introspective empiricism throws particular emphases on the ethical issues involving the individual self.[3] These emphases are placed on the following: on a rigorous inspection of concrete, primary experience, experience, that is, as it presents itself to the individual, as opposed to the interpreted, secondary data of science and abstractive reflection; on the actual situation in which the individual finds himself, *la condition humaine;* on the individual's personal commitment or lack of commitment of himself to that situation, his willingness or lack thereof to become *engagé;* on the peculiarly human character of pledges, promises, and loyalties, which commit a human being to the ethical life in contrast to the life of the lower animals; on the individual's relationship to fate and freedom; on the emergence or nonemergence of what may be called a Self.[4] Hence, because of their very method, emphasizing self-involvement as it does, certain existentialists are inclined to recognize the existence of mysteries, as distinct from the existence of problems or riddles, which alone are recognized by positivists and scientistic analysts. Gabriel Marcel says in *Being and Having:*

> A problem is something which I meet, which I find complete before me, but which I can therefore lay siege to and reduce. But a mystery is something in which I myself am involved, and it can therefore only be thought of as "a sphere where the distinction between what is in me and what is before me loses its meaning and its initial validity." A genuine problem is subject to an appropriate technique by the exercise of which it is defined; whereas a mystery, by definition,

---

[2]Even scientific studies in ancient times were pursued for ethical ends; cf. F. M. Cornford. "Greek Natural Philosophy and Modern Science," pp. 81-94 of *The Unwritten Philosophy and Other Essays* (Cambridge, 1950).

[3]For a discussion of the difficulties involved in defining existentialism and of the inadequacy of Jean-Paul Sartre's widely quoted definition. "Existentialism is the philosophy which declares as its first principle that existence is prior to essence," see Marjorie Grene. *Dreadful Freedom: A Critique of Existentialism* (Chicago, 1948) pp. 1–4. Actually the Sartrean definition smuggles in Sartre's peculiar doctrine of freedom; cf. Wilfrid Desan, *The Tragic Finale* (Cambridge, Mass., 1954) pp. 162 ff.

[4]Concise characterizations of existentialism may be found in H. J. Blackham, *Six Existentialist Thinkers* (London, 1952) esp. pp. 149–65, and in Jean Wahl, *A Short History of Existentialism*, tr. Forrest Williams and Stanley Maron (New York, 1949).

transcends every conceivable technique.[5] It is, no doubt, always possible (logically and psychologically) to degrade a mystery so as to turn it into a problem. But this is a fundamentally vicious proceeding, whose springs might perhaps be discovered in a kind of corruption of the intelligence. The problem of evil, as the philosophers have called it, supplies us with a particularly instructive example of its degradation.[6]

There is no intention in this paper of presenting Sophocles as an existentialist philosopher[7] But it would perhaps not be too anachronistic to maintain that Sophocles wrote at a time when the intellectual situation was somewhat analogous to our own, that his reaction to it was somewhat similar to that of our existentialists, and that consequently his works deal with issues that are substantially the same as those treated in modern existentialist literature. Oedipus, in *Oedipus Rex*, confronts the dilemmas of personal commitment as opposed to intellectual abstraction, of his own relationship to fate and freedom, of apparent existence and true being, of the acceptance or rejection of emergent selfhood: his story then, as handled by Sophocles, if it is not strictly existentialist, may at least be called existential.

That Sophocles was opposed to certain intellectual tendencies of his time, that he set himself against the trend toward a facile and narrow rationalism: these have become critical commonplaces.[8] He is usually contrasted with Euripi-

---

[5]Worth quoting is H. T. Wade-Grey, *The Poet of the Iliad* (Cambridge, 1952) p. 45: "With the death of Patroklos, or of Mercutio, we are suddenly, in General Mihailovich's phrase, caught in the gale of the world: no contrivance now will work, all contrivances are now insignificant. This is what we recognize as tragedy: it was the pattern of thought of Shakespeare's and Homer's mind. The greatness of life, to these two, is when intrigue, the moral or hedonistic calculus, is caught in the gale." That our culture is almost exclusively a contriving, intriguing. "problem-solving" one, with an almost total non-recognition of tragedy and mystery, a glance into any periodical, from the most popular to the most specialized, will confirm.

[6]Quoted by Marcel himself in *The Mystery of Being*, tr. G. S. Fraser, vol. 1 (Chicago' 1950) pp. 211–12.

[7]Max Pohlenz, *Die Griechische Tragödie*, 2nd ed., vol. 2 (Göttingen, 1954) p. 6, remarks of the existentialist (specifically Weinstock's) approach to Sophocles: "Es war gewiss eine zeitgebundene Illusion, wenn Schillers Humanismus sich die Griechen als ein seliges Geschlecht vorstellte, das von den Göttern an der Freude leichtem Gängelbände geführt wurde; aber ebenso einseitig und verfehlt ist es, wenn man heute eine nicht minder zeitgebundene Daseinssicht in das Griechentum hineinträgt." (Cf. also vol. 1, pp. 9–11.) There is some justice in this, yet Pohlenz himself is victim of an illusion equally "zeitgebundene," namely the Hegelian notion that cultures develop in the direction of greater freedom for the individual. As a matter of fact, this post-Enlightenment interest in personality-development constitutes the bulk of Sophoclean criticism; examples are to be found in T. B. L. Webster, *An Introduction to Sophocles* (Oxford, 1936); T. D. Goodell, *Athenian Tragedy* (New Haven, 1920); Gilbert Norwood, *Greek Tragedy* (London, 1928); J. T. Sheppard, *Greek Tragedy* (Cambridge, 1934); and many others.

[8]See, among many, John A. Moore, *Sophocles and Arete* (Cambridge, Mass., 1938) esp. chs. 2 and 3; Victor Ehrenberg, *Sophocles and Pericles* (Oxford, 1954) ch. 7; Enrico Turolla, *Saggio sulla Poesia di Sofocle*, 2nd ed. (Bari, 1948).

des[9] in this, frequently to the advantage of the latter, who is admired for his liberal-progressive spirit, whereas Sophocles is likely to be depicted as a somewhat dimwitted conservative, pietistic, obscurantist, devoted to the intuitive and the irrational. Such epithets are the usual weapons of rationalists in their quarrel with anyone who as Sophocles undoubtedly does in *Oedipus Rex*—attempts to point out the limitations of human reason. This quarrel is almost always conducted in false either-or terms: after all, there is no such person as an "irrationalist." No one has ever consistently argued for deliberately hampering the activity of reason, if only because he could not allow his own reason to be hampered in defense of his position; no thinker has ever thought that human reason should not be permitted to go as far as it can: there have simply been many to add that, having gone so far, it must not rest in the unreasonable conclusion that it has gone all the way, or that, having gone farther than it can, it must not conclude that it is any longer reasonable. Sophocles in the *Oedipus* surely attacks intellectual pride; he does not attack the intellect as such.

Intellectual pride arises from the exaltation of the intellect to the neglect of other parts of the soul, and seems most likely to be a common vice of ages when there prevails a system of psychology that treats human behavior in simple terms of appetite and of schemes for its satisfaction. The Sophistic psychology of Sophocles' day was like this, if we are to believe Aristophanes and Thucydides, and in a somewhat similar way modern psychological thinking virtually ignores the human will. And precisely here is the source of the difficulties encountered by modern commentators in applying Aristotle's *hamartia* theory to *Oedipus Rex*.[10] *Hamartia* must mean either a "moral flaw" (an isolated misdeed or a persistent defect of character) or an "error in judgement." Cedric Whitman sums up the controversy:

> There are two fundamental ways of explaining the tragedy, corresponding in general to the two possibilities involved in hamartia. One is to attribute Oedipus' fall to the rash, self-willed temper already mentioned. But others maintain that no such moral failing is involved, but rather an intellectual slip, an error, entailing no moral guilt, but merely the well-known cataclysmic sequel. This error—"trifling," as Aristotle said—occurred when Oedipus slew his father and married his mother. He was innocent, in that he acted in ignorance, but he was wrong in that he did these things. . . . The relative significance of these two views for tragedy itself is, of course, immense. But the important

---

[9]See Cedric Whitman, *Sophocles: A Study in Heroic Humanism* (Cambridge, Mass., 1951) p. 228. Whitman's "heroic humanism," incidentally, might also very properly be described as existentialist, in spite of Whitman's explicit rejection of Weinstock's and Reinhardt's approach (pp. 26–27) and aside from his advancement of a dubiously Sophoclean belief in the possiblity of apotheosis (ch. 11).

[10]It has become the fashion to repudiate Aristotle's theories about tragedy, either on the ground that they were tailored to fit only a few plays—or even this very play alone. *Oedipus Rex*—or on the ground that he followed the great tragedians by a century. To the first objection it should be answered that Aristotle had many more plays to examine than we have, and was thus better able to formulate the ideal toward which he thought the whole *genre* was striving; in reply to the second, one can only ask, "Then what price the criticism of us who are twenty-four times further removed?"

question for the present is, which did Aristotle mean? Did he intend us to find a morally culpable act or merely a mistake as the cause of tragic catastrophe?[11]

An either-or dilemma again. Whitman quite rightly decides that neither theory is adequate and rejects a *hamartia* explanation altogether.[12] But instead of answering "Neither" it is possible to answer "Both." Possession of knowledge or the lack of it, exercise of reason or the failure to exercise it, are never ethically neutral in all their aspects. Modern thought, with its fundamental neglect of the will, or rather its submergence of the will into desire, leads to a mere ethics of custom, *mores* instead of morality, which is impersonal and does not truly engage the individual will. Surely the relationship between the parts of the soul is more complex; there are an ethics of epistemology and an ethics of logic. *Hamartia* is neither mere intellectual error nor misconduct; it is blindness to a whole phase of universal reality, blindness to such a degree that it affects all of a man's attitudes and all of his behavior.

What is Oedipus' *hamartia* then? Obviously it is not bad temper, suspicion, hastiness in action—for his punishment does not fit these crimes; nor ignorance of who his parents are—for ignorance of this type is not culpable;[13] still less murder and incest—for these things are fated for him by the gods.

No, Oedipus' blind spot is his failure in existential commitment;[14] a failure to recognize his own involvement in the human condition; a failure to realize that not all difficulties are riddles, to be solved by the application of disinterested intellect, but that some are mysteries, not to be solved at all, but to be coped

---

[11]Pp. 32–33. Whitman discusses the chief rival theories fully. It will be seen that the present paper is not so much a contradiction as a reconciliation of these.

[12]Other interpreters have been reduced to far more desperate expedients than Whitman's. Most numerous of anti-critical critics are "The play's the thing" advocates, who evade the primary task of answering the obvious question. "Yes, but what kind of thing?" Most influential of these was Tycho von Wilamowitz, *Die Dramatische Technik des Sophokles* (Berlin, 1917) with his insistence on the essential disunity of the plays; most entertaining was A. J. A. Waldock, *Sophocles the Dramatist* (Cambridge, 1951) with some excellent demolitions of others' interpretations; most typically Romantic was Gennaro Perrotta, *Sofocle* (Messina-Milan, 1935), who vehemently denied that any of the plays is a "dramma a tesi" or any of the poetry "poesia di pensireo," affirming rather that all is "soltanto poesia" and Sophocles himself "sopratutto poeta," whatever that may mean; most recent perhaps is Herbert Musurillo, "Sunken Imagery in Sophocles' 'Oedipus,' " *AJP* 78 (1957) 36–51, who, after an analysis of the dominant images in the play—interesting, but rather pointless unless shown to be illustrative of an underlying theme—concludes rather surprisingly, "And thus it may be said that the *Oedipus*, in a sense, has no interpretation." The last word on such negative criticism has been said by Charles Williams, in regard to a similar non-interpretation of Dante (*The Figure of Beatrice* [London, 1943] p. 100): "It is a tender, ironic, and consoling view. It is consoling because it shows us that, though we cannot write like Dante, yet we shall not be taken in by Dante. It is also consoling *because it relieves us from the neccessity of supposing that Dante may be relevant to us.*" (Italics mine.)

[13]Though it becomes so of course, if the individual, on being apprised of his condition, refuses to acknowledge the truth.

[14]Cf. Weinstock (2nd ed., Berlin, 1937) p. 181.

with only by the engagement, active or passive, of the whole self.[15] Oedipus' punishment, then, is not really punishment at all, but the only means by which the gods may enlighten a blindness of such profundity.[16]

The action of the play begins when the King undertakes a project, the discovery of the murderer of Laius, and binds himself with the most solemn promises to carry this project to its fulfillment. The concept of the project and the promise is dear to the existentialists: only Man can so engage himself, for only Man, unlike the other animals, has knowledge of past and future as well as present.[17] Yet the celebrated irony of the scene, as has been obvious to every reader, consists in the fact that the engagement is far more real than Oedipus knows. From the audience's point of view, therefore, this commitment has something of falsity about it, of incompleteness; it becomes to them a symbol of our common human failing to look for evil everywhere but in ourselves.[18] This last is the prime temptation of the intellect, which in its essential direction points from the self to the exterior world. Oedipus is willing to avenge the death of Laius as though Laius were his own father (264–65); he is willing to suspect even a member of his own household (249–51): these ironies are obvious. He says that the griefs of his people are his own, that he feels them even more deeply than others do (60–64), speaking more truly than he knows. He undertakes to solve the riddle as a father would solve a difficulty for his children,[19] little realizing that, as Teiresias warns him, this very day is to make him and his children equal (425).[20] The project, then, has an air of dissociation about it, because it lacks the last full measure of personal commitment; a promise may not be a real promise, cannot, in fact, be

---

[15]See Hans Diller, *Göttliches und Menschliches Wissen bei Sophokles* (Kiel, 1950) esp. pp. 18 ff., where there is developed a very suggestive opposition between the analytic habits of human thought, "das seiner Natur nach trennende, isolierende menschliche Denken" (p. 22) and the unitary nature of reality, "die Eindeutigkeit der göttlichen Antwort." Cf. also p. 30: "Auch im sophokleischen Oedipus erscheint der Mensch als der Ratsellöser, der das Rätsel seines Daseins nicht lösen kann, solange er in Gegensätzlichkeit isoliert sieht, was doch zusammengehort. Ihm erscheint als fremd, was in Wahrheit seine eigenste Sache ist. . . . " All the way through the play there is a contrast between what is theoretically known and what is personally known—between what is perceived with the intellect alone and what has penetrated to the depth of the soul—between knowledge, in short, and wisdom: see, for an example, the interplay between Oedipus and Teiresias, 359 ff.

[16]That Sophocles was not interested in telling a crime-and-punishment story is shown by his leaving the "crimes" themselves out of the action, which begins years later; many commentators have remarked on this, e.g., Whitman, p. 125, and Perrotta, p. 199.

[17]Compare Heidegger's doctrine of the "Entwurf," and see Jean-Paul Sartre, *Being and Nothingness*, tr. Hazel E. Barnes (New York, 1956) esp, pp. 34–35, 39, 40–43, 367–71, 433–566 *passim*. It must be admitted, however, that the Sartrean "project" has very little in common with Oedipus' in regard to nobility and altruism.

[18]Tragedians love this ironic device; one thinks of Clytemnestra prating about justice, rash Hamlet commending the stoical Horatio, and Lear praying for Heaven to give him patience, which Heaven does by letting fall on his own top all the stored vengeances he wants poured on his daughters.

[19]Throughout the Prologue, beginning with the first line, Oedipus addresses the Thebans as "children."

[20]Imagery based on the idea of equation is scattered throughout and is fully discussed by Bernard M. W. Knox, *Oedipus at Thebes* (New Haven, 1957) pp. 147–58.

a real promise until it is fulfilled. That at the end Oedipus fulfills it to the letter is the measure of his moral grandeur.

It may be objected that Oedipus *is* personally interested in solving the murder. This is true, but not because he feels any real involvement of himself in the general human condition. Rather he feels his own external fortune affected by the threat to his power. "The man who did this to Laius has reason to do this to me" is a quite different attitude from "What Laius' murderer did I may have done." "We must punish criminals in order to protect ourselves" is only the beginning of morality, the end of which is "There, but for the grace of God, go I." Oedipus is involved only as regards his self-interest, not as regards his own self; hence his quickness in directing his suspicion toward Creon.[21]

The person who wholly projects morality into the outer world loses his own selfhood in the process. Sophocles does not waste his time and the reader's patience by making Oedipus lament at the last that he could not help doing what he did or being what he is.[22] To look upon oneself as the mere product of external causes is to make oneself a thing instead of a person, as the existentialist philosophers never tire of pointing out. Oedipus is horrified at having been his own self-accuser, but he does not therefore retract the accusation. He realizes that he is a scapegoat; he does not complain that he is a goat. Determinism, theories of heredity and environment, fatalism: all are devices, not for explaining guilt and evil, but for explaining them away, away from ourselves, at all costs; Oedipus disdains to avail himself of these devices. Rather he reaches his true moral stature at the end of the play. For a man is never more conscious of being a person and less conscious of being a thing than when the self is accusing itself and accepting its own guilt. The willingness to accept guilt is an indispensable step toward the goal of self-knowledge; an animal, a savage, or a child cannot fully grasp the concept of guilt; similarly an adult who falls into deterministic excuses for his behavior shuts the door on the possibility of self-development. But a person reaches his greatest intensity of self-consciousness when he simultaneously plays the part both of the accuser and the accused. To such intensity the individual will not rise as long as his external fortunes are in a condition of prosperity; herein lies the necessity of tragedy. Albert Camus remarks,[23] "The human heart has a tiresome tendency to label as fate only what crushes it. But happiness likewise,

---

[21]That Oedipus' suspicions of Creon begin quite early in the play is noticed by J. T. Sheppard, *The Oedipus Tyrannus of Sophocles* (Cambridge, 1920) p. 111. Probably the suspicions are first aroused by Creon's desire to report the oracular response in private.
[22]Oedipus is not merely passive in the last scene, as is amply shown by Knox, pp. 185 ff. This scene, far from being the protracted piece of sentimentality some critics have found it, is the *raison d'être* of the play. See Wolfgang Schadewaldt. *Sophokles und das Leid* (Potsdam, 1947) esp. pp. 28–29: "Im Leiden aber, welchës ihn zu sich selber bringt, wird er in der Vernichtung seines Menschseins inne, und während er zuvor im Genuss der Kraftentfaltung, nur immer unbekannter mit sich selbst, immer mehr den Grund seiner Existenz zu verlieren drohte, rückt er im Leiden nun mit dem richtigen Verhältnis zu sich selbst auch in das richtige Verhältnis zu seinem Gott, und tauscht für die "Hybris,' die ihn hinriss, die Nüchternheit der 'Sophrosyne' ein, welche, als eine Art Zusich-kommen, der festeste Grund des Menschseins ist."
[23]*The Myth of Sisyphus and Other Essays*, tr. Justin O'Brien (New York, 1955) p. 128. Camus has disavowed being an existentialist, but his so-called "Absurdism" is obviously Kierkegaardian in origin.

in its way, is without reason, since it is inevitable. Modern man, however, takes the credit for it himself, when he doesn't fail to recognize it." Sophocles, needless to say, knew better than the "modern men" of his day.

Even the recognition of an unpleasant truth is a moral act; if a man is hideously ugly, he deserves some praise for taking an honest and steady look in the mirror. Morality is not a matter of putting some goodness or wickedness into a slot and receiving in return a proportionate package of pleasure or pain. *Oedipus Rex* is not a crime-and-punishment play; it is a moral drama of self-recognition. That the recognition is neither prompt nor willing is natural, and increases our feelings of pity and fear. The view that represents Sophocles as an advocate of mere religious conventionality and ethical conformity is inadequate. Oedipus as a scapegoat is singled out,[24] but, by accepting the role, he singles himself out and differentiates himself from the mass, the Chorus. His acceptance of the wretched creature that he is makes him a hero. His life is henceforth to be unique, a life set apart, as he well recognizes, and in this respect it is to become the being of a Person in contrast to the existence of a Thing. But the Chorus are quite willing to dissociate themselves from him and to withdraw into the anonymity of convention, a withdrawal which, as Heidegger[25] repeatedly emphasizes, is one of the chief methods of evading human freedom. The Chorus say that they take Oedipus as their *parádeigma*, their model from whom they may learn a lesson, but their wish never to have known him shows that his is a lesson that they are not actually prepared to learn. Thus they fall into the same error from which Oedipus is emerging.

It is ambiguous, therefore, to say that Sophocles does not offer a solution to the problem of evil such as Aeschylus gives. This is usually taken to imply an attitude of pessimism on his part, at worst marked by befuddlement or bitterness, at best stoical or pietistic.[26] But, after all, evil by definition is that to which there is no ultimate solution. It is a mystery, for even exterior evil always has inextricable connections with the self. Any evil outside myself, once acknowledged, immediately offers an ineluctable challenge to me; if I refuse to act or react—and strictly speaking I can only apparently refuse—I compound it. And interior evil, the evil of my own limited destiny, is the precondition of my action or reaction. Let it be said again that Oedipus' prime *hamartia*, his blind spot, his moral ignorance, is precisely his tendency to suppose that evil is a problem rather than

---

[24]Which is not to deny that every man is similarly singled out in the gods' own time and way; otherwise Oedipus could not truly serve as a *parádeigma*. This lack of universal application seems to be the weakness of C. M. Bowra's theory in *Sophoclean Tragedy* (Oxford, 1944) pp. 209–11, that Oedipus' fate is something essentially unusual, that his catastrophe is a warning from gods to men, and that by taking heed the latter may somehow escape.

[25]Cf. Blackham (see note 4) pp. 92–98.

[26]The fullest discussion of this whole problem is J. C. Opstelten, *Sophocles and Greek Pessimism*, tr J. A. Ross (Amsterdam, 1952). Cf. also Schadewaldt (see note 22) who proposes an interesting theory about the necessity of suffering to effect the emergence of the self: e. g., p. 26: "Denn, das Leid *versammelt* den Menschen zu sich selbst, versammelt ihn zur Gestalt. Es ist darum plastisch im umfassenden Sinn (während der einseitige Ausdruck der Freude, die ausser sich bringt, erhebt, löckert, löst, exzentrisch und wider den Sinn der Plastik ist)." But Turolla (see note 8) pp. 110, 214, 215, 221, supposes that Sophocles brings a message of utter despair.

a mystery, a something exterior to the self that can be solved without involving the self. To quote Marcel again:

> A mystery is a problem which encroaches upon its own data, invading them, as it were, and thereby transcending itself as a simple problem. . . .
> It will be seen at once that there is no hope of establishing an exact frontier between problem and mystery. For in reflecting on a mystery we tend inevitably to degrade it to the level of a problem. This is particularly clear in the case of the problem of evil.[27]
> In reflecting upon evil, I tend, almost inevitably, to regard it as a disorder which I view from outside and of which I seek to discover the causes or the secret aims. Why is it that the "mechanism" functions so defectively? Or is the defect merely apparent and due to a real defect of my vision? In this case the defect is in myself, yet it remains objective in relation to my thought, which discovers it and observes it. But evil which is only stated or observed is no longer evil which is suffered: in fact, it ceases to be evil. In reality, I can only grasp it as evil in the measure in which it *touches* me—that is to say, in the measure in which I am *involved*, as one is involved in a lawsuit. Being "involved" is the fundamental fact; I cannot leave it out of account except by an unjustifiable fiction, for in doing so, I proceed as though I were God, and a God who is an onlooker at that.[28]

Sophocles found in the Oedipus myth the perfect material for his purposes; he it was, perhaps, who converted the peripety from a mere penalty for transgressing a taboo into a means of moral enlightenment.[29] Doubtless already in

---

[27]Whitman's interpretation of *Oedipus Rex* (ch. 7) as a tragedy of "irrational evil" is marred by vagueness in the use of the word "irrational." Sometimes evil appears to be "irrational in the way that any datum of experience is," i.e., nonrational; sometimes "irrational as an animal is," i.e., sub-rational; sometimes "irrational beyond the scope of human reason," i.e., super-rational. (Whitman is aware of the distinction, but fails to observe it). This confusion carries over into the discussions of Sophocles' religious beliefs (cf. pp. 235, 245 for example). If Sophocles believed at all that evil, though god sent, was "irrational" in the third sense, he was *ipso facto* committing himself to a theodicy and eschewing the utter pessimism that Whitman supposes he fell into in the *Oedipus Rex* and the *Trachiniae*. (Of irrational evil as a mystery Whitman has no hint.) Francis Ferguson in *The Idea of a Theater* (New York, 1953) p. 29, is similarly unclear: "For the peculiar virtue of Sophocles' presentation of the myth is that it preserves the ultimate mystery by focusing upon the tragic human at a level beneath, or prior to any rationalization whatever."

[28]*The Philosophy of Existence*, tr. Manya Harari (London, 1948) pp. 8–9.

[29]It is interesting to note that in some versions of the myth Oedipus continued to rule in Thebes for many years after the disclosure of his transgressions, apparently unaffected by Jocasta's suicide. For the development of the myth see Carl Robert, *Oedipus* (Berlin 1915); Opstelten (see note 26) pp. 102, 103; Lord Raglan, *Jocasta's Crime* (London, 1933) chs. 22, 23, 26. Perhaps the most teasing puzzle about myth—and one that our increasing anthropological knowledge has done little to solve—is the provenance of its ethical and spiritual elements. It seems pretty well established by now that the story of Oedipus must have been originally a fictionalization of some sort of murderous contest wherein a new aspirant to the hand of the incarnate Great Mother, the Lady of the Crossways where the three roads met, had to kill his predecessor and undergo death or expulsion as

the myth as he received it the solution of the Sphinx's riddle was the cause of the King's prosperity and intellectual pride.[30] Sophocles' contribution was to bring out the fact that Oedipus' apparent success at explaining away the evil of the Sphinx was to mislead him into supposing that he could similarly explain all evil away. But the answer to the Sphinx's riddle was a mere abstraction.[31] "What is it that goes on four feet in the morning, two feet at noon, and three feet at eventide?" The answer is "Man," but Man in General means nothing to the Individual Man. So the success of this answer led inevitably to the marriage with Jocasta and the obligation to track down the murderer of Laius. As the drama unfolds, Oedipus finds himself doomed in his own person to live out his abstract answer: his own day's journey is to be the journey that the Sphinx's riddle hinted at:[32] the Sphinx has her revenge. "This day shall bring you to birth and destroy you," Teiresias tells him (438): and this day, at the height of his manhood, he shall first truly learn what he was as an infant and what he shall be as an old man (454–60):

> Out of the man of sight shall be made a blind man, out of the rich man a beggar, and he shall make his way into an alien land testing the ground ahead of him with his staff. And he shall be shown to be in like case with his children, brother to them and father; to the woman from whom he sprang he shall be seen to be son and husband; the seed of the father shall have sown seed where the father sowed,[33] and he shall have cut his father down.[34]

The solver of all problems is himself the problem beyond all solution. What appeared to Oedipus as a riddle—Man—is in reality a mystery—Myself.

---

a community scapegoat in his turn. All done, we are told, to ensure fat crops and full bellies for the tribe. And we can object only when assured that this explanation explains all. If this is all, whence come these ideas of atonement, of altruistic self sacrifice, of kinship with nature, this striking symbolism of man's ineluctable fate and circumscribed existence? Astounding coincidence that these bumbling aetiologies called myths should be so hospitable to profundities of philosophical and theological interpretation! Shocking as the thought is to our post-Enlightenment sense of intellectual superiority, could it be that such ideas were already present in "primitive" religion?

[30]Cf. lines 440–42: the source of Oedipus' intellectual greatness is at the same time the source of his foolishness.

[31]The significance of the answer to the riddle is remarked upon only, to my knowledge, by Erich Fromm, *The Forgotten Language* (New York, 1951) p. 212.

[32]Hence the frequent references to journeying and wandering. For the play on the word *poús* cf. Knox (see note 20) pp. 182–84. (I venture the suggestion that *Oedipus*, "Swollen Foot," may originally have been a euphemism for the ithyphallos or its wearer in a fertility rite.)

[33]For the translation of *honósporos* here, see Knox, p. 115.

[34]Admittedly the last phrase is not a translation, but a paraphrase. The "cutting down" idea is imported in order to complete the "sowing" imagery.

From the Director

David Welker of Wake Forest University approached Oedipus Rex *by asking two questions: What experience should the play render for the audience? and How may that be accomplished? He answers the first by saying that the play should transfer the universal teachings inherent in it, that the "humanness" of Oedipus must be made evident so each audience member is able to see a bit of himself. To achieve this effect, in answer to his second question, Dr. Welker proposes the production methods be more in tune with what the contemporary audience is used to, since, he feels, the attempt to recreate the elements common to ancient productions would serve more to confuse than produce the effect sought. The achievement of the play's universals can more effectively be accomplished by subordinating traditional classical production techniques.*

Directing Oedipus Rex

In thinking back over my experiences in directing *Oedipus the King*, I was startled by the realization of how large a part the play had had in my life as theater student and artist. Reading it for the first time, a third of a century ago, made me a permanent Greek enthusiast. I checked out every book at the University of Illinois library which had anything to do with Greek drama, read them all, as well as all of the extant plays, and wrote four papers on the subject. Later I served as guest lecturer on Greek drama at another university, and since have given major attention to the period in my courses in theater history. I have acted in *Oedipus*, have seen it as a movie, and have read it countless times. No play has had a larger part in my esthetic experience. Consequently, when one of my scene design students, Mr. Michael David, created a superb set for *Oedipus*, it seemed as though the ancient fates had made it inevitable that I direct the play.

It would be possible to discuss the directorial problems and procedures for this great play with some hope of adequacy in three or four hundred pages; a brief essay provides space only for a few footnotes.

With *Oedipus*, as with any play, the director must begin by asking two fundamental questions: What experience is the production intended to create for the audience? and What methods will contribute most to creating that experience? The first question is essentially esthetic, the second technical. All of the director's planning consists of the development of answers to those questions, and his work with his actors and technical staff represents the application of the answers he has found.

But although this procedure is standard and familiar, applying it to Sophocles' play is especially difficult because of the vast differences in the culture of the original audiences and the audiences the director must plan for. What experience did Sophocles intend his audiences to have? What were their attitudes toward the theatrical spectacle, the familiar story, the playwright's development and interpretation of it, the emotional responses he has created for his characters? What is the function of the chorus in the play?

Different directors would answer those questions in many different ways. One theory sees the plays as almost exclusively ritualistic—the movement of a group of puppet-like characters through a familiar pattern, ending in a predetermined denouement. Advocates of this theory emphasize the force of religion in the historical development of Greek drama. They tend to ascribe great authority to the source myths, and to see the plots as essentially divine, serving as illustrations of men and women moved about in complex paths like pieces on a chessboard, as willed by fate and the gods. Tragic characters are seen as suffering, but passive rather than active, seldom resisting or defying, helpless victims of fate, whose defects and errors are themselves willed by the gods and hence are without meaningful causal function. Such theorists view ancient conventions—the mask, the chorus, the use of messengers—as fundamental parts of the dramatic experience, and they attempt to preserve and emphasize them in their own productions.

But other theories, other approaches, other interpretations are possible. We cannot hope to achieve general agreement on which method is best. The relevant evidence is scattered, fragmentary, apparently contradictory, and puzzling; even to analyze it in detail would require a large book. But although a theorist may enjoy the luxury of uncertainty and indecision, of the suspension of judgment, the practical director must be decisive and unambiguous. Effective productions of *Oedipus the King* can be developed on various bases, but it is essential that each director define his own point of view with complete clarity. What follows, then, makes no attempt to trace through my own reasoning or my own analysis of the evidence, but simply describes the conclusions which served as the preliminary ground-clearing for planning the production, without any implication that this approach is necessarily right, or even the most practical.

To the Greek of Sophocles' time, the story of Oedipus was history, although from a period unimaginably ancient. In its basic outline, the plot was fixed. But even supposedly factual details were subject to the playwright's control. Thus, at the end of *Oedipus the King*, Creon becomes king without any suggestion that Oedipus's sons have any rights to the throne. In *Oedipus at Colonus*, Theban history has been rewritten, and we discover that a violent struggle has taken place for control of the kingdom (Sophocles' attempt to harmonize these discrepancies is clumsy, confusing, and unconvincing). But the playwright's handling of his characters' motivations, emotions, arguments, and thinking is still freer; Oedipus, Jocasta, Creon, and Teiresias are individual personalities, and the character of each is primarily what Sophocles has chosen to make it: it must be determined from the play itself, not from the legend which served as his source.

The divine machinery was an integral part of the myth; it is de-emphasized in the play. The machinations of the gods are important at four points in the plot. The oracular predictions of Oedipus's fate were necessary to his exposure in infancy, and to his fleeing from Corinth. On his own initiative, Oedipus has asked the advice of Apollo in dealing with the current plague. And the blasphemous attacks on the credibility of oracles by both Oedipus and Jocasta strengthen the case against them and provide the only clear example of guilt on their part, creating a justification, however feeble and incidental, for their ultimate tragedy.

But it is surely significant that of these four points at which the gods are involved in the story, three have occurred before the play begins, two of them in the distant past. Sophocles has reduced divine control, as compared with the source myth, not emphasized. The focus of the play is human. Individualized personalities are presented, complexly blended of faults and virtues, wisdom and folly, pride and humility, affection and hatred. What happens to them is the result of their own natures. If Oedipus (or Laius) had been cooler-headed, even simply better mannered, the initial murder would never have occurred. Oedipus might have avoided his incestuous marriage simply by refusing to marry a woman older than himself, even though the marriage was demanded as a condition of his enthronement. At most, only foreknowledge can be ascribed to the gods; dramaturgically, Oedipus is himself the creator of his fate.

This, then, is a human story. It presents a gracious and regal woman, a statesmanlike king, whose virtues are almost precisely balanced by his faults, yet whose rashness, ungoverned temper, and folly engulf them in ruin. The story like the myth, is dramatic; the characters are real. Each member of the audience can see in himself the same blend of strengths and weaknesses; the theatrical display of the characters' struggles, hopes, and sufferings can evoke intense empathy on the part of the audience, leading to the Aristotelian pattern of pity and fear. This is the experience that the director must struggle to create.

The long stretch of time, nearly two and a half millenniums, between the first production of *Oedipus the King* and today, makes the technical problems at least as difficult as the esthetic. For the modern audience in America, almost every word of the original script must be altered—the play must be translated into contemporary English, if it is to be intelligible. In the same way, the production methods must undergo a technical translation, that is, they must be restated in terms of the theatrical techniques which are available to us today, not in order to alter the experience as Sophocles intended it, but to preserve it. Few of us have a precise copy of an ancient theater for our performance of the play. But even if it were possible to reproduce the original production in every detail, such a copy of ancient techniques would, psychologically and esthetically, constitute almost the extreme falsification of the experience the production was intended to produce in the audience.

Audience attitudes, even the pattern of audience attention, have changed. By definition, a theatrical convention is an unrealistic element which the audience accepts because of its established familiarity, and which consequently receives the least attention. For the ancient audience, the masks, the cothurnus, the choral circle were to be expected, and largely ignored; instead, their attention was focused on those elements in each play which were fresh and new. A modern audience, exposed to an antiquarian copy of such a performance, would respond with a reversed pattern of attention; precisely because they were unfamiliar, these elements would attract major attention, and would distract from the human drama which should stand at the focus of view. And so the play must be handled in modern technical terms.

The most difficult problem concerns the treatment of the chorus. Attempts are sometimes made to define the function of the chorus in Greek drama by means of a simple formula. In fact, the chorus serves uniquely in every play; even in the two related Oedipus plays the choral function varies.

In *Oedipus the King* the chorus is active at approximately twelve points. Five of these consist of choral odes, with the chorus alone on stage; in a sixth, the chorus delivers a brief epilog.

The six other choral passages are in dialog, and involve also the major characters in the play, Jocasta in one scene, Creon in a second, Oedipus and the second messenger in another, and Oedipus alone in the remaining three.

The choral dialogs are a useful part of Sophocles' dramaturgical technique. They provide transitions between isolated scenes involving different sets of characters, and they supply expository information against which the characters can react. Thus, they describe the Oedipus-Creon quarrel to Jocasta, and they report Oedipus's charges to Creon. In other passages, they take part in much the same way as the major characters. They indentify the shepherd of Laius and vouch for his reliability; they react with some spirit to Oedipus's proclamation against the murderer, and give him advice on conducting the investigation. Throughout these passages their responses are individual, not formal or stereotyped. They reply to Creon, and even to Oedipus, with considerable sharpness; they express opinions and attitudes which are at variance with those of the major characters, and they represent a point of view which is individual and their own.

I have used the pronoun "they," but it is clear that in these passages the chorus does not speak as a group. Probably the simplest and most comfortable treatment of the dialog speeches ascribed to "chorus" is to assign them to a single actor. Where successive speeches are not clearly spoken by the same person, they can, if preferred, be given to other individual members of the chorus. But such passages cannot be chanted by the group in unison without seeming ridiculous.

The primary purpose of the odes, during which the chorus is alone on stage, is to express an emotional response, not to carry the plot forward. Five of these passages occur in the play (six, if we include the epilog, which has similar function). There is evidence that these odes were sung, and that they were accompanied by patterned movement which may have approached the pitch of dance. Their function then is essentially musical—they form bridges between key scenes, heightening the emotions, and preparing for later developments.

The director is faced with the practical question of how all these scenes are to be handled. The chorus is present throughout the entire play, but they move into the area of the audience's attention only at intervals. In the ancient theater they were restricted, in this as well as most Greek tragedies, to the orchestra circle, an area clearly distinguished from that occupied by the major actors. Their placement in the modern theater will depend greatly on the architecture of the theater and the design of the scenery, but a sound handling requires that their spatial arrangement match their esthetic function in the play, and their relationships with the other characters. They must be kept in the weaker areas of the stage throughout the passages of dialog, since even when they take part in the discussion they are never at the focus of attention. Within these areas, however, it is important for the director to block them so that they are able to move into stronger positions when, for example, they take part in a free exchange with Oedipus, and then back into weaker positions as a new character enters and the audience's attention is intended to turn more exclusively to the major actors.

During the choral odes, the chorus move at the focus of attention: they must consequently be given stronger positions. However, it seems desirable to maintain the separation of choral area from acting area which was so sharply marked in the ancient theaters. Probably the areas cannot be as clearly divided in the modern theater, but the director should attempt to create a feeling of separation; certainly, the chorus should not swarm over the entire stage, and up to the doors of the palace, even if they are alone on stage.

Probably the ideal treatment of delivery would be to set the odes to music, and have them at least half-sung or chanted. This is a dangerous technique however; the line between effectiveness and absurdity is very narrow. Not only must the music be effective, but it must be written so as not to obscure the words. The choral odes are less denotatively communicative than the dialog, but to reduce their clarity still further would destroy them.

Full choreography is also possible, but even more dangerous. The use of ballet positions, or even the more communicative gestures of modern dance, seems more likely to lead to humor than tragedy. Probably the best handling of choral movement is to design blocking so as to create group patterns of arrangement, without adding emotional gestures or business. Especially if the movements can be motivated, the group shift'ng from a random arrangement to a more orderly one, express'ng tension or agitation by their static and dynamic patterns, the blocking may contribute effectively to the performance without distracting attention from the lines and without falling into bathos or mannered preciosity.

The passages of choral dialog present real human beings; they are not drawn in full detail, but their outlines are individual, not stereotyped. The major characters are equally unique; Oedipus is not "a king," Teiresias is not "a prophet"; even the unnamed messenger from Corinth is a sharply defined idiosyncratic individual. The actors' realization of the characters may be hampered by their unfamiliarity with the Greek style. Since the Renaissance, dramatic characterization has been handled very differently. The kind of introspective self-anaysis expressed in the soliloquies of Hamlet or Antony, the minute detail of modern plays, are not to be found in this script. Sophocles paints individualized portraits, but with broad strokes of the brush; details are highly selected, and many are suggested indirectly.

As a result, actors are likely to feel that Sophocles has underinstructed them, that the script is thin and bare, and that there is little for them to work with. The director must encourage them to analyze the script with the greatest care, in order to discover all the information about their characters that Sophocles has given them—and it is likely to be fuller than appears at first glance. Further, they must be encouraged to enrich and complete the picture, in harmony with that drawn in the script. Creon's coldness is clearly indicated at the end of the play, in the formality with which he treats Oedipus; even his acts of kindness are embedded in an impersonal, legalistic context which dehumanizes them. His defense against the charge of treason is expressed in equally legalistic language; his argument is convincing, but it is based on pride and self-interest, and devoid of any comfortable emotion. The old man from Corinth, who appears only briefly, is a sharply silhouetted and individual figure. His playing with paradox, his sententiousness, his use of cryptic statements, his ready admission that he came in the hope of getting a reward, all create the impression of a self-consciously humorous old country wiseacre. These hints can be amplified by the actors into fully developed portraits.

The key figure is of course Oedipus himself. Wise, foolish, suspicious, hot-headed, affectionate, ruthless, rash and fearful, he is a very human tangle of contradictions. The actors should perhaps be warned against overinterpreting the word "king." His country is the city of Thebes, smaller than any kingdom now in existence. His power is distinctly limited; Creon, Teiresias, the priest, and even the leader of the chorus remind him of his personal and political limitations, advise and argue with him, and defend themselves against him with complete freedom. He is in fact more like the mayor of a small modern city than anyone we might think of as a king.

At the beginning of the play he is seen in his public function. A serious health problem has developed, and like any modern mayor he has sent for advice from the best source, in this case the oracle of Apollo. When confronted with an unsolved murder, he quickly sets the investigation in motion, beginning, again exactly like a modern mayor, with an official proclamation. It is stated in formal legalisms, offering rewards for information and threatening prosecution for the withholding of aid; it is exactly the kind of statement a modern mayor might release to the press in a similar situation. His early investigation might equally well have taken place in the police department of any contemporary town. Clearly Oedipus is a good office-holder, respected but not reverenced.

In emotional terms, the play might be graphed by a descending line. At the beginning Oedipus appears in full authority, concerned by the civic problem but handling it with calm decisiveness and assurance. At the end of the play, he has been reduced to the lowest degradation, blinded, widowed, branded not simply a criminal but a monster of crime, cast out of the country to wander as a beggar. The line is not entirely straight; moments of hope interrupt his growing fear; but the descent is swift and clear. The actor's primary problem is to trace this disintegration, showing a steady alteration in emotion, and making each moment believable.

Sophocles has developed this pattern by a series of short scenes in which Oedipus is contrasted with the other characters, the priest, Teiresias, Creon, Jocasta, the messenger from Corinth, Laius' old herdsman, and finally Creon again, and each brings new information; against these Oedipus reacts, moving step by step along the path toward disintegration.

Oedipus's relation with each character is unique, and the actor must identify and express the various tones. But one aspect of the scenes is especially important: that is, the degree and direction of dominance between the characters. If this quality were graphed, it would also show a descending line, but much less uniform than the emotional pattern. In the opening scene Oedipus is clearly in charge, although it is the priest and the chorus who have sought the confrontation. Oedipus's authority is unchallenged through the first scene with Creon, and then on through his proclamation and the beginning of the discussion with Teiresias. The old prophet challenges Oedipus strongly, although in terms which are ambiguous for Oedipus; he is able to interpret them as evidence of bad temper and a plot against him, rather in their obvious sense. By the end of the scene, Oedipus's authority has been damaged by his violence and loss of control; at the least, he has come to feel threatened by enemies he had not previously suspected.

Creon's defiance of Oedipus in the following scene, and his spirited and convincing defense of himself, throw Oedipus still further off balance, and the combined pleas of Jocasta and the leader of the chorus persuade him to reverse his decision with regard to Creon, even though his beliefs and attitudes have not changed. The decisive and assured leader of the city has been made at least temporarily indecisive, and has lost command of himself and of his political policies.

The conference with Jocasta which follows suggests the basic warmth of their relationship, and reveals a more attractive aspect of Oedipus's personality—elements which the actor must express clearly to the audience. Oedipus's account of his early life, of his past and present fears, and Jocasta's reassurances show him for the first time in a situation in which he is not dominant. It would be excessive to describe him as submissive, and the two relate at levels very close to equality, but, however slightly, it is clear that Jocasta is in charge of the scene, not from any desire to dominate, but from a concern which even in another context might be sensed as maternal.

The scene with the man from Corinth provides a momentary upsurge for Oedipus, a reassurance that his fears are false, although it is significant that the direction of the conversation is controlled not by the king but by the old servant. Then at the revelation that Oedipus had been adopted, his apprehension returns. When Jocasta pleads with him passionately to let the investigation drop, he is able to misinterpret her demands, and brushes them aside: he has become dominant again.

At the beginning of the scene with the herdsman, Oedipus supports his dominance through the intensity of his determination and anger. He presses the old man ruthlessly, even having him tortured when he becomes reluctant to testify. But as Oedipus forces the information from him, each item makes clearer the case against the king. With each one, his command of himself weakens, until finally his self-possession has been utterly destroyed. The herdsman has been fearful, suffering, reluctant, submissive; but in his final speech he suddenly rises to a calm, assured, firm judgment of Oedipus; the king responds in a speech demonstrating his disintegration. The positions of the two have been reversed; it is now the herdsman who is dominant, and the king who is dominated.

The final scene of the play shows Oedipus at the nadir of his life, utterly crushed. Theatrically he stands at the focus of attention, but emotionally he has become subordinate to all of the other characters in the play.

Structurally, then, the play is made up of a series of short scenes in which Oedipus confronts other characters in varying relationships and in various degrees and directions of dominance. The scenes are organized so as to form a pattern. Throughout the sequence, Oedipus moves from ignorance to self-knowledge, from assurance to hysteria, from authority to submission. In most cases, each scene matches the king with one other character; in a few, Jocasta, the choral leader, or some other character also take a significant part.

The expression of this pattern is an important responsibility of the actor who plays the title role. A major directorial problem is to design blocking which will assist him as much as possible. In my own production, this was greatly facilitated by Mr. David's set. Most of his time in working up the design was spent on planning an irregular series of platforms which led from stage-floor level to the entrance of the palace. The arrangement provided for three entrances and multiple paths with steps of varying height, cunningly arranged so that the relative elevation of actors could be altered with great freedom. At the beginning of the Oedipus-Teiresias scene, for instance, Oedipus stood at the edge of the highest platform, as Teiresias was led on from stage left. As Oedipus expressed his gracious formal greeting, a few short steps moved him down level with the prophet, and then another step took him to one level below Teiresias as Oedipus pleaded for his help. As the discussion turned into a quarrel, Oedipus was able to express his assumption of dominance by a single step toward Teiresias which raised him to a higher level, and to facilitate the prophet's momentary rise to dominance by stepping back to one or more levels below him. Similarly, when the old slave was brought on and interrogated, Oedipus was able to move so as to tower over him, or to fall back level with him; and at the end, by a headlong rush across the platforms he moved to a position on the stage floor which assisted the actor in expressing Oedipus's own disintegration, and which left the slave high above him, reinforcing the authority of his final statement. The actors, in other words, were able to play the platforms and steps almost like a musical instrument, producing a constantly changing melody of dominance and submission, as well as other emotional relationships. Obviously very great actors might be able to make such relationships equally clear on a single level, but the assistance which Mr. David gave them by his design was of the greatest value, and made the work of blocking the play much easier.

One minor problem for the actors is the handling of the long speeches in the play. It is a modern convention that people do not talk for long periods without interruption. Ordinary observation proves that that is not correct, and the practice of a thousand playwrights, including Shakespeare and Shaw, demonstrates that the long speech is not necessarily ineffective in the theater. Nevertheless, the modern fashion for something resembling stychomythia may produce a feeling of alarm among the actors when they first read through Sophocles' script.

But even in this play, the impression that the script is loaded with monologs is inaccurate. The speeches vary greatly in length, from a single word to sixty-three lines; their average (in the original Greek, and ignoring the choral odes) is only three lines. In fact, speech length is used with variety and realism; when a character would normally speak at length without interruption, as in Oedipus's official proclamation, he is given time for the message; when fast interchange would be more natural, the dialog is written in short speeches.

With a little encouragement from the director, the actors should be able to take the longer speeches in stride. Tension and interest must not be allowed to sag, and providing continuing excitement in these speeches is a challenge to the actor, but a challenge which is perfectly legitimate and dramaturgically sound, and which he can be expected to meet.

There is only one speech which constitutes a real problem, and that is the account of Jocasta's death and Oedipus's blinding, delivered by the second messenger. Here actor and director run afoul of the Greek convention that violent deaths must not be shown on stage. Even though the rule seems to have been based on the perfectly sound theatrical fact that such deaths can seldom be made convincing, the use of a messenger at this point produces real awkwardness. Before the entrance of the messenger, the tension of the play has been raised to its highest pitch; even with the best reading, the scene seems momentarily to interrupt and delay the progress of the play.

The actor, who has no other lines in the play, is likely to be tempted to try to make the most of his single scene, and the speeches are easy to ham. But the passage is essentially transitional and expository; if the emotions are played to the full, especially if they are reinforced by dramatic pauses, gestures, and physical reactions, the scene can easily become bathetic. Probably the best handling is to instruct the actor to read the lines at top speed, communicating their meaning and maintaining a high level of excitement, but not milking them of every possible drop of emotion.

Every play presents its own problems. *Oedipus the King* sounds a gong from an alien culture and a distant time. And yet Sophocles supports the actors with his superb dramaturgy, with the humanity of his philosophy, and the warmth of his feeling. If the actors can be persuaded to avoid treating the play as a wooden ceremony, and instead to meet it on its own terms, developing an empathic understanding of the roles, and enriching them with their own imaginations, the play can be an unforgettable theatrical and esthetic experience.

Source Materials for *Oedipus the King*

BY THE CRITICS

Ferguson, Francis. *Idea of a Theatre: A Study of Ten Plays*. Princeton: Princeton University Press, 1949, pp. 13–41.

Harshbarger, Karl. "Who Killed Lais?" *Tulane Drama Review* 9 (1965): 120–131.

Hathorn, Richmond Y. "The Existential Oedipus." *Classical Journal* 53 (1958): 223–230.

Lesser, Simon. "Oedipus the King: The Two Dramas, The Two Conflicts." *College English* 29 (December 1967).

O'Brein, Michael J., ed. *Twentieth Century Interpretations of Oedipus Rex*. Englewood Cliffs: Prentice-Hall, 1968.

Paolucci, A. "The Oracles Are Dumb: A Study of the Meaning of Oedipus Rex." *Classical Journal* 58 (1963): 241–247.

Vellacott, Philip. *Sophocles and Oedipus*. University of Michigan Press, 1971.

Woodward, T., ed. *Sophocles: A Collection of Critical Essays.* Englewood Cliffs: Prentice-Hall, 1966.

BY THE DIRECTOR

"Directing the Classics," Author Hopkins, in *Reference Point*, Samuel French, 1948, pp. 27–32.

AUDIO-VISUAL SOURCES

1. *Oedipus Series:* Four 30-minute, color films by Encyclopedia Britannica.
2. *Oedipus the King:* Full length film with Lili Palmer and Orson Wells, by Universal Kinetic.

The costumes of *Hamlet* may confine him to no one particular historical period. Syracuse Repertory Theatre, Syracuse University. Rex Henriot, director; set and costumes by Otto Theurer; starring Michael McGuire.

Robert Vaughn in the role of Hamlet. California State College at Los Angeles. Walter eaver, director; Edward C. Fitzpatrick, Jr., designer; costumes and makeup by Marjorie Smith; lighting by Maris Ubans; associate producers: Louis Gardenmal and Ted Delay.

The King and his Queen prepare for the "play within a play." University of California at Berkeley. William I. Oliver, director.

George Grizzard in the title role of
Hamlet, the modern dress version
performed by the Minnesota
Theatre Company, Tyrone Guthrie,
director; Tanya Moiseiwitch,
designer. (See "Costuming
Hamlet".)

Hamlet done in a constructivist
setting. McNeese State College.

One of the many times Hamlet
considers murdering his uncle,
Claudius. Asolo State Theatre,
Eberle Thomas, director.

Hamlet's strange behavior confuses Ophelia, who clings fearfully to the prince. Wayne State University. Directed by Leonard Leone; setting by William Rowe; costumes by Stephanie Schoelzel; lighting by Gary M. Witt; Ophelia: Michelle Deszeran; Hamlet: Earl D. A. Smith.

Revenge, at first thought sweet, bitterer ere long back on itself recoils.

John Milton

Hamlet

William Shakespeare

Hamlet

Characters   FRANCISCO, *a soldier*
BERNARDO ⎱ *officers*
MARCELLUS ⎰
HORATIO, *friend to* HAMLET
GHOST OF HAMLET'S FATHER
CLAUDIUS, *King of Denmark*
GERTRUDE, *Queen of Denmark and mother of* HAMLET
HAMLET, *son to the former, and nephew to the present, King*
POLONIUS, *Lord Chamberlain*
LAERTES, *son to* POLONIUS
VOLTIMAND ⎱ *courtiers*
CORNELIUS ⎰
OPHELIA, *daughter to* POLONIUS
REYNALDO, *servant to* POLONIUS
ROSENCRANTZ ⎱ *courtiers*
GUILDENSTERN ⎰
PLAYERS
FORTINBRAS, *Prince of Norway*
A CAPTAIN
A GENTLEMAN
TWO CLOWNS, *grave-diggers*
A PRIEST
OSRIC, *a courtier*
ENGLISH AMBASSADORS
LORDS, LADIES, OFFICERS, SOLDIERS, SAILORS, MESSENGERS, *and other* ATTENDANTS

Scene   *The castle of Elsinore in Denmark*

Act One

SCENE ONE

Elsinore. A platform before the castle.
            (FRANCISCO *at his post. Enter to him* BERNARDO)
BERNARDO   Who's there?
FRANCISCO   Nay, answer me: stand, and unfold yourself.
BERNARDO   Long live the king!
FRANCISCO   Bernardo?

BERNARDO   He.

FRANCISCO   You come most carefully upon your hour.

BERNARDO   'Tis now struck twelve; get thee to bed, Francisco.

FRANCISCO   For this relief much thanks: 'tis bitter cold,
     And I am sick at heart.

BERNARDO   Have you had quiet guard?

FRANCISCO   Not a mouse stirring.

BERNARDO   Well, good-night.
     If you do meet Horatio and Marcellus,
     The rivals of my watch, bid them make haste.

FRANCISCO   I think I hear them.—Stand, ho! Who is there?
          (*Enter* HORATIO *and* MARCELLUS)

HORATIO   Friends to this ground.

MARCELLUS   And liegemen to the Dane.

FRANCISCO   Give you good-night.

MARCELLUS   O, farewell, honest soldier:
     Who hath reliev'd you?

FRANCISCO   Bernardo has my place.
     Give you good-night.
          (*Exit*)

MARCELLUS   Holla! Bernardo!

BERNARDO   Say.
     What, is Horatio there?

HORATIO   A piece of him.

BERNARDO   Welcome, Horatio:—welcome, good Marcellus.

MARCELLUS   What, has this thing appear'd again to-night?

BERNARDO   I have seen nothing.

MARCELLUS   Horatio says 'tis but our fantasy,
     And will not let belief take hold of him
     Touching this dreaded sight, twice seen of us:
     Therefore I have entreated him along
     With us to watch the minutes of this night;
     That, if again this apparition come
     He may approve our eyes and speak to it.

HORATIO   Tush, tush, 'twill not appear.

BERNARDO   Sit down awhile,
     And let us once again assail your ears,
     That are so fortified against our story,
     What we two nights have seen.

HORATIO   Well, sit we down,
     And let us hear Bernardo speak of this.

BERNARDO   Last night of all,
     When yon same star that's westward from the pole
     Had made his course to illume that part of heaven
     Where now it burns, Marcellus and myself,
     The bell then beating one,—

MARCELLUS   Peace, break thee off; look where it comes again!
          (*Enter* GHOST, *armed*)

BERNARDO   In the same figure, like the king that's dead.

MARCELLUS   Thou art a scholar; speak to it, Horatio.

BERNARDO   Looks it not like the king? mark it, Horatio.

HORATIO   Most like:—it harrows me with fear and wonder.

BERNARDO   It would be spoke to.

MARCELLUS   Question it, Horatio.

HORATIO   What art thou, that usurp'st this time of night,
    Together with that fair and warlike form
    In which the majesty of buried Denmark
    Did sometimes march? by heaven I charge thee, speak!

MARCELLUS   It is offended.

BERNARDO   See, it stalks away!

HORATIO   Stay! speak, speak! I charge thee, speak!
    (*Exit* GHOST)

MARCELLUS   'Tis gone, and will not answer.

BERNARDO   How now, Horatio! you tremble and look pale:
    Is not this something more than fantasy?
    What think you on't?

HORATIO   Before my God, I might not this believe
    Without the sensible and true avouch
    Of mine own eyes.

MARCELLUS   It it not like the king?

HORATIO   As thou art to thyself:
    Such was the very armor he had on
    When he the ambitious Norway combated;
    So frown'd he once when, in an angry parle,
    He smote the sledded Polacks on the ice.
    'Tis strange.

MARCELLUS   Thus twice before, and just at this dead hour,
    With martial stalk hath he gone by our watch.

HORATIO   In what particular thought to work I know not;
    But, in the gross and scope of my opinion,
    This bodes some strange eruption to our state.

MARCELLUS   Good now, sit down, and tell me, he that knows,
    Why this same strict and most observant watch
    So nightly toils the subject of the land;
    And why such daily cast of brazen cannon,
    And foreign mart for implements of war;
    Why such impress of shipwrights, whose sore task
    Does not divide the Sunday from the week;
    What might be toward, that this sweaty haste
    Doth make the night joint-laborer with the day:
    Who is't that can inform me?

HORATIO   That can I;
    At least, the whisper goes so. Our last king,
    Whose image even but now appear'd to us,
    Was, as you know, by Fortinbras of Norway,
    Thereto prick'd on by a most emulate pride,

Dar'd to the combat; in which our valiant Hamlet,—
For so this side of our known world esteem'd him,—
Did slay this Fortinbras; who, by a seal'd compact,
Well ratified by law and heraldry,
Did forfeit, with his life, all those his lands,
Which he stood seiz'd of, to the conqueror:
Against the which, a moiety competent
Was gagéd by our king; which had return'd
To the inheritance of Fortinbras,
Had he been vanquisher; as by the same cov'nant
And carriage of the article design'd,
His fell to Hamlet. Now, sir, young Fortinbras,
Of unimproved mettle hot and full,
Hath in the skirts of Norway, here and there,
Shark'd up a list of landless resolutes,
For food and diet, to some enterprise
That hath a stomach in't: which is no other,—
As it doth well appear unto our state,—
But to recover of us by strong hand,
And terms compulsatory, those foresaid lands
So by his father lost: and his, I take it,
Is the main motive of our preparations,
The source of this our watch, and the chief head
Of this post-haste and romage in the land.

BERNARDO   I think it be no other, but e'en so:
Well may it sort that this portentous figure
Comes armed through our watch; so like the king
That was and is the question of these wars.

HORATIO   A mote it is to trouble the mind's eye.
In the most high and palmy state of Rome,
A little ere the mightiest Julius fell,
The graves stood tenantless, and the sheeted dead
Did squeak and gibber in the Roman streets:
As, stars with trains of fire and dews of blood,
Disasters in the sun; and the moist star,
Upon whose influence Neptune's empire stands,
Was sick almost to doomsday with eclipse:
And even the like precurse of fierce events,—
As harbingers preceding still the fates,
And prologue to the omen coming on,—
Have heaven and earth together demonstrated
Unto our climature and countrymen.—
But, soft, behold! lo, where it comes again!
        (*Re-enter* GHOST)
I'll cross it, though it blast me.—Stay, illusion!
If thou hast any sound or use of voice,
Speak to me:
If there be any good thing to be done,

That may to thee do ease, and grace to me,
Speak to me:
If thou art privy to thy country's fate,
Which, happily, foreknowing may avoid,
O, speak!
Or if thou has uphoarded in thy life
Extorted treasure in the womb of earth,
For which, they say, you spirits oft walk in death
        (*Cock crows*)
Speak of it:—stay, and speak!—Stop it, Marcellus.

MARCELLUS   Shall I strike at it with my partisan?

HORATIO   Do, if it will not stand.

BERNARDO   'Tis here!

HORATIO   'Tis here!

MARCELLUS   'Tis gone!
        (*Exit* GHOST)
We do it wrong, being so majestical,
To offer it the show of violence;
For it is, as the air, invulnerable,
And our vain blows malicious mockery.

BERNARDO   It was about to speak when the cock crew.

HORATIO   And then it started like a guilty thing
Upon a fearful summons. I have heard,
The cock, that is the trumpet to the morn,
Doth with his lofty and shrill-sounding throat
Awake the god of day; and at his warning,
Whether in sea or fire, in earth or air,
The extravagant and erring spirit hies
To his confine: and of the truth herein
This present object made probation.

MARCELLUS   It faded on the crowing of the cock.
Some say that ever 'gainst that season comes
Wherein our Saviour's birth is celebrated,
The bird of dawning singeth all night long:
And then, they say, no spirit can walk abroad;
The nights are wholesome; then no planets strike,
No fairy takes, nor witch hath power to charm;
So hallow'd and so gracious is the time.

HORATIO   So have I heard, and do in part believe.
But, look, the morn, in russet mantle clad,
Walks o'er the dew of yon high eastern hill:
Break we our watch up: and, by my advice,
Let us impart what we have seen to-night
Unto young Hamlet; for, upon my life,
This spirit, dumb to us, will speak to him:
Do you consent we shall acquaint him with it,
As needful in our loves, fitting our duty?

MARCELLUS   Let's do't, I pray; and I this morning know
Where we shall find him most conveniently.
(*Exeunt*)

SCENE TWO

Elsinore. A room of state in the castle.
(*Enter the* KING, QUEEN, HAMLET, POLONIUS, LAERTES,
VOLTIMAND, CORNELIUS, LORDS, *and* ATTENDANTS)

KING   Though yet of Hamlet our dear brother's death
The memory be green; and that it us befitted
To bear our hearts in grief, and our whole kingdom
To be contracted in one brow of woe;
Yet so far hath discretion fought with nature
That we with wisest sorrow think on him,
Together with remembrance of ourselves.
Therefore our sometime sister, now our queen,
The imperial jointress of this warlike state,
Have we, as 'twere with defeated joy,—
With one auspicious and one dropping eye,
With mirth and funeral, and with dirge in marriage,
In equal scale weighing delight and dole,—
Taken to wife: nor have we herein barr'd
Your better wisdoms, which have freely gone
With this affair along:—for all, our thanks.
Now follows that you know, young Fortinbras,
Holding a weak supposal of our worth,
Or thinking by our late dear brother's death
Our state to be disjoint and out of frame,
Colleagued with the dream of his advantage,
He hath not fail'd to pester us with message,
Importing the surrender of those lands
Lost by his father, with all bonds of law,
To our most valiant brother. So much for him.—
Now for ourself, and for this time of meeting:
Thus much the business is:—we have here writ
To Norway, uncle of young Fortinbras,—
Who, impotent and bed-rid, scarcely hears
Of this his nephew's purpose,—to suppress
His further gait herein; in that the levies,
The lists, and full proportions, are all made
Out of his subject:—and we here despatch
You, good Cornelius, and you, Voltimand,
For bearers of this greeting to old Norway;
Giving to you no further personal power
To business with the king more than the scope
Of these dilated articles allow.
Farewell; and let your haste commend your duty.

CORNELIUS *and* VOLTIMAND   In that and all things will we show our duty.

KING   We doubt it nothing: heartily farewell.

> (*Exeunt* VOLTIMAND *and* CORNELIUS)

And now, Laertes, what's the news with you?
You told us of some suit; what is't, Laertes?
You cannot speak of reason to the Dane,
And lose your voice: what wouldst thou beg, Laertes,
That shall not be my offer, nor thy asking?
The head is not more native to the heart,
The hand more instrumental to the mouth,
Than is the throne of Denmark to thy father.
What wouldst thou have, Laertes?

LAERTES   Dread my lord,
Your leave and favor to return to France;
From whence though willingly I came to Denmark,
To show my duty in your coronation;
Yet now, I must confess, that duty done,
My thoughts and wishes bend again toward France,
And bow them to your gracious leave and pardon.

KING   Have you your father's leave? What says Polonius?

POLONIUS   He hath, my lord, wrung from me my slow leave
By laborsome petition; and at last
Upon his will I seal'd my hard consent:
I do beseech you, give him leave to go.

KING   Take thy fair hour, Laertes; time be thine,
And thy best graces spend it at thy will!—
But now, my cousin Hamlet, and my son,—

HAMLET (*Aside*)   A little more than kin, and less than kind.

KING   How is it that the clouds still hang on you?

HAMLET   Not so, my lord; I am too much i' the sun.

QUEEN   Good Hamlet, cast thy nighted color off,
And let thine eye look like a friend on Denmark.
Do not for ever with thy vailed lids
Seek for thy noble father in the dust:
Thou know'st 'tis common,—all that live must die,
Passing through nature to eternity.

HAMLET   Ay, madam, it is common.

QUEEN   If it be,
Why seems it so particular with thee?

HAMLET   Seems, madam! nay, it is; I know not seems.
'Tis not alone my inky cloak, good mother,
Nor customary suits of solemn black,
Nor windy suspiration of forc'd breath,
No, nor the fruitful river in the eye,
Nor the dejected 'havior of the visage,
Together with all forms, moods, shows of grief,
That can denote me truly: these, indeed, seem;
For they are actions that a man might play:

But I have that within which passeth show;
These but the trappings and the suits of woe.

KING 'Tis sweet and commendable in your nature, Hamlet,
To give these mourning duties to your father:
But, you must know, your father lost a father;
That father lost, lost his; and the survivor bound,
In filial obligation, for some term
To do obsequious sorrow: but to persever
In obstinate condolement is a course
Of impious stubbornness; 'tis unmanly grief:
It shows a will most incorrect to heaven;
A heart unfortified, a mind impatient;
An understanding simple and unschool'd:
For what we know must be, and is as common
As any the most vulgar thing to sense,
Why should we, in our peevish opposition,
Take it to heart? Fie! 'tis a fault to heaven,
A fault against the dead, a fault to nature,
To reason most absurd; whose common theme
Is death of fathers, and who still hath cried,
From the first corse till he that died to-day,
This must be so. We pray you, throw to earth
This unprevailing woe; and think of us
As of a father: for let the world take note
You are the most immediate to our throne;
And with no less nobility of love
Than that which dearest father bears his son
Do I impart toward you. For your intent
In going back to school in Wittenberg,
It is most retrograde to our desire:
And we beseech you bend you to remain
Here, in the cheer and comfort of our eye,
Our chiefest courtier, cousin, and our son.

QUEEN Let not thy mother lose her prayers, Hamlet:
I pray thee, stay with us; go not to Wittenberg.

HAMLET I shall in all my best obey you, madam.

KING Why, 'tis a loving and a fair reply:
Be as ourself in Denmark.—Madam, come;
This gentle and unforc'd accord of Hamlet
Sits smiling to my heart; in grace whereof,
No jocund health that Denmark drinks to-day
But the great cannon to the clouds shall tell;
And the king's rouse the heavens shall bruit again,
Re-speaking earthly thunder. Come away.
        (*Exeunt all but* HAMLET)

HAMLET O, that this too too solid flesh would melt,
Thaw, and resolve itself into a dew!
Or that the Everlasting had not fix'd

His canon 'gainst self-slaughter! O God! O God!
How weary, stale, flat, and unprofitable
Seem to me all the uses of this world!
Fie on't! O fie! 'tis an unweeded garden,
That grows to seed; things rank and gross in nature
Possess it merely. That it should come to this!
But two months dead!—nay, not so much, not two:
So excellent a king; that was, to this,
Hyperion to a satyr: so loving to my mother,
That he might not beteem the winds of heaven
Visit her face too roughly. Heaven and earth!
Must I remember? why, she would hang on him
As if increase of appetite had grown
By what it fed on: and yet, within a month,—
Let me not think on't,—Frailty, thy name is woman!—
A little month; or ere those shoes were old
With which she follow'd my poor father's body
Like Niobe, all tears;—why she, even she,—
O God! a beast, that wants discourse of reason,
Would have mourn'd longer,—married with mine uncle,
My father's brother; but no more like my father
Than I to Hercules: within a month;
Ere yet the salt of most unrighteous tears
Had left the flushing in her galled eyes,
She married:—O, most wicked speed, to post
With such dexterity to incestuous sheets!
It is not, nor it cannot come to good;
But break, my heart,—for I must hold my tongue!
          (*Enter* HORATIO, MARCELLUS, *and* BERNARDO)

HORATIO   Hail to your lordship!
HAMLET   I am glad to see you well:
    Horatio,—or I do forget myself.
HORATIO   That same, my lord, and your poor servant ever.
HAMLET   Sir, my good friend; I'll change that name with you:
    And what make you from Wittenberg, Horatio?—Marcellus?
MARCELLUS   My good lord,—
HAMLET   I am very glad to see you.—Good even, sir.—
    But what, in faith, make you from Wittenberg?
HORATIO   A truant disposition, good my lord.
HAMLET   I would not hear your enemy say so;
    Nor shall you do mine ear that violence,
    To make it truster of your own report
    Against yourself: I know you are no truant.
    But what is your affair in Elsinore?
    We'll teach you to drink deep ere you depart.
HORATIO   My lord, I came to see your father's funeral.
HAMLET   I pray thee, do not mock me, fellow-student;
    I think it was to see my mother's wedding.

HORATIO   Indeed, my lord, it follow'd hard upon.

HAMLET   Thrift, thrift, Horatio! the funeral-bak'd meats
Did coldly furnish forth the marriage tables.
Would I had met my dearest foe in heaven
Ere I had ever seen that day, Horatio!—
My father,—methinks I see my father.

HORATIO   Where, my lord?

HAMLET   In my mind's eye, Horatio.

HORATIO   I saw him once; he was a goodly king.

HAMLET   He was a man, take him for all in all,
I shall not look upon his like again.

HORATIO   My lord, I think I saw him yesternight.

HAMLET   Saw who?

HORATIO   My lord, the king your father.

HAMLET   The king my father!

HORATIO   Season your admiration for awhile
With an attent ear, till I may deliver,
Upon the witness of these gentlemen,
This marvel to you.

HAMLET   For God's love, let me hear.

HORATIO   Two nights together had these gentlemen,
Marcellus and Bernardo, in their watch,
In the dead vast and middle of the night,
Been thus encounter'd. A figure like your father,
Arm'd at all points exactly, cap-a-pe,
Appears before them, and with solemn march
Goes slow and stately by them; thrice he walk'd
By their oppress'd and fear-surprised eyes,
Within his truncheon's length; whilst they, distill'd
Almost to jelly with the act of fear,
Stand dumb, and speak not to him. This to me
In dreadful secrecy impart they did;
And I with them the third night kept the watch:
Where, as they had deliver'd, both in time,
Form of the thing, each word made true and good,
The apparition comes: I knew your father;
These hands are not more like.

HAMLET   But where was this?

MARCELLUS   My lord, upon the platform where we watch'd.

HAMLET   Did you not speak to it?

HORATIO   My lord, I did;
But answer made it none: yet once methought
It lifted up its head, and did address
Itself to motion, like as it would speak:
But even then the morning cock crew loud,
And at the sound it shrunk in haste away,
And vanish'd from our sight.

HAMLET   'Tis very strange.

HORATIO   As I do live, my honor'd lord, 'tis true;
    And we did think it writ down in our duty
    To let you know of it.
HAMLET   Indeed, indeed, sirs, but this troubles me.
    Hold you the watch to-night?
MARCELLUS *and* BERNARDO   We do, my lord.
HAMLET   Arm'd, say you?
MARCELLUS *and* BERNARDO   Arm'd, my lord.
HAMLET   From top to toe?
MARCELLUS *and* BERNARDO   My lord, from head to foot.
HAMLET   Then saw you not his face?
HORATIO   O yes, my lord; he wore his beaver up.
HAMLET   What, look'd he frowningly?
HORATIO   A countenance more in sorrow than in anger.
HAMLET   Pale or red?
HORATIO   Nay, very pale.
HAMLET   And fix'd his eyes upon you?
HORATIO   Most constantly.
HAMLET   I would I had been there.
HORATIO   It would have much amaz'd you.
HAMLET   Very like, very like. Stay'd it long?
HORATIO   While one with moderate haste might tell a hundred.
MARCELLUS *and* BERNARDO   Longer, longer.
HORATIO   Not when I saw't.
HAMLET   His beard was grizzled,—no?
HORATIO   It was, as I have seen it in his life,
    A sable silver'd.
HAMLET   I will watch to-night;
    Perchance 'twill walk again.
HORATIO   I warrant it will.
HAMLET   If it assume my noble father's person
    I'll speak to it, though hell itself should gape
    And bid me hold my peace. I pray you all,
    If you have hitherto conceal'd this sight,
    Let it be tenable in your silence still;
    And whatsoever else shall hap to-night,
    Give it an understanding, but no tongue:
    I will requite your loves. So, fare ye well:
    Upon the platform, 'twixt eleven and twelve,
    I'll visit you.
ALL   Our duty to your honor.
HAMLET   Your loves, as mine to you: farewell.
        (*Exeunt* HORATIO, MARCELLUS, *and* BERNARDO)
    My father's spirit in arms; all is not well;
    I doubt some foul play: would the night were come!
    Till then sit still, my soul: foul deeds will rise,
    Though all the earth o'erwhelm them, to men's eyes.
        (*Exit*)

SCENE THREE

A room in POLONIUS' *house.*
            (*Enter* LAERTES *and* OPHELIA)

LAERTES   My necessaries are embark'd: farewell:
        And, sister, as the winds give benefit,
        And convoy is assistant, do not sleep,
        But let me hear from you.
OPHELIA   Do you doubt that?
LAERTES   For Hamlet, and the trifling of his favor,
        Hold it a fashion and a toy in blood:
        A violet in the youth of primy nature,
        Forward, not permanent, sweet, not lasting,
        The perfume and suppliance of a minute;
        No more.
OPHELIA   No more but so?
LAERTES   Think it no more:
        For nature, crescent, does not grow alone
        In thews and bulk; but as this temple waxes,
        The inward service of the mind and soul
        Grows wide withal. Perhaps he loves you now;
        And now no soil nor cautel doth besmirch
        The virtue of his will: but you must fear,
        His greatness weigh'd, his will is not his own;
        For he himself is subject to his birth:
        He may not, as unvalu'd persons do,
        Carve for himself; for on his choice depends
        The safëty and the health of the whole state;
        And therefore must his choice be circumscrib'd
        Unto the voice and yielding of that body
        Whereof he is the head. Then if he says he loves you,
        It fits your wisdom so far to believe it
        As he in his particular act and place
        May give his saying deed; which is no further
        Than the main voice of Denmark goes withal.
        Then weigh what loss your honor may sustain
        If with too credent ear you list his songs,
        Or lose your heart, or your chaste treasure open
        To his unmaster'd importunity.
        Fear it, Ophelia, fear it, my dear sister;
        And keep within the rear of your affection,
        Out of the shot and danger of desire.
        The chariest maid is prodigal enough
        If she unmask her beauty to the moon:
        Virtue itself scapes not calumnious strokes:
        The canker galls the infants of the spring
        Too oft before their buttons be disclos'd;

And in the morn and liquid dew of youth
Contagious blastments are most imminent.
Be wary, then; best safety lies in fear:
Youth to itself rebels, though none else near.

OPHELIA   I shall the effect of this good lesson keep
As watchman to my heart. But, good my brother,
Do not, as some ungracious pastors do,
Show me the steep and thorny way to heaven;
Whilst like a puff'd and reckless libertine,
Himself the primrose path of dalliance treads,
And recks not his own rede.

LAERTES   O, fear me not.
I stay too long:—but here my father comes.
        (*Enter* POLONIUS)
A double blessing in a double grace;
Occasion smiles upon a second leave.

POLONIUS   Yet here, Laertes! Aboard, aboard, for shame!
The wind sits in the shoulder of your sail,
And you are stay'd for. There,—my blessing with you!
        (*Laying his hand on* LAERTES' *head*)
And these few precepts in thy memory
See thou charácter. Give thy thoughts no tongue,
Nor any unproportion'd thought his act.
Be thou familiar, but by no means vulgar.
The friends thou hast, and their adoption tried,
Grapple them to thy soul with hoops of steel;
But do not dull thy palm with entertainment
Of each new-hatch'd, unfledg'd comrade. Beware
Of entrance to a quarrel; but, being in,
Bear't that the opposèd may beware of thee.
Give every man thine ear, but few thy voice:
Take each man's censure, but reserve thy judgment.
Costly thy habit as thy purse can buy,
But not express'd in fancy; rich, not gaudy:
For the apparel oft proclaims the man;
And they in France of the best rank and station
Are most select and generous chief in that.
Neither a borrower nor a lender be:
For a loan oft loses both itself and friend;
And borrowing dulls the edge of husbandry.
This above all,—to thine own self be true;
And it must follow, as the night the day,
Thou canst not then be false to any man.
Farewell: my blessing season this in thee!

LAERTES   Most humbly do I take my leave, my lord.

POLONIUS   The time invites you; go, your servants tend.

LAERTES   Farewell, Ophelia; and remember well
What I have said to you.

OPHELIA   'Tis in my memory lock'd,
   And you yourself shall keep the key of it.
LAERTES   Farewell. (*Exit*)
POLONIUS   What is't, Ophelia, he hath said to you?
OPHELIA   So please you, something touching the Lord Hamlet.
POLONIUS   Marry, well bethought:
   'Tis told me he hath very oft of late
   Given private time to you; and you yourself
   Have of your audience been most free and bounteous:
   If it be so,—as so 'tis put on me,
   And that in way of caution,—I must tell you,
   You do not understand yourself so clearly
   As it behoves my daughter and your honor.
   What is between you? give me up the truth.
OPHELIA   He hath, my lord, of late made many tenders
   Of his affection to me.
POLONIUS   Affection! pooh! you speak like a green girl,
   Unsifted in such perilous circumstance.
   Do you believe his tenders, as you call them?
OPHELIA   I do not know, my lord, what I should think.
POLONIUS   Marry, I'll teach you: think yourself a baby;
   That you have ta'en these tenders for true pay,
   Which are not sterling. Tender yourself more dearly;
   Or,—not to crack the wind of the poor phrase,
   Wronging it thus,—you'll tender me a fool.
OPHELIA   My lord, he hath impórtun'd me with love
   In honorable fashion.
POLONIUS   Ay, fashion you may call it; go to, go to.
OPHELIA   And hath given countenance to his speech, my lord,
   With almost all the holy vows of heaven.
POLONIUS   Ay, springes to catch woodcocks. I do know,
   When the blood burns, how prodigal the soul
   Lends the tongue vows: these blazes, daughter,
   Giving more light than heat,—extinct in both,
   Even in their promise, as it is a-making,—
   You must not take for fire. From this time
   Be somewhat scanter of your maiden presence;
   Set your entreatments at a higher rate
   Than a command to parley. For Lord Hamlet,
   Believe so much in him, that he is young;
   And with a larger tether may he walk
   Than may be given you: in few, Ophelia,
   Do not believe his vows; for they are brokers,—
   Not of that die which their investments show,
   But mere implorators of unholy suits,
   Breathing like sanctified and pious bawds,
   The better to beguile. This is for all,—
   I would not, in plain terms, from this time forth,

Have you so slander any moment leisure
As to give words or talk with the Lord Hamlet.
Look to't, I charge you; come your ways.
OPHELIA   I shall obey, my lord. (*Exeunt*)

SCENE FOUR

The platform.
                    (*Enter* HAMLET, HORATIO, *and* MARCELLUS)
HAMLET   The air bites shrewdly; it is very cold.
HORATIO   It is a nipping and an eager air.
HAMLET   What hour now?
HORATIO   I think it lacks of twelve.
MARCELLUS   No, it is struck.
HORATIO   Indeed? I heard it not: then it draws near the season
    Wherein the spirit held his wont to walk.
            (*A flourish of trumpets, and ordnance shot off within*)
    What does this mean, my lord?
HAMLET   The king doth wake to-night, and takes his rouse,
    Keeps wassail, and the swaggering upspring reels;
    And, as he drains his draughts of Rhenish down,
    The kettle-drum and trumpet thus bray out
    The triumph of his pledge.
HORATIO   Is it a custom?
HAMLET   Ay, marry, is't:
    But to my mind,—though I am native here,
    And to the manner born,—it is a custom
    More honor'd in the breach than the observance.
    This heavy-headed revel east and west
    Makes us traduc'd and tax'd of other nations:
    They clepe us drunkards, and with swinish phrase
    Soil our addition; and, indeed, it takes
    From our achievements, though perform'd at height,
    The pith and marrow of our attribute.
    So oft it chances in particular men
    That, for some vicious mole of nature in them,
    As in their birth,—wherein they are not guilty,
    Since nature cannot choose his origin,—
    By the o'ergrowth of some complexion,
    Oft breaking down the pales and forts of reason;
    Or by some habit, that too much o'erleavens
    The form of plausive manners;—that these men,—
    Carrying, I say, the stamp of one defect,
    Being nature's livery or fortune's star,—
    Their virtues else,—be they as pure as grace,
    As infinite as man may undergo,—
    Shall in the general censure take corruption

From that particular fault: the dram of evil
Doth all the noble substance of a doubt
To his own scandal.

HORATIO   Look, my lord, it comes!
          (*Enter* GHOST)

HAMLET   Angels and ministers of grace defend us!—
          Be thou a spirit of health or goblin damn'd,
          Bring with thee airs from heaven or blasts from hell.
          Be thy intents wicked or charitable,
          Thou com'st in such a questionable shape
          That I will speak to thee: I'll call thee Hamlet,
          King, father, royal Dane: O, answer me!
          Let me not burst in ignorance; but tell
          Why thy canóniz'd bones, hearsèd in death,
          Have burst their cerements; why the sepulchre,
          Wherein we saw thee quietly in-urn'd,
          Hath op'd his ponderous and marble jaws
          To cast thee up again! What may this mean,
          That thou, dead corse, again in còmplete steel,
          Revisit'st thus the glimpses of the moon,
          Making night hideous and we fools of nature
          So horridly to shake our disposition
          With thoughts beyond the reaches of our souls?
          Say, why is this? wherefore? what should we do?
          (GHOST *beckons* HAMLET)

HORATIO   It beckons you to go away with it,
          As if it some impartment did desire
          To you alone.

MARCELLUS   Look, with what courteous action
          It waves you to a more removed ground:
          But do not go with it.

HORATIO   No, by no means,

HAMLET   It will not speak; then will I follow it.

HORATIO   Do not, my lord.

HAMLET   Why, what should be the fear?
          I do not set my life at a pin's fee;
          And for my soul, what can it do to that,
          Being a thing immortal as itself?
          It waves me forth again;—I'll follow it.

HORATIO   What if it tempt you toward the flood, my lord.
          Or to the dreadful summit of the cliff
          That beetles o'er his base into the sea,
          And there assume some other horrible form,
          Which might deprive your sovereignty of reason,
          And draw you into madness? think of it:
          The very place puts toys of desperation,
          Without more motive, into every brain

That looks so many fathoms to the sea
And hears it roar beneath.
HAMLET   It waves me still.—
Go on; I'll follow thee.
MARCELLUS   You shall not go, my lord.
HAMLET   Hold off your hands.
HORATIO   Be rul'd; you shall not go.
HAMLET   My fate cries out,
And makes each petty artery in this body
As hardy as the Némean lion's nerve.—
           (GHOST *beckons*)
Still am I call'd;—unhand me, gentlemen;—(*Breaking from them*)
By heaven, I'll make a ghost of him that lets me.
I say, away!—Go on; I'll follow thee.
           (*Exeunt* GHOST *and* HAMLET)
HORATIO   He waxes desperate with imagination.
MARCELLUS   Let's follow; 'tis not fit thus to obey him.
HORATIO   Have after.—To what issue will this come?
MARCELLUS   Something is rotten in the state of Denmark.
HORATIO   Heaven will direct it.
MARCELLUS   Nay, let's follow him. (*Exeunt*)

SCENE FIVE

A more remote part of the platform.
           (*Enter* GHOST *and* HAMLET)
HAMLET   Where wilt thou lead me? speak, I'll go no further.
GHOST   Mark me.
HAMLET   I will.
GHOST   My hour is almost come,
When I to sulphurous and tormenting flames
Must render up myself.
HAMLET   Alas, poor ghost!
GHOST   Pity me not, but lend thy serious hearing
To what I shall unfold.
HAMLET   Speak; I am bound to hear.
GHOST   So art thou to revenge, when thou shalt hear.
HAMLET   What?
GHOST   I am thy father's spirit;
Doom'd for a certain term to walk the night,
And, for the day, confin'd to waste in fires
Till the foul crimes done in my days of nature
Are burnt and purg'd away. But that I am forbid
To tell the secrets of my prison-house,
I could a tale unfold whose lightest word
Would harrow up thy soul; freeze thy young blood;
Make thy two eyes, like stars, start from their spheres;

Thy knotted and combined locks to part,
And each particular hair to stand on end,
Like quills upon the fretful porcupine:
But this eternal blazon must not be
To ears of flesh and blood.—List, list, O, list!—
If thou didst ever thy dear father love,—

HAMLET   O God!

GHOST   Revenge his foul and most unnatural murder.

HAMLET   Murder!

GHOST   Murder—most foul, as in the best it is;
But this most foul, strange, and unnatural.

HAMLET   Haste me to know't, that I, with wings as swift
As meditation or the thoughts of love,
May sweep to my revenge.

GHOST   I find thee apt;
And duller shouldst thou be than the fat weed
That rots itself in ease on Lethe wharf,
Wouldst thou not stir in this. Now, Hamlet,
'Tis given out that, sleeping in mine orchard,
A serpent stung me; so the whole ear of Denmark
Is by a forged process of my death
Rankly abus'd: but know, thou noble youth,
The serpent that did sting thy father's life
Now wears his crown.

HAMLET   O my prophetic soul! mine uncle!

GHOST   Ay, that incestuous, that adulterate beast,
With witchcraft of his wit, with traitorous gifts,—
O wicked wit and gifts that have the power
So to seduce!—won to his shameful lust
The will of my most seeming virtuous queen:
O Hamlet, what a falling-off was there!
From me, whose love was of that dignity
That it went hand in hand even with the vow
I made to her in marriage: and to decline
Upon a wretch whose natural gifts were poor
To those of mine!
But virtue, as it never will be mov'd,
Though lewdness court it in a shape of heaven;
So lust, though to a radiant angel link'd,
Will sate itself in a celestial bed
And prey on garbage.
But, soft! methinks I scent the morning air;
Brief let me be.—Sleeping within mine orchard,
My custom always in the afternoon,
Upon my secure hour thy uncle stole,
With juice of cursed hebenon in a vial,
And in the porches of mine ears did pour

The leperous distilment; whose effect
Holds such an enmity with blood of man
That, swift as quicksilver, it courses through
The natural gates and alleys of the body;
And with a sudden vigor it doth posset
And curd, like eager droppings into milk,
The thin and wholesome blood: so did it mine;
And a most instant tetter bark'd about,
Most lazar-like, with vile and loathsome crust,
All my smooth body.
Thus was I, sleeping, by a brother's hand,
Of life, of crown, of queen, at once despatch'd:
Cut off even in the blossoms of my sin,
Unhousel'd, unanointed, unanel'd;
No reckoning made, but sent to my account
With all my imperfections on my head:
O, horrible! O, horrible! most horrible!
If thou hast nature in thee, bear it not;
Let not the royal bed of Denmark be
A couch for luxury and damned incest.
But, howsoever thou pursu'st this act,
Taint not thy mind, nor let thy soul contrive
Against thy mother aught: leave her to heaven,
And to those thorns that in her bosom lodge,
To prick and sting her. Fare thee well at once!
The glowworm shows the matin to be near,
And 'gins to pale his uneffectual fire:
Adieu, adieu! Hamlet, remember me. (*Exit*)

HAMLET   O all you host of heaven! O earth! what else?
And shall I couple hell?—O, fie!—Hold, my heart;
And you, my sinews, grow not instant old,
But bear me stiffly up.—Remember thee!
Ay, thou poor ghost, while memory holds a seat
In this distracted globe. Remember thee!
Yea, from the table of my memory
I'll wipe away all trivial fond recórds,
All saws of books, all forms, all pressures past,
That youth and observation copied there;
And thy commandment all alone shall live
Within the book and volume of my brain,
Unmix'd with baser matter: yes, by heaven.—
O most pernicious woman!
O villain, villain, smiling, damned villain!
My tables,—meet it is I set it down,
That one may smile, and smile, and be a villain;
At least, I am sure, it may be so in Denmark:
       (*Writing*)
So, uncle, there you are. Now to my word;

It is, *Adieu, adieu! remember me:*
I have sworn't.

HORATIO (*Within*)   My lord, my lord,—

MARCELLUS (*Within*)   Lord Hamlet,—

HORATIO (*Within*)   Heaven secure him!

MARCELLUS (*Within*)   So be it!

HORATIO (*Within*)   Illo, ho, ho, my lord!

HAMLET   Hillo, ho, ho, boy! come, bird, come.

(*Enter* HORATIO *and* MARCELLUS)

MARCELLUS   How is't, my noble lord?

HORATIO   What news, my lord?

HAMLET   O, wonderful!

HORATIO   Good my lord, tell it.

HAMLET   No; you'll reveal it.

HORATIO   Not I, my lord, by heaven.

MARCELLUS   Nor I, my lord.

HAMLET   How say you, then; would heart of man once think it?—
But you'll be secret?

HORATIO *and* MARCELLUS   Ay, by heaven, my lord.

HAMLET   There's ne'er a villain dwelling in all Denmark
But he's an arrant knave.

HORATIO   There needs no ghost, my lord, come from the grave
To tell us this.

HAMLET   Why, right; you are i' the right;
And so, without more circumstance at all,
I hold it fit that we shake hands and part:
You, as your business and desire shall point you,—
For every man has business and desire,
Such as it is;—and for mine own poor part,
Look you, I'll go pray.

HORATIO   These are but wild and whirling words, my lord.

HAMLET   I'm sorry they offend you, heartily;
Yes, faith, heartily.

HORATIO   There's no offence, my lord.

HAMLET   Yes, by Saint Patrick, but there is, Horatio,
And much offence too. Touching this vision here,—
It is an honest ghost, that let me tell you:
For you desire to know what is between us,
O'ermaster't as you may. And now, good friends,
As you are friends, scholars, and soldiers,
Give me one poor request.

HORATIO   What is't, my lord? we will.

HAMLET   Never make known what you have seen to-night.

HORATIO *and* MARCELLUS   My lord, we will not.

HAMLET   Nay, but swear't.

HORATIO   In faith,
My lord, not I.

MARCELLUS   Nor I, my lord, in faith.

HAMLET   Upon my sword.

MARCELLUS   We have sworn, my lord, already.

HAMLET   Indeed, upon my sword, indeed.

GHOST (*Beneath*)   Swear.

HAMLET   Ha, ha, boy! say'st thou so? art thou there, truepenny?—
    Come on,—you hear this fellow in the cellarage,—
    Consent to swear.

HORATIO   Propose the oath, my lord.

HAMLET   Never to speak of this that you have seen,
    Swear by my sword.

GHOST (*Beneath*)   Swear.

HAMLET   *Hic et ubique?* then we'll shift our ground.—
    Come hither, gentlemen,
    And lay your hands again upon my sword:
    Never to speak of this that you have heard,
    Swear by my sword.

GHOST (*Beneath*)   Swear.

HAMLET   Well said! old mole! canst work i' the earth so fast?
    A worthy pioneer!—Once more remove, good friends.

HORATIO   O day and night, but this is wondrous strange!

HAMLET   And therefore as a stranger give it welcome.
    There are more things in heaven and earth, Horatio,
    Than are dreamt of in your philosophy.
    But come;—
    Here, as before, never, so help you mercy,
    How strange or odd soe'er I bear myself,—
    As I, perchance, hereafter shall think meet
    To put an antic disposition on,—
    That you, at such times seeing me, never shall,
    With arms encumber'd thus, or this headshake,
    Or by pronouncing of some doubtful phrase,
    As, *Well, well, we know;*—or, *We could, an if we would;*—
    Or, *If we list to speak;*—or, *There be, an if they might;*—
    Or such ambiguous giving out, to note
    That you know aught of me:—this not to do,
    So grace and mercy at your most need help you,
    Swear.

GHOST (*Beneath*)   Swear.

HAMLET   Rest, rest, perturbed spirit!—So, gentlemen,
    With all my love I do commend to you:
    And what so poor a man as Hamlet is
    May do, to express his love and friending to you,
    God willing, shall not lack. Let us go in together;
    And still your fingers on your lips, I pray.
    The time is out of joint:—O cursed spite,
    That ever I was born to set it right!—
    Nay, come, let's go together. (*Exeunt*)

Act Two

SCENE ONE

A room in POLONIUS' *house.*
            (*Enter* POLONIUS *and* REYNALDO)
POLONIUS   Give him this money and these notes, Reynaldo.
REYNALDO   I will, my lord.
POLONIUS   You shall do marvelous wisely, good Reynaldo,
      Before you visit him, to make inquiry
      On his behavior.
REYNALDO   My lord, I did intend it.
POLONIUS   Marry, well said; very well said. Look you, sir,
      Inquire me first what Danskers are in Paris;
      And how, and who, what means, and where they keep,
      What company, at what expense; and finding,
      By this encompassment and drift of question,
      That they do know my son, come you more nearer
      Than your particular demands will touch it:
      Take you, as 'twere, some distant knowledge of him;
      As thus, *I know his father and his friends,*
      And in part him;—do you mark this, Reynaldo?
REYNALDO   Ay, very well, my lord.
POLONIUS   *And in part him;*—*but,* you may say, *not well:*
      But if't be he I mean, he's very wild;
      Addicted so and so; and there put on him
      What forgeries you please; marry, none so rank
      As may dishonor him; take heed of that;
      But, sir, such wanton, wild, and usual slips
      As are companions noted and most known
      To youth and liberty.
REYNALDO   As gaming, my lord.
POLONIUS   Ay, or drinking, fencing, swearing, quarreling,
      Drabbing:—you may go so far.
REYNALDO   My lord, that would dishonor him.
POLONIUS   Faith, no; as you may season it in the charge.
      You must not put another scandal on him,
      That he is open to incontinency;
      That's not my meaning: but breathe his faults so quaintly
      That they may seem the taints of liberty;
      The flash and outbreak of a fiery mind;
      A savageness in unreclaimed blood,
      Of general assault.
REYNALDO   But, my good lord,—
POLONIUS   Wherefore should you do this?
REYNALDO   Ay, my lord,
      I would know that.
POLONIUS   Marry, sir, here's my drift;

And I believe it is a fetch of warrant:
You laying these slight sullies on my son,
As 'twere a thing a little soil'd i' the working,
Mark you,
Your party in converse, him you would sound,
Having ever seen in the prenominate crimes
The youth you breathe of guilty, be assur'd
He closes with you in this consequence;
Good sir, or so; or *friend,* or *gentleman,*—
According to the phrase or the addition
Of man and country.

REYNALDO   Very good, my lord.

POLONIUS   And then, sir, does he this,—he does,—
What was I about to say?—By the mass, I was
About to say something:—where did I leave?

REYNALDO   At *closes in the consequence,*
At *friend or so,* and *gentleman.*

POLONIUS   At—closes in the consequence,—ay, marry;
He closes with you thus:—*I know the gentleman;*
I saw him yesterday, or t'other day,
Or then, or then; with such, or such; and, as you say,
There was he gaming; there o'ertook in's rouse;
There falling out at tennis: or perchance,
I saw him enter such a house of sale,—
Videlicet, a brothel,—or so forth.—
See you now;
Your bait of falsehood takes this carp of truth:
And thus do we of wisdom and of reach,
With windlasses, and with assays of bias,
By indirections find directions out:
So, by my former lecture and advice,
Shall you my son. You have me, have you not?

REYNALDO   My lord, I have.

POLONIUS   God b' wi' you; fare you well.

REYNALDO   Good my lord!

POLONIUS   Observe his inclination in yourself.

REYNALDO   I shall, my lord.

POLONIUS   And let him ply his music.

REYNALDO   Well, my lord.

POLONIUS   Farewell!
        (*Exit* REYNALDO)
        (*Enter* OPHELIA)
How now, Ophelia! what's the matter?

OPHELIA   Alas, my lord, I have been so affrighted!

POLONIUS   With what, i' the name of God?

OPHELIA   My lord, as I was sewing in my chamber,
Lord Hamlet,—with his doublet all unbrac'd;
No hat upon his head; his stockings foul'd,
Ungarter'd, and down-gyved to his ankle;

Pale as his shirt; his knees knocking each other;
And with a look so piteous in purport
As if he had been loosed out of hell
To speak of horrors,—he comes before me.

POLONIUS   Mad for thy love?

OPHELIA   My lord, I do not know;
But truly I do fear it.

POLONIUS   What said he?

OPHELIA   He took me by the wrist, and held me hard;
Then goes he to the length of all his arm;
And with his other hand thus o'er his brow,
He falls to such perusal of my face
As he would draw it. Long stay'd he so;
At last,—a little shaking of mine arm,
And thrice his head thus waving up and down,—
He rais'd a sigh so piteous and profound
That it did seem to shatter all his bulk
And end his being; that done, he lets me go:
And, with his head over his shoulder turn'd,
He seem'd to find his way without his eyes;
For out o' doors he went without their help,
And to the last bended their light on me.

POLONIUS   Come, go with me: I will go seek the king.
This is the very ecstasy of love;
Whose violent property fordoes itself,
And leads the will to desperate undertakings,
As oft as any passion under heaven
That does afflict our nature. I am sorry,—
What, have you given him any hard words of late?

OPHELIA   No, my good lord; but, as you did command,
I did repel his letters, and denied
His access to me.

POLONIUS   That hath made him mad.
I am sorry that with better heed and judgment
I had not quoted him: I fear'd he did but trifle,
And meant to wreck thee; but, beshrew my jealousy!
It seems it is as proper to our age
To cast beyond ourselves in our opinions
As it is common for the younger sort
To lack discretion. Come, go we to the king:
This must be known; which, being kept close, might move
More grief to hide than hate to utter love.
            (*Exeunt*)

SCENE TWO

A room in the castle.
            (*Enter* KING, QUEEN, ROSENCRANTZ, GUILDENSTERN, *and*
            ATTENDANTS)

KING   Welcome, dear Rosencrantz and Guildenstern!
    Moreover that we much did long to see you,
    The need we have to use you did provoke
    Our hasty sending. Something have you heard
    Of Hamlet's transformation; so I call it,
    Since nor the exterior nor the inward man
    Resembles that it was. What it should be,
    More than his father's death, that thus hath put him
    So much from the understanding of himself,
    I cannot dream of: I entreat you both,
    That being of so young days brought up with him,
    And since so neighbor'd to his youth and humor,
    That you vouchsafe your rest here in our court
    Some little time: so by your companies
    To draw him on to pleasures, and to gather,
    So much as from occasion you may glean,
    Whether aught, to us unknown, afflicts him thus,
    That, open'd, lies within our remedy.
QUEEN   Good gentlemen, he hath much talk'd of you;
    And sure I am two men there are not living
    To whom he more adheres. If it will please you
    To show us so much gentry and good-will
    As to expend your time with us awhile,
    For the supply and profit of our hope,
    Your visitation shall receive such thanks
    As fits a king's remembrance.
ROSENCRANTZ   Both your majesties
    Might, by the sovereign power you have of us,
    Put your dread pleasures more into command
    Than to entreaty.
GUILDENSTERN   We both obey,
    And here give up ourselves, in the full bent,
    To lay our service freely at your feet,
    To be commanded.
KING   Thanks, Rosencrantz and gentle Guildenstern.
QUEEN   Thanks, Guildenstern and gentle Rosencrantz:
    And I beseech you instantly to visit
    My too-much-changed son.—Go, some of you,
    And bring these gentlemen where Hamlet is.
GUILDENSTERN   Heavens make our presence and our practices
    Pleasant and helpful to him!
QUEEN   Ay, amen!
        (*Exeunt* ROSENCRANTZ, GUILDENSTERN, *and some*
        ATTENDANTS)
        (*Enter* POLONIUS)
POLONIUS   The ambassadors from Norway, my good lord,
    Are joyfully return'd.
KING   Thou still has been the father of good news.

POLONIUS   Have I, my lord? Assure you, my good liege,
    I hold my duty, as I hold my soul,
    Both to my God and to my gracious king:
    And I do think,—or else this brain of mine
    Hunts not the trail of policy so sure
    As it hath us'd to do,—that I have found
    The very cause of Hamlet's lunacy.
KING   O, speak of that; that do I long to hear.
POLONIUS   Give first admittance to the ambassadors;
    My news shall be the fruit to that great feast.
KING   Thyself do grace to them, and bring them in.
       (*Exit* POLONIUS)
    He tells me, my sweet queen, that he hath found
    The head and source of all your son's distemper.
QUEEN   I doubt it is no other but the main,—
    His father's death and our o'erhasty marriage.
KING   Well, we shall sift him.
      (*Re-enter* POLONIUS, *with* VOLTIMAND *and* CORNELIUS)
      Welcome, my good friends!
    Say, Voltimand, what from our brother Norway?
VOLTIMAND   Most fair return of greetings and desires.
    Upon our first, he sent out to suppress
    His nephew's levies; which to him appear'd
    To be a preparation 'gainst the Polack;
    But, better look'd into, he truly found
    It was against your highness: whereat griev'd,—
    That so his sickness, age, and impotence
    Was falsely borne in hand,—sends out arrests
    On Fortinbras; which he, in brief, obeys;
    Receives rebuke from Norway; and, in fine,
    Makes vows before his uncle never more
    To give the assay of arms against your majesty.
    Whereon old Norway, overcome with joy,
    Gives him three thousand crowns in annual fee;
    And his commission to employ those soldiers,
    So levied as before, against the Polack:
    With an entreaty, herein further shown, (*gives a paper*)
    That it might please you to give quiet pass
    Through your dominions for this enterprise,
    On such regards of safety and allowance
    As therein are set down.
KING   It likes us well;
    And at our more consider'd time we'll read,
    Answer, and think upon this business.
    Meantime we thank you for your well-took labor:
    Go to your rest; at night we'll feast together:
    Most welcome home!
      (*Exeunt* VOLTIMAND *and* CORNELIUS)

POLONIUS   This business is well ended.—
My liege, and madam,—to expostulate
What majesty should be, what duty is,
Why day is day, night night, and time is time,
Were nothing but to waste night, day, and time.
Therefore, since brevity is the soul of wit,
And tediousness the limbs and outward flourishes,
I will be brief:—your noble son is mad:
Mad call I it; for to define true madness,
What is't but to be nothing else but mad?
But let that go.
QUEEN   More matter with less art.
POLONIUS   Madam, I swear I use no art at all.
That he is mad, 'tis true 'tis pity;
And pity 'tis 'tis true: a foolish figure;
But farewell it, for I will use no art.
Mad let us grant him, then: and now remains
That we find out the cause of this effect;
Or rather say, the cause of this defect,
For this effect defective comes by cause:
Thus it remains, and the remainder thus.
Perpend.
I have a daughter,—have whilst she is mine,—
Who, in her duty and obedience, mark,
Hath given me this: now gather, and surmise
        (*Reads*)
To the celestial, and my soul's idol, the most beautified Ophelia,—
That's an ill phrase, a vile phrase,—*beautified* is a vile phrase: but you
shall hear. Thus:
        (*Reads*)
In her excellent white bosom, these, &c.
QUEEN   Came this from Hamlet to her?
POLONIUS   Good madam, stay a while; I will be faithful.
        (*Reads*)
        Doubt thou the stars are fire;
            Doubt that the sun doth move;
        Doubt truth to be a liar;
            But never doubt I love.
    O dear Ophelia, I am ill at these numbers,
    I have not art to reckon my groans: but that I love
            thee best, O most best, believe it. Adieu.
        Thine evermore, most dear lady, whilst this machine is to him,
                                                        Hamlet
This, in obedience, hath my daughter show'd me:
And more above, hath his solicitings,
As they fell out by time, by means, and place,
All given to mine ear.
KING   But how hath she
Receiv'd his love?

POLONIUS   What do you think of me?

KING   As of a man faithful and honorable.

POLONIUS   I would fain prove so. But what might you think,
When I had seen this hot love on the wing,—
As I perceiv'd it, I must tell you that,
Before my daughter told me,—what might you,
Or my dear majesty your queen here, think,
If I had play'd the desk or table-book;
Or given my heart a winking, mute and dumb;
Or look'd upon this love with idle sight;—
What might you think? No, I went round to work,
And my young mistress thus I did bespeak:
Lord Hamlet is a prince out of thy sphere;
This must not be: and then I precepts gave her,
That she should lock herself from his resort,
Admit no messengers, receive no tokens.
Which done, she took the fruits of my advice;
And he, repulsed,—a short tale to make,—
Fell into a sadness; then into a fast;
Thence to a watch; thence into a weakness;
Thence to a lightness; and, by this declension,
Into the madness wherein now he raves
And all we wail for.

KING   Do you think 'tis this?

QUEEN   It may be, very likely.

POLONIUS   Hath there been such a time,—I'd fain know that,—
That I have positively said, *'Tis so,*
When it prov'd otherwise?

KING   Not that I know.

POLONIUS   Take this from this, if this be otherwise: (*Pointing to his head and*
        shoulder)
If circumstances lead me, I will find
Where truth is hid, though it were hid indeed
Within the center.

KING   How may we try it further?

POLONIUS   You know, sometimes he walks for hours together
Here in the lobby.

QUEEN   So he does, indeed.

POLONIUS   At such a time I'll loose my daughter to him:
Be you and I behind an arras then;
Mark the encounter: if he love her not,
And be not from his reason fall'n thereon,
Let me be no assistant for a state,
But a keep a farm and carters.

KING   We will try it.

QUEEN   But look, where sadly the poor wretch comes reading.

POLONIUS   Away, I do beseech you, both away:
I'll board him presently:—O, give me leave.

(*Exeunt* KING, QUEEN, *and* ATTENDANTS)
(*Enter* HAMLET, *reading*)
How does my good Lord Hamlet?

HAMLET   Well, God-a-mercy.

POLONIUS   Do you know me, my lord?

HAMLET   Excellent, excellent well; you're a fishmonger.

POLONIUS   Not I, my lord.

HAMLET   Then I would you were so honest a man.

POLONIUS   Honest, my lord!

HAMLET   Ay, sir; to be honest, as this world goes, is to be one man picked out of ten thousand.

POLONIUS   That's very true, my lord.

HAMLET   For if the sun breed maggots in a dead dog, being a god kissing carrion,—Have you a daughter?

POLONIUS   I have, my lord.

HAMLET   Let her not walk i' the sun: conception is a blessing; but not as your daughter may conceive: friend, look to't.

POLONIUS   How say you by that?—(*Aside*) Still harping on my daughter:— yet he knew me not at first; he said I was a fishmonger: he is far gone, far gone: and truly in my youth I suffered much extremity for love; very near this. I'll speak to him again.—What do you read, my lord?

HAMLET   Words, words, words.

POLONIUS   What is the matter, my lord?

HAMLET   Between who?

POLONIUS   I mean, the matter that you read, my lord.

HAMLET   Slanders, sir: for the satirical slave says here that old men have gray beards; that their faces are wrinkled; their eyes purging thick amber and plum-tree gum; and that they have a plentiful lack of wit, together with most weak hams: all which, sir, though I most powerfully and potently believe, yet I hold it not honesty to have it thus set down; for you yourself, sir, should be old as I am, if, like a crab, you could go backward.

POLONIUS (*Aside*)   Though this be madness, yet there is method in't.—Will you walk out of the air, my lord?

HAMLET   Into my grave?

POLONIUS   Indeed, that is out o' the air.—(*Aside*) How pregnant sometimes his replies are! a happiness that often madness hits on, which reason and sanity could not so prosperously be delivered of. I will leave him, and suddenly contrive the means of meeting between him and my daughter.— More honorable lord, I will most humbly take my leave of you.

HAMLET   You cannot, sir, take from me anything that I will more willingly part withal,—except my life, except my life, except my life.

POLONIUS   Fare you well, my lord.

HAMLET   These tedious old fools!
(*Enter* ROSENCRANTZ *and* GUILDENSTERN)

POLONIUS   You go to seek the Lord Hamlet; there he is.

ROSENCRANTZ (*To* POLONIUS)   God save you, sir! (*Exit* POLONIUS)

GUILDENSTERN   Mine honored lord!

ROSENCRANTZ   My most dear lord!

HAMLET   My excellent good friends! How dost thou, Guildenstern? Ah,
Rosencrantz? Good lads, how do ye both?

ROSENCRANTZ   As the indifferent children of the earth.

GUILDENSTERN   Happy in that we are not over-happy; on fortune's cap we
are not the very button.

HAMLET   Nor the soles of her shoe?

ROSENCRANTZ   Neither, my lord.

HAMLET   Then you live about her waist, or in the middle of her favors?

GUILDENSTERN   Faith, her privates we.

HAMLET   In the secret parts of fortune? O, most true; she is a strumpet.
What's the news?

ROSENCRANTZ   None, my lord, but that the world's grown honest.

HAMLET   Then is doomsday near: but your news is not true. Let me question
more in particular: what have you, my good friends, deserved at the
hands of fortune, that she sends you to prison hither?

GUILDENSTERN   Prison, my lord!

HAMLET   Denmark's a prison.

ROSENCRANTZ   Then is the world one.

HAMLET   A goodly one; in which there are many confines, wards, and dun-
geons, Denmark being one o' the worst.

ROSENCRANTZ   We think not so, my lord.

HAMLET   Why, then, 'tis none to you; for there is nothing either good or bad,
but thinking makes it so: to me it is a prison.

ROSENCRANTZ   Why, then, your ambition makes it one; 'tis too narrow for
your mind.

HAMLET   O God, I could be bounded in a nutshell, and count myself a king
of infinite space, were it not that I have bad dreams.

GUILDENSTERN   Which dreams, indeed, are ambition; for the very substance
of the ambitious is merely the shadow of a dream.

HAMLET   A dream itself is but a shadow.

ROSENCRANTZ   Truly, and I hold ambition of so airy and light a quality that
it is but a shadow's shadow.

HAMLET   Then are our beggars bodies, and our monarchs and outstretched
heroes the beggars' shadows. Shall we to the court? for, by my fay, I
cannot reason.

ROSENCRANTZ and GUILDENSTERN   We'll wait upon you.

HAMLET   No such matter: I will not sort you with the rest of my servants;
for, to speak to you like an honest man, I am most dreadfully attended.
But, in the beaten way of friendship, what make you at Elsinore?

ROSENCRANTZ   To visit you, my lord; no other occasion.

HAMLET   Beggar that I am, I am even poor in thanks; but I thank you: and
sure, dear friends, my thanks are too dear a halfpenny. Were you not
sent for? Is it your own inclining? Is it a free visitation? Come, deal justly
with me: come, come; nay, speak.

GUILDENSTERN   What should we say, my lord?

HAMLET   Why, anything—but to the purpose. You were sent for; and there
is a kind of confession in your looks, which your modesties have not craft

enough to color: I know the good king and queen have sent for you.

ROSENCRANTZ   To what end, my lord?

HAMLET   That you must teach me. But let me conjure you, by the rights of
our fellowship, by the consonancy of our youth, by the obligation of
our ever-preserved love, and by what more dear a better proposer could
charge you withal, be even and direct with me, whether you were sent
for or no?

ROSENCRANTZ   What say you? (*To* GUILDENSTERN)

HAMLET (*Aside*)   Nay, then, I have an eye of you.—If you love me, hold
not off.

GUILDENSTERN   My lord, we were sent for.

HAMLET   I will tell you why; so shall my anticipation prevent your discovery,
and your secrecy to the king and queen moult no feather. I have of late,—
but wherefore I know not,—lost all my mirth, forgone all custom of
exercises; and, indeed, it goes so heavily with my disposition that this
goodly frame, the earth, seems to me a sterile promontory; this most
excellent canopy, the air, look you, this brave o'erhanging firmament,
this majestical roof fretted with golden fire,—why, it appears no other
thing to me than a foul and pestilent congregation of vapors. What a piece
of work is man! How noble in reason! how infinite in faculties! in form
and moving, how express and admirable! in action, how like an angel!
in apprehension, how like a god! the beauty of the world! the paragon of
animals! And yet, to me, what is this quintessence of dust? man delights not
me; no, nor woman neither, though by your smiling you seem to say so.

ROSENCRANTZ   My lord, there was no such stuff in my thoughts.

HAMLET   Why did you laugh, then, when I said, *Man delights not me?*

ROSENCRANTZ   To think, my lord, if you delight not in man, what lenten entertainment the players shall receive from you: we coted them on the way;
and hither are they coming, to offer you service.

HAMLET   He that plays the king shall be welcome,—his majesty shall have
tribute of me; the adventurous knight shall use his foil and target; the
lover shall not sigh gratis; the humorous man shall end his part in peace;
the clown shall make those laugh whose lungs are tickled o' the sere; and
the lady shall say her mind freely, or the blank verse shall halt for't.—
What players are they?

ROSENCRANTZ   Even those you were wont to take delight in,—the tragedians
of the city.

HAMLET   How chances it they travel? their residence, both in reputation and
profit, was better both ways.

ROSENCRANTZ   I think their inhibition comes by the means of the late innovation.

HAMLET   Do they hold the same estimation they did when I was in the city?
Are they so followed?

ROSENCRANTZ   No, indeed, they are not.

HAMLET   How comes it? do they grow rusty?

ROSENCRANTZ   Nay, their endeavor keeps in the wonted pace; but there is,
sir, an aery of children, little eyases, that cry out on the top of question,
and are most tyrannically clapped for't: these are now the fashion; and
so berattle the common stages,—so they call them,—that many wearing
rapiers are afraid of goose-quills, and dare scarce come thither.

HAMLET   What, are they children? who maintains 'em? how are they escoted? Will they pursue the quality no longer than they can sing? will they not say afterwards, if they should grow themselves to common players,—as it is most like, if their means are not better,—their writers do them wrong, to make them exclaim against their own succession?

ROSENCRANTZ   Faith, there has been much to do on both sides; and the nation holds it no sin to tarre them to controversy: there was for awhile no money bid for argument, unless the poet and the player went to cuffs in the question.

HAMLET   Is't possible?

GUILDENSTERN   O, there has been much throwing about of brains.

HAMLET   Do the boys carry it away?

ROSENCRANTZ   Ay, that they do, my lord; Hercules and his load too.

HAMLET   It is not strange; for mine uncle is king of Denmark, and those that would make mouths at him while my father lived, give twenty, forty, fifty, an hundred ducats a-piece for his picture in little. 'Sblood, there is something in this more than natural, if philosophy could find it out.
   (*Flourish of trumpets within*)

GUILDENSTERN   There are the players.

HAMLET   Gentlemen, you are welcome to Elsinore. Your hands, come: the appurtenance of welcome is fashion and ceremony: let me comply with you in this garb; lest my extent to the players, which, I tell you, must show fairly outward, should more appear like entertainment than yours. You are welcome: but my uncle-father and aunt-mother are deceived.

GUILDENSTERN   In what, my dear lord?

HAMLET   I am but mad north-north-west: when the wind is southerly I know a hawk from a handsaw.
   (*Enter* POLONIUS)

POLONIUS   Well be with you, gentlemen!

HAMLET   Hark you, Guildenstern;—and you too;—at each ear a hearer: that great baby you see there is not yet out of his swathing-clouts.

ROSENCRANTZ   Happily he's the second time come to them: for they say an old man is twice a child.

HAMLET   I will prophesy he comes to tell me of the players; mark it.—You say right, sir: o' Monday morning; 'twas so indeed.

POLONIUS   My lord, I have news to tell you.

HAMLET   My lord, I have news to tell you. When Roscius was an actor in Rome,—

POLONIUS   The actors are come hither, my lord.

HAMLET   Buzz, buzz!

POLONIUS   Upon mine honor,—

HAMLET   Then came each actor on his ass,—

POLONIUS   The best actors in the world, either for tragedy, comedy, history, pastoral, pastoral-comical, historical-pastoral, tragical-historical, tragical-comical-historical-pastoral, scene individable, or poem unlimited: Seneca cannot be too heavy nor Plautus too light. For the law of writ and the liberty, these are the only men.

HAMLET   O Jephthah, judge of Israel, what a treasure hadst thou!

POLONIUS   What a treasure had he, my lord?

HAMLET   Why—

> One fair daughter and no more,
> The which he loved passing well.

POLONIUS (*Aside*)   Still on my daughter.

HAMLET   Am I not i' the right, old Jephthah?

POLONIUS   If you call me Jephthah, my lord, I have a daughter that I love
passing well.

HAMLET   Nay, that follows not.

POLONIUS   What follows, then, my lord?

HAMLET   Why—

> As by lot, God wot,

and then, you know,

> It came to pass, as most like it was—,

the first row of the pious chanson will show you more; for look where
my abridgement comes.

> (*Enter four or five* PLAYERS)

You are welcome, masters; welcome, all:—I am glad to see thee well:—
welcome, good friends.—O, my old friend! Thy face is valanced since I
saw thee last; comest thou to beard me in Denmark?—What, my young
lady and mistress! By'r lady, your ladyship is nearer heaven than when
I saw you last, by the altitude of a chopine. Pray God, your voice, like a
piece of uncurrent gold, be not cracked within the ring.—Masters, you are
all welcome. We'll e'en to't like French falconers, fly at anything we see:
we'll have a speech straight: come, give us a taste of your quality; come,
a passionate speech.

1ST PLAYER   What speech, my lord?

HAMLET   I heard thee speak me a speech once,— but it was never acted; or, if
it was, not above once; for the play, I remember, pleased not the million;
'twas caviare to the general: but it was,—as I received it, and others
whose judgments in such matters cried in the top of mine,—an excellent
play, well digested in the scenes, set down with as much modesty as cunning. I remember, one said there were no sallets in the lines to make the
matter savory, nor no matter in the phrase that might indite the author
of affectation; but called it an honest method, as wholesome as sweet,
and by very much more handsome than fine. One speech in it I chiefly
loved: 'twas Æneas' tale to Dido; and thereabout of it especially where
he speaks of Priam's slaughter: if it live in your memory, begin at this
line;—let me see, let me see:—
The rugged Pyrrhus, like the Hyrcanian beast,
—it is not so:—it begins with Pyrrhus:—
The rugged Pyrrhus,—he whose sable arms,
Black as his purpose, did the night resemble
When he lay couched in the ominous horse,—
Hath now this dread and black complexion smear'd
With heraldry more dismal; head to foot
Now is he total gules; horridly trick'd
With blood of fathers, mothers, daughters, sons,
Bak'd and impasted with the parching streets,

That lend a tyrannous and damned light
To their vile murders: roasted in wrath and fire,
And thus o'er-sized with coagulate gore,
With eyes like carbuncles, the hellish Pyrrhus
Old grandsire Priam seeks.—
So proceed you.

POLONIUS 'Fore God, my lord, well spoken, with good accent and good discretion.

1ST PLAYER Anon he finds him
Striking too short at Greeks; his antique sword,
Rebellious to his arm, lies where it falls,
Repugnant to command: unequal match'd,
Pyrrhus at Priam drives; in rage strikes wide;
But with the whiff and wind of his fell sword
The unnerved father falls. Then senseless Ilium,
Seeming to feel this blow, with flaming top
Stoops to his base; and with a hideous crash
Takes prisoner Pyrrhus' ear: for, lo! his sword,
Which was declining on the milky head
Of reverend Priam, seem'd i' the air to stick:
So, as painted tyrant, Pyrrhus stood;
And, like a neutral to his will and matter,
Did nothing.
But as we often see, against some storm,
A silence in the heavens, the rack stand still,
The blood winds speechless, and the orb below
As hush as death, anon the dreadful thunder
Doth rend the region; so, after Pyrrhus' pause,
A roused vengeance sets him new a-work;
And never did the Cyclops' hammers fall
On Mars his armor, forg'd for proof eterne,
With less remorse than Pyrrhus' bleeding sword
Now falls on Priam.—
Out, out, thou strumpet, Fortune! All you gods,
In general synod, take away her power;
Break all the spokes and fellies from her wheel,
And bowl the round knave down the hill of heaven,
As low as to the fiends!

POLONIUS This is too long.

HAMLET It shall to the barber's, with your beard.—Pr'ythee, say on.—He's
for a jig, or a tale of bawdry, or he sleeps:—say on; come to Hecuba.

1ST PLAYER But who, O, who had seen the mobled queen,—

HAMLET *The mobled queen?*

POLONIUS That's good; *mobled queen* is good.

1ST PLAYER Run barefoot up and down, threatening the flames
With bissom rheum; a clout upon that head
Where late the diadem stood; and, for a robe,
About her lank and all o'er-teemed loins,

A blanket, in the alarm of fear caught up;—
Who this had seen, with tongue in venom steep'd,
'Gainst Fortune's state would treason have pronounc'd:
But if the gods themselves did see her then,
When she saw Pyrrhus make malicious sport
In mincing with his sword her husband's limbs,
The instant burst of clamor that she made,—
Unless things mortal move them not at all,—
Would have made milch the burning eyes of heaven,
And passion in the gods.

POLONIUS   Look, whether he has not turn'd his color, and has tears in's
eyes.—Pray you, no more.

HAMLET   'Tis well; I'll have thee speak out the rest soon.—Good my lord,
will you see the players well bestowed? Do you hear, let them be well
used; for they are the abstracts and brief chronicles of the time; after
your death you were better have a bad epitaph than their ill report while
you live.

POLONIUS   My lord, I will use them according to their desert.

HAMLET   Odd's bodikin, man, better: use every man after his desert, and who
should scape whipping? Use them after your own honor and dignity:
the less they deserve the more merit is in your bounty. Take them in.

POLONIUS   Come, sirs.

HAMLET   Follow him, friends: we'll hear a play to-morrow.
        (*Exit* POLONIUS *with all the* PLAYERS *but the* FIRST)
Dost thou hear me, old friend; can you play the Murder of Gonzago?

1ST PLAYER   Ay, my lord.

HAMLET   We'll ha't to-morrow night. You could, for a need, study a speech
of some dozen or sixteen lines which I would set down and insert in't?
could you not?

1ST PLAYER   Ay, my lord.

HAMLET   Very well.—Follow that lord; and look you mock him not.
        (*Exit* FIRST PLAYER)
—My good friends (*to* ROSENCRANTZ *and* GUILDENSTERN) I'll leave you
till night: you are welcome to Elsinore.

ROSENCRANTZ   Good my lord!
        (*Exeunt* ROSENCRANTZ *and* GUILDENSTERN)

HAMLET   Ay, so God b' wi' ye!—Now I am alone.
O, what a rogue and peasant slave am I!
Is it not monstrous that this player here,
But in a fiction, in a dream of passion,
Could force his soul so to his own conceit
That from her working all his visage wan'd;
Tears in his eyes, distraction in's aspéct,
A broken voice, and his whole function suiting
With forms to his conceit? And all for nothing!
For Hecuba?
What's Hecuba to him or he to Hecuba,
That he should weep for her? What would he do,

Had he the motive and the cue for passion
That I have? He would drown the stage with tears,
And cleave the general ear with horrid speech;
Make mad the guilty, and appal the free;
Confound the ignorant, and amaze, indeed,
The very faculties of eyes and ears.
Yet I,
A dull and muddy-mettled rascal, peak,
Like John-a-dreams, unpregnant of my cause,
And can say nothing; no, not for a king
Upon whose property and most dear life
A damn'd defeat was made. Am I a coward?
Who calls me villain? breaks my pate across?
Plucks off my beard and blows it in my face?
Tweaks me by the nose? gives me the lie i' the throat,
As deep as to the lungs? who does me this, ha?
'Swounds, I should take it: for it cannot be
But I am pigeon-liver'd, and lack gall
To make oppression bitter; or ere this
I should have fatted all the region kites
With this slave's offal:—bloody, bawdy villain!
Remorseless, treacherous, lecherous, kindless villain!
O, vengeance!
Why, what an ass am I! This is most brave,
That I, the son of a dear father murder'd,
Prompted to my revenge by heaven and hell,
Must, like a whore, unpack my heart with words,
And fall a-cursing like a very drab,
A scullion!
Fie upon't, foh!—About, my brain! I have heard
That guilty creatures, sitting at a play,
Have by the very cunning of the scene
Ben struck so to the soul that presently
They have proclaim'd their malefactions;
For murder, though it have no tongue, will speak
With most miraculous organ. I'll have these players
Play something like the murder of my father
Before mine uncle: I'll observe his looks;
I'll tent him to the quick: if he but blench,
I know my course. The spirit that I have seen
May be the devil: and the devil hath power
To assume a pleasing shape; yea, and perhaps
Out of my weakness and my melancholy,—
As he is very potent with such spirits,—
Abuses me to damn me: I'll have grounds
More relative than this:—the play's the thing
Wherein I'll catch the conscience of the king. (*Exit*)

Act Three

SCENE ONE

A room in the castle.

(*Enter* KING, QUEEN, POLONIUS, OPHELIA, ROSENCRANTZ, *and* GUILDENSTERN)

KING   And can you, by no drift of circumstance,
     Get from him why he puts on this confusion,
     Grating so harshly all his days of quiet
     With turbulent and dangerous lunacy?
ROSENCRANTZ   He does confess he feels himself distracted;
     But from what cause he will by no means speak.
GUILDENSTERN   Nor do we find him forward to be sounded;
     But, with a crafty madness, keeps aloof
     When we would bring him on to some confession
     Of his true state.
QUEEN   Did he receive you well?
ROSENCRANTZ   Most like a gentleman.
GUILDENSTERN   But with much forcing of his disposition.
ROSENCRANTZ   Niggard of question; but, of our demands,
     Most free in his reply.
QUEEN   Did you assay him
     To any pastime?
ROSENCRATZ   Madam, it so fell out that certain players
     We o'er-raught on the way: of these we told him;
     And there did seem in him a kind of joy
     To hear of it: they are about the court;
     And, as I think, they have already order
     This night to play before him.
POLONIUS   'Tis most true:
     And he beseech'd me to entreat your majesties
     To hear and see the matter.
KING   With all my heart, and it doth much content me
     To hear him so inclin'd.
     Good gentlemen, give him a further edge,
     And drive his purpose on to these delights.
ROSENCRANTZ   We shall, my lord. (*Exeunt* ROSENCRANTZ *and* GUILDENSTERN)
KING   Sweet Gertrude, leave us too;
     For we have closely sent for Hamlet hither
     That he, as 'twere by accident, may here
     Affront Ophelia:
     Her father and myself,—lawful espials,—
     Will so bestow ourselves that, seeing, unseen,
     We may of their encounter frankly judge;
     And gather by him, as he is behav'd,

If't be the affliction of his love or no
That thus he suffers for.

QUEEN   I shall obey you:—
    And for your part, Ophelia, I do wish
    That your good beauties be the happy cause
    Of Hamlet's wildness: so shall I hope your virtues
    Will bring him to his wonted way again,
    To both your honors.

OPHELIA   Madam, I wish it may.
          (*Exit* QUEEN)

POLONIUS   Ophelia, walk you here.—Gracious, so please you,
    We will bestow ourselves.—(*To* OPHELIA) Read on this book;
    That show of such an exercise may color
    Your loneliness.—We are oft to blame in this,—
    'Tis too much prov'd,—that with devotion's visage
    And pious action we do sugar o'er
    The devil himself.

KING (*Aside*)   O, 'tis too true!
    How smart a lash that speech doth give my conscience!
    The harlot's cheek, beautied with plastering art,
    Is not more ugly to the thing that helps it
    Than is my deed to my most painted word:
    O heavy burden!

POLONIUS   I hear him coming: let's withdraw, my lord.
          (*Exeunt* KING *and* POLONIUS)
          (*Enter* HAMLET)

HAMLET   To be, or not to be,—that is the question:—
    Whether 'tis nobler in the mind to suffer
    The slings and arrows of outrageous fortune,
    Or to take arms against a sea of troubles,
    And by opposing end them?—To die,—to sleep,—
    No more; and by a sleep to say we end
    The heart-ache and the thousand natural shocks
    That flesh is heir to,—'tis a consummation
    Devoutly to be wish'd. To die,—to sleep;—
    To sleep! perchance to dream:—ay, there's the rub;
    For in that sleep of death what dreams may come,
    When we have shuffled off this mortal coil,
    Must give us pause: there's the respect
    That makes calamity of so long life;
    For who would bear the whips and scorns of time,
    The oppressor's wrong, the proud man's contumely,
    The pangs of déspis'd love, the law's delay,
    The insolence of office, and the spurns
    That patient merit of the unworthy takes,
    When he himself might his quietus make
    With a bare bodkin? who would fardels bear,
    To grunt and sweat under a weary life,

But that the dread of something after death,—
The undiscover'd country, from whose bourn
No traveler returns,—puzzles the will,
And makes us rather bear those ills we have
Than to fly to others that we know not of?
Thus conscience does make cowards of us all;
And thus the native hue of resolution
Is sicklied o'er with the pale cast of thought;
And enterprises of great pith and moment,
With this regard, their currents turn awry,
And lose the name of action.—Soft you now!
The fair Ophelia.—Nymph, in thy orisons
Be all my sins remember'd.

OPHELIA   Good my lord,
How does your honor for this many a day?

HAMLET   I humbly thank you; well, well, well.

OPHELIA   My lord, I have remembrances of yours,
That I have longed long to re-deliver;
I pray you, now receive them.

HAMLET   No, not I;
I never gave you aught.

OPHELIA   My honor'd lord, you know right well you did;
And with them, words of so sweet breath compos'd
As made the things more rich: their perfume lost,
Take these again; for to the noble mind
Rich gifts wax poor when givers prove unkind.
There, my lord.

HAMLET   Ha, ha! are you honest?

OPHELIA   My lord?

HAMLET   Are you fair?

OPHELIA   What means your lordship?

HAMLET   That if you be honest and fair, your honesty should admit no discourse to your beauty.

OPHELIA   Could beauty, my lord, have better commerce than with honesty?

HAMLET   Ay, truly; for the power of beauty will sooner transform honesty from what it is to a bawd than the force of honesty can translate beauty into his likeness: this was sometime a paradox, but now the time gives it proof. I did love you once.

OPHELIA   Indeed, my lord, you made me believe so.

HAMLET   You should not have believed me; for virtue cannot so inoculate our old stock but we shall relish of it: I loved you not.

OPHELIA   I was the more deceived.

HAMLET   Get thee to a nunnery: why wouldst thou be a breeder of sinners? I am myself indifferent honest; but yet I could accuse me of such things that it were better my mother had not borne me: I am very proud, revengeful, ambitious; with more offences at my beck than I have thoughts to put them in, imagination to give them shape, or time to act them in. What should such fellows as I do crawling between heaven and earth?

We are arrant knaves, all; believe none of us. Go thy ways to a nunnery.
Where's your father?

OPHELIA   At home, my lord.

HAMLET   Let the doors be shut upon him, that he may play the fool nowhere
but in's own house. Farewell.

OPHELIA   O, help him, you sweet heavens!

HAMLET   If thou dost marry, I'll give thee this plague for thy dowry,—be thou
as chaste as ice, as pure as snow, thou shalt not escape calumny. Get
thee to a nunnery, go: farewell. Or, if thou wilt needs marry, marry a
fool; for wise men know well enough what monsters you make of them.
To a nunnery, go; and quickly too. Farewell.

OPHELIA   O heavenly powers, restore him!

HAMLET   I have heard of your paintings too, well enough; God has given you
one face and you make yourselves another: you jig, you amble, and
you lisp, and nickname God's creatures, and make your wantonness
your ignorance. Go to, I'll no more on't; it hath made me mad. I say,
we will have no more marriages: those that are married already, all but
one, shall live; the rest shall keep as they are. To a nunnery, go. (*Exit*)

OPHELIA   O, what a noble mind is here o'erthrown!
The courtier's, soldier's, scholar's eye, tongue, sword:
The expectancy and rose of the fair state,
The glass of fashion and the mould of form,
The observ'd of all observers,—quite, quite down!
And I, of ladies most deject and wretched
That suck'd the honey of his music vows,
Now see that noble and most sovereign reason,
Like sweet bells jangled, out of tune and harsh;
That unmatch'd form and feature of blown youth
Blasted with ecstasy: O, woe is me,
To have seen what I have seen, see what I see!
(*Re-enter* KING *and* POLONIUS)

KING   Love! his affections do not that way tend;
Nor what he spake, though it lack'd form a little,
Was not like madness. There's something in his soul
O'er which his melancholy sits on brood;
And I do doubt the hatch and the disclose
Will be some danger: which for to prevent,
I have in quick determination
Thus set it down:—he shall with speed to England
For the demand of our neglected tribute:
Haply, the seas and countries different,
With variable objects, shall expel
This something-settled matter in his heart;
Whereon his brains still beating puts him thus
From fashion of himself. What think you on't?

POLONIUS   It shall do well: but yet do I believe
The origin and commencement of his grief
Sprung from neglected love.—How now, Ophelia!

You need not tell us what Lord Hamlet said;
We heard it all.—My lord, do as you please;
But if you hold it fit, after the play,
Let his queen mother all alone entreat him
To show his grief: let her be round with him;
And I'll be plac'd, so please you, in the ear
Of all their conference. If she finds him not,
To England send him; or confine him where
Your wisdom best shall think.

KING   It shall be so:
Madness in great ones must not unwatch'd go. (*Exeunt*)

SCENE TWO

A hall in the castle.
                    (*Enter* HAMLET *and certain* PLAYERS)

HAMLET   Speak the speech, I pray you, as I pronounced it to you, trippingly
on the tongue: but if you mouth it, as many of your players do, I had as
lief the town-crier spoke my lines. Nor do not saw the air too much with
your hand, thus; but use all gently: for in the very torrent, tempest, and,
as I may say, the whirlwind of passion, you must acquire and beget a
temperance that may give it smoothness. O, it offends me to the soul, to
hear a robustious periwig-pated fellow tear a passion to tatters, to very
rags, to split the ears of the groundlings, who, for the most part, are
capable of nothing but inexplicable dumb shows and noise: I could have
such a fellow whipped for o'erdoing Termagant; it out-herods Herod:
pray you, avoid it.

1ST PLAYER   I warrant your honor.

HAMLET   Be not too tame neither, but let your own discretion be your tutor:
suit the action to the word, the word to the action; with this special observance, that you o'erstep not the modesty of nature: for anything so
overdone is from the purpose of playing, whose end, both at the first and
now, was and is, to hold, as 'twere, the mirror up to nature; to show virtue
her own feature, scorn her own image, and the very age and body of the
time his form and pressure. Now, this overdone or come tardy off, though
it make the unskilful laugh, cannot but make the judicious grieve; the
censure of the which one must, in your allowance, o'erweigh a whole
theater of others. O, there be players that I have seen play,—and heard
others praise, and that highly,—not to speak it profanely, that, neither
having the accent of Christians, nor the gait of Christian, pagan, nor man,
have so strutted and bellowed that I have thought some of nature's journey-
men had made men, and not made them well, they imitated humanity so
abominably.

1ST PLAYER   I hope we have reformed that indifferently with us, sir.

HAMLET   O, reform it altogether. And let those that play your clowns speak no
more than is set down for them: for there be of them that will themselves
laugh, to set on some quantity of barren spectators to laugh too; though,
in the meantime, some necessary question of the play be then to be con-

sidered: that's villainous, and shows a most pitiful ambition in the fool
that uses it. Go, make you ready.

(*Exeunt* PLAYERS)

(*Enter* POLONIUS, ROSENCRANTZ, *and* GUILDENSTERN)

How now, my lord! will the king hear this piece of work?

POLONIUS   And the queen, too, and that presently.

HAMLET   Bid the players make haste.

(*Exit* POLONIUS)

Will you two help to hasten them?

ROSENCRANTZ *and* GUILDENSTERN   We will, my lord. (*Exeunt*)

HAMLET   What, ho, Horatio! (*Enter* HORATIO)

HORATIO   Here, sweet lord, at your service.

HAMLET   Horatio, thou art e'en as just a man
As e'er my conversation cop'd withal.

HORATIO   O, my dear lord,—

HAMLET   Nay, do not think I flatter;
For what advancement may I hope from thee,
That no revénue hast, but thy good spirits,
To feed and clothe thee? Why should the poor be flatter'd?
No, let the candied tongue lick ábsurd pomp;
And crook the pregnant hinges of the knee
Where thrift may follow fawning. Dost thou hear?
Since my dear soul was mistress of her choice,
And could of men distinguish, her election
Hath seal'd thee for herself: for thou hast been
As one, in suffering all, that suffers nothing;
A man that Fortune's buffets and rewards
Hast ta'en with equal thanks: and bless'd are those
Whose blood and judgment are so well commingled
That they are not a pipe for Fortune's finger
To sound what stop she please. Give me that man
That is not passion's slave, and I will wear him
In my heart's core, ay, in my heart of heart,
As I do thee.—Something too much of this.—
There is a play to-night before the king;
One scene of it comes near the circumstance
Which I have told thee of my father's death:
I pr'ythee, when thou see'st that act a-foot,
Even with the very comment of thy soul
Observe mine uncle: if this his occulted guilt
Do not itself unkennel in one speech,
It is a damned ghost that we have seen;
And my imaginations are as foul
As Vulcan's stithy. Give him heedful note:
For I mine eyes will rivet to his face;
And, after, we will both our judgments join
In censure of his seeming.

HORATIO   Well, my lord:

If he steal aught the whilst this play is playing,
And scape detecting, I will pay the theft.
HAMLET   They are coming to the play; I must be idle:
Get you a place.
(*Danish march. A flourish. Enter* KING, QUEEN,
POLONIUS, OPHELIA, ROSENCRANTZ, GUILDENSTERN, *and
others*)
KING   How fares our cousin Hamlet?
HAMLET   Excellent, i'faith; of the chameleon's dish: I eat the air, promise-
crammed: you cannot feed capons so.
KING   I have nothing with this answer, Hamlet; these words are not mine.
HAMLET   No, nor mine now. (*To* POLONIUS) My lord, you played once i'the
university, you say?
POLONIUS   That did I, my lord, and was accounted a good actor.
HAMLET   And what did you enact?
POLONIUS   I did enact Julius Cæsar: I was killed i' the Capitol; Brutus
killed me.
HAMLET   It was a brute part of him to kill so capital a calf there.—Be the
players ready.
ROSENCRANTZ   Ay, my lord; they stay upon your patience.
QUEEN   Come hither, my good Hamlet, sit by me.
HAMLET   No, good mother, here's metal more attractive.
POLONIUS   O, ho! do you mark that? (*To the* KING)
HAMLET   Lady, shall I lie in your lap? (*Lying down at* OPHELIA's *feet*)
OPHELIA   No, my lord.
HAMLET   I mean, my head upon your lap?
OPHELIA   Ay, my lord.
HAMLET   Do you think I meant country matters?
OPHELIA   I think nothing, my lord.
HAMLET   That's a fair thought to lie between maids' legs.
OPHELIA   What is, my lord?
HAMLET   Nothing.
OPHELIA   You are merry, my lord.
HAMLET   Who, I?
OPHELIA   Ay, my lord.
HAMLET   O, your only jig-maker. What should a man do but be merry? for,
look you, how cheerfully my mother looks, and my father died within's
two hours.
OPHELIA   Nay, 'tis twice two months, my lord.
HAMLET   So long? Nay, then, let the devil wear black, for I'll have a suit of
sables. O heavens! die two months ago, and not forgotten yet? Then there's
hope a great man's memory may outlive his life half a year: but, by'r
lady, he must build churches, then; or else shall he suffer not thinking on,
with the hobby-horse, whose epitaph is, *For, O, for, O, the hobby-horse
is forgot.*
(*Trumpets sound. The dumb show enters*)
(*Enter a* KING *and a* QUEEN, *very lovingly; the* QUEEN
embracing him and he her. She kneels, and makes show

of protestation unto him. He takes her up, and declines
his head upon her neck: lays him down upon a bank of
flowers: she, seeing him asleep, leaves him. Anon comes
in a fellow, takes off his crown, kisses it, and pours
poison in the KING'S *ears, and exit. The* QUEEN *returns;*
finds the KING *dead, and makes passionate action. The*
POISONER, *with some two or three* MUTES, *comes in again,*
seeming to lament with her. The dead body is carried
away. The POISONER *woos the* QUEEN *with gifts: she*
seems loth and unwilling awhile, but in the end ac-
cepts his love)
    (*Exeunt*)

OPHELIA   What means this, my lord?
HAMLET   Marry, this is miching mallecho; it means mischief.
OPHELIA   Belike this show imports the argument of the play.
    (*Enter* PROLOGUE)
HAMLET   We shall know by this fellow: the players cannot keep counsel;
    they'll tell all.
OPHELIA   Will he tell us what this show meant?
HAMLET   Ay, or any show that you'll show him: be not you ashamed to show,
    he'll not shame to tell you what it means.
OPHELIA   You are naught, you are naught: I'll mark the play.
PROLOGUE   *For us, and for our tragedy,*
        Here stooping to your clemency,
        We beg your hearing patiently.
HAMLET   Is this a prologue, or the posy of a ring?
OPHELIA   'Tis brief, my lord.
HAMLET   As woman's love.
    (*Enter a* KING *and a* QUEEN)
PROLOGUE KING   Full thirty times hath Phœbus' cart gone round
    Neptune's salt wash and Tellus' orbed ground,
    And thirty dozen moons with borrow'd sheen
    About the world have times twelve thirties been,
    Since love our hearts, and Hymen did our hands
    Unite commutual in most sacred bands.
PROLOGUE QUEEN   So many journeys may the sun and moon
    Make us again count o'er ere love be done!
    But, woe is me, you are so sick of late,
    So far from cheer and from your former state
    That I distrust you. Yet, though I distrust,
    Discomfort you, my lord, it nothing must:
    For women's fear and love holds quantity,
    In neither aught, or in extremity.
    Now, what my love is, proof hath made you know;
    And as my love is siz'd, my fear is so:
    Where love is great, the littlest doubts are fear;
    Where little fears grow great, great love grows there.
PROLOGUE KING   Faith, I must leave thee, love, and shortly too;

My operant powers their functions leave to do:
And thou shalt live in this fair world behind,
Honor'd, belov'd; and haply one as kind
For husband shalt thou,—
PROLOGUE QUEEN   O, confound the rest!
Such love must needs be treason in my breast:
In second husband let me be accurst!
None wed the second but who kill'd the first.
HAMLET (*Aside*)   Wormwood, wormwood.
PROLOGUE QUEEN   The instances that second marriage move
Are base respects of thrift, but none of love:
A second time I kill my husband, dead,
When second husband kisses me in bed.
PROLOGUE KING   I do believe you think what now you speak;
But what we do determine oft we break.
Purpose is but the slave to memory;
Of violent birth, but poor validity:
Which now, like fruit unripe, sticks on the tree;
But fall unshaken when they mellow be.
Most necessary 'tis that we forget
To pay ourselves what to ourselves is debt:
What to ourselves in passion we propose,
The passion ending, doth the purpose lose.
The violence of either grief or joy
Their own enactures with themselves destroy:
Where joy most revels grief doth most lament;
Grief joys, joy grieves, on slender accident.
This world is not for aye; nor 'tis not strange
That even our loves should with our fortunes change;
For 'tis a question left us yet to prove
Whether love lead fortune or else fortune love.
The great man down, you mark his favorite flies;
The poor advanc'd makes friends of enemies.
And hitherto doth love on fortune tend:
For who not needs shall never lack a friend;
And who in want a hollow friend doth try,
Directly seasons him his enemy.
But, orderly to end where I begun,—
Our wills and fates do so contráry run
That our devices still are overthrown;
Our thoughts are ours, their ends none of our own:
So think thou wilt no second husband wed;
But die thy thoughts when thy first lord is dead.
PROLOGUE QUEEN   Nor earth to me give food, nor heaven light!
Sport and repose lock from me day and night!
To desperation turn my trust and hope!
An anchor's cheer in prison be my scope!
Each opposite, that blanks the face of joy,

Meet what I would have well, and it destroy!
Both here and hence, pursue me lasting strife,
If, once a widow, ever I be wife!
HAMLET   If she should break it now! (*To* OPHELIA)
PROLOGUE KING   'Tis deeply sworn. Sweet, leave me here awhile;
My spirits grow dull, and fain I would beguile
The tedious day with sleep. (*Sleeps*)
PROLOGUE QUEEN   Sleep rock thy brain,
And never come mischance between us twain! (*Exit*)
HAMLET   Madam, how like you this play?
QUEEN   The lady doth protest too much, methinks.
HAMLET   O, but she'll keep her word.
KING   Have you heard the argument? Is there no offence in't?
HAMLET   No, no, they do but jest, poison in jest; no offence i' the world.
KING   What do you call the play?
HAMLET   The Mouse-trap. Marry, how? Tropically. This play is the image of
a murder done in Vienna: Gonzago is the duke's name: his wife Baptista:
you shall see anon; 'tis a knavish piece of work: but what o' that? your
majesty, and we that have free souls, it touches us not: let the galled
jade wince, our withers are unwrung.
(*Enter* LUCIANUS)
This is one Lucianus, nephew to the king.
OPHELIA   You are a good chorus, my lord.
HAMLET   I could interpret between you and your love, if I could see the
puppets dallying.
OPHELIA   You are keen, my lord, you are keen.
HAMLET   It would cost you a groaning to take off my edge.
OPHELIA   Still better, and worse.
HAMLET   So you must take your husbands.—Begin, murderer; pox, leave thy
damnable faces and begin. Come:—*The croaking raven doth bellow for
revenge.*
LUCIANUS   Thoughts black, hands apt, drugs fit and time agreeing;
Confederate season, else no creature seeing;
Thou mixture rank, of midnight weeds collected,
With Hecate's ban thrice blasted, thrice infected,
Thy natural magic and dire property
On wholesome life usurp immediately.
(*Pours the poison into the sleeper's ears*)
HAMLET   He poisons him i' the garden for's estate. His name's Gonzago: the
story is extant, and writ in choice Italian: you shall see anon how the
murderer gets the love of Gonzago's wife.
OPHELIA   The king rises.
HAMLET   What, frighted with false fire!
QUEEN   How fares my lord?
POLONIUS   Give o'er the play.
KING   Give me some light:—away!
ALL   Lights, lights, lights! (*Exeunt all but* HAMLET *and* HORATIO)
HAMLET   Why, let the stricken deer go weep,

The hart ungalled play;
For some must watch, while some must sleep:
So runs the world away.—
Would not this, sir, and a forest of feathers,
If the rest of my fortunes turn Turk with me,
With two Provencial roses on my razed shoes,
Get me a fellowship in a cry of players, sir?

HORATIO   Half a share.

HAMLET   A whole one, I.

For thou dost know, O Damon dear,
This realm dismantled was
Of Jove himself; and now reigns here
A very, very—pajock.

HORATIO   You might have rhymed.

HAMLET   O good Horatio, I'll take the ghost's word for a thousand pound,
Didst perceive?

HORATIO   Very well, my lord.

HAMLET   Upon the talk of the poisoning,—

HORATIO   I did very well note him.

HAMLET   Ah, ha!—Come, some music! come, the recorders!—
For if the king like not the comedy,
Why, then, belike,—he likes it not, perdy. Come, some music!

(*Re-enter* ROSENCRANTZ *and* GUILDENSTERN)

GUILDENSTERN   Good my lord, vouchsafe me a word with you.

HAMLET   Sir, a whole history.

GUILDENSTERN   The king, sir,—

HAMLET   Ay, sir, what of him?

GUILDENSTERN   Is, in his retirement, marvelous distempered.

HAMLET   With drink, sir!

GUILDENSTERN   No, my lord, rather with choler.

HAMLET   Your wisdom should show itself more richer to signify this to his
doctor; for, for me to put him to his purgation would perhaps plunge him
into far more choler.

GUILDENSTERN   Good my lord, put your discourse into some frame, and start
not so wildly from my affair.

HAMLET   I am tame, sir:—pronounce.

GUILDENSTERN   The queen, your mother, in most great affliction of spirit, hath
sent me to you.

HAMLET   You are welcome.

GUILDENSTERN   Nay, good my lord, this courtesy is not of the right breed. If it
shall please you to make me a wholesome answer. I will do your mother's
commandment: if not, your pardon and my return shall be the end of my
business.

HAMLET   Sir, I cannot.

GUILDENSTERN   What, my lord?

HAMLET   Make you a wholesome answer; my wit's diseas'd: but, sir, such
answer as I can make, you shall command; or, rather, as you say, my
mother: therefore no more, but to the matter: my mother, you say,—

ROSENCRANTZ   Then thus she says: your behavior hath struck her into amazement and admiration.

HAMLET   O wonderful son, that can so astonish a mother!—But is there no sequel at the heels of this mother's admiration?

ROSENCRANTZ   She desires to speak with you in her closet ere you go to bed.

HAMLET   We shall obey, were she ten times our mother. Have you any further trade with us?

ROSENCRANTZ   My lord, you once did love me.

HAMLET   So I do still, by these pickers and stealers.

ROSENCRANTZ   Good, my lord, what is your cause of distemper? you do, surely, bar the door upon your own liberty if you deny your griefs to your friend.

HAMLET   Sir, I lack advancement.

ROSENCRANTZ   How can that be, when you have the voice of the king himself for your succession in Denmark?

HAMLET   Ay, but *While the grass grows,*—the proverb is something musty.
    (*Re-enter the* PLAYERS, *with recorders*)
    O, the recorders:—let me see one.—To withdraw with you:—why do you go about to recover the wind of me, as if you would drive me into a toil?

GUILDENSTERN   O, my lord, if my duty be too bold, my love is too unmannerly.

HAMLET   I do not well understand that. Will you play upon this pipe?

GUILDENSTERN   My lord, I cannot.

HAMLET   I pray you.

GUILDENSTERN   Believe me, I cannot.

HAMLET   I do beseech you.

GUILDENSTERN   I know no touch of it, my lord.

HAMLET   'Tis as easy as lying: govern these ventages with your finger and thumb, give it breath with your mouth, and it will discourse most eloquent music. Look you, these are the stops.

GUILDENSTERN   But these cannot I command to any utterance of harmony; I have not the skill.

HAMLET   Why, look you now, how unworthy a thing you make of me! You would play upon me; you would seem to know my stops; you would pluck out the heart of my mystery; you would sound me from my lowest note to the top of my compass: and there is much music, excellent voice, in this little organ; yet cannot you make it speak. 'Sblood, do you think that I am easier to be played on than a pipe? Call me what instrument you will, though you can fret me you cannot play upon me.
    (*Enter* POLONIUS)
    God bless you, sir!

POLONIUS   My lord, the queen would speak with you, and presently.

HAMLET   Do you see yonder cloud that's almost in shape of a camel?

POLONIUS   By the mass, and 'tis like a camel indeed.

HAMLET   Methinks it is like a weasel.

POLONIUS   It is backed like a weasel.

HAMLET   Or like a whale?

POLONIUS   Very like a whale.

HAMLET   Then will I come to my mother by and by.—They fool me to the top of my bent.—I will come by and by.

POLONIUS   I will say so.

HAMLET   By and by is easily said.
    (*Exit* POLONIUS)
  Leave me, friends.
    (*Exeunt* ROSENCRANTZ, GUILDENSTERN, HORATIO, *and*
    PLAYERS)
  'Tis now the very witching time of night,
  When churchyards yawn, and hell itself breathes out
  Contagion to this world: now could I drink hot blood,
  And do such bitter business as the day
  Would quake to look on. Soft! now to my mother.—
  O heart, lose not thy nature; let not ever
  The soul of Nero enter this firm bosom:
  Let me be cruel, not unnatural:
  I will speak daggers to her, but use none;
  My tongue and soul in this be hypocrites,—
  How in my words soever she be shent,
  To give them seals never, my soul, consent! (*Exit*)

SCENE THREE

A room in the castle.
    (*Enter* KING, ROSENCRANTZ, *and* GUILDENSTERN)

KING   I like him not; nor stands it safe with us
  To let his madness range. Therefore prepare you;
  I your commission will forthwith despatch,
  And he to England shall along with you:
  The terms of our estate may not endure
  Hazard so dangerous as doth hourly grow
  Out of his lunacies.

GUILDENSTERN   We will ourselves provide:
  Mostly holy and religious fear it is
  To keep those many many bodies safe
  That live and feed upon your majesty.

ROSENCRANTZ   The single and peculiar life is bound,
  With all the strength and armor of the mind,
  To keep itself from 'noyance; but much more
  That spirit upon whose weal depend and rest
  The lives of many. The cease of majesty
  Dies not alone; but like a gulf doth draw
  What's near it with it: it is a massy wheel,
  Fix'd on the summit of the highest mount,
  To whose huge spokes ten thousand lesser things
  Are mortis'd and adjoin'd; which, when it falls,
  Each small annexment, petty consequence,
  Attends the boisterous ruin. Never alone
  Did the king sigh, but with a general groan.

KING   Arm you, I pray you, to this speedy voyage;

For we will fetters put upon this fear,
Which now goes too free-footed.
ROSENCRANTZ *and* GUILDENSTERN: We will haste us.
        (*Exeunt* ROSENCRANTZ *and* GUILDENSTERN)
        (*Enter* POLONIUS)
POLONIUS   My lord, he's going to his mother's closet:
        Behind the arras I'll convey myself
        To hear the process; I'll warrant she'll tax him home:
        And, as you said, and wisely was it said,
        'Tis meet that some more audience than a mother,
        Since nature makes them partial, should o'erhear
        The speech, of vantage. Fare you well, my liege:
        I'll call upon you ere you go to bed,
        And tell you what I know.
KING   Thanks, dear my lord.
            (*Exit* POLONIUS)
        O, my offence is rank, it smells to heaven;
        It hath the primal eldest curse upon't,—
        A brother's murder!—Pray can I not,
        Though inclination be as sharp as will:
        My stronger guilt defeats my strong intent;
        And, like a man to double business bound,
        I stand in pause where I shall first begin,
        And both neglect. What if this cursed hand
        Were thicker than itself with brother's blood,—
        Is there not rain enough in the sweet heavens
        To wash it white as snow? Whereto serves mercy
        But to confront the visage of offence?
        And what's in prayer but this twofold force,—
        To be forestalled ere we come to fall,
        Or pardon'd being down? Then I'll look up;
        My fault is past. But, O, what form of prayer
        Can serve my turn? Forgive me my foul murder?—
        That cannot be; since I am still possess'd
        Of those effects for which I did the murder,—
        My crown, mine own ambition, and my queen.
        May one be pardon'd and retain the offence?
        In the corrupted currents of this world
        Offence's gilded hand may shove by justice;
        And oft 'tis seen the wicked prize itself
        Buys out the law: but 'tis not so above;
        There is no shuffling,—there the action lies
        In his true nature; and we ourselves compell'd,
        Even to the teeth and forehead of our faults,
        To give in evidence. What then? what rests?
        Try what repentance can: what can it not?
        Yet what can it when one can not repent?
        O wretched state! O bosom black as death!

O limed soul, that, struggling to be free,
Art more engag'd! Help, angels! make assay:
Bow, stubborn knees; and, heart, with strings of steel,
Be soft as sinews of the new-born babe!
All may be well. (*Retires and kneels*)
     (*Enter* HAMLET)

HAMLET   Now might I do it pat, now he is praying;
And now I'll do't—and so he goes to heaven;
And so am I reveng'd:—that would be scann'd:
A villain kills my father; and for that,
I, his sole son, do this same villain send
To heaven.
O, this is hire and salary, not revenge.
He took my father grossly, full of bread;
With all his crimes broad blown, as flush as May;
And how his audit stands who knows save heaven?
But in our circumstance and course of thought
'Tis heavy with him: and am I, then, reveng'd,
To take him in the purging of his soul,
When he is fit and season'd for his passage?
No.
Up, sword; and know thou a more horrid hent:
When he is drunk, asleep, or in his rage;
Or in the incestuous pleasure of his bed;
At gaming, swearing; or about some act
That has no relish of salvation in't;—
Then trip him, that his heels may kick at heaven;
And that his soul may be as damn'd and black
As hell, whereto it goes. My mother stays:
This physic but prolongs thy sickly days. (*Exit*)
     (*The* KING *rises and advances*)

KING   My words fly up, my thoughts remain below:
Words without thoughts never to heaven go. (*Exit*)

SCENE FOUR

Another room in the castle.
     (*Enter* QUEEN *and* POLONIUS)

POLONIUS   He will come straight. Look you lay home to him:
Tell him his pranks have been too broad to bear with,
And that your grace hath screen'd and stood between
Much heat and him. I'll silence me e'en here.
Pray you, be round with him.

HAMLET (*Within*)   Mother, mother, mother!

QUEEN   I'll warrant you:
Fear me not:—withdraw, I hear him coming.
     (POLONIUS *goes behind the arras*)
     (*Enter* HAMLET)

HAMLET   Now, mother, what's the matter?

QUEEN   Hamlet, thou hast thy father much offended.

HAMLET   Mother, you have my father much offended.

QUEEN   Come, come, you answer with an idle tongue.

HAMLET   Go, go, you question with a wicked tongue.

QUEEN   Why, how now, Hamlet!

HAMLET   What's the matter now?

QUEEN   Have you forgot me?

HAMLET   No, by the rood, not so:
 You are the queen, your husband's brother's wife;
 And,—would it were not so!—you are my mother.

QUEEN   Nay, then, I'll set those to you that can speak.

HAMLET   Come, come, and sit you down; you shall not budge;
 You go not till I set you up a glass
 Where you may see the inmost part of you.

QUEEN   What wilt thou do? thou wilt not murder me?—
 Help, help, ho!

POLONIUS (*Behind*)   What, ho! help, help, help!

HAMLET   How now! a rat? (*Draws*)
 Dead, for a ducat, dead! (*Makes a pass through the arras*)

POLONIUS (*Behind*)   O, I am slain! (*Falls and dies*)

QUEEN   O me, what hast thou done?

HAMLET   Nay, I know not:
 Is it the king? (*Draws forth* POLONIUS)

QUEEN   O, what a rash and bloody deed is this!

HAMLET   A bloody deed!—almost as bad, good mother,
 As kill a king and marry with his brother.

QUEEN   As kill a king!

HAMLET   Ay, lady, 'twas my word,—
 Thou wretched, rash, intruding fool, farewell! (*To* POLONIUS)
 I took thee for thy better: take thy fortune;
 Thou find'st to be too busy is some danger.—
 Leave wringing of your hands: peace; sit you down,
 And let me wring your heart: for so I shall,
 If it be made of penetrable stuff;
 If damned custom have not braz'd it so
 That it is proof and bulwark against sense.

QUEEN   What have I done, that thou dar'st wag thy tongue
 In noise so rude against me?

HAMLET   Such an act
 That blurs the grace and blush of modesty;
 Calls virtue hypocrite; takes off the rose
 From the fair forehead of an innocent love,
 And sets a blister there; makes marriage-vows
 As false as dicers' oaths: O, such a deed
 As from the body of contraction plucks
 The very soul, and sweet religion makes
 A rhapsody of words: heaven's face doth glow;

Yea, this solidity and compound mass,
With tristful visage, as against the doom,
Is thought-sick at the act.
QUEEN   Ah me, what act,
That roars so loud, and thunders in the index?
HAMLET   Look here upon this picture and on this,—
The counterfeit presentment of two brothers.
See what grace was seated on this brow;
Hyperion's curls; the front of Jove himself;
An eye like Mars, to threaten and command;
A station like the herald Mercury
New-lighted on a heaven-kissing hill;
A combination and a form, indeed,
Where every god did seem to set his seal,
To give the world assurance of a man:
This was your husband.—Look you now, what follows:
Here is your husband, like a mildew'd ear
Blasting his wholesome brother. Have you eyes?
Could you on this fair mountain leave to feed,
And batten on this moor? Ha! have you eyes?
You cannot call it love; for at your age
The hey-day in the blood is tame, it's humble,
And waits upon the judgment: and what judgment
Would step from this to this? Sense, sure, you have,
Else could you not have motion: but sure that sense
Is apoplex'd: for madness would not err;
Nor sense to ecstasy was ne'er so thrill'd
But it reserv'd some quantity of choice
To serve in such a difference. What devil was't
That thus hath cozen'd you at hoodman-blind?
Eyes without feeling, feeling without sight,
Ears without hands or eyes, smelling sans all,
Or but a sickly part of one true sense
Could not so mope.
O shame! where is thy blush! Rebellious hell,
If thou canst mutine in a matron's bones,
To flaming youth let virtue be as wax,
And melt in her own fire: proclaim no shame
When the compulsive ardor gives the charge,
Since frost itself as actively doth burn,
And reason panders will.
QUEEN   O Hamlet, speak no more:
Thou turn'st mine eyes into my very soul;
And there I see such black and grained spots
As will not leave their tinct.
HAMLET   Nay, but to live
In the rank sweat of an enseamed bed,
Stew'd in corruption, honeying and making love
Over the nasty sty,—

QUEEN   O, speak to me no more;
These words like daggers enter in mine ears;
No more, sweet Hamlet.
HAMLET   A murderer and a villain;
A slave that is not twenticth part the tithe
Of your precedent lord; a vice of kings;
A cutpurse of the empire and the rule,
That from a shelf the precious diadem stole,
And put it in his pocket!
QUEEN   No more.
HAMLET   A king of shreds and patches,—
          (*Enter* GHOST)
Save me, and hover o'er me with your wings,
You heavenly guards!—What would your gracious figure?
QUEEN   Alas, he's mad!
HAMLET   Do you not come your tardy son to chide,
That, laps'd in time and passion, lets go by
The important acting of your dread command? O, say!
GHOST   Do not forget: this visitation
Is but to whet thy almost blunted purpose.
But, look, amazement on thy mother sits:
O, step between her and her fighting soul,—
Conceit in weakest bodies strongest works,—
Speak to her, Hamlet.
HAMLET   How is it with you, lady?
QUEEN   Alas, how is't with you,
That you do bend your eye on vacancy,
And with the incorporal air do hold discourse?
Forth at your eyes your spirits wildly peep;
And, as the sleeping soldiers in the alarm,
Your bedded hair, like life in excrements,
Starts up and stands on end. O gentle son,
Upon the heat and flame of thy distemper
Sprinkle cool patience. Whereon do you look?
HAMLET   On him, on him! Look you, how pale he glares!
His form and cause conjoin'd, preaching to stones,
Would make them capable.—Do not look upon me;
Lest with this piteous action you convert
My stern effects: then what I have to do
Will want true color; tears perchance for blood.
QUEEN   To whom do you speak this?
HAMLET   Do you see nothing there?
QUEEN   Nothing at all; yet all that is I see.
HAMLET   Nor did you nothing hear?
QUEEN   No, nothing but ourselves.
HAMLET   Why, look you there! look, how it steals away!
My father, in his habit as he liv'd!
Look, where he goes, even now, out at the portal!
          (*Exit* GHOST)

QUEEN   This is the very coinage of your brain:
    This bodiless creation ecstasy
    Is very cunning in.
HAMLET   Ecstasy!
    My pulse, as yours, doth temperately keep time.
    And makes as healthful music: it is not madness
    That I have utter'd: bring me to the test,
    And I the matter will re-word; which madness
    Would gambol from. Mother, for love of grace,
    Lay not that flattering unction to your soul,
    That not your trespass, but my madness speaks:
    It will but skin and film the ulcerous place,
    Whilst rank corruption, mining all within,
    Infects unseen. Confess yourself to Heaven;
    Repent what's past; avoid what is to come;
    And do not spread the compost on the weeds,
    To make them ranker. Forgive me this my virtue;
    For in the fatness of these pursy times
    Virtue itself of vice must pardon beg,
    Yea, curb and woo for leave to do him good.
QUEEN   O Hamlet, thou hast cleft my heart in twain.
HAMLET   O, throw away the worser part of it,
    And live the purer with the other half.
    Good-night: but go not to mine uncle's bed;
    Assume a virtue, if you have it not.
    That monster custom, who all sense doth eat,
    Of habits devil, is angel yet in this,—
    That to the use of actions fair and good
    He likewise gives a frock or livery
    That aptly is put on. Refrain to-night;
    And that shall lend a kind of easiness
    To the next abstinence: the next more easy;
    For use almost can change the stamp of nature,
    And either curb the devil, or throw him out
    With wondrous potency. Once more, good-night:
    And when you are desirous to be bless'd,
    I'll blessing beg of you.—For this same lord (*pointing to* POLONIUS)
    I do repent: but Heaven hath pleas'd it so,
    To punish me with this, and this with me,
    That I must be their scourge and minister.
    I will bestow him, and will answer well
    The death I gave him. So, again, good-night.—
    I must be cruel only to be kind:
    Thus bad begins and worse remains behind.—
    One word more, good lady.
QUEEN   What shall I do?
HAMLET   Not this, by no means, that I bid you do:
    Let the bloat king tempt you again to bed;

Pinch wanton on your cheek; call you his mouse;
And let him, for a pair of reechy kisses,
Or paddling in your neck with his damn'd fingers,
Make you to ravel all this matter out,
That I essentially am not in madness,
But mad in craft. 'Twere good you let him know;
For who that's but a queen, fair, sober, wise,
Would from a paddock, from a bat, a gib,
Such dear concernings hide? who would do so?
No, in despite of sense and secrecy,
Unpeg the basket on the house's top,
Let the birds fly, and, like the famous ape,
To try conclusions, in the basket creep,
And break your own neck down.

QUEEN   Be thou assur'd, if words be made of breath
And breath of life, I have not life to breathe
What thou hast said to me.

HAMLET   I must to England; you know that?

QUEEN   Alack,
I had forgot: 'tis so concluded on.

HAMLET   There's letters seal'd: and my two school-fellows,—
Whom I will trust as I will adders fang'd,
They bear the mandate; they must sweep my way,
And marshal me to knavery. Let it work;
For 'tis the sport to have the éngineer
Hoist with his own petard: and't shall go hard
But I will delve one yard below their mines,
And blow them at the moon: O, 'tis most sweet,
When in one line two crafts directly meet,—
This man shall set me packing:
I'll lug the guts into the neighbor room.—
Mother, good-night.—Indeed, this counsellor
Is now most still, most secret, and most grave,
Who was in life a foolish prating knave.
Come, sir, to draw toward an end with you:—
Good-night, mother.

          (*Exeunt severally;* HAMLET *dragging out* POLONIUS)

Act Four

SCENE ONE

A room in the castle.
          (*Enter* KING, QUEEN, ROSENCRANTZ, *and* GUILDENSTERN)

KING   There's matter in these sighs, these prófound heaves:
You must translate: 'tis fit we understand them.
Where is your son?

QUEEN   Bestow this place on us a little while.
            (*To* ROSENCRANTZ *and* GUILDENSTERN, *who go out*)
        Ah, my good lord, what have I seen to-night!
KING   What, Gertrude? How does Hamlet?
QUEEN   Mad as the sea and wind, when both contend
        Which is the mightier: in his lawless fit,
        Behind the arras hearing something stir,
        He whips his rapier out, and cries, *A rat, a rat!*
        And, in this brainish apprehension, kills
        The unseen good old man.
KING   O heavy deed!
        It had been so with us had we been there:
        His liberty is full of threats to all;
        To you yourself, to us, to every one.
        Alas, how shall this bloody deed be answer'd?
        It will be laid to us, whose providence
        Should have kept short, restrain'd, and out of haunt
        This mad young man: but so much was our love,
        We would not understand what was most fit;
        But, like the owner of a foul disease,
        To keep it from divulging, let it feed
        Even on the pith of life. Where is he gone?
QUEEN   To draw apart the body he hath kill'd:
        O'er whom his very madness, like some ore
        Among a mineral of metals base,
        Shows itself pure; he weeps for what is done.
KING   O Gertrude, come away!
        The sun no sooner shall the mountains touch
        But we will ship him hence: and this vile deed
        We must, with all our majesty and skill,
        Both countenance and excuse.—Ho, Guildenstern!
            (*Enter* ROSENCRANTZ *and* GUILDENSTERN)
        Friends both, go join you with some further aid:
        Hamlet in madness hath Polonius slain,
        And from his mother's closet hath he dragg'd him:
        Go seek him out; speak fair, and bring the body
        Into the chapel. I pray you, haste in this.
            (*Exeunt* ROSENCRANTZ *and* GUILDENSTERN)
        Come, Gertrude, we'll call up our wisest friends;
        And let them know both what we mean to do
        And what's untimely done: so haply slander,—
        Whose whisper o'er the world's diameter,
        As level as the cannon to his blank,
        Transports his poison'd shot,—may amiss our name,
        And hit the woundless air.—O, come away!
        My soul is full of discord and dismay.
            (*Exeunt*)

SCENE TWO

Another room in the castle.

(*Enter* HAMLET)

HAMLET   Safely stowed.

ROSENCRANTZ *and* GUILDENSTERN (*Within*)   Hamlet! Lord Hamlet!

HAMLET   What noise? who calls on Hamlet?

O, here they come.

(*Enter* ROSENCRANTZ *and* GUILDENSTERN)

ROSENCRANTZ   What have you done, my lord, with the dead body?

HAMLET   Compounded it with dust, whereto 'tis kin.

ROSENCRANTZ   Tell us where 'tis, that we may take it thence,

And bear it to the chapel.

HAMLET   Do not believe it.

ROSENCRANTZ   Believe what?

HAMLET   That I can keep your counsel, and not mine own. Besides, to be demanded of a sponge!—what replication should be made by the son of a king?

ROSENCRANTZ   Take you me for a sponge, my lord?

HAMLET   Ay, sir; that soaks up the king's countenance, his rewards, his authorities. But such officers do the king best service in the end: he keeps them, like an ape, in the corner of his jaw; first mouthed, to be last swallowed: when he needs what you have gleaned, it is but squeezing you, and, sponge, you shall be dry again.

ROSENCRANTZ   I understand you not, my lord.

HAMLET   I am glad of it: a knavish speech sleeps in a foolish ear.

ROSENCRANTZ   My lord, you must tell us where the body is, and go with us to the king.

HAMLET   The body is with the king, but the king is not with the body. The king is a thing,—

GUILDENSTERN   A thing, my lord!

HAMLET   Of nothing: bring me to him.

Hide fox, and all after.

(*Exeunt*)

SCENE THREE

Another room in the castle.

(*Enter* KING, *attended*)

KING   I have sent to seek him, and to find the body.

How dangerous is it that this man goes loose!

Yet must not we put the strong law on him:

He's lov'd of the distracted multitude,

Who like not in their judgment, but their eyes;

And where 'tis so, the offender's scourge is weigh'd,

But never the offence. To bear all smooth and even,

This sudden sending him away must seem

Deliberate pause: diseases desperate grown
By desperate appliance are reliev'd,
Or not at all.
    (*Enter* ROSENCRANTZ)
How now! what hath befallen!

ROSENCRANTZ   Where the dead body is bestow'd, my lord,
    We cannot get from him.

KING   But where is he?

ROSENCRANTZ   Without, my lord; guarded, to know your pleasure.

KING   Bring him before us.

ROSENCRANTZ   Ho, Guildenstern! bring in my lord.
    (*Enter* HAMLET *and* GUILDENSTERN)

KING   Now, Hamlet, where's Polonius?

HAMLET   At supper.

KING   At supper! where?

HAMLET   Not where he eats, but where he is eaten: a certain convocation of
    politic worms are e'en at him. Your worm is your only emperor for diet:
    we fat all creatures else to fat us, and we fat ourselves for maggots: your
    fat king and your lean beggar is but variable service,—two dishes, but to
    one table: that's the end.

KING   Alas, alas!

HAMLET   A man may fish with the worm that hath eat of a king, and eat of the
    fish that hath fed of that worm.

KING   What dost thou mean by this?

HAMLET   Nothing but to show you how a king may go a progress through the
    guts of a beggar.

KING   Where is Polonius?

HAMLET   In heaven; send thither to see: if your messenger find him not there,
    seek him i' the other place yourself. But, indeed, if you find him not
    within this month, you shall nose him as you go up the stairs into the
    lobby.

KING   Go seek him there. (*To some* ATTENDANTS)

HAMLET   He will stay till ye come.
    (*Exeunt* ATTENDANTS)

KING   Hamlet, this deed, for thine especial safety,—
    Which we do tender, as we dearly grieve
    For that which thou hast done,—must send thee hence
    With fiery quickness: therefore prepare thyself;
    The bark is ready, and the wind at help,
    The associates tend, and everything is bent
    For England.

HAMLET   For England!

KING   Ay, Hamlet.

HAMLET   Good.

KING   So is it, if thou knew'st our purposes.

HAMLET   I see a cherub that sees them.—But, come; for England!—Farewell,
    dear mother.

KING   Thy loving father, Hamlet.

HAMLET   My mother: father and mother is man and wife; man and wife is one
flesh; and so, my mother.—Come, for England! (*Exit*)

KING   Follow him at foot; tempt him with speed aboard;
Delay it not; I'll have him hence to-night:
Away! for everything is seal'd and done
That else leans on the affair, pray you, make haste.
            (*Exeunt* ROSENCRANTZ *and* GUILDENSTERN)
And, England, if my love thou hold'st at aught,—
As my great power thereof may give thee sense,
Since yet thy cicatrice looks raw and red
After the Danish sword, and thy free awe
Pays homage to us,—thou mayst not coldly set
Our sovereign process; which imports at full,
By letters conjuring to that effect,
The present death of Hamlet. Do it, England;
For like the hectic in my blood he rages,
And thou must cure me: till I know 'tis done,
Howe'er my haps, my joys will ne'er begin. (*Exit*)

SCENE FOUR

A plain in Denmark.
            (*Enter* FORTINBRAS, *and* FORCES *marching*)

FORTINBRAS   Go, from me greet the Danish king:
Tell him that, by his license, Fortinbras
Craves the conveyance of a promis'd march
Over his kingdom. You know the rendezvous,
If that his majesty would aught with us,
We shall express our duty in his eye,
And let him know so.

CAPTAIN   I will do't, my lord.

FORTINBRAS   Go softly on.
            (*Exeunt* FORTINBRAS *and* FORCES)
            (*Enter* HAMLET, ROSENCRANTZ, GUILDENSTERN, *&c.*)

HAMLET   Good sir, whose powers are these?

CAPTAIN   They are of Norway, sir.

HAMLET   How purpos'd, sir, I pray you?

CAPTAIN   Against some part of Poland.

HAMLET   Who commands them, sir?

CAPTAIN   The nephew to old Norway, Fortinbras.

HAMLET   Goes it against the main of Poland, sir,
Or for some frontier?

CAPTAIN   Truly to speak, and with no addition,
We go to gain a little patch of ground
That hath in it no profit but the name.
To pay five ducats, five, I would not farm it;
Nor will it yield to Norway or the Pole
A ranker rate should it be sold in fee.

HAMLET   Why, then the Polack never will defend it.
CAPTAIN   Yes, it is already garrison'd.
HAMLET   Two thousand souls and twenty thousand ducats
     Will not debate the question of this straw:
     This is the imposthume of much wealth and peace,
     That inward breaks, and shows no cause without
     Why the man dies.—I humbly thank you, sir.
CAPTAIN   God b' wi' you, sir. (*Exit*)
ROSENCRANTZ   Will't please you go, my lord?
HAMLET   I'll be with you straight. Go a little before.
          (*Exeunt all but* HAMLET)
     How all occasions do inform against me,
     And spur my dull revenge! What is a man,
     If his chief good and market of his time
     Be but to sleep and feed? a beast, no more.
     Sure he that made us with such large discourse,
     Looking before and after, gave us not
     That capability and godlike reason
     To fust in us unus'd. Now, whether it be
     Bestial oblivion or some craven scruple
     Of thinking too precisely on the event,—
     A thought which, quarter'd, hath but one part wisdom
     And ever three parts coward,—I do not know
     Why yet I live to say, *This thing's to do;*
     Sith I have cause, and will, and strength, and means
     To do't. Examples, gross as earth, exhort me:
     Witness this army, of such mass and charge,
     Led by a delicate and tender prince;
     Whose spirit, with divine ambition puff'd,
     Makes mouths at the invisible event;
     Exposing what is mortal and unsure
     To all that fortune, death, and danger dare,
     Even for an egg-shell. Rightly to be great
     Is not to stir without great argument,
     But greatly to find quarrel in a straw
     When honor's at the stake. How stand I, then,
     That have a father kill'd, a mother stain'd,
     Excitements of my reason and my blood,
     And let all sleep? while, to my shame, I see
     The imminent death of twenty thousand men,
     That, for a fantasy and trick of fame,
     Go to their graves like beds; fight for a plot
     Whereon the numbers cannot try the cause,
     Which is not tomb enough and continent
     To hide the slain?—O, from this time forth,
     My thoughts be bloody, or be nothing worth! (*Exit*)

SCENE FIVE

Elsinore. A room in the castle.
   (*Enter* QUEEN *and* HORATIO)
QUEEN I will not speak with her.
HORATIO She is importunate; indeed, distract:
  Her mood will needs be pitied.
QUEEN   What would she have?
HORATIO She speaks much of her father; says she hears
  There's tricks i' the world; and hems, and beats her heart;
  Spurns enviously at straws; speaks things in doubt,
  That carry but half sense: her speech is nothing,
  Yet the unshapéd use of it doth move
  The hearers to collection; they aim at it,
  And botch the words up fit to their own thoughts;
  Which, as her winks, and nods, and gestures yield them,
  Indeed would make one think there might be thought,
  Though nothing sure, yet much unhappily.
  'Twere good she were spoken with; for she may strew
  Dangerous conjectures in ill-breeding minds.
QUEEN Let her come in.
    (*Exit* HORATIO)
  To my sick soul, as sin's true nature is,
  Each toy seems prologue to some great amiss:
  So full of artless jealously is guilt,
  It spills itself in fearing to be spilt.
    (*Re-enter* HORATIO *and* OPHELIA)
OPHELIA Where is the beauteous majesty of Denmark?
QUEEN How now, Ophelia!
OPHELIA (*Sings*)
     How should I your true love know
      From another one?
     By his cockle hat and staff,
      And his sandal shoon.
QUEEN Alas, sweet lady, what imports this song?
OPHELIA Say you? nay, pray you, mark. (*Sings*)
     He is dead and gone, lady,
      He is dead and gone;
     At his head a grass green turf,
      At his heels a stone.
QUEEN Nay, but, Ophelia,—
OPHELIA   Pray you, mark. (*Sings*)
     White his shroud as the mountain snow,
    (*Enter* KING)
QUEEN Alas, look here, my lord.
OPHELIA (*Sings*)
     Larded with sweet flowers;

Which bewept to the grave did go
With true-love showers.

KING How do you, pretty lady?

OPHELIA Well, God 'ild you! They say the owl was a baker's daughter. Lord, we know what we are, but know not what we may be. God be at your table!

KING Conceit upon her father.

OPHELIA Pray you, let's have no words of this; but when they ask you what it means, say you this: (*Sings*)

To-morrow is Saint Valentine's day
All in the morning betime,
And I a maid at your window,
To be your Valentine.

Then up he rose, and donn'd his clothes,
And dupp'd the chamber-door;
Let in the maid, that out a maid
Never departed more.

KING Pretty Ophelia!

OPHELIA Indeed, la, without an oath, I'll make an end on't; (*Sings*)

By Gis and by Saint Charity,
Alack, and fie for shame!
Young men will do't, if they come to't;
By cock, they are to blame.

Quoth she, before you tumbled me,
You promis'd me to wed.
So would I ha' done, by yonder sun,
An thou hadst not come to my bed.

KING How long hath she been thus?

OPHELIA I hope all will be well. We must be patient: but I cannot choose but weep, to think they should lay him i' the cold ground. My brother shall know of it: and so I thank you; for your good counsel.—Come, my coach!—Good-night, ladies; good-night, sweet ladies; good-night, good-night. (*Exit*)

KING Follow her close; give her good watch, I pray you.
(*Exit* HORATIO)
O, this is the poison of deep grief; it springs
All from her father's death. O Gertrude, Gertrude,
When sorrows come, they come not single spies,
But in battalions! First, her father slain:
Next, your son gone: and he most violent author
Of his own just remove: the people muddied,
Thick and unwholesome in their thoughts and whispers
For good Polonius' death; and we have done but greenly
In hugger-mugger to inter him: poor Ophelia
Divided from herself and her fair judgment,
Without the which we are pictures, or mere beasts:
Last, and as much containing as all these,
Her brother is in secret come from France;

Feeds on his wonder, keeps himself in clouds,
And wants not buzzers to infect his ear
With pestilent speeches of his father's death;
Wherein necessity, of matter beggar'd,
Will nothing stick our person to arraign
In ear and ear. O my dear Gertrude, this,
Like to a murdering piece, in many places
Gives me superfluous death.
        (A noise within)

QUEEN   Alack, what noise is this?

KING   Where are my Switzers? let them guard the door.
        (Enter a GENTLEMAN*)*
What is the matter?

GENTLEMAN   Save yourself, my lord:
The ocean, overpeering of his list,
Eats not the flats with more impetuous haste
Than young Laertes, in a riotous head,
O'erbears your officers. The rabble call him lord;
And, as the world were now but to begin,
Antiquity forgot, custom not known,
The ratifiers and props of every word,
They cry, *Choose we, Laertes shall be king!*
Caps, hands, and tongues applaud it to the clouds,
Laertes shall be king, Laertes king!

QUEEN   How cheerfully on the false trail they cry!
O, this is counter, you false Danish dogs!

KING   The doors are broke.
        (Noise within)
        (Enter LAERTES *armed;* DANES *following)*

LAERTES   Where is this king?—Sirs, stand you all without.

DANES   No, let's come in.

LAERTES   I pray you, give me leave.

DANES   We will, we will. *(They retire without the door)*

LAERTES   I thank you:—keep the door.—O thou vile king,
Give me my father!

QUEEN   Calmly, good Laertes.

LAERTES   That drop of blood that's calm proclaims me bastard;
Cries cuckold to my father; brands the harlot
Even here, between the chaste unsmirched brow
Of my true mother.

KING   What is the cause, Laertes,
That thy rebellion looks so giant-like?—
Let him go, Gertrude; do not fear our person:
There's such divinity doth hedge a king,
That treason can but peep to what it would,
Acts little of his will.—Tell me, Laertes,
Why thou art thus incens'd.—Let him go, Gertrude:—

Speak, man.

LAERTES   Where is my father?

KING   Dead.

QUEEN   But not by him.

KING   Let him demand his fill.

LAERTES   How came he dead? I'll not be juggled with:
To hell, allegiance! vows, to the blackest devil!
Conscience and grace, to the profoundest pit!
I dare damnation:—to this point I stand,—
That both the worlds I give to negligence,
Let come what comes; only I'll be reveng'd
Most thoroughly for my father.

KING   Who shall stay you?

LAERTES   My will, not all the world:
And for my means, I'll husband them so well,
They shall go far with little.

KING   Good Laertes,
If you desire to know the certainty
Of your dear father's death, is't writ in your revenge
That, sweepstake, you will draw both friend and foe,
Winner or loser?

LAERTES   None but his enemies.

KING   Will you know them, then?

LAERTES   To his good friends thus wide I'll ope my arms;
And, like the kind life-rendering pelican,
Repast them with my blood.

KING   Why, now you speak
Like a good child and a true gentleman.
That I am guiltless of your father's death,
And am most sensible in grief for it,
It shall as level to your judgment pierce
As day does to your eye.

DANES (*Within*)   Let her come in.

LAERTES   How now! what noise is that?

      (*Re-enter* OPHELIA, *fantastically dressed with straws and
      flowers*)

O heat, dry up my brains; tears seven times salt
Burn out the sense and virtue of mine eyes!—
By heaven, thy madness shall be paid by weight
Till our scale turn the beam. O rose of May!
Dear maid, kind sister, sweet Ophelia!—
O heavens! is't possible a young maid's wits
Should be as mortal as an old man's life!
Nature is fine in love; and where 'tis fine
It sends some precious instance of itself
After the thing it loves.

OPHELIA (*Sings*)

> They bore him barefac'd on the bier;
> Hey no nonny, nonny, hey nonny;
> And on his grave rain'd many a tear,—
> Fare you well, my dove!

LAERTES   Hadst thou thy wits, and didst persuade revenge,
It could not move thus.

OPHELIA   You must sing, *Down-a-down, an you call him a-down-a.* O, how
the wheel becomes it! It is the false steward, that stole his master's
daughter.

LAERTES   This nothing's more than matter.

OPHELIA   There's rosemary, that's for remembrance; pray, love, remember:
and there is pansies that's for thoughts.

LAERTES   A document in madness,—thoughts and remembrance fitted.

OPHELIA   There's fennel for you, and columbines:—there's rue for you; and
here's some for me:—we may call it herb-grace o' Sundays:—O, you must
wear your rue with a difference.—There's a daisy:—I would give you some
violets, but they withered all when my father died:—they say, he made
a good end,—(*Sings*)

> For bonny sweet Robin is all my joy,—

LAERTES   Thoughts and affliction, passion, hell itself,
She turns to favor and to prettiness.

OPHELIA (*Sings*)

> And will he not come again?
> And will he not come again?
>   No, no, he is dead,
>   Go to thy death-bed,
> He never will come again.
>
> His beard was as white as snow
> All flaxen was his poll:
>   He is gone, he is gone,
>   And we cast away moan:
> God ha' mercy on his soul!

And of all Christian souls, I pray God.—God b' wi' ye. (*Exit*)

LAERTES   Do you see this, O God?

KING   Laertes, I must commune with your grief,
Or you deny me right. Go but apart,
Make choice of whom your wisest friends you will,
And they shall hear and judge 'twixt you and me:
If by direct or by collateral hand
They find us touch'd, we will our kingdom give,
Our crown, our life, and all that we call ours,
To you in satisfaction; but if not,
Be you content to lend your patience to us,
And we shall jointly labor with your soul
To give it due content.

LAERTES   Let this be so;
His means of death, his óbscure burial,—
No trophy, sword, nor hatchment o'er his bones

No noble rite nor formal ostentation,—
Cry to be heard, as 'twere from heaven to earth,
That I must call't in question.

KING   So you shall;
And where the offence is, let the great axe fall.
I pray you, go with me.
        (*Exeunt*)

SCENE SIX

Another room in the castle.
        (*Enter* HORATIO *and a* SERVANT)
HORATIO   What are they that would speak with me?
SERVANT   Sailors, sir: they say they have letters for you.
HORATIO   Let them come in.—
        (*Exit* SERVANT)
I do not know from what part of the world
I should be greeted, if not from Lord Hamlet.
        (*Enter* SAILORS)
1ST SAILOR   God bless you, sir.
HORATIO   Let him bless thee too.
1ST SAILOR   He shall, sir, an't please him. There's a letter for you, sir; it comes
    from the ambassador that was bound for England; if your name be
    Horatio, as I am let to know it is.
HORATIO (*Reads*)   *Horatio, when thou shalt have overlooked this, give these
    fellows some means to the king: they have letters for him. Ere we were
    two days old at sea, a pirate of very warlike appointment gave us chase.
    Finding ourselves too slow of sail, we put on a compelled valor; and in
    the grapple I boarded them; on the instant they got clear of our ship; so
    I alone became their prisoner. They have dealt with me like thieves of
    mercy: but they knew what they did; I am to do a good turn for them.
    Let the king have the letters I have sent; and repair thou to me with as
    much haste as thou wouldst fly death. I have words to speak in thine
    ear will make thee dumb; yet are they much too light for the bore of the
    matter. These good fellows will bring thee where I am. Rosencrantz
    and Guildenstern hold their course for England: of them I have much to
    tell thee. Farewell. He that thou knowest thine.*   Hamlet
Come, I will give you way for these your letters;
And do't the speedier, that you may direct me
To him from whom you brought them.
        (*Exeunt*)

SCENE SEVEN

Another room in the castle.
        (*Enter* KING *and* LAERTES)
KING   Now must your conscience my acquittance seal,

And you must put me in your heart for friend,
Sith you have heard, and with a knowing ear,
That he which hath your noble father slain
Pursu'd my life.

LAERTES   It well appears: but tell me
Why you proceeded not against these feats,
So crimeful and so capital in nature,
As by your safety, wisdom, all things else,
You mainly were stirr'd up.

KING   O, for two special reasons;
Which may to you, perhaps, seem much unsinew'd,
But yet to me they are strong. The queen his mother
Lives almost by his looks; and for myself,—
My virtue or my plague, be it either which,—
She's so conjunctive to my life and soul,
That, as the star moves not but in his sphere,
I could not but by her. The other motive,
Why to a public count I might not go,
Is the great love the general gender bear him;
Who, dipping all his faults in their affection,
Would, like the spring that turneth wood to stone,
Convert his gyves to graces; so that my arrows,
Too slightly timber'd for so loud a wind,
Would have reverted to my bow again,
And not where I had aim'd them.

LAERTES   And so have I a noble father lost;
A sister driven into desperate terms,—
Whose worth, if praises may go back again,
Stood challenger on mount of all the age
For her perfections:—but my revenge will come.

KING   Break not your sleeps for that: you must not think
That we are made of stuff so flat and dull
That we can let our beard be shook with danger,
And think it pastime. You shortly shall hear more:
I lov'd your father, and we love ourself:
And that, I hope, will teach you to imagine,—
       (*Enter a* MESSENGER)
How now! what news?

MESSENGER   Letters, my lord, from Hamlet:
This to your majesty; this to the queen.

KING   From Hamlet! Who brought them?

MESSENGER   Sailors, my lord, they say; I saw them not:
They were given me by Claudio,—he receiv'd them
Of him that brought them.

KING   Laertes, you shall hear them.—Leave us.
       (*Exit* MESSENGER)
(*Reads*) *High and mighty,— You shall know I am set naked on your*
kingdom. To-morrow shall I beg leave to see your kingly eyes: when I

*shall, first asking your pardon thereunto, recount the occasions of my sud-
den and more strange return.*   Hamlet
What should this mean? Are all the rest come back?
Or is it some abuse, and no such thing?

LAERTES   Know you the hand?

KING   'Tis Hamlet's character:—*Naked*,—
And in a postscript here, he says, *alone*.
Can you advise me?

LAERTES   I am lost in it, my lord. But let him come;
It warms the very sickness in my heart,
That I shall live, and tell him to his teeth,
Thus diddest thou.

KING   If it be so, Laertes,—
As how should it be so? how otherwise?—
Will you be rul'd by me?

LAERTES   Ay, my lord:
So you will not o'errule me to a peace.

KING   To thine own peace. If he be now return'd,—
As checking at his voyage, and that he means
No more to undertake it,—I will work him
To an exploit, now ripe in my device,
Under the which he shall not choose but fall:
And for his death no wind of blame shall breathe;
But even his mother shall uncharge the practice
And call it accident.

LAERTES   My lord, I will be rul'd;
The rather if you could devise it so
That I might be the organ.

KING   It falls right.
You have been talk'd of since your travel much,
And that in Hamlet's hearing, for a quality
Wherein they say you shine: your sum of parts
Did not together pluck such envy from him
As did that one; and that, in my regard,
Of the unworthiest siege.

LAERTES   What part is that, my lord?

KING   A very riband in the cap of youth,
Yet needful too; for youth no less becomes
The light and careless livery that it wears
Than settled age his sables and his weeds,
Importing health and graveness.—Two months since,
Here was a gentleman of Normandy,—
I've seen myself, and serv'd against, the French,
And they can well on horseback: but this gallant
Had witchcraft in't; he grew unto his seat;
And to such wondrous doing brought his horse,
As he had been incorps'd and demi-natur'd
With the brave beast: so far he topp'd my thought,

That I, in forgery of shapes and tricks,
Come short of what he did.

LAERTES   A Norman was't?

KING   A Norman.

LAERTES   Upon my life, Lamond.

KING   The very same.

LAERTES   I know him well: he is the brooch, indeed,
And gem of all the nation.

KING   He made confession of you;
And gave you such a masterly report
For art and exercise in your defence,
And for your rapier most especially,
That he cried out, 'twould be a sight indeed
If one could match you: the scrimers of their nation,
He swore, had neither motion, guard, nor eye,
If you oppos'd them. Sir, this report of his
Did Hamlet so envenom with his envy,
That he could nothing do but wish and beg
Your sudden coming o'er, to play with him.
Now, out of this,—

LAERTES   What out of this, my lord?

KING   Laertes, was your father dear to you?
Or are you like the painting of a sorrow,
A face without a heart?

LAERTES   Why ask you this?

KING   Not that I think you did not love your father;
But that I know love is begun by time;
And that I see, in passages of proof,
Time qualifies the spark and fire of it.
There lives within the very flame of love
A kind of wick or snuff that will abate it;
And nothing is at a like goodness still;
For goodness, growing to a pleurisy,
Dies in his own too much: that we would do
We should do when we would; for this *would* changes,
And hath abatements and delays as many
As there are tongues, or hands, or accidents;
And then this *should* is like a spendthrift sigh
That hurts by easing. But to the quick o' the ulcer:—
Hamlet comes back: what would you undertake
To show yourself your father's son in deed
More than in words?

LAERTES   To cut his throat i' the church.

KING   No place, indeed, should murder sanctuarize;
Revenge should have no bounds. But, good Laertes,
Will you do this, keep close within your chamber.
Hamlet return'd shall know you are come home:
We'll put on those shall praise your excellence,

And set a double varnish on the fame
The Frenchman gave you; bring you, in fine, together,
And wager on yours heads: he, being remiss,
Most generous, and free from all contriving,
Will not peruse the foils; so that, with ease,
Or with a little shuffling, you may choose
A sword unbated, and, in a pass of practice,
Requite him for your father.

LAERTES   I will do't it:
And, for that purpose, I'll anoint my sword.
I bought an unction of a mountebank,
So mortal that but dip a knife in it,
Where it draws blood no cataplasm so rare,
Collected from all simples that have virtue
Under the moon, can save the thing from death
That is but scratch'd withal: I'll touch my point
With this contagion, that, if I gall him slightly,
It may be death.

KING   Let's further think of this;
Weigh what convenience both of time and means
May fit us to our shape: if this should fail,
And that our drift look through our bad performance,
'Twere better not assay'd: therefore this project
Should have a back or second, that might hold
If this should blast in proof. Soft! let me see:—
We'll make a solemn wager on your cunnings,—
I ha't:
When in your motion you are hot and dry,—
As make your bouts more violent to that end,—
And that he calls for drink, I'll have prepar'd him
A chalice for the nonce; whereon but sipping,
If he by chance escape your venom'd stuck
Our purpose may hold there.
              (*Enter* QUEEN)
                    How now, sweet queen!

QUEEN   One woe doth tread upon another's heel,
         So fast they follow:—your sister's drown'd, Laertes.

LAERTES   Drown'd! O, where?

QUEEN   There is a willow grows aslant a brook,
         That shows his hoar leaves in the glassy stream;
         There with fantastic garlands did she come
         Of crowflowers, nettles, daisies, and long purples,
         That liberal shepherds give a grosser name,
         But our cold maids do dead men's fingers call them.
         There, on the pendant boughs her coronet weeds
         Clambering to hang, an envious sliver broke;
         When down her weedy trophies and herself
         Fell in the weeping brook. Her clothes spread wide;

And, mermaid-like, awhile they bore her up:
Which time she chanted snatches of old tunes;
As one incapable of her own distress,
Or like a creature native and indu'd
Unto that element: but long it could not be
Till that her garments, heavy with their drink,
Pull'd the poor wretch from her melodious lay
To muddy death.

LAERTES   Alas, then, she is drown'd?

QUEEN   Drown'd, drown'd.

LAERTES   Too much of water hast thou, poor Ophelia,
And therefore I forbid my tears: but yet
It is our trick; nature her custom holds,
Let shame say what it will: when these are gone,
The woman will be out.—Adieu, my lord:
I have a speech of fire, that fain would blaze,
But that this folly douts it. (*Exit*)

KING   Let's follow, Gertrude;
How much I had to do to calm his rage!
Now fear I this will give it start again;
Therefore let's follow.
            (*Exeunt*)

Act Five

SCENE ONE

A churchyard.
            (*Enter two* CLOWNS *with spades, &c.*)

1ST CLOWN   Is she to be buried in Christian burial that wilfully seeks her own
    salvation?

2ND CLOWN   I tell thee she is; and therefore make her grave straight: the
    crowner hath sat on her, and finds it Christian burial.

1ST CLOWN   How can that be, unless she drowned herself in her own defence?

2ND CLOWN   Why, 'tis found so.

1ST CLOWN   It must be *se offendendo;* it cannot be else. For here lies the point:
    if I drown myself wittingly, it argues an act: and an act hath three
    branches; it is to act, to do, and to perform: argal, she drowned herself
    wittingly.

2ND CLOWN   Nay, but hear you, goodman delver,—

1ST CLOWN   Give me leave. Here lies the water; good: here stands the man;
    good: if the man go to this water and drown himself, it is, will he, nill he,
    he goes,—mark you that: but if the water come to him and drown him,
    he drowns not himself: argal, he that is not guilty of his own death
    shortens not his own life.

2ND CLOWN   But is this law?

1ST CLOWN   Ay, marry, is't; crowner's quest law.

2ND CLOWN   Will you ha' the truth on't? If this had not been a gentlewoman
she should have been buried out of Christian burial.

1ST CLOWN   Why, there thou say'st: and the more pity that great folks should
have countenance in this world to drown or hang themselves more than
their even-Christian.—Come, my spade. There is no ancient gentlemen
but gardeners, ditchers, and gravemakers; they hold up Adam's profession.

2ND CLOWN   Was he a gentleman?

1ST CLOWN   He was the first that ever bore arms.

2ND CLOWN   Why, he had none.

1ST CLOWN   What, art a heathen? How dost thou understand the Scripture?
The Scripture says, Adam digged: could he dig without arms? I'll put
another question to thee: if thou answerest me not to the purpose, confess thyself,—

2ND CLOWN   Go to.

1ST CLOWN   What is he that builds stronger than either the mason, the shipwright, or the carpenter?

2ND CLOWN   The gallows-maker; for that frame outlives a thousand tenants.

1ST CLOWN   I like thy wit well, in good faith: the gallows does well; but how
does it well? it does well to those that do ill: now thou dost ill to say the
gallows is built stronger than the church: argal, the gallows may do well
to thee. To't again, come.

2ND CLOWN   Who builds stronger than a mason, a shipwright, or a carpenter?

1ST CLOWN   Ay, tell me that, and unyoke.

2ND CLOWN   Marry, now I can tell.

1ST CLOWN   To't.

2ND CLOWN   Mass, I cannot tell.

(*Enter* HAMLET *and* HORATIO, *at a distance*)

1ST CLOWN   Cudgel thy brains no more about it, for your dull ass will not
mend his pace with beating; and when you are asked this question next,
say a grave-maker; the houses that he makes last till doomsday. Go, get
thee to Yaughan: fetch me a stoup of liquor.

(*Exit* SECOND CLOWN)

(*Digs and sings*)

In youth, when I did love, did love,
  Methought it was very sweet,
To contract, O, the time, for, ah, my behove,
  O, methought there was nothing meet.

HAMLET   Has this fellow no feeling of his business, that he sings at grave-
making?

HORATIO   Custom hath made it in him a property of easiness.

HAMLET   'Tis e'en so: the hand of little employment hath the daintier sense.

1ST CLOWN (*Sings*)

But age, with his stealing steps,
  Hath claw'd me in his clutch,
And hath shipp'd me intil the land,
  As if I had never been such.

(*Throws up a skull*)

HAMLET   That skull had a tongue in it, and could sing once: how the knave
joels it to the ground, as if it were Cain's jawbone, that did the first murder!
This might be the pate of a politician, which this ass now o'erreaches;
one that would circumvent God, might it not?

HORATIO   It might, my lord.

HAMLET   Or of a courtier; which could say, *Good-morrow, sweet lord! How
dost thou, good lord?* This might be my lord such-a-one, that praised my
lord such-a-one's horse, when he meant to beg it,—might it not?

HORATIO   Ay, my lord.

HAMLET   Why, e'en so: and now my Lady Worm's; chapless, and knocked
about the mazard with a sexton's spade: here's fine revolution, an we had
the trick to see't. Did these bones cost no more the breeding but to play
at loggats with 'em? Mine ache to think on't.

1ST CLOWN (*Sings*)

> A pick-axe and a spade, a spade,
> For and a shrouding sheet:
> O, a pit of clay for to be made
> For such a guest is meet.

> *(Throws up another)*

HAMLET   There's another: why may not that be the skull of a lawyer? Where
be his quiddits now, his quillets, his cases, his tenures, and his tricks?
why does he suffer this rude knave now to knock him about the sconce
with a dirty shovel, and will not tell him of his action of battery? Hum!
This fellow might be in's time a great buyer of land, with his statutes,
his recognizances, his fines, his double vouchers, his recoveries: is this the
fine of his fines, and the recovery of his recoveries, to have his fine pate
full of dirt? will his vouchers vouch him no more of his purchases, and
double ones too, than the length and breadth of a pair of indentures? The
very conveyances of his lands will hardly lie in this box; and must the
inheritor himself have no more, ha?

HORATIO   Not a jot more, my lord.

HAMLET   Is not parchment made of sheep-skins?

HORATIO   Ay, my lord, and of calf-skins too.

HAMLET   They are sheep and calves which seek out assurance in that. I will
speak to this fellow.—Whose grave's this, sir?

1ST CLOWN   Mine, sir.   (*Sings*)

> O, a pit of clay for to be made
> For such a guest is meet.

HAMLET   I think it be thine indeed; for thou liest in't.

1ST CLOWN   You lie out on't, sir, and therefore it is not yours: for my part,
I do not lie in't, and yet it is mine.

HAMLET   Thou dost lie in't, to be in't, and say it is thine: 'tis for the dead, not
for the quick; therefore thou liest.

1ST CLOWN   'Tis a quick lie, sir; 'twill away again from me to you.

HAMLET   What man dost thou dig it for?

1ST CLOWN   For no man, sir.

HAMLET   What woman, then?

1ST CLOWN   For none, neither.

HAMLET   Who is to be buried in't?

1ST CLOWN   One that was a woman, sir; but, rest her soul, she's dead.

HAMLET   How absolute the knave is! we must speak by the card, or equivocation will undo us. By the Lord, Horatio, these three years I have taken note of it; the age is grown so picked that the toe of the peasant comes so near the heel of the courtier, he galls his kibe.—How long hast thou been a grave-maker?

1ST CLOWN   Of all the days i' the year, I came to't that day that our last King Hamlet o'ercame Fortinbras.

HAMLET   How long is that since?

1ST CLOWN   Cannot you tell that? every fool can tell that: it was the very day that young Hamlet was born,—he that is mad, and sent into England.

HAMLET   Ay, marry, why was he sent into England?

1ST CLOWN   Why, because he was mad: he shall recover his wits there; or, if he do not, it's no great matter there.

HAMLET   Why?

1ST CLOWN   'Twill not be seen in him there; there the men are as mad as he.

HAMLET   How came he mad?

1ST CLOWN   Very strangely, they say.

HAMLET   How strangely?

1ST CLOWN   Faith, e'en with losing his wits.

HAMLET   Upon what ground?

1ST CLOWN   Why, here in Denmark: I have been sexton here, man and boy, thirty years.

HAMLET   How long will a man lie i' the earth ere he rot?

1ST CLOWN   Faith, if he be not rotten before he die,—as we have many pocky corses now-a-days, that will scarce hold the laying in,—he will last you some eight year or nine year: a tanner will last you nine year.

HAMLET   Why he more than another?

1ST CLOWN   Why, sir, his hide is so tanned with his trade that he will keep out water a great while; and your water is a sore decayer of your whoreson dead body. Here's a skull now; this skull has lain in the earth three-and-twenty years.

HAMLET   Whose was it?

1ST CLOWN   A whoreson mad fellow's it was: whose do you think it was?

HAMLET   Nay, I know not.

1ST CLOWN   A pestilence on him for a mad rogue! 'a poured a flagon of Rhenish on my head once. This same skull, sir, was Yorick's skull, the king's jester.

HAMLET   This?

1ST CLOWN   E'en that.

HAMLET   Let me see. (*Takes the skull*)—Alas, poor Yorick!—I knew him, Horatio; a fellow of infinite jest, of most excellent fancy: he hath borne me on his back a thousand times; and now, how abhorred in my imagination it is! my gorge rises at it. Here hung those lips that I have kissed I know not how oft. Where be your gibes now? your gambols? your songs? your flashes of merriment, that were wont to set the table on a roar? Not one now, to mock your own grinning? quite chap-fallen? Now

get you to my lady's chamber, and tell her, let her paint an inch thick,
to this favor she must come; make her laugh at that.—Pr'ythee, Horatio,
tell me one thing.

HORATIO   What's that, my lord?

HAMLET   Dost thou think Alexander looked o' this fashion i' the earth?

HORATIO   E'en so.

HAMLET   And smelt so? pah! (*Throws down the skull*)

HORATIO   E'en so, my lord.

HAMLET   To what base uses we may return, Horatio! Why may not imagination
trace the noble dust of Alexander till he find it stopping a bung-hole?

HORATIO   'Twere to consider too curiously to consider so.

HAMLET   No, faith, not a jot; but to follow him thither with modesty enough,
and likelihood to lead it: as thus; Alexander died, Alexander was buried,
Alexander returneth into dust; the dust is earth; of earth we make loam;
and why of that loam whereto he was converted might they not stop a
beer-barrel?

> Imperious Caesar, dead and turn'd to clay,
> Might stop a hole to keep the wind away:
> O, that that earth which kept the world in awe
> Should patch a wall to expel the winter's flaw!—

But soft! but soft! aside.—Here comes the king.

> (*Enter* PRIESTS, &c., *in procession; the corpse of*
> OPHELIA, LAERTES *and* MOURNERS *following;* KING, QUEEN,
> *their* TRAINS, &c.)

The queen, the courtiers: who is that they follow?
And with such maimed rites? This doth betoken
The corse they follow did with desperate hand
Fordo its own life: 'twas of some estate.
Couch we awhile and mark. (*Retiring with* HORATIO)

LAERTES   What ceremony else?

HAMLET   That is Laertes,
A very noble youth: mark.

LAERTES   What ceremony else?

1ST PRIEST   Her obsequies have been as far enlarg'd
As we have warrantise: her death was doubtful,
And, but that great command o'ersways the order,
She should in ground unsanctified have lodg'd
Till the last trumpet; for charitable prayers,
Shards, flints, and pebbles, should be thrown on her,
Yet here she is allowed her virgin rites,
Her maiden strewments, and the bringing home
Of bell and burial.

LAERTES   Must there no more be done?

1ST PRIEST   No more be done:
We should profane the service of the dead
To sing a *requiem,* and such rest to her
As to peace-parted souls.

LAERTES   Lay her i' the earth;—

And from her fair and unpolluted flesh
May violets spring!—I tell thee, churlish priest,
A ministering angel shall my sister be
When thou liest howling.

HAMLET   What, the fair Ophelia!

QUEEN   Sweets to the sweet: farewell! (*Scattering flowers*)
I hop'd thou shouldst have been my Hamlet's wife;
I thought thy bride-bed to have deck'd, sweet maid,
And not have strew'd thy grave.

LAERTES   O, treble woe
Fall ten times treble on that cursed head
Whose wicked deed thy most ingenious sense
Depriv'd thee of!—Hold off the earth awhile,
Till I have caught her once more in mine arms:
          (*Leaps into the grave*)
Now pile your dust upon the quick and dead,
Till of this flat a mountain you have made,
To o'er-top old Pelion or the skyish head
Of blue Olympus.

HAMLET (*Advancing*)   What is he whose grief
Bears such an emphasis? whose phrase of sorrow
Conjures the wandering stars, and makes them stand
Like wonder-wounded hearers? this is I, Hamlet the Dane. (*Leaps into
          the grave*)

LAERTES   The devil take thy soul! (*Grappling with him*)

HAMLET   Thou pray'st not well.
I pr'ythee, take thy fingers from my throat;
For, though I am not splenetive and rash,
Yet have I in me something dangerous,
Which let thy wiseness fear: away thy hand.

KING   Pluck them asunder.

QUEEN   Hamlet! Hamlet!

ALL   Gentlemen,—

HORATIO   Good my lord, be quiet.
          (*The* ATTENDANTS *part them, and they come out of the
          grave*)

HAMLET   Why, I will fight with him upon this theme
Until my eyelids will no longer wag.

QUEEN   O my son, what theme?

HAMLET   I lov'd Ophelia; forty thousand brothers
Could not, with all their quantity of love,
Make up my sum.—What wilt thou do for her?

KING   O, he is mad, Laertes.

QUEEN   For love of God, forbear him.

HAMLET   'Swounds, show me what thou'lt do:
Woul't weep? woul't fight? woul't fast? woul't tear thyself?
Woul't drink up eisel? eat a crocodile?
I'll do't.—Dost thou come here to whine?

To outface me with leaping in her grave?
Be buried quick with her, and so will I:
And, if thou prate of mountains, let them throw
Millions of acres on us, till our ground,
Singeing his pate against the burning zone,
Make Ossa like a wart! Nay, an thou'lt mouth,
I'll rant as well as thou.

QUEEN   This is mere madness:
And thus awhile the fit will work on him;
Anon, as patient as the female dove,
When that her golden couplets are disclos'd,
His silence will sit drooping.

HAMLET   Hear you, sir;
What is the reason that you use me thus?
I lov'd you ever: but it is no matter;
Let Hercules himself do what he may,
The cat will mew, and dog will have his day. (*Exit*)

KING   I pray thee, good Horatio, wait upon him.—
          (*Exit* HORATIO)
          (*To* LAERTES)
Strengthen your patience in our last night's speech;
We'll put the matter to the present push.—
Good Gertrude, set some watch over your son.—
This grave shall have a living monument:
An hour of quiet shortly shall we see;
Till then, in patience our proceeding be.
          (*Exeunt*)

SCENE TWO

A hall in the castle.
          (*Enter* HAMLET *and* HORATIO)
HAMLET   So much for this, sir: now let me see the other;
     You do remember all the circumstance?

HORATIO   Remember it, my lord!

HAMLET   Sir, in my heart there was a kind of fighting
     That would not let me sleep: me thought I lay
     Worse than the mutines in the bilboes. Rashly,
     And prais'd be rashness for it,—let us know,
     Our indiscretion sometimes serves us well,
     When our deep plots do fail: and that should teach us
     There's a divinity that shapes our ends,
     Rough-hew them how we will.

HORATIO   This is most certain.

HAMLET   Up from my cabin,
     My sea-gown scarf'd about me, in the dark
     Grop'd I to find out them: had my desire;

Finger'd their packet; and, in fine, withdrew
To mine own room again: making so bold,
My fears forgetting manners, to unseal
Their grand commission; where I found, Horatio,
O royal knavery! an exact command,—
Larded with many several sorts of reasons,
Importing Denmark's health and England's too,
With, ho! such bugs and goblins in my life,—
That, on the supervise, no leisure bated,
No, not to stay the grinding of the axe,
My head should be struck off.

HORATIO   Is't possible?

HAMLET   Here's the commission: read it at more leisure.
But wilt thou hear me how I did proceed?

HORATIO   I beseech you.

HAMLET   Being thus benetted round with villainies,—
Ere I could make a prologue to my brains,
They had begun the play,—I sat me down;
Devis'd a new commission; wrote it fair:
I once did hold it, as our statists do,
A baseness to write fair, and labor'd much
How to forget that learning; but, sir, now
It did me yeoman's service. Wilt thou know
The effect of what I wrote?

HORATIO   Ay, good my lord.

HAMLET   An earnest conjuration from the king,—
As England was his faithful tributary;
As love between them like the palm might flourish;
As peace should still her wheaten garland wear
And stand a comma 'tween their amities;
And many such like as's of great charge,—
That, on the view and know of these contents,
Without debatement further, more or less,
He should the bearers put to sudden death,
Not shriving-time allow'd.

HORATIO   How was this seal'd?

HAMLET   Why, even in that was heaven ordinant.
I had my father's signet in my purse,
Which was the model of that Danish seal:
Folded the writ up in form of the other;
Subscrib'd it; gav't the impression; plac'd it safely,
The changeling never known. Now, the next day
Was our sea-fight; and what to this was sequent
Thou know'st already.

HORATIO   So Guildenstern and Rosencrantz go to't.

HAMLET   Why, man, they did make love to this employment;
They are not near my conscience; their defeat
Does by their own insinuation grow:

'Tis dangerous when the baser nature comes
Between the pass and fell incensed points
Of mighty opposites.
HORATIO   Why, what a king is this!
HAMLET   Does it not, think'st thee, stand me now upon,—
He that hath kill'd my king and whor'd my mother;
Popp'd in between the election and my hopes;
Thrown out his angle for my proper life,
And with such cozenage,—is't not perfect conscience
To quit him with this arm? and is't not to be damn'd,
To let this canker of our nature come
In further evil?
HORATIO   It must be shortly known to him from England
What is the issue of the business there.
HAMLET   It will be short: the interim is mine;
And a man's life's no more than to say One.
But I am very sorry, good Horatio,
That to Laertes I forgot myself;
For by the image of my cause I see
The portraiture of his: I'll court his favors:
But, sure, the bravery of his grief did put me
Into a towering passion.
HORATIO   Peace; who comes here?
            (*Enter* OSRIC)
OSRIC   Your lordship is right welcome back to Denmark.
HAMLET   I humbly thank you, sir.—Dost know this water-fly?
HORATIO   No, my good lord.
HAMLET   Thy state is the more gracious; for 'tis a vice to know him. He
hath much land, and fertile: let a beast be lord of beasts, and his crib shall
stand at the king's mess: 'tis a chough; but, as I say, spacious in the pos-
session of dirt.
OSRIC   Sweet lord, if your lordship were at leisure, I should impart a thing to
you from his majesty.
HAMLET   I will receive it with all diligence of spirit. Put your bonnet to his
right use; 'tis for the head.
OSRIC   I thank your lordship, 'tis very hot.
HAMLET   No, believe me, 'tis very cold; the wind is northerly.
OSRIC   It is indifferent cold, my lord, indeed.
HAMLET   Methinks it is very sultry and hot for my complexion.
OSRIC   Exceedingly, my lord; it is very sultry,— as't were,—I cannot tell how.—
But, my lord, his majesty bade me signify to you that he has laid a great
wager on your head. Sir, this is the matter,—
HAMLET   I beseech you, remember,—(HAMLET *moves him to put on his hat*)
OSRIC   Nay, in good faith; for mine ease, in good faith. Sir, here is newly come
to court Laertes; believe me, an absolute gentleman, full of most excellent
differences, of very soft society and great showing: indeed, to speak
feelingly of him, he is the card or calendar of gentry, for you shall find
in him the continent of what part a gentleman would see.

HAMLET   Sir, his definement suffers no perdition in you;—though, I know, to
divide him inventorially would dizzy the arithmetic of memory, and yet
but yaw neither, in respect of his quick sail. But, in the verity of extol-
ment, I take him to be a soul of great article; and his infusion of such
dearth and rareness as, to make true diction of him, his semblable is his
mirror; and who else would trace him, his umbrage, nothing more.

OSRIC   Your lordship speaks most infallibly of him.

HAMLET   The concernancy, sir? why do we wrap the gentleman in our more
rawer breath?

OSRIC   Sir?

HORATIO   Is't not possible to understand in another tongue? You will do't
sir, really.

HAMLET   What imports the nomination of this gentleman?

OSRIC   Of Laertes?

HORATIO   His purse is empty already; all's golden words are spent.

HAMLET   Of him, sir.

OSRIC   I know, you are not ignorant,—

HAMLET   I would you did, sir; yet, in faith, if you did, it would not much
approve me.—Well, sir.

OSRIC   You are not ignorant of what excellence Laertes is,—

HAMLET   I dare not confess that, lest I should compare with him in excellence;
but to know a man well were to know himself.

OSRIC   I mean, sir, for his weapon; but in the imputation laid on him by them,
in his meed he's unfellowed.

HAMLET   What's his weapon?

OSRIC   Rapier and dagger.

HAMLET   That's two of his weapons: but, well.

OSRIC   The king, sir, hath wagered with him six Barbary horses: against the
which he has imponed, as I take it, six French rapiers and poniards, with
their assigns, as girdle, hangers, and so: three of the carriages, in faith,
are very dear to fancy, very responsive to the hilts, most delicate carriages,
and of very liberal conceit.

HAMLET   What call you the carriages?

HORATIO   I knew you must be edified by the margent ere you had done.

OSRIC   The carriages, sir, are the hangers.

HAMLET   The phrase would be more german to the matter if we could carry
cannon by our sides: I would it might be hangers till then. But, on: six
Barbary horses against six French swords, their assigns, and three liberal
conceited carriages; that's the French bet against the Danish: why is this
imponed, as you call it?

OSRIC   The king, sir, hath laid, that in a dozen passes between you and him he
shall not exceed you three hits: he hath laid on twelve for nine; and it
would come to immediate trial if your lordship would vouchsafe the
answer.

HAMLET   How if I answer no?

OSRIC   I mean, my lord, the opposition of your person in trial.

HAMLET   Sir, I will walk here in the hall: if it please his majesty, it is the
breathing time of day with me: let the foils be brought, the gentleman

willing, and the king hold his purpose, I will win for him if I can; if not,
I will gain nothing but my shame and the odd hits.

OSRIC   Shall I re-deliver you e'en so?

HAMLET   To this effect, sir; after what flourish your nature will.

OSRIC   I commend my duty to your lordship.

HAMLET   Yours, yours.

     (*Exit* OSRIC)

He does well to commend it himself; there are no tongues else for's turn.

HORATIO   This lapwing runs away with the shell on his head.

HAMLET   He did comply with his dug before he sucked it. Thus has he,—and
many more of the same bevy, that I know the drossy age dotes on,—only
got the tune of the time, and outward habit of encounter; a kind of
yesty collection, which carries them through and through the most fanned
and winnowed opinions; and do but blow them to their trial, the bubbles
are out.

     (*Enter a* LORD)

LORD   My lord, his majesty commended him to you by young Osric, who
brings back to him that you attend him in the hall: he sends to know if
your pleasure hold to play with Laertes, or that you will take longer time.

HAMLET   I am constant to my purposes; they follow the king's pleasure: if his
fitness speaks, mine is ready; now or whensoever, provided I be so able
as now.

LORD   The king and queen and all are coming down.

HAMLET   In happy time.

LORD   The queen desires you to use some gentle entertainment to Laertes before you fall to play.

HAMLET   She well instructs me.

     (*Exit* LORD)

HORATIO   You will lose this wager, my lord.

HAMLET   I do not think so; since he went into France I have been in continual
practice: I shall win at the odds. But thou wouldst not think how ill all's
here about my heart: but it is no matter.

HORATIO   Nay, good my lord,—

HAMLET   It is but foolery; but it is such a kind of gain-giving as would perhaps
trouble a woman.

HORATIO   If your mind dislike anything, obey it: I will forestall their repair
hither, and say you are not fit.

HAMLET   Not a whit, we defy augury: there's a special providence in the fall
of a sparrow. If it be now, 'tis not to come; if it be not to come, it will be
now; if it be not now, yet it will come: the readiness is all. Since no man
has aught of what he leaves, what is't to leave betimes?

     (*Enter* KING, QUEEN, LAERTES, LORDS, OSRIC, *and*
     ATTENDANTS *with foils, &c.*)

KING   Come, Hamlet, come, and take this hand from me.

     (*The* KING *puts* LAERTES' *hand into* HAMLET'S)

HAMLET   Give me your pardon, sir: I have done you wrong:
But pardon't, as you are a gentleman.
This presence knows, and you must needs have heard,

How I am punish'd with sore distraction.
What I have done,
That might your nature, honor, and exception
Roughly awake, I here proclaim was madness.
Was't Hamlet wrong'd Laertes? Never Hamlet:
If Hamlet from himself be ta'en away,
And when he's not himself does wrong Laertes,
Then Hamlet does it not, Hamlet denies it.
Who does it, then? His madness: if't be so,
Hamlet is of the faction that is wrong'd;
His madness is poor Hamlet's enemy.
Sir, in this audience,
Let my disclaiming from a purpos'd evil
Free me so far in your most generous thoughts
That I have shot mine arrow o'er the house
And hurt my brother.

LAERTES   I am satisfied in nature,
Whose motive, in this case, should stir me most
To my revenge: but in my terms of honor
I stand aloof; and will no reconcilement
Till by some elder masters of known honor
I have a voice and precedent of peace
To keep my name ungor'd. But till that time
I do receive your offer'd love like love,
And will not wrong it.

HAMLET   I embrace it freely;
And will this brother's wager frankly play.—
Give us the foils; come on.

LAERTES   Come, one for me.

HAMLET   I'll be your foil, Laertes; in mine ignorance
Your skill shall, like a star in the darkest night,
Stick fiery off indeed.

LAERTES   You mock me, sir.

HAMLET   No, by this hand.

KING   Give them the foils, young Osric.
Cousin Hamlet,
You know the wager?

HAMLET   Very well, my lord;
Your grace hath laid the odds o' the weaker side.

KING   I do not fear it; I have seen you both;
But since he's better'd, we have therefore odds.

LAERTES   This is too heavy, let me see another.

HAMLET   This likes me well. These foils have all a length?
            (*They prepare to play*)

OSRIC   Ay, my good lord.

KING   Set me the stoups of wine upon that table,—
If Hamlet give the first or second hit,
Or quit in answer of the third exchange,

Let all the battlements their ordnance fire;
The king shall drink to Hamlet's better breath;
And in the cup an union shall he throw,
Richer than that which four successive kings
In Denmark's crown have worn. Give me the cups;
And let the kettle to the trumpet speak,
The trumpet to the cannoneer without,
The cannons to the heavens, the heavens to earth,
Now the king drinks to Hamlet.—Come, begin;—
And you, the judges, bear a wary eye.

HAMLET   Come on, sir.
LAERTES   Come, my lord.
          (*They play*)
HAMLET   One.
LAERTES   No.
HAMLET   Judgment.
OSRIC   A hit, a very palpable hit.
LAERTES   Well;—again.
KING   Stay, give me a drink.—Hamlet, this pearl is thine;
          Here's to thy health.—
              (*Trumpets sound, and cannon shot off within*)
          Give him the cup.
HAMLET   I'll play this bout first; set it by awhile.—
          Come.—Another hit; what say you?
              (*They play*)
LAERTES   A touch, a touch, I do confess.
KING   Our son shall win.
QUEEN   He's fat, and scant of breath.—
          Here, Hamlet, take my napkin, rub thy brows:
          The queen carouses to thy fortune, Hamlet.
HAMLET   Good madam!
KING   Gertrude, do not drink.
QUEEN   I will, my lord; I pray you, pardon me.
KING (*Aside*)   It is the poison'd cup; it is too late.
HAMLET   I dare not drink yet, madam; by and by.
QUEEN   Come, let me wipe thy face.
LAERTES   My lord, I'll hit him now.
KING   I do not think't.
LAERTES (*Aside*)   And yet 'tis almost 'gainst my conscience.
HAMLET   Come, for the third, Laertes: you but dally;
          I pray you, pass with your best violence:
          I am afeard you make a wanton of me.
LAERTES   Say you so? come on.
              (*They play*)
OSRIC   Nothing, neither way.
LAERTES   Have at you now!
              (LAERTES *wounds* HAMLET; *then, in scuffling, they change
              rapiers, and* HAMLET *wounds* LAERTES)

KING   Part them; they are incens'd.
HAMLET   Nay, come, again.
            (*The* QUEEN *falls*)
OSRIC   Look to the queen there, ho!
HORATIO   They bleed on both sides.—How is it, my lord?
OSRIC   How is't, Laertes?
LAERTES   Why, as a woodcock to my own springe, Osric;
      I am justly kill'd with mine own treachery.
HAMLET   How does the queen?
KING   She swoons to see them bleed.
QUEEN   No, no, the drink, the drink,—O my dear Hamlet,—
      The drink, the drink!—I am poison'd. (*Dies*)
HAMLET   O villainy!—Ho! let the door be lock'd:
      Treachery! seek it out.
            (LAERTES *falls*)
LAERTES   It is here, Hamlet: Hamlet, thou art slain;
      No medicine in the world can do thee good;
      In thee there is not half an hour of life;
      The treacherous instrument is in thy hand,
      Unbated and envenom'd: the foul practice
      Hath turn'd itself on me; lo, here I lie,
      Never to rise again: thy mother's poison'd:
      I can no more:—the king, the king's to blame.
HAMLET   The point envenom'd too!—
      Then venom to thy work. (*Stabs the* KING)
OSRIC *and* LORDS   Treason! treason!
KING   O, yet defend me, friends; I am but hurt.
HAMLET   Here, thou incestuous, murderous, damned Dane,
      Drink off this potion.—Is thy union here?
      Follow my mother.
            (*King dies*)
LAERTES   He is justly serv'd;
      It is a poison temper'd by himself.—
      Exchange forgiveness with me, noble Hamlet:
      Mine and my father's death come not upon thee,
      Nor thine on me! (*Dies*)
HAMLET   Heaven make thee free of it! I follow thee.—
      I am dead, Horatio.—Wretched queen, adieu!—
      You that look pale and tremble at this chance,
      That art but mutes or audience to this act,
      Had I but time,—as this fell sergeant, death,
      Is strict in his arrest,—O, I could tell you,—
      But let it be.—Horatio, I am dead;
      Thou liv'st; report me and my cause aright
      To the unsatisfied.
HORATIO   Never believe it:
      I am more an antique Roman than a Dane,—
      Here's yet some liquor left.

HAMLET As thou'rt a man,
Give me the cup; let go; by heaven, I'll have't.—
O good Horatio, what a wounded name,
Things standing thus unknown, shall live behind me!
If thou didst ever hold me in thy heart,
Absent thee from felicity awhile,
And in this harsh world draw thy breath in pain,
To tell my story.—
(*March afar off, and shot within*)
What warlike noise is this?
OSRIC Young Fortinbras, with conquest come from Poland,
To the ambassadors of England gives
This warlike volley.
HAMLET O, I die, Horatio;
The potent poison quite o'er-crows my spirit:
I cannot live to hear the news from England;
But I do prophesy the election lights
On Fortinbras: he has my dying voice;
So tell him, with the occurrents, more and less,
Which have solicited.—The rest is silence. (*Dies*)
HORATIO Now cracks a noble heart.—Good-night, sweet prince,
And flights of angels sing thee to thy rest!
Why does the drum come hither?
(*March within. Enter* FORTINBRAS, *the* ENGLISH
AMBASSADORS, *and others*)
FORTINBRAS Where is this sight?
HORATIO What is it you would see?
If aught of woe or wonder, cease your search.
FORTINBRAS This quarry cries on havoc.—O proud death,
What feast is toward in thine eternal cell,
That thou so many princes at a shot
So bloodily hast struck?
1ST AMBASSADOR The sight is dismal;
And our affairs from England come too late:
The ears are senseless that should give us hearing,
To tell him his commandment is fulfill'd,
That Rosencrantz and Guildenstern are dead:
Where should we have our thanks?
HORATIO Not from his mouth,
Had it the ability of life to thank you:
He never gave commandment for their death.
But since, so jump upon this bloody question,
You from the Polack wars, and you from England,
Are here arriv'd, give order that these bodies
High on a stage be placed to the view;
And let me speak to the yet unknowing world
How these things came about: so shall you hear
Of carnal, bloody, and unnatural acts;

Of accidental judgments, casual slaughters;
Of deaths put on by cunning and forc'd cause;
And, in this upshot, purposes mistook
Fall'n on the inventors' heads: all this can I
Truly deliver.

FORTINBRAS   Let us haste to hear it,
And call the noblest to the audience.
For me, with sorrow I embrace my fortune:
I have some rights of memory in this kingdom,
Which now to claim my vantage doth invite me.

HORATIO   Of that I shall have also cause to speak,
And from his mouth whose voice will draw on more:
But let this same be presently perform'd,
Even while men's minds are wild: lest more mischance
On plots and errors happen.

FORTINBRAS   Let four captains
Bear Hamlet like a soldier to the stage;
For he was likely, had he been put on,
To have prov'd most royally: and, for his passage,
The soldier's music and the rites of war
Speak loudly for him.—
Take up the bodies.—Such a sight as this
Becomes the field, but here shows much amiss.
Go, bid the soldiers shoot.

     (*A dead march*)
     (*Exeunt, bearing off the dead bodies: after which a*
     peal of ordnance is shot off)

From the Playwright

So much controversy surrounds Shakespeare's Hamlet, *resolution seems doubtful. It is, however, generally agreed that Quarto 2 (there are two Quartos and one Folio in addition to the Globe text) is the version transcribed directly from Shakespeare's original script, and since no notes or letters of the author concerning Hamlet survive him pointing otherwise, critics agree the stage directions found in Quarto 2 are from Shakespeare's hand. What follows, then, are those directions. (Comparisons with other transcriptions of HAMLET, including the one in this text, will reveal that scribes have added more detailed and sometimes more explicit stage directions in an effort to make the drama more "playable." In addition, various sentences have been altered.)*

Act One

Scene One

Enter Barnardo, and Francisco, two Centinels.
Enter Horatio, and Marcellus. (l. 13.)
Exit Fran.
Hora. What, ha's this thing. . . .
Enter Ghost.

Exit Ghost.

Enter Ghost. (l. 125.)

It spreads his armes.
The cocke crowes.
(l. 138.)

Exeunt.

Scene Two

Florish. Enter Claudius, King of Denmarke, Gertrad the Queene, Counsaile: as Polonius, and his Sonne Laertes, Hamlet, Cum Alijs.

Cor. Vo. In that, and. . . .

Florish. Exeunt all, but Hamlet.

Enter Horatio, Marcellus, and Bernardo.
Exeunt. (l. 253.)
Exit.

Scene Three

Enter Laertes, and Ophelia his Sister.
Enter Polonius. (l. 51, middle.)
Exit Laertes.
Exeunt.

Scene Four

Enter Hamlet, Horatio and Marcellus.
A florish of trumpets and 2. peeces goes of.
Enter Ghost.
Beckins.
Exit Ghost and Hamlet.

Exeunt.

Scene Five

Enter Ghost, and Hamlet.

Enter Horatio, and Marcellus.
Hora. My Lord,. . . .

Ham. So be it.
Mar. Illo, ho, ...

Ghost cries vnder the Stage.
Ghost. Sweare.

Exeunt.

Act Two

Scene One
Enter old Polonius,
with his man or two.
Exit Rey. (l. 73.)
Enter Ophelia.
Exeunt.

Scene Two
Florish. Enter King
and Queene,
Rosencraus and
Guyldensterne.

Exeunt Ros. and Guyld.

Enter Polonius.

Enter Embassadors.
(l. 57.)

Exeunt Embassadors.

Letter. (l. 116.)

Exit King and Queene.
(l. 169.)
Enter Hamlet. (l. 167.)

Enter Guyldersterne,
and Rosencraus
(l. 221.)

A Florish.

Enter Polonius.
Enter the Players.

Player. What
speech. . . .

Exeunt Pol. and
Players. (l. 573.)

Exeunt. (l. 574.)

Exit.

Act Three

Scene One
Enter King, Queene,
Polonius, Ophelia,
Rosencraus,
Guyldensterne, Lords.
Exeunt Ros. & Guyl.
Enter Hamlet. (l. 54.)

Exit.
Exit.
Enter King and
Polonius.

Exeunt.

Scene Two
Enter Hamlet, and
three of the Players.

Enter Polonius,
Guyldensterne, and
Rosencraus. (l. 52.)

Ros. I my Lord.

Exeunt they two.
Enter Horatio.
Nay. . . .
Enter Trumpets and
Kettle Drummes,

Scene Three
Enter King and
Queene.

Quee. So many
iourneyes. . . .
Quee. O confound. . . .

Quee. Nor earth. . . .

Quee. Sleepe rock. . . .
Exeunt.
Enter Lucianus.
(l. 254.)

Scene Two

King, Queene,
Polonius, Ophelia.
(l. 94.)

The Trumpets sounds.
Dumbe show followes.
Enter a King and a
Queene, the Queene
embracing him, and he
her, he takes her vp,
and declines his head
vpon her necke, he
lyes him downe vpon
a bancke of flowers,
she seeing him asleepe,
leaues him: anon come
in an other man, takes
off his crowne, kisses
it, pours poyson in the
sleepers eares, and
leaues him: the
Queene returnes, finds
the King dead, makes
passionate action, the
poysner with some
three or foure come in
againe, seeme to
condole with her, the
dead body is carried
away, the poysner
wooes the Queene with
gifts, she seemes harsh
awhile, but in the end
accepts loue.

Enter Prologue.
(l. 151.)

Scene Three

Pol. Lights, lights,
lights.

Exeunt all but Ham.
& Horatio.

Enter Rosencraus and
Guyldensterne.

Ros. What my Lord.

Enter the Players with
Recorders. (l. 357.)

Enter Polonius.
(l. 390.)

Then I will. . . .

I will. . . .

By and by. . . .

Exit.

Enter King,
Rosencraus, and
Guyldensterne.

Ros. We will. . . .

Exeunt Gent.

Enter Polonius.
Exit.

Enter Hamlet.
Exit.
Exit.

Scene Four

Enter Gertraid and
Polonius.

Enter Hamlet. (l. 5.)

Ham. That roares. . . .
(l. 52.)

Enter Ghost. (l. 101.)

Exit Ghost.
Exit.

Act Four

Scene One
Enter King, and
Queene, with
Rosencraus and
Guyldensterne.
Enter Ros. and Guild.
(l. 31.)
Exeunt.

Scene Two
Enter Hamlet,
Rosencraus, and others.
Exeunt. (l. 32.)

Scene Three
Enter King, and two
or three.
Enter Rosencraus and
all the rest.
They enter.
Exit.
Exit.

Scene Four
Enter Fortinbrasse
with his Army ouer
the stage.
Enter Hamlet,
Rosencraus, &c.
Exit.

Scene Five
Enter Horatio,
Gertrard, and a
Gentleman.
Gent. Shee is
importunat. . . .
Gent. She speakes
much. . . .
Hora. Twere good. . . .
Let her. . . .
Quee. To my. . . .
Enter Ophelia. (l. 16.)
shee sings. (l. 22.)
Song.
Enter King.
Song. (l. 38.)
Song.
A noise within.
Enter a Messenger.
(l. 96.)
Messem. Saue your
selfe. . . .
A noise within.
(l. 109.)
Enter Laertes with
others. (l. 110.)
A noyse within. Enter
Ophelia.
Laer. Let her. . . .
Song.
Song.
Exeunt.

Scene Six
Enter Horatio and
others.
Enter Saylers.
Exeunt.

Scene Seven
Enter King and
Laertes.
Enter a Messenger
with Letters.
Enter Queene.
Exit.
Exeunt.

Act Five

Scene One

Enter two Clownes.

Enter Hamlet and Horatio. (l. 72.)

Song.
Song.
Song.

Enter K. Q. Laertes and the corse.

Doct. Her obsequies. . . .

Doct. No more.

All. Gentlemen.

Hora. Good my Lord. . . .

Quee. This is meere madnesse, ...

Exit Hamlet and Horatio.

Exeunt.

Scene Two

Enter Hamlet and Horatio.

Enter a Courtier. (l. 67.)

Enter a Lord.

A table prepard, Trumpets, Drums and officers with Cushions, King, Queene, and all the state, Foiles, daggers, and Laertes.

Trumpets the while.

Drum, trumpets and shot. Florish, a peece goes off. (l. 292.)

A march a tarre off. (l. 359.)

Enter Osrick.

Enter Fortenbrasse, with the Embassadors.

Exeunt.

From the Critic

As one of the greatest critics in the history of drama, **William Hazlitt** *discusses the complex Hamlet in his famous* Characters in Shakespeare's Plays, *concluding that a bit of Hamlet exists in all of us.*

On the Character Hamlet

Hamlet is a name; his speeches and sayings but the idle coinage of the poet's brain. What then, are they not real? They are as real as our own thoughts. Their reality is in the reader's mind. It is *we* who are Hamlet. This play has a prophetic truth, which is above that of history. Whoever has become thoughtful and melancholy through his own mishaps or those of others; whoever has borne about with him the clouded brow of reflection, and thought himself 'too much i' th' sun'; whoever has seen the golden lamp of day dimmed by envious mists rising in his own breast, and could find in the world before him only a dull blank with nothing left remarkable in it; whoever has known 'the pangs of despised love, the insolence of office, or the spurns which patient merit of the unworthy takes'; he who has felt his mind sink within him, and sadness cling to his heart like a malady, who has had his hopes blighted and his youth staggered by the apparitions of strange things; who cannot be well at ease, while he sees evil hovering near him like a spectre; whose powers of action have been eaten up by thought, he to whom the universe seems infinite, and himself nothing; whose bitterness of soul makes him careless of consequences, and who goes to play as his best resource to shove off, to a second remove, the evils of life by a mock representation of them—this is the true Hamlet.

We have been so used to this tragedy that we hardly know how to criticise it any more than we should know how to describe our own faces. But we must make such observations as we can. It is the one of Shakespeare's plays that we think of the oftenest, because it abounds most in striking reflections on human life, and because the distresses of Hamlet are transferred, by the turn of his mind, to the general account of humanity. Whatever happens to him we apply to ourselves, because he applies it so himself as a means of general reasoning. He is a great moraliser; and what makes him worth attending to is, that he moralises on his own feelings and experience. He is not a common-place pedant. If *Lear* is distinguished by the greatest depth of passion, HAMLET is the most remarkable for the ingenuity, originality, and unstudied developement of character. Shakespeare had more magnanimity than any other poet, and he has shewn more of it in this play than in any other. There is no attempt to force an interest: every thing is left for time and circumstances to unfold. The attention is excited without effort, the incidents succeed each other as matters of course, the characters think and speak and act just as they might do, if left entirely to themselves. There is no set purpose, no straining at a point. The observations are suggested by the passing scene—the gusts of passion come and go like sounds of music borne on the wind. The whole play is an exact transcript of what might be supposed to have taken place at the court of Denmark, at the remote period of time fixed upon, before the modern refinements in morals and manners were heard of. It would have been interesting enough to have been admitted as a by-stander in such a scene, at such a time, to have heard and witnessed something of what was going on. But here we are more than spectators. We have not only 'the outward pageants and the signs of grief'; but 'we have that within which passes shew.' We read the thoughts of the heart, we catch the passions living as they rise. Other dramatic writers give us very fine versions and paraphrases of nature; but Shakespeare, together with his own comments, gives us the original text, that we may judge for ourselves. This is a very great advantage.

The character of Hamlet stands quite by itself. It is not a character marked by strength of will or even of passion, but by refinement of thought and sentiment. Hamlet is as little of the hero as a man can well be: but he is a young and princely novice, full of high enthusiasm and quick sensibility—the sport of circumstances, questioning with fortune and refining on his own feelings, and forced from the natural bias of his disposition by the strangeness of his situation. He seems incapable of deliberate action, and is only hurried into extremities on the spur of the occasion, when he has no time to reflect, as in the scene where he kills Polonius, and again, where he alters the letters which Rosencraus and Guildenstern are taking with them to England, purporting his death. At other times, when he is most bound to act, he remains puzzled, undecided, and sceptical, dallies with his purposes, till the occasion is lost, and finds out some pretence to relapse into indolence and thoughtfulness again. For this reason he refuses to kill the King when he is at his prayers, and by a refinement in malice, which is in truth only an excuse for his own want of resolution, defers his revenge to a more fatal opportunity, when he shall be engaged in some act 'that has no relish of salvation in it.'

> 'He kneels and prays,
> And now I'll do't, and so he goes to heaven,
> And so am I reveng'd: *that would be scann'd.*
> He kill'd my father, and for that,
> I, his sole son, send him to heaven.
> Why this is reward, not revenge.
> Up sword and know thou a more horrid time,
> When he is drunk, asleep, or in a rage.'

He is the prince of philosophical speculators; and because he cannot have his revenge perfect, according to the most refined idea his wish can form, he declines it altogether. So he scruples to trust the suggestions of the ghost, contrives the scene of the play to have surer proof of his uncle's guilt, and then rests satisfied with this confirmation of his suspicions, and the success of his experiment, instead of acting upon it. Yet he is sensible of his own weakness, taxes himself with it, and tries to reason himself out of it.

. . . . .

Still he does nothing; and this very speculation on his own infirmity only affords him another occasion for indulging it. It is not from any want of attachment to his father or of abhorrence of his murder that Hamlet is thus dilatory, but it is more to his taste to indulge his imagination in reflecting upon the enormity of the crime and refining on his schemes of vengeance, than to put them into immediate practice. His ruling passion is to think, not to act: and any vague pretext that flatters this propensity instantly diverts him from his previous purposes.

From the Director

In his planning for the production, the theatre director has among his multitude of responsibilities overseeing the choice and construction of costumes, hoping at all times to remain appropriate as well as inventive. In this capacity, **Tyrone Guthrie** *of the renowned Minnesota Theatre Company chose to present Shakespeare's* Hamlet *in modern dress, and in the process, aroused quite a furor. What follows is his rationale for this choice.*

Costuming Hamlet

At ten on Monday morning March 11, 1963, the Minnesota Theatre Company met in the rehearsal room of the theatre. We were quite a large group—thirty-five actors; the stage manager, Rex Partington, and his two assistants; Tanya Moiseiwitsch and her two attendants; the McKnight Fellows; Douglas Campbell and myself; and, in addition, ten men and two women, hired locally, who were to be courtiers, soldiers, and so on, in Hamlet.

The model of the set for Hamlet was on view, also the sketches for the dresses—modern dresses. Miss Moiseiwitsch and I had decided to dress this production as though the play were taking place in a contemporary European royal court. Since this decision aroused some controversy, I shall briefly explain our reasons.

In modern clothes it is possible at a glance to infer a number of things about the characters of the play, which are not apparent in period dress; the time of day, for instance, and the weather; who is a civilian and who a soldier.

The time of day is particularly important in the middle section of the play. It is valuable for the audience to realise that there is no time lapse from Hamlet's advice to the Players, right through the play scene and the subsequent scenes in the King's room and the Queen's, the chase through the palace after Hamlet has murdered Polonius, the meeting hastily convened by Claudius just before dawn when Hamlet is sent to England, right through to the final scene of this sequence (Act 4, Scene IV), where in the first light of dawn Hamlet, escorted by Rosencrantz and Guildenstern, encounters, on his way to take ship for England, the invading army of Fortinbras. All these events occur during one terrible night. This dramatic point does not really emerge when the players are in "costume," but in modern dress it is clear. We see them change for the play into spectacular and elaborate evening dresses. Not only does this mark the time of day, it also implies that the Command Performance of The Murder of Gonzago is a Gala Occasion. During the following scenes of confusion and panic, the finery gradually falls apart—hair gets ruffled, ties crumple; when Claudius calls up his "wisest friends" the hour of the day is indicated, and the emergency stressed, by the fact that some of them have obviously just been dug up out of their beds.

This is but one instance of many where we believed that contemporary clothes could help to clarify a complicated story. Since we knew that a large proportion of our audience would be seeing the play for the first time, it seemed a good idea to make the story as clear as we could.
. . . . .

Perhaps it is impertinent, but as a Director I feel it is my duty to try to protect Shakespeare, and to try to protect all of us, from our passionate addiction to Romance and to Stereotype.

Therefore in Hamlet it seemed a good idea to dress the characters in a manner which accords with the text but does not necessarily accord with the stereotype.

How, it may be argued, can a modern-dress production accord with a text which describes Hamlet as appearing to Ophelia with "his doublet all unbraced, no hat upon his head, his stockings fouled, ungartered and down-gyved to his ankle." It cannot. But this, I think, is the single instance where modern dress does not support the text; and to condemn the use of modern dress simply for this one departure does not seem reasonable, if it be admitted that there are adequate compensatory reasons for its use.

I suppose the arch-stereotype of all theatrical stereotypes is the figure of Hamlet himself. I would venture to assume that for most people the name Hamlet conjures up a vision of a very mournful, distempered-looking young person in a black velvet tam-o'-shanter with a drooping ostrich feather, black velvet tunic trimmed with black beads, black tights. The figure is addressing itself to a skull. It is the incarnation of the Gloomy Dane and derives, I suspect, from numerous engravings of old actors in the role.

In fact, to my mind, the evidence that Hamlet is a gloomy fellow, who is "constitutionally incapable of decisive action," is entirely outweighed by contrary evidence in the text. Further, there is no reason to suppose that the "traditional" costume is any more right than a modern suit, rather the contrary. The "traditional" black bonnet and tunic does not accord with the costume worn in Shakespeare's own day, nor with the textual evidence of doublet, stockings, garters and so on. There is reason to believe, though no one knows for certain, that Burbage, the original interpreter of Hamlet, will, according to theatrical custom of his day, have worn contemporary dress, to which will have been added a certain amount of fancywork and feathers to denote royalty and make a show.

There would therefore be some logic in producing the play in late Elizabethan dress. This is very rarely done, for several excellent reasons. If the clothes of this period are to look either authentic or handsome, they must be made of very stiff, heavy and expensive material; they demand a high degree of craftsmanship from the tailor and an inordinate amount of his time; they need a great deal of maintenance and laundry work; and, when finally achieved, are exceedingly uncomfortable and difficult to wear.

Failing Elizabethan dress, it seems to me that modern clothes are the next most logical choice, though I admit logic is not necessarily the right basis for deciding how to dress a play.

The "traditional" costume is not logical at all; it is based upon styles seen in early sixteenth-century Italian painting, which are then freely adapted to suit the figure of the actor, the taste of the designer and the purse of the management. There are, however, good arguments in its favour; it is cheap, comfortable, becoming and, because it is so usual in the context of Hamlet, it excites no undue comment, it is accepted as "right." The single good reason against using it seems to me unanswerable; it encourages the audience, almost obliges it, to accept the romantic stereotype.

We figured that if the characters looked recognisable, like the sort of people with whom we are familiar and whom we can place in the context of our own experience, it would be easier to accept them as real people, not just as remote beings from another era. We believed that by so doing we need not necessarily make the stage look drab and ordinary. The fact that the play is set in a royal court permitted us to dress the men either in formal clothes or handsome, colourful full-dress uniforms, and to deck the women out with long gloves, plenty of jewelry and dignified, long dresses. Some of our critics objected that the full-dress uniforms were nineteenth-century and did not "go" with modern civilian suits. In this they were mistaken. In all European courts, military full dress has hardly changed in the last hundred years, and is seen in the same rooms and at the same functions as completely modern civilian clothes.

Our final reason for producing this particular Hamlet in modern dress was that we believed it would better suit an American cast, less at home with "period" plays than British actors who get more opportunities to appear in them. American actors are apt to be inhibited and self-conscious in the clothes of other days. They feel that they must grope for something called "style," which consists of getting into elegant attitudes, tapping snuffboxes, waving fans and lace handkerchiefs and in general carrying-on in a very fancy way. In fact, style is not something which can be assumed externally. It consists of knowledge, of knowing what the play you are doing is about, which involves not just a knowledge of the story and the characters but of their whole environment. Only so can you be sure of why your speeches are written as they are, why your character behaves as he does; only in the light of such knowledge can you wear your clothes, move, speak, think and feel truly. Style, therefore, in a period play is the knowledge which enables your acting to bear the stamp of truth.

Moreover, style does not only apply to period plays, or to plays about grand and elegant people. There is a style to Westerns, for instance, which totally eludes British actors, but comes easily to actors who have the right knowledge; the knowledge, in this case, of the relevant environment. If competent British actors can make the complete hash, which I have seen them do, of Oklahoma! or Room Service, it ought not to be strange if no less competent American actors approach Shakespeare with the accent on values other than Renaissance splendour and high style.

. . . . .

I have digressed at some length on this matter because it seems relevant in any consideration of a classical repertoire. If classics are to be fresh and not preserved in a sort of aspic of uncritical reverence, then there must be constant experiment with their production. Yet it must be faced that such experiment will be conducted in the teeth of furious opposition by a considerable section of just that public who will be the support of a classic theatre. It is a pity in some ways; but on the whole I welcome such opposition. It is a sign of life. Controversy is far healthier than acquiescence. . . .

Source Materials for *Hamlet*

BY THE CRITICS

Bradley, A. C. *Shakespearean Tragedy: Lectures on* Hamlet. 1904.

Draper, J. W. *The* Hamlet *of Shakespeare's Audience*. New York: Octagon Books, 1966.

Granville-Barker, H. *Prefaces to Shakespeare*. Princeton University Press, 1965.

Levin, H. *The Question of* Hamlet. New York: Oxford University Press, 1959.

Weitz, M. Hamlet *and the Philosophy of Literary Criticism*. Chicago: University of Chicago Press, 1964.

Wilson, J. D. *What Happens in* Hamlet. New York: Cambridge University Press, 1951.

BY THE DIRECTORS

Flatter, Richard. *Shakespeare's Producing Hand*. William Heinemann, Ltd.

Gielgud, John, and Gilder, Rosamond. *John Gielgud's* Hamlet: *A Record of Performance with Notes on Costume, Scenery and Stage Business*. New York: Oxford University Press, 1937.

Guthrie, Tyrone. "Hidden Motives in Five Shakespearean Plays." In *In Various Directions*. New York: Macmillan, 1965, pp. 73–82.

King, T. J. *Shakespearean Staging, 1599–1642*. Cambridge: Harvard University Press, 1971.

Lawrence, W. J. "The Staging of *Hamlet*." In *Pre-Restoration Stage Studies*. New York: Benjamin Blom, 1967.

Rossi, Alfred. *Minneapolis Rehearsals: Guthrie Directs Hamlet*. Berkeley: University of California Press, 1970.

Watkins, R. *On Producing Shakespeare*. New York: Benjamin Blom, 1964.

Webster, Margaret. *Shakespeare Without Tears*. New York: Fawcett World Library, 1957.

Wilson, Dover. *The Manuscript of Shakespeare's* Hamlet, 1934.

AUDIO-VISUAL SOURCES

Hamlet, Shakespeare Recording Society. Caedmon Records.

Hamlet, Burton and Broadway Cast. Columbia Records (dol-302).

Hamlet, 16mm, B & W, (Lawrence Olivier), Contemporary Films, Inc.

HAMLET SERIES (Four films, 28 min. each, color)
1. *Hamlet*—The Age of Elizabeth
2. *Hamlet*—The Readiness is All
3. *Hamlet*—The Poisoned Kingdom
4. *Hamlet*—What Happens in *Hamlet*

Shakespeare—Soul of An Age, 16mm, Color, Parts I and II, 56 min. each, NBC.

Shakespeare's Theatre—The Globe Playhouse—B & W, 18 min., University of Indiana.

Comedy

Comedy is the most elusive of the dramatic modes to define. Trying to hazard a definition is like trying to grab a bowl of jello—its shape keeps changing. We can say that comedy is a lighter form of drama than tragedy, offering amusement as its primary goal. The level of amusement comedy evokes can vary from a slight chuckle to uproarious laughter. Whatever the reaction of the audience, comedy most often achieves its effect through presenting some incongruity of speech, action, or character. Though serious subject matter can be treated in comedy, as well as in tragedy, comedy's treatment is lighter, merrier, and generally irreverent.

Definition

Professor Alan Thompson[1] sees comedy as a ladder, ranging from the very lowest rung, obscenity, to the very highest, satire. These graduated scales serve to distinguish the kinds of comedy:

| FARCE | HIGH COMEDY |

        FARCE   HIGH COMEDY
                      6.   Comedy of ideas and satire
                  5.   Inconsistencies of character
              4.   Verbal wit
          3.   Plot device
      2.   Physical mishaps
  1.   Obscenity

For our purposes, we can draw the dividing line between comedy and farce between rungs three and four. That is, we shall consider a play farce if it primarily concerns or contains either obscenity or physical mishaps, or is founded on plot devices. Thus Shakespeare's *Comedy of Errors*, despite its title, is really farce. It is founded on a rather unlikely plot device, dealing with double mistaken identity and the ensuing entanglements. While Molière's *Tartuffe* is comedy (as we will see), his *Physician in Spite of Himself* is farce. A casual reading of *Physician* is enough to reveal mistaken identities, disguises, and beatings. Although farce can present occasional flashes of wit or even satire (*Physician* ridicules the medical profession), these attempts at higher purposes are subordinate to the action and effect. The action often is contrived and unreal, and the effect is usually pure entertainment. To be sure, a basic criterion for comedy is that it be honest in its portrayal of life, something farce is not.

---

[1] Alan Reynolds Thompson, *The Anatomy of Drama* (Berkeley: University of California Press, 1942).

Purpose

Behind the laughter comedy evokes is a purpose, an idea or a protest that provokes thought. Bergson[2] believed comedy had a social, or critical, function. In each culture, there are those who deviate from the norm. Laughter and ridicule are a way for the audience to "keep the character in line" and return him to the status quo. In *Tartuffe*, for example, Molière, commenting on religious hypocrisy, attempts to expose and ridicule an individual who is trying to capitalize on one of society's institutions, religion; and Molière's purpose, like Sophocles', transcends the printed page.

Traditionally, the role of comedy has been to produce laughter at someone or something that stands out, apart from the social norm, in order to perpetuate the prevailing social order. (Molière's comments will attest to this.) A function of comedy, then, may be to correct "man's vices and follies." Ideally, the audience identifies with the comic events, and their laughter serves as a sort of comic catharsis, purging feelings of ridicule or dissonance. The laughter caused by comedy, unlike that evoked by farce, is a *genuine* laughter stemming from *probable* events, which allows fuller audience identification, and thus a more complete purging. In pre-modern comedies, audiences felt genuine laughter for the foibles of a comic individual in a proper society.

It is interesting to note, however, that contemporary comedy (from Shaw to the present) seems to have switched the roles of society and the individual. *Society* is now the comic figure. It is *society*, and not the individual, that is sick and must be cured. Because our society can be seen as impersonal, mechanized, and repressive, its failings must be exposed, ridiculed, damned, and satirized. George Bernard Shaw was perhaps the first great playwright to use comedy to achieve this end. Plays like *Man and Superman* and *Arms and the Man* are social commentary. (Indeed, his plays, at least to some, are unique enough to be given a separate listing— Shavian Comedy.) In the twentieth century, many of Noel Coward's plays succeed in satirizing society's upper classes. And the playwrights of the theatre of the absurd have labelled their works tragi-comedies and tragi-farces (see section on theatre of the absurd).

There are other theories about the purpose of comedy that we haven't the room to discuss here.

---

[2] Henri Bergson, *Laughter*, translated by C. Brereton and F. Rothwell (New York: The Macmillan Co., 1917).

Language

Whatever comedy's purpose or type (be it sentimental or romantic comedy, or comedy of manners or ideas), we must keep in mind that it still can be distinguished from farce—by its language, as well as by purpose. Language is to comedy what action is to farce. It is the vehicle by which the purpose is achieved. Comedy's language tools may include epigrams (terse, pointed statements or poems often carrying a definite meaning) or puns (plays on words). An example of an epigram, found in *Tartuffe*, is: "Those whose conduct gives room to talk are always the first to attack their neighbors." In Richard B. Sheridan's *School for Scandal*, Sir Harry is raising a toast to Maria and to women in general:

> Here's to the maiden of bashful fifteen;
> Here's to the widow of fifty;
> Here's to the flaunting, extravagant queen,
> And here's to the housewife that's thrifty.
> > Let the toast pass;
> > Drink to the lass;
> I'll warrant she'll prove an excuse for the glass.

In another of Sheridan's plays, *The Rivals*, pun is exemplified when Mrs. Malaprop says, "Illiterate him, I say, quite from your memory."

Other language tools used by the playwright include imagery (vivid, imaginative, rather than literal, expressions), or antithesis (juxtaposition of opposing terms for comic effect, such as "your naked coverings"). Sheridan, again in *The Rivals*, gives us a good example of another tool, alliteration (repetition of the same sound in successive or closely associated words or syllables), when Sir Ben says, "where a neat rivulet of text shall meander through a meadow of margin." Other than these tools, the author may choose to use irony (the opposite of what is expected), or perhaps, repartee (rapid instances of wit, bounced back and forth in conversation). An excellent example of this occurs in Sheridan's *School for Scandal:*

LADY TEAZLE   What's the matter Mrs. Candour?
MRS. CANDOUR   They'll not allow our friend Mrs. Vermillion
    to be handsome.
LADY TEAZLE   Oh, surely, she's a pretty woman.
CRAB   I'm very glad you think so ma'am.
MRS. CANDOUR   She has a charming fresh color.
LADY TEAZLE   Yes, when it is fresh put on.
MRS. CANDOUR   Oh fie! I'll swear her color is
    natural: I have seen it come and go.

LADY TEAZLE   I dare say you have, ma'am: it goes off at night
    and comes again in the morning.
SIR BEN   True, ma'am, it not only comes and goes; but, what's
    more, egad, her maid can fetch and carry it.

It is through language that comedy comes to life. Its appeal, most
often, is intellectual; and its subject matter serious. The language of comedy,
more often than not, is witty and light. And the laughter evoked is usually
at or with a character, rarely because of him. The play included here as a
representative of comedy presents an example of the purposes of comedy,
and is replete with the tools of language that are necessary for achieving
those purposes.

Tartuffe assures Orgon his intentions are totally benign. San Diego City College.

Tartuffe begins to display his true nature in the first scene with Elmire. Stratford Shakespearean Festival, Ontario. Jean Gascon, director. Photo courtesy Douglas Spillane.

Orgon's patience is worn thin from hearing about Tartuffe. University of Denver.

Mariane politely listens while Mme. Pernell expounds Tartuffe's virtues. Central Florida Junior College, George Statler, director.

Tartuffe feigns innocence as his hypocrisy shines through. Austin Peay State University, I. J. Filippo, director.

Just before his arrest, Tartuffe kneels in the 1860 version by the Asolo State Theatre Co. Photo by Wayne Manley. Robert Strane, director. (See "Notes on Transplanting a Classic.")

Mme. Pernell refuses to believe that Tartuffe could be such a scoundrel. Boston University.

One of the most memorable moments of the theatre, as Orgon hides while Tartuffe attempts to seduce Elmire. Seattle Repertory Theatre, Allen Fletcher, director. Tartuffe: Joseph Sommer; Orgon: George Vogel; Elmire: Kay Doubleday.

Hypocrisy is a homage vice pays to virtue.
Duc De La Rochefoucauld

Tartuffe

Molière

Translated by James L. Rosenberg

Tartuffe

Characters   MADAME PERNELLE, *mother of Orgon*
ORGON
ELMIRE, *Orgon's wife*
DAMIS, *son of Orgon, stepson of Elmire*
MARIANE, *daughter of Orgon and stepdaughter of Elmire*
VALÈRE
CLÉANTE, *brother-in-law of Orgon, brother of Elmire*
TARTUFFE
DORINE, *companion of Mariane*
MONSIEUR LOYAL, *bailiff*
A POLICE OFFICER
FLIPOTE, *Madame Pernelle's servant*

Scene   *The setting thoughout is the salon of* ORGON'S *house in
Paris. The furnishings are those of a well-to-do bourgeois.*

Act One

SCENE ONE

MADAME PERNELLE, FLIPOTE, ELMIRE, MARIANE, DORINE, DAMIS,
and CLÉANTE.
MME. PERNELLE   Come on, Flipote, away from their mad chatter.
ELMIRE   Heavens, Madame! Now what can be the matter?
MME. PERNELLE   Enough, enough; spare me their smiling faces.
    I can well dispense with certain airs and graces.
ELMIRE   Madame, no one has given you cause to grieve;
    Why, I pray, are you so resolved to leave?
MME. PERNELLE   I cannot stand this place a minute more;
    My every wish is trampled and spurned to the floor.
    I leave your house no wiser, but much sadder,
    And now—heigh ho!—you ask me what's the matter.
    None honors age, all speak with impudence,
    This house has become like a Court of Insolence.
DORINE   If . . .
MME. PERNELLE   You are, my girl, a humble maid, a minion,
    And yet you talk and give us your free opinion
    Like the veriest, blabbiest, gabbling hobbledehoy!
DAMIS   But . . .
MME. PERNELLE   In words of single syllables, my boy,

You are a fool. And that's all there is to that.
You've no more common sense than my old cat.
I've warned your father, not once, but a hundred times
That in the end you'd not be worth a dime.

MARIANE   I think . . .

MME. PERNELLE   And you, his sister, so demure and shy!
But I suspect that sparkle in your eye;
I note the adage about waters running deep
When I hear you sweetly sigh and softly weep.

ELMIRE   But, mother . . .

MME. PERNELLE   And you who should above all play the role
Of modesty and grace; upon the whole
I find your conduct shocking. Is it your place
To squander your husband's money, paint your face,
And boldly parade your charms before the world
Like a golden galleon with all her sails unfurled?
A woman who only seeks to attract her spouse
Does not so gaily decorate the house!

CLÉANTE   But, madame, after all . . .

MME. PERNELLE   And you, my lad,
I honor, love and respect you, need I add?
But if I were in my son her husband's place
I'd earnestly ask you not to show your face
Ever again in my house. It seems you preach
Tireless moral maxims, but what you teach
And what you live do not precisely agree.
Foregive my bluntness; my manner of speech is free.

DAMIS   I'm sure, madame, your Tartuffe is fortunate . . .

MME. PERNELLE   He is a man you might well imitate,
And it makes me furious through and through
To hear him maligned by a fool and a dolt like you.

DAMIS   What the devil? (Pardon the expression!)
Am I to live at the bigoted discretion
Of a puritanical tyrant and beg his consent
To live or breathe in my father's establishment?

DORINE   According to him and his maxims, we can't begin
To wiggle a toe without committing a sin.
He's got his nose in everything, sniffing out wrongs.

MME. PERNELLE   Wherever his nose is, there, I'm sure, it belongs.
He seeks to lead you with him on Heaven's path,
And you, like silly geese, just sit and laugh.

DAMIS   Neither the due respect I owe to my father
Nor anything else could make me go to the bother
Of trying to like that unctuous hypocrite,
And I cannot live at ease with myself and sit
At the table with him, smiling and wishing him well,
Or wishing, in short, he were anywhere else but in Hell!

DORINE   Indeed, I say it's a monstrous and scandalous thing
    To see a stranger come and put a ring
    In the master's nose and lead him around like a bull—
    A penniless tramp whose belly was seldom full,
    Whose shoes and coat were as holy as now he allows
    His precious soul is—having the run of the house!

MME. PERNELLE   Ah! mercy on us! how happy we would be
    If we all obeyed his wise and pious decrees.

DORINE   He's a shining saint in your imagination
    But a hypocrite in our frank estimation.

MME. PERNELLE   Hold your tongue!

DORINE   I wouldn't trust him, by the book,
    As far as I could throw a ten-ton rock.

MME. PERNELLE   All your malicious lies leave me unmoved.
    In my opinion, Tartuffe stands approved
    In every way. You hate him, you foolish things,
    Because he tells you of your faults and brings
    A message calling your souls away from sin.
    Heaven's all he's interested in.

DORINE   Oh, yes indeed! But tell me why, I pray,
    He wants to drive all visitors away.
    When someone calls, is Heaven so offended
    That he must rave as though the world had ended?
    Do you know what I think of the affair? (*pointing to* ELMIRE)
    I think he's jealous of Madame—so there!

MME. PERNELLE   Hold your tongue and mind what you are saying.
    He's not alone in finding your giddy playing
    And all your social life a bit too much:
    These carriages and servants, crowds and such,
    Disturb the neighborhood with an uproar
    The like of which has not been heard before
    By decent folk. No doubt there's no harm done,
    But gossip breeds like flies in the summer sun.

CLÉANTE   Ah, madame, would you cure the human race
    Of gossiping or showing the double face?
    And what a sorry world now this would be
    If every little lie that touched on me
    Forced me to lose a friend. The fact
    Is, no one's ever legislated tact.
    No one's safe against the tongue of slander
    Or those malicious souls who long to pander
    To the mob's desire for scandal. No, each man
    Must merely live as wisely as he can.

DORINE   Isn't it old Daphne and that shrimp
    Of a husband of hers—the little pimp!—
    Who've been busy spreading their gossip and lies
    About us? We're sinners in their eyes,

Or so they say. But why, pray, is it those
Whose own inane behavior, Heaven knows,
Is always most ridiculous or suspect
Who seem to feel it's their duty to inflict
Their stupid opinions upon the rest of us?
Can it be these peccadilloes they discuss
Are exactly the things they're up to on the sly
And they think the insinuating lie
Of who was seen ascending someone's stairs
Will leave them free to conduct their own affairs?

MME PERNELLE   All this chitchat's quite beside the point.
You all, I'm sure, know my dear friend Orante,
A good and saintly woman, full of grace;
She's not pleased with what goes on in this place.

DORINE   A fine example, and a most chaste wife!
It's true indeed she lives an austere life,
But age has waked that cold reforming zeal;
The fire dies down when one runs out of fuel.
Many a prude's born when youth's beauty dies
And looks perforce on life with saintly eyes.
Orante now hides beneath discretion's veil
Those fading charms that from henceforth must fail
To win esteem. These veteran coquettes
Revenge themselves on a world that soon forgets
Their fast-decaying beauty and retire
To rectitude, renouncing all desire;
Cheated of love, they turn to criticism
And make Morality their catechism;
They censure all who taste the joy of life
And concentrate on stirring endless strife.
Not principle, but envy, activates
Their tireless tongues and bitterly creates
That twisted malice which insanely drives them
To hate those pleasures of which age deprives them.

MME. PERNELLE (*to* ELMIRE)   These are the things that you delight to hear,
And it seems this gracious lady has your ear
And is allowed to go on talking all the day
While I must keep my peace and go my way.
Alas, the sins of this world! Yet I'll be heard
And give you, will-you nill-you, this last word:
The wisest decision my son has ever made
Was in taking this holy man to be his guide;
God has sent him here to redeem your sins
And show you where the road to Heaven begins.
All those balls and dances, conversations,
Those goings to and fro, those visitations
Are surely inspired by the Evil One's decrees;

One never hears a pious word or sees
A modest action; all come in for their share
In the tide of malicious gossip running there.
In short, all sensible people lose their sense
In that sea of shallow frippery and pretense.
A thousand silly stories spread in a day,
And I heard a certain noted doctor say
This house has become a virtual Tower of Babel
Where everyone talks as fast and loud as he's able.
And to explain how this comment came to be . . . (*pointing to*
    CLÉANTE)
But I see yon gentleman secretly smiling at me.
Eh bein, go find the fools who make you gay. (*to* ELMIRE)
To you, my daughter, I've nothing more to say,
Except that I disapprove of your home and friends;
Good-bye. Farewell. Here our acquaintance ends. (*giving* FLIPOTE
    a box on the ear)
Come on, wake up, you silly gaping goose!
I'll fetch you a wallop will knock your senses loose!
Come on, away, away!

SCENE TWO

CLÉANTE *and* DORINE.

CLÉANTE   I'll not go rushing
    After her, for fear of more tongue-lashing.
    That old battle-axe . . .
DORINE   Ah, it's a pity
    She can't hear you. What a lively ditty
    She would sing you now—she'd shout and scold
    To let you know she's not so awfully old!
CLÉANTE   How angry she was with us, and all for nothing!
    Tartuffe has got her poor old brain a-buzzing.
DORINE   All this is a minor situation
    Compared to the master's infatuation.
    If you could only see him, you'd say he's turned
    An utter fool. In recent years he'd earned
    The reputation of a man of sense,
    But since Tartuffe's bewitched him, all pretense
    Of plain intelligence has left his head.
    He calls him "brother" and has often said
    He loves him more than daughter, son, or wife.
    He makes him the director of his life
    And his secret soul's true confidant;
    A mistress or a sweetheart couldn't want
    More tender demonstrations of his love;
    At the dining table, Tartuffe sits above

In the place of honor, like a greedy glutton
Devouring vast slabs of beef and mutton;
The choicest cuts are his, let him but "hic"
The master cries "God bless you!" double quick.
In short, he dotes upon him like a fool;
Tartuffe's his hero, and he's the villian's tool.
He quotes him with the wildest admiration
And praises him on every least occasion.
Tartuffe, who knows a sucker when he sees him,
Employs a hundred little arts to please him;
He steals him blind, meanwhile, with pious maxims,
While criticizing all the family's actions.
Even that sneering jackanapes of a boy
Who serves him as a page seems to enjoy
The freedom of the house and has the power
To lecture and correct us hour by hour.
A handkerchief of mine drew his complaints
Because he found it pressed in a Book of Saints.

SCENE THREE

ELMIRE, MARIANE, DAMIS, CLÉANTE, *and* DORINE.
ELMIRE   You're lucky, brother, your ears were not made sore
    By her haranguing all the way to the door.
    But I saw my husband as I was passing the stair;
    I'll be in my room, if he wishes to see me there.
CLÉANTE   Thanks. I'll wait, despite your friendly warning,
    And try at least to wish him a "Good morning."

SCENE FOUR

CLÉANTE, DAMIS *and* DORINE.
DAMIS   Speak to him, if you will, about Mariane.
    You know I'm interested in her plan
    To marry Valère. I fear my father's delay
    Is based on Tartuffe's dislike of the wedding day.
    If Valère and my sister marry, it may be
    My own joy with his sister I may see
    Quite soon . . .
CLÉANTE   Here he comes.

SCENE FIVE

ORGON, CLÉANTE, *and* DORINE.
ORGON   Ah, good morning, brother.
CLÉANTE   Dear Orgon, I am glad to have another
    Chance to speak to you. The fields are drying . . .

ORGON   Forgive me, brother, but I'm dying
   To hear the latest news about the household
   From the greatest drawing-room to the smallest mousehole. (*to*
     DORINE)
   Has all gone happily since yesterday?
   How's everybody's health? Tell me, I pray!
DORINE   Madame was feverish and had to take
   A medicine to cure a vile headache.
ORGON   And Tartuffe?
DORINE   Tartuffe? Healthy, stout and merry,
   Bright as paint and ruddy as a cherry.
ORGON   Poor man!
DORINE   Last night, her headache grew so bad
   She scarce could stir out of her bed
   And could not eat a bit of dinner.
ORGON   And Tartuffe?
DORINE   He ate—that well-fed sinner—
   A brace of good plump partridges, done brown,
   With a bottle of red wine to wash them down.
ORGON   Poor man!
DORINE   She passed a tortured, sleepless night
   In endless pain; the morning's cold gray light
   At last relieved her fever, but we sat
   Beside her all night long; just think of that!
ORGON   And Tartuffe?
DORINE   Replete and sleepy, satisfied,
   He drifted from the meal to his fireside,
   Crept thence into his warm and cozy bed
   And snored till dawn, the comfy sleepy-head.
ORGON   Poor man!
DORINE   Madame, agreeing to our fond persuasions,
   Consented to the doctor's ministrations
   And, bled and physicked, felt somewhat relieved.
ORGON   And Tartuffe?
DORINE   Not, I must confess, unduly grieved
   By Madame's illness, but right valiantly
   Took arms against foul trouble's surging sea
   And drank some wine to replace the blood she'd lost.
ORGON   Poor man!
DORINE   I'm happy to report the danger's past,
   And now I'll hasten to inform my mistress
   How pleased you are she's cured of her distress.

SCENE SIX

ORGON *and* CLÉANTE.
CLÉANTE   Brother, she's laughing in your very face

And, though I'm far from wishing you disgrace,
I must say that she's right in her estimation.
Who ever saw such a mad infatuation?
Is it possible this man has charmed you so
That you can forget all else for him, and go
Running about to do his commands? I swear
I've never seen such nonsense . . .

ORGON   Stop right there;
For you don't know the man of whom you speak.

CLÉANTE   All right, then. I don't know him, if you like,
But I know various things that I have heard.

ORGON   To know him is to love him, take my word.
I model myself on him whenever I can;
He is a man who . . . well, in short, a man.
Whoever follows his precepts lives in peace
And sees the rest of the world as so much dross.
Yes, I have changed since he came into my life;
He's taught me not to waste my love on my wife
Or on any mortal thing; what's more,
I could see my children turned away from my door,
Thanks to him, without the least concern.

CLÉANTE   These are surely humane truths to learn!

ORGON   Ah, if you could have seen him when at first
We met, in the days when my life was still accursed!
Each day in church he came and, if you please,
Fell with a crash before me to his knees.
He drew the attention of everybody there
With the ardency and loudness of his prayer.
He sighed, stretched flatly forth on his abdomen,
And kissed the floor with every passing moment.
When I departed, he ran along before me
And lightly sprinked holy water o'er me.
I made inquiries of his servant, and he
Told me of who he was, and his poverty
Described so movingly, I could not choose
But offer gifts to him, which he'd refuse,
Forever crying, "No, no, it's too much;
I am unworthy, no, I dare not touch
A penny of it!" And, if I persisted,
He'd give it to the poor. Oh, he assisted
Many a one that way. Chaste Heaven, at last,
Moved me to take him in here as my guest.
Since then, all prospers. Sternly he reproves
All sinful and suspect behavior, moves
Particularly to guard my sacred honor
Where my wife's concerned. He keeps upon her
A most strict watch, and is indeed more jealous

Of all those coxcombs and conceited fellows
Who hang around her than *I* am, I feel;
You'd scarce believe the extent of his pious zeal.
One day he killed a flea with too much pique,
Then scourged himself and fasted for a week.

CLÉANTE   Brother, I swear, there's something wrong with your head.
Are you laughing at me with all this that you've said?
What does it mean? This madness worries me . . .

ORGON   Your language, brother, savors of heresy.
Your thinking's somewhat tainted by that vice,
And, as I've had to warn you once or twice,
You're liable to a judgment on your head.

CLÉANTE   To think like you is worse than being dead.
You voluntary blind men always call
The rest of us "freethinkers," whereas all
We're guilty of is scorning empty shows
And faithlessness. And now do you suppose
Your veiled denunciations frighten me?
My heart is open for all men to see.
I am no dupe of formalistic panders;
Religion, like the throne, has false pretenders.
And as the truly brave aren't always those
Who trumpet loudest or with gaudy shows
Paint their performance, so the true devout
Don't always pray the loudest or go about
With piously exaggerated gestures;
True worth does not reside in outward vestures,
Hypocrisy too often masks religion,
And men like you confuse life's true condition
By judging that the mask must be the face;
But don't you see such judgment's a disgrace?
The shadow, not the substance, is your God;
The false coin's what you worship, not the good.
Man must be, indeed, a curious creature
Who can't obey the simple laws of nature.
Reason seems to hem him in too tightly,
And so he never plays his part quite rightly.
He ruins every act by exaggeration
In trying to advance in estimation.
And, brother, by the way, a word to the wise . . .

ORGON   Well, you must be a scholar in disguise,
For clearly all the wisdom of the ages
Has found its home in you; the greatest sages
Are nothing unto you—you are a Cato,
A Socrates, a Zeno, or a Plato!

CLÉANTE   I'm not a doctor of philosophy,
And all life's wisdom doesn't reside in me.

My science lies in being able to see
Distinctions between truth and falsity.
And as I know of nothing more commendable
Than the honest piety of dependable
And devoted holy men, so too I find
Nothing's worse than those whose double mind
Betrays true holiness, those hypocrites
Upon whose subtle faces triumph sits
In smiling sacrilegious impudence,
Whose lives are nothing but one long pretense
Of piousness, the while they make a mock
Of all that's good, and while they fleece the flock
Of silly sheep by various devices
Designed to line their pockets; all their vices
Masquerade as virtue; on their way
To Heaven they contrive to jest and play
In secrecy, maintaining the disguise
Of holiness by lifting up their eyes
In pious, zealous ardor; who, in short,
While living in the luxury of Court,
Dryly preach abstinence, plain living,
And retirement; who, without misgiving,
Can reconcile their vices and their zeal;
Passionate, revengeful, they conceal
Their petty jealousies beneath the cloak
Of piety and goodness and invoke
God's name to consecrate their evils,
So bold and fearless are these subtle devils.
They place themselves upon the side of Heaven
And assassinate their foes with a sacred weapon.
This modern age, I fear, too rankly teems
With such pretenders, but although it seems
Hard to detect them, still true piety
Is never really difficult to see:
Look at Ariston, look at Périandre,
Oronte, Alcidamas, Polydore, and Clitandre
No one would dare deny to them the title
Of honesty in any true recital
Of virtue's servants; never do they show
This ostentatious righteousness or go
Meddling into other folk's affairs
And giving themselves these smug and holy airs.
Their goodness is direct and free and simple
And only by their own benign example
Do they ever even so much as venture
To subject others unto moral censure.
They do not trust the face that evil shows

But are the first to think the best of those
Whom lying slander villainously attacks.
We find no intrigues or no secret pacts
Among them; virtue's what they're interested in;
They love the sinner, though they hate the sin.
Above all, they're embarrassed to disclose
Toward Heaven greater zeal than Heaven shows
Toward them. Such people truly share my heart.

ORGON   And have you finally spoken all your part?

CLÉANTE   Yes.

ORGON   Your servant, sir. I bid you a good day.

CLÉANTE   A moment, brother. Please don't run away.
    Do you recall your promise to Valère?

ORGON   Yes.

CLÉANTE   And that you'd blessed the happy, loving pair?

ORGON   That's true.

CLÉANTE   Why, then, is there this great delay?

ORGON   I don't know.

CLÉANTE   You're planning for another day?

ORGON   Perhaps.

CLÉANTE   You mean you'd break your word?

ORGON   I don't say that.

CLÉANTE   From what I've heard,
    You have no reason to delay things thus.

ORGON   That depends.

CLÉANTE   There certainly should be no fuss.

ORGON   I suppose not.

CLÉANTE   What shall I tell Valère?

ORGON   Whatever you please.

CLÉANTE   But don't you care
    To make your wishes clear?

ORGON   I care
    Only to do what Heaven wills.

CLÉANTE   Come, now,
    You gave the lad your sacred vow.

ORGON   Farewell. (*Exits.*)

CLÉANTE   I fear the worst in this affair.
    I must speak further quickly with Valère.

Act Two

SCENE ONE

ORGON *and* MARIANE.

ORGON   Mariane.

MARIANE   Father?

ORGON   Come closer; let me speak
    To you.
MARIANE   (*to* ORGON, *who is peering off stage*)   What is it there
    that you seek?
ORGON   I'm looking to see if anyone's eavesdropping.
    This is a likely place for tricksy snooping.
    There now. All's well. Now then, my dear,
    There's something that I wish for you to hear;
    You know I've always held you in my heart.
MARIANE   You've always played a loving father's part.
ORGON   Well said! And to deserve that love, my treasure,
    You should think of nothing but your father's pleasure.
MARIANE   I hope I never merit your reproof.
ORGON   Splendid! Tell me, what do you think of Tartuffe?
MARIANE   Who, I?
ORGON   You. Take care with your answer, pray.
MARIANE   Alas! I'll say whatever you wish me to say.
            (DORINE *enters quietly and stands behind* ORGON *without his
            seeing her.*)

SCENE TWO

ORGON, MARIANE, *and* DORINE.
ORGON   Ah, wisely spoken. Then say, my dearest dove,
    He has inspired your heart with tender love
    And that the crown of joy upon your life
    Descends the day that you become his wife.
MARIANE   What?
ORGON   Eh?
MARIANE   What did you say?
ORGON   Me?
MARIANE   Heavens above!
    Who is it that's inspired my heart with love?
    Who'll place the crown of joy upon my life
    The day that I agree to be his wife?
ORGON   Tartuffe.
MARIANE   But, father, I feel nothing of the sort.
    Would you have me betray the truth of my true heart?
ORGON   But I *want* it to be true. It should suffice
    That my wishes in this matter are precise.
MARIANE   What? You wish . . . ?
ORGON   I intend, you see,
    To firmly unite Tartuffe to my family
    By marrying him to you. With that in view,
    I'm resolved this marriage must . . . (*sees* DORINE) Ha! You!
    Your curiosity must be a powerful passion
    To make you come and eavesdrop in this fashion.

DORINE   I must say, sir, I don't know whether I can
  Tell whether the rumor arose by careful plan
  Or accident, but when somebody spoke
  Of such a marriage, I treated it all as a joke.
ORGON   And what is so incredible, I pray?
DORINE   I'm sorry. I can't believe a word that you say.
ORGON   I know how to make you believe it, I'll tell you that.
DORINE   Ha! What a tale! You're talking through your hat!
ORGON   I'm telling you what will very soon prove true.
DORINE   Nonsense!
ORGON   Now daughter, I mean what I say, I'm warning you.
DORINE   Ha, ha! Don't believe him! He's only laughing!
ORGON   I tell you . . .
DORINE   What stuff! Get out! You must be chaffing?
ORGON   I warn you now, take care; my anger's rising!
DORINE   Well, I must say, it's surely most surprising.
  Are we to believe a man as wise as you
  With that splendid beard and eyes of baby blue
  Would be so big a fool . . .
ORGON   Now listen here!
  You're taking certain liberties, my dear,
  Which do not please me at all, I can't deny.
DORINE   Come, let's speak calmly, sir, if we can, and try
  To understand each other. Of course, you're joking.
  Your daughter to marry a bigot, whose manner of speaking
  Would scarce melt butter? And explain, if you can,
  What such an alliance would bring to you, a man
  Of notable wealth—to corrupt your daughter's love
  By marrying her off to a beggar . . .
ORGON   That's enough!
  I tell you that's the reason I revere him.
  His poverty is honest. If you could hear him
  Spurning worldly wealth and vulgar rank
  As gross deceptions, then, my girl, you'd thank
  Your father for marrying you to a saint,
  A man who never has a word of complaint,
  Whatever his woes. But with modest aid
  He'll soon regain the splendid role he played
  In happier days. He once owned property
  And was a landed squire in his home county.
DORINE   Yes, so he says; I say his vanity
  Does not sort well with all his piety.
  When you set up in business as a saint,
  You shouldn't boast and brag without restraint.
  Humility and love and true devotion
  Are strange bedmates, indeed, for gross ambition.
  Why be so haughty? But I see that you

Don't care at all for this. Then let's turn to
His person, not his claims to noble rank;
Doesn't it make you sometimes shudder or shrink
To think of a hypocritical fool
Like that corrupting the innocent soul
Of a girl like this? Stop and consider
The consequences, if you commit her
To such a loathesome and revolting marriage.
You'd better save your breath to cool your porridge
Than try to lecture a young and ardent wife
Who's bound by marriage to a hateful life.
Those husbands who wear horns upon their heads
Have driven their wives away from their weary beds
By their stupidities; and woe to those fathers
Who make such marriages for their poor daughters!
Beware of driving her to be a wife.

ORGON   It's nice of you to tell me about life!

DORINE   You could do worse than follow my advice.

ORGON   I'm sure these learned strictures are very nice.
But, daughter, you will do what I command.
Obey your father: that's the law of the land.
At one time, true, I'd pledged you to Valère,
But now I'm much disturbed by what I hear
Of that young man: free-thinking, playing cards, and such.

DORINE   And next you'll say you don't see him in church
Like those who go for advertising's sake.

ORGON   May I remind you that I didn't make
A special request for *your* precise advice
I don't intend to speak to you more than twice.
The other man of whom we speak, I say,
Has made his peace with Heaven. That's the way
To build a marriage rich in every blessing.
You'll love each other. There'll be no transgressing.
You'll coo and gurgle like two doting turtles
And grow to be the happiest of mortals.
You'll make of him whatever you wish to make.

DORINE   She'll furnish him with horns within a week.

ORGON   What? What's that?

DORINE   He's got the head for it,
And I fear the melancholy aspect of his planet,
Despite your daughter's virtue, will prove too strong.

ORGON   *I* say stop interrupting and hold your tongue!
Mind your business; stop this damnable meddling.

DORINE   I'm only trying to stop your foolish fiddling.

ORGON   That's very kind of you. Now please be silent.

DORINE   If I didn't love you, sir . . .

ORGON   I'm growing violent.

DORINE   I want to help you, sir, despite your ire.

ORGON   Ha!

DORINE   It's true. Believe me, I can't bear
All the mocking you'd be subject to.

ORGON   You won't shut up?

DORINE   Whatever else, I'm true,
True-blue, to my employer all the way.

ORGON   Serpent! Silence! The next word you say . . . !

DORINE   A holy man like you, in such a temper?

ORGON   You plague me so, I find I can't remember
What I started to say. Not one more squawk!

DORINE   All right, but I can think, if I can't talk.

ORGON   Think, if you like, but see that you don't dare
To utter a word (*to* MARIANE) I'll grant you that Valère
Is a handsome chap . . .

DORINE   It drives me simply crazy
Not to be able to speak.

ORGON   Though no fop or daisy,
Tartuffe has looks . . .

DORINE   Indeed! To stop a clock.

ORGON   And, too, he comes of very ancient stock.
His other gifts . . .

DORINE   Oh, you fortunate girl!
If I were forced to marry such a churl,
I'd have my sweet revenge already planned
And prove a woman always has at hand
Those weapons that will give her the last hit.

ORGON   You won't obey my orders? Is that it?

DORINE   What's your trouble? I'm not talking to you.

ORGON   To whom, pray tell?

DORINE   Why, to myself, that's who.

ORGON (*aside*)   *Eh bien.* There's only one recourse in such a case.
And that's to give her a slap across the face.
        (*Raises his hand to give her a blow, but whenever he looks
        at her, she stands mute and motionless.*)

ORGON   Daughter, you ought to think well of my scheme;
Tartuffe's the answer to a maiden's dream (*to* DORINE)
Why don't you speak?

DORINE   I've nothing more to say.

ORGON   Go on. One little word.

DORINE   Thanks, not today.

ORGON   I'm all ready for you.

DORINE   I'm not *that* dumb.

ORGON (*to* MARIANE)   It's not that I want my daughter under my
        thumb,
But you must learn to accept a father's rule.

DORINE (*fleeing*)   I'd die before I'd marry that fat fool!

*(Orgon tries to slap her but misses and falls down as she
runs out.)*

ORGON   I can't live any longer with that pest
Or I'll suffer the sin of anger. I must rest.
I'm not in any state to go on with our talk.
Excuse me while I go and take a walk.
(Exit ORGON. DORINE *re-enters cautiously.)*

SCENE THREE

MARIANE *and* DORINE.

DORINE   Mariane—ye gods—have you nothing to say?
And must I play the part that you should play?
A proposition utterly absurd,
And yet you don't defend yourself with a word!

MARIANE   His power is absolute. What can I do?

DORINE   Anything, except what he wants you to.

MARIANE   What?

DORINE   Tell him that a girl can't love by proxy,
And when it comes to marrying a foxy
And bigoted old hypocrite—*mon Dieu!*—
Your wishes ought to count for something, too.
If he loves Tartuffe dearer than a brother,
Then—Devil take it!—Let them marry each other!

MARIANE   I know, but father is so overbearing,
I don't dare raise my voice within his hearing.

DORINE   Look here. Let's think this through. Valère, you know,
Has offered you his hand. Is that not so?

MARIANE   Stop it, Dorine! Of course I love Valère
More than words can tell, and I can't bear
To think of looking at another lover;
But I've repeated all this ten times over.

DORINE   I'm sometimes doubtful of such a coy admission
And wonder if you're merely feigning passion.

MARIANE   You do me wrong in doubting me, my dear.
I'd thought that you believed I was sincere.

DORINE   In short, you love the boy?

MARIANE   Oh, yes, with passion!

DORINE   And it would seem he loves you in like fashion?

MARIANE   I think so.

DORINE   And the way to happiness
For both of you is marriage?

MARIANE   Yes, oh, yes!

DORINE   And what about Tartuffe, love's adversary?

MARIANE   I'll kill myself, if that seems necessary.

DORINE   Oh, fine! "I'll kill myself," the maid replied.
The answer to life's grief is suicide.

A sovereign cure! It makes me mad clear through
To hear that kind of crazy talk from you.
MARIANE   Good heavens, what a temper! There you go!
You don't much sympathize with others' woe.
DORINE   I don't much sympathize with those who drivel,
Like you; then, when the test comes, shrivel.
MARIANE   You know I've always been a timid sort.
DORINE   But love demands a strong, courageous heart.
MARIANE   Loyalty to Valère's my firm intent,
But he must ask, and gain, Papa's consent.
DORINE   But if your father is an utter goof.
Who's so infatuated with Tartuffe
He'll break the promise that he's pledged you to,
What is there left for poor Valère to do?
MARIANE   If I confess my true scorn for Tartuffe,
Won't I reveal unconsciously the truth
Of my affections? Though I love Valère,
Should I abandon modesty and dare
To flaunt my love for all the world to see?
DORINE   Oh, never mind. At least it's clear to me
You really want to be Madame Tartuffe,
And I was wrong to offer my reproof.
Why should I argue with two loving hearts?
The match would be ideal on both your parts.
Monsieur Tartuffe! a pretty pouter pigeon!
Tartuffe the Great! A man of high position!
A lucky girl she is who is his wife!
She royally has fixed herself for life.
Every day, each hour, you hear his praises
Sung by choirs in half a dozen places;
His ears are red as is the richest rose,
Only surpassed in glory by his nose.
MARIANE   Oh, God!
DORINE   What ecstasy will fill your loving breast
When you go home to share his little nest.
MARIANE   Stop this agonizing talk! Not one more word!
I cannot stand it any more. I've heard
Enough. Tell me how I can escape his clutches.
DORINE   A daughter should obey her father's wishes,
Although he choose a monkey for her mate.
I'd like to help, but really, it's too late.
Just think, you'll have a splendid horse and carriage
To help you ease the boredom of your marriage.
You can go calling on aunts, uncles, cousins,
Whom you'll find round the city by the dozens.
You'll call upon the Lord High Mayoress
And on the tax-collector's wife, no less,

Who'll seat you on a stool, the place of honor,
And might invite you to stay on for dinner;
A round of balls—as much as once a year—
Two bagpipes for a band, some watery beer;
Perhaps a puppet show, complete with monkey.
However, if your husband . . .

MARIANE   Oh, that donkey!
Dorine, for heaven's sake, I need advice.

DORINE   You must excuse me.

MARIANE   Please, I've asked you twice.

DORINE   To punish you, this marriage must go through.

MARIANE   Dorine!

DORINE   No!

MARIANE   I'll speak to father, as you wish me to.

DORINE   You've made your choice. It's clear Tartuffe's your man.

MARIANE   No more, Dorine. I've done all that I can.
My tears and sighs don't even leave you ruffled.

DORINE   As far as I'm concerned, you'll be Tartuffled.

MARIANE   Since my unhappiness can't move your heart,
I must surrender to despair and start
To search out methods of escaping life:
A little vial of poison or a knife.

DORINE   Here, here, come back. I'll put aside my ire
And help you to attain your true desire.

MARIANE   Dorine, if they insist on martyring me,
I'll simply die. I'll end my life. You'll see.

DORINE   Don't worry. We can find a way to spare
Your life, I'm sure. But look, here comes Valère.
        (*Enter* VALÈRE. *He speaks at first jestingly.*)

SCENE FOUR

VALÈRE, MARIANE, *and* DORINE.

VALÈRE   Mademoiselle, a story's reached my ears
Confirming all my wildest doubts and fears.

MARIANE   What's that?

VALÈRE   You're marrying Tartuffe.

MARIANE   That's true.
My father wishes . . . What else can I do?

VALÈRE   Your father, mademoiselle . . .

MARIANE   Has changed his mind.
Tartuffe's the man for whom I am designed.

VALÈRE   Is he serious?

MARIANE   As serious as serious can be.
He just was urging this affair to me.

VALÈRE   What's your opinion of this serious prank,
Pray tell?

MARIANE   I just don't know.
VALÈRE   Well, at least, that's frank.
    You don't know?
MARIANE   No.
VALÈRE   No?
MARIANE   What's your advice?
VALÈRE   Accept this splendid husband. Don't think twice.
MARIANE   That's your advice?
VALÈRE   Yes.
MARIANE   Really?
VALÈRE   Absolutely.
    You must pursue this rare chance resolutely.
MARIANE   I'm much obliged to you for this sage counsel.
VALÈRE   No thanks are due. I scarcely strained a tonsil.
MARIANE   I'll ponder your advisements at my leisure.
VALÈRE   I gave the counsel but to give you pleasure.
DORINE (*aside*)   I wonder how this all is going to end?
VALÈRE   I owe you thanks for frankness, at least, my friend.
    When you . . .
MARIANE   I beg you not to talk like that.
    You told me in so many words I should accept
    The man my father chose to pledge me to;
    I'm saying that's what I intend to do;
    I'm simply following your own advice.
VALÈRE   Don't fob me off with that antique device.
    Before I ever spoke, your mind was fixed
    And now you're seizing on some frivolous pretext
    To justify your falsehood to my face.
MARIANE   Well put! Quite true.
VALÈRE   The plain facts of the case
    Are that you've never loved me for a minute.
MARIANE   Think what you will, if you take pleasure in it.
VALÈRE   Pleasure? Ha! The hurt you've dealt my heart
    Is deep, but I'll learn to make a second start
    And find more sympathy and warmth than I do here.
MARIANE   I don't doubt that. What girl would not admire
    Your character?
VALÈRE   Forget my character.
    It's not so hot. I'm crooked as a barrister,
    Blind as a fool in love, yes, even blinder,
    But there's a girl somewhere who may be kinder
    Than you. She'll take me on the rebound, if she must.
MARIANE   The loss is not so great. Somehow, I trust,
    I'll manage to sustain it stoically.
VALÈRE   I'm sure you will comport yourself heroically.
    And, as for me, it's never very pleasant
    To find oneself forgotten. For the present,

I'll do my best to sigh, smile and forget,
Or, if I can't forget, pretend. And yet
There's something weak and pitiful and wilted
About a man who weeps when he's been jilted.

MARIANE   A lofty sentiment, indeed, if true.

VALÈRE   More people should approve it, as you do.
What! Would you have me keep within my heart
My love for you unchanging from the start,
See you go happy to another's arms
And not seek solace in a lady's charms?

MARIANE   Why, not at all! That's what I most desire—
A new romance to set your heart afire!

VALÈRE   You'd like that?

MARIANE   Yes.

VALÈRE   Enough of this detraction!
I'll try to give you instant satisfaction. (*starts to leave and returns
through the next few speeches.*)

MARIANE   Good.

VALÈRE   Kindly remember that, for good or ill,
I follow your example.

MARIANE   As you will.

VALÈRE   Your wishes are quite clear. I will comply.

MARIANE   Fine!

VALÈRE   Enough. You get no more of me. Good-by.

MARIANE   Excellent!

VALÈRE   Eh?

MARIANE   What?

VALÈRE   I thought I heard my name.

MARIANE   You must be hearing things.

VALÈRE   This game
Begins to weary me. Farewell.

MARIANE   Adieu.

DORINE   May I
Speak up now as a humble stander-by
And say I think you both are addled
And ought to have your backsides paddled?
Monsieur Valère!
        (*She takes him by the arm; he feigns resistance.*)

VALÈRE   What do you want, Dorine?

DORINE   Come here!

VALÈRE   No, no! I'm in a rage. You've seen
I'm doing what she wants. Don't interfere.

DORINE   Stop!

VALÈRE   The matter is all settled, that's quite clear.

DORINE   Ha!

MARIANE   My presence here clearly annoys someone.
It's wiser if I leave him quite alone.

(DORINE *leaves* VALÈRE *and runs to* MARIANE.)
DORINE   Where are you going?
MARIANE   Let me alone!
DORINE   Come back!
MARIANE   No use, Dorine. You try another tack.
VALÈRE   It's clear it tortures her to look at me.
     I'll just remove myself and set her free.
DORINE (*leaving* MARIANE *and running to* VALÈRE)   What the
     deuce? What's all this that I hear?
     Now stop this nonsense! Both of you come here! (*She pulls at
     them, one with each hand.*)
VALÈRE   What are you up to?
MARIANE   What do you think you're doing?
DORINE   Trying to get you two to billing and cooing.
VALÈRE   You must be crazy, as far as I can see.
     Didn't you hear the way she talked to me?
DORINE (*to* MARIANE)   You act as if you're going off your head.
MARIANE   Didn't you hear the awful things he said?
DORINE   You're crazy, both of you. (*to* VALÈRE) Now I am sure
     The only thing she wants is to be yours.
     (*to* MARIANE) He loves you only; I'm prepared to swear
     That marriage—and to you—is his desire.
MARIANE (*to* VALÈRE)   Why did you give me, then, your vile advice?
VALÈRE (*to* MARIANE)   Your asking for it wasn't exactly nice.
DORINE   I said you both were crazy. Give me your hand.
     Yours, now.
VALÈRE   Why give you my hand?
DORINE   You'll understand.
MARIANE   What *is* all this?
DORINE   Just this. You're both in love
     More than you're either of you conscious of.
VALÈRE   Well, there's no harm—at least once in a while— ·
     In giving a man a little friendly smile.
               (MARIANE *looks at* VALÈRE *and smiles feebly.*)
DORINE   The fact is, lovers are completely daft.
VALÈRE   *I've* reason to complain, you know. You laughed
     At me and scorned me with reproof
     Because I thought you'd said "Yes" to Tartuffe.
MARIANE   But you yourself . . . it really is a shame . . .
DORINE   Let's leave this issue for another time.
     The thing we need now is a cunning plan.
MARIANE   Speak up, Dorine. We'll do all that we can.
DORINE   There are a lot of tricks that we can play.
     Your father's bluffing, surely, but the way
     For you to get around him is to feign
     Complete compliance with his mad design,
     So that, in case of crisis, you can manage

To keep postponing this unwelcome marriage.
Time has many virtues; it can heal
Many a wound that seems beyond repeal.
And there are many tricks. Say you fell ill;
No one can force you then against your will.
Or maybe some dire omen greets your eyes:
A funeral in the street (a grim surprise),
A broken mirror, auguring the worst,
A black cat, which suggests your life is cursed—
A dozen dodges. But I would much rather
You two would not be seen like this together.
(*to* VALÈRE) Now go and use the help of all your friends
To win the girl that clearly Fate intends
For you. (*to* MARIANE) I'm sure you'll get your brother
To help you, not to mention your stepmother.
Good-by!

VALÈRE (*to* MARIANE)   We all will do whatever we can do,
But my best hope and love resides in you.

MARIANE   I don't know what my father may decide.
I only know I'll not be Tartuffe's bride.

VALÈRE   You make me very happy. And if ever . . .

DORINE   Lovers are never tired. They talk forever.
Come on, get going!

VALÈRE   Farewell . . .

DORINE   Oh, talk, talk, talk!
You that way, and you this. Come on, now! Walk!

Act Three

SCENE ONE

DAMIS *and* DORINE.

DAMIS   Let Heaven strike me with a lightning bolt,
Let all the world call me a rogue, a dolt;
No talk of filial respect, no father's power
Will hold me back; I'll act within the hour!

DORINE   For Heaven's sake, enough of this mad chatter;
Your father's merely talked about the matter.
Need I remind you that there's many a slip
Betwixt the smooth cup and the slippery lip?

DAMIS   I'll stop that fat conspirator's career;
I'll speak a word or two into his ear.

DORINE   Easy does it, boy; let your stepmother
Handle him, the way she does your father.
Tartuffe becomes like putty in her hands
And easily agrees to her demands.

I think he eyes her with a secret yen;
Lord knows, I hope that that's the case, for then
She'll come to interview him, for your sake,
Learn what his feelings are and make
Him understand what troubles will be brewing
If he continues as he has been doing.
His valet tells me that he's at his prayers;
No one can see him; he's alone upstairs.
But he'll be coming down in a minute or two,
So beat it, please; I'll see what I can do.

DAMIS   I must be present when he talks to her.

DORINE   Never! Beat it!

DAMIS   I won't speak or stir.

DORINE   Nonsense! I know how you fly off the handle,
And that's the surest way to snuff the candle.
Go on!

DAMIS   I promise I won't rage or shout.

DORINE   Oh, what a pest you are! Look, here he comes! Get out!
          (DORINE *pushes him out.* TARTUFFE *enters and, seeing*
          DORINE, *calls off stage.*)

SCENE TWO

TARTUFFE *and* DORINE.

TARTUFFE (*calls off stage*)   Put away my hair shirt and my scourge
          And pray perpetually that Heaven may purge
          Our souls of sin. If someone asks for me,
          I've gone to bless the poor with charity.

DORINE (*aside*)   What hogwash! What a stupid thing to say!

TARTUFFE   What do you want?

DORINE   I . . .

TARTUFFE (*drawing out a kerchief*)   Wait! I pray,
          Take this handkerchief before you speak.

DORINE   Why?

TARTUFFE   Cover that bosom which demurely peeks
          Above your bodice. Such forbidden sights
          May well give rise to slightly carnal thoughts.

DORINE   You must be quite concupiscently queasy
          If a little flesh can make you so uneasy.
          Of course, I don't know how you're stimulated
          But I'm not quite so easily elated.
          Why, I could see you nude without a qualm;
          In fact, I think I'd stay supremely calm.

TARTUFFE   A bit more modesty in speech, my dear,
          Or I'll withdraw and leave you standing here.

DORINE   No, I will go and leave you here alone,
          But first, there's something that you should have known;

Madame Elmire will soon come into view.
   She'd like to have a word or two with you.
TARTUFFE   Delighted!
DORINE (*aside*)   He leaps and bleats just like a woolly lamb.
   I'm right, he has a hankering for madame.
TARTUFFE   She's coming soon?
DORINE   Yes, here she comes this way;
   I'll leave you two together, if I may. (*Exit*.)

SCENE THREE

ELMIRE *and* TARTUFFE.
TARTUFFE   May Heaven's grace, madame, preserve you whole
   And sound in mind, in body, and in soul,
   And bless your days according to the prayers
   Of one who's much concerned with your affairs.
ELMIRE   I'm deeply grateful for your pieties.
   Let us sit down and chat more at our ease.
TARTUFFE   I trust, madame, your fever's not persisted?
ELMIRE   I'm feeling well; the fever's quite arrested.
TARTUFFE   My poor and humble prayers here in this place
   Seem all too small to have brought down such grace
   Upon you from on high; yet I confess
   My constant thoughts are of your happiness.
ELMIRE   Your pious zeal is rather overpowering.
TARTUFFE   Pray Heaven that the heavens keep on showering
   Blessings on you; I'd give my life for yours.
ELMIRE   There's no need for such drastic overtures.
   But I'm indebted to you for your prayers.
TARTUFFE   Dear lady, *any*thing to ease your cares . . .
            (DAMIS *enters unseen behind them.*)
ELMIRE   I wanted to speak privately to you.
   I'm glad we're here out of the public view.
TARTUFFE   And so am I! Dear Heaven, but it's sweet
   To be beside you, madame, on this seat.
   This is a chance for which I've often prayed;
   It seems a stroke of luck that Fate has made.
ELMIRE   I know, my friend, exactly what you mean.
   I've often longed for a chat like this, unseen.
TARTUFFE   Oh, how I've prayed that we could freely share
   Our thoughts and words, that I could boldly bare
   My soul unto you, that I might explain
   My distaste for the friends you entertain
   Springs not from my dislike of your devotion
   To them, but rather from my own profound emotion
   Which fairly chokes me . . .
ELMIRE   Well, your zeal

Is something, sir, that you need not conceal.

TARTUFFE (*taking her hand and squeezing her fingers*)   How hard
　I pray for you, and even harder . . .

ELMIRE   Ouch! You're hurting me!

TARTUFFE   Forgive my ardor!
　I had no idea of hurting you, I swear!
　It's just . . . (*puts his hand on her knee*)

ELMIRE   Your hand. What is it doing there?

TARTUFFE   Just feeling the material; it's nice!

ELMIRE   I'm ticklish. Please, don't make me ask you twice.
　　　　　(*She moves her chair away;* TARTUFFE *brings his closer. This
　　　　　continues throughout the scene.*)

TARTUFFE   I am a great admirer of fine lace.
　The workmanship, the beauty, and the grace
　Of the design. What lovely decoration!

ELMIRE   Perhaps. But now, sir, to our conversation.
　I hear my husband wants to marry you
　To Mariane. Pray tell me, is that true?

TARTUFFE   He's mentioned it. But, lady, need I say
　That's not the joy I dream of night and day?
　It's elsewhere that I see the lovely fire
　Which blazes with the beauties I desire.

ELMIRE   You mean you don't love earthly things alone?

TARTUFFE   I mean, madame, my heart's not made of stone.

ELMIRE   I see. You mean your thoughts are turned to Heaven,
　Toward which your yearning spirit long has striven.

TARTUFFE   The love which draws us toward eternal beauty
　Does not release us from our earthly duty
　To love each other. Heaven often forms
　A vessel whose supernal beauty warms
　Our earthly blood. And such a one are you;
　My spirit soars when you come into view.
　Heaven's glories shine within your face;
　Your form and figure testify to Grace.
　O perfect beauty, perfect in each feature!
　In you I worship great creating Nature.
　Fair goddess! wondrous woman; in your eyes
　I see the will of Heaven and am wise.
　At first I trembled, lest my sacred passion
　For you prove false, a hindrance to salvation,
　Perhaps—who knows?—a horrid stratagem
　Of the Evil One, a trap to catch me in.
　I even thought to flee in foolish fashion,
　But then I came to see that such a passion,
　Inspired by Heaven as it is, undoubtedly,
　Need not be inconsistent with true modesty.
　And so I gave my eager heart full rein.

I know I should not hope that you will deign
To smile with condescension on my suit;
But still, when Heaven calls, dare man be mute?
In you is all my hope, my good, my peace;
In you rests my damnation or release.
I may taste bliss or be tormented still;
It all will be according to your will.

ELMIRE This is indeed a gallant declaration.
I must confess, though, to some consternation.
You should have steeled your feelings somewhat better;
Why, what would happen if my husband ever
Heard words like this from such a pious man? . . .

TARTUFFE Though I am pious, I am still a man,
An erring, mortal man, and when your beauties
Flame on my sight, all my religious duties
Grow somewhat blurred. I know such an appraisal
May shock you somewhat. Still, I'm not an angel.
And if you view my conduct with alarm,
You must accuse your own bewitching charm.
Since I first viewed your beauty's flawless art,
You've been the sovereign of my secret heart.
My poor soul struggled, but alas! in vain
Against your distant beauty and disdain;
In vain, in vain my fasting, prayers and tears.
Each soft breeze blew your sweet name to my ears.
How long I've sought to say this with my eyes;
Now hear it in my words and in my sighs.
And if you look with pity and compassion
Upon this poor unworthy slave of passion,
If you consent to bring me consolation
And bring about my yearning soul's salvation,
I'll swear to you with most profound emotion
Unending service and a true devotion.
And in my hands be sure a lady's honor
Is safe, no danger that there'll come upon her
The smallest breath of scandal. These young sparks
That ladies dote on are unsafe. Their larks,
Their jokes, their boasts about the wars of love
Leave ladies' reputations not above
Reproach, and many ladies have been tarnished
By faithless gallants whose careers have furnished
Examples of betrayal and deceit.
But fear me not, dear lady; I'm discreet.
The care a man like me takes of his name
Is guarantee that you need fear no shame;
You buy, if you accept my heart, my dear,
Love without scandal, pleasure without fear.

ELMIRE   I'm fascinated; and your rhetoric
    Effectively removes all the inveterate
    Fears I might have felt; but don't *you* fear
    That I might speak a word in Orgon's ear
    About your strange behavior here today?
    If I did, what do you think he'd say?
TARTUFFE   I know you are too merciful and good
    And that my love is not misunderstood
    Pity for human frailty will excuse
    My over-ardent voicing of such views.
    Although I yearn toward the True and Good,
    Still I am human, merely flesh and blood.
ELMIRE   Another woman might, indeed, repeat
    This story; but I too can be discreet.
    I'll not tell Orgon of your strange behavior;
    In turn I'll beg of you a certain favor:
    I want you to speak boldly and declare
    That you support the marriage of Valère
    And Mariane, that you renounce the claim
    By which you would usurp another's name,
    And . . .

SCENE FOUR

ELMIRE, DAMIS *and* TARTUFFE.

DAMIS (*emerging*)   No, madame, no! This news must come to light!
    I've been this while concealed there, within sight
    And hearing. Heaven's favor led me there
    To trap this hypocrite in his own snare
    And place within my hands at last the power
    Of sweet revenge. Aha! Within the hour
    I'll undeceive my father and he'll know
    The gross sins of that fat Lothario!
ELMIRE   No, Damis, it's enough if he repents.
    I'll count that a sufficient recompense
    I've promised it; don't make me break a vow.
    No nasty scenes; I'm willing to allow
    The whole affair to pass and not displease
    My husband's ears with such absurdities.
DAMIS   You may have reason, madame, to be lenient,
    But I do not consider it convenient
    To lose this chance of pricking his fat bubble
    And plunging him up to the ears in trouble.
    His sanctimonious impudence too long
    Has stirred up trouble in our home; too long
    He's bilked my father, led him by the nose.
    And now with vengeance sure, do you suppose
    I'll overlook my opportunity?

It is a grace that Heaven's conferred on me.
Now and henceforth I am Heaven's debtor,
And Heaven knows when I will find a better
Chance to give this slippery fox a jolt.
If I passed up this chance, I'd be a dolt.

ELMIRE   Damis . . .

DAMIS   I must do what I think is justified.
I've never felt so richly satisfied.
Please don't deter me. Try to understand
My joy in holding vengeance in my hand.
I'll have full satisfaction, I vow,
And see, here comes my opportunity, right now.

SCENE FIVE

ORGON, ELMIRE, DAMIS, *and* TARTUFFE.

DAMIS (*continuing, to* ORGON, *who enters*)   Father, I've got a bit of a surprise
For you; some news to open up your eyes.
Your kindnesses have here been well repaid;
This gentleman, behind your back, has made
Proposals to madame which cast upon her
A curious light and work to your dishonor.
In short, I've just surprised this monstrous beast
In making love to her and, sir, he ceased
Only when I spoke. Madame implored
I spare you this recital, but I've stored
A thirst for vengeance in my hungry heart,
And I don't choose to play a forgiving part.

ELMIRE   I think a wife ought never to annoy
Her husband with such silly tales. My boy,
A woman likes to handle such affairs
In her own way, so that nobody shares
The knowledge of the circumstances. You'd be
Silent now if you were ruled by me. (*Exit.*)

SCENE SIX

ORGON, DAMIS, *and* TARTUFFE.

ORGON   Oh, gracious Heavens! Can I trust my ears?

TARTUFFE   Alas, the case is just as it appears:
I am a sinner lost in deep iniquity,
One who would let mere physical propinquity
Corrupt his holy purposes and stain
His spotless shield of honor; don't refrain
From heaping censure on me. I'm a beast.
My life's a mass of crime; there's not the least
Extenuation possible for me.
Heaven has contrived all this, I see,

As punishment for my most rank misdeeds
And Heaven has ordained that no one pleads
For me. Let no man speak. Let me be driven
Out of your house, out of the sight of Heaven.

ORGON (*to* DAMIS)   Traitor! How do you dare, with nasty lies,
To bring the innocent tears into his eyes?

DAMIS   Don't tell me all this blubbering and bluster
Is going to make you think . . .

ORGON   Be silent, monster!

TARTUFFE   Ah, let him speak! How wrongly you accuse him!
Believe his words! It's wrong if you refuse him
Your trusting ears. Why put your faith in me?
How do you know what sort of man I might be?
Brother, how can you trust my outward seeming?
Perhaps when you look at me you're merely dreaming.
No, no, my outward semblance may deceive;
Within, I am far worse than you believe.
Although I commonly pass for a man of virtue,
You sadly let my outer surface cheat you. (*to* DAMIS)
Speak, dear boy, call me a vile traitor,
Perfidious, a liar, a betrayer
Of friendship's trust; call me the vilest term
You can imagine; I'm lower than a worm (*on his knees*)
Let me acknowledge here upon my knees
My horrid crimes. Comdemn me, if you please.

ORGON   Brother, this is too much! (*to* DAMIS) So—your heart
Remains unmoved?

DAMIS   He's merely playing a part!

ORGON   Silence, scoundrel! (*to* TARTUFFE) My brother, I beg you,
stand! (*to* DAMIS)
Rascal!

DAMIS   He can . . .

ORGON   Silence!

DAMIS   Don't you understand?

ORGON   Just one more word, and I'll punch you in the nose!

TARTUFFE   Do not be angry, brother. Do you suppose
I would not rather suffer indignity
Than have him suffer the slightest scratch for me?

ORGON (*to* DAMIS)   Ingrate!

TARTUFFE   Leave him in peace! See, I'm kneeling
To ask you for his pardon.

ORGON   Oh, what feeling! (*falling on his knees and embracing* TARTUFFE)
Observe his goodness!

DAMIS   But . . .

ORGON   Peace!

DAMIS   But, I . . .

ORGON   Quiet!

I understand why you're raising all this riot.
You hate him, all of you: my faithful wife,
My children, servants—why, upon my life!
It's a conspiracy to drive this saint
Out of my house. And this absurd complaint
Against him doesn't move me, not a whit.
I'll stand with him forever; you can sit
And spin your lies; I'll hasten with my plan
To marry this wronged saint to Mariane.

DAMIS You think you'll force her into such a plight?

ORGON Yes, and, to spite you all, this very night!
Oh, I defy you! Defy you, do you hear?
I'll show you, mark my words, who's master here!
Take back your wicked words, you monster, and entreat
His pardon. I command you, fall at his feet!

DAMIS What? Fall at the feet of this repulsive liar?

ORGON Ah, you resist my will? You've roused my ire!
Give me a stick, a stick! Don't hold me back!
Out of my sight! I'll deal you such a crack
Your ears will ring! Out! Out of my place!

DAMIS All right, I'll go, but . . .

ORGON   Don't let me see your face!
Reptile, I'll remove you from my will!
Take my curse, and go—wherever you will.
            (*Exit* DAMIS.)

SCENE SEVEN

ORGON *and* TARTUFFE.

ORGON (*continuing, to* TARTUFFE) Think of offering such insults to you!

TARTUFFE May Heaven pardon him, as I would do.
Ah, could you know how bitterly I suffer
To hear such words spoken to my brother . . .

ORGON Alas!

TARTUFFE Merely to think of such ingratitude
Makes my heart ache. Words so rough and crude
Fill my soul with a horror that's so deep
I can do nothing but beat my breast and weep!

ORGON (*runs to the door where he has driven* DAMIS) Villain!
I'm sorry I didn't knock you down
When I had the chance! Liar! Monster! Clown!

TARTUFFE Brother, compose yourself. Don't be distressed.
Let's have no more of this. I think it best
That I should leave your home, dear friend, right now.
I'll never return to bother you, I vow.

ORGON You're jesting!

TARTUFFE   No, no, they all hate me here.

They'd even question my sincerity, I fear.
ORGON   Do you think I listen to anything they say?
TARTUFFE   But they'll go on with their tales, day after day.
These stories that today have left you grieved
Tomorrow may be readily believed.
ORGON   Oh, never, brother, never!
TARTUFFE   Brother, a wife
May sway a husband's mind and rule his life.
ORGON   You shall not go! Never! I will not hear it!
TARTUFFE   Well, I'll remain, to mortify my spirit.
Still, if you desired it . . .
ORGON   Oh!
TARTUFFE   Well, no more.
I'll not behave as I have done before.
Honor is delicate, and, like Caesar's wife,
I must be past suspicion. On my life,
I'll flee the presence of madame and call . . .
ORGON   No, you'll attend her, to defy them all.
My one desire now is to fully spite them;
You must be with her constantly—we'll fight them,
Fire with fire, slander with suspicion,
To keep their tongues a-wagging. In addition,
I'm firm resolved that you must be my heir.
I'll change my will today, and I'll declare
That all my wealth is yours by legal right.
I tell you, brother, I take more delight
In you, my heir, than in all my family.
TARTUFFE   May Heaven's will be done eternally.
ORGON   Come, let's change the document; meanwhile,
Let the jealous choke on their own bile!

Act Four

SCENE ONE

CLÉANTE *and* TARTUFFE.
CLÉANTE   Everywhere I go I hear this story;
It's one that doesn't add unto your glory;
And I am glad, sir, I've run into you
So I can tell you briefly what my view
Of the matter is. I won't weigh right and wrong;
In any case, the evidence is strong.
But let's assume the tale Damis propounded
Was false, and the whole thing was unfounded.
Should not a Christian pardon the mistake,
Turning the other cheek for charity's sake?

Should such a quarrel, by purpose or by chance
Be cause for Damis' disinheritance?
In perfect frankness, sir, let me repeat:
The story's spreading; everyone you meet
Is talking of it. Look at what you've done!
It's not too late for father and for son
To reconcile; if you promote this union,
You'll bring yourself back into good opinion.

TARTUFFE   Alas, how happy I would be, if this could be!
God knows, my heart of rancor is quite free.
I would not harm him, bless you, if I could;
I long with all my heart to do him good.
But Heaven's will doesn't always fit my heart;
If he returns to the house, I must depart.
No, no, I couldn't stay with him in this place,
Not without a sense of complete disgrace;
It would be an intolerable situation;
Why, people might accuse me of calculation.
They'd say I was pretending, as a ruse, sir,
False charity to silence my accuser.
They'd say I kept him here beneath surveillance
Merely to ensure his guilty silence.

CLÉANTE   Your statements have some plausibility,
But still it all sounds quite far-fetched to me.
Since when are you the self-appointed judge
Of who must cringe beneath great Heaven's scourge?
Let God decide on matters of election
And let him implement his own correction,
And he who's moved by Heaven, not his humors,
Should not be sensitive to idle rumors.
No need, I'm sure, for fearing idle tongues
When you act truly to correct great wrongs,
And he who would take justice in his hands
Should first be sure he's tuned to God's commands.

TARTUFFE   My one desire's to be obedient
To God, whenever it's expedient.
But, after Damis' recent rude behavior,
I'd not forgive him, no, were I the Savior.

CLÉANTE   And does God order you to punish him
By aiding and abetting Orgon's whim
To disinherit him? And does God know
How you will profit by his overthrow?

TARTUFFE   No one who's plumbed the true depths of my spirit
Could think a thing like that of me, or fear it.
The riches of this world are dross to me;
Their gleaming superficiality
Does not seduce me; and if I accept

Something of the wealth Orgon has kept
Hidden away, my motives are quite pure:
To keep it out of the hands of an evildoer,
Someone who might, alas! make evil use
Of it, or squander it without excuse;
How better, then, to give it to one who swore he
Would dedicate its use to Heaven's glory?

CLÉANTE   Your reasons are somewhat sophistical,
If not, indeed, a trifle egotistical.
Why not let Damis have his proper wealth,
As long as you have liberty and health?
Better, indeed, to let the lad misuse it
Than countenance the rumor you'd abuse it
For your own purposes. I'm amazed
You could have heard this plan and not have raised
Your voice in protest. As far as I'm aware,
God doesn't condone defrauding a son and heir.
And if God in truth your heart has steeled
Against Damis, then why not quit the field
As any honorable adversary should
And leave the house to him? I'm sure I would.
Believe me, sir, it does you no great credit
To have this story spread, and if you let it
Gain further credence, your basic piety
Will seem . . .

TARTUFFE   Excuse me, sir, it's half-past three;
I must retire to prayers and meditations;
I leave you with my best felicitations. (*Exit.*)

SCENE TWO

ELMIRE, MARIANE, CLÉANTE *and* DORINE.

DORINE   Sir, can't you help her soul gain some relief,
For she is suffering a most cruel grief?
This hateful marriage pledge her father's made
Has sickened her poor heart, and it's betrayed
Her fondest hopes. He's coming now. Let's try
To undermine this project on the sly,
And unite this poor maid and Valère.
        (*Enter* ORGON.)

SCENE THREE

ORGON, ELMIRE, MARIANE, CLÉANTE, *and* DORINE.

ORGON   I'm glad to find you all assembled here. (*to* MARIANE)
There's something in this deed to make you smile,
And I'll reveal it in a little while.

MARIANE   Father, I call on Heaven, which knows my grief!
    Look in your heart and offer me relief
    From this oppressive sorrow; oh, relax
    The rights of fatherhood, I pray. Don't tax
    My frail forbearance, so that I must cry
    In bitter protest unto God on high.
    Don't make a senseless tragedy
    Out of that life which you have given me.
    Though you forbid my wedding the one I love,
    At least, I beg, by all the powers above,
    Don't bring me to this miserable estate
    By forcing me to marry one I hate.
    Don't drive me to an act of blind despair
    By bringing all your legal powers to bear.
ORGON (*aside*)   Be strong, my heart! Don't yield to human frailty!
MARIANE   I'm not distressed by your continued loyalty
    To him. Give him your wealth, if that's what you want to do
    And, if that's not enough, why, take mine too.
    Give him all that I have; it cannot worsen
    My grief. But don't consign to him my person!
    Just spare me that. Then, when the deed is done,
    Let me retire to spend my life as a nun.
ORGON   You think, by waxing weepy and despondent,
    And talking crazily about a convent,
    You'll frighten me? Get up! I say, the more
    Your heart recoils, the more you'll answer for.
    So mortify your senses by your yielding
    Meekly to the power that I'm wielding.
DORINE   But what . . .?
ORGON   Be silent! Speak when you're spoken to!
    I don't want to hear a syllable out of you!
CLÉANTE   If you'll permit me to offer some advice . . .
ORGON   Your words, dear brother, always are quite nice,
    And your advice is always full of merit,
    So much so, I'd perfer just not to hear it.
ELMIRE (*to* ORGON)   Seeing all this, I find myself struck dumb.
    I can't believe how blind you have become.
    You must be hypnotized, or else insane,
    To doubt our word about this recent scene.
ORGON   I believe your words, dear, one by one,
    And I know how fond you are of my rascal son.
    Clearly you were afraid to disavow
    The fraud he tried to perpetrate just now.
    And you were, I must protest, a shade too calm;
    A woman in your place should have showed alarm.
ELMIRE   Should a woman's honor be so stirred
    If someone offers her a wicked word?

And does a mere suggestion then require
Denunciations and a tongue of fire?
Why, all I do is laugh at such advances;
To me, they're unimportant circumstances.
I try to wear my virtue modestly
And not like some protesting prudes I see
Whose virtue comes full-armed with teeth and claws
Ready to scratch and bite at the slightest cause.
Heaven preserve me from such purity!
True Virtue needs no arms and need not be
Masked by scowls. A firm and simple "No"
Will tell unwelcome lovers where to go.

ORGON   You needn't try to make a dupe of me.

ELMIRE   I can't believe your gullibility!
Could I shake your blind, unthinking faith
By making you witness to the truth?

ORGON   Witness?

ELMIRE   Yes.

ORGON   Nonsense!

ELMIRE   Suppose
I show you the fact before your very eyes?

ORGON   Balderdash!

ELMIRE   Oh, what a man! It's too absurd!
You obviously won't believe a word.
Suppose we could place you here concealed
Where you could see what would be revealed,
And you saw the truth? Then what would you do?

ORGON   I'd say in that case . . . well, I'd say "Pooh pooh!"
For it cannot be.

ELMIRE   You've been too long unwise,
And you've accused me for too long of telling lies.
Now, for my satisfaction and your proof,
I'll make you witness to the living truth.

ORGON   I'll take you up on that! Let's see your scheme.
The truth will be far stranger than you dream.

ELMIRE (to DORINE)   Send him in here.

DORINE   He's clever as a fox
And he won't be easily trapped within a box.

ELMIRE   Some men are easily fooled by infatuation;
Such blindness must be cured by illumination.
Have him come down. (to CLÉANTE and MARIANE) And, you two, please go.
(Exeunt DORINE, CLÉANTE, and MARIANE.)

SCENE FOUR

ELMIRE and ORGON.

ELMIRE (continuing, to ORGON)   See that table? There's your
place—below.

ORGON   What?

ELMIRE   You'll have to hide yourself, that's clear.

ORGON   But why beneath the table?

ELMIRE   Get under here!
    I have my plan; You'll see how it works out;
    Under the table, quick, and when you're set,
    Not a whisper. Don't make any comments.

ORGON   I must say, I'm most patient with your nonsense.
    Well, let me see you wiggle out of this one.

ELMIRE   Remember, there are one or two conditions:
    Since this is a rather ticklish situtation,
    I must behave according to the occasion;
    Pray don't be scandalized if I seem to behave
    Quite forwardly; I do it for you, to save
    Your sanity; some questions I may ask
    Are merely traps to tempt him to unmask,
    And if I smile upon his lewd desires
    It's merely to arouse his amorous fires.
    Remember: for your sake and his confusion
    I have consented here in this seclusion
    To meet with him. The action will subside
    As soon as you feel fully satisfied.
    Your task will be, concealed there as you are,
    To call a halt if things have gone too far.
    A husband, after all, should shield his wife
    From the unpleasant perils of this life;
    You are the master in the house, and your will
    Should be obeyed . . . Sh! Here he comes! Be still!

SCENE FIVE

TARTUFFE, ELMIRE, *and* ORGON. ORGON *is under the table.*

TARTUFFE   They said, dear lady, you were waiting here.

ELMIRE   Yes. I've a secret for your private ear.
    But close that door first, please, and peep
    About the room. Let's not be caught asleep.
        (TARTUFFE *shuts the door and looks about.*)

ELMIRE   We certainly don't want again, you know,
    The sort of scene we had a while ago.
    That was most disagreeable, it's true,
    And I was in a panic because of you.
    You saw I did my best to keep him quiet.
    But he was clearly determined to raise a riot.
    Of course, I was so alarmed—I was nearly dead!—
    I didn't think to deny the things he'd said.
    But, Heaven be praised, it all worked out ideally
    And everything is understood—yes, really!
    Your reputation's so strong, it cannot fall,

And my husband does not suspect you, not at all.
In fact, to still the voice of slander, he
Wants us to be together continually.
So now we're able to be sequestered here
Behind locked doors and free of blame or fear,
And I can reveal what my true feelings are
About you, sir—but perhaps I go too far.

TARTUFFE   This talk is rather baffling, I'll admit;
You've changed, madame, since the last time we met.

ELMIRE   Why, if you're angry at my earlier rebuff,
You don't know women's hearts quite well enough.
You don't know our hearts are trying to speak
When our defense seems languid, slow, and weak.
And ever our modesty must make a show
Of struggling valiantly to overthrow
Our feelings, which, the while we're yielding,
We blush to find our words have been revealing.
At first we fight against them, but our tender
Sighs betray our swift complete surrender.
For honor's sake, we put our hearts on trial
And promise everything with a denial.
I fear I'm speaking much too honestly
And overlooking proper modesty.
But, since I'm speaking frankly, don't you see
Why I didn't struggle to restrain Damis?
And would I, pray, so graciously, so long,
Have listened to your offer, and so long
Have let you pour your heart out in full measure
If the affair did not afford me pleasure?
And when I argued with such force and courage
To get you to renounce your coming marriage
Why would my claims have been so strongly pressed
Except for my own selfish interest?
In short, I feared this marriage might divide
A heart I wanted whole, and near my side.

TARTUFFE   Ah, madame, it gives me joy extreme
To hear such words from you. It's like a dream!
Their honey pours into my tortured brain;
Their liquid sweetness flows through every vein.
My aim's to please you, all things else above;
My heart's beatitude lies in your love.
And yet I hope you'll not think me suspicious
To dare to doubt my joys are so delicious.
I could almost suspect a sly arrangement
To get me to break off my late engagement.
And so, madame, to put the matter bluntly,
And much as I enjoy your lovely company,

I'll dare to doubt your tender words until
Some tangible favors indicate your will,
Implanting in my wavering soul a faith
That your dear bounty's not a vagrant wraith.

ELMIRE (*coughing to warn* ORGON) What do you mean? Don't
    tell me that you think
You can rush love to its climax in a wink!
I've forced myself to make a rash admission,
But now you'd add, I see, another condition,
And you won't be satisfied until you win
Love's final favors almost before you begin.

TARTUFFE The less one merits, the less one dares to hope;
    Where talk is cheap, each parish priest's a Pope.
One easily mistrusts a promised bliss
And can't believe it till it's really his.
Knowing how little I am worthy of you,
I doubt I'll ever be allowed to love you.
In short, madame, I'll not believe a word
Till facts confirm these promises I've heard.

ELMIRE Dear me! Your love is really quite tyrannical.
    I'd hate to think I'm being puritanical,
But, mercy me! love drives men quite insane,
So powerful and violent is its reign;
Can I not raise my hands in weak defense?
Is there no way to curb your violence?
Take pity on a lady, sir, and send her
Reprieve. Complete, abject surrender
Is frightening, you know, and it may cost
You a regard you'd rather not have lost.

TARTUFFE If you receive my homage with compassion,
    Then why withhold love's tangible expression?

ELMIRE But, if I consent, won't Heaven be offended?
    This is your constant theme, and I commend it.

TARTUFFE Pooh! If Heaven's all that's worrying you,
    I'll take care of that, and easily too;
I can remove such obstacles with ease.

ELMIRE And yet they threaten us so with Heaven's decrees!

TARTUFFE I can banish such superstitious fear.
    There is an art, you know, in making clear
Heaven's will, and though Heaven may proscribe
Certain joys, a bit of a spiritual bribe
Can clear the path sometimes. There is a science
Of loosening the conscience so compliance
Is easy, and the evil of an action
Is rectified to Heaven's satisfaction.
I'll teach you all these secrets; you will see.
But you must put your confidence in me.

Content my longings, lady; do not fear.
The risk is mine; don't hesitate, my dear.
          (ELMIRE *coughs*.)
TARTUFFE   You have a nasty cough . . .
ELMIRE   It's most distressing.
TARTUFFE   I have some cough drops. Try one, with my blessing.
ELMIRE   I've had this cough for weeks, would you believe it?
     I fear that all your cough drops can't relieve it.
TARTUFFE   Very annoying.
ELMIRE   Yes, it's quite severe.
TARTUFFE   Well, at least I can dispel your fear.
     Your secret is known to us alone,
     And evil's not evil until it's known
     To the world at large, and, as for sin,
     To sin in silence is not to sin.
ELMIRE (*coughs*)   In short, I see that I shall have to yield
     And, fleeing, leave you master of the field
     Of my poor honor, for I can't convince
     A man who demands such tangible evidence.
     I must admit I fear to go so far,
     But who cares what my foolish scruples are?
     And since I'm driven to it cruelly
     By one who seems to find my pleas unduly
     Quibbling and demands complete conviction
     I must decide to render satisfaction
     Unto his claims. If there is any crime
     In such consent, it's clear the blame's not mine.
     Surely I am not responsible.
TARTUFFE   Of course not, lady! Why the thought's impossible!
ELMIRE   But first, please open the door—but not too wide—
     And see if my husband's lurking there outside.
TARTUFFE   Pooh! Why worry about dolts like those?
     He's the type you can lead around by the nose,
     The type to abet our little intimacies;
     Why, we can make him believe whatever we please.
ELMIRE   All the same, I'd feel much more secure
     If you'd take a look around just to be sure.
          (*Exit* TARTUFFE.)

SCENE SIX

ORGON *and* ELMIRE.
ORGON (*emerging from under the table*)   Such wickedness is inconceivable!
     I'm thunderstruck! It's unbelievable!
ELMIRE   What, crawling out so soon? Don't be absurd!
     Creep in again and wait. You haven't heard
     A fraction yet. Wait, and you'll correct your

Ideas further, and it won't be mere conjecture.
ORGON   Nothing more wicked has ever come out of hell!
ELMIRE   Don't be too quick to believe the tales they tell
About him. Perhaps you are mistaken
And you've let your faith be far too lightly shaken . . .
     (*As* TARTUFFE *re-enters,* ELMIRE *quickly hides* ORGON
     behind her.)

SCENE SEVEN

TARTUFFE, ELMIRE, *and* ORGON.

TARTUFFE   Everything's working out, madame, for the best.
The coast is clear. It seems that Heaven has blessed
This moment. My senses are delighted . . .
     (*As he advances to embrace* ELMIRE, *she steps aside, and
     he walks into the arms of* ORGON.)
ORGON   Hold on a minute! Don't get so excited!
Don't let your passions carry you away!
Aha! You pious soul, you thought to betray
Your benefactor by seducing his wife,
Wedding his daughter and fixing yourself for life!
I've long suspected that some day I would see
You're not all that you're cracked up to be.
But now I've seen enough, yes, and I've heard
More than enough. No, not another word.
ELMIRE (*to* TARTUFFE)   It's not my manner to tease and betray,
But I've been forced to treat you in this way.
TARTUFFE (*to* ORGON)   What, can you believe . . . ?
ORGON   Let no more be said.
Get out of here before I lose my head.
TARTUFFE   I only sought . . .
ORGON   To secretly seduce my spouse!
I know. This minute—get out of my house!
TARTUFFE   But, just a moment—*you* are the one to leave.
This house belongs to me, I do believe.
There's no use trying to pick a quarrel with me
On such a poor excuse. You wait! You'll see!
You're in a poor position to evict me,
When *you're* the one to pack and leave—and quickly!
I have the power to avenge offended Heaven;
Please be gone by quarter past eleven. (*Exit.*)

SCENE EIGHT

ELMIRE *and* ORGON.

ELMIRE   What's he talking about? It's all a bluff.
ORGON   I wish it were. I fear he's serious enough.

ELMIRE   What is it?

ORGON   This is a pretty mess, indeed.
 I made a great mistake when I gave him that deed.

ELMIRE   A deed?

ORGON   Yes, and it's signed and sealed.
 But there may be even more to be revealed.

ELMIRE   What's that?

ORGON   I'll tell you later; first, I want to see
 If my strongbox still is where it used to be.

Act Five

SCENE ONE

ORGON *and* CLEANTE.

CLÉANTE   Where are you going?

ORGON   I don't know.

CLÉANTE   It's clear
 We need to talk about this dreadful affair.

ORGON   The strongbox mainly weighs upon my mind,
 More than all the other matters combined.

CLÉANTE   This strongbox is an important mystery?

ORGON   It has a most unusual history.
 My good friend Argas gave it to me in trust,
 Impressing on me, come what may, I must
 Keep it a secret; his life, his property
 Depended on that box he gave to me.

CLÉANTE   Then why, pray tell, did you give it to Tartuffe?

ORGON   I know, dear brother; I merit your reproof.
 I hoped to keep my conscience easy, though,
 And he persuaded me to let it go
 By telling me that, in case of investigation,
 I might deny then any imputation
 Of guilty knowledge and could take an oath
 That would not be contrary to the truth.

CLÉANTE   I must confess, I fear you're on the rocks.
 The deed of gift, the transfer of the box—
 I speak the truth, I cannot deal in lies—
 To put the matter gently, were most unwise.
 With these as evidence, it's clear he's got you
 Exactly where he wants you. You forgot you
 Were dealing with a man of many schemes;
 You never should have pushed him to extremes.

ORGON   Oh! Under such an outward show of piety
 To hide such wickedness and impropriety!
 To think I rescued him from sheer disgrace!

From now on, I renounce the human race.
Henceforth I'll shun them utterly and call
Myself a fool if I don't hate them all!
CLÉANTE Now there you go, flying off the handle!
Won't you ever learn to burn the candle
At just one end? You waver wildly, brother,
From one grotesque extreme back to the other.
You see your error now and recognize
That you were taken in by pious lies,
Buy why correct your error and confusion
By falling into greater disillusion
And lump all mankind in one category
As though that told the full facts of the story?
Because a rascal cuts truth on the bias,
Pretending to be holy, good, and pious,
You would conclude that Chaos is upon us
And that the human race has turned dishonest.
Let the freethinkers think that, if they choose,
But learn to separate the external views
From the inner truth. And then don't rush away
Too hastily, but keep to the middle way.
Try not to be the dupe of charlatans,
But don't brand truly pious men as harlequins
And if you must make one or the other choice,
Then let excessive leniency be your vice.

SCENE TWO

ORGON, CLÉANTE, *and* DAMIS.
DAMIS Father, is it true this brazen rogue,
Forgetting all the favors you've bestowed,
Has grown presumptuous and threatens
To use your benefits against you as his weapons?
ORGON My son, I'm sorry to say it's all too true.
DAMIS Give me the word, and I'll run him through and through
With a carving knife. One should never waver
Before the impudence of that soul-saver!
I'll fix him so he'll never bother us again!
CLÉANTE Ah, that's the speech of youth. But now and then
It's necessary to be more composed.
We're men, not beasts; the course that you've proposed
Is surely no way to resolve the matter.

SCENE THREE

MADAME PERNELLE, ORGON, ELMIRE, CLÉANTE, MARIANE, DAMIS, *and* DORINE.
MME. PERNELLE Good Heavens, what's the meaning of all this chatter?

ORGON   Strange things indeed I've seen with my own eyes,
    And a strange and most unpleasant kind of surprise!
    I rescue a man from abject poverty,
    Give him my home, my daughter, my property,
    Treat him, in short, better than my brother,
    Crown every benefit I give him with another,
    And what is my reward, upon my life?
    He seeks beneath my nose to seduce my wife,
    And, still not fully satisfied with this,
    He dares to use against me my own gifts,
    Trying to bring me down by using the hold
    I've given him by my kindness, and he's bold
    Enough to kick me from under this roof that's covered him
    And leave me in the gutter where I discovered him!
DORINE   The poor man!
MME. PERNELLE   My son, I can't imagine
    He could behave in such a fashion.
ORGON   What!
MME. PERNELLE   People always envy pious men.
ORGON   Do I have to tell you all of this again?
MME. PERNELLE   I know that people here don't love him;
    I know they're all quite jealous of him.
ORGON   And what's that got to do with this affair?
MME. PERNELLE   When you were a boy, I warned you to take care,
    For virtue's always slandered by a lie;
    Though envy perishes, the envious won't die.
ORGON   I don't see how any of this is apropos.
MME. PERNELLE   Liars will tirelessly spread their lies, you know.
ORGON   I tell you I saw it all with my very own eyes!
MME. PERNELLE   Ah, alas! that this world is so full of lies!
ORGON   You'll make me sin through anger. For the last time,
    I tell you I *saw* his shameless attempt at crime!
MME. PERNELLE   This world is ever full of slanderous tongues
    Ready to make up tales of imagined wrongs.
ORGON   What you are saying is absolute nonsense!
    I *saw* the man! He hasn't the slightest defense!
    I *saw* him try to do it! Do I have to yell
    The simple truth in your ear or ring a bell?
MME. PERNELLE   Mercy me! Appearances often deceive.
    Don't be overly rash in what you believe.
ORGON   You're driving me crazy!
MME. PERNELLE   False suspicion
    Is common to one in your condition.
ORGON   Then he piously sought to improve my life
    By making infamous love to my wife?
MME. PERNELLE   You need *facts* to support an accusation
    Which might destroy a good man's reputation.

ORGON   *Facts?* How in the hell can I be more factual
    Than to catch the scoundrel in the actual
    Act of . . . no, you almost made me say it.
MME. PERNELLE   If there's evil in him, he doesn't betray it,
    Not by the slightest glance or sneer;
    I just can't believe these stories I hear.
ORGON   Good Lord, I'm so mad I could jump on my hat!
    If you weren't my mother, I'd do worse than that!
DORINE (*to* ORGON)   You wouldn't believe a word we'd say;
    Now turn about, I'm afraid, is fair play.
CLÉANTE   We're wasting time here babbling like silly sheep;
    When the wolf is on the prowl, one shouldn't sleep.
    How are we going to meet that scoundrel's scheme?
DAMIS   He wouldn't have the nerve! He wouldn't dream . . . !
ELMIRE   I really doubt if he'd take legal action
    Merely to obtain his satisfaction.
CLÉANTE   Don't be too sure. He's got tricks up his sleeve,
    And we know he's slyer than anyone dare believe.
    For less than this, men have served a spell
    With bread and water in a prison cell.
    And I repeat, since we know what his weapons are,
    You made a mistake in pushing him so far.
ORGON   All right, all right, but what else could I do?
    His impudence simply angered me through and through.
CLÉANTE   I wish with all my heart we could arrange
    Some kind of fair and equitable exchange.
ELMIRE   If I had known he held such trumps in hand,
    I'd have thought twice about the trick I planned.
                (M. LOYAL *appears at the door;* DORINE *goes to meet him.*)

SCENE FOUR

ORGON, MADAME PERNELLE, ELMIRE, MARIANE, CLÉANTE, DAMIS, DORINE,
and MONSIEUR LOYAL.
ORGON   Who's that fellow? Tell him to go away.
    I'm in no state to deal with callers today
M. LOYAL   Sister, good morning. Your master, pray, where is he?
    I must speak to him at once.
DORINE   He's busy.
    He can't see anyone, I fear.
M. LOYAL   I shouldn't like to intrude upon him here.
    But I don't think my business will upset him;
    He can hear my news, if you will let him.
DORINE   Your name?
M. LOYAL   Just say I've come to bring him proof
    Of the warm regard of Monsieur Tartuffe.
DORINE (*to* ORGON)   He is a messenger, and quite soft-spoken,

From our old friend. He says he brings a token
Of Tartuffe's regard.
CLÉANTE   You'd better see
Who he is and what his news can be.
ORGON   Maybe he's coming to offer apologies.
Should I greet him politely and put him at his ease?
CLÉANTE   Speak softly, but don't vouchsafe any admission.
If he offers peace, though—better listen.
M. LOYAL   Greetings, good sir! May Heaven confound your foes
And shower you with love and sweet repose!
ORGON (to CLÉANTE)   A most polite beginning! An indication
He wants a reconciliation.
M. LOYAL   Your family's interests have long been mine.
I served your worthy father many a time.
ORGON   I beg your pardon, sir, but to my shame
I must confess I don't recall your name.
M. LOYAL   My name is Loyal. I too have a confession.
I am a process server by profession.
For forty years it's been my pride and joy
To hold that honorable office, man and boy.
You asked my business here, sir? This is it:
To serve upon you this judicial writ.
ORGON   What!
M. LOYAL   Now, please, let's talk without unseemly friction.
It's just a little notice of eviction.
You and your family must get out,
Remove your goods and furniture, and in about—
Let's say, an hour—sooner, if you could.
ORGON   What, leave my house!
M. LOYAL   If you would be so good.
This house belongs, as you are well aware,
To good Monsieur Tartuffe. A deed I bear
Attests unto the fact beyond dispute,
So please don't force him, good sir, to bring suit
And call upon the law in his defense.
DAMIS   I'm simply staggered by such insolence!
M. LOYAL   Young man, my business here is not with you,
But with your father, a good man and true,
Who knows his legal duties, you may trust us,
And wouldn't dream of contravening justice.
ORGON   But . . .
M. LOYAL   Yes, I know that not for a fortune
Would you protest or would you importune
The court to contradict its stern commands
And remove this writ from out of your hands.
DAMIS   You might get a wholesome beating on the end
Of your black and gloomy coat, my friend!

M. LOYAL   Sir, bid your son be silent and retire.
  I'd hate to have to report his ire
  And his threats of violence and fits of pique.
DORINE (*aside*)   He says his name is Loyal? I'd say, Sneak.
M. LOYAL   I have a great respect for honesty,
  And I agreed to serve this writ, you see,
  Just to oblige you and to give you pleasure,
  For others might not execute the seizure
  Of your goods with such consideration
  As I, who feel for you such admiration.
ORGON   What could be worse, or could be a greater crime
  Than evicting a man?
M. LOYAL   But, you see, I'm giving you time.
  I will suspend till tomorrow, if you need
  Some extra time, the service of the deed.
  I'll merely come, with a dozen of my men,
  To quietly spend the night with you, and then
  I'll ask you to deliver to me the keys
  Of the house before you go to bed, if you please.
  Please be assured, we'll not trouble your repose;
  It's just a matter of form, you know how it goes.
  Tomorrow morning early you'll move out
  All your furniture. I've picked some stout
  And husky fellows; you'll find they're quite discreet,
  As well as skilled at moving things out on the street.
  No one, I think, could possibly act more fairly,
  Nor put the matter before you more sincerely,
  And as I'm giving you all this kind assistance
  I must beg you to offer no resistance.
ORGON (*aside*)   How happy I would be to give my last
  Hundred louis for the chance to blast
  This monster of pure impudence and clout
  Him violently and squarely on the snout!
CLÉANTE   Easy, don't lose your head.
DAMIS   Oh, I insist.
  Just one punch. I've got an itching fist.
DORINE   That noble back, monsieur, seems to demand
  A good sound beating from a lady's hand.
M. LOYAL   Beware, my dear; the law makes no distinction
  Regarding sex when it comes to legal action.
CLÉANTE   No more of this, sir; whatever the law allows,
  Just give us the writ, and then get out of the house.
M. LOYAL   Au revoir, gentlemen! May God content you! (*Exit.*)

SCENE FIVE

ORGON, MADAME PERNELLE, ELMIRE, CLEANTE, MARIANE, DAMIS, *and* DORINE.
ORGON   May He confound you and the man who sent you! (*to* MME. PERNELLE)

Well, Mother, tell me, was I right
About this monster who is your delight?
MME. PERNELLE   I'm flabbergasted! I can't believe my ears!
DORINE   Well, maybe it's all better than it appears.
His goal is good; he's doing all he can
To demonstrate how he loves his fellow-man.
He knows the soul's corrupted by the love
Of money, so he'll lovingly remove
Temptation from his friends, for their salvation.
ORGON   Oh, shut up! Stop this bickering! Damnation!
CLÉANTE   Let's try to think of the proper course to take.
ELMIRE   Let's tell the world he's a hypocritical fake.
These despicable tricks he has employed
Would render any contract null and void.
Public opinion, once his deeds are known,
Will surely rise, and its power will be shown.

SCENE SIX

VALÈRE, ORGON, MADAME PERNELLE, ELMIRE, CLÉANTE, MARIANE, DAMIS,
and DORINE.
VALÈRE   I'm sorry, sir, to cause you any distress,
But I feel obliged to by the present mess
You're in; a very old and trusted friend
Who knows my interest has dared to send
Me word of your affairs, in violation
Of that high secrecy belonging to his station.
The news he sends is bitter, curt, and tight:
Your only possible recourse is flight.
He who has swindled you of everything
Has made an accusation to the King,
And has supported his charges, sad to relate,
With the strongbox of an outlaw of the state,
The which he found, he says, in your possession.
Proof of your most traitorous transgression.
I don't know whether you're innocent or not,
But you're ordered to be arrested on the spot,
And Tartuffe himself has been commended
And charged to see that you are apprehended.
CLÉANTE   Thus armed might assists him in his schemes
And helps him realize his evil dreams.
ORGON   Oh, that man is wicked past man's thought!
VALÈRE   Any delay will be fatal, so I've brought
My carriage round to whisk you safely away
And a thousand louis to help you on your way.
So don't waste time; this is a fearful blow;
Escape is the only answer that I know.

I'll find you a hiding-place with another friend
And I'll stay by your side until the end.

ORGON   I owe so much to your kind consideration,
But that can wait for a happier occasion;
I only pray that Heaven gives me the power
To fitly remember your goodness in this hour.
Good-bye, my friends . . .

CLÉANTE   Hurry! No delays! Don't fear,
We'll take care of everything right here.

(*Enter* TARTUFFE *and a* POLICE OFFICER. *As* ORGON *starts
to exit*, TARTUFFE *seizes him.*)

SCENE SEVEN

TARTUFFE, *a* POLICE OFFICER, MADAME PERNELLE, ORGON, ELMIRE, CLÉANTE,
MARIANE, VALÈRE, DAMIS, *and* DORINE.

TARTUFFE   Here now, good sir! Don't run away so fast!
A lodging's ready for you. No need for haste.
I take you prisoner, in the name of the King.

ORGON   Villain, you are guilty of everything;
You duped me into listening to your counsel
So that you might bring about my utter downfall!

TARTUFFE   I will not flinch, although you rave quite wildly.
Heaven has taught me to suffer insults mildly.

CLÉANTE   So these are the lessons your religion has given!

DAMIS   How impudently he plays with the name of Heaven!

TARTUFFE   You cannot move me by your enmity;
To do my duty means everything to me.

MARIANE   Much glory you will draw from this affair,
And maybe more honor than even you can bear!

TARTUFFE   Glory only accrues unto an action
Blessed and commanded by the royal sanction.

ORGON   Have you forgotten it was my charity
That rescued you from the depths of poverty?

TARTUFFE   True, you helped me with an occasional loan,
But my highest duty is to the royal throne.
This sacred and compelling obligation
Extinguishes all small considerations
Of petty gratitude. Upon my life,
I place it ahead of children, family, or wife!

ELMIRE   Imposter!

DORINE   This treacherous, sly snake would
Twist and mock all values we hold sacred!

CLÉANTE   But if this noble and religious zeal
Is quite as perfect as you'd have us feel,
How is it that it waited to appear
Till you were caught embracing Madame here?

Why did you delay your denunciation
Till you were trapped in that curious situation?
I won't allege, though it might have played a part,
That deed of gift from the goodness of his heart,
But why accept the money, then and later,
Of a man whom you denounce now as a traitor?

TARTUFFE (*to the* POLICE OFFICER)   Deliver me, monsieur, from attacks like these
And execute your orders, if you please.

OFFICER   Yes, I've delayed too long now, at the best;
And, aptly enough, you're the one who makes the request.
So here's the order: kindly follow me
To the prison cell that is your home-to-be.

TARTUFFE   Who, me?

OFFICER   Yes, you.

TARTUFFE   What do you mean? You must be insane!

OFFICER   You're not the one to whom I must explain. (*to* ORGON)
You've had a nasty scare, but, praised be God,
Our present King is an enemy of fraud;
His eyes can penetrate his subjects' hearts
And he's not deluded by a trickster's arts.
His great spirit, mighty, calm, and wise,
Watches his kingdom with discerning eyes.
Charlatans and practicers of treason
Cannot delude or shake his sovereign reason.
To worthy men he gives due recompense,
Yet he's not blind to fraud and false pretense.
His love for truth, however, does not eclipse
The horror one should feel for hypocrites.
Tartuffe was not the type who could hoodwink him:
The King is more perceptive than men think him.
Immediately and subtly he divined
The vile conniving of an evil mind.
This man betrayed himself by his accusation
And by a process of due retribution
The King identified him as a thief
With a criminal record almost past belief,
A man of various names, whose numerous crimes
Have been recorded a good many times.
In short, His Majesty found so abhorrent
This man's career, that it was ample warrant
For his arrest. This additional crime
Only sealed his fate. That's why I'm
With him today. The King commanded me
To accompany him today and see
What impudence he would dare as a last evasion.
Now I shall force him to make you reparation,
Seizing the powers that he might have destroyed;

The King declares the contract null and void
Which might have made Tartuffe your legal heir
And he pardons that transgression where
You erred but to protect a friend.
Thus he rewards you, thus does he commend
Your past fidelity in the civil wars,
Proving his heart remembers and rewards
A loyal subject; like the King of paradise,
He's mindful more of virtue than of vice.

DORINE   May Heaven be praised!

MME. PERNELLE   Ah, I'm so relieved!

ELMIRE   All's well again!

MARIANE   This scarcely can be believed!

ORGON (*to* TARTUFFE)   So now we've got you, villain . . .

        (*The* OFFICER *drags* TARTUFFE *away.*)

SCENE EIGHT

MADAME PERNELLE, ORGON, ELMIRE, MARIANE, CLÉANTE, VALÈRE, DAMIS,
and DORINE.

CLÉANTE   Please; moderation.
Don't yield to an unworthy exultation.
Leave the wretched man to his wretched fate;
He's already bowed beneath the heavy weight
Of his own remorse. Why not hope, rather,
That his heart may undergo a change, dear brother,
And by progressing to better from the worse, he
May move the King to temper justice with mercy,
The while you kneel before the royal throne
To beg that Tartuffe's fate might be like your own.

ORGON   Well said, indeed. So let us, at his feet,
Thank him for his kindness and entreat
Mercy for our enemies. This done,
There's one more crown of joy left to be won,
And that's for me to happily declare
Mariane shall be the bridge of Valère.

From the Playwright

In the history of drama, possibly only Ibsen's Ghosts *and Hugo's* Hernani *created more of a furor than* Tartuffe. *After its initial presentation (1664), the play aroused enough antagonism in France to result in its banishment for five years. In the "Preface to* Tartuffe," *written during this interim,* **Molière** *replies to his critics and defends the role of comedy as a necessary tool for unmasking the pompous and exposing the dishonorable.*

From Preface to Tartuffe

This is a comedy which has been persecuted for a long time and one about which people have made much fanfare. Those of whom it makes fun have indeed demonstrated that they were more powerful in France than those whom I have ridiculed to date. The marquis, the affected ladies, the cuckolds and the doctors have graciously accepted the fact that they have been spoofed. They pretended that they were amused, along with everyone else, by the portrait made of them. The hypocrites, however, could not take the kidding. At first they were shocked and thought it strange that I was so bold as to make fun of their gestures and to want to lampoon a profession of which so many fine people were members. It was a crime for which they could not pardon me, and they banded together against my play with frightful fury. They were careful not to attack it in the parts that concerned them most. They are too shrewd for that and know all too well how not to reveal their true thoughts. Proceeding in their usual praiseworthy manner, they cloaked their personal interest in the cause of God; and Tartuffe, according to them, is a play that offends piety. The play is, from beginning to end, full of abominable things and deserves to be burned. Every syllable is irreverent; even the gestures of the actors are criminal; and the slightest glance, the least nod of the head, the slightest motion to the right or left, contains hidden mysteries which they contrive to explain to my disadvantage.

In vain I have submitted the play to the examination of my friends and the consideration of all. This included the corrections I was able to make in it, the opinion of the king and queen who saw it, the approbation of great princes and high-ranking ministers of government who publicly honored it with their presence and the testimony of cultivated and wealthy people who found it profitable. All this served no good purpose. They do not want to back down from their stand, and every day they have their zealous followers publicly shout their pious slander. In the name of charity they condemn me to eternal damnation.

I would care little about all they say were it not for the guile they employ in making enemies of people whom I respect, fine people whom they attract to their side and whose good faith they take advantage of. These are people who are genuinely religious and easily swayed by ideas that others want to give them. It is this that forces me to defend myself. It is the truly devout for whom I most desire to justify myself in the handling of my play. I beg them not to condemn things before seeing them, to rid themselves of bias and not to serve the eager desire of those who dishonor them with fancy maneuvers.

If one takes the trouble to examine my play in good faith, he will undoubtedly see that my intentions are innocent throughout, and that it in no way tends to make fun of things that should be revered. One will further see that I have handled it with all the care that the delicacy of the subject demands, and that I have used all my talent and taken all precautions possible to separate the character of the hypocrite from that of the true devotee. To do this, I have used two entire acts preparing for the arrival of my scoundrel. He does not keep, even for a single moment, the audience in doubt! First of all, people recognize him by the traits I give him; and, from beginning to end, he does not speak a word or make a move which does not indicate to the spectators the character of an evil man, especially in contrast to the truly fine man I employ. . . .

I well know that, by way of reply, these gentlemen are trying to insinuate that it is not in the theater that these matters should be mentioned. With their permission I ask them on what they base this fine thought. It is a proposition based only on supposition and one which they can in no way prove. Undoubtedly it would not be difficult to show them that drama in ancient times had its origin in religion and was a part of religious plays, that the Spaniards, our neighbors, celebrate few religious holidays in which drama does not play a part, and that even, among ourselves, it owes its beginning to the work of a religious brotherhood to which the Hotel de Bourgogne belongs. It was a place donated for the purpose of presenting the most important mystery plays of our faith. One can still see plays printed in gothic letters under the mane of a doctor of the Sorbonne; and without straying too great a distance, holy plays of Monsieur de Corneille have been presented there during our own time. These have gained the admiration of all France.

If the purpose of comedy is to correct the vices of men, I do not see in any way why some should be privileged. Politically, this is of a far more dangerous consequence than all the rest, and we have seen that the theater has a great virtue in the area of correction. The greatest points of a serious moral conception are, most often, less powerful than those of satire. Nothing affects most men more than the painting of their faults. There is no greater blow to vice than exposing it to the ridicule of everyone. One can stand criticism, but he cannot put up with ridicule. One is willing to appear evil, but he does not want to seem ridiculous.

People reproach me for having put words of piety in the mouth of my imposter. But how else could this be prevented if one wants to depict the character of a hypocrite? It is sufficient, it seems to me, that I reveal the criminal motives which make him speak the words he does, and that I have not employed holy words that would have caused embarrassment if he had spoken them—but in the fourth act he delivers evil words on morality. And yet, has not this kind of morality already been dinned into our ears? Is anything new said in my play? And can one fear that things so generally hated will make an impression on people's minds? Do I make such things dangerous by presenting them in the theater? Do they gain authority for being spoken by a scoundrel? This is in no way the case, and one should either approve the play Tartuffe or condemn all plays in general.

For some time people have been trying to do just this, and never has there been so great an outburst against the theater. I cannot deny that there have been Church Fathers who have condemned plays, but it also cannot be denied that there have been some who have treated them more amiably. In this fashion the authority on which they base their censure is destroyed by this division. The only consequence that can be drawn from this diversity of opinion among people of similar intelligence is that they have looked at the theater from different points of view. Some have considered it in its pure state while others have viewed it in its corruption. The latter have confused it with evil spectacles that should be considered depraved.

And, in fact, since one ought to offer opinions about things and not about words, and since most misunderstandings are the result of not being understood and of using a single word for things that are entirely different, one should only remove the curtain of equivocation and consider what the play is, standing on its own merits, to see if it deserves to be condemned. People will undoubtedly realize that being nothing more than a clever poem which, through pleasant lessons considers men's faults, they will not censure it unjustly. If we wish to listen to the testimony of antiquity, it will tell us that the most famous philosophers—those who professed so austere a wisdom and who cried unceasingly against the evils of their century—praised the theater. It will be revealed to us that Aristotle spent many a night in his consideration of the theater, and that he took it upon himself to draw up precepts on the art of writing plays. It will tell us that the greatest and most dignified men gloried in composing plays themselves; and that there were others who were not opposed to reciting in public ones they had composed. Greece showed her esteem for this art with wonderful prizes and superb theaters. In Rome, too, this same art also received extraordinary honors; and I am not speaking of that debauched Rome during the time of the licentious emperors, but of the well-disciplined Rome of the wise consuls during the vigorous, virtuous times.

I admit that there were times when the theater was corrupt. What in the world is there that is not corrupt at one time or another? There is nothing so innocent that cannot be spoiled by men, no art so beneficial that aims cannot be upset, nothing so good that it cannot be put to evil uses. Medicine is a worthy art, and all revere it as one of the most excellent that we possess. And yet there were times when it was in ill-repute, when it was an art to poison people. Philosophy is a gift from Heaven. It was given to us to lift our minds to the understanding of a God through the contemplation of nature's marvels, and yet we realize that often it has been shunted from its real use and been publicly used to support impiety. Even the holiest of things are not safe from the corruption of man, and we see scoundrels who, everyday, abuse piety and employ it for the greatest of evil crimes. Even in this matter we do not fail to make the necessary distinctions. We do not conceal the best of the things that have been corrupted by the evil acts of the corrupters. We always separate the basic intention of the art from evil uses of the same. We do not forbid the practice of medicine because it had been banned in Rome, nor philosophy for having been publicly condemned in Athens. We ought not, for the same reason, want to ban a play because it was censured at some time or other. This censuring had its reasons, but they no longer apply. It pertained to what could be seen at that time and we ought not apply it to present cases. We ought not extend it any farther than necessary and should not permit it to include both the innocent and the guilty. The theater that it planned to attack is not at all the theater we want to defend. We must take care not to confuse one with the other. They are as two people whose ways are entirely opposite. They have no connection with each other except the name; and it would be a horrible injustice to want to condemn Olympia, who is a good woman, because there was an Olympia who was a dissolute. Such judgments would undoubtedly cause much misunderstanding in society. In this manner, everything would be condemned; and as people are not so strict about everyday abuses, we should be just as fair to the theater by approving those plays in which both decency and learning appear.

I know that there are those people whose refinement cannot bear any type of play, those who say that the most decent plays are the most dangerous; that the passions represented are all the more pertinent because they are virtuous, and that people are affected by this type of performance. I do not see what great crime it is to be moved by an honest passion; and how virtuous it is that this indifference is what they want us to aim for! I doubt that such great perfection lies in the realm of human nature, and I do not know but that it is better to work toward the correction and alleviation of men's passions rather than to cut them off completely. I admit that there are some places that are better to frequent than the theater; and, if one does not wish to blame everything which is not directly concerned with God and our salvation, it is certain that the theater should be included. I do not find it out of order that the theater be condemned with the rest, however, let us suppose, as is the case, that pious practices are permitted at intervals and that men do have a need for diversion. I maintain that one cannot find anything more innocent than the theater. I have gone on at too great a length. Let us finish with a few words of a great prince about the play *Tartuffe*.

A week after *Tartuffe* had been forbidden, a play entitled *Scaramouche the Hermit* was performed before the court. The king, upon leaving, said to the great prince: "I should like to know why those who are so scandalized by Molière's play say nothing about *Scaramouche*." The prince replied: "The reason for this is that the play *Scaramouche* makes fun of holy and religious matters about which these gentlemen do not have the least concern. Molière's play, however, ridicules them personally and that is what they cannot bear."

FIRST PETITION
ADDRESSED TO THE KING
ABOUT THE PLAY *TARTUFFE*

Sire,
The duty of comedy being to correct men's vices while amusing them, I believed that, in my present profession, I could do no better than to attack the ridiculous portraits of vice common to my century. As hypocrisy is undoubtedly one of the most common, disagreeable and dangerous vices, it occurred to me, Sire, that I would render some service to all the honest people in your kingdom

by writing a play which discredited hypocrites by featuring, as is necessary, all the feigned facial expressions of these ultra-fine people, all the hidden trickery of these counterfeiters of devotion who desire to ensnare men with pretended zeal and sophisticated charity.

I wrote this play, Sire, with all the care, I believe, and all the caution that the delicacy of the subject could possibly call for. In order to better maintain the esteem and the respect that one owes to true believers, I have emphasized as much as I possibly could the character I was depicting. I have left no doubt, and I have removed anything that could confuse good with evil. In this portrait I have used only those express colors and essential features which are immediately recognized as those of an outright hypocrite.

Nevertheless all my cares have been useless. People have profited, Sire, from the kindness of your heart concerning matters of religion, and they knew how to reach you in the only place you could be reached—I mean through your respect for holy things. The Tartuffes were underhandedly skillful enough to gain favor from Your Majesty; and the original ones finally succeeded in getting the copy suppressed, however innocent it may have been and whatever resemblance it may have contained.

Although the suppression of this work was a damaging blow, my misfortune was, nevertheless, lessened by the way in which Your Majesty explained your views on the subject. I thought, Sire, that I had no reason to complain when you so kindly declared that you found nothing wrong in this play that you forbade me to present in public.

But, in spite of this fine declaration of the greatest and most enlightened king in the world, in spite of the approval of the Papal Legate and of most of our prelates all of whom, during the private readings of my work which I gave them, were in complete accord with the feelings of Your Majesty; in spite of all this there is a book written by a parish priest which completely belies all these wise testimonies. In vain Your Majesty speaks, in vain the legate and the prelates give their opinions, and still my play, which he hasn't even seen, is as diabolical as I am myself. I am a devil in human form, a libertine, a blasphemer worthy of exemplary punishment. It is not enough that eternal damnation atone for my offense in public. I would be getting off too easily. The charitable zeal of this fine, outstanding man is not content to stop there. He does not even want me to even attain God's mercy. He absolutely desires that I be eternally damned, and that is it in short. . . .

From
SECOND PETITION
ADDRESSED TO THE KING
ABOUT THE PLAY *TARTUFFE*

Sire,
. . . My play, Sire, has not profited from the kindness of Your Majesty. In vain I have produced it under the title of *The Imposter* and disguised the main character beneath the cloak of a worldly man. In vain I gave him a small hat, long hair, a stiff collar, a sword and lace all over . . .

I do not doubt, Sire, that the people whom I depict in my play will move heaven and earth to influence Your Majesty. . . . This they have sufficiently revealed in the plays they have so many times allowed to be presented in public without uttering the slightest word. These were the plays that attacked piety and religion about which they were hardly concerned. Mine both attacks and makes fun of them, and this is what they cannot stand. . . .

From the Critic

That Molière was attempting to expose religious hypocrisy in Tartuffe *is an unmistakable fact, according to critic* **Henry Trollope.** *But in order to gain a complete realization of Molière's purpose, it is also necessary to understand that the* character *Tartuffe was drawn from the pretentious and dishonest "directors of conscience" known to France at that time, and that they too were the target of Molière's stinging criticism.*

What Was Tartuffe?

There have been hypocrites in every time and in every country, but the forms of society under which they have lived have not always been the same. Other people, other manners. The wiles of hypocrisy will vary according to the conditions favorable to their existence. Everybody knows that Tartuffe was a hypocrite, but everybody does not know to what class he belonged. He was one of the directors of conscience—a class of men either in the Church or connected with it, but not to be confounded with the confessors, who had always been admitted into holy orders. I shall have something to say about the directors later on. Adaptations of Molière's play have been made in England to suit our notions, but the most important character has been altered, because the reasons for his existence are not familiar to us. Tartuffe is not a scoundrel of English growth, like Pecksniff, nor could he be easily transplanted to our soil. We have had our hypocrites, but our imaginative literature does not supply us with a Tartuffe. For us he must remain a foreigner. It is not the enormity of the man's offence that differentiates him from our own native-born scoundrels, but its kind. The circumstances under which we live, our customs and habits of thought, do not leave a ready opening for his schemes. Our form of Protestantism debars his entrance into our households. But in France, in the seventeenth century, everything lay ready to his hands; the will only on his part was wanting. If a man in his position did not scruple to become a villain, he could find a scope for his talents.

As the 'Provincial Letters' (January 1656 to March 1657) was an event in literary history, so was 'Le Tartuffe' (first written in 1664) an event in the annals of the stage. Like Pascal's Letters, Molière's comedy was at the time an actuality. It spoke of matters that were of daily occurrence in well-to-do households, and was therefore likely to excite strong interest. People thought very differently about it. The public as a whole enjoyed the comedy; but men in high places, those in authority, decried it, and said that it was immoral. Pascal had to hide himself while his Letters were being printed clandestinely, and Molière was denounced in terms that now might make us smile did we not know that ignorant-minded men commonly make use of very violent language in speaking of their opponents. But in spite of all the invective shown by the ablest advocates that the enemies of each could bring forward, neither the Letters nor the comedy were refuted. They were both written for the public, and by the public they were both accepted and believed. In both cases time has ratified the popular verdict.

Molière did not draw his picture of a *faux devot* from any one of his contemporaries. The Abbé Roquette was commonly said to have been his model; but there were two other names which tradition has handed down to us as furnishing materials for his character. If there were three churchmen whose likeness to Tartuffe was remarked, there were probably others who afforded points of resemblance that were noticeable. One of these points was the Jesuitical doctrine of "directing the intention," which Tartuffe tries to teach Elmire in the fourth act; another was the doctrine of "mental restrictions," which Orgon shows that Tartuffe had succeeded in teaching him in act v. sc. 1. Pascal had previously satirised both of these deceitful practices.

. . . . .

. . . The play was then regarded by the Church, by the Bench, and by many in private life, as an impious theological pamphlet, holding up to scorn and ridicule devout people—the teacher and his pupil—who were to be reprobated and laughed at by everybody who wished to see them travestied. We who live now can see more clearly than those who were alive at the time, that Molière was actuated by a broader and a truer religion than his opponents. We can see now that he was bold enough to tell the world, with all earnestness and reverence, how a wicked man can scoff at religious practices and invoke heaven for his own bad ends. We can see now that Molière's intentions may have been mistaken at the time, and that moderate-minded people may have regarded his play as dangerous. Yet Tartuffe's villainy is perfectly transparent. It is quite impossible, one would say, to confound him with a sincere or a God-fearing man. To any one who knows the meaning of words, his baseness is as clear as the sun; no ingenuity, no special pleading, can make it otherwise. He does not appear on the stage until the third act; by that time his character is plainly established. His first words, spoken to his valet as soon as he sees Dorine, form a most admirable dramatic *début*: "Laurent, lock up my hair shirt with my scourge, and pray that heaven may always shine upon you. If any one comes to see me, I am going to the prisoners to divide amongst them my small alms of charity." In the next scene he makes a strong protestation of love to Orgon's wife.

The province of comedy has always been to laugh at the follies and attack the vices of the age, and the dramatist felt himself justified in exposing to derision and contempt the double-facedness of some members of a class of men who were increasing in numbers, and whose influence was gaining strength in the households of good families. Molière knew that the charge he was making was very serious, and I cannot think that he undertook it lightly; nor can I quite agree with those who hold that he bravely threw his gauntlet into the arena as the champion reformer of a grave abuse. He was not a reformer by nature. He had no wish to constitute himself a literary or stage policeman over his fellow-creatures. Such work was not to his taste. And he was not an enthusiast like Pascal. But his sensitive and sympathetic nature was pained to see men in places of deep responsibility and of emolument walking through the world with a lie continually on their faces and on their tongues. I interpret in the same way, though in a lesser degree, his attacks upon the doctors; but against the Tartuffes the accusation was much more serious. If there are any who think that he was trifling in solemn matters, they will do well to read the play again. It is not difficult to imagine that he enjoyed his own fun as he was writing the 'Amour Médecin' or the 'Médecin malgré lui,' but there is much less inward enjoyment to be discovered in the composition of 'Le Tartuffe.' If his mirth is infectious, so also are his cares; and there is in this play an earnestness of feeling he has not shown elsewhere, unless it be in the character of Alceste in the 'Misanthrope.'

. . . . .

It has not been my intention to speak of Tartuffe's character at large, to repeat or to repel the charge that he was overdrawn, that it is against nature to suppose that any man in his position could have been so black as he has been painted. . . . My concern has been with one side of Tartuffe's character. I have tried to show that, besides drawing the picture of a hypocrite, which was doubtless Molière's chief object, the dramatist wished to direct his satire against the dishonest directors of conscience. I repeat—what everybody knows—that Molière's chief desire was to satirise hypocrisy—"all the studied grimaces of those outrageously good men, all the dissembling tricks of those false coiners of devotion, who wish to ensnare men with counterfeit zeal and deceitful charity." These are Molière's words. But there is, I think, a side to the character of Tartuffe not very well known in England, and it is about this particular or special feature that I have made my remarks.

From the Director

*As co-artistic director of one of America's great repertory theatres—the Asolo Theatre of Florida—***Robert Strane** *in 1968 transformed the classical* Tartuffe *into a robust "Southernized" American comedy. His comments serve not only as a justification of this approach, but also enable us a first hand glimpse of the "creative license" the theatre director has.*

Notes on Transplanting a Classic

"Theatre," writes critic Gordon Rogoff, "occurs only for one reason: to bring a group of people together for a commonly received experience. . . . The story it has to tell . . . must act out the events that most vividly concern us." It is too often blandly assumed that classics so-called by their very existence as such concern us—or at any rate, because they are classics they *ought* to concern us. However, when one has to face up to the professional theatre's implicit demand that each production be at least potentially a "commonly received," and therefore commercially viable, experience, it is not long before he begins to challenge the validity of that assumption to the limit of his capability.

That assumption was challenged in the case of Molière's *Tartuffe* for its revival by the Asolo State Theatre in its spring repertory season, 1968. *Tartuffe* is certainly one of the great classics of world theatre, a fact to which the immense frequency of its appearance on the American stage alone powerfully attests. To judge from such evidence, together with its generally handsome boxoffice return, it would seem sufficient merely to "do" the play once again, while banking on its prestige as a classic to supply its own justification. The Asolo Theatre had in fact done that in the summer of 1961, and with reasonably gratifying results. But why risk running a good thing into the ground, especially since such artistic passivity and the law of diminishing returns are ever on the most intimate of terms.

So we challenged this classic as to its real capacity for generating "events that most vividly concern us." Its main event is the concerted attempt on the part of a family to undeceive its head (idolator/victim) as to the truth about his relationship with his star boarder (idol/con-man). A family is being tyrannized by a sanctimonious sponger and must free itself quickly lest it be permanently deprived of its cohesion and vitality. That, we readily agreed, is an event that potentially would "most vividly concern us." (Recall the impact of another play with an analogous event, Joseph Hayes' *The Desperate Hours*.)

The stellar presence of Tartuffe, and to only a somewhat lesser extent that of Orgon, notwithstanding, the real star of this play, and of Molière's other "bourgeois" comedies, is the *family*. This accepted, we viewed our first task as producers of the play to make that family immediately recognizable and possessed of a highly specified, richly textured onstage and offstage life of its own. We had to supply the text with a sub-text in which all of us, actors and audience alike, could share. This task seemed unlikely to be accomplished in demonstrable terms as long as we confined ourselves to the world of Molière, mid-seventeenth century Paris, the world of the *faux devots*. The only thing left of that world in which to share today is a pale residue—so much is lost, so much is meaningless in altered value contexts—and it seemed futile to attempt anything like a burgeoning growth within a pale residue.

Mindful of British director Jonathan Miller's observation that classics "invite you to make some sort of imaginative movement," we moved at once to the obvious solution of defining a family experience of our own—American—and one located within a world of our own making and remembrance. Following an intuitive principle of theatre that directs the seeker after the "commonly received" and immediately recognizable to myth, we turned to one of the most recent periods of our own history that still retains the bold contours and secure convictions of myth, the American Civil War.

This choice aligned itself happily with some of the salient data of Molière's text. For example, Orgon had, at the time of the *Fronde*, or French Civil War, sided with the prince (Louis XIV) and had stuck by him through thick and thin. The peril in his possession of the mysterious strongbox derived from the fact that he had received it from a fugitive traitor. In our blank verse adaptation, which places Orgon in a border state amidst a heavy concentration of Confederate sympathizers, the maid Dorine alludes to her master's having shown good "judgement" all through the war—meaning the Civil War which in our version ended four years prior to the time of the action—and having "courageously stood up to the rebels." Argas, the traitor, logically became a Confederate spy in the guise of a commercial traveller, or some such. Minor concerns perhaps, but they amounted to bright encouragements to us in our assessment of the play's transplantability.

The members of the family then, difficult to specify recognizably in the play's original world, became readily specifiable in our redefined one: Dorine, the bustling, sassy, capable and domineering mammy, actual head of the house in the interim between Orgon's wives and during his fatuous obsession with Tartuffe; Elmira (or Elmire), chic, young, city-bred widow with a highly sophisticated understanding of people, the perfect antipode of the fairy-tale stepmother; Damis, hot-headed young glory hound with an itchy trigger-finger and a John Wilkes Booth fixation, probably bent on a stage career; Marianne, an immensely vital teenager with her head in a romantic novel and her heart in a stable; her lover Valery (or Valère), leaping off the early pages of *Gone With the Wind*, riding bareback furiously to Marianne's front porch on the merest hint of her disloyalty and his dishonor; Mrs. Pernelle, neglected and therefore mayhem-prone southern matriarch, spouting banal maxims as panaceas for all the world; Judge Cleance (or Cléante), honorary judge, man of the world, genial skeptic and indefatigable advice-giver, the avuncular ideal; and finally Organ (or Orgon) Pernelle himself, perennial nose-to-the-grindstone *pater familias*, public strong man, domestic weakling, who carries his office about him as a turtle carries his shell, and whom affluence and permission for ease have panicked into a desperate search for an eleventh-hour spiritual revival, a "warm, thrilling cry of hallelujah."

The choice of persona for Tartuffe was no less obvious or folkloric: he became a Bible-thumping mountain preacher man, to a "T" the fellow Dorine describes early in the play as red-necked, ruby-lipped, rosy-cheeked and healthy as a horse. Something of a Humbert Humbert too, with his brain and his febrile body never quite plugged into the same switchboard, prone like Nabokov's tormented non-hero to "secure his retreat by neutral means of locomotion." Perhaps the pleasantest result of our insistence on starring the family was that now Tartuffe, relieved of the usual extremely onerous distinction of being the only vivid personage in the play, could "cool it" as he is supposed to do, could bide his time with respect both to the family and the audience, and save his frantic aggression for the few really big payoffs in his two scenes with Elmira. Instead of coming on at the end of Act III, as he often must, to "save the show," he could fully utilize his permission to be an enigma and allow the audience the pleasure of making discoveries about him as he improvises his way toward worldly riches and bodily bliss.

Our answer to the powerful strain of eroto-religiosity in the play was to select and play a strongly identifiable image of that active ingredient in Orgon's and Tartuffe's relationship. This came intuitively to be Michelangelo's *Pieta*, with Orgon the sustainer and Tartuffe the sustained. This image, we decided, reposes deep in Orgon's bosom, and we let it gradually surface from the subtext until at the end of Act III, and just before our one intermission, it was engaged in literally —and beneath the same beam of blue light used at the New York's World's Fair to illuminate the Michelangelo.

Our major change in adapting Molière's text came at the end of the play when we substituted the President of the United States (U. S. Grant) for *Le Roi*, and altered the Officer's speech (delivered, as we would have it, by a Major Nelson of the White House Guard) accordingly. (The resulting experience for the audience consisted, incidentally, though powerfully, of hilarious and telling political spoofery at the expense, it so happened, of Lyndon Baines Johnson, who at that time just before his surprising valedictory on TV was at the nadir of his popularity as President.) Following Orgon's last speech, a blaring town band at the rear of the house struck up "Hail to the Chief," and U. S. Grant himself, smoking a huge cigar and lit by a fireworks display, strode to the stage to congratulate the characters and lead them into their curtain calls.

It was at this point in our production where we at the Asolo who have made Molière's comedies a staple of our repertory had a particular axe to grind. Literary savants often accuse Molière of slapdash plot-making. We don't agree. Far from regarding the ending of *Tartuffe*, which has come in for an especially heaping share of abuse, as a perfunctory device, we saw it as a *coup de theatre* of the most exciting variety. (The fact that Molière may in fact have written it as a gesture of thanks to his royal patron for sparing his infamous piece of work struck us as pertinent only as a program note.) This finale should be managed— as we attempted to do—in as sensational, spectacular—and yes, phony—a way as possible, for the point is this: rather than a denouement it is the apt climax to a spiralling hallucination which begins with the last moments of the play's Act IV. It explodes the whole mad affair into outer space—which is the only place for a nightmare to go—and leads audience and cast to wakefulness, a condition to which we are entitled for our $4.50. It marks the transition from the premises of the play to those of theatre itself, and carries with it the fiendish reminder that whereas theatre will serve up deliverance from nightmares, life will not. Count this piece of patent absurdity a boon, the author bids us, for it is probably the only sort you are ever going to get.

Source Materials for *Tartuffe*

BY THE CRITICS

Gossman, Lionel. *Men and Masks: A Study of Molière*. Baltimore: Johns Hopkins Press, 1969, pp. 100–145.
Guicharnaud, J., ed. *Molière: A Collection of Critical Essays*. Englewood Cliffs: Prentice-Hall, 1964.
Lewis, D. B. Wyndham. *Molière: The Comic Mask*.
Nelson, R. J. "The Unreconstructed Heroes of Molière." *Tulane Drama Review* 4 (1959–60):14–37.
Orwen, Gifford P. *"Tartuffe* Reconsidered." *French Review* 41 (1968):611/617.
Peyre, Henri. "Tartuffe." In *Theatre: The Annual of the Lincoln Repertory Theatre of Lincoln Center*, Vol. 2. New York: Hill and Wang, 1965.

BY THE DIRECTOR

Gascon, Jean. "Director's Notes." In *The Stratford Scene 1958–1968*. Clarke, Irwin and Co., Ltd.

AUDIO-VISUAL SOURCES

Tartuffe. Stratford National Theatre of Canada. Caedmon Records.

Farce

Farce is our most popular form of comedy.* A glance at today's television listings or a community theatre's repertory will usually reveal an almost equal offering of melodrama and farce. For farce is entertaining, and the theatre director or program executive realizes one of their choice drawing cards is laughter—which farce produces. They comprehend that our oldest form of comedy still remains our most appealing form of drama. Television, for instance, has long recognized that this equal diet of humor and pathos—farce and melodrama—establishes the balance necessary for holding an evening's attention. In the theatre the game is the same. For us, laughter is enjoyable, and as a people we are constantly seeking that which we enjoy. This is what farce is about.

Purpose of Farce

Most critics maintain that farce is to comedy what melodrama is to tragedy: that is, a baser form of each, dealing with somewhat the same subjects in a story of much less significance, usually designed to produce no lasting change in the audience. There are critics who dissent from this view and argue that farce ought not to be assigned the bottom position on the ladder of comedy; many farces, they feel, are intended to embarrass or criticize some tenets of society, serving a function similar to that of comedy, as we have discussed it. Charlie Chaplin, for example, often lampooned society in his pantomimes, and did quite well without a word. Many more contemporary farces seemingly ridicule other societal institutions such as social class or sex roles. Based on the above and other examples, these critics maintain that farce "is used to provoke ideas as well as laughter."

While this may be true to a limited degree, the problem remains that this "idea" can never be anything but subordinate to laughter. The rollicking characters, physical mishaps, ridiculous situations, and burlesqued language can leave but little time for thoughtful response. Our eyes are being bombarded by the visual, our ears by the hilarious—our response is unrestrained laughter. The stage happenings cannot help but become a means to evoke laughter, not a technique for provoking thought. The physical situations farce employs are destined to produce an equal physical reaction—laughter—and it is difficult to exercise our intellect while drying the tears from our eyes. The audience does not leave the theatre saying:

---

*Together with farce, melodrama is our most popular form of theatre. See Appendix, which contrasts melodrama and tragedy.

"What can we do to correct our follies?" Instead they leave saying: "That was a funny play." Chaplin's motives may have been social, but his results were totally entertaining. Any vestige of intellectual content becomes a by-product.

Like satire, farce *can* pick at tradition, but unlike satire, it is destined to become entertainment in the purest sense—for any thought farce deals with is presented in a more base and counterfeit way. No lasting thought can come from the slapstick antics of a buffoon. No real social ills can be cured when reality has been stretched to its limits and man reduced to the ridiculous. The attitude of the audience is, "I want to be entertained," and the effect, as Eric Bentley calls it, is a farcical "catharsis"—the incomplete catharsis of tragedy (or even comedy), "because the audience watches without taking the responsibility or suffering the guilt because its effects are only immediate."[1] For the audience of tragedy and comedy, the play has meaning. For the audience of melodrama and farce, the play becomes an end in itself.

Since farce can be considered a lower form of comedy, a word about their differences is in order. The major distinctions between farce and comedy reside in the plot devices and physical situations farce employs, and in its use of language. At first glance, most comedies contain what could be considered farcical elements. In *Tartuffe*, for example, Orgon's hiding beneath the table is destined to cause the loudest of laughs. These elements, however, always remain subsidiary to the play's purpose, and the techniques of language used (as discussed in the section on comedy) are the much more elevated techniques. In viewing comedies, our laughter is "thoughtful laughter," for comedies are designed to produce an intellectual as well as a sensual response. Comedy, no matter how light, provokes thought—it exercises our intellect in, at least, a brief way; it criticizes social ills; it has some redeeming social value. Farce, for the most part, cannot do this. The characteristics it employs result only in producing amusement and laughter, while the chief desire of its wide and indiscriminating audience is only to be entertained. G. B. Tennyson, in his *Introduction to Drama*, sums up the distinguishing characteristics of farce:

> (Just) as melodrama satisfies the central human inclination toward serious drama, that is, the desire to experience in concentrated forms the intense and exciting moments of life, so farce satisfies the widespread human urge to be amused by ludicrous situations and undignified and robust behavior. We would be far less happy without them both.[2]

---

[1] Eric Bentley, "Farce," in *The Life of the Drama* (New York: Atheneum, 1964), p. 225.
[2] G. B. Tennyson, *Introduction to Drama* (New York: Holt, Rinehart and Winston, 1966), pp. 75–76.

Devices of Farce

The function of farce, then, is to entertain, and this entertainment is produced principally through laughter, the more the better. How is this laughter produced?—through jokes, slapstick, buffoonery, verbal insults, wisecracks, ludicrous physical action, and situations that are of more consequence than ideas (it is interesting to note that many of today's television programs are labeled "situation comedies"). In farce, man is reduced to his basics, characters are burlesqued, language is derisive, behavior is ridiculous and visual humor is at a peak. Other devices utilized may be violent or sudden action or behavior, uproarious misunderstandings, or even physical or verbal obscenities.

Whatever the method, however, human beings are out of control on a collision course with laughter. The wild ensuing merriment becomes the result of these devices, and the enjoyment they produce becomes the ultimate outcome. In Shakespeare's *Comedy of Errors*, the ridiculous situation of mistaken identity compounded by verbal insults, physical beatings, and foolish behavior are all devices for provoking uproarious laughter. The "imaginary invalid" of Hart and Kaufman's *The Man Who Came to Dinner* generates a riotous situation that becomes the basis from which all of the above devices spring.

The entire structure of farce is a series of complications, each usually founded on the preceding one. In *The Servant of Two Masters*, each mistaken identity increases the troubles for its characters. In Goldsmith's *She Stoops to Conquer*, Tony Lumpkin's prank—misinforming Marlow and Hastings as to their real destination—becomes a situation that serves as the foundation for all future predicaments. Truffaldino, in *The Servant of Two Masters*, sets all on their ears by taking on two identities. The variety of entanglements that result all exploit the basic situation and produce a never-ending stream of laughter from a thoroughly primed audience. Like melodrama, each farce is presented in a series of episodes which become a method of presentation designed least for provoking thought. If laughter is the desired response, then the means to that end must be present in abundance. And coupled with the above devices, this episodic and complicated story development becomes a preventive pill for mental stimulation.

Characters

The characters of farce are not of vital importance in themselves. They serve, rather, as tools manipulated to evoke laughter, which for farce is an end in itself, and it rarely matters who provokes that laugh or speaks that line. For unlike comedy, where humor exists so many times to help shape or define a character, farcical characters most often are unreal and exist only to manufacture laughter—so it may matter not from whom the gag comes. Marlow and Hastings could so many times be reversed, while the two mistaken servants in *Comedy of Errors* are hardly defined at all (Shakespeare not only gives them the same name, but the same face!).

What may also make farce more enjoyable is that the characters involved in these ridiculous and ludicrous situations approach them with sincerity. The incongruous behavior of the character, coupled with our knowledge of what is about to happen, becomes a prime source of laughter. We howl with delight as we watch the wrong Dromio seriously approach his mistaken master. His sincerity plus our knowledge doubly increases our enjoyment and prepares us for laughter.

Language of Farce

Just as physical action and complicated situations form a basis for farce, so does the exploitation of language. The use of wisecracks, repetition, puns, obscenity, and insults—the baser forms of language—becomes central for evoking laughter (the best examples of these are found in an evening's television). Hence, good timing, shrewdness, and a knowledge of his audience's tastes is what the author of farce requires to make this language successful. In *Comedy of Errors*, for example, Antipholus concludes beating his supposed servant, Dromio, who cries:

DROMIO . . . why am I beaten?
ANT.   Dost thou not know?
DROMIO   Nothing, sir, but that I am beaten.
ANT.   Shall I tell you why?
DROMIO   Ay, sir, and wherefor; for every why hath a wherefor.
ANT.   Why, first—for flouting me; and then, wherefor—for urging it the second time for me.
DROMIO   Was there any man thus beaten out of season, when in the why and wherefor is neither rhyme nor reason. Well, sir, I thank you.
ANT.   Thank me sir, for what?
DROMIO   Marry, sir, for this something that you gave me for nothing.
ANT.   I'll make amends next, to give you nothing for something.

While no one can deny some wit in the preceding, the language still remains quite basic and is designed solely for laughter, with no residual thought intended; the laugh exists for itself. In addition, the rather outrageous physical beating (action) serves as a focal point and impetus for the ensuing conversation. Most language devices in farce are founded on contrived situations, and it doubles the potential for humor when one occurs with the other. Both occurring almost simultaneously becomes, for farce, its most effective tool in provoking laughter.

Farce and Reality

One final word about the credibility of farce. It is necessary for us to attach at least a semblance of reality to the rather far-fetched and unreal stage events, lest we be unresponsive to the play (all drama requires us to "believe" what is happening is a replica of reality, but farce, like melodrama, requires more of this effort on our part). At heart, and when concluded, we realize that these events, situations, and characters are highly unlikely, but while they *are happening* we require ourselves to give them some shade of credibility. Since we, as an audience, have come to be entertained, we are willing to grant this minimum of credence to the stage in order to achieve that effect. The more basic our desire to be entertained or to laugh, in fact, the less real the stage has to be.

In watching a play or a movie, we are well aware that grown men (the Three Stooges or the Marx Brothers, for instance) don't *actually* participate in continual face-slapping, verbal insults, or constant tripping and falling. In reading farcical plays, we realize that the events and predicaments are rather improbable. But we require ourselves to bestow a close degree of reality to those situations and/or characters in order to be entertained. This is the concession we must make, the price we must pay; for in farce, this reality is never assumed, it is only a pretense. As Downs says: "If comedy is both possible and probable, farce is possible but not very probable."[3] The success of farce, then, can become dependent on the degree of actuality we are willing to give it—and we are usually willing to give it credence.

---

[3] E. Wright and L. Downs, *A Primer for Playgoers* (Englewood Cliffs: Prentice-Hall, 1958).

The good actor and Pantalone receive the wrath of Truffaldino. Note traditional contrasting body types of Lombardi and Pantalone. University of Akron. Directed by Wallace Sterling; designed by Susannah Lane; costumes by Nancy Wynn Zucchero.

Clarice does not want to marry Federigo Rasponi, while her father will have none of it. Note stylized mask. Polk Junior College, Norman M. Small, director.

Truffaldino is about to become the servant of both masters.
University of Maine. J. Norman Wilkinson, director; E. A.
Cyrus, designer.

Utilization of satire in costume and action. An unusual and
highly flamboyant production of Servant from the University
of Minnesota, M. W. Loppnow, director.

Pantalone is informed by Truffaldino that Federigo Rasponi is
alive! University of Arkansas.

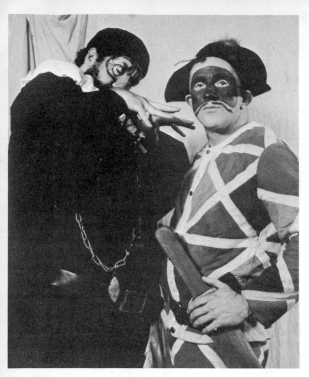

Dr. Lombardi attempts to hex Truffaldino in the Asolo State
Theatre production of the play.

STREET
WITH

Truffaldino laments to the audience about his serving two
masters. Polk Junior College. Norman M. Small, director.

The servant or the master?
at times we cannot tell.
Anonymous

The Servant of Two Masters

Carlo Goldoni

English Version by Edward J. Dent

The Servant of Two Masters

Characters

> PANTALONE DEI BISOGNOSI, *a Venetian merchant*
> CLARICE, *his daughter*
> DR. LOMBARDI
> SILVIO, *his son*
> BEATRICE RASPONI, *a lady of Turin, disguised as her brother*
>   FEDERIGO RASPONI
> FLORINDO ARETUSI, *of Turin, lover of* BEATRICE
> BRIGHELLA, *an innkeeper*
> SMERALDINA, *maidservant to* CLARICE
> TRUFFALDINO, *servant first to* BEATRICE, *and afterward to* FLORINDO
> FIRST WAITER
> SECOND WAITER
> FIRST PORTER
> SECOND PORTER

Scene

> *The scene is laid in Venice.*
> *The action takes place within a single day.*

Act One

SCENE ONE

A Room in the House of PANTALONE

PANTALONE, THE DOCTOR, CLARICE, SILVIO, BRIGHELLA, SMERALDINA.

SILVIO (*offering his hand to* CLARICE)   Here is my hand, and with it I give
     you my whole heart.
PANTALONE (*to* CLARICE)   Come, come, not so shy, give him your hand too.
     Then you will be betrothed, and very soon you will be married.
CLARICE   Dear Silvio, here is my hand. I promise to be your wife.
SILVIO   And I promise to be your husband.
          (*They take hands.*)
DR. LOMBARDI   Well done. Now that is settled, and there's no going
     back on it.

SMERALDINA (*aside*)   There's luck for you! And me just bursting to get married!

PANTALONE (*to* BRIGHELLA *and* SMERALDINA)   You two shall be witnesses of this betrothal of my daughter Clarice to Signor Silvio, the worthy son of our good Dr. Lombardi!

BRIGHELLA (*to* PANTALONE)   We will, sir, and I thank you for the honor.

PANTALONE   Look you, I was witness at your wedding, and now you are a witness to my daughter's. I have asked no great company of friends and relations, for the doctor too is a man of my sort. We will have dinner together; we will enjoy ourselves and nobody shall disturb us.
(*To* CLARICE *and* SILVIO)
What say you, children, does that suit you?

SILVIO   I desire nothing better than to be near my beloved bride.

SMERALDINA (*aside*)   Yes, that's the best of all foods.

DR. LOMBARDI   My son is no lover of vanities. He is an honest lad; he loves your daughter and thinks of nothing else.

PANTALONE   Truly we may say that this marriage was made in Heaven, for had it not been for the death of Federigo Rasponi, my correspondent at Turin, you know, I had promised my daughter to him.
(*To* SILVIO)
I could not then have given her to my dear son-in-law.

SILVIO   I can call myself fortunate indeed, sir; I know not if Signora Clarice will say the same.

CLARICE   You wrong me, dear Silvio. You should know if I love you. I should have married Signor Rasponi in obedience to my father; but my heart has always been yours.

DR. LOMBARDI   'Tis true indeed, the will of Heaven is wrought in unexpected ways.
(*To* PANTALONE)
Pray, sir, how did Federigo Rasponi come to die?

PANTALONE   Poor wretch, I hardly know. He was killed one night on account of some affair about his sister. Someone ran a sword through him and that was the end of him.

BRIGHELLA   Did that happen at Turin, sir?

PANTALONE   At Turin.

BRIGHELLA   Alas, poor gentleman! I am indeed sorry to hear it.

PANTALONE (*to* BRIGHELLA)   Did you know Signor Federigo Rasponi?

BRIGHELLA   Indeed and I did, sir. I was three years at Turin. I knew his sister too—a fine high-spirited young woman—dressed like a man and rode a-horseback; and he loved her more than anyone in the world. Lord! Who'd ha' thought it?

PANTALONE   Well, misfortune waits for all of us. But come, let us talk no more of sad things. Do you know what I have in mind, good master Brighella? I know you love to show your skill in the kitchen. Now, I would have you make us a few dishes of your best.

BRIGHELLA   'Tis a pleasure to serve you, sir. Though I say it that shouldn't, customers are always well contented at my house. They say there's no place where they eat as they do there. You shall taste something fine, sir.

PANTALONE   Good, good. Let's have something with plenty of gravy that we can sop the bread in.

(*A knock at the door*)

Oh! Someone is knocking. Smeraldina, see who it is.

SMERALDINA   Yes, sir.

(*Goes to door*)

CLARICE (*wishing to retire*)   Sir, may I beg your leave?

PANTALONE   Wait; we are all coming. Let us hear who is there.

SMERALDINA (*coming back*)   Sir, there is a gentleman's servant below who desires to give you a message. He would tell me nothing. He says he would speak to the master.

PANTALONE   Tell him to come up. We'll hear what he has to say.

SMERALDINA   I'll fetch him, sir.

(*Exit*)

CLARICE   May I not go, sir?

PANTALONE   Whither then, madam?

CLARICE   I know not—to my own room—

PANTALONE   No, madam, no; you stay here.

(*Aside to* DR. LOMBARDI)

These lovebirds can't be left alone just yet for a while.

DR. LOMBARDI (*aside to* PANTALONE)   Prudence above all things!

(SMERALDINA *brings in* TRUFFALDINO.)

TRUFFALDINO   My most humble duty to the ladies and gentlemen. And a very fine company too, to be sure! Ve-ry fine, indeed!

PANTALONE   Who are you, my good friend? And what is your business?

TRUFFALDINO (*to* PANTALONE, *pointing to* CLARICE)   Who is this fair gentlewoman?

PANTALONE   That is my daughter.

TRUFFALDINO   Delighted to hear it.

SMERALDINO (*to* TRUFFALDINO)   What's more, she is going to be married.

TRUFFALDINO   I'm sorry to hear it. And who are you?

SMERALDINA   I am her maid, sir.

TRUFFALDINO   I congratulate her.

PANTALONE   Come, sir, have done with ceremony. What do you want with me? Who are you? Who sends you hither?

TRUFFALDINO   Patience, patience, my good sir, take it easy. Three questions at once is too much for a poor man.

PANTALONE (*aside to* DR. LOMBARDI)   I think the man's a fool.

DR. LOMBARDI (*aside to* PANTALONE)   I think he's playing the fool.

TRUFFALDINO (*to* SMERALDINA)   Is it you that are going to be married?

SMERALDINA (*sighs*)   No, sir.

PANTALONE   Will you tell me who you are, or will you go about your business?

TRUFFALDINO   If you only want to know who I am, I'll tell you in two words. I am the servant of my master.

(*Turns to* SMERALDINA)

To go back to what I was saying—

PANTALONE   But who is your master?

TRUFFALDINO (*to* PANTALONE)   He is a gentleman who desires the honor of
paying his respects to you.

(*To* SMERALDINA)

We must have a talk about this marriage.

PANTALONE   Who is this gentleman, I say? What is his name?

TRUFFALDINO   Oh, that's a long story. Si'or Federigo Rasponi of Turin,
that's my master, and he sends his compliments, and he has come to
see you, and he's down below, and he sends me to say that he would like
to come up and he's waiting for an answer. Anything else, or will
that do?

(*All look surprised.*)

(*To* SMERALDINA, *as before*)

Let's begin again.

PANTALONE   Come here˙and talk to me. What the devil do you mean?

TRUFFALDINO   And if you want to know who I am, I am Truffaldin'
Battocchio from Bergamo.

PANTALONE   I don't care who *you* are. Tell me again, who is this master of
yours? I fear I did not understand you rightly.

TRUFFALDINO   Poor old gentleman! He must be hard of hearing. My master
is Si'or Federigo Rasponi of Turin.

PANTALONE   Away! You must be mad. Signor Federigo Rasponi of Turin
is dead.

TRUFFALDINO   Dead?

PANTALONE   To be sure he's dead, worse luck for him.

TRUFFALDINO (*aside*)   The devil! My master dead? Why, I left him alive
downstairs!

(*To* PANTALONE)

You really mean he is dead?

PANTALONE   I tell you for an absolute certainty, he is dead.

DR. LOMBARDI   'Tis the honest truth; he is dead; we can have no doubt
about it.

TRUFFALDINO (*aside*)   Alas, my poor master! He must have met with an
accident.

(*To* PANTALONE *as if retiring*)

Your very humble servant, sir.

PANTALONE   Can I do nothing more for you?

TRUFFALDINO   If he's dead, there's nothing more to do.

(*Aside*)

But I'm going to see if it's true or not.

(*Exit*)

PANTALONE   What are we to make of this fellow? Is he knave or fool?

DR. LOMBARDI   I really don't know. Probably a little of both.

BRIGHELLA   I should say he was just a zany. He comes from Bergamo; I can't
think he is a knave.

SMERALDINA He's not such a fool, neither.
        (*Aside*)
    I like that little dark fellow.
PANTALONE But what is this nightmare about Signor Federigo?
CLARICE If 'tis true indeed that he is here, it would be the worst of news
    for me.
PANTALONE What nonsense! Did not you see the letters yourself?
SILVIO If he *is* alive and here after all, he has come too late.
        (*Re-enter* TRUFFALDINO)
TRUFFALDINO Gentlemen, I am surprised at you. Is that the way to treat a
    poor man? Is that the way you deceive strangers? Is that the behavior of
    a gentleman? I shall insist upon satisfaction.
PANTALONE (*to* DR. LOMBARDI) We must be careful, the man's mad.
        (*To* TRUFFALDINO)
    What's the matter? What have they done to you?
TRUFFALDINO To go and tell me that Si'or Federigo Rasponi was dead!
PANTALONE Well, what then?
TRUFFALDINO What then? Well, he's here, safe and sound, in good health
    and spirits, and he desires to pay his respects to you, with your kind
    permission.
PANTALONE Signor Federigo?
TRUFFALDINO Si'or Federigo.
PANTALONE Rasponi?
TRUFFALDINO Rasponi.
PANTALONE Of Turin?
TRUFFALDINO Of Turin.
PANTALONE Be off to Bedlam, my lad; that's the place for you.
TRUFFALDINO The Devil take *you* there, sir! You'll make me swear like a Turk·
    I tell you he's here, in the house, in the next room, bad luck to you.
PANTALONE If you say any more I'll break your head.
DR. LOMBARDI No, no, Signor Pantalone; I tell you what to do. Tell him to
    bring in this person whom he thinks to be Federigo Rasponi.
PANTALONE Well, bring in this man that is risen from the dead.
TRUFFALDINO He may have been dead and risen from the dead, for all I
    know. That's no affair of mine. But he's alive now, sure enough, and you
    shall see him with your own eyes. I'll go and tell him to come.
        (*Angrily to* PANTALONE)
    And 'tis time you learned how to behave properly to strangers, to
    gentlemen of my position, to honorable citizens of Bergamo.
        (*To* SMERALDINA)
    Young woman, we will have some talk together when you will.
        (*Exit*)
CLARICE Silvio, I am all of a tremble.
SILVIO Have no fear; whatever happens, you shall be mine.
DR. LOMBARDI Now we shall discover the truth.
PANTALONE Some rogue, I dare say, come to tell me a string of lies.
BRIGHELLA Sir, as I told you just now, I knew Signor Federigo; we shall see
    if it be he.

SMERALDINA (*aside*) That little dark fellow doesn't look like a liar. I wonder, now, if—

(*Curtsy to* PANTALONE)

By your good leave, sir.

(*Exit*)

(*Enter* BEATRICE, *dressed as a man*)

BEATRICE Signor Pantalone, that courtesy which I have so much admired in your correspondence is but ill matched in the treatment which I have received from you in person. I send my servant to pay you my respects, and you keep me standing in the street for half an hour before you condescend to allow me to enter.

PANTALONE (*nervously*) I ask your pardon. But, sir, who are you?

BEATRICE Your obedient servant, sir, Federigo Rasponi of Turin.

(*All look bewildered*)

PANTALONE Extraordinary!

BRIGHELLA (*aside*) What does this mean? This is not Federigo, this is his sister Beatrice.

PANTALONE I rejoice to see you sir, alive and in health, after the bad news which we had received.

(*Aside to* DR. LOMBARDI)

I tell you, I am not convinced yet.

BEATRICE I know; 'twas reported that I was killed in a duel. Heaven be praised, I was but wounded; and no sooner was I restored to health than I set out for Venice, according to our previous arrangement.

PANTALONE I don't know what to say. You have the appearance of an honest man, sir, but I have sure and certain evidence that Signor Federigo is dead, and you will understand that if you cannot give us proof of the contrary—

BEATRICE Your doubt is most natural; I recognize that I must give you proof of my identity. Here are four letters from correspondents of yours whom you know personally; one of them is from the manager of our bank. You will recognize the signatures and you will satsify yourself as to who I am.

(*Gives four letters to* PANTALONE, *who reads them to himself*)

CLARICE Ah, Silvio, we are lost.

SILVIO I will lose my life before I lose you.

BEATRICE, *noticing* BRIGHELLA, *aside.* Heavens! Brighella! How the devil does he come to be here? If he betrays me—

(*Aloud to* BRIGHELLA)

Friend, I think I know you.

BRIGHELLA Indeed yes, sir; do you not remember Brighella Cavicchio at Turin?

BEATRICE Ah, yes, now I recognize you.

(*Goes up to him*)

And what are you doing in Venice, my good fellow?

(*Aside to* BRIGHELLA)

For the love of heaven do not betray me.

BRIGHELLA (*aside to* BEATRICE) Trust me.

(*Aloud*)

I keep an inn, sir, at your service.

BEATRICE   The very thing for me; as I have the pleasure of your acquaintance, I shall come to lodge at your inn.

BRIGHELLA   You do me honor, sir.

>   (*Aside*)

Running contraband, I'll be bound.

PANTALONE   I have read the letters. Certainly they present Signor Federigo Rasponi to me, and if you present them, I am bound to believe that you are–the person named therein.

BEATRICE   If you are still in doubt, here is Master Brighella; he knows me, he can assure you as to who I am.

BRIGHELLA   Of course, sir, I am happy to assure you.

PANTALONE   Well, if that be so, and my good friend Brighella confirms the testimony of the letters, then, dear Signor Federigo, I am delighted to see you and I ask your pardon for having doubted your word.

CLARICE   Then, sir, this gentleman is indeed Signor Federigo Rasponi?

PANTALONE   But of course he is.

CLARICE (*aside to* SILVIO)   Oh misery, what will happen to us?

SILVIO (*aside to* CLARICE)   Don't be frightened; you are mine and I will protect you.

PANTALONE (*aside to* DR. LOMBARDI)   What do you say to it, Doctor? He has come just in the nick of time.

DR. LOMBARDI   *Accidit in puncto, quod non contingit in anno.*

BEATRICE (*pointing to* CLARICE)   Signor Pantalone, who is that young lady?

PANTALONG.   That is my daughter Clarice.

BEATRICE.   The one who was promised in marriage to me?

PANTALONE.   Precisely, sir; that is she.

>   (*Aside*)

Now I am in a pretty mess.

BEATRICE (*to* CLARICE)   Madam, permit me to have the honor.

CLARICE (*stiffly*)   Your most humble servant, sir.

BEATRICE (*to* PANTALONE)   She receives me somewhat coldly.

PANTALONE   You must forgive her, she is shy by nature.

BEATRICE (*to* PANTALONE, *pointing at* SILVIO)   And this gentleman is a relative of yours?

PANTALONE   Yes, sir; he is a nephew of mine.

SILVIO (*to* BEATRICE)   No, sir, I am not his nephew at all; I am the promised husband of Signora Clarice.

DR. LOMBARDI (*aside to* SILVIO)   Well said, my boy! Don't lose your chance! Stand up for your rights, but do nothing rash.

BEATRICE   What? You the promised husband of Signora Clarice? Was she not promised to me?

PANTALONE   There, there, I'll explain the whole matter. My dear Signor Federigo, I fully believed that the story of your accident was true, that you were dead, in fact, and so I had promised my daughter to Signor Silvio; but there is not the least harm done. You have arrived at last, just in time. Clarice is yours, if you will have her, and I am here to keep my word. Signor Silvio, I don't know what to say; you can see the position yourself. You remember what I said to you; and you will have no cause to bear me ill-will.

SILVIO But Signor Federigo will never consent to take a bride who has given her hand to another.

BEATRICE Oh, I am not so fastidious. I will take her in spite of that.
(*Aside*)
I mean to have some fun out of this.

DR. LOMBARDI (*sarcastically*) There's a fine fashionable husband! I like him.

BEATRICE I hope Signora Clarice will not refuse me her hand.

SILVIO Sir, you have arrived too late. Signora Clarice is to be *my* wife, and you need have no hope that I will yield her to you. If Signor Pantalone does me wrong, I will be avenged upon him; and whoever presumes to desire Clarice will have to fight for her against this sword.

DR. LOMBARDI (*aside*) That's a fine boy, by the Lord!

BEATRICE (*aside*) Thank you, but I don't mean to die just yet.

DR. LOMBARDI Sir, I must beg to inform you that you are too late. Signora Clarice is to marry my son. The law, the law, sir, is clear on the point. *Prior in tempore, potior in jure.*
(*Exeunt* DR. LOMBARDI *and* SILVIO)

BEATRICE (*to* CLARICE) And you, madam bride, do you say nothing?

CLARICE I say—I say—I'd sooner marry the hangman.
(*Exit*)

PANTALONE. What, you minx! What did you say?
(*Starts to run after her*)

BEATRICE Stay, Signor Pantalone; I am sorry for her. It is not the moment for severity. In course of time I hope I may deserve her favor. Meanwhile let us go into our accounts together, for, as you know, that is one of the two reasons that have brought me to Venice.

PANTALONE Everything is in order for your inspection. You shall see the books; your money is ready for you, and we will make up the account whenever you like.

BEATRICE I will call on you at some more convenient time. Now, if you will allow me, I will go with Brighella to settle some little business which I have to do.

PANTALONE You shall do as you please, and if you have need of anything, I am at your service.

BEATRICE Well, if you could give me a little money, I should be greatly obliged; I did not bring any with me, for fear of being robbed on the way.

PANTALONE I am delighted to serve you; but the cashier is not here just now. The moment he comes I will send the money to your lodgings. Are you not staying at my friend Brighella's?

BEATRICE Yes, I lie there. But I will send my servant; he is entirely honest. You can trust him with anything.

PANTALONE Very well. I will carry out your wishes, and if you may be pleased to take pot luck with me, I am yours to command.

BEATRICE   For today I thank you. Another day I shall be happy to wait upon you.

PANTALONE   Then I shall expect you.

(*Enter* SMERALDINA)

SMERALDINA (*to* PANTALONE)   Sir, you are asked for.

PANTALONE   Who is it?

SMERALDINA   I couldn't say, sir.

PANTALONE   I will come directly. Sir, I beg you to excuse me. Brighella, you are at home here; be good enough to attend Signor Federigo.

BEATRICE   Pray do not put yourself about for me, sir.

PANTALONE   I must go. Farewell, sir.

(*Aside*)

I don't want to have trouble in my house.

(*Exit with* SMERALDINA)

BRIGHELLA   May I ask, Signora Beatrice——?

BEATRICE   Hush, for the love of Heaven, don't betray me. My poor brother is dead. 'Twas thought Florindo Aretusi killed him in a duel. You remember, Florindo loved me, and my brother would not have it. They fought, Federigo fell, and Florindo fled from justice. I heard he was making for Venice, so I put on my brother's clothes and followed him. Thanks to the letters of credit, which are my brother's, and thanks still more to you, Signor Pantalone takes me for Federigo. We are to make up our accounts; I shall draw the money, and then I shall be able to help Florindo too, if he has need of it. Be my friend, dear Brighella, help me, please! You shall be generously rewarded.

BRIGHELLA   That's all very well, but I don't want to be responsible for Signor Pantalone paying you out money in good faith and then finding himself made a fool of.

BEATRICE   Made a fool of? If my brother is dead, am I not his heir?

BRIGHELLA   Very true. Then why not say so?

BEATRICE   If I do that, I can do nothing. Pantalone will begin by treating me as if he were my guardian; then they will all worry me and say my conduct is unbecoming and all that sort of thing. I want my liberty. Help me to it. 'Twill not last long.

BRIGHELLA   Well, well, you were always one for having your own way. Trust me, and I'll do my best for you.

BEATRICE   Thank you. And now let us go to your inn.

BRIGHELLA   Where is your servant?

BEATRICE   I told him to wait for me in the street.

BRIGHELLA   Wherever did you get hold of that idiot? He cannot even speak plain.

BEATRICE   I picked him up on the journey. He seems a fool at times; but he isn't really a fool and I can rely on his loyalty.

BRIGHELLA   Yes, loyalty's a fine thing. Well, I am at your service. To think what love will make people do!

BEATRICE   Oh, this is nothing. Love makes people do far worse things than this.

BRIGHELLA   Well, here's a good beginning. If you go on that way, Lord knows what may come of it!

(*Exeunt* BEATRICE *and* BRIGHELLA)

SCENE TWO

A Street with BRIGHELLA'S *Inn*

TRUFFALDINO *solus.*

TRUFFALDINO   I'm sick of waiting; I can hold out no longer. With this master of mine there's not enough to eat, and the less there is the more I want it. The town clock struck twelve half an hour ago, and my belly struck two hours ago at least. If I only knew where we were going to lodge! With my other masters the first thing they did, as soon as they came to a town, was to go to a tavern. This gentleman—Lord no! He leaves his trunks in the boat at the landing stage, goes off to pay visits, and forgets all about his poor servant. When they say we ought to serve our masters with love, they ought to tell the masters to have a little charity toward their servants.

Here's an inn. I've half a mind to go in and see if I could find something to tickle my teeth; but what if my master comes to look for me? His own fault; he ought to know better. I'll go in—but now I come to think of it, there's another little difficulty that I hadn't remembered: I haven't a penny. Oh poor Truffaldin'! Rather than be a servant, devil take me, I'd—what indeed? By the grace of Heaven there's nothing I *can* do.

Enter FLORINDO *in traveling dress with a* PORTER *carrying a trunk on his shoulder*).

PORTER   I tell you, sir, I can go no farther; the weight's enough to kill me.

FLORINDO   Here is the sign of an inn. Can't you carry it these few steps?

PORTER   Help! The trunk is falling.

FLORINDO   I told you you could not carry it; you're too weak; you have no strength at all.

FLORINDO *rearranges the trunk on the* PORTER'S *shoulder*.)

TRUFFALDINO   Here's a chance for sixpence.

(*To* FLORINDO)

Sir, can I do anything for you?

FLORINDO   My good man, be so good as to carry this trunk into the inn there.

TRUFFALDINO   Yes, sir, let me take it, sir. See how I do it.

(*To the* PORTER)

You be off!

TRUFFALDINO *puts his shoulder under the trunk and takes it by himself, knocking the* PORTER *down at the same time.*)

FLORINDO   Well done!

TRUFFALDINO   It weighs nothing. A mere trifle.

(*Goes into the inn with the trunk*)

FLORINDO (*to* PORTER)   There! You see how it's done.

PORTER   I can do no more. I work as a porter for my misfortune, but I am the son of a respectable person.

FLORINDO   What did your father do?

PORTER   My father? He skinned lambs in the town.

FLORINDO   The fellow's mad.
        (*To* PORTER)
    That will do.
        (*Going towards the inn*)

PORTER   Please your honor——

FLORINDO   What do you want?

PORTER   The money for the porterage.

FLORINDO   How much am I to give you for ten yards? There's the landing stage!
        (*Pointing off*)

PORTER   I didn't count them. I want my pay.
        (*Holds out his hand*)

FLORINDO   There's twopence.
        (*Gives money*)

PORTER   I want my pay.
        (*Still holding out his hand*)

FLORINDO   Lord, what obstinacy! Here's twopence more.
        (*Gives money*)

PORTER   I want my pay.

FLORINDO (*kicks him*)   Go and be hanged!

PORTER   Thank you, sir, that's enough.
        (*Exit*)

FLORINDO   There's a humorous fellow! He was positively waiting for me to kick him. Well, let us go and see what the inn is like——
        (*Re-enter* TRUFFALDINO)

TRUFFALDINO   Sir, everything is ready for you.

FLORINDO   What lodging is there here?

TRUFFALDINO   'Tis a very good place, sir. Good beds, fine looking glasses, and a grand kitchen with a smell to it that is very comforting. I have talked with the waiter. You will be served like a king.

FLORINDO   What's *your* trade?

TRUFFALDINO   Servant.

FLORINDO   Are you a Venetian?

TRUFFALDINO   Not from Venice, but of the State. I'm from Bergamo, at your service.

FLORINDO   Have you a master now?

TRUFFALDINO   At the moment—to tell the truth, I have not.

FLORINDO   You are without a master?

TRUFFALDINO   You see me, sir. I am without a master.
        (*Aside*)
    My master is not here, so I tell no lies.

FLORINDO   Will you come and be *my* servant?

TRUFFALDINO   Why not?

(*Aside*)

If his terms are better.

FLORINDO At any rate, for as long as I stay in Venice.

TRUFFALDINO Very good, sir. How much will you give me?

FLORINDO How much do you want?

TRUFFALDINO I'll tell you: another master I had, who is here no more, he gave me a shilling a day and all found.

FLORINDO Good, I will give you as much.

TRUFFALDINO You must give me a little more than that.

FLORINDO How much more do you want?

TRUFFALDINO A halfpenny a day for snuff.

FLORINDO Oh, I'll give you that and welcome.

TRUFFALDINO If that's so, I'm your man, sir.

FLORINDO But I should like to know a little more about you.

TRUFFALDINO If you want to know all about me, you go to Bergamo; anyone there will tell you who I am.

FLORINDO Have you nobody in Venice who knows you?

TRUFFALDINO I only arrived this morning, sir.

FLORINDO Well, well, I take you for an honest man. I will give you a trial.

TRUFFALDINO You give me a trial and you shall see.

FLORINDO First of all, I am anxious to know if there are letters at the Post for me. Here's half a crown; go to the Turin Post and ask if there are letters for Florindo Aretusi; if there are, take them and bring them at once. I shall wait for you.

TRUFFALDINO Meanwhile you will order dinner, sir?

FLORINDO Yes, well said! I will order it.

(*Aside*)

He is a wag, I like him. I'll give him a trial.

(FLORINDO *goes into the inn.*)

TRUFFALDINO A halfpenny more a day, that's fifteen pence a month. 'Tis not true that the other gentleman gave me a shilling; he gives me six pennies. Maybe six pennies make a shilling, but I'm not quite sure. And this gentleman from Turin is nowhere to be seen. He's mad. He's a young fellow without a beard and without any sense neither. He may go about his business; I shall go to the Post for my new gentleman.

(*As he is going,* BEATRICE *enters with* BRIGHELLA *and meets him.*)

BEATRICE That's a nice way to behave! Is that the way you wait for me?

TRUFFALDINO Here I am, sir. I am still waiting for you.

BEATRICE And how do you come to be waiting for me here, and not in the street where I told you? 'Tis a mere accident that I have found you.

TRUFFALDINO I went for a bit of a walk to take away my appetite.

BEATRICE Well, go at once to the landing stage; fetch my trunk and take it to the inn of Master Brighella.

BRIGHELLA There's my inn, you cannot mistake it.

BEATRICE Very well, then, make haste, and I will wait for you.

TRUFFALDINO The devil! In *that* inn?

BEATRICE   Here, you will go at the same time to the Turin Post and ask if
there are any letters for me. You may ask if there are letters for
Federigo Rasponi and also for Beatrice Rasponi. That's my sister.
Some friend of hers might perhaps write to her; so be sure to see if
there are letters either for her or for me.

TRUFFALDINO (*aside*)   What *am* I to do? Here's a pretty kettle of fish!

BRIGHELLA (*to* BEATRICE)   Why do you expect letters in your real name if you
left home secretly?

BEATRICE   I told the steward to write to me; and I don't know which name
he may use. I'll tell you more later.

   (*To* TRUFFALDINO)

Make haste, be off with you to the Post and the landing stage. Fetch
the letters and have the trunk brought to the inn; I shall be there.

   (*Exit* BEATRICE *into the inn*)

TRUFFALDINO   Are you the landlord?

BRIGHELLA   Yes, I am. You behave properly and you need have no fear, I
will do you well.

   (*Exit* BRIGHELLA *into the inn*)

TRUFFALDINO   There's luck! There are many that look in vain for a master,
and I have found two. What the devil am I to do? I cannot wait upon
them both. No? Why not? Wouldn't it be a fine thing to wait upon both
of them, earn two men's wages and eat and drink for two? 'Twould be a
fine thing indeed, if neither of them found out. And if they did? What
then? No matter! If one sends me away, I stay with the other. I swear
I'll try it. If it last but a day, I'll try it. Whatever happens I shall have
done a fine thing. Here goes. Let's go to the Post for both of 'em.

   (*Enter* SILVIO *and meets* TRUFFALDINO)

SILVIO (*aside*)   That is the servant of Federigo Rasponi.

   (*To* TRUFFALDINO)

My good man.

TRUFFALDINO   Sir?

SILVIO   Where is your master?

TRUFFALDINO   My master? He's in that inn there.

SILVIO   Go at once and tell your master that I wish to speak to him; if he
be a man of honor let him come down; I wait for him.

TRUFFALDINO   My dear sir——

SILVIO (*angrily*)   Go at once.

TRUFFALDINO   But I must tell you, my master——

SILVIO   Don't answer me; or, by Heaven, I'll——

TRUFFALDINO   But which do you want?

SILVIO   At once, I say, or I'll beat you.

TRUFFALDINO (*aside*)   Well, I don't know—I'll send the first I can find.

   (*Exit* TRUFFALDINO *into the inn*)

SILVIO   No, I will never suffer the presence of a rival. Federigo may have got
off once with his life, but he shall not always have the same fortune.
Either he shall renounce all claims to Clarice, or he shall give me the
satisfaction of a gentleman. Here are some more people coming out of

the inn. I don't want to be disturbed.

(*Retires to the opposite side*)

(*Enter* TRUFFALDINO *with* FLORINDO)

TRUFFALDINO (*points out* SILVIO *to* FLORINDO) There's the fire-eating gentleman, sir.

FLORINDO   I do not know him. What does he want with me?

TRUFFALDINO   I don't know. I go to fetch the letters, with your good leave, sir.

(*Aside*)

I don't want any more trouble.

(*Exit*)

SILVIO (*aside*) Federigo does not come?

FLORINDO (*aside*)   I must find out what the truth is.

(*To* SILVIO)

Sir, are you the gentleman who inquired for me?

SILVIO   I, sir? I have not even the honor of your acquaintance.

FLORINDO   But that servant who has just gone told me that with a loud and threatening voice you made bold to challenge me.

SILVIO   He misunderstood. I said I wished to speak to his master.

FLORINDO   Very well, I am his master.

SILVIO   You his master?

FLORINDO   Certainly. He is in my service.

SILVIO   Then I ask your pardon. Either your servant is exactly like another whom I saw this morning, or he waits on another person.

FLORINDO   You may set your mind at rest; he waits on me.

SILVIO   If that be so, I ask your pardon again.

FLORINDO   No harm done. Mistakes often occur.

SILVIO   Are you a stranger here, sir?

FLORINDO   From Turin, sir, at your service.

SILVIO   The man whom I would have provoked was from Turin.

FLORINDO   Then perhaps I may know him; if he has given you offence, I shall gladly assist you to obtain just satisfaction.

SILVIO   Do you know one Federigo Rasponi?

FLORINDO   Ah! I knew him only too well.

SILVIO   He makes claim, on the strength of her father's word, to the lady who this morning swore to be my wife.

FLORINDO   My good friend, Federigo Rasponi cannot take your wife away from you. He is dead.

SILVIO   Yes, we all believed that he was dead; but this morning to my disgust he arrived in Venice safe and sound.

FLORINDO   Sir, you petrify me.

SILVIO   No wonder! I was petrified myself.

FLORINDO   I assure you Federigo Rasponi is dead.

SILVIO   I assure you that Federigo Rasponi is alive.

FLORINDO   Take care you are not deceived.

SILVIO   Signor Pantalone dei Bisognosi, the young lady's father, has made all possible inquiries to assure himself and is in possession of incontestable proofs that he is here in person.

FLORINDO (*aside*)   Then he was not killed in the duel, as everybody believed!

SILVIO   Either he or I must renounce claim of the love of Clarice or to life.

FLORINDO (*aside*)   Federigo here?

SILVIO   I am surprised that you have not seen him. He was to lodge at this very inn.

FLORINDO   I have not seen him. They told me that there was no one else at all staying there.

SILVIO   He must have changed his mind. Forgive me, sir, if I have troubled you. If you see him, tell him that for his own welfare he must abandon the idea of this marriage. Silvio Lombardi is my name; I am your most obedient servant, sir.

FLORINDO   I shall be greatly pleased to have the honor of your friendship.
(*Aside*)
I am confounded.

SILVIO   May I beg to know your name, sir?

FLORINDO (*aside*)   I must not discover myself.
(*To* SILVIO)
Your servant, sir, Orazio Ardenti.

SILVIO   Signor Orazio, I am yours to command.
(*Exit* SILVIO)

FLORINDO   I was told he died on the spot. Yet I fled so hurriedly when accused of the crime that I had no chance of finding out the truth. Then, since he is not dead, it will be better for me to go back to Turin and console my beloved Beatrice, who is perhaps in suffering and sorrow for my absence.
(*Enter* TRUFFALDINO, *with another* PORTER *who carries* BEATRICE'S *trunk.* TRUFFALDINO *comes forward a few steps, sees* FLORINDO *and, fearing to be seen himself, makes the* PORTER *retire.*)

TRUFFALDINO   Come along. This way—— The devil! There's my other master. Go back, friend, and wait for me at that corner.
(*Exit* PORTER)

FLORINDO (*continuing to himself*)   Yes, without delay. I will go back to Turin.

TRUFFALDINO   Here I am, sir.

FLORINDO   Truffaldino, will you come to Turin with me?

TRUFFALDINO   When?

FLORINDO   Now; at once.

TRUFFALDINO   Before dinner?

FLORINDO   No, we will have dinner, and then we will go.

TRUFFALDINO   Very good sir. I'll think it over at dinner.

FLORINDO   Have you been to the Post?

TRUFFALDINO   Yes, sir.

FLORINDO   Have you found my letters?

TRUFFALDINO   I have, sir.

FLORINDO   Where are they?

TRUFFALDINO   I will give you them.

(Takes three letters out of his pocket. Aside)

The devil! I have mixed up one master's letters with the other's. How shall I find out which are his? I cannot read.

FLORINDO Come, give me my letters.

TRUFFALDINO Directly, sir.

(Aside)

Here's a muddle.

(To FLORINDO)

I must tell you, sir; these three letters are not all for your honor. I met another servant, who knows me; we were in service together at Bergamo; I told him I was going to the Post, and he asked me to see whether there was anything for *his* master. I think there was one letter, but I don't know which of them it was.

FLORINDO Let me see; I will take mine and give you the other back.

TRUFFALDINO There, sir; I only wanted to do my friend a good turn.

FLORINDO *(aside)* What is this? A letter addressed to Beatrice Rasponi? To Beatrice Rasponi at Venice?

TRUFFALDINO Did you find the one that belongs to my mate?

FLORINDO Who is this mate of yours who asked you to do this for him?

TRUFFALDINO He is a servant his name is Pasqual'——

FLORINDO Whom does he wait upon?

TRUFFALDINO I do not know, sir.

FLORINDO But if he told you to fetch his master's letters, he must have told you his name.

TRUFFALDINO Of course he did.

(Aside)

The muddle's getting thicker.

FLORINDO Well, what name did he tell you?

TRUFFALDINO I don't remember.

FLORINDO What?

TRUFFALDINO He wrote it down on a bit of paper.

FLORINDO And where is the paper?

TRUFFALDINO I left it at the Post.

FLORINDO *(aside)* Confusion! What does this mean?

TRUFFALDINO *(aside)* I am learning my part as I go along.

FLORINDO Where does this fellow Pasquale live?

TRUFFALDINO Indeed, sir, I haven't the slightest idea.

FLORINDO How will you be able to give him the letter?

TRUFFALDINO He said he would meet me in the Piazza.

FLORINDO *(aside)* I don't know what to make of it.

TRUFFALDINO *(aside)* If I get through this business clean 'twill be a miracle.

(To FLORINDO)

Pray give me the letter, sir, and I shall find him somewhere.

FLORINDO No; I mean to open this letter.

TRUFFALDINO Oh, sir, do not do that, sir. Besides, you know how wrong it is to open letters.

FLORINDO I care not; this letter interests me too much. It is addressed to a

person on whom I have a certain claim. I can open it without scruple.
(*Opens letter*)

TRUFFALDINO   As you will, sir.

(*Aside*)

He has opened it!

FLORINDO (*reads*)   "Madam, your departure from this city has given rise to much talk, and all understand that you have gone to join Signor Florindo. The Court of Justice has discovered that you have fled in man's dress and intends to have you arrested. I have not sent this letter by the courier from Turin to Venice, so as not to reveal the place whither you were bound, but I have sent it to a friend at Genoa to be forwarded to Venice. If I have any more news to tell you, I will not fail to send it by the same means. Your most humble servant, Antonio."

TRUFFALDINO   That's a nice way to behave! Reading other people's letters!

FLORINDO (*aside*)   What is all this? Beatrice has let home? In man's dress? To join me? Indeed she loves me. Heaven grant I may find her in Venice.

(*To* TRUFFALDINO)

Here, my good Truffaldino, go and do all you can to find Pasquale; find out from him who his master is, and if he be man or woman. Find out where he lodges, and if you can, bring him here to me, and both he and you shall be handsomely rewarded.

TRUFFALDINO   Give me the letter; I will try to find him.

FLORINDO   There it is. I count upon you. This matter is of infinite importance to me.

TRUFFALDINO   But am I to give him the letter open like this?

FLORINDO   Tell him it was a mistake, an accident. Don't make difficulties.

TRUFFALDINO   And are you going to Turin now?

FLORINDO   No, not for the present. Lose no time. Go and find Pasquale.

(*Aside*)

Beatrice in Venice, Federigo in Venice! If her brother finds her, unhappy woman! I will do all I can to discover her first!

(*Exit toward the town*)

TRUFFALDINO   Upon my word, I hope he is not going away. I want to see how my two jobs will work out. I'm on my mettle. This letter, now, which I have to take to my other master—I don't like to have to give it him opened. I must try to fold it again.

(*Tries various awkward folds*)

And now it must be sealed. If I only knew how to do it! I have seen my grandmother sometimes seal letters with chewed bread. I'll try it.

(*Takes a piece of bread out of his pocket*)

It's a pity to waste this little piece of bread, but still something must be done.

(*Chews a little bread to seal the letter and accidentally swallows it.*)

The devil! It has gone down. I must chew another bit.

(*Same business*)

No good, nature rebels. I'll try once more.

*(Chews again; would like to swallow the bread, but
restrains himself and with great difficulty removes the
bread from his mouth.)*

Ah, here it is; I'll seal the letter.

(Seals the letter with the bread.)

I think that looks quite well. I'm always a great man for doing things
cleanly.

Lord! I have forgotten the porter.

(Calls off)

Friend, come hither; take the trunk on your shoulder.

(Re-enter PORTER)

PORTER   Here I am; where am I to carry it?

TRUFFALDINO   Take it into that inn; I am coming directly.

(BEATRICE comes out of the inn.)

BEATRICE   Is this my trunk?

TRUFFALDINO   Yes, sir.

BEATRICE *(to PORTER)*   Carry it into my room.

PORTER   Which is your room?

BEATRICE   Ask the waiter.

PORTER   There's one and threepence to pay.

BEATRICE   Go on, I will pay you.

PORTER   Please be quick about it.

BEATRICE   Don't bother me.

PORTER   I've half a mind to throw the trunk down in the middle of the street.

(Goes into the inn)

TRUFFALDINO   Great folk for politeness, these porters!

BEATRICE   Have you been to the Post?

TRUFFALDINO   Yes, sir.

BEATRICE   Any letters for me?

TRUFFALDINO   One for your sister.

BEATRICE   Good; where is it?

TRUFFALDINO   Here.

(Gives letter)

BEATRICE   This letter has been opened.

TRUFFALDINO   Opened? No! Impossible!

BEATRICE   Yes, opened, and then sealed with bread.

TRUFFALDINO   I can't think how that can have happened.

BEATRICE   You cannot think, eh? Rascal, who has opened this letter? I
must know.

TRUFFALDINO   Sir, I'll tell you, I'll confess the truth. We are all liable to make
mistakes. At the Post there was a letter for me; I can't read very much,
and by mistake, instead of opening my letter, I opened yours. I ask
your pardon——

BEATRICE   If that was all, there's no great harm done.

TRUFFALDINO   'Tis true, on the word of a poor man.

BEATRICE   Have you read this letter? Do you know what is in it?

TRUFFALDINO   Not a word. I can't read the handwriting.

BEATRICE   Has anyone else seen it?

TRUFFALDINO (*with an air of great indignation*)   Oh!

BEATRICE   Take care now——

TRUFFALDINO (*same business*)   Sir!

BEATRICE (*aside*)   I hope he is not deceiving me.
> (*Reads to herself*)

TRUFFALDINO   That's all put straight.

BEATRICE (*aside*)   Antonio is a faithful servant and I am obliged to him.
> (*To* TRUFFALDINO)

Listen; I have some business to do close by. You go into the inn, open the trunk—here are my keys—and unpack my things. When I come back, we will have dinner.
> (*Aside*)

I have seen nothing of Signor Pantalone, and I am anxious to have my money.
> (*Exit*)

TRUFFALDINO   Come, that all went well; it couldn't have gone better. I'm a great fellow; I think a deal more of myself than I did before.
> (*Enter* PANTALONE)

PANTALONE   Tell me, my good man, is your master in the house?

TRUFFALDINO   No, sir, he is not there.

PANTALONE   Do you know where he may be?

TRUFFALDINO   Not that neither.

PANTALONE   Is he coming home to dinner?

TRUFFALDINO   Yes, I should think so.

PANTALONE   Here, as soon as he comes home give him this purse with these hundred guineas. I cannot stay, I have business. Good day to you.
> (*Exit* PANTALONE)

TRUFFALDINO   And good day to you, sir! He never told me to which of my masters I was to give it.
> (*Enter* FLORINDO)

FLORINDO   Well, did you find Pasquale?

TRUFFALDINO   No, sir, I did not find Pasqual', but I found a gentleman who gave me a purse with a hundred guineas in it.

FLORINDO   A hundred guineas? What for?

TRUFFALDINO   Tell me truly, sir, were you expecting money from anyone?

FLORINDO   Yes; I had presented a letter of credit to a merchant.

TRUFFALDINO   Then this money will be for you.

FLORINDO   What did he say when he gave it to you?

TRUFFALDINO   He told me to give it to my master.

FLORINDO   Then of course it is mine. Am I not your master? What doubt could you have?

TRUFFALDINO (*aside*)   Yes, but what about t'other one?

FLORINDO   And you do not know who gave you the money?

TRUFFALDINO   No, sir; I think I have seen his face somewhere, but I don't remember exactly.

FLORINDO   It will have been the merchant to whom I had a letter.

TRUFFALDINO   Yes, of course, sir.

FLORINDO   You won't forget Pasquale.

TRUFFALDINO   I'll find him after dinner.

FLORINDO   Then let us go and order our meal.

> (*Goes into the inn*)

TRUFFALDINO   We will. Lucky I made no mistake this time. I've given the purse to the right one.

SCENE THREE

A Room in the House of PANTALONE

PANTALONE *and* CLARICE.

PANTALONE   That's the long and short of it; Signor Federigo is to be your husband. I have given my word and I am not to be cozened.

CLARICE   You have my obedience, sir; but I beseech you, this is tyranny.

PANTALONE   When Signor Federigo first asked for your hand, I told you; you never replied that you did not wish to marry him. You should have spoken then; now it is too late.

CLARICE   My fear of you, sir, and my respect, made me dumb.

PANTALONE   Then your fear and respect should do the same now.

CLARICE   Indeed I cannot marry him, sir.

PANTALONE   No? And why not?

CLARICE   Nothing shall induce me to marry Federigo.

PANTALONE   You dislike him so much?

CLARICE   He is odious in my eyes.

PANTALONE   And supposing I were to show you how you might begin to like him a little?

CLARICE   What do you mean, sir?

PANTALONE   Put Signor Silvio out of your mind, and you will soon like Federigo well enough.

CLARICE   Silvio is too firmly stamped upon my heart; and your own approval, sir, has rooted him there the more securely.

PANTALONE (*aside*)   In some ways I am sorry for her.

> (*To* CLARICE)

You have got to make a virtue of necessity.

CLARICE   My heart is not capable of so great an effort.

PANTALONE   Come, come; you shall!

> (*Enter* SMERALDINA)

SMERALDINA   Sir, Signor Federigo is here and desires to speak with you.

PANTALONE   Tell him to come in; I am at his service.

CLARICE (*weeping*)   Alas! What torture!

SMERALDINA   What is it, madam? You are weeping? Truly you do wrong. Have you not noticed how handsome Signor Federigo is? If I had such luck, I would not cry; no, I would laugh with the whole of my mouth.

> (*Exit* SMERALDINA)

PANTALONE   There, there, my child; you must not be seen crying.

CLARICE   But if I feel my heart bursting!
    (*Enter* BEATRICE *in man's dress*)
BEATRICE   My respects to Signor Pantalone.
PANTALONE   Your servant, sir. Did you receive a purse with a hundred guineas
    in it?
BEATRICE   No.
PANTALONE   But I gave it to your servant just now. You told me he was a
    trustworthy man.
BEATRICE   Yes, indeed; there is no danger. I did not see him. He will give me
    the money when I come home again.
        (*Aside to* PANTALONE)
    What ails Signora Clarice that she is weeping?
PANTALONE (*aside to* BEATRICE)   Dear Signor Federigo, you must have pity
    on her. The news of your death was the cause of this trouble. I hope it
    will pass away in time.
BEATRICE (*to* PANTALONE)   Do me a kindness, Signor Pantalone, and leave
    me alone with her a moment, to see if I cannot obtain a kind word
    from her.
PANTALONE   With pleasure, sir. I will go, and come back again.
        (*To* CLARICE)
    My child, stay here, I will be back directly. You must entertain your
    promised husband awhile.
        (*Softly to* CLARICE)
    Now, be careful.
        (*Exit* PANTALONE)
BEATRICE   Signora Clarice, I beg you——
CLARICE   Stand away, and do not dare to importune me.
BEATRICE   So severe with him who is your destined husband?
CLARICE   They may drag me by force to the altar, but you will have only my
    hand, never my heart.
BEATRICE   You disdain me, but I hope to appease you.
CLARICE   I shall abhor you to all eternity.
BEATRICE   But if you knew me, you would not say so.
CLARICE   I know you well enough as the destroyer of my happiness.
BEATRICE   But I can find a way to comfort you.
CLARICE   You deceive yourself; there is no one who can comfort me
    but Silvio.
BEATRICE   'Tis true, I cannot give you the same comfort as your Silvio might,
    but I can at least contribute to your happiness.
CLARICE   I think it is quite enough, sir, that although I speak to you as
    harshly as I can, you should continue to torture me.
BEATRICE (*aside*)   Poor girl! I can't bear to see her suffer.
CLARICE (*aside*)   I'm so angry, I don't care how rude I am.
BEATRICE   Signora Clarice, I have a secret to tell you.
CLARICE   I make no promise to keep it; you had better not tell it me.
BEATRICE   Your severity deprives me of the means to make you happy.
CLARICE   You can never make me anything but miserable.

BEATRICE You are wrong, and to convince you I will speak plainly. You have no desire for me, I have no use for you. You have promised your hand to another, I to another have already pledged my heart.

CLARICE Oh! Now you begin to please me.

BEATRICE Did I not tell you that I knew how to comfort you?

CLARICE Ah, I feared you would deceive me.

BEATRICE Nay, madam, I speak in all sincerity; and if you promise me that discretion which you refused me just now, I will confide to you a secret, which will ensure your peace of mind.

CLARICE I vow I will observe the strictest silence.

BEATRICE I am not Federigo Rasponi, but his sister Beatrice.

CLARICE What! I am amazed. You a woman?

BEATRICE I am indeed. Imagine my feelings when I claimed you as my bride!

CLARICE And what news have you of your brother?

BEATRICE He died indeed by the sword. A lover of mine was thought to have killed him, and 'tis he whom I am seeking now in these clothes. I beseech you by all the holy laws of friendship and of love not to betray me.

CLARICE Won't you let me tell Silvio?

BEATRICE No; on the contrary I forbid you absolutely.

CLARICE Well, I will say nothing.

BEATRICE Remember I count upon you.

CLARICE You have my promise. I will be silent.

BEATRICE Now, I hope, you will treat me more kindly.

CLARICE I will be your friend indeed; and if I can be of service to you, dispose of me.

BEATRICE I too swear eternal friendship to you. Give me your hand.

CLARICE I don't quite like to——

BEATRICE Are you afraid I am not a woman after all? I will give you proof positive.

CLARICE It all seems just like a dream.

BEATRICE Yes. 'Tis a strange business.

CLARICE 'Tis indeed fantastic.

BEATRICE Come, I must be going. Let us embrace in sign of honest friendship and loyalty.

CLARICE There! I doubt you no longer.
        (*Enter* PANTALONE)

PANTALONE. Well done, well done; I congratulate you.
        (*To* CLARICE)
My child, you have been very quick in adapting yourself.

BEATRICE. Did I not tell you, Signor Pantalone, that I should win her round?

PANTALONE Magnificent! You have done more in four minutes than I should have done in four years.

CLARICE (*aside*) Now I am in a worse tangle than ever.

PANTALONE (*to* CLARICE) Then we will have the wedding at once.

CLARICE Pray do not be in too much haste, sir.

PANTALONE What? Holding hands on the sly and kissing, and then in no haste about it? No, no, I don't want you to get yourself into trouble. You shall be married tomorrow.

BEATRICE   Signor Pantalone, 'twill be necessary first of all to arrange the settlement and to go into our accounts.

PANTALONE   We will do all that. These things can be done in a couple of hours.

CLARICE   Sir, I beseech you——

PANTALONE   Madam, I am going straight away to say a word to Signor Silvio.

CLARICE   For the love of Heaven do not anger him.

PANTALONE   What, what? Do you want two husbands?

CLARICE   Not exactly—but——

PANTALONE   Butt me no buts. 'Tis all settled. Your servant, sir.
          (*Going*)

BEATRICE (*to* PANTALONE)   Listen, sir——

PANTALONE   You are husband and wife.
          (*Going*)

CLARICE   Had you not better——

PANTALONE   We will talk about it this evening.
          (*Exit*)

CLARICE   Oh, Signora Beatrice, 'tis worse than it was before!

Act Two

SCENE ONE

The Courtyard of PANTALONE'S *House*

SILVIO *and the* DOCTOR.

SILVIO   Sir, I entreat you to leave me alone.

DR. LOMBARDI   Stay, answer me.

SILVIO   I am beside myself.

DR. LOMBARDI   What are you doing in the courtyard of Signor Pantalone?

SILVIO   I intend either that he should keep his word that he has given me, or that he should render me account for his intolerable insult.

DR. LOMBARDI   But you cannot do this in Pantalone's own house. You are a fool to let yourself be so transported with anger.

SILVIO   A man who behaves so abominably deserves no consideration.

DR. LOMBARDI   True; but that is no reason why you should be so rash. Leave him to me, my dear boy, leave him to me; let me talk to him; maybe I can bring him to reason and make him see where his duty lies. Go away somewhere and wait for me; leave this courtyard; do not let us make a scene. I will wait for Signor Pantalone.

SILVIO   But sir, I——

DR. LOMBARDI   But, sir, I will have you obey me.

SILVIO   I obey you, sir. I will go. Speak to him. I wait for you at the apothecary's. But if Signor Pantalone persists, he will have to settle with me.

(*Exit* SILVIO)

DR. LOMBARDI   Poor dear boy, I feel truly sorry for him. Signor Pantalone ought never to have led him on so far before he was quite certain that man from Turin was dead. I must see him quietly; I must not let my temper get the better of me.

(*Enter* PANTALONE)

PANTALONE (*aside*)   What is the doctor doing in my house?

DR. LOMBARDI   Oh, Signor Pantalone, your servant.

PANTALONE   Your servant, Doctor. I was just going to look for you and your son.

DR. LOMBARDI   Indeed? Good! I suppose you were coming to give us your assurance that Signora Clarice is to be Silvio's wife.

PANTALONE (*much embarrassed*)   Well, the fact is, I was coming to tell you——

DR. LOMBARDI   No, no; there is no need for explanations. You have my sympathy in a very awkward situation. But we are old friends and we will let bygones be bygones.

PANTALONE (*still hesitating*)   Yes, of course, in view of the promise made to Signor Federigo——

DR. LOMBARDI   He took you by surprise, and you had no time for reflection; you did not think of the affront you were giving to our family.

PANTALONE   You can hardly talk of an affront, when a prevoius contract——

DR. LOMBARDI   I know what you are going to say. It seemed at first sight out of the question that your promise to the Turin gentleman could be repudiated, because it was a formal contract. But that was a contract merely between you and him; whereas ours is confirmed by the girl herself.

PANTALONE   Very true, but—

DR. LOMBARDI   And as you know, in matrimonial cases, *consensus, et non concubitus, facit virum.*

PANTALONE   I am no Latin scholar; but I must tell you—

DR. LOMBARDI   And girls must not be sacrificed.

PANTALONE   Have you anything more to say?

DR. LOMBARDI   I have nothing more to say.

PANTALONE   Have you finished?

DR. LOMBARDI   I have finished.

PANTALONE   May I speak?

DR. LOMBARDI   You may.

PANTALONE   My dear Doctor, with all your learning—

DR. LOMBARDI   As regards the dowry, we can easily arrange matters. A little more or a little less, I will make no difficulties.

PANTALONE   I must begin all over again. Will you allow me to speak?

DR. LOMBARDI   With pleasure.

PANTALONE   I must tell you; I have the greatest respect for your legal learning, but in this case it does not apply.

DR. LOMBARDI   And you mean to tell me that this other marriage is to take place?

PANTALONE   For my part I have given my word and I cannot go back upon it. My daughter is content; what impediment can there be? I was just coming to look for you or Signor Silvio, to tell you this. I am extremely sorry, but I see no help for it.

DR. LOMBARDI   I am not surprised at your daughter's behavior. But I am surprised at yours, sir, at your treating me in this disgraceful way. If you were not perfectly certain about the death of Signor Federigo, you had no business to enter into an engagement with my son; and having entered into an engagement with him, you are bound to maintain that engagement whatever it may cost you. The news of Federigo's death was quite sufficient to justify, even to Federigo, your new intention; he could have no right to reproach you, still less to demand compensation. The marriage which was contracted this morning between Signora Clarice and my son *coram testibus* cannot be dissolved by a mere word given by you to another party. If I were to listen to my son I should insist upon the annulment of the new contract and compel your daughter to marry him; but I should be ashamed to receive into my house so disreputable a daughter-in-law, the daughter of a man who breaks his word as you do. Signor Pantalone, you have done me an injury, you have done an injury to the house of Lombardi. The time will come when you will have to pay for it; yes, sir, the time will come—*ominia tempus habent.*

(*Exit* DOCTOR)

PANTALONE   You may go to the devil for all I care. I don't care a fig, I'm not afraid of you. The Rasponis are worth a hundred of the Lombardis. An only son, and as rich as he is—you won't find that every day. It has got to be.

(*Enter* SILVIO)

SILVIO (*aside*)   'Tis all very fine for my father to talk. Let him keep his temper who can.

PANTALONE (*seeing* SILVIO, *aside*)   Here comes the other.

SILVIO (*rudely*)   Your servant, sir.

PANTALONE   Yours to command, sir.

(*Aside*)

He is boiling.

SILVIO   I have just heard something from my father; am I to believe that it is true?

PANTALONE   If your father said it, it must certainly be true.

SILVIO   Then the marriage is settled between Signora Clarice and Signor Federigo?

PANTALONE   Yes, sir, settled and concluded.

SILVIO   I am amazed that you should have the face to tell me so. You are a man of no reputation, you are no gentleman.

PANTALONE   What is all this? Is that the way you speak to a man of my age?

SILVIO   I don't care how old you are; I have a mind to run you straight through the body.

PANTALONE   I am not a frog, sir, to be spitted. Do you come into my own house to make all this turmoil?

SILVIO   Come outside then.

PANTALONE   I am surprised at you, sir.

SILVIO   Come on, if you are a man of honor.

PANTALONE   I am accustomed to be treated with respect.

SILVIO   You are a low fellow, a coward, and a villain.

PANTALONE   You are a most impertinent young puppy.

SILVIO   I swear to Heaven——

> (*Lays his hand to his sword*)

PANTALONE   Help! Murder!

> (*Draws a pistol*)
>
> (*Enter* BEATRICE *with a drawn sword*)

BEATRICE   I am here to defend you.

> (*To* PANTALONE)

PANTALONE   My dear son-in-law, I am much obliged to you.

SILVIO (*to* BEATRICE)   You are the very man I want to fight.

BEATRICE (*aside*)   I am in for it now.

SILVIO (*to* BEATRICE)   Come on, sir.

PANTALONE (*frightened*)   My dear son-in-law——

BEATRICE   It is not the first time that I have been in danger.

> (*To* SILVIO)

I am not afraid of you.

> (*Presents sword*)

PANTALONE   Help! Help!

> (PANTALONE *runs toward the street.* BEATRICE *and*
> SILVIO *fight.* SILVIO *falls and drops his sword.* BEATRICE
> *holds her point to his heart.*)
> (*Enter* CLARICE)

CLARICE (*to* BEATRICE)   Stop, stop!

BEATRICE   Fair Clarice, at your request I grant Silvio his life, and in
consideration of my mercy, I beg you to remember your oath.

> (*Exit* BEATRICE)

CLARICE   Dear Silvio, are you hurt?

SILVIO   Dear Silvio! Faithless deceiver! Dear Silvio! To a lover disdained, to
a betrayed husband!

CLARICE   No, Silvio, I do not deserve your reproaches. I love you, I adore
you, I am indeed faithful.

SILVIO   Oh, lying jade! Faithful to me, forsooth! You call that fidelity, to
plight your troth to another?

CLARICE   I never did so, nor will I ever. I will die rather than desert you.

SILVIO   I heard just now that you have given your oath.

CLARICE   My oath does not bind me to marry him.

SILVIO   Then what did you swear?

CLARICE   Dear Silvio, have mercy on me; I cannot tell you.

SILVIO   Why not?

CLARICE   Because I am sworn to silence.

SILVIO   That proves your guilt.

CLARICE   No, I am innocent.

SILVIO   Innocent people have no secrets.

CLARICE   Indeed I should be guilty if I spoke.

SILVIO   And to whom have you sworn this silence?

CLARICE   To Federigo.

SILVIO   And you will observe it so jealously?

CLARICE   I will observe it, rather than be a perjuress.

SILVIO   And you tell me you do not love him? He's a fool that believes you.
I do not believe you, cruel deceiver! Begone from my sight!

CLARICE   If I did not love you, I should not have run hither in all haste to
save your life.

SILVIO   Then I loathe my life, if I must own it to one so ungrateful.

CLARICE   I love you with all my heart.

SILVIO   I abhor you with all my soul.

CLARICE   I will die, if you are not to be appeased.

SILVIO   I would sooner see you dead than unfaithful.

CLARICE   Then you shall have that satisfaction.
(*Picks up his sword*)

SILVIO   Yes, that sword should avenge my wrongs.

CLARICE   Are you so cruel to your Clarice?

SILVIO   'Twas you that taught me cruelty.

CLARICE   Then you desire my death?

SILVIO   I know not what I desire.

CLARICE   I do.
(*Points the sword at her breast*)
(*Enter* SMERALDINA)

SMERALDINA   Stop, stop! What on earth are you doing?
(*Takes the sword away from* CLARICE)
And you, you dog, you would have let her die?
(*To* SILVIO)
Have you the heart of a tiger, of a hyena, of a devil? Look at you,
you're a pretty little fellow, that expects ladies to disembowel themselves
for you! You are much too kind to him, madam. He doesn't want you
any more, I suppose? The man that doesn't want you doesn't deserve
you. Let this murderer go to the devil; and you come along with me.
There's no shortage of men; I'll promise to find you a dozen before
evening.
(*She throws down the sword,* SILVIO *picks it up.*)

CLARICE (*weeping*)   Ungrateful! Can it be that my death should cost you not
a single sigh? But I *shall* die, and die of grief. I shall die, and you will
be content. But one day you will know that I am innocent, and then,
when it is too late, you will be sorry you did not believe me, you will
weep for my misfortune and for your own barbarous cruelty.
(*Exit* CLARICE)

SMERALDINA   Here's something I really don't understand. Here's a girl on the
point of killing herself, and you sit there looking on, just as if you
were at a play.

SILVIO   Nonsense, woman! Do you suppose she really meant to kill herself?

SMERALDINA   How should I know? I know that if I had not arrived in time, she would have gone, poor thing.

SILVIO   The point was nowhere near her heart.

SMERALDINA   Did you ever hear such a lie? It was just ready to pierce her.

SILVIO   You women always invent things.

SMERALDINA   We should indeed, if we were like you. It's as the old saw says; we get the kicks and you the halfpence. They say women are unfaithful, but men are committing infidelities all day long. People talk about the women, and they never say a word about the men. We get all the blame, and you are allowed to do as you please. Do you know why? Because 'tis the men who have made the laws. If the women had made them, things would be just the other way. If I were a queen, I'd make every man who was unfaithful carry a branch of a tree in his hand, and I know all the towns would look like forests.

(*Exit* SMERALDINA)

SILVIO   Clarice faithless! Clarice a traitress! Her pretense at suicide was a trick to deceive me, to move my compassion. But though fate made me fall before my rival, I will never give up the thought of revenge. That wretch shall die, and my ungrateful Clarice shall see her lover wallowing in his own gore.

(*Exit* SILVIO)

SCENE TWO

A Room in BRIGHELLA'S *Inn, with a door at each side and two doors at the back, facing the audience.*

TRUFFALDINO *solus.*

TRUFFALDINO   Just my luck! Two masters and neither of them comes home to dinner. 'Tis two o'clock, and not one to be seen. Sure enough they will both come at the same time, and I shall be in a mess; I shall not be able to wait on both together, and the whole thing will be found out. Hush, here comes one. All the better.

(*Enter* FLORINDO)

FLORINDO   Well, did you find that fellow Pasquale?

TRUFFALDINO   Didn't we say, sir, that I was to look for him after dinner?

FLORINDO   I am impatient to see him.

TRUFFALDINO   You should have come back to dinner a little sooner.

FLORINDO (*aside*)   I can find no way of making certain whether Beatrice is here.

TRUFFALDINO   You told me to go and order dinner, and then you go out. The dinner will have been spoiled.

FLORINDO   I don't want to eat anything.

(*Aside*)

I shall go to the Post; I must go myself; then perhaps I shall find out something.

TRUFFALDINO   You know, sir, at Venice you must eat; if you do not, you will fall sick.

FLORINDO   I must go out; I have important business. If I come back to dinner, well and good; if not, I shall eat in the evening. You can get yourself some food, if you like.

TRUFFALDINO   Very good, sir; just as you please, sir; you're the master.

FLORINDO   This money is heavy; here, put it in my trunk. There is the key.
    (*Gives* TRUFFALDINO *the purse and his keys*)

TRUFFALDINO   Certainly, sir; I'll bring the key back at once.

FLORINDO   No, no, you can give it me later. I can't stop. If I do not come back to dinner come to the Piazza; I can't rest till you have found Pasquale.
    (*Exit* FLORINDO)

TRUFFALDINO   Well, anyway, he said I could get myself some food; we are agreed about that. If he won't eat his dinner, he can leave it. My complexion was not for fasting. I'll just put away this purse, and then—
    (*Enter* BEATRICE)

BEATRICE   Oh, Truffaldino!

TRUFFALDINO (*aside*)   The devil!

BEATRICE   Did Signor Pantalone dei Bisognosi give you a purse of a hundred guineas?

TRUFFALDINO   Yes, indeed he did.

BEATRICE   Then why did you not give it to me?

TRUFFALDINO   Was it meant for your honor?

BEATRICE   Was it meant for me? What did he say when he gave you the purse?

TRUFFALDINO   He told me I was to give it to my master.

BEATRICE   Well, and who is your master?

TRUFFALDINO   Your honor.

BEATRICE   Then why do you ask if the purse is mine?

TRUFFALDINO   Then it will be yours.

BEATRICE   Where is it?

TRUFFALDINO   Here, sir.
    (*Gives* BEATRICE *the purse.*)

BEATRICE   Is the money all there?

TRUFFALDINO   I never touched it, sir.

BEATRICE (*aside*)   I shall count it.

TRUFFALDINO (*aside*)   I made a mistake over the purse; but that puts it straight. I wonder what the other gentleman will say? Oh well, if the money wasn't his, he'll say nothing at all.

BEATRICE   Is the landlord in?

TRUFFALDINO   Yes, sir.

BEATRICE   Tell him I shall have a friend to dinner with me, and he must get it ready as soon as ever he can.

TRUFFALDINO   What do you want for dinner, sir? How many dishes?

BEATRICE   Oh, Signor Pantalone dei Bisognosi is not a man who expects a great deal. Tell him to give us five or six dishes; something good.

TRUFFALDINO   You leave it all to me, sir?

BEATRICE   Yes, you order it, do the best you can. I am going to fetch the

gentleman, he is not far off; see that all is ready by the time we come back.
  (*Going*)

TRUFFALDINO You shall see how they serve you here.

BEATRICE Look! Take this paper; put it in my trunk. Be careful with it;
  'tis a bill for exchange for four thousand crowns.

TRUFFALDINO Be sure of it, sir, I'll put it away at once.

BEATRICE See that everything is ready.
  (*Aside*)
  Poor Signor Pantalone—I gave him a terrible fright! I must cheer him
up a little.
  (*Exit* BEATRICE)

TRUFFALDINO Now's time to do myself proud. 'Tis the first time this master of
  mine has told me to order him a dinner. I'll show him I am a man of
  good taste. I'll just put away this paper and then—no, I'll put it away
  afterward, I must not waste time. Ho there! Is nobody at home?
  (*Calling into the inn*)
  Call Master Brighella, tell him I want to talk to him.
  (*Returning*)
  Now with a really good dinner 'tis not the having such and such dishes,
  but the way it is served. A properly laid table is worth more than a
  mountain of dishes.
  (*Enter* BRIGHELLA)

BRIGHELLA What is it, Si'or Truffaldin'? What can I do for you?

TRUFFALDINO My master has got a gentleman to dine with him. He wants a
  good dinner, and that quickly. Have you got enough in the kitchen?

BRIGHELLA I always have plenty of everything. In half an hour I can put on
  any sort of dinner you like.

TRUFFALDINO Very well, then. Tell me what you can give us.

BRIGHELLA For two persons, we will have two courses of four dishes each;
  will that do?

TRUFFALDINO He said five or six dishes—better say six or eight. That will do.
  What will you give us?

BRIGHELLA For the first course, I shall give you soup, fried, boiled, and a
  fricandeau.

TRUFFALDINO Three of the dishes I know, but I do not know the last.

BRIGHELLA 'Tis a French dish—a ragout very tasty indeed.

TRUFFALDINO Very well, that will do for the first course; now the second.

BRIGHELLA For the second course the roast, the salad, a meat pie—and a trifle.

TRUFFALDINO (*indignant*) What's that? A trifle? My master and his guest are
  gentlemen of substance; they won't be satisfied with a mere trifle. A trifle
  indeed!

BRIGHELLA You don't understand. I said
  (*Impressively*)
  a trifle! That's an English dish, a pudding, my very own specialty;
  there's not another man in Venice knows how to make it!

TRUFFALDINO (*nonchalantly*) Oh well, I dare say it will do. But how are you
  going to arrange the table?

BRIGHELLA   Oh, that's easy enough. The waiter will see to that.

TRUFFALDINO   No, my good friend, laying the table is a very important matter; that's the first thing about a dinner, to have the table properly laid.

BRIGHELLA   Well, you might put the soup here, the fried there, there the boiled and here the fricandeau.
   (*Makes an imaginary arrangement*)

TRUFFALDINO   I don't like that. Don't you put something in the middle?

BRIGHELLA   Then we should want five dishes.

TRUFFALDINO   Good, then let us have five.

BRIGHELLA   We can put the gravy in the middle.

TRUFFALDINO   No, no, friend, you know nothing about laying a table; you can't put the gravy in the middle; soup always goes in the middle.

BRIGHELLA   Then the meat on one side, and the gravy on the other.

TRUFFALDINO   Lord, lord, that won't do at all. You innkeepers may know how to cook, but you have no idea of butlering. Now I'll show you.
   (*Kneels down on one knee and points to the floor*)
Suppose this is the table. Now you look how we arrange the five dishes. Like this: here in the middle the soup.
   (*He tears off a piece of the bill of exchange and puts it on the floor to represent a dish*)
Now the boiled meat.
   (*Same business*)
Here we put the fried opposite,
   (*Same business*)
here the gravy and here that—what-d'ye-call-it. There now! Won't that look fine?

BRIGHELLA   H'm, 'twill do; but you have put the gravy too far away from the meat.

TRUFFALDINO   Very well, we must see if we can't put it a little nearer.
   (*Enter* BEATRICE *and* PANTALONE)

BEATRICE   What are you doing on your knees?

TRUFFALDINO (*stands up*)   I was just planning how to have the table laid.

BEATRICE   What is that paper?

TRUFFALDINO (*aside*)   The devil! The letter that he gave me!

BEATRICE   That is my bill of exchange.

TRUFFALDINO   I am very sorry, sir; I will stick it together again.

BEATRICE   You rascal! Is that the way you look after my things? Things of such value too! You deserve a good thrashing. What say you, Signor Pantalone? Did you ever see such a piece of folly?

PANTALONE   To tell the truth, I cannot help laughing. 'Twould be a serious matter if it could not be mended, but I will write you out another and then all will be in order.

BEATRICE   But just think if the bill had been made out not here but in some place a long way off!
   (*To* TRUFFALDINO)
You ignorant fool!

TRUFFALDINO   This has all come about because Brighella doesn't know how
    to lay a table.

BRIGHELLA   He finds fault with everything I do.

TRUFFALDINO   I am a man that knows his business.

BEATRICE (*to* TRUFFALDINO)   Go away.

TRUFFALDINO   Things must be done properly.

BEATRICE   Be off, I tell you.

TRUFFALDINO   In the matter of pantry work I won't give way to the first butler
    in the land.
        (*Exit* TRUFFALDINO)

BRIGHELLA   I don't understand that fellow; sometimes he is a knave and
    sometimes a fool.

BEATRICE   This tomfoolery is all put on. Well, is dinner ready?

BRIGHELLA   If you will have five dishes to each course, 'twill take a little time.

PANTALONE   What's this about courses of five dishes? We'll take pot luck—a
    risotto, a couple of other dishes, and I shall be most obliged to you. My
    tastes are simple.

BEATRICE (*to* BRIGHELLA)   You hear that? That will do nicely.

BRIGHELLA   Very good, sir; but will you please to tell me if there might be
    anything you would particularly fancy?

PANTALONE   I should like some rissoles if you have them; my teeth are not very
    good nowadays.

BEATRICE   You hear? Rissoles.

BRIGHELLA   Very good, sir. If you will sit down here for a moment,
    gentlemen, dinner will be ready directly.

BEATRICE   Tell Truffaldino to come and wait on us.

BRIGHELLA   I'll tell him, sir.
        (*Exit* BRIGHELLA)

BEATRICE   Signor Pantalone, I fear you will indeed have to be content with
    pot luck.

PANTALONE   My dear sir, I am overcome with all the attention you show me;
    in fact you are doing for me what I ought to be doing for you. But, you
    see, I have that girl of mine at home, and until everything is finally
    settled it would not be proper for you to be together. So I accept your
    kind hospitality to raise my spirits a little; indeed I still feel quite upset.
    Had it not been for you, that young scoundrel would have done for me.

BEATRICE   I am glad that I arrived in time.
        (WAITERS *enter from the kitchen and carry glasses, wine,*
        bread, etc., into the room where BEATRICE *and* PANTALONE
        are to dine.)

PANTALONE   They are very quick about their business here.

BEATRICE   Brighella is a smart fellow. He was servant to a great nobleman at
    Turin, and still wears his livery.

PANTALONE   There's a very good tavern on the other side of the Grand Canal
    opposite the Rialto where you can eat very well; I have often been there
    with various good friends of mine, very sound men, too; I often think
    of that place. They had some wonderful Burgundy wine there too—'twas

a wine for the gods.

BEATRICE   There's nothing one enjoys more than good wine in good company.

PANTALONE   Good company! Ah, if you had known them! That was good company! Good honest fellows, with many a good story to tell. God bless them. Seven or eight of them there were, and there wasn't the like of them in all the world.

(*The* WAITERS *come out of the room and return to the kitchen.*)

BEATRICE   You often had a merry time with these gentlemen, eh?

PANTALONE   And I hope I may live to have many more.

(*Enter* TRUFFALDINO *carrying the soup tureen*)

TRUFFALDINO (*to* BEATRICE)   Dinner is ready for you in that room, sir.

BEATRICE   Go and put the soup on the table.

TRUFFALDINO (*makes a bow*)   After you, sir.

PANTALONE   A queer fellow, that servant of yours.

(*Goes in*)

BEATRICE (*to* TRUFFALDINO)   I want less wit and more attention.

(*Goes in*)

TRUFFALDINO   Call that a dinner! One dish at a time! They have money to spend, but they get nothing good for it. I wonder if this soup is worth eating; I'll try it.

(*Takes a spoon out of his pocket and tastes the soup*)

I always carry my weapons about me. Not bad; it might be worse.

(*Goes into room with soup*)

(*Enter* FIRST WAITER *with a dish*)

FIRST WAITER   When is that man coming to take the dishes?

TRUFFALDINO (*re-entering*)   Here I am, friend. What have you got for me?

FIRST WAITER   Here's the boiled meat. There's another dish to follow.

(*Exit* FIRST WAITER)

TRUFFALDINO   Mutton? Or veal? Mutton, I think. Let's taste it.

(*Tastes*)

No, 'tis neither mutton nor veal; 'tis lamb, and very good, too.

(*Goes toward* BEATRICE'S *room*)

(*Enter* FLORINDO)

FLORINDO   Where are you going?

TRUFFALDINO (*aside*)   Oh dear, oh dear!

FLORINDO   What are you doing with that dish?

TRUFFALDINO   I was just putting it on the table, sir.

FLORINDO   For whom?

TRUFFALDINO   For you, sir.

FLORINDO   Why do you serve dinner before I come in?

TRUFFALDINO   I saw you from the window.

(*Aside*)

I must find some excuse.

FLORINDO   And you begin with boiled meat instead of soup?

TRUFFALDINO   You must know, sir, at Venice soup is always taken last.

FLORINDO   I have other habits. I want my soup. Take that back to the kitchen.

TRUFFALDINO   Yes, sir, as you wish, sir.

FLORINDO   Make haste; afterward I want to have a nap.

TRUFFALDINO   Yes, sir.
>   (*Makes as if going to the kitchen*)

FLORINDO   (*aside*) Shall I never find Beatrice again?

FLORINDO *goes into the other room. As soon as he is in,*
>   TRUFFALDINO *quickly takes the dish in to* BEATRICE. *Enter*
>   FIRST WAITER *with another dish.* FLORINDO *calls from his*
>   *room.*)

FLORINDO   Truffaldino! Truffaldino! Am I always to be kept waiting?

TRUFFALDINO   (*coming out of* BEATRICE'S *room*)   Coming, sir.
>   (*To* FIRST WAITER)

Quick, go and lay the table in that other room, the other gentleman
has arrived; bring the soup at once.

FIRST WAITER   Directly.
>   (*Exit* FIRST WAITER)

TRUFFALDINO   What may this dish be? This must be the "fricandeau."
>   (*Tastes it*)

That's good, upon my word.
>   (*Takes it in to* BEATRICE)
>   WAITERS *enter and carry glasses, wine, bread, etc., into*
>   FLORINDO'S *room*)

TRUFFALDINO (*to* WAITERS)   Good lads, that's right.
>   (*Aside*)

They're as lively as kittens. Well, if I can manage to wait at table on two
masters at once, 'twill be a great accomplishment indeed.
>   (*The* WAITERS *come back out of* FLORINDO'S *room and go*
>   *toward the kitchen*)

TRUFFALDINO   Hurry up, lads, the soup!

FIRST WAITER   You look after your own table; we'll take care of this one.
>   (*Exeunt* WAITERS)

TRUFFALDINO   I want to look after both, if I can.
>   (*Re-enter* FIRST WAITER *with* FLORINDO'S *soup*)

TRUFFALDINO   Here, give me that; I'll take it. Go and get the stuff for the
other room.
>   (*Takes soup from* FIRST WAITER *and carries it into*
>   FLORINDO'S *room*)

FIRST WAITER   That's a strange fellow. He wants to wait on everyone. Let him.
They will have to give me *my* tip all the same.
>   (TRUFFALDINO *comes out of* FLORINDO'S *room*)

BEATRICE (*calling from her room*)   Truffaldino!

FIRST WAITER (*to* TRUFFALDINO)   Your master's calling.

TRUFFALDINO   Coming, sir.
>   (*Goes into* BEATRICE'S *room*)
>   (SECOND WAITER *brings the boiled meat for* FLORINDO.
>   TRUFFALDINO *brings the dirty plates out of* BEATRICE'S
>   *room*)

TRUFFALDINO   Here, give it to me.
   (*Exit* SECOND WAITER)
FLORINDO (*calls*)   Truffaldino!
TRUFFALDINO (*wishes to take the meat from* WAITER)   Give it to me.
FIRST WAITER   No, I'm taking this.
TRUFFALDINO   Didn't you hear him call for me?
   (*Takes meat from him and carries it in to* FLORINDO)
FIRST WAITER   Well, that's fine! He wants to do everything.
   (SECOND WAITER *brings in a dish of rissoles, gives it to*
   the FIRST WAITER *and exit*)
I would take this in myself, but I don't want to have words with that
fellow.
   (*Re-enter* TRUFFALDINO *from* FLORINDO'S *room with dirty*
   plates)
Here, master Jack-of-all-trades; take these rissoles to your master.
TRUFFALDINO (*takes dish*)   Rissoles?
FIRST WAITER   Yes, the rissoles he ordered.
   (*Exit* FIRST WAITER)
TRUFFALDINO   Oh, fine! Now which table are these to go to? I wonder which
the devil of my two masters can have ordered them? If I go to the kitchen
and ask, they'll begin to suspect; if I make a mistake and carry them to
the one who didn't order them, then the other will ask for them and
I shall be found out. I know what I'll do; I'll divide them on two plates,
take half to each, and then I shall see who ordered them.
   (*Takes plates and divides the rissoles*)
That's four and that's four. There's one over. Who's to have that? We
mustn't cause ill-feeling; I'll eat that one myself.
   (*Eats it*)
Now. We'll take the rissoles to this gentleman.
   (TRUFFALDINO *puts one plate of rissoles on the floor and*
   takes the other in to BEATRICE. FIRST WAITER *enters*
   with an English pudding (*trifle*))
FIRST WAITER   Truffaldino!
TRUFFALDINO (*comes out of* BEATRICE'S *room*)   Coming!
FIRST WAITER   Take this pudding—
TRUFFALDINO   Wait a moment, I'm coming.
   (*Takes the other dish of rissoles and is going to*
   FLORINDO'S *room*)
FIRST WAITER   That's not right, the rissoles belong there.
TRUFFALDINO   I know they do, sir; I have carried them there; and my master
sends these four as a courtesy to this gentleman.
   (*Goes into* FLORINDO'S *room*)
FIRST WAITER   I see, they know each other—friends, you might say? They
might as well have dined together.
TRUFFALDINO (*re-entering*)   What's this affair?
FIRST WAITER   That's an English pudding.
TRUFFALDINO   Who is it for?
FIRST WAITER   For your master.

(*Exit* FIRST WAITER)

TRUFFALDINO   What the devil is this "pudding"? It smells delicious, and looks like polenta. Oh! If it is polenta, that would be good indeed. I'll taste it.
>   (*Brings a fork out of his pocket and tries the pudding*)

It's not polenta, but it's very much like it.
>   (*Eats*)

Much better than polenta.
>   (*Goes on eating*)

BEATRICE (*calling*)   Truffaldino!

TRUFFALDINO (*with mouth full*)   Coming, sir.

FLORINDO (*calling*)   Truffaldino!

TRUFFALDINO (*with mouth full*)   Coming, sir.
>   (*To himself*)

Oh what wonderful stuff! Just another mouthful and then I'll go.
>   (*Goes on eating*)
>   BEATRICE *comes out of her room, sees* TRUFFALDINO
>   *eating, kicks him, and says:*)

BEATRICE   You come and wait on me.
>   (*She goes back to her room.*)

Truffaldino!

TRUFFALDINO   Coming!
>   (TRUFFALDINO *puts the pudding on the floor and goes
>   into* BEATRICE'S *room.* FLORINDO *comes out of his.*)

FLORINDO (*calling*)   Truffaldino! Where the devil is he?
>   (TRUFFALDINO *comes out of* BEATRICE'S *room*)

TRUFFALDINO   Here, sir.
>   (*Seeing* FLORINDO)

FLORINDO   What are you doing? Where have you been?

TRUFFALDINO   I just went to fetch the next course, sir.

FLORINDO   Is there anything more to eat?

TRUFFALDINO   I'll go and see.

FLORINDO   Make haste, I tell you, because I want to have a nap afterward.
>   (*Goes back into his room*)

TRUFFALDINO   Very good, sir.
>   (*Calling*)

Waiter, is there anything more to come?
>   (*Aside*)

I'll put this pudding aside for myself.
>   (*Hides it*)
>   (*Enter* FIRST WAITER *with dish*)

FIRST WAITER   Here's the roast.

TRUFFALDINO (*takes the roast.*)   Quick, the dessert!

FIRST WAITER   Lord, what a fluster! In a minute.
>   (*Exit* FIRST WAITER)

TRUFFALDINO   I'll take the roast to this gentleman.
>   (*Takes it to* FLORINDO)
>   (*Re-enter* FIRST WAITER)

FIRST WAITER (*with plate of fruit*) Here's the dessert; where are you?

TRUFFALDINO (*re-entering from* FLORINDO's *room*) Here.

FIRST WAITER (*gives him the fruit*) There. Anything more?

TRUFFALDINO Wait.

> (*Takes the dessert to* BEATRICE)

FIRST WAITER He jumps about here and there like the devil himself.

TRUFFALDINO (*re-entering*) That will do. Nobody wants any more.

FIRST WAITER I'm glad to hear it.

TRUFFALDINO And now lay the table for *me*.

FIRST WAITER In a moment.

> (*Exit* FIRST WAITER)

TRUFFALDINO Now for my pudding! Hurrah! I've got through it all, they are all content, they want nothing more, they've had a very good dinner. I have waited at table on two masters at once, and neither of 'em knew anything about the other. But if I have waited for two, now I am going to eat for four.

SCENE THREE

A Street with BRIGHELLA's *Inn*

Enter SMERALDINA.

SMERALDINA A very proper sort of young lady my mistress is! To send me all alone with a letter to a tavern, a young girl like me! Waiting on a woman in love is a sad business. This young lady of mine does a thousand crazy things, and what I cannot understand is this—if she is so much in love with Signor Silvio as to be ready to disembowel herself for him, why does she send letters to another gentleman? One for summer and one for winter, I suppose! Well, there it is!

I am not going inside that tavern. I'll call; somebody will come out. Hey there! Anyone at home?

> (FIRST WAITER *comes out of the inn.*)

FIRST WAITER Now, young woman, what do you want?

SMERALDINA (*aside*) I feel thoroughly ashamed.

> (*To* WAITER)

Tell me—a certain Signor Federigo Rasponi lodges here, does he not?

FIRST WAITER Yes, indeed. He has just this moment finished dinner.

SMERALDINA I have something to say to him.

FIRST WAITER A message? You can come inside.

SMERALDINA And what sort of a girl do you take me for? I am the waiting maid of the lady he is to marry.

FIRST WAITER (*more politely*) Well then, pray step this way.

SMERALDINA Oh, but I don't like to go in there.

FIRST WAITER Do you expect me to bring him out into the street for you? That would not be at all the right thing; more especially as he has Signor Pantalone dei Bisognosi with him.

SMERALDINA What, my master? Worse and worse! I'll not come in.

FIRST WAITER I can send his servant, if you like.

SMERALDINA   The little dark man?

FIRST WAITER   Exactly so.

SMERALDINA   Yes, do send him.

FIRST WAITER (*aside*)   I understand. She fancies the little dark man, and is ashamed to come inside. She is not ashamed to be seen with him in the middle of the street.

(*Goes in*)

SMERALDINA   If the master sees me, whatever shall I say? I'll tell him I came to look for *him;* that will do nicely. I'm never short of an answer.

(*Enter* TRUFFALDINO *with a bottle in his hand, a glass and a napkin.*)

TRUFFALDINO   Who sent for me?

SMERALDINA   I did, sir. I ask pardon if I have troubled you.

TRUFFALDINO   Not a bit of it. I am here to receive your commands.

SMERALDINA   I fear I must have taken you from your dinner.

TRUFFALDINO   I was having dinner, but I can go back to it.

SMERALDINA   I am truly sorry.

TRUFFALDINO   I am delighted. The fact is, I have had my bellyful, and your bright eyes are just the right thing to make me digest it.

SMERALDINA (*aside*)   Very gallant!

TRUFFALDINO   I'll just set down this bottle, and then I'm with you, my dear.

SMERALDINA (*aside*)   He called me "my dear"!

(*To* TRUFFALDINO)

My mistress sends this letter to Signor Federigo Rasponi; I do not like to come into the tavern, so I thought I might put you to this trouble, as you are his man.

TRUFFALDINO   I'll take it with pleasure; but first, you must know that I have a message for *you.*

SMERALDINA   From whom?

TRUFFALDINO   From a very honest man. Tell me, are you acquainted with one Truffaldin' Battocchio?

SMERALDINA   I think I have heard him spoken of, but I am not sure.

(*Aside*)

It must be himself.

TRUFFALDINO   He's a good-looking man; short, thickset, with plenty of wit to his talk. Understands butlering too—

SMERALDINA   I don't know him from Adam.

TRUFFALDINO   Yes, you do; and what's more, he's in love with you.

SMERALDINA   Oh! You are making fun of me.

TRUFFALDINO   And if he could only have just a little hope that his affections were returned, he would make himself known.

SMERALDINA   Well, sir, if I were to see him, and he took my fancy, it might possibly be that I should return his affection.

TRUFFALDINO   Shall I show him to you?

SMERALDINA   I should like to see him.

TRUFFALDINO   Just a moment.

(*Goes into the inn*)

SMERALDINA   Then 'tis not he.

> (TRUFFALDINO *comes out of the inn, makes low bows to* SMERALDINA, *passes close to her, sighs, and goes back into the inn.*)

SMERALDINA   I do not understand this play-acting.

TRUFFALDINO (*re-entering*)   Did you see him?

SMERALDINA   See whom?

TRUFFALDINO   The man who is in love with your beauty.

SMERALDINA   I saw no one but you.

TRUFFALDINO (*sighs*   Well!

SMERALDINA   It is you, then, who profess to be in love with me?

TRUFFALDINO   It is.

> (*Sighs*)

SMERALDINA   Why did you not say so before?

TRUFFALDINO   Because I am rather shy.

SMERALDINA (*aside*)   He would make a stone fall in love with him.

TRUFFALDINO   Well, and what do you say?

SMERALDINA   I say——

TRUFFALDINO   Come, tell me.

SMERALDINA   Oh—I am rather shy too.

TRUFFALDINO   Then if we were joined up, 'twould be a marriage of two people who are rather shy.

SMERALDINA   I must say, you are just my fancy.

TRUFFALDINO   Are you a maid?

SMERALDINA   Need you ask?

TRUFFALDINO   I suppose that means "certainly not."

SMERALDINA   On the contrary, it means "certainly I am."

TRUFFALDINO   I am a bachelor too.

SMERALDINA   I could have been married fifty times, but I never found the man I really fancied.

TRUFFALDINO   Do you think there is any hope for me?

SMERALDINA   Well—to tell the truth—really—I must say—there's a— something about you—— No, I won't say another word.

TRUFFALDINO   If somebody wanted to marry you, what would he have to do?

SMERALDINA   I have neither father nor mother. He would have to speak to my master, or to my mistress.

TRUFFALDINO   And if I speak to them, what will they say?

SMERALDINA   They will say, that if I am content——

TRUFFALDINO   And what will you say?

SMERALDINA   I shall say—that if they are content too——

TRUFFALDINO   That will do. We shall all be content. Give me the letter and when I bring you back the answer, we will have a talk.

SMERALDINA   Here's the letter.

TRUFFALDINO   Do you know what is in it?

SMERALDINA   No—if you only knew how curious I am to know!

TRUFFALDINO   I hope it is not a disdainful letter, or I shall get my face spoiled.

SMERALDINA   Who knows? It can't be a love letter.

TRUFFALDINO I don't want to get into trouble. If I don't know what is in the letter, I am not going to take it.

SMERALDINA We could open it—but how are we to seal it again?

TRUFFALDINO Leave it to me; sealing letters is just my job. No one will ever know anything.

SMERALDINA Then let us open it.

TRUFFALDINO Can you read?

SMERALDINA A little. But you can read quite well, I'm sure.

TRUFFALDINO Yes, I too can read just a little.

SMERALDINA Then let us hear.

TRUFFALDINO We must open it cleanly.
      (*Tears off a piece*)

SMERALDINA Oh! What have you done?

TRUFFALDINO Nothing. I've a secret way to mend it. Here it is, open.

SMERALDINA Quick, read it.

TRUFFALDINO *You* read it. You will know your young lady's handwriting better than I do.

SMERALDINA (*looking at the letter*) Really, I can't make out a word.

TRUFFALDINO (*same business*) Nor I neither.

SMERALDINA Then what was the good of opening it?

TRUFFALDINO (*takes the letter*) Wait; let me think; I can make out some of it.

SMERALDINA Oh I know some of the letters too.

TRUFFALDINO Let us try one by one. Isn't that an M?

SMERALDINA No! That's an R!

TRUFFALDINO Between R and M there is very little difference.

SMERALDINA *Ri, ri, o.* No, no; keep quiet; I think it *is* an M—*Mi, mi, o—mio!*

TRUFFALDINO It's not *mio*, it's *mia*.

SMERALDINA But it is, there's the hook—

TRUFFALDINO That proves it is *mia.*
      (BEATRICE *comes out of the inn with* PANTALONE.)

PANTALONE (*to* SMERALDINA) What are you doing here?

SMERALDINA (*frightened*) Nothing, sir; I came to look for *you.*

PANTALONE (*to* SMERALDINA) What do you want with me?

SMERALDINA The mistress wants you, sir.

BEATRICE (*to* TRUFFALDINO) What is this paper?

TRUFFALDINO (*frightened*) Nothing, just a bit of paper—

BEATRICE Let me see.

TRUFFALDINO (*gives paper, trembling*) Yes, sir.

BEATRICE What? This is a letter addressed to me. Villain, will you open all my letters?

TRUFFALDINO I know nothing about it, sir—

BEATRICE Look, Signor Pantalone, here is a letter from Signora Clarice, in which she tells me of Silvio's insane jealousy—and this rascal has the impudence to open it!

PANTALONE (*to* SMERALDINA) And you helped him to do so?

SMERALDINA I know nothing about it, sir.

BEATRICE Who opened this letter?

TRUFFALDINO   Not I.

SMERALDINA   Nor I.

PANTALONE   Well, who brought it?

SMERALDINA   Truffaldino brought it to his master.

TRUFFALDINO   And Smeraldina brought it to Truffaldino.

SMERALDINA (*aside*)   Sneak! I don't like you any more.

PANTALONE   You meddlesome little hussy, so you are the cause of all this trouble, are you? I've a good mind to smack your face.

SMERALDINA   I've never had my face smacked by any man; I'm surprised at you.

PANTALONE (*coming near her*)   Is that the way you answer me?

SMERALDINA   You won't catch me. You're too rheumatic, you can't run.
            (*Exit running*)

PANTALONE   You saucy minx, I'll show you if I can run; I'll catch you.
            (*Runs after her*)

TRUFFALDINO (*aside*)   If I only knew how to get out of this!

BEATRICE (*looking at the letter, aside*)   Poor Clarice! She is in despair over Silvio's jealousy; 'twill be best for me to discover myself and set her mind at rest.

TRUFFALDINO (*tries to steal away quietly*)   I don't think he is looking. I'll try to get away.

BEATRICE   Where are you off to?

TRUFFALDINO   Nowhere.
            (*Stops*)

BEATRICE   Why did you open this letter?

TRUFFALDINO   It was Smeraldina; I had nothing to do with it.

BEATRICE   Smeraldina, forsooth! You did it, you rascal. One and one make two. That's the second letter of mine you have opened today. Come here.

TRUFFALDINO (*approaching timidly*)   Oh, for mercy's sake, sir—

BEATRICE   Come here, I say.

TRUFFALDINO (*same business*)   Oh, for the love of Heaven—
            (BEATRICE *takes the stick which* TRUFFALDINO *has at his flank (i.e., Harlequin's wooden sword or baton) and beats him well, she standing with her back to the inn.*
            FLORINDO *appears at the window and sees the beating.*)

FLORINDO   What's this? Beating my servant?
            (*Leaves window*)

TRUFFALDINO   Stop, stop, sir, for pity's sake.

BEATRICE   Take that, rascal, and learn to open my letters.
            (*Throws stick on the ground, and exit to street*)

TRUFFALDINO (*after* BEATRICE *has gone*)   My blood! My body! Is that the way to treat a man of my sort? Beat a man like me? If a servant is no good, you can send him away, but you don't beat him.
            (FLORINDO *comes out, unseen by* TRUFFALDINO)

FLORINDO   What's that?

TRUFFALDINO (*seeing* FLORINDO)   Oh! I said people had no business to beat other people's servants like that. This is an insult to my master.

(*Looking toward direction of* BEATRICE'S *exit*)

FLORINDO   Yes, 'tis an affront put upon *me*. Who was it gave you a thrashing?

TRUFFALDINO   I couldn't say, sir; I do not know him.

FLOR NDO   Why did he thrash you?

TRUFFALDINO   Because I—I spat on his shoe.

FLORINDO   And you let yourself be beaten like that? Did nothing? Made no
attempt to defend yourself? And you expose your master to insult, with
perhaps serious consequences? Ass! Poltroon!

(*Picks up the stick*)

Since you enjoy being thrashed, I'll give you your pleasure, I'll thrash
you myself as well.

(*Thrashes him and exit into inn*)

TRUFFALDINO   Well, there's no mistake about my being the servant of two
masters. They have both paid me my wages.

(*Exit into the inn*)

Act Three

SCENE ONE

A Room in BRIGHELLA'S *Inn*

TRUFFALDINO *solus.*

TRUFFALDINO   I don't care that for my beating! I have eaten well, I've dined
well, and this evening I shall sup still better; and as long as I can serve
two masters, there's this at least, that I draw double wages.

And now what's to be done? Master number one is out of doors,
master number two is fast asleep; why, it's just the moment to give those
clothes an airing—take them out of the trunks and see if there's anything
wants doing. Here are the keys. This room will do nicely. I'll get the
trunks out and make a proper job of it. I must have someone to help
me though.

(*Calls*)

Waiter!

(*Enter* WAITERS)

FIRST WAITER   What do you want?

TRUFFALDINO   I want you to lend a hand to bring some trunks out of those
rooms, to give the clothes an airing.

FIRST WAITER (*to* SECOND WAITER)   Go and help him.

TRUFFALDINO (*to* SECOND WAITER)   Come along, and I'll give you a good
handful of what my masters gave me.

(TRUFFALDINO *and* SECOND WAITER *go into* BEATRICE'S
room.)

FIRST WAITER   He looks like a rare good servant—quick, ready, and most
attentive; but I'll warrant he has his faults somewhere. I've been a
servant myself and I know the ropes. Nobody does anything just for love.
Whatever they do, either they are robbing their masters or they are

throwing dust in their eyes.

> (TRUFFALDINO *comes out of the room with the* SECOND
> WAITER *carrying a trunk.*)

TRUFFALDINO   Gently! Let's put it down here.

> (*They put the trunk in the middle of the room.*)

Now let's fetch the other. But quietly, for my master is in there asleep.

> (TRUFFALDINO *and* SECOND WAITER *go into* FLORINDO'S
> *room.*)

FIRST WAITER   Either he's a real first-rate fellow, or he's a real knave; I never saw anybody wait on two gentlemen at once like that. I shall just keep my eyes open; maybe, under the pretense of waiting on two gentlemen at once, he means to rob them both.

> (TRUFFALDINO *and* SECOND WAITER *re-enter with the
> other trunk.*)

TRUFFALDINO   And we'll put this one here.

> (*They put it down a little way off from the other.*)
>
> (*To* SECOND WAITER)

There! You can run along now, if you like. I don't want anything more.

FIRST WAITER (*to* SECOND WAITER)   Go on; off with you to the kitchen.

> (*Exit* SECOND WAITER)
>
> (*To* TRUFFALDINO)

Can I help you?

TRUFFALDINO   No, thank you; I can do my work myself.

FIRST WAITER   I must say, you are a giant for work; it's a marvel to me how you get through it all.

> (*Exit* FIRST WAITER)

TRUFFALDINO   Now I'm going to do my work properly, in peace and quiet, with no one to worry me.

> (*Takes a key out of his pocket*)

Now which key is this, I wonder? Which trunk does it fit? Let's try.

> (*Opens one trunk*)

I guessed right at once. I'm the cleverest man on earth. And this other will open t'other trunk.

> (*Takes out second key and opens second trunk*)

Now they are both open. Let's take everything out.

> (*He takes all the clothes out of both trunks and puts
> them on the table. In each trunk there must be a black
> suit, books and papers, and anything else ad lib.*)

I'll just see if there is anything in the pockets. You never know, sometimes they leave biscuits or sweets in them.

> (*Searches the pockets of* BEATRICE'S *suit and finds a
> portrait*)

My word, what a pretty picture! There's a handosme man! Who can it be? A queer thing, I seem to know him, but yet I can't remember. He is just the least little bit like my other master; but no, *he* never wears clothes like that, nor that wig neither.

> (FLORINDO *calls from his room.*)

FLORINDO   Truffaldino!

TRUFFALDINO Oh, plague take him! He has woken up. If the devil tempts him to come out and he sees this other trunk, he'll want to know—quick, quick—I'll lock it up and say I don't know whose it is.

> (*Begins putting clothes in again*)

FLORINDO (*calling*) Truffaldino!

TRUFFALDINO Coming, sir!

> (*Aside*)

I must put these things away first. But I can't remember which trunk this coat came from, nor these papers neither.

FLORINDO (*calling*) Come here, I say; or must I fetch a stick to you?

TRUFFALDINO In a minute, sir.

> (*Aside*)

Quick, before he comes! I'll put all straight when he goes out.

> (*Stuffs the things into the trunks anyhow and locks them.*
> FLORINDO *comes out in a dressing gown.*)

FLORINDO What the devil are you doing?

TRUFFALDINO Pray, sir, didn't you tell me to give your clothes an airing? I was just about to do it here.

FLORINDO And this other trunk, whose is that?

TRUFFALDINO I couldn't say, sir; 'twill belong to some other gentleman.

FLORINDO Give me my black coat.

TRUFFALDINO Very good, sir.

> (*Opens* FLORINDO'S *trunk and gives him the black suit.*
> FLORINDO *takes off his dressing gown with* TRUFFALDINO'S
> *help and puts on the black coat; then puts his hand into
> the pockets and finds the portrait*)

FLORINDO (*much surprised*) What is this?

TRUFFALDINO (*aside*) Oh Lord, I've made a mistake. I ought to have put it into the other gentleman's pocket. 'Tis the color made me go wrong.

FLORINDO (*aside*) Heavens! There can be no mistake. This is my own portrait; the one I gave to my beloved Beatrice.

> (*To* TRUFFALDINO)

Tell me, how ever did this portrait come to be in the pocket of my coat? It wasn't there before.

TRUFFALDINO (*aside*) Now what's the answer to that? I don't know. Let me think—

FLORINDO Come on, out with it, answer me. How did this portrait come to be in my pocket?

TRUFFALDINO Sir, be kind and forgive me for taking a liberty. The portrait belongs to me, and I hid it there for safety, for fear I might lose it.

FLORINDO How did you come by this portrait?

TRUFFALDINO My master left it to me.

FLORINDO Left it to you?

TRUFFALDINO Yes, sir; I had a master who died, and he left me a few trifles which I sold, all except this portrait, sir.

FLORINDO Great heavens! And how long is it since this master of yours died?

TRUFFALDINO 'Twill be just about a week ago, sir.

> (*Aside*)

I say the first thing that comes into my head.

FLORINDO   What was your master's name?

TRUFFALDINO   I do not know, sir; he lived incognito.

FLORINDO   Incognito? How long were you in his service?

TRUFFALDINO   Only a short time, sir; ten or twelve days.

FLORINDO (*aside*)   Heavens! More and more do I fear that it was Beatrice.
   She escaped in man's dress; she concealed her name—Oh, wretched me,
   if it be true!

TRUFFALDINO (*aside*)   As he believes it all, I may as well go on with the fairytale.

FLORINDO (*despairingly*)   Tell me, was your master young?

TRUFFALDINO   Yes, sir, quite a young gentleman.

FLORINDO   Without a beard?

TRUFFALDINO   Without a beard, sir.

FLORINDO (*aside, with a sigh*)   'Twas she, doubtless.

TRUFFALDINO (*aside*)   I hope I'm not in for another thrashing.

FLORINDO   At least, you know where your late master came from?

TRUFFALDINO   I did know, sir, but I can't now call it to mind.

FLORINDO   Was he from Turin?

TRUFFALDINO   Turin it was, sir.

FLORINDO (*aside*)   Every word he speaks is a sword thrust in my heart.
      (*To* TRUFFALDINO)
   Tell me again, this young gentleman from Turin, is he really dead?

TRUFFALDINO   He is dead indeed, sir.

FLORINDO   Of what did he die?

TRUFFALDINO   He met with an accident, and that was the end of him.
      (*Aside*)
   That seems to be the best way out.

FLORINDO   Where was he buried?

TRUFFALDINO (*aside*)   I wasn't ready for that one.
      (*To* FLORINDO)
   He wasn't buried, sir.

FLORINDO   What!

TRUFFALDINO   No, sir, another servant from the same place got permission to
   have him put into a coffin and sent home, sir.

FLORINDO   And was it, by any chance, the same servant who got you to fetch
   his letters for him from the Post this morning?

TRUFFALDINO   Exactly so, sir; it was Pasqual'.

FLORINDO (*aside*)   Then all hope is lost. Beatrice is dead. Unhappy Beatrice!
   The discomforts of the journey and the tortures of her heart must have
   killed her. Oh, I can no longer endure the agony of my grief!
      (*Exit into his room*)

TRUFFALDINO   That portrait has touched him in the guts. He must have known
   the gentleman. Well, I had better take the trunks back to the rooms
   again, or I shall be in for more trouble of the same sort. Oh dear! Here
   comes my other master.
      (*Enter* BEATRICE *and* PANTALONE)

BEATRICE   I assure you, Signor Pantalone, the last consignment of mirrors and
   wax candles has been put down twice over.

PANTALONE   Maybe my young men have made a mistake. We will go through the books again, and then we shall find out exactly how things stand.

BEATRICE   I too have a list copied from my own books. We will compare them. Perhaps that may decide the point either in your favor or mine. Truffaldino!

TRUFFALDINO   Here, sir.

BEATRICE   Have you the key of my trunk?

TRUFFALDINO   Yes, sir; here it is.

BEATRICE   Why have you brought my trunk in here?

TRUFFALDINO   To air your clothes, sir.

BEATRICE   Have you aired them?

TRUFFALDINO   I have, sir.

BEATRICE   Open the trunk and give me—Whose is that other trunk?

TRUFFALDINO   It belongs to another gentleman who has just come.

BEATRICE   G ve me the memorandum book which you will find there.

TRUFFALDINO   Yes, sir.
> (*Aside*)
The Lord help me this time!
> (*Opens trunk and looks for the book*)

PANTALONE   As I say, they may have made a mistake; of course, if there is a mistake, you will not have to pay.

BEATRICE   We may find that all is in order; we shall see.

TRUFFALDINO   Is this the book, sir?
> (*Holding out a book to* BEATRICE)

BEATRICE   I expect so.
> (*Takes the book without looking carefully and opens it*)
No, this is not—Whose is this book?

TRUFFALDINO (*aside*)   I've done it now!

BEATRICE (*aside*)   These are two letters which I wrote to Florindo. Alas, these notes, these accounts belong to him. I tremble, I am in a cold sweat, I know not where I am.

PANTALONE   What ails you, Signor Federigo? Are you unwell?

BEATRICE   'Tis nothing.
> (*Aside to* TRUFFALDINO)
Truffaldino, how did this book come to be in my trunk? It is not mine.

TRUFFALDINO   I hardly know, sir—

BEATRICE   Come, out with it—tell me the truth.

TRUFFALDINO   I ask your pardon for the liberty I took, sir, putting the book into your trunk. It belongs to me, and I put it there for safety.
> (*Aside*)
That was a good enough story for the other gentleman, I hope 'twill do for this one too.

BEATRICE   The book is your own, you say, and yet you gave it to me instead of mine, without noticing?

TRUFFALDINO (*aside*)   He's much too clever.
> (*To* BEATRICE)
I'll tell you, sir; I have only had the book a very short time, so I did not recognize it at once.

BEATRICE   And how came you by this book?

TRUFFALDINO   I was in service with a gentleman at Venice, and he died and left the book to me.

BEATRICE   How long ago?

TRUFFALDINO   I don't remember exactly—ten or twelve days.

BEATRICE   How can that be, when I met you at Verona?

TRUFFALDINO   I had just come away from Venice on account of my poor master's death.

BEATRICE   (aside)   Alas for me!
     (To TRUFFALDINO)
     Your master—was his name—Florindo?

TRUFFALDINO   Yes, sir; Florindo.

BEATRICE   And his family name Aretusi?

TRUFFALDINO   That was it, sir; Aretusi.

BEATRICE   And you are sure he is dead?

TRUFFALDINO   As sure as I stand here.

BEATRICE   Of what did he die? Where was he buried?

TRUFFALDINO   He tumbled into the canal and was drowned and never seen again.

BEATRICE   Oh, wretched that I am! Florindo is dead, my beloved is dead; my one and only hope is dead. All is lost. Love's strategems are fruitless! I leave my home, I leave my relatives, I dress as a man, I confront danger, I hazard my very life, all for Florindo—and Florindo is dead. Unhappy Beatrice! Was the loss of my brother so little to me that Fate must make me lose my lover as well? Oh! Grief overwhelms me, I can no longer bear the light of day. My adored one, my beloved, I will follow you to the tomb.
     (Exit into her room, raving)

PANTALONE (who has listened to her speech with astonishment)
     Truffaldino!

TRUFFALDINO   Si'or Pantalon'?

PANTALONE   A woman!

TRUFFALDINO   A female!

PANTALONE   Most extraordinary!

TRUFFALDINO   Who'd have thought it?

PANTALONE   I'm struck all of a heap.

TRUFFALDINO   You might knock me down with a feather.

PANTALONE   I shall go straight home and tell my daughter.
     (Exit)

TRUFFALDINO   It seems I am not the servant of two masters but of a master and a mistress.
     (Exit)

SCENE TWO

A Street
Enter DR. LOMBARDI *meeting* PANTALONE.

DR. LOMBARDI   (aside)   This doddering old villain Pantalone sticks in my gizzard. The more I think about him, the more I abominate him.

PANTALONE (*cheerfully*)   Good day, my dear Doctor, your servant.

DR. LOMBARDI   I am surprised that you have the effrontery to address me.

PANTALONE   I have news for you. Do you know——

DR. LOMBARDI   You are going to tell me that the marriage has already been performed? I care not a fig if it has.

PANTALONE   The whole story is untrue. Let me speak, plague take you.

DR. LOMBARDI   Speak on then, pox on you.

PANTALONE (*aside*)   I should like to give him a good doctoring with my fists.
        (*To* DR. LOMBARDI)
My daughter shall marry your son whenever you please.

DR. LOMBARDI   I am vastly obliged to you. Pray do not put yourself to inconvenience. My son is not prepared to stomach that, sir. You may give her to the Turin gentleman.

PANTALONE   If you knew who the Turin gentleman is, you would say differently.

DR. LOMBARDI   He may be who he will. Your daughter has been seen with him, *et hoc sufficit.*

PANTALONE   But 'tis not true that he is——

DR. LOMBARDI   I will not hear another word.

PANTALONE   If you won't hear me, 'twill be the worse for you.

DR. LOMBARDI   We shall see for whom it will be the worse.

PANTALONE   My daughter is a girl of unblemished reputation, and——

DR. LOMBARDI   The devil take you.

PANTALONE   The devil take you, sir.

DR. LOMBARDI   You disreputable old villain!
        (*Exit* DR. LOMBARDI)

PANTALONE   Damn you! He is more like a beast than a man. Why, how could I ever tell him that the man was a woman? Not a bit of it, he wouldn't let me speak. But here comes that young lout of a son of his; now I shall be in for more impertinence.
        (*Enter* SILVIO)

SILVIO (*aside*)   There is Pantalone. I should like to run a sword through his paunch.

PANTALONE   Signor Silvio, if you will give me leave, I should like to give you a piece of good news, if you will condescend to allow me to speak, and not behave like that windmill of a father of yours.

SILVIO   What have you to say to me? Pray speak, sir.

PANTALONE   You must know, sir, that the marriage of my daughter to Signor Federigo has come to nothing.

SILVIO   Indeed? Do not deceive me.

PANTALONE   'Tis true indeed, and if you are still of your former mind, my daughter is ready to give you her hand.

SILVIO   Oh, heavens! You bring me back from death to life.

PANTALONE (*aside*)   Well, well, he is not quite such a bear as his father.

SILVIO   But heavens! How can I clasp to my bosom her who has for so long been the bride of another?

PANTALONE   To cut a long story short, Federigo Rasponi has turned into
    Beatrice his sister.

SILVIO   What? I do not understand you.

PANTALONE   Then you are very thickheaded. The person whom we thought to
    be Federigo has been discovered to be Beatrice.

SILVIO   Dressed as a man?

PANTALONE   Dressed as a man.

SILVIO   At last I understand.

PANTALONE   About time you did.

SILVIO   How did it happen? Tell me.

PANTALONE   Let us go to my house. My daughter knows nothing of it. I
    need only tell the story once to satisfy you both.

SILVIO   I will come, sir; and I most humbly beg your forgiveness, for having
    allowed myself to be transported by passion——

PANTALONE   'Twas a mere nothing; I appreciate your feelings. I know what
    love is. Now, my dear boy, come along with me.
        (Going)

SILVIO *(aside)*   Who is happier than I am? What heart could be more
    contented?
        (Exit with PANTALONE*)*

SCENE THREE

A Room in BRIGHELLA'S *Inn*

        BEATRICE *and* FLORINDO *come out of their rooms
        simultaneously; each holds a sword or dagger and is on
        the point of committing suicide.* BRIGHELLA *is restraining
        *BEATRICE *and the* FIRST WAITER *restraining* FLORINDO.
        They all come forward in such a way that BEATRICE *and
        *FLORINDO *are unaware of each other's presence)*

BRIGHELLA *(seizing* BEATRICE'S *hand)*   Stop, stop!

BEATRICE *(trying to break loose)*   For pity's sake, let me go.

FIRST WAITER *(holding* FLORINDO*)*   This is madness.

FLORINDO *(breaks away from* WAITER*)*   Go to the devil.

BEATRICE *(breaking away from* BRIGHELLA*)*   You shall not hinder me.
        *(Both come forward, determined to kill themselves, they
        see each other, recognize each other, and stand dazed.)*

FLORINDO   What do I see?

BEATRICE   Florindo!

FLORINDO   Beatrice!

BEATRICE   Are you alive?

FLORINDO   Are you too living?

BEATRICE   Oh, destiny!

FLORINDO   Oh, my adored one!
        (They drop their weapons and embrace)

BRIGHELLA *(jokingly to the* WAITER*)*   You had better mop up the blood; we
    don't want a mess here.

(Exit BRIGHELLA)

FIRST WAITER *(aside)*   Anyway I'll pick up the weapons and I shall not give them back again.

(Picks up the daggers and exits)

FLORINDO   What brought you to attempt such an act of madness?

BEATRICE   The false news of your death.

FLORINDO   Who told you that I was dead?

BEATRICE   My servant.

FLORINDO   And mine gave me to believe that you were dead; and I too, carried away by the same agony of grief, intended to take my life.

BEATRICE   It was this book caused me to believe the story.

FLORINDO   That book was in my trunk. How came it into your hands? Ah, now I know. By the same means, no doubt, as the portrait I found in my coat pocket. Here it is. The one I gave you at Turin.

BEATRICE   Those rascally servants of ours—Heaven only knows what they have been up to.

FLORINDO   Where are they, I wonder?

BEATRICE   Nowhere to be seen.

FLORINDO   Let us find them and confront them.

(Calling)

Ho there! Is nobody there?

(Enter BRIGHELLA)

BRIGHELLA   Did you call, sir?

FLORINDO   Where are our servants?

BRIGHELLA   I don't know, sir. Shall I send to look for them?

FLORINDO   Find them at once if you can and send them to us here.

BRIGHELLA   For myself I only know one of them; I will ask the waiters, they will know them both. I congratulate you, sir, and madam, on having made such a satisfactory end of yourselves; if you want to get yourselves buried, you must try some other establishment; that's more than we can undertake. Your servant, madam and sir.

(Exit BRIGHELLA)

FLORINDO   Then you too are lodged in this inn?

BEATRICE   I arrived this morning.

FLORINDO   I too this morning. And yet we never saw each other.

BEATRICE   Fate has been pleased to torment us a little.

FLORINDO   Tell me: your brother Federigo—is he dead?

BEATRICE   Have you any doubt? He died on the spot.

FLORINDO   I was told he was alive and here in Venice.

BEATRICE   It was I who traveled in his name and in these clothes to follow—

FLORINDO   To follow me—I know, my dearest; I read it in a letter from your servant at Turin.

BEATRICE   How came it into your hands?

FLORINDO   My servant gave it me by mistake and seeing it was addressed to you, I could not help opening it.

BEATRICE   I suppose a lover's curiosity is always legitimate.

FLORINDO   But where are these servants of ours? Ah!

(*Sees* TRUFFALDINO *approaching*)

Here is one.

BEATRICE   He looks like the worse knave of the two.

FLORINDO   I think you are not far wrong.

(*Enter* TRUFFALDINO *brought in by force by* BRIGHELLA *and the* FIRST WAITER)

FLORINDO   Come here, come here, don't be frightened.

BEATRICE   We shall do you no harm.

TRUFFALDINO (*aside*)   H'm, I still remember the thrashing.

BRIGHELLA   We have found this one; if we can find the other, we will bring him.

FLORINDO   Yes, we *must* have them both here together.

BRIGHELLA (*aside to* WAITER)   Do you know the other?

FIRST WAITER (*to* BRIGHELLA)   Not I.

BRIGHELLA   We'll ask in the kitchen. Someone there will know him.

FIRST WAITER   If he had been there, I should have known him too.

(*Exeunt* FIRST WAITER *and* BRIGHELLA)

FLORINDO (*to* TRUFFALDINO)   Come, now, tell us what happened about that changing of the portrait and the book, and why you and that other rascal conspired to drive us distracted.

TRUFFALDINO, *signs to both with his finger to keep silence.*

Hush!

(*To* FLORINDO)

Pray, sir, a word with you in private.

(*To* BEATRICE *just as he turns to speak to* FLORINDO)

I will tell you everything directly.

(*To* FLORINDO)

You must know, sir, I am not to blame for anything that has happened; it's all Pasqual's fault, the servant of that lady there.

(*Cautiously pointing at* BEATRICE)

It was he mixed up the things, and put into one trunk what belonged to the other, without my knowledge. The poor man begged and prayed me to take the blame, for fear his master should send him away, and as I am a kindhearted fellow that would let himself be drawn and quartered for his friends, I made up all these stories to see if I could help him. I never dreamed it was a portrait of you or that you would be so much upset at hearing of the death of the owner. Now I have told you the whole truth, sir, as an honest man and a faithful servant.

BEATRICE (*aside*)   'Tis a very long story he is telling. I am curious to know what the mystery is about.

FLORINDO (*aside to* TRUFFALDINO)   Then the man who got you to fetch that letter from the Post was the servant of Signora Beatrice?

TRUFFALDINO (*aside to* FLORINDO)   Yes, sir, that was Pasqual'.

FLORINDO   Then why conceal from me a fact I so urgently desired to know?

TRUFFALDINO   He begged me not to tell anyone, sir.

FLORINDO   Who?

TRUFFALDINO   Pasqual'.

FLORINDO   Why didn't you obey your master?

TRUFFALDINO   For the love of Pasqual'.

FLORINDO   You and Pasquale deserve a sound thrashing together.

TRUFFALDINO (*aside to himself*)   In that case I should get both.

BEATRICE   Have you not yet finished this long cross-examination?

FLORINDO   This fellow has been telling me—

TRUFFALDINO (*aside to* FLORINDO)   For the love of Heaven, your honor, do not say it was Pasqual'. I'd rather you told the lady it was me. You can give me a beating if you like, but don't let any trouble come to Pasqual'.

FLORINDO   (*aside to* TRUFFALDINO)   Are you so devoted a friend to Pasquale?

TRUFFALDINO   I love him as if he were my very own self. Now I am going to the lady, and I am going to tell her that it was all my fault; she may scold me as she pleases and do what she will to me, but I *will* protect Pasqual'.

(TRUFFALDINO *moves toward* BEATRICE.)

FLORINDO (*aside*)   Well, he's certainly a very loyal and affectionate character.

TRUFFALDINO (*to* BEATRICE)   Here I am, madam.

BEATRICE (*aside to* TRUFFALDINO)   What is all this long story you've been telling Signor Florindo?

TRUFFALDINO (*aside to* BEATRICE)   You must know, madam, that that gentleman has a servant called Pasqual'; he is the most arrant noddy in the world; it was he made all that mess of things; but because the poor man was afraid his master would send him away, I made up all the story about the book and the master who was dead and drowned, and all the rest of it. And just now I've been telling Si'or Florindo that I was the cause of it all.

BEATRICE   But why accuse yourself of faults which you have never committed?

TRUFFALDINO   Madam, 'tis all for the love I bear Pasqual'.

FLORINDO (*aside*)   This seems a very long business.

TRUFFALDINO (*to* BEATRICE *as before*)   Dear madam, I beg of you, don't get him into trouble.

BEATRICE   Whom?

TRUFFALDINO   Pasqual'.

BEATRICE   Pasquale and you are a pretty pair of rascals.

TRUFFALDINO (*aside to himself*)   I fear I'm the only one.

FLORINDO   Come. That's enough. Signora Beatrice, our servants certainly deserve to be punished; but in consideration of our own great happiness, we surely may forgive what is past.

BEATRICE   True; but your servant——

TRUFFALDINO (*aside to* BEATRICE)   For the love of Heaven don't mention Pasqual'.

BEATRICE (*to* FLORINDO)   Well, I must go and call upon Signor Pantalone dei Bisognosi; will you accompany me?

FLORINDO   I would do so with pleasure, but I have to wait here and see my banker. I will come later, if you are in haste.

BEATRICE   I am, I must go at once. I shall expect you at Signor Pantalone's; and shall stay there till you come.

FLORINDO   I don't know where he lives.

TRUFFALDINO   I know, sir, I'll show you the way.

BEATRICE   Very well, and now I must go to my room and tidy myself up.

TRUFFALDINO (*aside to* BEATRICE)   Very good, madam; I am at your service directly.

BEATRICE   Dear Florindo! What torments have I not endured for love of you!

(BEATRICE *goes into her room.*)

FLORINDO   Mine have been no less.

TRUFFALDINO   Sir, Pasqual' is not here, and Si'ora Beatrice has no one to help her dress; will you give me leave to wait upon her instead of Pasqual'?

FLORINDO   Yes, by all means. Wait upon her with diligence; I am delighted.

TRUFFALDINO (*aside*)   For invention, for promptness and for intrigue I will challenge the attorney general.

(TRUFFALDINO *goes into* BEATRICE'S *room.*)

FLORINDO   What strange things have happened in the course of this one day! Tears, lamentations, and anguish, and then at last consolation and happiness. From tears to laughter is a happy step, which makes us forget our agonies, but when we pass from pleasure to pain the change is even yet more acutely perceptible.

(*Re-enter* BEATRICE *followed by* TRUFFALDINO.)

BEATRICE   Here I am, have I not been quick?

FLORINDO   When will you change these clothes?

BEATRICE   Do I not look well in them?

FLORINDO   I long to see you in a woman's dress. Your beauties ought not to be so completely disguised.

BEATRICE   Well, I shall expect you at Signor Pantalone's; make Truffaldino show you the way.

FLORINDO   I must wait for the banker; if he does not come soon another time will do.

BEATRICE   Show me your love in your anxiety to attend me.

(*About to go*)

TRUFFALDINO (*aside to* BEATRICE)   Do you wish me to stay and wait upon this gentleman?

BEATRICE   Yes, you will show him the way to Signor Pantalone's.

TRUFFALDINO   Yes, madam, certainly, as Pasqual' is not here.

BEATRICE   Wait upon him, I shall be pleased indeed.

(*Aside to herself*)

I love him more than my very self.

(*Exit* BEATRICE)

TRUFFALDINO   The fellow's nowhere to be seen. His master wants to dress, and he goes out on his own and is nowhere to be found.

FLORINDO   Of whom are you speaking?

TRUFFALDINO   Of Pasqual'. I love him, he is a good friend of mine, but he's a lazy dog. Now I am a servant worth two.

FLORINDO   Come and dress my wig. The banker will be here directly.

TRUFFALDINO   Please your honor, I hear your honor has to go to Si'or Pantalon's.

FLORINDO   Yes, what then?

TRUFFALDINO   I want to ask a favor of you.

FLORINDO   Well, you deserve it after all you have done.

TRUFFALDINO   If there has been any trouble, you know, sir, 'tis all the fault of Pasqual'.

FLORINDO   But where on earth *is* this cursed Pasquale? Can't one see him?

TRUFFALDINO   He'll come, the knave. And so, sir, I want to ask you this favor.

FLORINDO   What do you want?

TRUFFALDINO   You see, sir, I'm in love too.

FLORINDO   In love?

TRUFFALDINO   Yes, sir, and my young woman is maidservant to Si'or Pantalon'; and it would be very kind if your honor——

FLORINDO   How do I come into it?

TRUFFALDINO   I won't say, sir, that you come into it; but I being your servant, you might say a word for me to Si'or Pantalon'.

FLORINDO   We must see first whether the girl wants you.

TRUFFALDINO   The girl wants me, no mistake. All I want is a word to Si'or Pantalon'; I beg you, sir, of your charity.

FLORINDO   Certainly, I will speak for you, but how can you keep a wife?

TRUFFALDINO   I shall do what I can. I shall ask for help from Pasqual'.

FLORINDO   You had better ask help from someone with more sense.

(FLORINDO *goes into his room.*)

TRUFFALDINO   Well, if I don't show sense this time, I shall never show it again.

(TRUFFALDINO *follows* FLORINDO *into his room.*)

SCENE FOUR

A Room in the House of PANTALONE

PANTALONE, *the* DOCTOR, CLARICE, SILVIO *and* SMERALDINA.

PANTALONE   Come, Clarice, pull yourself together. You see that Signor Silvio has repented and asks your forgiveness. If he acted foolishly, it was all for love of you; I have forgiven him his extravagances, you ought to forgive him too.

SILVIO   Measure my agony by your own, Signora Clarice, and rest assured that I most truly love you, since 'twas the fear of losing you that rendered me distracted. Heaven desires our happiness; do not be ungrateful for the blessings of Providence. Do not let the idea of revenge spoil the most beautiful day of your life.

DR. LOMBARDI   I join my prayers to those of my son; Signora Clarice, my dear daughter-in-law, have pity on the poor young man; he nearly went out of his mind.

SMERALDINA   Come, dear madam, what would you? Men are all cruel to us, some more, some less. They demand the most absolute fidelity, and on the least shadow of suspicion they bully us, ill-treat us and are like to murder us. Well, you have got to marry one or another of them someday, so I say to you as one says to sick people—since you have got to take your nasty medicine, take it.

PANTALONE   There, do you hear that? Smeraldina calls matrimony medicine.
You must not think it is poison.

>   (*Aside to* DR. LOMBARDI)

We must try to cheer her up.

DR. LOMBARDI   Certainly, 'tis not poison, nor even nasty medicine. Matrimony
is a lollipop, a jujube, a lozenge!

SILVIO   But dear Clarice, won't you say a word? I know I deserve to be
punished by you, but, of your mercy, punish me with hard words rather
than with silence. Behold me at your feet; have pity upon me.

CLARICE (*to* SILVIO *with a sigh*)   Cruel!

PANTALONE (*aside to* DR. LOMBARDI)   You heard that little sigh? A good sign.

DR. LOMBARDI (*aside to* SILVIO)   Strike while the iron is hot.

SMERALDINA (*aside*)   A sign is like lightning; it promises rainfall.

SILVIO   If I could think that you desired my blood to avenge my supposed
cruelty, I give it you with all my heart. But, oh God! instead of the blood
of my veins, accept, I beg you, that which gushes from my eyes.

>   (*Weeps*)

PANTALONE   Bravo! Bravo! Well said!

DR. LOMBARDI   Capital! Capital!

CLARICE (*sighing as before, but more tenderly*)   Cruel!

DR. LOMBARDI (*aside to* PANTALONE)   She's done to a turn.

PANTALONE   Here, come up with you.

>   (*He raises* SILVIO, *takes by him the hand.*)

Stand over there.

>   (*Takes* CLARICE'S *hand*)

And you come here too, madam. Now, join your hands together again;
and make peace. So no more tears, be happy, no more nonsense and
Heaven bless you both.

DR. LOMBARDI   There; 'tis done.

SMERALDINA   'Tis done, 'tis done.

SILVIO (*holding* CLARICE'S *hand*)   Oh, Signora Clarice, for pity's sake——

CLARICE   Ungrateful!

SILVIO   Dearest!

CLARICE   Inhuman!

SILVIO   Beloved!

CLARICE   Monster!

SILVIO   Angel!

CLARICE (*sighs*)   Ah!

PANTALONE (*aside*)   Going, going——

SILVIO   Forgive me, for the love of Heaven.

CLARICE (*sighs*)   I forgive you.

PANTALONE (*aside*)   Gone!

DR. LOMBARDI   Come, Silvio, she has forgiven you.

SMERALDINA   The patient is ready; give her her medicine.

>   (*Enter* BRIGHELLA)

BRIGHELLA   By your leave, sir, may I come in?

PANTALONE   Pray come in, good friend Brighella. 'Twas you, was it not, that told me all these pretty stories, who assured me that that party was Signor Federigo—eh?

BRIGHELLA   My dear sir, who would not have been deceived? They were twin brother and sister, as like as two peas. In those clothes I would have wagered my head that it was he.

PANTALONE   Enough. That's all done with. What is the news?

BRIGHELLA   Signora Beatrice is here, and desires to pay her respects.

PANTALONE   Let her come in; she is most welcome.

CLARICE   Poor Signora Beatrice, I am happy to think that her troubles are over.

SILVIO   You are sorry for her?

CLARICE   I am indeed.

SILVIO   And for me?

CLARICE   Oh, cruel!

PANTALONE (*aside to* DR. LOMBARDI)   You hear these loving words?

DR. LOMBARDI (*aside to* PANTALONE)   Ah, my son has a way with him.

PANTALONE   My daughter, poor dear child, has a very good heart.

SMERALDINA   Yes, they will both of them do their duty by each other.

(*Enter* BEATRICE)

BEATRICE   Ladies and gentlemen, I come to ask your pardon and forgiveness, that you should on my account have been put to inconvenience——

CLARICE   No, no, my dear; come to me.

(*Embraces her*)

SILVIO (*annoyed at the embrace*)   How now?

BEATRICE (*to* SILVIO)   What! May she not even embrace a woman?

SILVIO (*aside*)   'Tis those clothes again.

PANTALONE   Well, well, Signora Beatrice, I must say, for a young woman of your age you have a wonderful courage.

DR. LOMBARDI (*to* BEATRICE)   Too much spirit, madam.

BEATRICE   Love makes one do great things.

PANTALONE   And you have found your young gentleman at last? So I hear.

BEATRICE   Yes, Heaven has made us happy.

DR. LOMBARDI   A nice reputation you have made yourself!

BEATRICE   Sir, you have no business with my affairs.

SILVIO (*to* DR. LOMBARDI)   Sir, I beg you, let everyone do as they will; do not be so put out about it. Now that I am happy, I want all the world to be happy too. Is anyone else going to be married? Let them all get married!

SMERALDINA (*to* SILVIO)   What about me, sir?

SILVIO   Whom are you going to marry?

SMERALDINA   The first man that comes along, sir.

SILVIO   Find him then, here am I.

CLARICE (*to* SILVIO)   You? What for?

SILVIO   To give her a wedding present.

CLARICE   That is no affair of yours.

SMERALDINA (*aside*)   She's afraid everybody will eat him. She likes the taste of him, I see.

(*Enter* TRUFFALDINO)

TRUFFALDINO   My respects to the company.

BEATRICE (*to* TRUFFALDINO)   Where is Signor Florindo?

TRUFFALDINO   He is here and would like to come in, by your leave.

BEATRICE   Signor Pantalone, will you give Signor Florindo leave?

PANTALONE   Is that your young gentleman?

BEATRICE   He is going to marry me.

PANTALONE   I shall be pleased to meet him.

BEATRICE (*to* TRUFFALDINO)   Show him in.

TRUFFALDINO (*aside to* SMERALDINA)   Young woman, my respects to you.

SMERALDINA (*aside to* TRUFFALDINO)   Pleased to see you, my little darkie.

TRUFFALDINO   We will have a talk.

SMERALDINA   What about?

TRUFFALDINO (*makes as though giving her a wedding ring*)   Are you willing?

SMERALDINA   Why not?

TRUFFALDINO   We'll have a talk.

(*Exit* TRUFFALDINO)

SMERALDINA (*to* CLARICE)   Madam, with the company's leave, I want a favor
    of you.

CLARICE (*going aside to listen to* SMERALDINA)   What is it?

SMERALDINA (*to* CLARICE)   I too am a poor young girl that would like to settle
    myself; there's the servant of Signora Beatrice who wants to marry me;
    now if you would say a kind word to his mistress, and get her to allow
    him to take me to wife, I should be the happiest girl in the world.

CLARICE   Dear Smeraldina, with all the pleasure in life; as soon as I can speak
    freely to Beatrice, I will certainly do so.

PANTALONE (*to* CLARICE)   What is all this whispering about?

CLARICE   Nothing, sir. She had something to say to me.

SILVIO (*to* CLARICE)   May I not know?

CLARICE   How inquisitive they all are! And then they talk about us women!

(*Enter* FLORINDO *shown in by* TRUFFALDINO.)

FLORINDO   Your most humble servant, ladies and gentlemen.

(*All bow and curtsy.*)

(*To* PANTALONE)

Are you the master of the house, sir?

PANTALONE   Yours to command, sir.

FLORINDO   Allow me, sir, to have the honor of waiting upon you this
    evening; I present myself by command of the Signora Beatrice, whose
    adventures will be known to you, and mine too.

PANTALONE   I am happy to know you, sir, and to see you here; I congratulate
    you most heartily on your good fortune.

FLORINDO   Signora Beatrice is to be my wife, and if you will not disdain to do
    us the honor, I hope you will give away the bride.

PANTALONE   Whatever has to be done, let it be done at once. Give her your
    hand.

FLORINDO   Signora Beatrice, I am willing.

BEATRICE   Here is my hand, Signor Florindo.

SMERALDINA (*aside*)   *They* don't want pressing.

PANTALONE   Afterward we will settle up our accounts. You will put yours in order; then we will settle ours.

CLARICE (*to* BEATRICE)   Dear friend, I congratulate you.

BEATRICE (*to* CLARICE)   And I you, with all my heart.

SILVIO (*to* FLORINDO)   Sir, do you know me again?

FLORINDO (*to* SILVIO)   Indeed I do, sir; you would have provoked me to a duel.

SILVIO   'Twas to my own disaster. Here is the adversary
        (*Pointing to* BEATRICE)
who disarmed me and very nearly killed me.

BEATRICE   And gave you your life too, you might say.

SILVIO   'Tis true.

CLARICE   At my entreaty.

SILVIO   That is very true.

PANTALONE   Everything is in order, everything is settled.

TRUFFALDINO   The best is yet to come, ladies and gentlemen.

PANTALONE   What is yet to come?

TRUFFALDINO (*to* FLORINDO, *taking him apart*)   With your good leave, sir, one word.

FLORINDO   What do you want?

TRUFFALDINO   You remember what you promised me, sir?

FLORINDO   What did I promise? I do not recollect.

TRUFFALDINO   To ask Si'or Pantalon' for Smeraldina as my wife.

FLORINDO   Of course, now I remember; I will do so at once.

TRUFFALDINO (*aside*)   I, too, poor man, want to put myself right with the world.

FLORINDO   Signor Pantalone, although this is the first occasion on which I have had the honor of knowing you, I make bold to desire a favor of you.

PANTALONE   You may command me, sir; I will serve you to the best of my powers.

FLORINDO   My manservant desires to marry your maid; have you any objection to giving your consent?

SMERALDINA (*aside*)   Wonderful! Here's another who wants to marry me! Who the devil can he be? I wish I knew him.

PANTALONE   For my part I am agreed.
        (*To* SMERALDINA)
What say you, girl?

SMERALDINA   If I thought he would make a good husband——

PANTALONE   Is he a good honest man, this servant of yours?

FLORINDO   For the short time he has been with me he has certainly proved himself trusty, and he seems to be intelligent.

CLARICE   Signor Florindo, you have anticipated me in something that *I* ought to have done. I was to propose the marriage of my maid with the manservant of Signora Beatrice. You have asked for her for *your* servant, I can say no more.

FLORINDO   No, no; since you so earnestly desire this, I withdraw altogether and leave you completely free.

CLARICE   Indeed, sir, I could never permit myself to have my own wishes preferred to yours. Besides, I must admit that I am not fully authorized. Pray continue in your proposal.

FLORINDO   You say so out of courtesy, madam. Signor Pantalone, I withdraw all that I have said. I will not say another word on behalf of my servant; on the contrary, I am absolutely opposed to his marrying her.

CLARICE   If *your* man is not to marry her, no more shall the other man. We must be fair on both sides.

TRUFFALDINO (*aside*)   Here's a state of things! They pay each other compliments, and meanwhile I am left without a wife at all.

SMERALDINA (*aside*)   It looks as if I should have neither one nor the other.

PANTALONE   Come, we *must* settle it somehow; this poor girl wants to get married, let us give her either to the one or the other.

FLORINDO   Not to *my* man. Nothing shall induce me to do Signora Clarice an injustice.

CLARICE   Nor will I ever tolerate an injustice to Signor Florindo.

TRUFFALDINO   Sir, madam, I can settle the matter myself.
        (*With his usual air of great ingenuity*)
    Si'or Florindo, did you not ask the hand of Smeraldina for your servant?

FLORINDO   I did; did you not hear me?

TRUFFALDINO   And you, Si'ora Clarice, did you not intend Smeraldina to marry the servant of Si'ora Beatrice?

CLARICE   Most certainly I was to do so.

TRUFFALDINO   Good; then if that is so, give me your hand, Smeraldina.

PANTALONE   And pray what right have *you* to ask for her hand?

TRUFFALDINO   Because I am the servant of Si'or Florindo and of Si'ora Beatrice too.

FLORINDO   What?

BEATRICE   What do you say?

TRUFFALDINO   Pray be calm. Si'or Florindo, who asked you to ask Si'or Pantalon' for Smeraldina?

FLORINDO   You did.

TRUFFALDINO   And you, Si'ora Clarice, whom had you in mind as the intended husband of Smeraldina?

CLARICE   Yourself.

TRUFFALDINO   *Ergo*, Smeraldina is mine.

FLORINDO   Signora Beatrice, where is your servant?

BEATRICE   Why, here! Truffaldino, of course.

FLORINDO   Truffaldino? He is *my* servant!

BEATRICE   Is not yours called Pasquale?

FLORINDO   Pasquale? I thought Pasquale was *yours!*

BEATRICE (*to* TRUFFALDINO)   How do you explain this?
        (TRUFFALDINO *makes silent gestures asking for forgiveness.*)

FLORINDO   You rascal!

BEATRICE   You knave!

FLORINDO   So you waited on two masters at once?

TRUFFALDINO   Yes, sir, I did, that was the very trick. I took on the job without thinking; just to see what I could do. It did not last long, 'tis true; but at any rate I can boast that nobody would ever have found me out, if I had not given myself away for love of this girl here. I have done a hard day's work, and I dare say I had my shortcomings, but I hope that in consideration of the fun of the thing, all these ladies and gentlemen will forgive me.

From the Playwright

The Servant of Two Masters *was a decisive turning point in* **Goldoni's** *personal battle between a career in law or the theatre. Finding law lucrative and comedy disappointing, Goldoni was at once ready to abandon attempts at the latter until the noted Italian actor Sacchi requested otherwise (circa* 1749). *The result was* The Servant of Two Masters, *a farce that retained four of the characters of the previously universally popular* Commedia del arte—*Brighella, Pantalone, Lombardi, and Truffaldino (Harlequin). Thereafter, Goldoni continued to make use of the masked characters of the* Commedia *in many of his later comedies, sometimes to lampoon the aristocracy.*

From Memoirs   edited by William Drake

I saw all the Arcadian shepherds who were that day assembled in succession: I dined with some and supped with others. The Pisans are very kind and obliging to strangers, and they conceived a great friendship and consideration for me. I announced myself as a Venetian advocate; I told them part of my adventures; they saw that I was a man without employment, but capable of it; they proposed to me to resume the gown which I had quitted, and they promised me clients and books. Any foreign licentiate may practise at the bar of Pisa; and I undertook boldly to plead as a civil and criminal advocate.

The Pisans were in every way as good as their word, and I was fortunate enough to satisfy them. I laboured night and day; I had more causes than I could undertake; I found out the secret of diminishing the burden to the satisfaction of my clients; I demonstrated to them the folly of litigation, and endeavoured to bring about a reconciliation with adverse parties. They paid me for my consultations, and we were all of us satisfied.

Whilst my affairs were going on prosperously, and my closet was in such a flourishing state as to inspire my brethren with jealousy, the devil, I believe, sent a company of comedians to Pisa. I could not abstain from seeing them, and I was seized with a strong desire to give them something of mine. They were too indifferent actors for me to think of confiding a comedy of character to them; but I abandoned to them my outline of a comedy called the "Hundred and Four Accidents in One Night"; and it was on this occasion I experienced the disagreeable circumstances mentioned in a former part of these memoirs.

Mortified at the failure of my piece, I resolved never more to go near the comedians, or to think of comedy. I redoubled my legal assiduity, and I gained three law-suits the same month.

I also derived infinite honour from a criminal defence. A young man of family had robbed his neighbour. A door had been forced, and the young man was on the point of being condemned to the galleys.

The family was respectable, he was an only son, his sisters were unmarried; all these circumstances stimulated me to endeavour to save him.

After satisfying the party complaining, I caused the lock of his apartments to be changed, so that the key of the other party could not open it. The young man had taken one floor for another; he had opened the door by mistake: and seeing the money spread out, the opportunity had tempted him.

I began my memorial with the seventh verse of the twenty-fifth Psalm: "*Delicta juventutis mea et ignorantias meas ne memineris, Domine,*" "Remember not the sins of my youth, nor my transgressions, O Lord." I strengthened my pleading with classical quotations, decisions of the Roman law and of the Criminal Chamber of Florence, called Il Magistrato degli Otto, the Tribunal of Eight. I employed both reasoning and pathos; he was not a criminal inured to crimes, who endeavoured to palliate his guilt, but a rash and inconsiderate young man who owned his fault, and only asked forgiveness for the sake of the honour of a respectable father and two interesting young women of quality who were fit for marriage.

My youthful robber was at length condemned to remain in prison for three months; the family were very well satisfied with me, and the criminal judge was pleased to compliment me on the occasion.

This attached me more and more to a profession which was at once productive of both honour and pleasure, and a very reasonable profit.

In the midst of my labours and occupations, I received a letter from Venice, which threw all my blood and spirits into commotion. It was a letter from Sacchi.

This comedian had returned to Italy; he knew I was at Pisa; he asked me for a comedy; he even sent me the subject of one, which he left me at freedom to work on as I pleased.

What a temptation for me! Sacchi was an excellent actor; comedy had been my passion; I felt my old taste, my old fire and enthusiasm reviving within me. The subject proposed was "The Servant of Two Masters"; and I easily saw what might be made of it with such an actor as Sacchi. I was therefore devoured with a desire of trying my hand again ... I knew not what to do ... law-suits and clients crowded on me ... but my poor Sacchi ... but the servant with two masters ... Well, for this time ... but I cannot ... yes I can ... At length I wrote in answer that I would undertake it.

I laboured by day for the bar, and by night at my play: I finished the piece, and sent it to Venice. Nobody knew the circumstance; my wife only was in the secret: and she suffered as much as myself. Alas! I passed the nights ...

While I worked at my piece, my doors were closed at night-fall, and I did not pass my evenings in the coffee-house of the Arcadi.

The first time I made my appearance there, I was reproached for my neglect, and I excused myself on account of my increase of business. These gentlemen were very glad to see me employed; but still they were unwilling that I should forget the delightful amusement of poetry.

M. Fabri arrived, and was delighted to see me. He drew a large packet from his pocket, and presented me with two diplomas which he had procured for me; the one was my charter of aggregation to the Arcadi of Rome, under the name of Polisseno; the other gave me the investiture of the Fegean fields. I was on this saluted by the whole assembly in chorus under the name of Polisseno Fegeio, and embraced by them as a fellow-shepherd and brother.

The Arcadians are very rich, as you may perceive, my dear reader; we possess estates in Greece; we water them with our labours for the sake of reaping branches of laurels; and the Turks sow them with grain and plant them with vines, and laugh at both our titles and our songs.

Notwithstanding my occupations, I still composed sonnets, odes, and other pieces of lyrical poetry from time to time for the sittings of our academy.

But however much the Pisans might be satisfied with me, I was not satisfied myself. I must do myself justice; I have never been a good poet. In point of invention perhaps I have not been defective, and the theatre is a proof of it; for my genius took that turn.

Some time afterwards, Sacchi communicated to me the success of my piece. "The Servant of Two Masters" was applauded and drew immense crowds, and he sent me a present which I did not expect; but he demanded another piece still, the subject of which he left entirely to me. He wished, however, as my last comedy had a comic foundation, that this should have an interesting fable for basis, susceptible of sentiment and all the pathos compatible with a comedy.

This was the language of a man; I knew him well; I was very desirous of satisfying him, and his mode of acting engaged me still more to him; but then my closet . . . this kept my mind on the rack again. At my last piece I had said, "Only this once." I had three days to answer him in. During those three days, walking, dining, or sleeping, I thought of nothing but Sacchi; and I was obliged to get this object out of my head to be good for anything else.

In addition to his comments surrounding the authoring of Servant, *Goldoni also offers us a glimpse into the playwright's mind through the below observations on his own dramatic techniques and ideas.*

There are, it seems to me, two kinds of comedy, pure comedy and comedy of intrigue. The first can be written while observing the unity of the place, the second cannot thus be constructed without crudity and incongruity. The ancients had not, as we have, a way to shift scenery, and for this reason they observed all the unities. We comply with the unity of place when the action occurs in the same city, and all the more when it remains in the same house. I conclude, therefore, that if comedy can be constructed in compliance with the unity of place without hairsplitting and unseemliness, it should be done; but if, because of it, absurdities must be introduced, it is better to change the plot and observe the rules of probability.

To make a play succeed, many things of beauty must be united. The least flaw may make it a failure. Though lacking an interesting story, a comedy may have nevertheless many beautiful details; yet, if there is no complication and suspense in the action, it cannot be other than a poor play. The style, too, must be proper to comedy, that is to say, simple and natural, not academic or elevated. The great art lies in adhering to nature in all things, never deviating from it. Sentiments must be true, not affected; expression within the comprehension of all. The commonest traits please more than delicate conceits. Moreover, it is with national morals and customs, with our own foibles and absurdities, that Comedy should be concerned.

Indeed, writing comedies is a difficult business, and I do not flatter myself with the illusion that I shall ever learn just in what comic perfection consists. But this I know, that in order to create wholesome laughter, one must first laugh oneself. When things are said and done with grace, they get a double value. The shorter, therefore, and the more unexpected comic scenes are, the more they please. The principal comedian should act copiously and speak sparingly. When he speaks, he should deliver his thrust pungently and at the right time, not cynically as if under stress. He may be allowed to mutilate expressions naturally, as in dialect, but he must not twist and murder words. Especially should he beware of that cheap innuendo in which so many would-be comedies abound. In order to succeed, you must create something of your own, and to create you must study.

I have also learned not to seek my subject in the associations of crime, but rather to choose it among the merely ridiculous; and to know that while improbability will kill a play, an artistic mixture of the pathetic and the comical is ever an element of surprise. The catastrophe, too, must be in accordance with human nature. Although one may ridicule changes in fashion, head-dress, or summer life in the country, in order to make woman a fit subject for comic attack, the ridicule must be supplied by the vagaries of her mind, not by the whimsies of her heart. Even so, though the presentation of a female character may thus be comic in its own right, it has to be propt up by interesting and pleasing situations, else it may easily bore.

I used to go through four processes before taking up the construction and final polishing of a play. The first step was the making of the outline with its division into the three principal parts: the exposition, the arch of the plot, and the catastrophe. The second step consisted in the apportioning of the action among acts and scenes; the third in the dialoguing of the most interesting incidents, the fourth in the general dialoguing of the whole.

It often happened that, when the last process was reached, I had by that time changed everything I had done in the second and third, for ideas succeed one another, one scene produces the next, a word found by chance suggests a new thought. After a time, therefore, I came to combine the four operations into one. With the plot and the three divisions constantly in mind, I now begin at once: Act One, Scene One; so I proceed to the end, ever remembering that the lines must converge toward a single point, determined beforehand, that is to say, toward the climax of the action, which is the principal part of the play, and for which it appears that all the machinery of planning and constructing has been set in motion.

In my climaxes I have rarely been mistaken. I can say this with assurance, for the whole world has told me so. Besides, the problem does not seem difficult to me. It is, on the contrary, quite easy to find a satisfying solution when you provide for it at the beginning of the play and do not lose sight of it in the course of the work. Tastes, however, keep on changing from day to day, and my comedies, which are now triumphant, will surely become mere rubbish in the course of time.

Indeed, all comedy becomes old-fashioned in the long run, however well it may have been written, or revamped and revived. But the manner of writing it, I hope, always has room in which to improve. True and recognizable characters never grow stale, and although their number is not infinite in kind, it is infinite in species, since every virtue, every vice, every custom, every defect assumes its hue from the continuously varying circumstances which surround it.

From the Critic

In Goldoni and the Venice of His Time, **Joseph Spencer Kennard's** *exhaustive study of Italy's most prolific playwright, the author makes the point that Goldoni was no real reformer in the manner of Molière. Though believing in reform, Kennard says, Goldoni nevertheless chided more universal wrongdoings—evil, greed—rather than concentrating on his native Venice. This, in part, is responsible for the huge appeal of a Goldoni play, offering a broader base of identity. When Kennard wrote the biography (1920), "farce" was not a popular word, but much of his description of Goldoni's style reflects this style.*

From
Goldoni and the Venice of His Time

Furthermore Goldoni is above all a playwright, conscious of the absolute necessity of satisfying his audience. "Let us even agree that, according to natural principles, virtue is to be preferred to birth and wealth, there still remains the impellent duty to proclaim on the stage that morality which is more generally approved and practised."

Could he do more than suggest those changes which he thought might raise the common level? Could he have done more without jeopardising his position in Venice, his literary fame?

Before settling this point one should remember Goldoni's sunny nature and natural optimism, his respect for aristocracy as a caste, and his personal obligation to some of its members, and, above all, Goldoni's literary principles and the conception he adopted of comedy, comedy reformed but still a continuation of ancient comedy.[1]

Neither the aristocratic origin of the classical comedy, nor the literary development of the popular comedy tended to a transformation which, in any case, Goldoni would not have accepted. He was neither philosopher nor politician; and the Italian comedy was not a vehicle for abstract thesis, or for the propaganda of social doctrines. Goldoni was not a satirist, and the role of the Italian comedy was not satire. Every attempt made in later times, in imitation of foreign methods, adds evidence to this assertion. Goldoni, obeying his natural propensity, adhering to the teachings of example and tradition, never allowed his comedy to stray into forbidden paths.

He knew what aim and what means were proper to his art and what object he must keep in view, a lay sermon about the ways of the world, a mild chiding of frivolities and petty sins, a forcible picture of things that he considered pernicious. He is an optimist and believes in the possibility of reform. When family tyranny is pilloried in his plays, he expects the household tyrant to relax; when he has vividly painted the hateful sin of avarice, he believes that purse-strings will be loosened; when cicisbeism has been ridiculed he feels sure that some *cavaliere servente* will be converted to more manly feelings.

Of such stuff no satirist, no humourist is made. Goldoni pursued his work, not aiming very high, not aspiring at great results, but satisfied that some good must come of his teachings. Hence the benevolence of his representation in almost every case; hence his vigour in attacking those sins which he thinks are most likely to be corrected.

---

[1]Francesco De Sanctis in *Storia della Letteratura Italiana*, vol. ii, page 384 and *passim*, thus qualifies Goldoni's work: " His scanty classical training secured him the advantage of keeping his mind free from anything that was not modern and contemporary. That which he aims at is not the classical comedy obedient to the literary rules of the Latin or the Tuscans but that which he called good comedy . . . which conception of good comedy he summed in these words: 'All the application I spend on the construction of my plays tends merely to reproduce nature without spoiling her.' "

Further on, De Sanctis adds: "His character was idyllic, superior to all backbiting and petty rivalries common among Italian men of letters; he accepted good or evil luck with the same unruffled spirits and lived out his span of full eighty-six years and died in Paris a few years after Metastasio's death in Venice. He used to say of himself, 'My moral is like my physical temper; I fear neither cold nor warm weather, I never take fire in anger, nor do I allow joy to inebriate me.' With such a temperament qualifying him rather for the role of spectator than of actor, while others acted Goldoni observed and painted from the life. He believed that nature well observed is richer than all the compositions of fantasy. Art was for him nature; it was the imitation of reality. He is the Galileo of a renovated literature. His telescope was the clear and immediate intuition of reality; his guide was common sense. As Galileo proscribed from the study of science all occultism, all conjectures, all supernaturalism, thus Goldoni would have banished out of the dominion of art all that is fantastic, grotesque, emphatic, and rhetorical. That which Molière had done for France, he wished to do for Italy, the classical land of rhetoric. His reform was far more important than it seems at first sight, because starting from comedy it was grounded on a universal principle; namely naturalness as opposed to mannerism and conventionalism . . . "

In the analysis of his plays we have seen that Goldoni directs his hardest blows against abuse of power, against meanness and every form of selfishness. Another general tendency of his is to encourage the civic virtues that make life's burden easier to bear. Thus Goldoni's ideal manhood is not merely kindness, benevolence, the absence of vice, but it is the man who works hard, and yet does not complain. Il Cortesan, il Cavaliere, l'Avvacato, Pantalone, his favourites, are gay, active, eager to enjoy life and make life enjoyable for those who depend on them. The miser, the grumbler, the gossip, his peculiar bugbears, are miserable people and make life a burden to their dependents. Even in women he admires the active spirit, the mirthful disposition, that blesses all those that come within reach; while his blackest sin is the mixture of extravagance and shrewishness which characterises Beatrice.

Altogether the most unassuming program and the most modest aim a reformer ever proposed; but one which he has better fulfilled than the more magniloquent declarations and more presuming aims of any of his predecessors, obtaining more lasting effects than any one of his contemporaries, effects that have not only outlived his time but which seem to be still growing. While every other playwright barely keeps his rank in handbooks of literature, or, at best, finds at long intervals a flash of glory in some official recital; whilst even Molière is relegated within the sanctuary of appointed nights à la Comedie Francaise whenever it pleases a famous actor to measure his force in the pieces du rèpertoire, and while Shakespeare is the bugbear of the manager who thinks chiefly of box office receipts, Goldoni is continually performed all over Italy in every possible manner. He is a household god, an old acquaintance, a friend for every Italian-speaking man, woman, or child. In villages and in schools he is as welcome as in the greatest theatres. The best and the humblest among Italian players are glad to impersonate Goldonian characters, and troupes that specialise in this performance are increasing every day, and they are sure to find moderate gains and satisfactory welcome wherever they appear.

It would be interesting to show the very great influence exerted by Goldoni, not only on the Italian modern comedy, but on the whole literary evolution of his country and also in the remodelling of the Italian national character, out of the blending and mixing of regional and racial elements; to measure the quality of Goldoni's realism as compared to Manzoni's and his humour so curiously akin to the slyly satirical vein pervading immortal Promessi Sposi. But such a study would require a full development.

From the Director

I directed Goldoni's The Servant of two Masters *myself in June of 1971. It proved to be a worthwhile adventure. For many of us in the community college (and other small colleges), undertaking a directing assignment also involves acting as designer, costumer, technical director, etc., with student help. This involves more work but fewer problems with coordination. Thus I am able to offer my comments below on aspects of the entire production, having been in charge of each respective area.*

Directing for Laughter

The first task a director faces in producing a play is how to fall in love with it. And since in academia, at least, farce never really gained a firm footing in the collegiate door, the college director might be hesitant to attempt such "unworthy stuff." To perform *Medea* and *Charley's Aunt* the same year may have once seemed imbalanced, but not any longer. Plays such as *A Flea in Her Ear*, *An Italian Straw Hat*, and *A Servant of Two Masters* (and some of Molière) are cropping up continually in seasonal junior and senior college listings. And with good reason, for "thoughtless laughter" is not only enjoyable, it is necessary—necessary that an audience relax, at least for one night, and have their funnybones tickled.

Of all the plays available, a period farce or comedy has always remained my favorite. It is a director's manna, a gift from the playwright's heaven. Add a dash of direction to a riotous script and an audience's love for laughter, and you head for success. Such is the case with *The Servant of Two Masters*. (Modern farce, say, Neil Simon's, does not lend itself at all to most of the techniques to be discussed.) Hence, I proceeded on the premise that laughter was my goal, despite the fact that Goldoni was vaguely moral in intention when writing *Servant*.

BACKGROUND

When Goldoni sat down to write *Servant*, he was heavily influenced by the *Commedia del arte*, the theatre of improvisation which had been existing since about 1550. Goldoni had been writing scenarios for various troupes of the *Commedia* (brief plot outlines the actors followed while improvising action, business, and dialogue), but about 1745 he began experimenting with the inclusion of the stock *Commedia* characters into a totally written script. Into *Servant* he incorporared four of the traditional masked *Commedia* characters—Pantalone, Brighella, Lombardi (Dottore) and Truffaldino (Harlequin), but altered some of the usual characterization. Pantalone had appeared miserly and sinister; Goldoni makes him a respectable, if somewhat lightheaded, merchant. Brighella was usually portrayed as a conniving and cunning scoundrel; Goldoni underplays this characteristic.

MASKS

Goldoni also called for the discontinuation of the *Commedia* mask, and most American directors will agree. For me, any use of three-dimensional masks would have three disadvantages. Their use somewhat confuses the audience (though this is surely the weakest argument against them); they make the actors feel awkward, forever wondering if the masks will stay on while never really having a full range of vision; and their use eliminates the comic response to the facial expressions of the actors, which is the greatest drawback.

To remedy this, we used make-up masks. This technique tred a middle ground by staying true to the *Commedia* while also defining the character without inhibiting facial expressions (see photos).

The *Commedia* itself, besides giving us such terms as "zanny" and "slapstick" plus broadening the base of all farce, also directly contributed to the character "Punch" of the English Punch and Judy shows and our own circus clowns. We were able to make use of the latter to bridge each scene change, a potential headache. Rather than simply dimming out with each character taking his place in the dark, we created two "clowns" in full costume and make-up who served to move each character in place and draw or undraw the curtains as needed. In the beginning of the play they utilized two huge "keys" to "wind up" each character and give them life. As a transitory device, it solved our problem; as an adjunct to the pace and spontaniety of the entire play, the use of the clowns proved our most successful innovation.

SETTING

The play is ideally suited for any type stage, proscenium, arena, or thrust. In our case we utilized our modified proscenium and attempted to simulate the "makeshift" stage common to the traveling *Commedia* companies. This was accomplished by two sets of canvas "curtains" hung on wooden poles, rather than by using the act curtain. On the back set was painted a Venetian street scene, serving as Pantalone's courtyard and a street. When opened the area became a room in Brighella's Inn. The front curtain, twelve feet from the apron, functioned as the background to Brighella's Inn, with the point at which the curtains met becoming the doorway. This forestage area also served as a room in Pantalone's house. Changes of locale in this area were undertaken by our clowns hanging the appropriate signs rather than by a painted scene (see photo). The setting, along with the play, was and ought to be highly "theatrical."

I would also suggest the use of music. A light, fast-paced harpsichord or string quartet might do. We made use of *Switched On Bach*, an electronic rendition, played during the scene shifts performed by the clowns.

COSTUME

Traditional costumes should be employed for the four masked characters. Pantalone should be dressed in red and/or pink, with a loose cap and turned-up slippers (nose putty, also, by all means!). Lombardi, the doctor of laws who brandishes his Latin like a sword, could be costumed in black with a large white ruffled collar. Some form of hat should also be used. Be certain to put Brighella in white or beige. We gave him a baker's hat and a rolling pin. The traditional checkerboard or diamond pattern costume ought to be worn by Truffaldino with a belt to hold his stick plus a goofy hat. Also, we found it effective to mirror the costumes of both the clowns and Truffaldino by dividing the ground cloth in varying rectangles and squares, and using about six different bright colors for the entire floor. The result was carnival, a fine reflection of the gaity of the play.

PACE

Any slowing of the pace in farce invites disaster. If any one overriding thought must be kept in mind, it's that the movement and pace must be kept quick. Have plenty of movement, spending extra time to rehearse those scenes where timing and pace serve to heighten laughter. We needed extra rehearsal time for the eating scene (and also found it necessary to stick down most of the dishes and plates). Entrances must be very close to the point of action in this scene since rapidity is so important. In addition, the many times Beatrice and Florindo "just miss" each other should be played almost overlapping.

BUSINESS AND LANGUAGE

In the *Commedia del arte, lazzi*, or comic business runs rampant. A wise director will make use of as much slapstick and buffoonery as possible. You will also find it to your advantage to encourage the cast to suggest any additional pieces of business or action that might raise a laugh. You may find some very inventive suggestions.

Latitude can be extended to many of the characters, depending, of course, on ability. We allowed our clowns room for much improvisation, and the four masked characters can, true to their *Commedia* heritage, add slight bits or business or alter various lines depending on their wit, the audience responsiveness, etc. Our Brighella developed a stutter one evening that could only be halted by shouting an expletive before his next word; Lombardi incorporated timely political barbs here and there during his tirades with Pantalone; Florindo kicked Truffaldino when he was handed his coat from the trunk that the prop girl had accidentally buttoned; and Truffaldino passed out pieces of bread to the audience during the curtain call.

Other small bits we found useful:

1. Play as much to the audience as possible: they adore it. For instance, when Truffaldino was beaten by both Beatrice and Florindo we had him leave the stage and run in front of the first row.
2. Change a number of lines beforehand so they become colloquial or topical.
3. Have the portrait of Florindo Truffaldino finds in the coat a caricature, or at least totally outlandish. Have him show it to the audience on the line, "There's a handsome man!"
4. Make Truffaldino's slap-stick out of two separate pieces of wood, fastened together so they "slap" together when he is beaten. The sound, and thus the humor, is magnified.
5. The first waiter should be an old man.
6. Be certain to have movement in the opening scene. The potential for any expository scene to become tedious is strong. Try to combat this with pace and movement, but do not sacrifice the seriousness of the betrothal. Wait for Truffaldino's entrance before really letting loose.

7. When Truffaldino chews the bread, make use of exaggerated facial expressions. We found it effective to have him sit on the edge of the stage apron. In fact, exaggerate as many facial and character reactions as possible. Farce allows for that.
8. Pasquale must be made to appear totally believable.
9. In Act Two, Scene One, when Smeraldina is berating Silvio for being so insensitive, let her become a literal pest to him.
10. Most audiences over ten years of age laugh heartily at anything even slightly risque. Truffaldino's relationship with Smeraldina can be handled this way, and since they are servants this is easier to accept. For example, we had Truffaldino constantly maneuvering to be kissed. The entire scene between these two is laden with comic possibilities.
11. Much can be made of Truffaldino's ravenous desire to eat.

The imaginative director will be able to add many more suggestions to the above list, aware at all times that he does so for the avowed purpose of making the audience laugh.

CHARACTER

A word of warning: the person who plays Truffaldino must be a fine comic actor, capable of much inventiveness, possessing a shrewd sense of timing and able to run through every emotion in the book. He must at all times be a lovable rascal, for it is not so much the dialogue that provokes the humor in *Servant*, but the character and situation. To be made most of, Truffaldino must be able to extract the maximum amount of humor from these situations.

Silvio and Clarice should be young and naive, while Smeraldina could be made saucy and temperamental, displaying no disrespect until the letter scene with Truffaldino and Pantalone. Pantalone himself would prove effectual by being a rapid talker, high pitched and "flitty," a contrast to Lombardi, whose Latin weighs him down occasionally like some great suit of armor. Beatrice and Florindo ought be played straight, although exaggeration may rear itself when each grieves for the death of the other. The porters and second waiter are self-explanatory, the former preferably barefooted, the latter in sandals or some similar footware.

CONCLUSION

Putting it all together, a director has chosen a winner with *The Servant of Two Masters*. The play is ripe for all sorts of comic complications, improvisations and imagination. The many asides are also a boon, and the lattitude with make-up, costume and staging offer much room for invention. The audience is certain to love your choice.

Source Materials for *The Servant of Two Masters*

BY THE PLAYWRIGHT

Memoirs of Goldoni, translated by John Black. New York and London: Knopf, 1926.

BY THE CRITICS

Kennard, J. S. *Goldoni and the Venice of His Time*. New York: Macmillan, 1920.
de Sanctis, F. *History of Italian Literature*, translated by Joan Redfern. New York: Harcourt, 1931.
Symonds, J. A. *Renaissance in Italy*. New York: Modern Library, 1935.

BY THE DIRECTORS

Dent, Edward. "Directorial Notes." In *The Classic Theatre, Vol. I*, edited by Eric Bentley. New York: Doubleday, pp. 378–381.

Realism

Realism has been the stage's most dominant mode of presentation. Most plays, even in the contemporary theatre, attempt to create an "illusion of reality"—meaning a belief in staging the play with concern for detail so as to give the impression of re-creating life. Realism began as a method of correcting the outmoded and outdated traditions of society, as well as a technique for staging. In combination, these two aspects of nineteenth century thought produced more revolutionary changes on the stage than any earlier dramatic period, with many of these changes remaining today.

The Beginnings

By the mid-nineteenth century a general dissatisfaction with Romanticism pervaded literary Europe, though it was to be twenty-five years before the *stage* reflected this view (the drama has many times lagged behind the rest of the literary world). Conditions caused by the Industrial Revolution were now fully realized, and the Continent had just seen another major revolution. The idealization of men and the escapist dreams the theatre provided no longer seemed close enough to reality for solving man's problems. These new directions were nurtured further by Charles Darwin and Auguste Comte—exponents of science and sociology—who preached that heredity and environment were the primary determinents of existence.

Taking his cue from these contributing factors, the realist believed that the behavior of man could be explained by the deterministic composition of man's ancestors and the environment in which he was born. It was not the individual who was so much at fault, but rather the society that perpetuated the existing outdated traditions. In the face of scientific data and objective observation, society could not be forgiven for the outmoded beliefs about man it fostered. Civilization, instead, must be blamed for allowing these abhorrent conditions to exist. This is why Anton Checkov could say, "My duty is to show the real so that we may change for the future." In addition, since man was not the superior being he claimed to be (if he was, how could he have allowed his surroundings to so deteriorate?), then he, too, was subject to the same scientific investigation and analysis as the lower forms of life. If man was indeed an animal, determined by factors outside his control, the application of science and the upsetting of tradition could now serve in the amelioration of his suffering.

This particular concept challenged even the existence of God, although indirectly. Since man's lot was determined by heredity and environment—conditions beyond the control of the individual—then God must exist as a dispassionate and unconcerned observer (if, indeed, he existed at all), having as little effect on men as they have on God. If this were the case, the realist reasoned, then it became the duty and obligation of science to improve the plight of men in their present world. *This* world should be made the better world, thus the physical, psychological, and sociological conditions of man demanded change—the change that only rational and corrective thought could give it. If romanticism dealt with man as he should be, realism would deal with man as he is. If melodrama portrayed men artificially, realism would picture him accurately. If classicism asked actors for grand and sweeping gestures, realism would request they mirror life—once removed. Since so many of the other kinds of drama *escaped* from reality, the realist would meet it head-on. Obviously, this approach generated much criticism, but the realist countered that he was simply representing the aspects of a daily world. Hence the critic, instead of denouncing the playwright who reported these conditions, ought to channel his efforts into improving them.

The Realistic Playwrights

Like most other modes of the drama, realism had its roots in literature, but the first realist of any significance on the stage was Alexandre Dumas *fils*. His *Camille*, dealing with a prostitute, was explicit enough to have its opening delayed five years. Despite the play's lifelike characterization (Dumas *fils* did know someone very much like his heroine) and its unhappy ending (Marguerite dies), *Camille* nevertheless displayed the romantic tendency to adorn its heroine with extraordinary virtue.

Dumas *fils*, nevertheless, was concerned with social problems, and his plays dealt with subjects such as divorce and illegitimate children. But the playwright could not discontinue moralizing, and his plays became "stage preaching," generally termed "thesis plays." In all, Dumas *fils* can be credited with more than just scratching the surface. His honesty in dealing with men as they actually are was uncommon in his day.

Henrik Ibsen of Norway was the giant among the realists. Realistic drama achieved its full maturity with Ibsen's iconoclastic attacks on society's false values. In his plays—particularly during the period 1880 to 1890—Ibsen castigated a society that forced the individual to live with false values, and criticized severely the people who perpetuated these faithless tenets. In *Ghosts*, for example, Mrs. Alving persuades herself (along with the help of Pastor Manders) that no matter how injurious it may prove to her family or herself, society demands a happy marriage of a woman. It therefore becomes necessary, at all costs, to maintain this facade. In *The Wild Duck*, Ibsen presents the belief that all men need certain illusions to live by. Any meddling by outside do-gooders seeking to destroy those illusions becomes more dangerous than the illusions.

In his attempt to capture reality, Ibsen painted lifelike characters who communicated in everyday language: no more asides or soliloquies, no more direct address to the audience. Furthermore, there was little overt action. Crisp dialogue, vivid characterization, and a damning theme replaced the romanticized staging the realist considered out of step with scientific man.

Paralleling Ibsen was Russia's greatest dramatist, Anton Chekhov. By extreme analysis and poignant characterization Chekhov sought to help his mother country advance toward the future. In *The Cherry Orchard*, where the aristocratic upper class is shown still clinging to old-fashioned values, Chekhov attempted to show the inability of these values "to cope with the modern world," as Chekhov himself stated. In other plays Chekhov reproved what he considered the outdated codes of morality and ideals of the Russian aristocracy. In effect, Chekhov was to Russia what Ibsen was to Norway.

As an early defender of Ibsen, George Bernard Shaw was later to work at upsetting his Victorian England. In *Mrs. Warren's Profession*, prostitution was, for the first time in a major work, dealt with not as a damning blot on the soul of humanity. And the belief that war was not as glorious as the English pretended it to be was presented in *Arms and the Man*. (It was Shaw's philosophy, more than his style of writing, that agreed with the ideas of the realists.) Shaw believed that the drama must have a purpose in examining the values of men. Hence, he always was ready to burst the bubble of obsolete tradition.

For the realists, then, change was the watchword. Realism sought to strip away the facade of sentimental escapism pervading the theatre and to objectively examine and present man as he is. Understanding replaced moralizing; science replaced metaphysics. These were plays of ideas, not action; of criticizing tradition instead of perpetuating it. Realism propounded "art for truth's sake," not "art for art's sake."

The Realist Directors

Even before the realistic dramatist began attacking the ideas of theatre, the director was questioning the drama's method of staging. Guided by their distaste for the artificial and regimented styles of acting and stage production common to the stage in the nineteenth century, theatre directors began to clamor for change. The first of these important men was a theatre-buff monarch, the Duke of Saxe-Meiningen, a small province in Germany. Though the Duke was a virtual dictator inside the playhouse, his contributions to the realistic stage were revolutionary. He insisted on long periods of rehearsal, himself in full command. His acting troupe toured Europe emphasizing "ensemble acting"—scenes in which the actors' groupings realistically simulated life, talking and moving normally, and playing their roles in conjunction with each other, rather than artificially strolling to the stage apron and directing lines to the audience.

The Duke also sought integration of the actors with the setting by designing realistic scenery and insisting the action take place within the set, which he considered a functional part of performance rather than a stage ornament. His work in the careful preparation of mob scenes led to a concern for the effect of "total performance," to the exclusion of the "star system" formerly familiar to the stage. He carefully planned all action and blocked all movement. The Duke's objective was to achieve complete verisimilitude, and to do this he adopted three-dimensional scenery and historically accurate settings in conjunction with "natural" acting.

The Duke and his followers transformed the idea of the "fourth wall"—the proscenium, or "picture frame" stage—into a doctrine basic to realism. The actor was to move behind this frame, in back of the proscenium arch, so that the setting would become the actor's environment. No longer would the players admit to the presence of the audience. Backs would be turned, furniture would now be placed facing three sides rather than toward front, and a physical and psychological barrier would be maintained. Dramatic action, not personal style, would be emphasized. The goal of each actor would be to create complete belief in the character he was portraying.

These techniques are as common to today's theatre as they were innovative to the theatre of the nineteenth century. Using the traditional plays of Shakespeare and Schiller, the Duke transformed a once artificial and bombastic portrayal into an electrifying performance on his tours throughout Europe. The director now was becoming the hub of the theatrical wheel, and the stage the mirror of life. Later directors, who saw or heard the Duke —Antoine of Paris, Brahm of Germany, Stanislavski of Russia—continued these revolutionary transitions to make the theatre once more a place of change.

Like naturalism, realism lost its appeal as a complete stage entity, but its effects on drama still are evident. The picture frame stage still dominates our college and community theatres (though a modified proscenium, or "thrust" stage, is becoming increasingly popular); ensemble acting still governs our stage groupings; and the director has emerged as the center around which all aspects of production revolve. Even most forms of the drama evolving this century still concern themselves with picturing man as he is (expressionism, theatre of the absurd), and though their orientation may differ, most believe it is their duty to analyze, examine, and report. Realism, then, has continued to influence and mold the theatre.

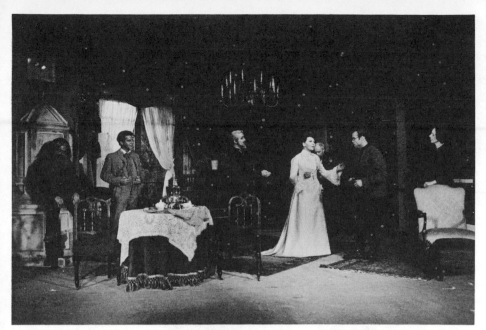

Note how posture and expression help define each easily recognizable character in *The Cherry Orchard*. IASTA production, University of Denver. Photo by Richard W. Purdie.

The futility of Ranevsky and her brother Gaev appear evident in this scene from *The Cherry Orchard*. Tyrone Guthrie, director; Tanya Moiseiwitsch designer; starring Jessica Tandy (Minnesota Theatre Company.)

Lopahin argues vainly with Gayev to sell the Cherry Orchard. Asolo State Theatre. Robert Strane, director.

Madam Ranevsky appears happy upon returning home to her cherry orchard. University of South Florida. Mesrop Kesdekian director; Russell G. Whaley, designer.

The Past is like a funeral gone by,
The Future comes like an unwelcome guest.
Edmund Goose

The Cherry Orchard

Anton Chekhov

The Cherry Orchard

Translated by Constance Garnett

Characters   MADAME RANEVSKY (LYUBOV ANDREYEVNA), *the owner of the Cherry Orchard*
ANYA, *her daughter, aged 17*
VARYA, *her adopted daughter, aged 24*
GAEV (LEONID ANDREYEVITCH), *brother of* MADAME RANEVSKY
LOPAHIN (YERMOLAY ALEXEYEVITCH), *a Merchant*
TROFIMOV (PYOTR SERGEYEVITCH), *a Student*
SEMYÓNOV-PISHTCHIK, *a Landowner*
CHARLOTTA IVANOVNA, *a Governess*
EPIHODOV (SEMYON PANTALEYEVITCH), *a Clerk*
DUNYASHA, *a Maid*
FIRS, *an old Valet, aged 87*
YASHA, *a young Valet*
A VAGRANT
THE STATION MASTER
A POST-OFFICE CLERK
VISITORS, SERVANTS

Scene   The action takes place on the estate of MADAME RANEVSKY.

Act One

A room, which has always been called the nursery. One of the doors leads into ANYA'S *room. Dawn, sun rises during the scene. May, the cherry trees in flower, but it is cold in the garden with the frost of early morning. Windows closed.*

    Enter DUNYASHA *with a candle and* LOPAHIN *with a book in his hand.*

LOPAHIN   The train's in, thank God. What time is it?

DUNYASHA   Nearly two o'clock (*puts out the candle*). It's daylight already.

LOPAHIN   The train's late! Two hours, at least (*yawns and stretches*). I'm a pretty one; what a fool I've been. Came here on purpose to meet them at the station and dropped asleep. . . . Dozed off as I sat in the chair. It's annoying. . . . You might have waked me.

DUNYASHA   I thought you had gone (*listens*). There, I do believe they're coming!

LOPAHIN (*listens*)   No, what with the luggage and one thing and another (*a pause*). Lyubov Andreyevna has been abroad five years; I don't know what she is like now. . . . She's a splendid woman. A good-natured, kind-hearted woman. I remember when I was a lad of fifteen, my poor father—he used to keep a little shop here in the village in those days—gave me a punch in the face with his fist and made my nose bleed. We were in the yard here, I forget what we'd come about—he had had a drop. Lyubov Andreyevna—I can see her now—she was a slim young girl then —took me to wash my face, and then brought me into this very room, into the nursery. "Don't cry, little peasant," says she, "it will be well in time for your wedding day" . . . (*a pause*). Little peasant. . . . My father was a peasant, it's true, but here am I in a white waistcoat and brown shoes, like a pig in a bun shop. Yes, I'm a rich man, but for all my money, come to think, a peasant I was, and a peasant I am (*turns over the pages of the book*). I've been reading this book and I can't make head or tail of it. I fell asleep over it (*a pause*).

DUNYASHA   The dogs have been awake all night, they feel that the mistress is coming.

LOPAHIN   Why, what's the matter with you, Dunyasha?

DUNYASHA   My hands are all of a tremble. I feel as though I should faint.

LOPAHIN   You're a spoilt soft creature, Dunyasha. And dressed like a lady too, and your hair done up. That's not the thing. One must know one's place.

> (*Enter* EPIHODOV *with a nosegay; he wears a pea-jacket and highly polished creaking topboots; he drops the nosegay as he comes in.*)

EPIHODOV (*picking up the nosegay*)   Here! the gardener's sent this, says you're to put it in the dining-room (*gives* DUNYASHA *the nosegay*).

LOPAHIN   And bring me some kvass.

DUNYASHA   I will (*goes out*).

EPIHODOV   It's chilly this morning, three degrees of frost, though the cherries are all in flower. I can't say much for our climate (*sighs*). I can't. Our climate is not often propitious to the occasion. Yermolay Alexeyevitch, permit me to call your attention to the fact that I purchased myself a pair of boots the day before yesterday, and they creak, I venture to assure you, so that there's no tolerating them. What ought I to grease them with?

LOPAHIN   Oh, shut up! Don't bother me.

EPIHODOV   Every day some misfortune befalls me. I don't complain, I'm used to it, and I wear a smiling face.

> (DUNYASHA *comes in, hands* LOPAHIN *the kvass.*)

EPIHODOV   I am going (*stumbles against a chair, which falls over*). There! (*As though triumphant*) There you see now, excuse the expression, an accident like that among others. . . . It's positively remarkable (*goes out*).

DUNYASHA   Do you know, Yermolay Alexeyevitch, I must confess, Epihodov has made me a proposal.

LOPAHIN   Ah!

DUNYASHA   I'm sure I don't know. . . . He's a harmless fellow, but sometimes when he begins talking, there's no making anything of it. It's all very fine and expressive, only there's no understanding it. I've a sort of liking for him too. He loves me to distraction. He's an unfortunate man; every day there's something. They tease him about it—two and twenty misfortunes they call him.

LOPAHIN (*listening*)   There! I do believe they're coming.

DUNYASHA   They are coming! What's the matter with me? . . . I'm cold all over.

LOPAHIN   They really are coming. Let's go and meet them. Will she know me? It's five years since I saw her.

DUNYASHA (*in a flutter*)   I shall drop this very minute. . . . Ah, I shall drop.

> (*There is a sound of two carriages driving up to the house.* LOPAHIN *and* DUNYASHA *go out quickly. The stage is left empty. A noise is heard in the adjoining rooms.* FIRS, *who has driven to meet* MADAME RANEVSKY, *crosses the stage hurriedly leaning on a stick. He is wearing old-fashioned livery and a high hat. He says something to himself, but not a word can be distinguished. The noise behind the scenes goes on increasing. A voice: "Come, let's go in here." Enter* LYUBOV ANDREYEVNA, ANYA, *and* CHARLOTTA IVANOVNA *with a pet dog on a chain, all in travelling dresses.* VARYA *in an out-door coat with a kerchief over her head,* GAEV, SEMYONOV-PISHTCHIK, LOPAHIN, DUNYASHA *with bag and parasol, servants with other articles. All walk across the room.*)

ANYA   Let's come in here. Do you remember what room this is, mamma?

LYUBOV (*joyfully, through her tears*)   The nursery!

VARYA   How cold it is, my hands are numb. (*To* LYUBOV ANDREYEVNA) Your rooms, the white room and the lavender one, are just the same as ever, mamma.

LYUBOV   My nursery, dear delightful room. . . . I used to sleep here when I was little . . . (*cries*). And here I am, like a little child . . . (*kisses her brother and* VARYA, *and then her brother again*). Varya's just the same as ever, like a nun. And I knew Dunyasha (*kisses* DUNYASHA).

GAEV   The train was two hours late. What do you think of that? Is that the way to do things?

CHARLOTTA (*to* PISHTCHIK)   My dog eats nuts, too.

PISHTCHIK (*wonderingly*)   Fancy that!

> (*They all go out except* ANYA *and* DUNYASHA.)

DUNYASHA   We've been expecting you so long (*takes* ANYA's *hat and coat*).

ANYA   I haven't slept for four nights on the journey. I feel dreadfully cold.

DUNYASHA   You set out in Lent, there was snow and frost, and now? My darling! (*Laughs and kisses her*) I *have* missed you, my precious, my joy. I must tell you . . . I can't put it off a minute. . . .

ANYA (*wearily*)   What now?

DUNYASHA   Epihodov, the clerk, made me a proposal just after Easter.

ANYA   It's always the same thing with you . . . (*straightening her hair*). I've lost all my hairpins . . . (*she is staggering from exhaustion*).

DUNYASHA   I don't know what to think, really. He does love me, he does love me so!

ANYA (*looking towards her door, tenderly*)   My own room, my windows just as though I had never gone away. I'm home! Tomorrow morning I shall get up and run into the garden. . . . Oh, if I could get to sleep! I haven't slept all the journey, I was so anxious and worried.

DUNYASHA   Pyotr Sergeyevitch came the day before yesterday.

ANYA (*joyfully*)   Petya!

DUNYASHA   He's asleep in the bath house, he has settled in there. I'm afraid of being in their way, says he. (*Glancing at her watch*) I was to have waked him, but Varvara Mihalovna told me not to. Don't you wake him, says she.

(*Enter* VARYA *with a bunch of keys at her waist.*)

VARYA   Dunyasha, coffee and make haste. . . . Mamma's asking for coffee.

DUNYASHA   This very minute (*goes out*).

VARYA   Well, thank God, you've come. You're home again (*petting her*). My little darling has come back! My precious beauty has come back again!

ANYA   I have had a time of it!

VARYA   I can fancy.

ANYA   We set off in Holy Week—it was so cold then, and all the way Charlotta would talk and show off her tricks. What did you want to burden me with Charlotta for?

VARYA   You couldn't have travelled all alone, darling. At seventeen!

ANYA   We got to Paris at last, it was cold there—snow. I speak French shockingly. Mamma lives on the fifth floor, I went up to her and there were a lot of French people, ladies, an old priest with a book. The place smelt of tobacco and so comfortless. I felt sorry, oh! so sorry for mamma all at once, I put my arms round her neck, and hugged her and wouldn't let her go. Mamma was as kind as she could be, and she cried. . . .

VARYA (*through her tears*)   Don't speak of it, don't speak of it!

ANYA   She had sold her villa at Mentone, she had nothing left, nothing. I hadn't a farthing left either, we only just had enough to get here. And mamma doesn't understand! When we had dinner at the stations, she always ordered the most expensive things and gave the waiters a whole rouble. Charlotta's just the same. Yasha too must have the same as we do; it's simply awful. You know Yasha is mamma's valet now, we brought him here with us.

VARYA   Yes, I've seen the young rascal.

ANYA   Well, tell me—have you paid the arrears on the mortgage?

VARYA   How could we get the money?

ANYA   Oh, dear! Oh, dear!

VARYA   In August the place will be sold.

ANYA   My goodness!

LOPAHIN (*peeps in at the door and moos like a cow*)   Moo! (*Disappears.*)

VARYA (*weeping*)   There, that's what I could do to him (*shakes her fist*).

ANYA (*embracing* VARYA, *softly*)   Varya, has he made you an offer? (VARYA *shakes her head*) Why, but he loves you. Why is it you don't come to an understanding? What are you waiting for?

VARYA   I believe that there never will be anything between us. He has a lot to do, he has no time for me . . . and takes no notice of me. Bless the man, it makes me miserable to see him. . . . Everyone's talking of our being married, everyone's congratulating me, and all the while there's really nothing in it; it's all like a dream! (*In another tone*) You have a new brooch like a bee.

ANYA (*mournfully*)   Mamma bought it. (*Goes into her own room and in a light-hearted childish tone*) And you know, in Paris I went up in a balloon!

VARYA   My darling's home again! My pretty is home again!

> (DUNYASHA *returns with the coffee-pot and is making*
> *the coffee.*)

VARYA (*standing at the door*)   All day long, darling, as I go about looking after the house, I keep dreaming all the time. If only we could marry you to a rich man, then I should feel more at rest. Then I would go off by myself on a pilgrimage to Kiev, to Moscow . . . and so I would spend my life going from one place to another. . . . I would go on and on. . . . What bliss!

ANYA   The birds are singing in the garden. What time is it?

VARYA   It must be nearly three. It's time you were asleep, darling (*going into* ANYA'S *room*). What bliss!

> (YASHA *enters with a rug and a travelling bag.*)

YASHA (*crosses the stage, mincingly*)   May one come in here, pray?

DUNYASHA   I shouldn't have known you, Yasha. How you have changed abroad.

YASHA   Hm! . . . And who are you?

DUNYASHA   When you went away, I was that high (*shows distance from floor*). Dunyasha, Fyodor's daughter. . . . You don't remember me!

YASHA   Hm! . . . You're a peach! (*Looks around and embraces her: she shrieks and drops a saucer.* YASHA *goes out hastily.*)

VARYA (*in the doorway, in a tone of vexation*)   What now?

DUNYASHA (*through her tears*)   I have broken a saucer.

VARYA   Well, that brings good luck.

ANYA (*coming out of her room*)   We ought to prepare mamma: Petya is here.

VARYA   I told them not to wake him.

ANYA (*dreamily*)   It's six years since father died. Then only a month later little brother Grisha was drowned in the river, such a pretty boy he was, only seven. It was more than mamma could bear, so she went away, went away without looking back (*shuddering*). . . . How well I understand her, if only she knew! (*A pause*) And Petya Trofimov was Grisha's tutor, he may remind her.

> (*Enter* FIRS: *he is wearing a pea-jacket and a white*
> *waistcoat.*)

FIRS (*goes up to the coffee-pot, anxiously*)   The mistress will be served here (*puts on white gloves*). Is the coffee ready? (*Sternly to* DUNYASHA) Girl! Where's the cream?

DUNYASHA   Ah, mercy on us! (*Goes out quickly.*)

FIRS (*fussing round the coffee-pot*)   Ech! you good-for-nothing! (*Muttering to himself*) Come back from Paris. And the old master used to go to Paris too . . . horses all the way (*laughs*).

VARYA   What is it, Firs?

FIRS   What is your pleasure? (*Gleefully*) My lady has come home! I have lived
to see her again! Now I can die (*weeps with joy*).

>   (*Enter* LYUBOV ANDREYEVNA, GAEV *and* SEMYONOV-
>   PISHTCHIK; *the latter is in a short-waisted full coat of fine
>   cloth, and full trousers.* GAEV, *as he comes in, makes a
>   gesture with his arms and his whole body, as though he
>   were playing billiards.*)

LYUBOV   How does it go? Let me remember. Cannon off the red!

GAEV   That's it—in off the white! Why, once, sister, we used to sleep together
in this very room, and now I'm fifty-one, strange as it seems.

LOPAHIN   Yes, time flies.

GAEV   What do you say?

LOPAHIN   Time, I say, flies.

GAEV   What a smell of patchouli!

ANYA   I'm going to bed. Good-night, mamma (*kisses her mother*).

LYUBOV   My precious darling (*kisses her hands*). Are you glad to be home?
I can't believe it.

ANYA   Good-night, uncle.

GAEV (*kissing her face and hands*)   God bless you! How like you are to your
mother! (*To his sister*) At her age you were just the same, Lyuba.

>   (ANYA *shakes hands with* LOPAHIN *and* PISHTCHIK, *then
>   goes out, shutting the door after her.*)

LYUBOV   She's quite worn out.

PISHTCHIK   Aye, it's a long journey, to be sure.

VARYA (*to* LOPAHIN *and* PISHTCHIK)   Well, gentlemen? It's three o'clock and
time to say good-bye.

LYUBOV (*laughs*)   You're just the same as ever, Varya (*draws her to her and
kisses her*). I'll just drink my coffee and then we will all go and rest.
(FIRS *puts a cushion under her feet*) Thanks, friend. I am so fond
of coffee, I drink it day and night. Thanks, dear old man (*kisses
FIRS*).

VARYA   I'll just see whether all the things have been brought in (*goes out*).

LYUBOV   Can it really be me sitting here? (*Laughs*) I want to dance about and
clap my hands. (*Covers her face with her hands*) And I could drop
asleep in a moment! God knows I love my country, I love it tenderly; I
couldn't look out of the window in the train, I kept crying so. (*Through
her tears*) But I must drink my coffee, though. Thank you, Firs, thanks,
dear old man. I'm so glad to find you still alive.

FIRS   The day before yesterday.

GAEV   He's rather deaf.

LOPAHIN   I have to set off for Harkov directly, at five o'clock. . . . It is annoying! I wanted to have a look at you, and a little talk. . . . You are
just as splendid as ever.

PISHTCHIK (*breathing heavily*)   Handsomer, indeed. . . . Dressed in Parisian
style . . . completely bowled me over.

LOPAHIN   Your brother, Leonid Andreyevitch here, is always saying that I'm
a low-born knave, that I'm a money-grubber, but I don't care one straw

for that. Let him talk. Only I do want you to believe in me as you used to. I do want your wonderful tender eyes to look at me as they used to in the old days. Merciful God! My father was a serf of your father and of your grandfather, but you—you—did so much for me once, that I've forgotten all that; I love you as though you were my kin . . . more than my kin.

LYUBOV   I can't sit still, I simply can't . . . (*jumps up and walks about in violent agitation*). This happiness is too much for me. . . . You may laugh at me, I know I'm silly. . . . My own bookcase (*kisses the bookcase*). My little table.

GAEV   Nurse died while you were away.

LYUBOV   (*sits down and drinks coffee*)   Yes, the Kingdom of Heaven be hers! You wrote me of her death.

GAEV   And Anastasy is dead. Squinting Petruchka has left me and is in service now with the police captain in the town (*takes a box of caramels out of his pocket and sucks one*).

PISHTCHIK   My daughter, Dashenka, wishes to be remembered to you.

LOPAHIN   I want to tell you something very pleasant and cheering (*glancing at his watch*). I'm going directly . . . there's no time to say much . . . well, I can say it in a couple of words. I needn't tell you your cherry orchard is to be sold to pay your debts; the 22nd of August is the date fixed for the sale; but don't you worry, dearest lady, you may sleep in peace, there is a way of saving it. . . . This is what I propose. I beg your attention! Your estate is not twenty miles from the town, the railway runs close by it, and if the cherry orchard and the land along the river bank were cut up into building plots and then let on lease for summer villas, you would make an income of at least 25,000 roubles a year out of it.

GAEV   That's all rot, if you'll excuse me.

LYUBOV   I don't quite understand you, Yermolay Alexeyevitch.

LOPAHIN   You will get a rent of at least 25 roubles a year for a three-acre plot from summer visitors, and if you say the word now, I'll bet you what you like there won't be one square foot of ground vacant by the autumn, all the plots will be taken up. I congratulate you; in fact, you are saved. It's a perfect situation with that deep river. Only, of course, it must be cleared—all the old buildings, for example, must be removed, this house too, which is really good for nothing and the old cherry orchard must be cut down.

LYUBOV   Cut down? My dear fellow, forgive me, but you don't know what you are talking about. If there is one thing interesting—remarkable indeed—in the whole province, it's just our cherry orchard.

LOPAHIN   The only thing remarkable about the orchard is that it's a very large one. There's a crop of cherries every alternate year, and then there's nothing to be done with them, no one buys them.

GAEV   This orchard is mentioned in the "Encyclopædia."

LOPAHIN   (*glancing at his watch*)   If we don't decide on something and don't take some steps, on the 22nd of August the cherry orchard and the whole estate too will be sold by auction. Make up your minds! There is no other way of saving it, I'll take my oath on that. No, No!

FIRS   In the old days, forty or fifty years ago, they used to dry the cherries, soak them, pickle them, make jam too, and they used . . .

GAEV   Be quiet, Firs.

FIRS   And they used to send the preserved cherries to Moscow and to Harkov by the wagon-load. That brought the money in! And the preserved cherries in those days were soft and juicy, sweet and fragrant. . . . They knew the way to do them then. . . .

LYUBOV   And where is the recipe now?

FIRS   It's forgotten. Nobody remembers it.

PISHTCHIK (*to* LYUBOV ANDREYEVNA)   What's it like in Paris? Did you eat frogs there?

LYUBOV   Oh, I ate crocodiles.

PISHTCHIK   Fancy that now!

LOPAHIN   There used to be only the gentlefolks and the peasants in the country, but now there are these summer visitors. All the towns, even the small ones, are surrounded nowadays by these summer villas. And one may say for sure, that in another twenty years there'll be many more of these people and that they'll be everywhere. At present the summer visitor only drinks tea in his verandah, but maybe he'll take to working his bit of land too, and then your cherry orchard would become happy, rich and prosperous. . . .

GAEV (*indignant*)   What rot!
    (*Enter* VARYA *and* YASHA.)

VARYA   There are two telegrams for you, mamma (*takes out keys and opens an old-fashioned bookcase with a loud crack*). Here they are.

LYUBOV   From Paris (*tears the telegrams, without reading them*). I have done with Paris.

GAEV   Do you know, Lyuba, how old that bookcase is? Last week I pulled out the bottom drawer and there I found the date branded on it. The bookcase was made just a hundred years ago. What do you say to that? We might have celebrated its jubilee. Though it's an inanimate object, still it is a *book* case.

PISHTCHIK (*amazed*)   A hundred years! Fancy that now.

GAEV   Yes. . . . It is a thing . . . (*feeling the bookcase*). Dear, honoured bookcase! Hail to thee who for more than a hundred years hast served the pure ideals of good and justice; thy silent call to fruitful labour has never flagged in those hundred years, maintaining (*in tears*) in the generations of man, courage and faith in a brighter future and fostering in us ideals of good and social consciousness (*a pause*).

LOPAHIN   Yes. . . .

LYUBOV   You are just the same as ever, Leonid.

GAEV (*a little embarrassed*)   Cannon off the right into the pocket!

LOPAHIN (*looking at his watch*)   Well, it's time I was off.

YASHA (*handing* LYUBOV ANDREYEVNA *medicine*)   Perhaps you will take your pills now.

PISHTCHIK   You shouldn't take medicines, my dear madam . . . they do no harm and no good. Give them here . . . honoured lady (*takes the pill-*

box, pours the pills into the hollow of his hand, blows on them, puts them in his mouth and drinks off some kvass). There!

LYUBOV (*in alarm*)   Why, you must be out of your mind!

PISHTCHIK   I have taken all the pills.

LOPAHIN   What a glutton! (*All laugh.*)

FIRS   His honour stayed with us in Easter week, ate a gallon and a half of cucumbers . . . (*mutters*).

LYUBOV   What is he saying?

VARYA   He has taken to muttering like that for the last three years. We are used to it.

YASHA   His declining years!

> (CHARLOTTA IVANOVNA, *a very thin, lanky figure in a white dress with a lorgnette in her belt, walks across the stage.*)

LOPAHIN   I beg your pardon, Charlotta Ivanovna, I have not had time to greet you (*tries to kiss her hand*).

CHARLOTTA (*pulling away her hand*)   If I let you kiss my hand, you'll be wanting to kiss my elbow, and then my shoulder.

LOPAHIN   I've no luck today! (*All laugh*) Charlotta Ivanovna, show us some tricks!

LYUBOV   Charlotta, do show us some tricks!

CHARLOTTA   I don't want to. I'm sleepy (*goes out*).

LOPAHIN   In three weeks' time we shall meet again (*kisses* LYUBOV ANDREYEVNA'S *hand*). Good-bye till then—I must go. (*To* GAEV) Good-bye. (*Kisses* PISHTCHIK) Good-bye. (*Gives his hand to* VARYA, *then to* FIRS *and* YASHA) I don't want to go. (*To* LYUBOV ANDREYEVNA) If you think over my plan for the villas and make up your mind, then let me know; I will lend you 50,000 roubles. Think of it seriously.

VARYA (*angrily*)   Well, do go, for goodness sake.

LOPAHIN   I'm going, I'm going (*goes out*).

GAEV   Low-born knave! I beg pardon, though . . . Varya is going to marry him, he's Varya's fiancé.

VARYA   Don't talk nonsense, uncle.

LYUBOV   Well, Varya, I shall be delighted. He's a good man.

PISHTCHIK   He is, one must acknowledge, a most worthy man. And my Dashenka . . . says too that . . . she says . . . various things (*snores, but at once wakes up*). But all the same, honoured lady, could you oblige me . . . with a loan of 240 roubles . . . to pay the interest on my mortgage tomorrow?

VARYA (*dismayed*)   No, no.

LYUBOV   I really haven't any money.

PISHTCHIK   It will turn up (*laughs*). I never lose hope. I thought everything was over, I was a ruined man, and lo and behold—the railway passed through my land and . . . they paid me for it. And something else will turn up again, if not today, then tomorrow . . . Dashenka'll win two hundred thousand . . . she's got a lottery ticket.

LYUBOV   Well, we've finished our coffee, we can go to bed.

FIRS (*brushes* GAEV, *reprovingly*)   You have got on the wrong trousers again! What am I to do with you?

VARYA (*softly*)   Anya's asleep. (*Softly opens the window*) Now the sun's risen, it's not a bit cold. Look, mamma, what exquisite trees! My goodness! And the air! The starlings are singing!

GAEV (*opens another window*)   The orchard is all white. You've not forgotten it, Lyuba? That long avenue that runs straight, straight as an arrow, how it shines on a moonlight night. You remember? You've not forgotten?

LYUBOV (*looking out of the window into the garden*)   Oh, my childhood, my innocence! It was in this nursery I used to sleep, from here I looked out into the orchard, happiness waked with me every morning and in those days the orchard was just the same, nothing has changed (*laughs with delight*). All, all white! Oh, my orchard! After the dark gloomy autumn, and the cold winter; you are young again, and full of happiness, the heavenly angels have never left you. . . . If I could cast off the burden that weighs on my heart, if I could forget the past!

GAEV   H'm! and the orchard will be sold to pay our debts; it seems strange. . . .

LYUBOV   See, our mother walking . . . all in white, down the avenue! (*Laughs with delight*) It is she!

GAEV   Where?

VARYA   Oh, don't, mamma!

LYUBOV   There is no one. It was my fancy. On the right there, by the path to the arbour, there is a white tree bending like a woman. . . .

> (*Enter* TROFIMOV *wearing a shabby student's uniform and spectacles.*)

LYUBOV   What a ravishing orchard! White masses of blossoms, blue sky. . . .

TROFIMOV   Lyubov Andreyevna! (*She looks round at him*) I will just pay my respects to you and then leave you at once (*kisses her hand warmly*). I was told to wait until morning, but I hadn't the patience to wait any longer. . . .

> (LYUBOV ANDREYEVNA *looks at him in perplexity.*)

VARYA (*through her tears*)   This is Petya Trofimov.

TROFIMOV   Petya Trofimov, who was your Grisha's tutor. . . . Can I have changed so much?

> (LYUBOV ANDREYEVNA *embraces him and weeps quietly.*)

GAEV (*in confusion*)   There, there, Lyuba.

VARYA (*crying*)   I told you, Petya, to wait till tomorrow.

LYUBOV   My Grisha . . . my boy . . . Grisha . . . my son!

VARYA   We can't help it, mamma, it is God's will.

TROFIMOV (*softly through his tears*)   There . . . there.

LYUBOV (*weeping quietly*)   My boy was lost . . . drowned. Why? Oh, why, dear Petya? (*More quietly*) Anya is asleep in there, and I'm talking loudly . . . making this noise. . . . But, Petya? Why have you grown so ugly? Why do you look so old?

TROFIMOV   A peasant-woman in the train called me a mangy-looking gentleman.

LYUBOV   You were quite a boy then, a pretty little student, and now your hair's thin—and spectacles. Are you really a student still? (*Goes towards the door.*)

TROFIMOV　I seem likely to be a perpetual student.

LYUBOV　(*kisses her brother, then* VARYA)　Well, go to bed. . . . You are older too, Leonid.

PISHTCHIK　(*follows her*)　I suppose it's time we were asleep. . . . Ugh! my gout. I'm staying the night! Lyubov Andreyevna, my dear soul, if you could . . . tomorrow morning . . . 240 roubles.

GAEV　That's always his story.

PISHTCHIK　240 roubles . . . to pay the interest on my mortgage.

LYUBOV　My dear man, I have no money.

PISHTCHIK　I'll pay it back, my dear . . . a trifling sum.

LYUBOV　Oh, well, Leonid will give it you. . . . You give him the money, Leonid.

GAEV　Me give it him! Let him wait till he gets it!

LYUBOV　It can't be helped, give it him. He needs it. He'll pay it back.

　　　　(LYUBOV ANDREYEVNA, TROFIMOV, PISHTCHIK *and* FIRS
　　　　go out. GAEV, VARYA *and* YASHA *remain.*)

GAEV　Sister hasn't got out of the habit of flinging away her money. (*To* YASHA) Get away, my good fellow, you smell of the hen-house.

YASHA　(*with a grin*)　And you, Leonid Andreyevitch, are just the same as ever.

GAEV　What's that? (*To* VARYA) What did he say?

VARYA　(*to* YASHA)　Your mother has come from the village; she has been sitting in the servants' room since yesterday, waiting to see you.

YASHA　Oh, bother her!

VARYA　For shame!

YASHA　What's the hurry? She might just as well have come tomorrow (*goes out*).

VARYA　Mamma's just the same as ever, she hasn't changed a bit. If she had her own way, she'd give away everything.

GAEV　Yes (*a pause*). If a great many remedies are suggested for some disease, it means that the disease is incurable. I keep thinking and racking my brains; I have many schemes, a great many, and that really means none. If we could only come in for a legacy from somebody, or marry our Anya to a very rich man, or we might go to Yaroslavl and try our luck with our old aunt, the Countess. She's very, very rich, you know.

VARYA　(*weeps*)　If God would help us.

GAEV　Don't blubber. Aunt's very rich, but she doesn't like us. First, sister married a lawyer instead of a nobleman. . . .

　　　　(ANYA *appears in the doorway.*)

GAEV　And then her conduct, one can't call it virtuous. She is good, and kind, and nice, and I love her, but, however one allows for extenuating circumstances, there's no denying that she's an immoral woman. One feels it in her slightest gesture.

VARYA　(*in a whisper*)　Anya's in the doorway.

GAEV　What do you say? (*A pause*) It's queer, there seems to be something wrong with my right eye. I don't see as well as I did. And on Thursday when I was in the district Court . . .

　　　　(*Enter* ANYA.)

VARYA Why aren't you asleep, Anya?

ANYA I can't get to sleep.

GAEV My pet (*kisses* ANYA'S *face and hands*). My child (*weeps*). You are not my niece, you are my angel, you are everything to me. Believe me, believe . . .

ANYA I believe you, uncle. Everyone loves you and respects you . . . but, uncle dear, you must be silent . . . simply be silent. What were you saying just now about my mother, about your own sister? What made you say that?

GAEV Yes, yes . . . (*puts his hand over his face*). Really, that was awful! My God, save me! And today I made a speech to the bookcase . . . so stupid! And only when I had finished, I saw how stupid it was.

VARYA It's true, uncle, you ought to keep quiet. Don't talk, that's all.

ANYA If you could keep from talking, it would make things easier for you, too.

GAEV I won't speak (*kisses* ANYA'S *and* VARYA'S *hands*). I'll be silent. Only this is about business. On Thursday I was in the district Court; well, there was a large party of us there and we began talking of one thing and another, and this and that, and do you know, I believe that it will be possible to raise a loan on an I.O.U. to pay the arrears on the mortgage.

VARYA If the Lord would help us!

GAEV I'm going on Tuesday; I'll talk of it again. (*To* VARYA) Don't blubber. (*To* ANYA) Your mamma will talk to Lopahin; of course, he won't refuse her. And as soon as you're rested you shall go to Yaroslavl to the Countess, your great-aunt. So we shall all set to work in three directions at once, and the business is done. We shall pay off arrears, I'm convinced of it (*puts a caramel in his mouth*). I swear on my honour, I swear by anything you like, the estate shan't be sold (*excitedly*). By my own happiness, I swear it! Here's my hand on it, call me the basest, vilest of men, if I let it come to an auction! Upon my soul I swear it!

ANYA (*her equanimity has returned, she is quite happy*) How good you are, uncle, and how clever! (*Embraces her uncle*) I'm at peace now! Quite at peace! I'm happy!

    (*Enter* FIRS.)

FIRS (*reproachfully*) Leonid Andreyevitch, have you no fear of God? When are you going to bed?

GAEV Directly, directly. You can go, Firs. I'll . . . yes, I will undress myself. Come, children, bye-bye. We'll go into details tomorrow, but now go to bed (*kisses* ANYA *and* VARYA). I'm a man of the eighties. They run down that period, but still I can say I have had to suffer not a little for my convictions in my life. It's not for nothing that the peasant loves me. One must know the peasant! One must know how . . .

ANYA At it again, uncle!

VARYA Uncle dear, you'd better be quiet!

FIRS (*angrily*) Leonid Andreyevitch!

GAEV I'm coming. I'm coming. Go to bed. Potted the shot—there's a shot for you! A beauty! (*Goes out,* FIRS *hobbling after him.*)

ANYA My mind's at rest now. I don't want to go to Yaroslavl, I don't like my great-aunt, but still my mind's at rest. Thanks to uncle (*sits down*).

VARYA   We must go to bed. I'm going. Something unpleasant happened while you were away. In the old servants' quarters there are only the old servants, as you know—Efimyushka, Polya and Yevstigney—and Karp too. They began letting stray people in to spend the night—I said nothing. But all at once I heard they had been spreading a report that I gave them nothing but pease pudding to eat. Out of stinginess, you know. . . . And it was all Yevstigney's doing. . . . Very well, I said to myself. . . . If that's how it is, I thought, wait a bit. I sent for Yevstigney . . . (*yawns*). He comes. . . . "How's this, Yevstigney," I said, "you could be such a fool as to? . . ." (*Looking at* ANYA) Anitchka! (*a pause*). She's asleep (*puts her arm round* ANYA). Come to bed . . . come along! (*Leads her*) My darling has fallen asleep! Come . . . (*They go.*)

>   (*Far away beyond the orchard a shepherd plays on a pipe.* TROFIMOV *crosses the stage and, seeing* VARYA *and* ANYA, *stands still.*)

VARYA   Sh! asleep, asleep. Come, my own.

ANYA (*softly, half asleep*)   I'm so tired. Still those bells. Uncle . . . dear . . . mamma and uncle. . . .

VARYA   Come, my own, come along.

>   (*They go into* ANYA'S *room.*)

TROFIMOV (*tenderly*)   My sunshine! My spring.

>   (*The Curtain Falls.*)

Act Two

The open country. An old shrine, long abandoned and fallen out of the perpendicular; near it a well, large stones that have apparently once been tombstones, and an old garden seat. The road to GAEV'S *house is seen. On one side rise dark poplars; and there the cherry orchard begins. In the distance a row of telegraph poles and far, far away on the horizon there is faintly outlined a great town, only visible in very fine clear weather. It is near sunset.* CHARLOTTA, YASHA *and* DUNYASHA *are sitting on the seat.* EPIHODOV *is standing near, playing something mournful on a guitar. All sit plunged in thought.* CHARLOTTA *wears an old forage cap; she has taken a gun from her shoulder and is tightening the buckle on the strap.*

CHARLOTTA (*musingly*)   I haven't a real passport of my own, and I don't know how old I am, and I always feel that I'm a young thing. When I was a little girl, my father and mother used to travel about to fairs and give performances—very good ones. And I used to dance *salto-mortale* and all sorts of things. And when papa and mamma died, a German lady took me and had me educated. And so I grew up and became a governess. But where I came from, and who I am, I don't know. . . . Who my parents were, very likely they weren't married . . . I don't know (*takes a cucumber out of her pocket and eats*). I know nothing at all (*a pause*). One wants to talk and has no one to talk to . . . I have nobody.

EPIHODOV (*plays on the guitar and sings*)   "What care I for the noisy world!

What care I for friends or foes!" How agreeable it is to play on the mandolin!

DUNYASHA   That's a guitar, not a mandolin (*looks in a hand-mirror and powders herself*).

EPIHODOV   To a man mad with love, it's a mandolin. (*Sings*) "Were her heart but aglow with love's mutual flame." (YASHA *joins in.*)

CHARLOTTA   How shockingly these people sing! Foo! Like jackals!

DUNYASHA (*to* YASHA)   What happiness, though, to visit foreign lands.

YASHA   Ah, yes! I rather agree with you there (*yawns, then lights a cigar*).

EPIHODOV   That's comprehensible. In foreign lands everything has long since reached full complexion.

YASHA   That's so, of course.

EPIHODOV   I'm a cultivated man, I read remarkable books of all sorts, but I can never make out the tendency I am myself precisely inclined for, whether to live or to shoot myself, speaking precisely, but nevertheless I always carry a revolver. Here it is . . . (*shows revolver*).

CHARLOTTA   I've had enough, and now I'm going (*puts on the gun*). Epihodov, you're a very clever fellow, and a very terrible one too, all the women must be wild about you. Br-r-r! (*Goes*) These clever fellows are all so stupid; there's not a creature for me to speak to. . . . Always alone, alone, nobody belonging to me . . . and who I am, and why I'm on earth, I don't know (*walks away slowly*).

EPIHODOV   Speaking precisely, not touching upon other subjects, I'm bound to admit about myself, that destiny behaves mercilessly to me, as a storm to a little boat. If, let us suppose, I am mistaken, then why did I wake up this morning, to quote an example, and look round, and there on my chest was a spider of fearful magnitude . . . like this (*shows with both hands*). And then I take up a jug of kvass, to quench my thirst, and in it there is something in the highest degree unseemly of the nature of a cockroach (*a pause*). Have you read Buckle? (*A pause*) I am desirous of troubling you, Dunyasha, with a couple of words.

DUNYASHA   Well, speak.

EPIHODOV   I should be desirous to speak with you alone (*sighs*).

DUNYASHA (*embarrassed*)   Well—only bring me my mantle first. It's by the cupboard. It's rather damp here.

EPIHODOV   Certainly. I will fetch it. Now I know what I must do with my revolver (*takes guitar and goes off playing on it*).

YASHA   Two and twenty misfortunes! Between ourselves, he's a fool (*yawns*).

DUNYASHA   God grant he doesn't shoot himself! (*A pause*) I am so nervous, I'm always in a flutter. I was a little girl when I was taken into our lady's house, and now I have quite grown out of peasant ways, and my hands are white, as white as a lady's. I'm such a delicate, sensitive creature, I'm afraid of everything. I'm so frightened. And if you deceive me, Yasha, I don't know what will become of my nerves.

YASHA (*kisses her*)   You're a peach! Of course a girl must never forget herself; what I dislike more than anything is a girl being flighty in her behaviour.

DUNYASHA   I'm passionately in love with you, Yasha; you are a man of culture —you can give your opinion about anything (*a pause*).

YASHA (*yawns*)   Yes, that's so. My opinion is this: if a girl loves anyone, that means that she has no principles (*a pause*). It's pleasant smoking a cigar in the open air (*listens*). Someone's coming this way . . . it's the gentle-folk (DUNYASHA *embraces him impulsively*). Go home, as though you had been to the river to bathe; go by that path, or else they'll meet you and suppose I have made an appointment with you here. That I can't endure.

DUNYASHA (*coughing softly*)   The cigar has made my head ache . . . (*goes off*).

(YASHA *remains sitting near the shrine. Enter* LYUBOV ANDREYEVNA, GAEV *and* LOPAHIN.)

LOPAHIN   You must make up your mind once for all—there's no time to lose. It's quite a simple question, you know. Will you consent to letting the land for building or not? One word in answer: Yes or no? Only one word!

LYUBOV   Who is smoking such horrible cigars here? (*Sits down.*)

GAEV   Now the railway line has been brought near, it's made things very convenient (*sits down*). Here we have been over and lunched in town. Cannon off the white! I should like to go home and have a game.

LYUBOV   You have plenty of time.

LOPAHIN   Only one word! (*Beseechingly*) Give me an answer!

GAEV (*yawning*)   What do you say?

LYUBOV (*looks in her purse*)   I had quite a lot of money here yesterday, and there's scarcely any left today. My poor Varya feeds us all on milk soup for the sake of economy; the old folks in the kitchen get nothing but pease pudding, while I waste my money in a senseless way (*drops purse, scattering gold pieces*). There, they have all fallen out! (*Annoyed.*)

YASHA   Allow me, I'll pick them up (*collects the coins*).

LYUBOV   Pray do, Yasha. And what did I go off to the town to lunch for? Your restaurant's a wretched place with its music and the tablecloth smelling of soap. . . . Why drink so much, Leonid? And eat so much? And talk so much? Today you talked a great deal again in the restaurant, and all so inappropriately. About the era of the 'seventies, about the decadents. And to whom? Talking to waiters about decadents!

LOPAHIN   Yes.

GAEV (*waving his hand*)   I'm incorrigible; that's evident. (*Irritably to* YASHA) Why is it you keep fidgeting about in front of us!

YASHA (*laughs*)   I can't help laughing when I hear your voice.

GAEV (*to his sister*)   Either I or he . . .

LYUBOV   Get along! Go away, Yasha.

YASHA (*gives* LYUBOV ANDREYEVNA *her purse*)   Directly (*hardly able to suppress his laughter*). This minute . . . (*goes off*).

LOPAHIN   Deriganov, the millionaire, means to buy your estate. They say he is coming to the sale himself.

LYUBOV   Where did you hear that?

LOPAHIN   That's what they say in town.

GAEV   Our aunt in Yaroslavl has promised to send help; but when, and how much she will send, we don't know.

LOPAHIN   How much will she send? A hundred thousand? Two hundred?

LYUBOV   Oh, well! . . . Ten or fifteen thousand, and we must be thankful to get that.

LOPAHIN   Forgive me, but such reckless people as you are—such queer, unbusiness-like people—I never met in my life. One tells you in plain Russian your estate is going to be sold, and you seem not to understand it.

LYUBOV   What are we to do? Tell us what to do.

LOPAHIN   I do tell you every day. Every day I say the same thing. You absolutely must let the cherry orchard and the land on building leases; and do it at once, as quick as may be—the auction's close upon us! Do understand! Once make up your mind to build villas, and you can raise as much money as you like, and then you are saved.

LYUBOV   Villas and summer visitors—forgive me saying so—it's so vulgar.

GAEV   There I perfectly agree with you.

LOPAHIN   I shall sob, or scream, or fall into a fit. I can't stand it! you drive me mad! (*To* GAEV) You're an old woman!

GAEV   What do you say?

LOPAHIN   An old woman! (*Gets up to go.*)

LYUBOV (*in dismay*)   No, don't go! Do stay, my dear friend! Perhaps we shall think of something.

LOPAHIN   What is there to think of?

LYUBOV   Don't go, I entreat you! With you here it's more cheerful, anyway (*a pause*). I keep expecting something, as though the house were going to fall about our ears.

GAEV (*in profound dejection*)   Potted the white! It fails—a kiss.

LYUBOV   We have been great sinners. . . .

LOPAHIN   You have no sins to repent of.

GAEV (*puts a caramel in his mouth*)   They say I've eaten up my property in caramels (*laughs*).

LYUBOV   Oh, my sins! I've always thrown my money away recklessly like a lunatic. I married a man who made nothing but debts. My husband died of champagne—he drank dreadfully. To my misery I loved another man, and immediately—it was my first punishment—the blow fell upon me, here, in the river . . . my boy was drowned and I went abroad—went away for ever, never to return, not to see that river again . . . I shut my eyes, and fled, distracted, and *he* after me . . . pitilessly, brutally. I bought a villa at Mentone, for *he* fell ill there, and for three years I had no rest day or night. His illness wore me out, my soul was dried up. And last year, when my villa was sold to pay my debts, I went to Paris and there he robbed me of everything and abandoned me for another woman; and I tried to poison myself. . . . So stupid, so shameful! . . . And suddenly I felt a yearning for Russia, for my country, for my little girl . . . (*dries her tears*). Lord, Lord, be merciful! Forgive my sins! Do not chastise me more! (*Takes a telegram out of her pocket*) I got this today from Paris. He implores forgiveness, entreats me to return (*tears up the telegram*). I fancy there is music somewhere (*listens*).

GAEV   That's our famous Jewish orchestra. You remember, four violins, a flute and a double bass.

LYUBOV   That still in existence? We ought to send for them one evening, and give a dance.

LOPAHIN (*listens*)   I can't hear. . . . (*Hums softly*) "For money the Germans will turn a Russian into a Frenchman." (*Laughs*) I did see such a piece at the theatre yesterday! It was funny!

LYUBOV   And most likely there was nothing funny in it. You shouldn't look at plays, you should look at yourselves a little oftener. How grey your lives are! How much nonsense you talk.

LOPAHIN   That's true. One may say honestly, we live a fool's life (*pause*). My father was a peasant, an idiot; he knew nothing and taught me nothing, only beat me when he was drunk, and always with his stick. In reality I am just another blockhead and idiot. I've learnt nothing properly. I write a wretched hand. I write so that I feel ashamed before folks, like a pig.

LYUBOV   You ought to get married, my dear fellow.

LOPAHIN   Yes . . . that's true.

LYUBOV   You should marry our Varya, she's a good girl.

LOPAHIN   Yes.

LYUBOV   She's a good-natured girl, she's busy all day long, and what's more, she loves you. And you have liked her for ever so long.

LOPAHIN   Well? I'm not against it. . . . She's a good girl (*pause*).

GAEV   I've been offered a place in the bank: 6,000 roubles a year. Did you know?

LYUBOV   You would never do for that! You must stay as you are.
        (*Enter* FIRS *with overcoat.*)

FIRS   Put it on, sir, it's damp.

GAEV (*putting it on*)   You bother me, old fellow.

FIRS   You can't go on like this. You went away in the morning without leaving word (*looks him over*).

LYUBOV   You look older, Firs!

FIRS   What is your pleasure?

LOPAHIN   You look older, she said.

FIRS   I've had a long life. They were arranging my wedding before your papa was born . . . (*laughs*). I was the head footman before the emancipation came. I wouldn't consent to be set free then; I stayed on with the old master . . . (*a pause*). I remember what rejoicings they made and didn't know themselves what they were rejoicing over.

LOPAHIN   Those were fine old times. There was flogging anyway.

FIRS (*not hearing*)   To be sure! The peasants knew their place, and the masters knew theirs; but now they're all at sixes and sevens, there's no making it out.

GAEV   Hold your tongue, Firs. I must go to town tomorrow. I have been promised an introduction to a general, who might let us have a loan.

LOPAHIN   You won't bring that off. And you won't pay your arrears, you may rest assured of that.

LYUBOV   That's all his nonsense. There is no such general.
        (*Enter* TROFIMOV, ANYA *and* VARYA.)

GAEV   Here come our girls.

ANYA   There's mamma on the seat.

LYUBOV (*tenderly*)   Come here, come along. My darlings! (*Embraces* ANYA *and* VARYA) If you only knew how I love you both. Sit beside me, there, like that. (*All sit down.*)

LOPAHIN   Our perpetual student is always with the young ladies.

TROFIMOV   That's not your business.

LOPAHIN   He'll soon be fifty, and he's still a student.

TROFIMOV   Drop your idiotic jokes.

LOPAHIN   Why are you so cross, you queer fish?

TROFIMOV   Oh, don't persist!

LOPAHIN   (*laughs*)   Allow me to ask you what's your idea of me?

TROFIMOV   I'll tell you my idea of you, Yermolay Alexeyevitch: you are a rich man, you'll soon be a millionaire. Well, just as in the economy of nature a wild beast is of use, who devours everything that comes in his way, so you too have your use.

(*All laugh.*)

VARYA   Better tell us something about the planets, Petya.

LYUBOV   No, let us go on with the conversation we had yesterday.

TROFIMOV   What was it about?

GAEV   About pride.

TROFIMOV   We had a long conversation yesterday, but we came to no conclusion. In pride, in your sense of it, there is something mystical. Perhaps you are right from your point of view; but if one looks at it simply, without subtlety, what sort of pride can there be, what sense is there in it, if man in his physiological formation is very imperfect, if in the immense majority of cases he is coarse, dull-witted, profoundly unhappy? One must give up glorification of self. One should work, and nothing else.

GAEV   One must die in any case.

TROFIMOV   Who knows? And what does it mean—dying? Perhaps man has a hundred senses, and only the five we know are lost at death, while the other ninety-five remain alive.

LYUBOV   How clever you are, Petya!

LOPAHIN   (*ironically*)   Fearfully clever!

TROFIMOV   Humanity progresses, perfecting its powers. Everything that is beyond its ken now will one day become familiar and comprehensible; only we must work, we must with all our powers aid the seeker after truth. Here among us in Russia the workers are few in numbers as yet. The vast majority of the intellectual people I know, seek nothing, do nothing, are not fit as yet for work of any kind. They call themselves intellectual, but they treat their servants as inferiors, behave to the peasants as though they were animals, learn little, read nothing seriously, do practically nothing, only talk about science and know very little about art. They are all serious people, they all have severe faces, they all talk of weighty matters and air their theories, and yet the vast majority of us—ninety-nine per cent—live like savages, at the least thing fly to blows and abuse, eat piggishly, sleep in filth and stuffiness, bugs everywhere, stench and damp and moral impurity. And it's clear all our fine talk is only to divert our attention and other people's. Show me where to find the crèches there's so much talk about, and the reading-rooms? They only exist in novels: in real life there are none of them. There is nothing but filth and vulgarity and Asiatic apathy. I fear and dislike very serious faces. I'm afraid of serious conversations. We should do better to be silent.

LOPAHIN   You know, I get up at five o'clock in the morning, and I work from morning to night; and I've money, my own and other people's, always passing through my hands, and I see what people are made of all round me. One has only to begin to do anything to see how few honest, decent people there are. Sometimes when I lie awake at night, I think: "Oh! Lord, thou hast given us immense forests, boundless plains, the widest horizons, and living here we ourselves ought really to be giants."

LYUBOV   You ask for giants! They are no good except in story-books; in real life they frighten us.

(EPIHODOV *advances in the background, playing on the guitar.*)

LYUBOV (*dreamily*)   There goes Epihodov.

ANYA (*dreamily*)   There goes Epihodov.

GAEV   The sun has set, my friends.

TROFIMOV   Yes.

GAEV (*not loudly, but, as it were, declaiming*)   O nature, divine nature, thou art bright with eternal lustre, beautiful and indifferent! Thou, whom we call mother, thou dost unite within thee life and death! Thou dost give life and dost destroy!

VARYA (*in a tone of supplication*)   Uncle!

ANYA   Uncle, you are at it again!

TROFIMOV   You'd much better be cannoning off the red!

GAEV   I'll hold my tongue, I will.

(*All sit plunged in thought. Perfect stillness. The only thing audible is the muttering of* FIRS. *Suddenly there is a sound in the distance, as it were from the sky—the sound of a breaking harp-string, mournfully dying away.*)

LYUBOV   What is that?

LOPAHIN   I don't know. Somewhere far away a bucket fallen and broken in the pits. But somewhere very far away.

GAEV   It might be a bird of some sort—such as a heron.

TROFIMOV   Or an owl.

LYUBOV (*shudders*)   I don't know why, but it's horrid (*a pause*).

FIRS   It was the same before the calamity—the owl hooted and the samovar hissed all the time.

GAEV   Before what calamity?

FIRS   Before the emancipation (*a pause*).

LYUBOV   Come, my friends, let us be going; evening is falling. (*To* ANYA) There are tears in your eyes. What is it, darling? (*Embraces her.*)

ANYA   Nothing, mamma; it's nothing.

TROFIMOV   There is somebody coming.

(*The wayfarer appears in a shabby white forage cap and an overcoat; he is slightly drunk.*)

WAYFARER   Allow me to inquire, can I get to the station this way?

GAEV   Yes. Go along that road.

WAYFARER   I thank you most feelingly (*coughing*). The weather is superb. (*Declaims*) My brother, my suffering brother! . . . Come out to the Volga! Whose groan do you hear? . . . (*To* VARYA) Mademoiselle, vouchsafe a hungry Russian thirty kopeks.

    (VARYA *utters a shriek of alarm.*)

LOPAHIN (*angrily*)   There's a right and a wrong way of doing everything!

LYUBOV (*hurriedly*)   Here, take this (*looks in her purse*). I've no silver. No matter—here's gold for you.

WAYFARER   I thank you most feelingly! (*Goes off.*)

    (*Laughter.*)

VARYA (*frightened*)   I'm going home—I'm going . . . Oh, mamma, the servants have nothing to eat, and you gave him gold!

LYUBOV   There's no doing anything with me. I'm so silly! When we get home, I'll give you all I possess. Yermolay Alexeyevitch, you will lend me some more . . . !

LOPAHIN   I will.

LYUBOV   Come, friends, it's time to be going. And Varya, we have made a match of it for you. I congratulate you.

VARYA (*through her tears*)   Mamma, that's not a joking matter.

LOPAHIN   "Ophelia, get thee to a nunnery!"

GAEV   My hands are trembling; it's a long while since I had a game of billiards.

LOPAHIN   "Ophelia! Nymph, in thy orisons be all my sins remember'd."

LYUBOV   Come, it will soon be supper-time.

VARYA   How he frightened me! My heart's simply throbbing.

LOPAHIN   Let me remind you, ladies and gentlemen: on the 22nd of August the cherry orchard will be sold. Think about that! Think about it!

    (*All go off, except* TROFIMOV *and* ANYA.)

ANYA (*laughing*)   I'm grateful to the wayfarer! He frightened Varya and we are left alone.

TROFIMOV   Varya's afraid we shall fall in love with each other, and for days together she won't leave us. With her narrow brain she can't grasp that we are above love. To eliminate the petty and transitory which hinders us from being free and happy—that is the aim and meaning of our life. Forward! We go forward irresistibly towards the bright star that shines yonder in the distance. Forward! Do not lag behind, friends.

ANYA (*claps her hands*)   How well you speak! (*A pause*) It is divine here today.

TROFIMOV   Yes, it's glorious weather.

ANYA   Somehow, Petya, you've made me so that I don't love the cherry orchard as I used to. I used to love it so dearly. I used to think that there was no spot on earth like our garden.

TROFIMOV   All Russia is our garden. The earth is great and beautiful—there are many beautiful places in it (*a pause*). Think only, Anya, your grandfather, and great-grandfather, and all your ancestors were slave-owners—the owners of living souls—and from every cherry in the orchard, from every leaf, from every trunk there are human creatures looking at you. Cannot you hear their voices? Oh, it is awful! Your orchard is a fearful thing, and when in the evening or at night one walks about the orchard, the old bark on the trees glimmers dimly in the dusk, and the old cherry trees seem to be dreaming of centuries gone by and tortured by fearful visions. Yes! We are at least two hundred years behind, we have really gained nothing yet, we have no definite attitude to the past, we do nothing but theorise or complain of depression or drink vodka. It is clear that to begin to live in the present we must first expiate our past, we must break with it; and we can expiate it only by suffering, by extraordinary unceasing labour. Understand that, Anya.

ANYA   The house we live in has long ceased to be our own, and I shall leave it, I give you my word.

TROFIMOV   If you have the house keys, fling them into the well and go away. Be free as the wind.

ANYA (*in ecstasy*)   How beautifully you said that!

TROFIMOV   Believe me, Anya, believe me! I am not thirty yet, I am young, I am still a student, but I have gone through so much already! As soon as winter comes I am hungry, sick, careworn, poor as a beggar, and what ups and downs of fortune have I not known! And my soul was always, every minute, day and night, full of inexplicable forebodings. I have a foreboding of happiness, Anya. I see glimpses of it already.

ANYA (*pensively*)   The moon is rising.

>   (EPIHODOV *is heard playing still the same mournful*
>   *song on his guitar. The moon rises. Somewhere near the*
>   *poplars* VARYA *is looking for* ANYA *and calling* "Anya!
>   where are you?")

TROFIMOV   Yes, the moon is rising (*a pause*). Here is happiness—here it comes! It is coming nearer and nearer; already I can hear its footsteps. And if we never see it—if we may never know it—what does it matter? Others will see it after us.

VARYA'S VOICE   Anya! Where are you?

TROFIMOV   That Varya again! (*Angrily*) It's revolting!

ANYA   Well, let's go down to the river. It's lovely there.

TROFIMOV   Yes, let's go. (*They go.*)

VARYA'S VOICE   Anya! Anya!

(*The Curtain Falls.*)

Act Three

A drawing-room divided by an arch from a larger drawing-room. A chandelier burning. The Jewish orchestra, the same that was mentioned in Act 2, is heard playing in the ante-room. It is evening. In the larger drawing-room they are dancing the grand chain. The voice of SEMYONOV-PISHTCHIK: "*Promenade à une paire!*" *Then enter the drawing-room in couples first* PISHTCHIK *and* CHARLOTTA IVANOVNA, *then* TROFIMOV *and* LYUBOV ANDREYEVNA, *thirdly* ANYA *with the Post-Office Clerk, fourthly* VARYA *with the Station Master, and other guests.* VARYA *is quietly weeping and wiping away her tears as she dances. In the last couple is* DUNYASHA. *They move across the drawing-room.* PISHTCHIK *shouts:* "Grand rond, balancez!" *and* "Les Cavaliers à genou et remerciez vos dames."

FIRS *in a swallow-tail coat brings in selzer water on a tray.* PISHTCHIK *and*
TROFIMOV *enter the drawing-room.*

PISHTCHIK I am a full-blooded man; I have already had two strokes. Dancing's
hard work for me, but as they say, if you're in the pack, you must bark
with the rest. I'm as strong, I may say, as a horse. My parent, who would
have his joke—may the Kingdom of Heaven be his!—used to say about
our origin that the ancient stock of the Semyonov-Pishtchiks was derived
form the very horse that Caligula made a member of the senate (*sits
down*). But I've no money, that's where the mischief is. A hungry dog
believes in nothing but meat . . . (*snores, but at once wakes up*). That's
like me . . . I can think of nothing but money.

TROFIMOV There really is something horsy about your appearance.

PISHTCHIK Well . . . a horse is a fine beast . . . a horse can be sold.
(*There is the sound of billiards being played in an
adjoining room.* VARYA *appears in the arch leading to
the larger drawing-room.*)

TROFIMOV (*teasing*) Madame Lopahin! Madame Lopahin!

VARYA (*angrily*) Mangy-looking gentleman!

TROFIMOV Yes, I am a mangy-looking gentleman, and I'm proud of it!

VARYA (*pondering bitterly*) Here we have hired musicians and nothing to pay
them! (*Goes out.*)

TROFIMOV (*to* PISHTCHIK) If the energy you have wasted during your
lifetime in trying to find the money to pay your interest, had gone to
something else, you might in the end have turned the world upside down.

PISHTCHIK Nietzsche, the philosopher, a very great and celebrated man . . .
of enormous intellect . . . says in his works, that one can make forged
bank-notes.

TROFIMOV Why, have you read Nietzsche?

PISHTCHIK What next . . . Dashenka told me . . . And now I am in such a
position, I might just as well forge bank-notes. The day after tomorrow I
must pay 310 roubles—130 I have procured (*feels in his pockets, in
alarm*). The money's gone! I have lost my money! (*Through his tears*)
Where's the money? (*Gleefully*) Why, here it is behind the lining. . . .
It has made me hot all over.
(*Enter* LYUBOV ANDREYEVNA *and* CHARLOTTA IVANOVNA.)

LYUBOV (*hums the Lezginka*) Why is Leonid so long? What can he be doing
in town? (*To* DUNYASHA) Offer the musicians some tea.

TROFIMOV The sale hasn't taken place, most likely.

LYUBOV It's the wrong time to have the orchestra, and the wrong time to give
a dance. Well, never mind (*sits down and hums softly*).

CHARLOTTA (*gives* PISHTCHIK *a pack of cards*) Here's a pack of cards. Think
of any card you like.

PISHTCHIK I've thought of one.

CHARLOTTA Shuffle the pack now. That's right. Give it here, my dear Mr.
Pishtchik. Ein, zwei, drei—now look, it's in your breast pocket.

PISHTCHIK (*taking a card out of his breast pocket*) The eight of spades!
Perfectly right! (*Wonderingly*) Fancy that now!

CHARLOTTA (*holding pack of cards in her hands, to* TROFIMOV)   Tell me quickly which is the top card.

TROFIMOV   Well, the queen of spades.

CHARLOTTA   It is! (*To* PISHTCHIK) Well, which card is uppermost?

PISHTCHIK   The ace of hearts.

CHARLOTTA   It is! (*Claps her hands, pack of cards disappears*) Ah! what lovely weather it is today!

      (*A mysterious feminine voice which seems coming out of the floor answers her.* "Oh, yes, it's magnificent weather, madam.")

CHARLOTTA   You are my perfect ideal.

VOICE   And I greatly admire you too, madam.

STATION MASTER (*applauding*)   The lady ventriloquist—bravo!

PISHTCHIK (*wonderingly*)   Fancy that now! Most enchanting Charlotta Ivanovna. I'm simply in love with you.

CHARLOTTA   In love? (*Shrugging shoulders*) What do you know of love, guter Mensch, aber schlechter Musikant?

TROFIMOV (*pats* PISHTCHIK *on the shoulder*)   You dear old horse. . . .

CHARLOTTA   Attention, please! Another trick! (*Takes a travelling rug from a chair*) Here's a very good rug; I want to sell it (*shaking it out*). Doesn't anyone want to buy it?

PISHTCHIK (*wonderingly*)   Fancy that!

CHARLOTTA   Ein, zwei, drei! (*Quickly picks up rug she has dropped; behind the rug stands* ANYA; *she makes a curtsey, runs to her mother, embraces her and runs back into the larger drawing-room amidst general enthusiasm.*)

LYUBOV (*applauds*)   Bravo! Bravo!

CHARLOTTA   Now again! Ein, zwei, drei! (*Lifts up the rug; behind the rug stands* VARYA, *bowing.*)

PISHTCHIK (*wonderingly*)   Fancy that now!

CHARLOTTA   That's the end. (*Throws the rug at* PISHTCHIK, *makes a curtsey, runs into the larger drawing-room*)

PISHTCHIK (*hurries after her*)   Mischievous creature! Fancy! (*Goes out*)

LYUBOV   And still Leonid doesn't come. I can't understand what he's doing in the town so long! Why, everything must be over by now. The estate is sold, or the sale has not taken place. Why keep us so long in suspense?

VARYA (*trying to console her*)   Uncle's bought it. I feel sure of that.

TROFIMOV (*ironically*)   Oh, yes!

VARYA   Great-aunt sent him an authorization to buy it in her name, and transfer the debt. She's doing it for Anya's sake, and I'm sure God will be merciful. Uncle will buy it.

LYUBOV   My aunt in Yaroslavl sent fifteen thousand to buy the estate in her name, she doesn't trust us—but that's not enough even to pay the arrears. (*Hides her face in her hands*) My fate is being sealed today, my fate. . . .

TROFIMOV (*teasing* VARYA)   Madame Lopahin.

VARYA (*angrily*)   Perpetual student! Twice already you've been sent down
from the University.

LYUBOV   Why are you angry, Varya? He's teasing you about Lopahin. Well,
what of that? Marry Lopahin if you like, he's a good man, and interesting;
if you don't want to, don't! Nobody compels you, darling.

VARYA   I must tell you plainly, mamma, I look at the matter seriously; he's
a good man, I like him.

LYUBOV   Well, marry him. I can't see what you're waiting for.

VARYA   Mamma. I can't make him an offer myself. For the last two years,
everyone's been talking to me about him. Everyone talks; but he says
nothing or else makes a joke. I see what it means. He's growing rich,
he's absorbed in business, he has no thoughts for me. If I had money,
were it ever so little, if I had only a hundred roubles, I'd throw
everything up and go far away. I would go into a nunnery.

TROFIMOV   What bliss!

VARYA (*to* TROFIMOV)   A student ought to have sense! (*In a soft tone with
tears*) How ugly you've grown, Petya! How old you look! (*To*
LYUBOV ANDREYEVNA, *no longer crying*) But I can't do without work,
mamma; I must have something to do every minute.
(*Enter* YASHA)

YASHA (*hardly restraining his laughter*)   Epihodov has broken a billiard
cue! (*Goes out*)

VARYA   What is Epihodov doing here? Who gave him leave to play billiards?
I can't make these people out. (*Goes out*)

LYUBOV   Don't tease her, Petya. You see she has grief enough without that.

TROFIMOV   She is so very officious, meddling in what's not her business.
All the summer she's given Anya and me no peace. She's afraid of a
love affair between us. What's it to do with her? Besides, I have given
no grounds for it. Such triviality is not in my line. We are above love!

LYUBOV   And I suppose I am beneath love. (*Very uneasily*) Why is it Leonid's
not here? If only I could know whether the estate is sold or not! It
seems such an incredible calamity that I really don't know what to
think. I am distracted . . . I shall scream in a minute . . . I shall
do something stupid. Save me, Petya, tell me something, talk to me!

TROFIMOV   What does it matter whether the estate is sold to-day or not?
That's all done with long ago. There's no turning back, the path is
overgrown. Don't worry yourself, dear Lyubov Andreyevna. You
mustn't deceive yourself; for once in your life you must face the truth!

LYUBOV   What truth? You see where the truth lies, but I seem to have lost
my sight, I see nothing. You settle every great problem so boldly, but
tell me, my dear boy, isn't it because you're young—because you haven't
yet understood one of your problems through suffering? You look
forward boldly, and isn't it that you don't see and don't expect anything
dreadful because life is still hidden from your young eyes? You're
bolder, more honest, deeper than we are, but think, be just a little
magnanimous, have pity on me. I was born here, you know, my father
and mother lived here, my grandfather lived here, I love this house. I
can't conceive of life without the cherry orchard, and if it really must

be sold, then sell me with the orchard. (*Embraces* TROFIMOV, *kisses him on the forehead*) My boy was drowned here. (*Weeps*) Pity me, my dear kind fellow.

TROFIMOV   You know I feel for you with all my heart.

LYUBOV   But that should have been said differently, so differently (*takes out her handkerchief, telegram falls on the floor*). My heart is so heavy today. It's so noisy here, my soul is quivering at every sound, I'm shuddering all over, but I can't go away; I'm afraid to be quiet and alone. Don't be hard on me, Petya . . . . I love you as though you were one of ourselves. I would gladly let you marry Anya—I swear I would—only, my dear boy, you must take your degree, you do nothing—you're simply tossed by fate from place to place. That's so strange. It is, isn't it? And you must do something with your beard to make it grow somehow (*laughs*). You look so funny!

TROFIMOV (*picks up the telegram*)   I've no wish to be a beauty.

LYUBOV   That's a telegram from Paris. I get one every day. One yesterday and one today. That savage creature is ill again, he's in trouble again. He begs forgiveness, beseeches me to go, and really I ought to go to Paris to see him. You look shocked, Petya. What am I to do, my dear boy, what am I to do? He is ill, he is alone and unhappy, and who'll look after him, who'll keep him from doing the wrong thing, who'll give him his medicine at the right time? And why hide it or be silent? I love him, that's clear. I love him! I love him! He's a millstone about my neck, I'm going to the bottom with him, but I love that stone and can't live without it (*presses* TROFIMOV's *hand*). Don't think ill of me, Petya, don't tell me anything, don't tell me . . .

TROFIMOV (*through his tears*)   For God's sake forgive my frankness: why, he robbed you!

LYUBOV   No! No! No! You mustn't speak like that (*covers her ears*).

TROFIMOV   He is a wretch! You're the only person that doesn't know it! He's a worthless creature! A despicable wretch!

LYUBOV (*getting angry, but speaking with restraint*)   You're twenty-six or twenty-seven years old, but you're still a schoolboy.

TROFIMOV   Possibly.

LYUBOV   You should be a man at your age! You should understand what love means! And you ought to be in love yourself. You ought to fall in love! (*Angrily*) Yes, yes, and it's not purity in you, you're simply a prude, a comic fool, a freak.

TROFIMOV (*in horror*)   The things she's saying!

LYUBOV   I am above love! You're not above love, but simply as our Firs here says, "You are a good-for-nothing." At your age not to have a mistress!

TROFIMOV (*in horror*)   This is awful! The things she is saying! (*Goes rapidly into the larger drawing-room clutching his head*) This is awful! I can't stand it! I'm going. (*Goes off, but at once returns*) All is over between us! (*Goes off into the ante-room.*)

LYUBOV (*shouts after him*)   Petya! Wait a minute! You funny creature! I was joking! Petya! (*There is a sound of somebody running quickly downstairs and suddenly falling with a crash.* ANYA *and* VARYA *scream, but there is a sound of laughter at once.)*

LYUBOV   What has happened?

(ANYA *runs in.*)

ANYA (*laughing*)   Petya's fallen downstairs! (*Runs out.*)

LYUBOV   What a queer fellow that Petya is!

(*The Station Master stands in the middle of the larger room and reads "The Magdalene," by Alexey Tolstoy. They listen to him, but before he has recited many lines strains of a waltz are heard from the ante-room and the reading is broken off. All dance.* TROFIMOV, ANYA, VARYA *and* LYUBOV ANDREYEVNA *come in from the ante-room.*)

LYUBOV   Come, Petya—come, pure heart! I beg your pardon. Let's have a dance! (*Dances with* PETYA.)

(ANYA *and* VARYA *dance.* FIRS *comes in, puts his stick down near the side door.* YASHA *also comes into the drawing-room and looks on at the dancing.*)

YASHA   What is it, old man?

FIRS   I don't feel well. In old days we used to have generals, barons and admirals dancing at our balls, and now we send for the post-office clerk and the station master and even they're not overanxious to come. I am getting feeble. The old master, the grandfather, used to give sealing-wax for all complaints. I have been taking sealing-wax for twenty years or more. Perhaps that's what's kept me alive.

YASHA   You bore me, old man! (*Yawns*) It's time you were done with.

FIRS   Ach, you're good-for-nothing! (*Mutters.*)

(TROFIMOV *and* LYUBOV ANDREYEVNA *dance in larger room and then on to the stage.*)

LYUBOV   *Merci.* I'll sit down a little (*sits down*). I'm tired.

(*Enter* ANYA.)

ANYA (*excitedly*)   There's a man in the kitchen has been saying that the cherry orchard's been sold today.

LYUBOV   Sold to whom?

ANYA   He didn't say to whom. He's gone away. (*She dances with* TROFIMOV, *and they go off into the larger room.*)

YASHA   There was an old man gossiping there, a stranger.

FIRS   Leonid Andreyevitch isn't here yet, he hasn't come back. He has his light overcoat on, *demi-saison,* he'll catch cold for sure. Ach! Foolish young things!

LYUBOV   I feel as though I should die. Go, Yasha, find out to whom it has been sold.

YASHA   But he went away long ago, the old chap (*laughs*).

LYUBOV (*with slight vexation*)   What are you laughing at? What are you pleased at?

YASHA   Epihodov is so funny. He's a silly fellow, two and twenty misfortunes.

LYUBOV   Firs, if the estate is sold, where will you go?

FIRS   Where you bid me, there I'll go.

LYUBOV   Why do you look like that? Are you ill? You ought to be in bed.

FIRS   Yes (*ironically*). Me go to bed and who's to wait here? Who's to see to things without me? I'm the only one in all the house.

YASHA (*to* LYUBOV ANDREYEVNA)   Lyubov Andreyevna, permit me to make a request of you; if you go back to Paris again, be so kind as to take me with you. It's positively impossible for me to stay here (*looking about him; in an undertone*). There's no need to say it, you see for yourself—an uncivilised country, the people have no morals, and then the dullness! The food in the kitchen's abominable, and then Firs runs after one muttering all sorts of unsuitable words. Take me with you, please do!
(*Enter* PISHTCHIK.)

PISHTCHIK   Allow me to ask you for a waltz, my dear lady. (LYUBOV ANDREYEVNA *goes with him*) Enchanting lady, I really must borrow of you just 180 roubles (*dances*), only 180 roubles. (*They pass into the larger room.*)

YASHA (*hums softly*)   "Knowest thou my soul's emotion."
(*In the larger drawing-room, a figure in a gray top hat and in check trousers is gesticulating and jumping about.* Shouts of "Bravo, Charlotta Ivanovna.")

DUNYASHA (*she has stopped to powder herself*)   My young lady tells me to dance. There are plenty of gentlemen, and too few ladies, but dancing makes me giddy and makes my heart beat. Firs, the post-office clerk said something to me just now that quite took my breath away.
(*Music becomes more subdued.*)

FIRS   What did he say to you?

DUNYASHA   He said I was like a flower.

YASHA (*yawns*)   What ignorance! (*Goes out.*)

DUNYASHA   Like a flower. I am a girl of such delicate feelings, I am awfully fond of soft speeches.

FIRS   Your head's being turned.
(*Enter* EPIHODOV.)

EPIHODOV   You have no desire to see me, Dunyasha. I might be an insect (*sighs*). Ah! life!

DUNYASHA   What is it you want?

EPIHODOV   Undoubtedly you may be right (*sighs*). But of course, if one looks at it from that point of view, if I may so express myself, you have, excuse my plain speaking, reduced me to a complete state of mind. I know my destiny. Every day some misfortune befalls me and I have long ago grown accustomed to it, so that I look upon my fate with a smile. You gave me your word, and though I . . .

DUNYASHA   Let us have a talk later, I entreat you, but now leave me in peace, for I am lost in reverie (*plays with her fan*).

EPIHODOV   I have a misfortune every day, and if I may venture to express myself, I merely smile at it, I even laugh.
(VARYA *enters from the larger drawing-room.*)

VARYA   You still have not gone, Epihodov. What a disrespectful creature you are, really! (*To* DUNYASHA) Go along, Dunyasha! (*To* EPIHODOV) First you play billiards and break the cue, then you go wandering about the drawing-room like a visitor!

EPIHODOV   You really cannot, if I may so express myself, call me to account like this.

VARYA   I'm not calling you to account. I'm speaking to you: You do nothing but wander from place to place and don't do your work. We keep you as a counting-house clerk, but what use you are I can't say.

EPIHODOV (*offended*)   Whether I work or whether I walk, whether I eat or whether I play billiards, is a matter to be judged by persons of understanding and my elders.

VARYA   You dare to tell me that! (*Firing up*) You dare! You mean to say I've no understanding. Begone from here! This minute!

EPIHODOV (*intimidated*)   I beg you to express yourself with delicacy.

VARYA (*beside herself with anger*)   This moment! get out! away! (*He goes toward the door, she following him*) Two and twenty misfortunes! Take yourself off! Don't let me set eyes on you! (EPIHODOV *has gone out, behind the door his voice*, "I shall lodge a complaint against you") What! You're coming back? (*Snatches up the stick* FIRS *has put down near the door*) Come! Come! Come! I'll show you! What! you're coming? Then take that! (*She swings the stick, at the very moment that* LOPAHIN *comes in.*)

LOPAHIN   Very much obliged to you!

VARYA (*angrily and ironically*)   I beg your pardon!

LOPAHIN   Not at all! I humbly thank you for your kind reception!

VARYA   No need of thanks for it. (*Moves away, then looks round and asks softly*) I haven't hurt you?

LOPAHIN   Oh, no! Not at all! There's an immense bump coming up, though!

VOICES FROM LARGER ROOM   Lopahin has come! Yermolay Alexeyevitch!

PISHTCHIK   What do I see and hear? (*Kisses* LOPAHIN) There's a whiff of cognac about you, my dear soul, and we're making merry here too!

(*Enter* LYUBOV ANDREYEVNA.)

LYUBOV   Is it you, Yermolay Alexeyevitch? Why have you been so long? Where's Leonid?

LOPAHIN   Leonid Andreyevitch arrived with me. He is coming.

LYUBOV (*in agitation*)   Well! Well! Was there a sale? Speak!

LOPAHIN (*embarrassed, afraid of betraying his joy*)   The sale was over at four o'clock. We missed our train—had to wait till half-past nine. (*Sighing heavily*) Ugh! I feel a little giddy.

(*Enter* GAEV. *In his right hand he has purchases, with his left hand he is wiping away his tears.*)

LYUBOV   Well, Leonid? What news? (*Impatiently, with tears*) Make haste, for God's sake!

GAEV (*makes her no answer, simply waves his hand. To* FIRS, *weeping*)   Here, take them; there's anchovies, Kertch herrings. I have eaten nothing all day. What I have been through! (*Door into the billiard room is open. There is heard a knocking of balls and the voice of* YASHA *saying* "Eighty-seven." GAEV's *expression changes, he leaves off weeping*) I am fearfully tired. Firs, come and help me change my things (*goes to his own room across the larger drawing-room*).

PISHTCHIK   How about the sale? Tell us, do!

LYUBOV   Is the cherry orchard sold?

LOPAHIN   It is sold.

LYUBOV   Who has bought it?

LOPAHIN   I have bought it. (*A pause.* LYUBOV *is crushed; she would fall down if she were not standing near a chair and table.*)

> (VARYA *takes keys from her waist-band, flings them on the floor in middle of drawing-room and goes out.*)

LOPAHIN   I have bought it! Wait a bit, ladies and gentlemen, pray. My head's a bit muddled, I can't speak (*laughs*). We came to the auction. Deriganov was there already. Leonid Andreyevitch only had 15,000 and Deriganov bid 30,000, besides the arrears, straight off. I saw how the land lay. I bid against him. I bid 40,000, he bid 45,000, I said 55, and so he went on, adding 5 thousands and I adding 10. Well . . . So it ended. I bid 90, and it was knocked down to me. Now the cherry orchard's mine! Mine! (*chuckles*) My God, the cherry orchard's mine! Tell me that I'm drunk, that I'm out of my mind, that it's all a dream (*stamps with his feet*). Don't laugh at me! If my father and my grandfather could rise from their graves and see all that has happened! How their Yermolay, ignorant, beaten Yermolay, who used to run about barefoot in winter, how that very Yermolay has bought the finest estate in the world! I have bought the estate where my father and grandfather were slaves, where they weren't even admitted into the kitchen. I am asleep, I am dreaming! It is all fancy, it is the work of your imagination plunged in the darkness of ignorance (*picks up keys, smiling fondly*). She threw away the keys; she means to show she's not the housewife now (*jingles the keys*). Well, no matter. (*The orchestra is heard tuning up*) Hey, musicians! Play! I want to hear you. Come, all of you, and look how Yermolay Lopahin will take the axe to the cherry orchard, how the trees will fall to the ground! We will build houses on it and our grandsons and great-grandsons will see a new life springing up there. Music! Play up!

> (*Music begins to play.* LYUBOV ANDREYEVNA *has sunk into a chair and is weeping bitterly.*)

LOPAHIN (*reproachfully*)   Why, why didn't you listen to me? My poor friend! Dear lady, there's no turning back now. (*With tears*) Oh, if all this could be over, oh, if our miserable disjointed life could somehow be changed!

PISHTCHIK (*takes him by the arm, in an undertone*)   She's weeping, let us go and leave her alone. Come (*takes him by the arm and leads him into the larger drawing-room*).

LOPAHIN   What's that? Musicians, play up! All must be as I wish it. (*With irony*) Here comes the new master, the owner of the cherry orchard! (*Accidentally tips over a little table, almost upsetting the candelabra*) I can pay for everything! (*Goes out with* PISHTCHIK. *No one remains on the stage or in the larger drawing-room except* LYUBOV, *who sits huddled up, weeping bitterly. The music plays softly.* ANYA *and* TROFIMOV *come in quickly.* ANYA *goes up to her mother and falls on her knees before her.* TROFIMOV *stands at the entrance to the larger drawing-room.*)

ANYA   Mamma! Mamma, you're crying, dear, kind, good mamma! My precious! I love you! I bless you! The cherry orchard is sold, it is gone, that's true, that's true! But don't weep, mamma! Life is still before you, you have still your good, pure heart! Let us go, let us go, darling, away from here! We will make a new garden, more splendid than this one; you will see it, you will understand. And joy, quiet, deep joy, will sink into your soul like the sun at evening! And you will smile, mamma! Come, darling, let us go!

(*The Curtain Falls.*)

Act Four

SCENE: *Same as in First Act. There are neither curtains on the windows nor pictures on the walls: only a little furniture remains piled up in a corner as if for sale. There is a sense of desolation; near the outer door and in the background of the scene are packed trunks, travelling bags, etc. On the left the door is open, and from here the voices of* VARYA *and* ANYA *are audible.* LOPAHIN *is standing waiting.* YASHA *is holding a tray with glasses full of champagne. In front of the stage* EPIHODOV *is tying up a box. In the background behind the scene a hum of talk from the peasants who have come to say good-bye. The voice of* GAEV: "Thanks, brothers, thanks!"*

YASHA   The peasants have come to say good-bye. In my opinion, Yermolay Alexeyevitch, the peasants are good-natured, but they don't know much about things.

(*The hum of talk dies away. Enter across front of stage* LYUBOV ANDREYEVNA *and* GAEV. *She is not weeping, but is pale; her face is quivering—she cannot speak.*)

GAEV   You gave them your purse, Lyuba. That won't do—that won't do!

LYUBOV   I couldn't help it! I couldn't help it!

(*Both go out.*)

LOPAHIN (*in the doorway, calls after them*)   You will take a glass at parting? Please do. I didn't think to bring any from the town, and at the station I could only get one bottle. Please take a glass. (*A pause*) What? You don't care for any? (*Comes away from the door*) If I'd known, I wouldn't have bought it. Well, and I'm not going to drink it. (YASHA *carefully sets the tray down on a chair*) You have a glass, Yasha, anyway.

YASHA   Good luck to the travellers, and luck to those that stay behind! (*Drinks*) This champagne isn't the real thing, I can assure you.

LOPAHIN   It cost eight roubles the bottle (*a pause*). It's devilish cold here.

YASHA   They haven't heated the stove today—it's all the same since we're going (*laughs*).

LOPAHIN   What are you laughing for?

YASHA   For pleasure.

LOPAHIN   Though it's October, it's as still and sunny as though it were summer. It's just right for building! (*Looks at his watch; says in doorway*) Take note, ladies and gentlemen, the train goes in forty-seven minutes; so you ought to start for the station in twenty minutes. You must hurry up!

(TROFIMOV *comes in from out of doors wearing a great-coat.*)

TROFIMOV   I think it must be time to start, the horses are ready. The devil only knows what's become of my goloshes; they're lost. (*In the doorway*) Anya! My goloshes aren't here. I can't find them.

LOPAHIN   And I'm getting off to Harkov. I am going in the same train with you. I'm spending all the winter at Harkov. I've been wasting all my time gossiping with you and fretting with no work to do. I can't get on without work. I don't know what to do with my hands, they flap about so queerly, as if they didn't belong to me.

TROFIMOV   Well, we're just going away, and you will take up your profitable labours again.

LOPAHIN   Do take a glass.

TROFIMOV   No, thanks.

LOPAHIN   Then you're going to Moscow now?

TROFIMOV   Yes. I shall see them as far as the town, and tomorrow I shall go on to Moscow.

LOPAHIN   Yes, I daresay, the professors aren't giving any lectures, they're waiting for your arrival.

TROFIMOV   That's not your business.

LOPAHIN   How many years have you been at the University?

TROFIMOV   Do think of something newer than that—that's stale and flat (*hunts for goloshes*). You know we shall most likely never see each other again, so let me give you one piece of advice at parting: don't wave your arms about—get out of the habit. And another thing, building villas, reckoning up that the summer visitors will in time become independent farmers— reckoning like that, that's not the thing to do either. After all, I am fond of you: you have fine delicate fingers like an artist, you've a fine delicate soul.

LOPAHIN (*embraces him*)   Good-bye, my dear fellow. Thanks for everything. Let me give you money for the journey, if you need it.

TROFIMOV   What for? I don't need it.

LOPAHIN   Why, you haven't got a halfpenny.

TROFIMOV   Yes, I have, thank you. I got some money for a translation. Here it is in my pocket, (*anxiously*) but where can my goloshes be!

VARYA (*from the next room*)   Take the nasty things! (*Flings a pair of goloshes onto the stage.*)

TROFIMOV   Why are you so cross, Varya? h'm! . . . but those aren't my goloshes.

LOPAHIN   I sowed three thousand acres with poppies in the spring, and now I have cleared forty thousand profit. And when my poppies were in flower, wasn't it a picture! So here, as I say, I made forty thousand, and I'm offering you a loan because I can afford to. Why turn up your nose? I am a peasant—I speak bluntly.

TROFIMOV   Your father was a peasant, mine was a chemist—and that proves absolutely nothing whatever. (LOPAHIN *takes out his pocketbook*) Stop that—stop that. If you were to offer me two hundred thousand I wouldn't take it. I am an independent man, and everything that all of you, rich and poor alike, prize so highly and hold so dear, hasn't the slightest power over me—it's like so much fluff fluttering in the air. I can get on without you. I can pass by you. I am strong and proud. Humanity is advancing towards the highest truth, the highest happiness, which is possible on earth, and I am in the front ranks.

LOPAHIN   Will you get there?

TROFIMOV   I shall get there (*a pause*). I shall get there, or I shall show others the way to get there.
(*In the distance is heard the stroke of an axe on a tree.*)

LOPAHIN   Good-bye, my dear fellow; it's time to be off. We turn up our noses at one another, but life is passing all the while. When I am working hard without resting, then my mind is more at ease, and it seems to me as though I too know what I exist for; but how many people there are in Russia, my dear boy, who exist, one doesn't know what for. Well, it doesn't matter. That's not what keeps things spinning. They tell me Leonid Andreyevitch has taken a situation. He is going to be a clerk at the bank—6,000 roubles a year. Only, of course, he won't stick to it—he's too lazy.

ANYA (*in doorway*)   Mamma begs you not to let them chop down the orchard until she's gone.

TROFIMOV   Yes, really, you might have the tact (*walks out across the front of the stage*).

LOPAHIN   I'll see to it! I'll see to it! Stupid fellows! (*Goes out after him.*)

ANYA   Has Firs been taken to the hospital?

YASHA   I told them this morning. No doubt they have taken him.

ANYA (*to* EPIHODOV, *who passes across the drawing-room*)   Semyon Pantale-yevitch, inquire, please, if Firs has been taken to the hospital.

YASHA (*in a tone of offense*)   I told Yegor this morning—why ask a dozen times?

EPIHODOV   Firs is advanced in years. It's my conclusive opinion no treatment would do him good; it's time he was gathered to his fathers. And I can only envy him (*puts a trunk down on a cardboard hat-box and crushes it*). There now, of course—I knew it would be so.

YASHA (*jeeringly*)   Two and twenty misfortunes!

VARYA (*through the door*)   Has Firs been taken to the hospital?

ANYA   Yes.

VARYA   Why wasn't the note for the doctor taken too?

ANYA   Oh, then, we must send it after them (*goes out*).

VARYA (*from the adjoining room*)   Where's Yasha? Tell him his mother's come to say good-bye to him.

YASHA (*waves his hand*)   They put me out of all patience!
(DUNYASHA *has all this time been busy about the luggage.*
Now, when YASHA *is left alone, she goes up to him.*)

DUNYASHA   You might just give me one look, Yasha. You're going away. You're leaving me (*weeps and throws herself on his neck*).

YASHA   What are you crying for? (*Drinks the champagne*) In six days I shall be in Paris again. Tomorrow we shall get into the express train and roll away in a flash. I can scarcely believe it! *Vive la France!* It doesn't suit me here —it's not the life for me; there's no doing anything. I have seen enough of the ignorance here. I have had enough of it (*drinks champagne*). What are you crying for? Behave yourself properly, and then you won't cry.

DUNYASHA (*powders her face, looking in a pocket-mirror*)   Do send me a letter from Paris. You know how I loved you, Yasha—how I loved you! I am a tender creature, Yasha.

YASHA   Here they are coming! (*Busies himself about the trunks, humming softly. Enter* LYUBOV ANDREYEVNA, GAEV, ANYA *and* CHARLOTTA IVANOVNA.)

GAEV   We ought to be off. There's not much time now (*looking at* YASHA). What a smell of herrings!

LYUBOV   In ten minutes we must get into the carriage (*casts a look about the room*). Farewell, dear house, dear old home of our fathers! Winter will pass and spring will come, and then you will be no more; they will tear you down! How much those walls have seen! (*Kisses her daughter passionately*) My treasure, how bright you look! Your eyes are sparkling like diamonds! Are you glad? Very glad?

ANYA   Very glad! A new life is beginning, mamma.

GAEV   Yes, really, everything is all right now. Before the cherry orchard was sold, we were all worried and wretched, but afterwards, when once the question was settled conclusively, irrevocably, we all felt calm and even cheerful. I am a bank clerk now—I am a financier—cannon off the red. And you, Lyuba, after all, you are looking better; there's no question of that.

LYUBOV   Yes. My nerves are better, that's true. (*Her hat and coat are handed to her*) I'm sleeping well. Carry out my things, Yasha. It's time. (*To* ANYA) My darling, we shall soon see each other again. I am going to Paris. I can live there on the money your Yaroslavl auntie sent us to buy the estate with—hurrah for auntie!—but that money won't last long.

ANYA   You'll come back soon, mamma, won't you? I'll be working up for my examination in the high school, and when I have passed that, I shall set to work and be a help to you. We will read all sorts of things together, mamma, won't we? (*Kisses her mother's hands*) We will read in the autumn evenings. We'll read lots of books, and a new wonderful world will open out before us (*dreamily*). Mamma, come soon.

LYUBOV   I shall come, my precious treasure (*embraces her*).
(*Enter* LOPAHIN. CHARLOTTA *softly hums a song.*)

GAEV   Charlotta's happy; she's singing!

CHARLOTTA (*picks up a bundle like a swaddled baby*)   Bye, bye, my baby. (*A baby is heard crying: "Ooah! ooah!"*) Hush, hush, my pretty boy! (*Ooah! ooah!*) Poor little thing! (*Throws the bundle back*) You must please find me a situation. I can't go on like this.

LOPAHIN   We'll find you one, Charlotta Ivanovna. Don't you worry yourself.

GAEV   Everyone's leaving us. Varya's going away. We have become of no use all at once.

CHARLOTTA   There's nowhere for me to be in the town. I must go away. (*Hums*) What care I . . .
(*Enter* PISHTCHIK.)

LOPAHIN   The freak of nature!

PISHTCHIK (*gasping*)   Oh! . . . let me get my breath. . . . I'm worn out . . . my most honoured . . . Give me some water.

GAEV   Want some money, I suppose? Your humble servant! I'll go out of the way of temptation (*goes out*).

PISHTCHIK   It's a long while since I have been to see you . . . dearest lady.

(*To* LOPAHIN) You are here . . . glad to see you . . . a man of immense intellect . . . take . . . here (*gives* LOPAHIN) 400 roubles. That leaves me owing 840.

LOPAHIN (*shrugging his shoulders in amazement*)   It's like a dream. Where did you get it?

PISHTCHIK   Wait a bit . . . I'm hot . . . a most extraordinary occurrence! Some Englishmen came along and found in my land some sort of white clay. (*To* LYUBOV ANDREYEVNA) And 400 for you . . . most lovely . . . wonderful (*gives money*). The rest later (*sips water*). A young man in the train was telling me just now that a great philosopher advises jumping off a house-top. "Jump!" says he; "the whole gist of the problem lies in that." (*Wonderingly*) Fancy that, now! Water, please!

LOPAHIN   What Englishmen?

PISHTCHIK   I have made over to them the rights to dig the clay for twenty-four years . . . and now, excuse me . . . I can't stay . . . .I must be trotting on. I'm going to Znoikovo . . . to Kardamanovo. . . . I'm in debt all round (*sips*) . . . To your very good health! . . . I'll come in on Thursday.

LYUBOV   We are just off to the town, and tomorrow I start for abroad.

PISHTCHIK   What! (*In agitation*) Why to the town? Oh, I see the furniture . . . the boxes. No matter . . . (*through his tears*) . . . no matter . . . men of enormous intellect . . . these Englishmen. . . . Never mind . . . be happy. God will succour you . . . no matter . . . everything in this world must have an end (*kisses* LYUBOV ANDREYEVNA's *hand*). If the rumour reaches you that my end has come, think of this . . . old horse, and say: "There once was such a man in the world . . . Semyonov-Pishtchik . . . the Kingdom of Heaven be his!" . . . most extraordinary weather . . . yes. (*Goes out in violent agitation, but at once returns and says in the doorway*) Dashenka wishes to be remembered to you (*goes out*).

LYUBOV   Now we can start. I leave with two cares in my heart. The first is leaving Firs ill. (*Looking at her watch*) We still have five minutes.

ANYA   Mamma, Firs has been taken to the hospital. Yasha sent him off this morning.

LYUBOV   My other anxiety is Varya. She is used to getting up early and working; and now, without work, she's like a fish out of water. She is thin and pale, and she's crying, poor dear! (*A pause*) You are well aware, Yermolay Alexeyevitch, I dreamed of marrying her to you, and everything seemed to show that you would get married (*whispers to* ANYA *and motions to* CHARLOTTA *and both go out*). She loves you—she suits you. And I don't know—I don't know why it is you seem, as it were, to avoid each other. I can't understand it!

LOPAHIN   I don't understand it myself, I confess. It's queer somehow, altogether. If there's still time, I'm ready now at once. Let's settle it straight off, and go ahead; but without you, I feel I shan't make her an offer.

LYUBOV   That's excellent. Why, a single moment's all that's necessary. I'll call her at once.

LOPAHIN   And there's champagne all ready too (*looking into the glasses*).

Empty! Someone's emptied them already. (YASHA *coughs*) I call that greedy.

LYUBOV (*eagerly*)   Capital! We will go out. Yasha, *allez!* I'll call her in. (*At the door*) Varya, leave all that; come here. Come along! (*Goes out with* YASHA.)

LOPAHIN (*looking at his watch*)   Yes.

(*A pause. Behind the door, smothered laughter and whispering, and, at last, enter* VARYA.)

VARYA (*looking a long while over the things*)   It is strange, I can't find it anywhere.

LOPAHIN   What are you looking for?

VARYA   I packed it myself, and I can't remember (*a pause*).

LOPAHIN   Where are you going now, Varvara Mihailova?

VARYA   I? To the Ragulins. I have arranged to go to them to look after the house—as a housekeeper.

LOPAHIN   That's in Yashnovo? It'll be seventy miles away (*a pause*). So this is the end of life in this house!

VARYA (*looking among the things*)   Where is it? Perhaps I put it in the trunk. Yes, life in this house is over—there will be no more of it.

LOPAHIN   And I'm just off to Harkov—by this next train. I've a lot of business there. I'm leaving Epihodov here, and I've taken him on.

VARYA   Really!

LOPAHIN   This time last year we had snow already, if you remember; but now it's so fine and sunny. Though it's cold, to be sure—three degrees of frost.

VARYA   I haven't looked (*a pause*). And besides, our thermometer's broken (*a pause*).

(*Voice at the door from the yard:* "Yermolay Alexeyevitch!")

LOPAHIN (*as though he had long been expecting this summons*)   This minute!

(LOPAHIN *goes out quickly.* VARYA *sitting on the floor and laying her head an a bag full of clothes, sobs quietly. The door opens.* LYUBOV ANDREYEVNA *comes in cautiously.*)

LYUBOV   Well? (*A pause*) We must be going.

VARYA (*has wiped her eyes and is no longer crying*)   Yes, mamma, it's time to start. I shall have time to get to the Ragulins today, if only you're not late for the train.

LYUBOV (*in the doorway*)   Anya, put your things on.

(*Enter* ANYA, *then* GAEV *and* CHARLOTTA IVANOVNA. GAEV *has on a warm coat with a hood. Servants and cabmen come in.* EPIHODOV *bustles about the luggage.*)

LYUBOV   Now we can start on our travels.

ANYA (*joyfully*)   On our travels!

GAEV   My friends—my dear, my precious friends! Leaving this house for ever, can I be silent? Can I refrain from giving utterance at leave-taking to those emotions which now flood all my being?

ANYA (*supplicatingly*)   Uncle!

VARYA   Uncle, you mustn't!

GAEV (*dejectedly*)   Cannon and into the pocket . . . I'll be quiet . . .

(*Enter* TROFIMOV *and afterwards* LOPAHIN.)

TROFIMOV   Well, ladies and gentlemen, we must start.

LOPAHIN   Epihodov, my coat!

LYUBOV   I'll stay just one minute. It seems as though I have never seen before what the walls, what the ceilings in this house were like, and now I look at them with greediness, with such tender love.

GAEV   I remember when I was six years old sitting in that window on Trinity Day watching my father going to church.

LYUBOV   Have all the things been taken?

LOPAHIN   I think all. (*Putting on overcoat, to* EPIHODOV) You, Epihodov, mind you see everything is right.

EPIHODOV (*in a husky voice*)   Don't you trouble, Yermolay Alexeyevitch.

LOPAHIN   Why, what's wrong with your voice?

EPIHODOV   I've just had a drink of water, and I choked over something.

YASHA (*contemptuously*)   The ignorance!

LYUBOV   We are going—and not a soul will be left here.

LOPAHIN   Not till the spring.

VARYA (*pulls a parasol out of a bundle, as though about to hit someone with it.* LOPAHIN *makes a gesture as though alarmed*)   What is it? I didn't mean anything.

TROFIMOV   Ladies and gentlemen, let us get into the carriage. It's time. The train will be in directly.

VARYA   Petya, here they are, your goloshes, by that box. (*With tears*) And what dirty old things they are!

TROFIMOV (*putting on his goloshes*)   Let us go, friends!

GAEV (*greatly agitated, afraid of weeping*)   The train—the station! Double baulk, ah!

LYUBOV   Let us go!

LOPAHIN   Are we all here? (*Locks the side-door on left*) The things are all here. We must lock up. Let us go!

ANYA   Good-bye, home! Good-bye to the old life!

TROFIMOV   Welcome to the new life!

(TROFIMOV *goes out with* ANYA. VARYA *looks round the room and goes out slowly.* YASHA *and* CHARLOTTA IVANOVNA, *with her dog, go out.*)

LOPAHIN   Till the spring, then! Come, friends, till we meet! (*Goes out.*)

(LYUBOV ANDREYEVNA *and* GAEV *remain alone. As though they had been waiting for this, they throw themselves on each other's necks, and break into subdued smothered sobbing, afraid of being overheard.*)

GAEV (*in despair*)   Sister, my sister!

LYUBOV   Oh, my orchard!—my sweet, beautiful orchard! My life, my youth, my happiness, good-bye! good-bye!

VOICE OF ANYA (*calling gaily*)   Mamma!

VOICE OF TROFIMOV (*gaily, excitedly*)   Aa-oo!

LYUBOV   One last look at the walls, at the windows. My dear mother loved to walk about this room.

GAEV   Sister, sister!

VOICE OF ANYA   Mamma!

VOICE OF TROFIMOV   Aa-oo!

LYUBOV   We are coming. (*They go out.*)

> (*The stage is empty. There is the sound of the doors
> being locked up, then of the carriages driving away.
> There is silence. In the stillness there is the dull stroke
> of an axe in a tree, clanging with a mournful lonely
> sound. Footsteps are heard.* FIRS *appears in the doorway
> on the right. He is dressed as always—in a pea-jacket
> and white waistcoat, with slippers on his feet. He is ill.*)

FIRS (*goes up to the doors, and tries the handles*)   Locked! They have gone
. . . (*sits down on sofa*). They have forgotten me. . . . Never mind
. . . I'll sit here a bit. . . . I'll be bound Leonid Andreyevitch hasn't put
his fur coat on and has gone off in his thin overcoat (*sighs anxiously*). I
didn't see after him. . . . These young people . . . (*mutters something
that can't be distinguished*). Life has slipped by as though I hadn't lived.
(*Lies down*) I'll lie down a bit. . . . There's no strength in you, nothing
left you—all gone! Ech! I'm good for nothing (*lies motionless*).

> (*A sound is heard that seems to come from the sky, like
> a breaking harp-string, dying away mournfully. All is
> still again, and there is heard nothing but the strokes of
> the axe far away in the orchard.*)

(*The Curtain Falls.*)

From the Playwright

Chekhov *had no doubts that he'd written a comedy with* The Cherry Orchard. *His initial plans for the play, plus his dissatisfaction with the Stanislavski-Danchenko production all attest to his desire to author not a serious play, but a gay and lively one. Througout the period from inception to production of* The Cherry Orchard (*April, 1901 to January, 1904*), *Chekhov was continually offering comments and answering questions about casting, meaning and interpretation—even some suggestions on the setting. These excerpts from his letters show the close concern the author had for* The Cherry Orchard, *the source of his greatest anxiety and most triumphant success.*

Notes on The Cherry Orchard

April, 1901   to Olga Knipper[1]
    I have a tremendous desire to write for the Moscow Art Theatre a comedy or vaudeville in four acts. They will have it before the end of 1903.

December 18, 1901   to Olga Knipper
    Writing a funny play is still in my dreams. Whether I do is uncertain.

December 22, 1902   to Olga Knipper
    I want very badly to write a vaudeville, but there is never time. I have this sensation that vaudeville will again be popular.

January 3, 1903   to Olga Knipper
    I did want the play to be in three acts, but four will do just as well. It will still remain the same play.

February 5, 1903   to Stanislavski[2]
    I have finished the play in my mind. It is called "The Cherry Orchard" in four acts. Through the first three can be seen cherry trees in blossom through the windows. Everything, including the ladies' gowns, is in white.

March 5 & 6, 1903   to Olga Knipper
    Varya is a comical part, and there is one for Stanislavski too. If the play doesn't work out the way I've planned it, you may punch my head.

---

[1]Olga Knipper was Chekov's wife, and an actress with the Moscow Art Theatre who was to play Madam Ranevsky.
[2]Stanislavski was co-director of the Moscow Art Theatre and eventually played Gayev.

March 21, 1903   to Olga Knipper
  I've tried to give *The Cherry Orchard* as few characters as possible—it will be more intimate.

April 11, 1903   to Olga Knipper
  Will you (the Moscow Art Theatre) have an actress for the part of the elderly lady in *The Cherry Orchard?* If not, there shall be no play. I will not write it.

September 2, 1903   to Nemirovich-Danchenko[3]
  My play (if I continue writing as I've worked today) will be finished soon. Writing the second act was difficult, very difficult. But I believe it went well. I shall call the play a comedy.

September 15, 1903   to Lilina[4]
  My dear Maria Petrovna, don't believe what anyone says. Not a living soul has read my play yet. Your part (Varya) was not written as a "prig," but as a very naive young girl with which, I hope, you'll be satisfied . . . It hasn't turned out as a drama, but as a comedy, and in spots even a farce. I'm afraid that may cause some friction with Danchenko and Stanislavski.

September 21, 1903   to Olga Knipper
  When I'm through I'll send a telegram. The last act will be gay, but actually the entire play is gay and frivolous.

September 27, 1903   to Olga Knipper
  It's true that the characters come out as real people. But how the play is as a whole I don't know.

October 12, 1903   to Olga Knipper
  The play's finished, at last, and tomorrow evening will be sent to Moscow. I will send some comments for you also. If any changes are needed I feel they shall be small ones. The worst thing about the play is that I didn't write it at one time but spent a long time, and it's sure to seem spun out. It worries me.

October 14, 1903   to Olga Knipper
  The house is an old manor. People once lived in great style there and this must be felt by the setting. It must be comfortable.
  Varya's a bit crude and somewhat stupid, but very good hearted.
  You must portray Ranevsky. I see no one else in the role. She dresses with good taste, but not stuffy. She's bright, gentle, but forgetful. Always with a smile on her face, she's nice to everyone. Anya can only be played by a young actress.
  Gayev is for Vishnevsky. Tell him to pay attention to people playing billiards and write down all the terms. I don't play. I'll settle it later when I see him. In Act

---

[3]Along with Stanislavski, Danchenko was co-director of the Moscow Art Theatre.
[4]Lilina was the stage name of Stanislavski's wife, who was to play Anya.

Four Charlotta plays a trick with Trofimov's galoshes. Ranevsky can't play it. What's needed here is an actress with some humor.

October 21, 1903   to Olga Knipper

Stanislavski sent a telegram and calls the play a work of genius. I think he overdoes it, and this may prove harmful. Danchenko is wrong about Anya. Anya is most of all a child, and she stays gay to the end. She's naive and doesn't cry except in Act Two, and then she only has tears in her eyes.

October 23, 1903   to Olga Knipper

You write that Vishnevsky can't play Gaev. Who then? Stanislavski? But who could then play Lopahin? . . . Danchenko writes that there are many tears in my play and some coarseness. Write and tell me what you find wrong. What are people saying about it? I can change it yet.

October 23, 1903   to Danchenko

I would very much like to look in on some rehearsals. I'm afraid Anya might become too weepy in tone, and I fear her being played by an actress who isn't young. Anya doesn't cry once in my play, she nowhere speaks in a weepy tone. In the second act there are tears in her eyes, but the tone is gay and light. Why do you say in your wire that the play is filled with crying people? Where are they? Varya is the only one, but this is only because Varya's a cry baby by nature, and her tears must not be depressing to the audience. Often you'll find the stage direction "through tears," but that is only the mood, not real tears. There is no cemetery in Act II.

October 28, 1903   to Olga Knipper

No, I never wanted Ranevsky to calm down. Only death can calm a woman such as her. . . . It's not difficult to play Ranevsky. But it is necessary to strike the right tone from the beginning. You'll need to find a smile and a manner of behaving, and it's necessary to know how to dress.

October 30, 1903   to Olga Knipper

Stanislavski will make an excellent and orginal Gayev, but then who's to play Lopahin? To be sure, the part of Lopahin is the central one. If it doesn't succeed the entire play will fail. Lopahin shouldn't be played by anyone loud, and it isn't necessary to mold him as a typical merchant.

October 30, 1903   to Stanislavski

I thought of Lopahin as your part when I wrote it. If it doesn't appeal to you for some reason, then take Gayev. Yes, Lopahin is a merchant, but he's a fine person beyond doubt. He's intelligent and totally dignified. There should be nothing petty about him, no games, and I thought you to be the best for this part which is central to the play. When you pick an actor for this part you must not forget that Lopahin was loved by Varya, who was quite religious and serious. She would never love some wicked money-grabbing peasant.

November 2, 1903   to Danchenko
    Let Stanislavski choose between Gayev and Lopahin. If he chooses Lopahin
the play will succeed. You see, if Lopahin's lifeless and is played by a lifeless actor
the play is bound to fail.
    Charlotta speaks good Russian—not broken. Only occasionally does she mix
up hard and soft consonants and confuses genders. Pishtchik is a Russian, an
elderly man hampered by gout, old age and good living. He is fat, and wears a
peasant's sleeveless coat. Lopahin wears a white waistcoat and brown boots. He
always waves his arms as he talks, and his steps are large. He thinks while he
walks, walking in a straight line. Absentmindedly he combs his beard from back to
front . . . The part of Trofimov's quite lucid, I feel. Varya wears a black dress and
broad belt.
    I spent three years preparing to write this play and for these three years I've
been telling you to get an actress to play Ranevsky. So don't complain if you find
yourselves having problems you can't resolve.

November 10, 1903   to Stanislavski
    The house is large with two stories, as there is a comment in Act III of a
staircase going downstairs.
    The house must be large and solid, and what it's made of isn't important.
It's the kind of house used to tear down and make summer cottages. The furniture
is stylish and old-fashioned. It hasn't been affected by the financial ruin.
    You may use the same sets for Acts III and IV. Don't hamper yourself
with scenery—I leave it to you. In your theatre I'm always awed anyway. Whatever you decide will be fine—many times better than what I might think of.

January 6, 1904   to V. F. Komissarzhevsky
    I'm convinced that my play doesn't fit you at all. The central female part in
The Cherry Orchard is of an elderly woman caught up in the past. She has nothing
to do with the present . . .

After the first performance, January 17, 1904

January 19, 1904   to F. D. Batyvskov
    As far as I can tell, it will be carnival time at least before our actors come to
their senses and start playing *The Cherry Orchard* less confusedly and silly than
now.

March 18, 1904   to Olga Knipper
    Inform Danchenko that the sounds in Acts II and IV have to be shorter, much
shorter. They must feel as if coming from quite far away. Too much concern has
been generated here over a small matter, a mere noise that is clearly described
in the text.

March 29, 1904   to Olga Knipper
    Some of your relatives saw the play in March. They say Stanislavski plays
horribly as Gayev in Act IV and drags the play out. This is really dreadful. The act

should last no more than twelve minutes and he drags it out for forty. He has ruined my play. I will say no more about Stanislavski.

April 10, 1904   to Olga Knipper
      Why do they insist on calling my play a drama in the playbills and advertisements? What Danchenko and Stanislavski see in my play is not what I wrote. I will swear neither of them has read my play carefully even once.

(Translated by David Cooney)

From the Critic

Chekov's The Cherry Orchard, *like Oscar Wilde's* The Importance of Being Earnest, *is a totally unique play, and as such invites many interpretations. One basic battle of the critics has been over the classification of the play: is it comedy or tragedy?* **D. C. Gerould** *views the play as comedy, saying that the substance and theme of Chekov is lost if we think of the play in tragic terms. Gerould examines the plot, character, language, and resolution and concludes that the beauty of* The Cherry Orchard *comes in the realization that the play can only be considered comedy, though certainly not the comedy that we of the 70's are used to.*

The Cherry Orchard *as a Comedy*

      The first reaction to any proposal to consider *The Cherry Orchard* as a comedy will probably be one of disbelief. This must be our starting point. How could anyone possibly call a comedy a play in which the heroine's husband dies of drink, her son drowns, her lover deserts her, and she returns to the one thing in the world she loves—her home and cherry orchard—only to have them taken from her and destroyed, only to be turned out into the unfriendly world again, all alone? Furthermore, the other characters, who also love the orchard, are scattered at the end of the play, and the faithful old servant Firce is left behind, locked up in the deserted house—perhaps to die. Wouldn't a person have to have a warped sense of humor to find this story comic? Here is the first objection to calling *The Cherry Orchard* a comedy. It is an objection in terms of the plot, which seems to be composed of unhappy events and to have an unhappy outcome.
      A further objection might be made in terms of the characters and their emotions. Practically every character in the play from Madame Ranévskaya to Dunyasha the maid is deeply sensitive. Hardly a page passes that someone doesn't weep or give voice to strong feelings. At the end of the play Madame Ranévskaya and her brother Gaieff fall into each other's arms and sob. Aren't these the reactions we expect from serious, not comic, characters? How could

we possibly reconcile the strength of feeling all the characters display toward the orchard with a comic point of view?

A final objection might then be formulated on the basis of our reaction as audience to what we see on the stage or to what we read. Don't we pity the central characters and feel sorry for them in their misfortunes? Then doesn't a play of this sort have a depressing effect rather than a comic one? Don't we close the book or leave the theater feeling sad?

It would seem, then, that neither the plot of the play, nor the characters, nor the effect of these two upon the audience is in any way comic. This is the problem and these are the questions that *The Cherry Orchard* raises. If we imagine for a moment that we are producing and directing a production of the play, it becomes of the greatest importance to answer these questions satisfactorily before attempting to tell the actors how to speak their lines. By making the problem as real and as difficult as possible through the use of these three objections, we can insure that our answers and explanations will involve us in a thoughtful examination of each of the elements of the play and be the result of a thorough reading. It will be appropriate to take up each of the objections in order.

The first objection is that the plot is made of unhappy events, has an unhappy outcome, and is thus not at all comic. However, in such a summary of the action of the play, we are telling the story as it might appear in a novel, starting with Madame Ranévskaya's unhappy marriage, following her through the death of her son Grisha, her unhappy love affair in Paris, and her desertion by the man who had lived off her money, and finally ending with her return home and the loss of her estate. Now the play itself presents only the last stages of this long story, and we learn what happened in the past, not by seeing it presented directly, but by having it narrated by various characters in the course of the play.

Thus we can say that *The Cherry Orchard* begins toward the end of a sequence of events which goes back over many years, instead of showing us directly that whole sequence. In this respect, *The Cherry Orchard* is unlike a play such as *Macbeth* which traces through the major events of the plot over a period of many years; and it resembles to some degree a Greek play like *Oedipus* which begins at the very end of a long story with the final moment of crisis. However, *The Cherry Orchard* does cover a period from May to October of one year and therefore presents not only the final moment in a long progression but also several selected stages leading up to the final moment. We shall return a little later to this question of time, and then we shall have to ask why Chekhov, concentrating as he does on the moment of crisis, wishes to present the elapsing of several months.

The important point for our present discussion is to fix the limits of the action in order to determine what sort of plot the play has. We notice now that the action of the play is inclosed within the arrivals of the first act and the departures of the last act. In Act I we see the various characters assemble about the cherry orchard—some coming from far off, some from nearby. In the last act we see all these characters dispersed and scattered, with the exception of old Firce, who is forgotten. The action of the play in some way brings about the change from arrival to departure, from gathering to dispersal.

What is it that brings about this change? Obviously, it is the selling of the estate and orchard. Most plays contain some basic problem or conflict which the characters must face; and the resolution of this problem or conflict, either successfully or unsuccessfully, will affect the lives of these characters. Clearly, the problem in *The Cherry Orchard* is the approaching sale of the property. Can the sale of the estate be avoided and the orchard saved? This is the central question for all the characters; the fact that they are unsuccessful in dealing with this problem brings about the end of the play, the departures in Act IV.

That people are unsuccessful in solving a problem involving the loss of what they love most may not yet strike us as comic, but at least we have a new and accurate formulation of the action of *The Cherry Orchard*, which we can now describe as the unsuccessful efforts of the owners of the orchard to save their property in the face of its approaching sale.

Then the plot of the play will be concerned with these efforts to save the orchard. What are these efforts? Gaieff has four different ideas: the first is that he might inherit a fortune from somebody; the second that his niece Varya might marry a rich man; the third that his rich aunt might give him enough money; the fourth that he might get a job in a bank. How sensible or practical are any of these hopes? When we consider that to pay their debts they need several hundred thousand rubles, we see that Gaieff's schemes are ridiculous and absurdly unrealistic daydreams. For example, in Act II, Gaieff says: "I have the promise of an introduction to a General who may lend me money on a note." His sister comments: "He's out of his head. There's no General at all."

And what does Madame Ranévskaya do herself to prevent the loss of her homestead? She lends money to Pishchik, a needy neighbor; she gives money to a tramp; she holds a ball and hires an orchestra the day of the auction. Here is plenty of action, but it is all of a sort not to save the orchard but rather to make its loss absolutely certain. Therefore, we can say that the characters act in such a way as to insure that what they are trying to prevent *will* take place. Their actions, supposedly designed to save the orchard, are so futile and ludicrous that either they are utterly useless or they even tend to impoverish the family still more.

In other words, the actions of the characters are inappropriate, inadequate, and irrelevant to the situation in which they find themselves and to the problem they face. It is for this reason that we can say the action of the play is purely a comic one and one of the most perfect comic plots ever created.

Very early in Act I Varya tells Anya, "The place will be sold in August," and a little later Lopákhin announces to all: "If we can't think of anything and don't make up our minds, then on August 22 both the cherry orchard and the whole estate will be sold at auction. Make up your mind! I swear there's no other way out."

As Dryden points out in his *Essay of Dramatic Poesy*, it is a highly effective dramatic device to set a long-awaited day when something decisive will take place, on which the action of the whole play hinges. Chekhov uses the ever present threat of the sale of the orchard to contrast with the ludicrous preoccupations of the characters and their ridiculous responses to the threat. They reveal themselves to be totally incapable of the necessary, practical activity.

Let us look a little more closely at Chekhov's technique. In Act II Lopákhin continues to plead with Madame Ranévskaya to make a decision. He says: "We must decide once and for all: time won't wait. After all, my question's quite a simple one. Do you consent to lease your land for villas, or don't you? You can answer in one word: yes or no? Just one word!" "Who's been smoking such abominable cigars here?" replies Madame Ranévskaya.

Those two speeches contain in miniature the essence of the whole play, its plot and its humor. Most of Chekhov's comedy comes from this kind of incongruity—the trivial response to a serious situation. Thus there are many references to petty, undignified objects which seem to obtrude upon the important problem of how to save the orchard. Trofímov can't find his galoshes, Gaieff continues to eat candy and play his imaginary billiard game, and all kinds of food keep popping up at what should be solemn moments—frogs legs and herring and nuts and pickled cherries. While Charlotta Ivanovna, the lonely German governess, delivers her soliloquy at the beginning of Act II, "I haven't anybody to talk to . . . I haven't anybody at all," she is munching on a cucumber. Likewise, when Gaieff returns from the auction, where he could do nothing to prevent the loss of his estate, he comes back not entirely empty-handed; he says, weeping, to old Firce: "Here, take this. Here are anchovies, herrings from Kertch. . . . I've had no food today." His heart is broken, but he remembered the anchovies.

I should like to suggest as a general axiom that such an incongruity between situation and response, between the serious and the trivial, is one of the fundamental sources of comedy. Nothing more quickly deflates the tragic dignity of a character and brings him down to the level of common humanity than a sudden annoyance at cigar smoke or a craving for a cucumber. Imagine Macbeth during his soliloquy: "I have lived long enough. My way of life/Is fall'n into the sear, the yellow leaf," all at once overcome with an urge to have a bowl of home-made Scotch broth with barley.

We are now in a position to look a little more closely at this type of comic plot and see whether we can describe precisely the kind of comic incongruity with which we are dealing. For example, in a comedy such as *Volpone* there is an incongruity between the wit, intelligence, and eloquence of Volpone and Mosca and the unworthy and degraded ends for which all their talent is expended.

In *The Cherry Orchard* the reverse is true. The end of saving the orchard is worthy, but the characters are unable to engage in even the simplest plans or schemes to raise money; they are incapable of managing any business affairs. Although both plays center around money problems, in *The Cherry Orchard* squandering, not greed, is the comic failing of Madame Ranévskaya and her brother. In Act II, Madame Ranévskaya tells her friends: "I've always scattered money about without being able to control myself, like a madwoman." *The Cherry Orchard* is the comedy of the spendthrift or the wastrel. With the exception of Lopákhin, the principal characters are too foolish and footless to hold on to their dearly beloved possessions.

A brief examination of the structure of *The Cherry Orchard* should confirm these observations about the nature of the plot and the incongruities which it presents. We might begin this discussion of the organization of the play with a simple question: Why does the action of the play begin with the return of Madame Ranévskaya from Paris? In order to answer this question, we must first ask about her motive for coming home.

Here the gradual unfolding of the past gives us the explanation. We learn that after running off to Paris with her lover, Madame Ranévskaya continued to spend money recklessly, even buying a villa at Mentone on the Riviera by mortgaging her Russian estate and getting head over heels in debt. Finally, the French villa was sold to pay her debts, her lover ran off with another woman after robbing her of everything she had, and Madame Ranévskaya was left penniless and unable to pay her debts on her Russian estate. At this point she comes home, and the action of the play begins.

We can now see that the reason why she returns is that she has no more money left; she must attempt to save the estate and solve her financial problem. Thus the action of the play begins with her coming home, since it is her return which poses this central financial problem.

The turning point in the play occurs in Act III, when we learn that the merchant Lopákhin has purchased the estate. What is the nature of this turning point? It is a complete reversal, a total upset, since the estate now passes into the hands of the man who seemed least likely ever to own it—Lopákhin, son of a former serf on that very property! Here is another aspect of the comic incongruity of *The Cherry Orchard:* Not only have the owners lost their estate through their own folly, but it now belongs to the man that no one could have imagined as the new owner. The incongruity is made doubly ludicrous by the fact that Lopákhin is the one character in the play who had sincerely made repeated efforts to save the estate for its rightful owners. Chekhov has made this reversal quite probable, yet at the same time comically surprising, by his careful development of the relationship between Madame Ranévskaya and Lopákhin.

In Lopákhin there is a constant alternation between his old self, the son of a serf, and his new self, the rich businessman. At the turning point in Act III, when Lopákhin arrives flushed with his purchase to announce that he is now owner of the estate, Chekhov reminds us of the incongruity of his new position by the fact that Varya, who has threatened to hit the pompous, insolent clerk Yepikhodov, actually strikes Lopákhin by chance as he enters. The new master of the estate is hit over the head with a stick as he arrives to proclaim his new power, and this incident recalls to us the other Lopákhin—the small peasant boy beaten by his drunken father.

If the announcement of the sale of the orchard represents the turning point in the play and the resolution of the central problem, what is the function of the final act? The last act presents the consequences of this solution; we must see how the failure to save the orchard will affect all the characters. Thus if the arrival of Madame Ranévskaya initiates the action and poses the basic problem, it is not until her departure that the action ends, that her failure to solve the problem is presented to us in its entirety. Thus the setting of Act IV parallels that of Act I, except that the room is now empty and dismantled. As before, the characters were waiting for the train to arrive, now they are waiting for it to depart.

II

These remarks will have to suffice as an examination of the plot, the structure, and the revelation of the past. Our observations about the inability of the characters to change and meet new circumstances bring us to our second point. We raised the objection that the emotions of the characters are of too great depth and seriousness to be comic. For example, there are the passionate outbursts of Trofímov, Madame Ranévskaya, and Gaieff. Perhaps these characters are incable of *acting* effectively in a given situation, but they can at least *feel* profoundly, and this makes them pathetic and moving rather than comic. After all, King Lear is incapable of acting effectively, yet he is deeply tragic. Couldn't a similar case be made for Madame Ranévskaya and the others?

In order to answer this question, we must return to an earlier problem we left unresolved: the elapsing of time in *The Cherry Orchard*. Why does the play cover a period of six months? We can see now that this period from May to October is necessary to show the characters' repeated and continuous failure to act intelligently in a situation that demands practical action. A more limited time-span would not have shown effectively the change in the circumstances of the family, and, at the same time, their complete inability to change themselves and to grasp the reality of what is happening to them. To estimate rightly their flagrant wasting of opportunity, we must feel the passing of time and experience the difference between the household bustling with activity in May and the deserted room in October, without curtains, furniture and with suitcases piled in the corner.

Here we touch on the central fact about the characters in *The Cherry Orchard*. Their responses are always the same. To Dunyasha's announcement about Yepikhodov's proposal, Anya says, "Always the same . . ."; Madame Ranévskaya tells Gaieff, "You're just the same as ever"; and Varya says of Madame Ranévskaya herself: "Mother hasn't altered a bit, she's just as she always was." Trofímov will always go on being a student—like all the others, he is growing old without growing up. The characters age but remain unchanged, learning nothing from life.

They share a common past which they love to talk about; they would really like to go back to those good old days. They wish to return to their childhood and be children again; they can't seem to realize that things aren't as they used to be, that they have to face certain responsibilities. Instead, they refuse to face reality. By living in the past, in a world of dreams, they hope to avoid having to live in the present and make hard decisions. Although the orchard will be sold in a few months, all they do is talk about the wonderful old days.

Naturally enough, the old servant Firce is an extreme of this type; he lives entirely in the past. He even regrets the emancipation of the serfs. He remembers in the happy old days of slavery, fifty years ago, they dried the cherries from the orchard and made them into a most wonderful jam—when he is asked how it was done, he mutters that the recipe is lost and no one remembers how. Old Firce lives his life in this foggy, imaginary past when everyone was happy and didn't know why. And so it is with all their past happiness: the recipe is lost, and no one remembers how.

Madame Ranévskaya and her brother are like Firce in that they recall without cease the nursery and their ecstatically happy childhood. But by the end of the play they seem to have learned nothing at all from their experiences and to have matured in no way as a result of all their emotions. We can well imagine that Madame Ranévskaya will feel the loss of the estate chiefly when she talks about it to others, that she will weep and gush sentimentally about the orchard and the nursery, about her girlhood and days of innocence, as she sits in that small smoke-filled room on the fifth floor in Paris. Likewise, her brother Gaieff will embarrass and bore the people at the bank with his repetitious effusions about the "dear and honored" hundred-year-old cupboard, instead of doing the least bit of work.

It is this fixity, this lack of adaptability of the characters' emotional responses that makes them comic. We soon come to assess the emotions of Madame Ranévskaya and Gaieff as sentimental and excessive rather than tragic. That we are to laugh at Gaieff's foolish sentimentality is clear because the other characters try to shut him up and make gentle fun of his outbursts. His continual stock response: "Red into the corner!" as though he were playing billiards, is an example of such comic fixity on a simple, mechanical level. The self-pitying, self-dramatized outbursts of Madame Ranévskaya represent the same source of comedy on a psychological level.

On the basis of the foregoing analysis, I should like to suggest another axiom: In comedy the characters do not change profoundly because of the experiences they undergo, but they continue making the same responses, repeating the same errors, committing the same follies. The more we learn about Madame Ranévskaya's past, the more we see that her present difficulties are a result of an incorrigible nature which has not changed. She is consistent in her behavior; having created the unpleasant situation in which she finds herself, she is unable to extricate herself from it for just the same reasons. Furthermore, we can easily picture a comic figure such as Madame Ranévskaya continuing to act in the same way even after we have left the theater or closed the book. This is just the opposite of the shattering experience of tragedy which either ends the hero's life or utterly transforms it.

On the other hand, Madame Ranévskaya has never come to grips with reality and never will; she will go on living in the world of illusion, talking about herself and weeping over herself. It is this contrast between illusion and reality which makes all the characters in *The Cherry Orchard* part of the same comic vision. Let us now look at the other characters and see the particular illusions in which they live.

The servants are caricatures of their masters, with whom they mingle in a ridiculous and incongruous fashion. Dunyaska is just a maid, but she dresses and acts like a lady, her hands are white and delicate, and she has become so sensitive that she almost faints from nerves. Yasha is only a footman, but he has turned into such a Frenchified fop in Paris that he feels quite superior to his masters and turns up his nose at Lopákhin's bottle of domestic champagne (although he manages to finish it single-handed).

Yepikhodov is a lazy clerk who has great intellectual pretensions because he has read Henry Thomas Buckle's *The History of English Civilization*, but his shoes squeak. He also accidentally tips over chairs, breaks dishes, and puts trunks on hatboxes, and these calamities lead him to proclaim grandiloquently: "Fate, so to speak, treats me absolutely without mercy, just as a small ship, as it were." He finds cockroaches in his wine glass and becomes a fatalist, threatening to commit suicide if Dunyasha throws him over for Yasha. As he strums his guitar lugubriously, he says: "Now I know what to do with my revolver." In other words, Yepikhodov is a pompous fool who imagines he is as poetic and mysterious as Hamlet.

Lopákhin is all dressed up "in a white vest and brown shoes," seemingly successful and cultured, but the reality is that he's a peasant in origin and in spirit, and his past keeps showing through the veneer. In Act II he confesses that he's really a fool and an idiot and that his handwriting is just like a pig's!

The one character who understands and explains this kind of contrast between illusion and reality is the student Trofímov. He points out to the others: "It's obvious that all our nice talk is only carried on to delude ourse ves and others." Trofímov sees clearly the contrast between ideals and facts, wishful thinking and actual practice. Because of this, we might suspect that Trofímov is a spokesman for the author and not a comic figure, and we might think that we are to take quite seriously his talk about the future.

Let us look at Trofímov a little more closely. His creed is expressed in the phrase: "We must work"—which is what none of the characters do, Trofímov included. In fact, he has been wasting his time for years with some vague and endless course of study at the university. Trofímov penetrates the delusions of everyone but himself. He is perceptive enough to recognize that by clinging to the orchard the others are refusing to face reality, but he doesn't see that he likewise is escaping from the present with his beautiful dreams of the future. His talk of the future is as much sentimental rhapsodizing as Madame Ranévskaya's gushing about the orchard and poor little Grisha her dead son.

Trofímov informs all the others: "Mankind goes on to the highest possible truths and happiness on earth, and I march in the front ranks!" But he's marching without his galoshes, which he still can't find. He is the perfect type of the seedy, balding bohemian with elaborate theories and very little common sense. His contemporary counterpart is well known to all of us.

From these observations about character, it would be possible to indicate as another axiom that one of the basic incongruities in comedy lies in the inability of the characters to tell illusion from reality. Here we can make a distinction between *The Cherry Orchard*, on the one hand, and earlier English comedies such as *Volpone* and *Twelfth Night*, on the other. In the two Elizabethan plays, one group of characters deliberately dupes or tricks another and helps to produce the delusion, whereas in *The Cherry Orchard* the characters are self-deluded. In fact, they wilfully resist any efforts made to enlighten them on their true characters and state of affairs; they prefer to remain oblivious to the real world.

Such self-delusion manifests itself in a variety of ways. One of the principal forms it takes is egotism or self-centeredness. Each character is so wrapped up in himself that he is hardly aware of those about him. Although all the characters are intimately connected to the family group through deep ties in the past and through their love of the estate and the orchard, preoccupation with self produces an isolation of each character from all the others. The comic separateness of characters who should be close to one another is emphasized by their disregard for and deafness to what others are saying and by their persistence in thinking their own thoughts aloud.

On the simplest level, this deafness is quite literal, as in the case of old Firce, who once again represents the extreme toward which all the other characters tend in varying degrees. Firce lives in a world of illusion all his own because he is hard of hearing. His comments are nearly always irrelevant because he does not know what the others are talking about, quite literally as well as figuratively. When Madame Ranévskaya first sees him after her return, she goes up to him and says emotionally, "Thank you, dear old man. I'm so glad you're still with us." Firce replies, "The day before yesterday." A little later on, a propos of nothing at all, he mumbles, "They were here in Easter week and ate half a pailful of cucumbers."

On a less obvious plane, all the characters are deaf and go on muttering irrelevant things to themselves, unheeded by the others. When Dunyasha tells Anya that Yepikhodov has proposed to her, Anya says, "I've lost all my hair pins . . ." and later Anya falls asleep while Varya is talking to her. Pishchik even falls asleep in the middle of his own conversation when he is talking! Just at the moment that Varya first announces to Anya that the estate will be sold in August, Lopákhin sticks his head in the door and, for a joke, moos like a cow. There is a special comic irony here in that this is the future owner of the estate commenting on the central problem of the play, the chances of saving the orchard. No one pays any real attention to anyone else. Gaieff even talks to waiters in restaurants about the decadents!

Thus the self-centered isolation of the characters produces a lack of communication, a failure in expression. This lack of communication is one of the principal sources of comedy in *The Cherry Orchard* and appropriately brings us to a discussion of the comic use of language. If, in tragedy, language is used for maximum eloquence and expressiveness, in comedy language is abused for maximum nonsense and confusion. I should like to propose as another axiom that in comedy the resources of language are deliberately misused. This misuse takes the form of excess in many English comedies of the Shakespearean period. For example, in *Volpone* we see eloquence and rhetoric pushed to ludicrous extremes and put to unworthy uses in Volpone's mountebank speeches and in his pleas and arguments to Celia.

In *The Cherry Orchard* there is also an abuse and misuse of language, but it is in the opposite direction. Rather than an excessive glibness, there is a deficiency in articulateness. Old Firce's disconnected mutterings give us the essence of the comic use of language in *The Cherry Orchard*. Each character talks to himself about something irrelevant to the present situation, usually about something in the past either trivial or personal to the speaker, the significance of which cannot be grasped by the other characters.

Characteristically, the non sequitur or meaningless remark which doesn't logically follow what has gone before is the primary source of humor in Chekhov's use of language. The non sequitur not only expresses a momentary illogicality but, in the comic world that Chekhov creates, expresses the characters' reaction of their situation. Their response to the approaching sale of the estate is a non sequitur indicating the world of illusion in which each lives.

III

Even if these answers to the first two objections to calling *The Cherry Orchard* a comedy are found to be satisfactory, won't it still be possible to assert that the spectacle of this group of foolish, bungling, impractical characters being dispossessed and cast out into a world with which they are not fit to cope is not a comic one? A perceptive reader may be willing to grant that the characters are as incompetent as we have described them and that their actions are futile and inappropriate, but he will insist that the effect of seeing lonely, irresponsible people come to an unhappy end is one of sadness, not comedy. He might well argue that we feel sympathy and even pity for Madame Ranévskaya, Gaieff, Varya, old Firce, and all the rest, and ask whether these emotions are compatible with the conception of comedy which we have been developing. It will then be necessary to investigate the problem of the unhappy ending and the matter of comic sympathy if we are to convince this perceptive reader that he is actually experiencing comic, not tragic, emotions.

As concerns the unhappy ending and its supposedly sad effect, there are two answers. The first is that the denouement of the play is not quite so unhappy as it may at first appear. Although Madame Ranévskaya and her brother dread the loss of the estate before it takes place, after it has happened they seem to be surprisingly indifferent to the reality. Gaieff comments gaily: "Yes, really, everything's all right now. Before the cherry orchard was sold we were all excited and worried, and then when the question was solved once and for all, we all calmed down, and even became cheerful. I'm a bank official now, and a financier . . . red in the center; and you, Liuba, look better for some reason or other, there's no doubt about it." Madame Ranévskaya replies: "Yes. My nerves are better, it's true. I sleep well. . . . I'm off to Paris. I'll live on the money your grandmother from Yaroslavl sent to buy the estate—bless her!—though it won't last long."

A fine use for grandmother's money—to go back to Paris and live with her lover! Here is the crowning irony and incongruity: the money that was to be used to save the beloved estate will actually be used so that Madame Ranévskaya can continue a little longer in her loose, shiftless life!

If we remember Madame Ranévskaya's resolve in the first act when she said, "I'm through with Paris" and tore up the telegrams from her lover, we see the comical nature of the denouement in which, after all her noble intentions to save the orchard and reform her life, she continues true to her unregenerate nature, throwing away her own and other people's money in a completely unworthy cause.

In the second place, it is a mistake to suppose that comedies always have happy endings for the comic or ridiculous figures. In fact, the reverse is usually true: the ridiculous figures do *not* achieve their ends, but they are in some way frustrated, chastised, or held up to laughter or scorn. Thus it is that the denouement of *The Cherry Orchard* is in some way frustrating for all the characters. It is this very frustration which unifies all the different lines of action in the play; everything goes wrong, no one accomplishes any of the things he sets out to. All the minor mishaps and failures are related to the loss of the estate as lesser frustrations around one central failure. For example, Lopákhin in Act I comes to meet the party at the train station, but he falls asleep and misses the train; Varya would like to marry Lopakhin and he her, but neither can ever get around to talking about it. Such misfortunes are even personified in one almost farcical figure, the clerk Yepikhodov, nicknamed "Two-and-Twenty Troubles."

This frustration of the purposes of ridiculous figures is of the very essence of comedy. Just a moment ago we saw that the unhappiness produced thereby is not so great or so deeply felt as to be tragic and bring about any radical change in the lives of the characters. Therefore, we can conclude that the so-called unhappy end of *The Cherry Orchard* produces a true comic effect.

As for the objection that we feel sympathy for the characters, I should say that there is no reason why a comic figure should not be sympathetic. If we think of Don Quixote or Falstaff or Charlie Chaplin, we see that many of the greatest comic creations are very sympathetic. If we take sympathy to mean an "affinity between persons," a "liking or understanding arising from sameness of feelings," and the "ability to enter into another person's mental state" (*Webster's New World Dictionary of the American Language*), then in one important aspect comic characters are much more sympathetic than tragic ones. We are more like comic figures. We admire and respect a man like Oedipus from a distance, and we are awed by Lear's sufferings; but we feel we share the same weaknesses and the same fallible human nature as comic characters like Madame Ranévskaya. We are close to them and do the same foolish things they do: we procrastinate, waste time, choose poor companions, spend money foolishly, and then feel sorry for ourselves and invent excuses. And many of us are like Trofímov: we've spent far too many years at the university over imaginary studies, until our hair has grown thin and we wear spectacles.

It is this sense that comedy is just as profound as tragedy and perhaps more universal. Tragedy presents only the exceptional cases, individuals whose experiences are unique; comedy deals with types, with those traits all men have in common: their pettiness, egotism, foolishness, weakness, and hypocrisy.

From this point of view, tragedy and comedy are not to be distinguished one from the other by an unhappy or a happy ending. Rather, they are two fundamentally different ways of looking at the world. In the tragic view we see nobility and relentless self-honesty even in the cornered murderer Macbeth; in the comic view we see an unkempt philosopher looking about on the floor for his galoshes and a middle-aged woman, ignobly in love, deceiving herself with sentimental lies. In this way, comedy sees the contrast between what man should be and what he is, between what he claims to be and what he actually does; and it exposes all imposture.

In these terms, comedy is a criticism of life and a critical view of human nature, and not merely a form. All the great comic writers from Aristophanes and Molière to Chekhov and Shaw have been interested not only in creating works of art but, first and foremost, in criticizing the foibles and extravagances and the faults and vices of men and women. Jonson wrote: "The office of a comic poet is to imitate justice and instruct to life ... to inform in the best reason of living." Chekhov says almost exactly the same thing: "All I wanted was to say honestly to people: 'Have a look at yourselves and see how bad and dreary your lives are!' The important thing is that people should realise that, for when they do, they will most certainly create another and better life for themselves."

Despite their similarity of purpose, Chekhov, unlike Jonson in *Volpone*, is not concerned with vices like greed, jealousy, and lust which lead to violence and crime. Rather Chekhov is submitting to comic scrutiny the lesser follies of the bunglers in life—the half-baked sentimentalities, the fatuous emotionalism, and the wasteful absurdities of Madame Ranévskaya and her family and servants. Because they are kind, gentle fools with generous hearts and good intentions, we can sympathize with them and even pity them at the same time that we laugh at their utter lack of sense.

Such is the main line of argument which I believe can be profitably followed in a presentation of *The Cherry Orchard* as a comedy. However, the enunciation of these general principles and theories will be chiefly useful insofar as they enable us to understand and to enjoy more fully the play itself. Therefore, as a conclusion to this analysis, it will be of the utmost importance to present a detailed examination of certain portions of the text as concrete illustration of all that we have been saying about *The Cherry Orchard*. I should like to offer the following explications of two short scenes as examples of what can be done to show exactly how Chekhov's comic view operates in practice.

The first scene is the quarrel between Madame Ranévskaya and Trofímov which occurs during the ball in Act III.

In the course of this quarrel, each tells the other painful truths. Trofímov tells Madame Ranévskaya that she is deceiving herself both about the orchard which must be sold and also about her lover in Paris, who is no better than a thief. In anger, Madame Ranévskaya answers that Trofímov is nothing but a schoolboy who has never grown up. She says: "You're not above love, you're just what our Firce calls a bungler. Not to have a mistress at your age!" Trofímov leaves in horror at the things that have been said, vowing, "All is over between us." It seems for a moment that there may have been a tragic realization of the truth of their accusations and hence a discovery leading to a final rupture between the two, which would be grave, since we know how much they care for each other.

But what actually happens? We hear a loud crash and learn that Trofímov has fallen downstairs in his haste to make an effective exit. A moment later he is back in the room dancing with Madame Ranévskaya, and the whole episode is forgotten. There could be no better illustration of the way in which comic characters bounce back and go on in their old unthinking manner, quite unchanged by what has happened. The fall downstairs ludicrously deflates Trofímov's solemn, "All is over between us," and his speedy return to dance with Madame Ranévskaya contradicts his words.

In this scene we see how Chekhov transforms what might have been a tragic quarrel into a ridiculous scene with an unmistakable comic effect by the use of the surprising anticlimax that terminates the scene. At just the most serious moment, the rug is almost literally yanked out from underneath Trofímov, and he falls flat on his face. The next moment he's back on his feet again—dancing!

The second scene I should like to examine comes at the very end of the play, the short scene in which we see old Firce locked up in the deserted house. I have mentioned this scene several times because I feel that it is of central importance to an understanding of the play. What is the effect of this scene which give us our final impression of *The Cherry Orchard?*

Before Firce appears, we have the departure of Madame Ranévskaya presented in the grand manner. She and her brother fall in each other's arms and sob. This seems to be the great emotional climax of the play. Madame Ranévskaya exclaims: "My dear, my gentle, my beautiful orchard! My life, my youth, my happiness, good-bye! Good-bye!" This is where the ordinary dramatist would end his play, with the exit of the leading actress, as beautiful, as tearful, as emotional as possible. In fact, this is where the author of *The Wisteria Trees* did end his play, and, in the terms of the trade, this is called "good theater."

But a great dramatist like Chekhov does something much more than that. What Chekhov has done in ending the play, not with the farewell of Madame Ranévskaya to her orchard, but with the appearance of old Firce is exactly the same kind of comic anticlimax which we saw in the quarrel scene. Nothing shows better the shallow sentimentality of Gaieff and his sister about the orchard than the fact that they've entirely forgotten to insure that Firce will be taken care of, Firce the one person who has been blindly faithful to his masters.

Madame Ranévskaya has just said, "We go away, and not a soul remains behind." As if to contradict her, to show her persistence in error, old Firce then comes shuffling in, wearing slippers and white vest and dress jacket, and we have the final comic surprise and incongruity of the play. Failure and frustration of purpose prevail to the very end. The contrast of the sound of the axes, practical and efficient in their destruction of the orchard, with the picture of the feeble old servant still in livery lying down and falling asleep in the empty house expresses the central contrast between reality and illusion which has run through the whole play.

Firce reacts as he always has, thinking that Gaieff has forgotten his overcoat. "Oh, these young people!" he exclaims. It is appropriate that Firce end the play and have the last words, since he represents the extreme obliviousness to reality; his falling asleep is the final lack of response to the external world.

His last words enforce the whole comic meaning of the play. He says: "Life's gone on as if I'd never lived. . . . Oh, you . . . bungler!" This word *bungler*, which is a favorite with Firce, is used to describe practically every character in the play. It is the key word in *The Cherry Orchard* because it portrays the bumbling, muddled, sentimental failures that all the characters are. Thus *The Cherry Orchard* ends with delusion triumphant: Madame Ranévskaya leaves, intoxicated with her own words but failing to realize that her one loyal follower has been abandoned, and Firce himself remains bunglingly devoted to his bungling masters. The comedy is complete.

Lest this reading of *The Cherry Orchard* be thought too personal and unconventional to be sound for the purposes of general education, I should like to point out that we have Chekhov's own words about the play to serve as a guide. The following remarks which appear in different letters Chekhov wrote concerning *The Cherry Orchard* support not only the contention that the play should be regarded as a comedy but also the view that failure to approach the work in terms of its proper genre will result in serious misinterpretation.

Chekhov writes: "I shall call the play a comedy. . . . It has turned out not a drama, but a comedy, in parts a farce . . . the last act is gay, the whole play is gay, light . . . why on the posters and in the advertisements is my play so per-sistently called a *drama?* Nemirovich and Stanislavsky see in it a meaning dif-ferent from what I intended. They never read it attentively, I am sure."

Therefore, what I am urging is that we restore *The Cherry Orchard* to the proper tradition, the humanistic tradition; only by treating it as a comedy, along with other comedies, shall we be able to understand the play as Chekhov wrote it. We must read the play attentively, as the author suggests we should and restore to the title the part most editors of *The Cherry Orchard* omit: *A Comedy in Four Acts.* In this way, I believe *The Cherry Orchard* can occupy an important position in any humanities course.

From the Director

Probably no other director in the decades since 1950 has achieved such international success as **Tyrone Guthrie.** *His death in 1971 was a lamentable loss to the world of the stage. In this essay Guthrie presents a myriad of ideas stemming from his work with* The Cherry Orchard, *not the least of which is his belief that a director has the right to interpret a play differently despite the playwright's avowed intentions. Guthrie also discusses the advantages and disadvantages of producing Chekhov on the open stage.*

A Director's View
of The Cherry Orchard

Like any other great play, in which the characters are more than superficially observed, *The Cherry Orchard* can be interpreted in many different ways.

At the first production in Moscow, as Leonid Kipnis has noted in the pre-ceding pages, there was some difference of opinion between the author and the directors, Stanislavsky and Nemirovich-Danchenko. Chekhov faulted their inter-pretation for being too "tragic" and insisted that what he had written was a comedy.

It is rather too easy to argue that an author must know better than anyone else how his work ought to be interpreted. Is it not more true that the author must know best about the work which he *meant* to write, and which he *hopes* he has written? But what an author hopes that he means and what he actually ex-presses are not always quite the same thing.

Stanislavsky and Nemirovich-Danchenko were highly intelligent and talented men; also they had far more theatrical experience than Chekhov. Therefore they were surely entitled to their view of what the script meant—to them; and, as directors of the production, were not only entitled, but bound, to interpret it in their way. No doubt they will have been very much influenced by the author's disagreement, and will have made many changes, often against their better judgment; but, without their being able to help it, the interpretation will have, in general, been what *they* made of the script.

This possible divergence of view between creator and interpreter is not confined to playwrights and directors. An analogous divergence is constantly arising between composers and conductors. And there is a less precise, but still close, analogy concerning the divergence between what a painter or sculptor tries to express and what is made of his work by the critics and the public. Or again, take a novel: is it what the author meant to write and believes he has written? Or is it the impression which the novel makes upon each individual reader? In that case *David Copperfield*, for instance, means one thing to me, another to you; and neither of our impressions may be very close to Dickens' intention. Or is the essence of a work of art, perhaps, to be sought in a kind of amalgam of impressions—the impressions of every reader "processed" into the Average Viewpoint, as colorless, featureless, and deadly as that dismal abstraction: The Average Man.

Before we decide too glibly that the meaning of a complex work of art can be finally determined to be so-and-so, and therefore before we condemn those interpreters who may venture to "improve" upon the conscious intention of the creator—before doing this, let us consider what widely different interpretations may be put upon the very simplest sentence: "The cat sat on the mat" means one thing to a cat-lover in Bukhara; quite another to a cat-hater with a fluff allergy.

There is every reason to believe that the original production of *The Cherry Orchard*, despite the disagreements with the author, was a remarkably fine one. It may be suspected that with its directors' particular background, and especially with Stanislavsky playing Gaev, it may have leaned a little toward sentimentality about the dispossessed owners of the estate.

After the Bolshevik revolution—that is twelve years later—the balance, so I have heard, swung the other way: Trofimov became the central character. He became a symbol of ardent, idealistic youth, in revolt against decadent aristocracy, personified by Ranevskaya and her family, and against bourgeois materialism personified by Lopahin.

This interpretation seems, if it ever really existed, to have been abandoned. In the Moscow Art Theatre's production which was seen in New York in February 1965, Trofimov was not accorded undue prominence. The actor looked suitably seedy and unprepossessing, and all the rodomontade about progress was absolutely not delivered as a clarion call to revolution, not even as a serious prophecy about a Soviet millennium. Equally, neither Ranevskaya nor Gaev was sentimentalized, though neither performance was, in my opinion, a portrait which accorded too well with the evidence of the text. The portrayal of Lopahin, on the other hand, would, I believe, have been very acceptable to Chekhov. The text indicates that Lopahin is a sensitive and intelligent man; Trofimov says: "You have the hands of an artist and the feelings of an artist." Furthermore, Chekhov, in one of his letters, makes it clear that the part is not to be played as a coarse and vulgar upstart. The actor in the Moscow Art Theatre production looked extremely handsome, was far better dressed than anyone else, and only at the climax of the third act behaved in at all a vulgar or rough way, and then only momentarily and not in an obvious or overemphatic style.

I guess it was naive of me to be surprised and a little disillusioned to find that this theatre, together with the Abbey Theatre in Dublin, had grown old-fashioned. Sixty years ago these two theatres were far ahead of their time. Their writers, directors, and actors were exploring new territory, discovering new ways which seemed the more touching and thrilling because they were so simple, so unartificial. But neither the Moscow Art Theatre nor the Abbey seems to have been able to maintain a place in the theatre's vanguard. Both seem to be, temporarily no doubt, floating in the stagnant pond of a once successful style, which has long since been copycatted, developed, elaborated, and vulgarized by brisker, more commercial people; until now the once lively style seems uninteresting, unmoving, stale. No doubt life will come back to these two noble institutions which have so greatly influenced us all. Meantime it was sad to see a play so minutely, intimately, and imaginatively naturalistic presented by this theatre, which was the cradle and nurse of such naturalism, in what was, in my opinion, not just an old-fashioned, but an unimaginative and even unnatural style.

Actors took center stage for Big Moments; furniture was set in quite artificial and old-fashioned arrangements, with chairs and sofas conveniently placed so that actors could sink into them effectively and obviously, rather than naturally. In general, the rhythms and patterns of movement were uninteresting and uninventive. The scenery was poor too; however, most of the shortcomings on the visual side should probably be attributed to the difficulties inseparable from touring. But I had been hearing for years of the extraordinary verisimilitude which through scenery, lighting, and offstage sound effects so marvelously reinforced the actors of this company. Therefore it was rather a shock to find things as they were.

What was immensely impressive, however, was the solid professional strength of the company. One may not have agreed with all the casting, or admired without qualification all the performers, but there could be no gainsaying the general impression that a group of intelligent, highly trained people knew just what they were trying to do and why. There was a solid sense of unified endeavor, which had nothing whatever to do with politics, but was concerned entirely with artistic purpose. This is the result partly of an economic security which membership in a permanent repertory company gives to the actors; partly of a tradition, and a solidarity of companionship in, and loyalty to, an institution, which the short-term policies and flimsy managerial structures of our Western theatre simply do not engender.

To present Chekhov the Western theatre must make some translation in manner as well as in language. Just as the Russian language is rather more emotional and effusive than our own, so is Russian acting. Again and again Chekhov's stage directions read "through tears" or "weeping," on occasions when no doubt a Russian man or woman would act so, but when we of the Western world would maintain far stiffer upper lips. My belief is that we should not try to force ourselves into the extreme expressions of grief and joy which come quite easily and naturally to Slavs; and that, keyed down to our more restrained behavior, the play can be no less poignant, and its meaning no less clear.

The Chekhov productions of the Minnesota Theatre Company have been given on an open stage—a platform surrounded on three sides by the audience—where there can really be no attempt at dramatic illusion. *Uncle Vanya* was produced at Chichester, by Sir Laurence Olivier and the British National Theatre, in similar circumstances and with outstanding success.

Something is lost on the open stage; and something is gained. There is a loss of dramatic illusion. But ought we to demand of drama that it create illusion? It is my view that no one beyond the mental age of nine believes that what is happening on the stage is "really" happening. You know perfectly well that you are sitting in a theatre watching somebody on a stage pretending to be Hamlet. You do not believe yourself really to be in Elsinore, any more than, when you are reading a novel, you believe that you are present with Pierre Bezukhov at the battle of Borodino, or with Alice at the Red Queen's croquet party. It is true that, if a novel is good enough, you can be completely lost, totally transported, taken, as they say, out of yourself into an imaginary world. This happens too when a theatrical experience is good enough. But then it also happens at a good concert; with music, however, there is no question of illusion. You are rapt, transported, rendered oblivious of time, place, and all mundane considerations. But this is not the same thing as being rendered incapable of distinguishing between plain fact and palpable fiction.

Therefore I do not feel that a reduction of dramatic illusion is fatal to Chekhov. There may, however, on an open stage be loss of "atmosphere," especially in the matters of scenery and lighting. This is partly counterbalanced by a gain in intimacy, since the open stage permits the audience to be physically nearer to the actors; and a gain in flexibility and naturalness of choreography. Above all, on an open stage the exterior scenes—and Chekhov sets many of his scenes out of doors—can be presented with just the same degree of realism, or unrealism, as the indoor scenes. In a proscenium theatre it is hard, if not impossible, to avoid a jolting change of convention, since interiors can be rendered with elaborate realistic accuracy, whereas the exterior scenes can be no more than highly stylized, painted landscapes, "masked" by "wings," with "borders" overhead, which, however beautifully painted, however skillfully lit, are still not very like whatever they are pretending to be.

English productions of *The Cherry Orchard* have tended to present Ranevskaya and Gaev rather more sentimentally than was, I believe, the author's intention. The pathos of the dispossessed upper classes struck sympathetic chords in an epoch when taxation was making the maintenance of large old country-houses and estates increasingly difficult, and when a universally hideous "suburban sprawl" rightly tended to discredit Lopahin's projected housing development. In London in 1963 Michel Saint-Denis directed a revival which deliberately aimed to avoid sentiment about the poor, dear upper classes. It was not received with unmixed praise. Dramatic critics cling with touching faithfulness to theatrical stereotypes. It will be many a year before critics abandon the idea that this is a sad play about a charming, gracious heroine, who suffers undeserved misfortune at the hands of an ungrateful and insensitive vulgarian.

Source Materials for *The Cherry Orchard*

BY THE CRITICS

Deer, Irving. "Speech as Action in *The Cherry Orchard*," *Educational Theatre Journal* 10 (March 1958):30–34.

Fergusson, Francis. *Idea of a Theatre*. Princeton: Princeton University Press, 1949, pp. 146–177.

Goldstone, H., ed. *Chekhov's The Cherry Orchard*. Boston: Allyn and Bacon, 1965.

Latham, J. *"The Cherry Orchard* As Comedy." *Educational Theatre Journal* 10 (March 1958):21–29.

Silverstein, N. "Chekhov's Comic Spirit and *The Cherry Orchard*," *Modern Drama* 1 (1958):91–100.

BY THE PLAYWRIGHT

Letters of A. Tchekov to His Family and Friends, translated by Constance Garnett, Doubleday & Co., 1920.

The Life and Letters of A. Tchekov, translated by P. Tomlinson, Cassell, London, 1925.

BY THE DIRECTORS

My Life in Russian Theatre, Vladimir Nemirovitch-Dantchenko, pp. 137–142, 161–164, 165–167.

My Life In Art, Constatin Stanislavski, Theatre Arts Books, translated by E. R. Hapgood, pp. 345–375, 420–424.

AUDIO-VISUAL

The Cherry Orchard, Parts I (21 minutes) and II (22 minutes), Encyclopedia Brittanica, color or B&W. Narrated by Norris Houghton.

The Cherry Orchard, The Tyrone Guthrie Production, starring Jessica Tandy, Caedmon Recordings.

Naturalism

Naturalism attempts to be the most honest of the dramatic modes. The plots are not contrived and the characters are not carved. No suffering is spared and no vices are hidden. The characters in a naturalistic play do not shine with virtue, ever ready to meet and conquer their foe, for the foe of the naturalistic character is so many times a mechanistic and deterministic society over which he has no control. The naturalist subjects man to scientific investigation, and the results are often unpleasant.

Naturalism began as a revolt against the sentimental and romanticized late eighteenth- and early nineteenth-century stage, with its artificial trappings and "well-made" plays. The naturalist believed that the theatre had an obligation to depict real life, using scientific tools for investigating and reporting its findings. Naturalism would reflect real life in a more radical and stark manner than realism had attempted.

Zola and the Naturalists

The most outspoken (and usually most vociferous) mouthpiece of naturalism was Emile Zola. In his essays and prefaces, Zola made well known his dissatisfaction with dramatic literature. He was incensed primarily with the melodramatic manufacturing of plot, the artificial creation of clever dialogue, and the unrealistic typing of characters, all of which he considered a perversion of what the stage should offer. In order to forestall this inevitable extinction of art, Zola felt, life must be reported with the unswerving honesty of science. What art should concern itself with, then, was the objective and uncolored reporting of the event, mincing no words in the necessary exposing of man's deterministic nature. This could be accomplished only by the marriage of science and art.

In his reporting, Zola believed it was paramount that the writer keep out his personal bias and philosophical message. No longer should the stage moralize or teach. No longer should the purpose of the drama be to provide shallow entertainment or cheap thrills. Rather, the function of the theatre must be to experiment and analyze—incorporate the new methods of science in objectively reporting the facts. The theatre should be used to expose, to let reality speak for itself.

"Observation should replace invention," Zola said, the playwright "should not imagine an adventure, complicating it, preparing stage surprises, which from scene to scene will bring it to a final conclusion." Instead the drama should deal in truth and fact—employing this "data"— and disguising nothing in the process. The writer should detach himself and record nothing but the objective facts. Did not Gorki and Stanislavski themselves journey to the "lower depths"? Had not Zola known a person very much like his *Thérèse Raquin*? It was the job of the dramatist to record and report through his senses the state of our being.

And if this state of our being so many times reflected life's squalid and somber aspects, this could not be avoided—for this was "as it was," and the naturalist was simply an objective observer, diligently reporting what he saw. If the subject matter so many times dealt with the lower classes, showing their degradation instead of idealizing them, this too could not be helped; reporting anything different, according to Zola, would have been "imagining an adventure." Naturalism should do as the science of medicine does, examine and define the sufferings and ills of man—and where but in the lower classes would most of this human misery be found?

To be successful (and it was not so much a box office as a personal success he was concerned with), the naturalist felt he must conscientiously reproduce his human environment. If Molière and Racine were so popular, it was because they had reproduced their "contemporaneous society." The nineteenth century naturalists felt they, too, should reproduce their contemporary society, stressing the Darwinian belief that man's environment is determined by natural selection and survival of the fittest.

Slice of Life

Since the object of naturalism was to faithfully reproduce the events of life, so many times somber and at all times real, an attempt to structure traditionally the reporting of these happenings would do more to disfigure truth than to reveal it. In adhering to the belief that an objective arrangement of the story was as imperative as the subject with which the story dealt, the naturalist worried little about building climaxes, creating complications, or resolving events. If the audience *were* looking at life through a "fourth wall," how real would this picture *be* all wrapped up in a neat little package of exposition, crisis, resolution, and denouement?

The result was a "slice of life"—as if a smaller part of the whole had been cut out and placed on the stage, with little concern for dramatic development. Was this not, the naturalist reasoned, life "as it is"? Was this not the objective reporting of an event, similar to the newspaper story of who, what, where, when, and why, usually lacking any clear beginning, middle, or end? *The Lower Depths*, for instance, opens not with two characters bouncing expository information off each other, but as if someone had suddenly turned on the lights on an already progressing segment of life. And though the play's ending may seem abrupt, it is no more abrupt than life. For Zola, Gorki, Strindberg, and the other naturalists, the story—like life—goes on.

Realistic staging was crucial to the naturalism. Thus, painstaking care was taken to accurately reproduce every detail of the scene, going so far as to bring real beehives and beef carcasses on the stage! Costumes, movement, and furniture arrangements were arranged not with an eye for theatrics, but with a loyalty for reporting things as the naturalist sees them. The stage tried to become not a replica of life, but life itself.[1]

The Fall of Naturalism

In essence, this fanatic concern for extreme detail drew too much of the audience's attention to the setting, since, ideally, the setting was supposed to provide a secondary environment for the primary action and story. Thus, as in medodrama, the visual, at times, became a novelty and an end in itself. Many of the naturalistic stage effects were incorporated into realism.

But there were two additional reasons for the demise of naturalism besides its physical eccentricities. The first was its subject matter. Audiences became satiated with the constant diet of human wretchedness and suffering served by the naturalists. Though the theatre had reached its lowest point with the sentimental escapism of melodrama, the audience was not ready to accept as a substitute the perpetual gloominess of naturalism.

Finally, naturalism failed as a lasting mode of drama because of its story structure (or, rather, "non-structure"). The stage could never be a photograph of life. As one critic said, "reality cannot be transformed to the stage; reality must be interpreted there." Naturalism's technique of reporting the facts—the "slice of life"—required of the audience too much effort. The lack of structure, though noble in its attempt at re-creating life, either failed to hold interest or resulted in confusion; and a building without a foundation soon crumbles. In its desire for "truth," naturalism would not compromise.

The Realist and the Naturalist

The realist's philosophy was similar to that of the naturalist. Each was concerned with exposing man's problems, utilizing scientific examination. But there were differences, too.

First, the realist believed in a selective style and arrangement for his material, similar to what had been called the "well-made" play. Clear exposition, crises building, creation of a climax, and story resolution were structural techniques utilized by these dramatists. While the naturalist maintained that in order to reflect life the play must "be life," with no absolute beginning, middle, or end ("slice of life"), the realist strove to

---

[1]August Strindberg, who later renounced naturalism, did not cling to the "slice-of-life" thesis, but his plays *The Father* and *Miss Julie* are powerful portraits.

assemble his material according to dramatic development, employing rising and falling action, climactic curtains, and so forth.

A more important difference resided in choice of subject matter. While the naturalist was intent on exhibiting the squalid aspects of life, dealing mostly with the lower classes, the realist took his subjects mostly from the middle and sometimes from the upper classes. The realist's characters were involved with antiquated traditions and obsolete values, not exclusively with the effects of biological and environmental determinism (one of the reasons Ibsen's *Ghosts* caused such an uproar was that its critics mistook it as treatise on venereal disease). The naturalist saw science as exposing only the sordid; the realist saw it as a tool for the perfectability of mankind.

One last difference between the naturalist and the realist rested in the staging of their works. While the realist *was* concerned with the play's setting, he did not feel as compelled as the naturalist to adorn the stage with detail. He was satisfied with creating the "illusion of reality"—using flats and properties designed around, but without being, the real thing. In effect, the realist was not as radical as the naturalist, believing society's ills could better be corrected by a more structured form.

Contributions

As a contributing force to drama, naturalism bequeathed some worthy gifts. Its concern for the details of stage production remains with us today in all kinds and forms of drama. Properties and costumes are selected with a more careful eye, and stage details are handled more honestly. Productions are well planned and, for the most part, meticulously analyzed.

More important, though, was naturalism's concern for portraying life honestly, and its focus on the deterministic effects of environment on man. Naturalism was the first of the dramatic modes to call on us to examine man with the objective eye of the reporter and the critical eye of the scientist.

Satine and The Actor return from the "other" world. Antelope Valley College. Jack Preston Held, director.

A rare moment of joy for an inhabitant of *The Lower Depths*. University of California at Berkeley. Robert Goldsby, director; Henry May, designer.

The women of *The Lower Depths* listen dreamily to Luka.
Carnegie-Mellon University. R. Finkel, designer; E. W.
Hickman, director, 1938.

Breaking the monotony of a joyless life, Luka paints a picture of idealism for the residents
of *The Lower Depths*. Boston University.

Stanislavski, as Satine, pours a drink, in the Moscow Art
Theatre's original production of *The Lower Depths,* 1903.

All hope abandon, ye who enter here . . .
Dante's *Canto*

The Lower Depths

Maxim Gorki

The Lower Depths

Characters   MIKHAIL IVANOVICH KOSTYLYOV, *54 years old, owner of*
a lodging-house
VASILISA KARPOVNA, *26 years old, his wife*
NATASHA, *20 years old, her sister*
ABRAM MEDVEDEV, *50 years old, their uncle, a policeman*
VASYA PEPEL, *28 years old*
ANDREI KLESHCH, *40 years old, a locksmith*
ANNA, *30 years old, his wife*
NASTYA, *24 years old, a streetwalker*
KVASHNYA, *40 years old, a woman who peddles dumplings*
BUBNOV, *45 years old, a hatter*
THE BARON, *33 years old*
SATIN ⎱
THE ACTOR ⎰ *Approximately the same age, about 40*
LUKA, *60 years old, a pilgrim*
ALYOSHKA, *20 years old, a cobbler*
KRIVOI ZOB ⎱
THE TATAR ⎰ *Dock hands*

Act One

*A cellar resembling a cave. The heavy vaulted ceiling is smoke-blackened and in
places the plaster has fallen off. Light descends from a square window upstage
right. A thin partition turns the right corner of the stage into a room for* PEPEL.
Near the door of this room is BUBNOV'S *bunk. A large Russian stove occupies
the upper left corner. A door in the stone wall to the left leads to the kitchen
where* KVASHNYA, *the* BARON, *and* NASTYA *live. A wide bed enclosed by dirty
cotton hangings stands against the wall between the stove and this door. Bunks
are built against all the walls. Downstage left stands an upturned log to which
are attached a vice and an anvil. Behind the anvil on a similar, but lower log,
sits* KLESHCH, *trying keys in an old lock. The floor about him is cluttered with
rings of miscellaneous keys, a battered tin samovar, a hammer and files, etc.
The centre of the lodging is occupied by a large table, two benches and a stool,
all of them dirty and unpainted.* KVASHNYA *is busy at a samovar standing on the
table, the* BARON *is chewing a piece of black bread, and* NASTYA *is sitting with
her elbows on the table, poring over a dog-eared novel.* ANNA *can be heard
coughing behind the curtains of the bed.* BUBNOV *is sitting on his bunk with a
hat block between his knees, calculating how to cut a cap out of strips of cloth
ripped from an old pair of trousers. Near him lie bits of rags and oilcloth and
pieces of cardboard for making the visors of caps.* SATIN, *who has just awakened,*

is lying on his bunk and snarling. The ACTOR *is coughing and moving about on top of the stove,* out of sight of the audience. It is a morning in early spring.*

BARON   What next?

KVASHNYA   Oh no, you don't, my darling, says I. Keep your distance, says I. I've already had my try at that sort of thing, and you couldn't drag me to the altar again for a hundred baked crawfish, says I.

BUBNOV (*to* SATIN)   What're you grunting about?

(SATIN *snarls again.*)

KVASHNYA   Me, a free woman as is her own boss, to go and have herself writ into somebody else's passport? says I. That I should become the slave of some man? Not on your life! Oh no! Not if he was the King of America himself!

KLESHCH   That's a lie!

KVASHNYA   What's that?

KLESHCH   That's a lie. You'll marry Abram!

BARON (*snatching* NASTYA's *book and reading the title*)   "Fatal Love." (*Laughs.*)

NASTYA (*reaching for the book*):   Here, give it back! Come on! No fooling! (*The* BARON *teases her by waving the book in the air.*)

KVASHNYA (*to* KLESHCH)   You're a red-headed old goat, that's what you are! A lie! How dare you insult me like that!

BARON (*striking* NASTYA *over the head with the book*)   You're a fool, Nastya!

NASTYA (*snatching the book away*)   Give it to me!

KLESHCH   What a fine lady! But you'll marry Abram all right! That's all you're waiting for!

KVASHNYA   Oh yes, of course! What else? The way you've rode your wife to death!

KLESHCH   Shut up, you bitch! That's none of your business!

KVASHNYA   O-ho! Don't like to hear the truth, eh?

BARON   There they go! Nastya, where are you?

NASTYA (*without raising her head*)   Oh, get out!

ANNA (*peering out from behind the curtains*)   The day's begun! For God's sake, don't shout. Don't quarrel!

KLESHCH   Whining again!

ANNA   Every blessed day! You might let a person at least die in peace!

BUBNOV   Can't scare death off with a little noise.

KVASHNYA (*going over to* ANNA)   How'd you ever live with that fiend, my poor dearie?

ANNA   Leave me alone. Go away.

KVASHNYA   Hm. There's a martyr for you! Any easier in your chest today?

BARON   Kvashnya! Time to go to market!

KVASHNYA   Just a minute! (*To* ANNA.) Wouldn't you like some nice hot dumplings?

ANNA   No, thanks. Why should I bother to eat?

---

*A Russian stove is so constructed that the space above the oven is large enough to serve as a bed.—*Tr.*

KVASHNYA   You just try them. Good and hot—they'll loosen up your cough. I'll leave them here in this bowl so's you can help yourself when you feel like it. Come on, me lord! (*To* KLESHCH.) Br-r-r! You hobgoblin!

      (*Goes into the kitchen.*)

ANNA (*coughing*)   Oh, Lord!

BARON (*slyly giving* NASTYA'S *head a push*)   Drop it, you little fool!

NASTYA (*muttering*)   Get out! I'm not in your way, am I?

      (BARON *whistles a tune as he goes out on the heels of* KVASHNYA.)

SATIN (*raising himself on his bed*)   Who gave me a beating last night?

BUBNOV   What difference does it make to you?

SATIN   None, I suppose. But what did they give me a beating for?

BUBNOV   Were you in a card game?

SATIN   I was.

BUBNOV   That explains the beating.

SATIN   The scoundrels!

ACTOR (*poking his head over the edge of the stove*)   They'll beat you to death one of these days.

SATIN   You're an ass.

ACTOR   Why?

SATIN   You can't kill a person twice.

ACTOR (*after a pause*)   Why not? I don't see why not.

KLESHCH (*to* ACTOR)   Get down off that stove and tidy up. Afraid of spoiling your hands?

ACTOR   That's none of your business.

KLESHCH   Wait till Vasilisa comes in. She'll show you whose business it is!

ACTOR   To hell with Vasilisa! It's the Baron's turn to tidy up today. Baron!

BARON (*entering from the kitchen*)   I haven't time to tidy up. I'm going to market with Kvashnya.

ACTOR   What do I care? You can go to jail for all I care, but it's your turn to sweep the floor. I'm not doing another man's job for him.

BARON   To hell with you! Nastya will sweep the floor. Hey there, "fatal love"! Wake up! (*Snatches the book out of her hands.*)

NASTYA (*getting up*)   What do you want? Give it back! Funny, aren't you? And you call yourself a gentleman!

BARON (*handing back the book*)   Sweep the floor for me, Nastya. That's a good girl.

NASTYA (*going into the kitchen*)   Oh, won't I just! I'd love to!

KVASHNYA (*at the kitchen door, to the* BARON)   Come on! They'll manage here without your help. Hey, there, Actor! It's you they're asking, so be so kind. It won't break your back.

ACTOR   Humph! Always me. I don't see why—

BARON (*entering from the kitchen with a wooden yoke on his shoulders from which are suspended two baskets containing crocks covered with dirty rags*)   Heavier than usual today.

SATIN   Was it worth getting yourself born a Baron?

KVASHNYA (*to the* ACTOR)   You begin that sweeping, now!
  (*She makes for the passage, letting the* BARON *go
  out first.*)

ACTOR (*climbing down off the stove*)   It's harmful for me to inhale dust.
  (*Proudly.*) My organism is poisoned with alcohol. (*He becomes
  meditative, sinking down on one of the bunks.*)

SATIN   Organism. . . . Organon. . . .

ANNA   Andrei Mitrich. . . .

KLESHCH   Now, what do you want?

ANNA   Kvashnya left me some dumplings. Take them and eat them.

KLESHCH (*going over to her*)   What about you? Don't you want them?

ANNA   No. Why should I eat? But you're a working man. You need food.

KLESHCH   Are you afraid? Don't be afraid. You can't tell, maybe—

ANNA   Go ahead and eat them. I'm feeling bad. I guess it'll be soon now.

KLESHCH (*going out*)   Don't fret. Maybe you'll get better. It sometimes
  happens. (*Goes into the kitchen.*)

ACTOR (*loudly, as though he had suddenly awakened*)   Yesterday the doctor
  in the clinic said to me: Your organism, he said, is completely poisoned
  with alcohol.

SATIN (*smiling*)   Organon. . . .

ACTOR (*insisting*)   Not organon. Or-gan-ism.

SATIN   Sicambri!

ACTOR (*waving his hand at him*)   Idiocy! But I'm talking serious. Yes, I am!
  If your organism is poisoned, it must be harmful to sweep the floor, to
  breathe that dust.

SATIN   Macrobiotics! Hah!

BUBNOV   What's that you're garbling?

SATIN   Words. Then there's that: trans-scen-dep-tal.

BUBNOV   What does that mean?

SATIN   Don't know. Forgot.

BUBNOV   Then what do you say it for?

SATIN   Just for fun. I'm sick of all the words people use, brother. I'm sick
  of all our words! I've heard them all a thousand times!

ACTOR   In "Hamlet" they say, "Words, words, words!" A wonderful play!
  I acted the part of the grave-digger.

KLESHCH (*entering from the kitchen*)   When are you going to start acting
  the part of the floor-sweep?

ACTOR   Mind your own business! (*Striking his breast.*)   "Ophelia! Nymph,
  in thy orisons be all my sins remembered!"
    (*At some distance off stage is heard a confusion of voices,
    cries, police whistles.* KLESHCH *sits down to work,
    making a rasping noise with his file.*)

SATIN   I love odd, incomprehensible words. When I was a boy working in a
  telegraph office I did a lot of reading.

BUBNOV   Were you a telegraph operator, too?

SATIN   I was. (*Gives a little laugh.*)   There are some fine books, and a great
  many curious words. I was once a well-educated man, did you know that?

BUBNOV   Heard it a hundred times. What if you were? A lot of difference it makes now! Take me, for instance. I was a furrier once. Had my own shop. My hands used to be all yellow from dyeing the fur—hands and arms, right up to the elbow. I thought they'd stay that way to the day of my death. I thought I'd die with those yellow arms, and now look at them. Just plain dirty. Humph!

SATIN   Well, what of it?

BUBNOV   Nothing. That's all.

SATIN   Then what was the point of your speech?

BUBNOV   There wasn't any. Just an idea. It turns out that no matter how carefully you paint the outside, it all rubs off. It all rubs off. Humph!

SATIN   Oh, how my bones ache!

ACTOR (*sits hugging his knees*)   Education is nothing; it's talent that counts. I once knew an actor who could only read out his role by syllables, but when he acted, the theatre rocked and roared with the rapture of his audience.

SATIN   Bubnov, lend me five kopeks!

BUBNOV   I've only got two.

ACTOR   I'm telling you it's talent you need to be an actor. And talent means believing in yourself, in your ability.

SATIN   Give me five kopeks and I'll believe you're a genius, a hero, a crocodile, a police officer! Kleshch, give me five kopeks!

KLESHCH   Go to the devil! Too many like you around.

SATIN   No swearing, if you please. Don't I know you haven't got a kopek to your name?

ANNA   Andrei Mitrich . . . I can't breathe . . . so stuffy. . . .

KLESHCH   What do you expect me to do about it?

BUBNOV   Open the door into the passage.

KLESHCH   Oh yes, of course. You up there on your bed and me down here on the floor. Change places with me and you can open the door. I've got a cold as it is.

BUBNOV (*calmly*)   It's not me that wants the door open. It's your wife that's asking.

KLESHCH (*sullenly*)   There are plenty of things a person can ask for.

SATIN   How my head's humming! Why should people lam each other over the bean?

BUBNOV   Not only over the bean, but over the whole remaining territory of the body. (*Getting up.*) I'm going out to buy some thread. Wonder what's keeping our landlord and his wife so long today? Maybe they've kicked the bucket. (*Goes out.*)

> (ANNA *coughs.* SATIN *lies motionless with his hands under his head.*)

ACTOR (*glancing miserably about him, goes over to* ANNA)   Feeling bad?

ANNA   It's so stuffy.

ACTOR   I'll take you out into the passage if you like. Come, get up. (*He helps her rise, throws some rags about her shoulders and leads her out.*) That's it. Steady. I'm sick myself—poisoned with alcohol.

KOSTYLYOV (*in the doorway*)   Out for a walk? How pretty the two, the lamb and the ewe!

ACTOR   Out of the way! Can't you see we're sick?

KOSTYLYOV   Oh, yes! By all means! (*Humming a church tune through his nose, he glances suspiciously about the lodging, turning his head as if listening for something in* PEPEL'S *room.* KLESHCH *viciously jangles the keys and rasps with his file, watching the movements of the landlord from under lowered brows.*)   Scratching away?

KLESHCH   What's that?

KOSTYLYOV   I say, scratching away? (*Pause.*) Hm. Now then, what was it I wanted to ask? (*Speaking quickly and in a low voice.*) Has my wife been here?

KLESHCH   Didn't see her.

KOSTYLYOV (*stealing toward the door to* PEPEL'S *room*)   You're taking up a lot of space for two rubles a month, aren't you? A bed, and a place to sit besides. Hm. Worth at least five rubles. I'll have to throw on another half ruble.

KLESHCH   Throw on a noose and choke me to death! On your last legs, and still wondering how you can snatch another half a ruble!

KOSTYLYOV   Why should I choke you? Who'd profit by that? Live on, and may the Lord help you. But I'll throw on that extra half-ruble just the same! I'll buy some oil for my icon lamp and let it burn before the holy image, a sacrifice in retribution for my sins, and for yours too. You never think of your sins, do you now? Oh, it's a wicked man you are, Andrei! Your wife has wasted away from your meanness. Nobody likes you, nobody respects you. Scraping away at that iron of yours, getting on everybody's nerves—

KLESHCH (*shouting*)   Did you come here just to poison my life?
     (SATIN *roars.*)

KOSTYLYOV (*with a start*)   Good gracious, my good man—

ACTOR (*entering*)   I fixed her up out there in the passage, wrapped her up.

KOSTYLYOV   You have a kind heart, brother. That's a good thing. It'll all be counted to your credit.

ACTOR   When?

KOSTYLYOV   In the next world, brother. There everything, every little deed, is counted.

ACTOR   Maybe you'll reward me for my kindness here and now?

KOSTYLYOV   How could I do that?

ACTOR   By crossing out half my debt.

KOSTYLYOV   Hee-hee! You will have your fun, your little jokes! As if a kind heart could be rewarded with money! Goodness is the highest of all blessings. But, a debt's a debt, which means it must be paid. As to the kindness you show an old man like me, you shouldn't seek reward for it!

ACTOR   A rapscallion, that's what you are, old man!
     (*Goes out into the kitchen.* KLESHCH *gets up and goes out into the passage.*)

KOSTYLYOV (*to* SATIN)   The scraper here, he ran away. Hee-hee! He don't like me.

SATIN   Who but the devil could like you?

KOSTYLYOV (*playfully*)   Now why should you say such things to me! Me, as
loves you all so! Don't I know you're all my brothers, my poor,
unfortunate, fallen brothers? (*Suddenly and quickly.*) Er . . . a . . . Vasya
—is he home?

SATIN   Go and look.

KOSTYLYOV (*going over and knocking at the door*)   Vasya!
(*The* ACTOR *appears in the kitchen door chewing
something.*)

PEPEL   Who's there?

KOSTYLYOV   It's me. Me, Vasya.

PEPEL   What do you want?

KOSTYLYOV (*moving away*)   Open the door.

SATIN (*without looking at* KOSTYLYOV)   He'll open the door, and there she is.
(*The* ACTOR *gives a snort.*)

KOSTYLYOV (*uneasily, in a lowered voice*)   What? Who's there? What did you
say?

SATIN   You speaking to me?

KOSTYLYOV   What was it you said?

SATIN   Nothing special. Talking to myself.

KOSTYLYOV   Watch your step, brother! A joke's a joke, but in the right place!
(*Knocks sharply at the door.*)   Vasya!

PEPEL (*opening the door*)   Well? What do you come here bothering me for?

KOSTYLYOV (*peeping into the room*)   I . . . you see . . . you. . . .

PEPEL   Did you bring the money?

KOSTYLYOV   I have some business with you.

PEPEL   Did you bring the money?

KOSTYLYOV   What money? Wait a minute.

PEPEL   The seven rubles for the watch. Where is it?

KOSTYLYOV   What watch, Vasya? My goodness, you—

PEPEL   Careful, careful! People saw me sell you that watch yesterday for
ten rubles—three rubles down, seven to come. Let's have it. Why do you
stand there gaping? Hanging around disturbing everybody instead of
going about your business!

KOSTYLYOV   Sh-h-h! Don't be angry, Vasya! The watch, it's—

SATIN   Stolen goods.

KOSTYLYOV   I don't handle stolen goods! How dare you—

PEPEL (*taking him by the shoulders*)   What are you pestering me for? What do
you want?

KOSTYLYOV   Me? Why, nothing. Nothing at all. I'll be going if you're like that.

PEPEL   Get out, and bring me that money!

KOSTYLYOV (*leaving*)   Bah! Such coarse people!

ACTOR   A real comedy!

SATIN   Good. That's what I like.

PEPEL   What was he doing here?

SATIN (*laughing*)   Can't you guess? Looking for his wife. Why don't you
bump him off, Vasya?

PEPEL   As though I'd ruin my life for a swine like him!

SATIN   Be smart about it. Then you could marry Vasilisa and collect our rents.

PEPEL   Wouldn't that be fun! Before I knew it you'd guzzle down all my property and me in the bargain, out of the goodness of my heart. (*Sitting down on one of the bunks.*) The old devil! He woke me up. And I was having such a nice dream! I dreamt I was fishing and caught a huge pike. Couldn't find a pike that size outside of a dream. There it was on the end of the line, and me scared the rod would snap, so I get a net ready—here, thinks I, I'll catch it now—

SATIN   That wasn't a pike. It was Vasilisa.

ACTOR   He caught Vasilisa long ago.

PEPEL   (*angrily*)   You can all go to the devil, and take her with you!

KLESHCH   (*entering from the passage*)   Devilishly cold!

ACTOR   Why didn't you bring Anna in? She'll freeze out there.

KLESHCH   Natasha took her into the kitchen.

ACTOR   The old man will chase her out.

KLESHCH   (*sitting down to work*)   Then Natasha will bring her back.

SATIN   Vasya! Lend me five kopeks!

ACTOR   (*to* SATIN)   Five kopeks? Vasya! Lend us twenty kopeks!

PEPEL   I'd better hurry and give it to them before they ask for a ruble. Here.

SATIN   Thermopylae! Thieves are the finest people in the world!

KLESHCH   (*sullenly*)   Money comes easy to them. They don't work.

SATIN   Lots of people get money easy, but not many give it up easy. Work? Find me work it's a pleasure to do, and maybe I'll do it. Hm. Maybe. When work is a pleasure, life is a joy. When work is a duty, life is slavery! (*To the* ACTOR.)   Come, O Sardanapalus! Let us be going!

ACTOR   Let us be going, oh Nebuchadnezzar! I'll get as soused as forty thousand sots!

(*They go out.*)

PEPEL   (*yawning*)   How's your wife?

KLESHCH   You can see it won't be long now.

(*Pause.*)

PEPEL   Why in the world do you keep on scraping away there?

KLESHCH   What else should I do?

PEPEL   Nothing.

KLESHCH   Then how'd I feed myself?

PEPEL   Other people manage.

KLESHCH   Who, these here? Do you call them people? Tramps! Ragamuffins! Scum of the earth! I'm a working man, and it makes me ashamed just to look at them. I've been working as long as I can remember. You think I won't pull myself out of here? I will! I may scrape all the skin off my body, but I'll crawl out of here. Just you wait—my wife will die soon. I've only been living here six months, but it seems like six years.

PEPEL   You're no better than the rest of us, so there's no sense in talking like that.

KLESHCH   No better! You have no honour, no conscience!

PEPEL (*indifferently*)   Who wants them—honour and conscience? You can't wear honour and conscience on your feet in place of boots. It's only those in power who need honour and conscience.

BUBNOV (*coming in*)   Br-r-r! I'm frozen.

PEPEL   Bubnov! Have you got a conscience?

BUBNOV   What's that? A conscience?

PEPEL   Yes, a conscience.

BUBNOV   Why should I? I'm not rich.

PEPEL   That's what I say: it's only the rich who need honour and conscience. But Kleshch here is bawling us out. Our conscience, he says—

BUBNOV   Would he like to borrow a conscience?

PEPEL   Oh no, he's got a fine one of his own.

BUBNOV (*to* KLESHCH)   So he's selling it? Well, he won't find a customer here. If it was some old cards now, I might be interested— and then only if he'd let me have them on credit.

PEPEL (*instructively*)   You're a fool, Andrei! When it comes to conscience, you'd do well to listen to Satin—or even the Baron.

KLESHCH   There's nothing they can teach me.

PEPEL   They've got more brains than you have, even if they are drunks.

BUBNOV   The man who's drunk as well as wise, has won himself a double prize.

PEPEL   Satin says everybody wants others to have a conscience, but nobody wants one himself. That's the truth.

> (NATASHA *comes in. She is followed by* LUKA *with a stick in his hand, a knapsack on his back, a pot and a tea-kettle tied to his belt.*)

LUKA   Greetings to you, honest folk.

PEPEL (*stroking his moustache*)   Ah, Natasha!

BUBNOV (*to* LUKA)   We were honest in the past, the year before last.

NATASHA   Here's a new lodger.

LUKA   It's all the same to me. I have respect for crooks too. Not a flea but has its merits, the way I look at it. They're all of them black, they all of them jump. Now where were you thinking to put me up, my dear?

NATASHA (*pointing to the kitchen door*)   In there, grandad.

LUKA   Thank you, my girl. If you say there, then it's there I go. Any place that's warm is home to old bones.

PEPEL   A queer old fellow you've brought in, Natasha.

NATASHA   He's better than you are. Andrei, your wife is sitting in our kitchen. Come and get her in a little while.

KLESHCH   All right. I will.

NATASHA   You might be a little gentler with her now. You can see it won't be long.

KLESHCH   I know.

NATASHA   It's not enough to know. You've got to understand. After all, it's dreadful to die.

PEPEL   I'm not afraid.

NATASHA   Aren't you now! Such a fine brave fellow!

BUBNOV (*giving a little whistle*)   The thread's rotten!

PEPEL   Honest to goodness I'm not. I'm ready to die this very minute! Take that knife and stick it in my heart. I'll die without so much as a gasp. I'll even be glad, because it's by a spotless hand.

NATASHA (*going out*)   Do you expect me to swallow that?

BUBNOV (*with a wail*)   The thread is rotten!

NATASHA (*at the door to the passage*)   Don't forget about your wife, Andrei.

KLESHCH   I won't.

PEPEL   There's a girl for you!

BUBNOV   Not bad.

PEPEL   Why is she like that with me? Always putting me off. She'll be ruined if she stays here.

BUBNOV   It's because of you she'll be ruined.

PEPEL   What makes you say that? I . . . I pity her.

BUBNOV   Like the wolf pities the lamb.

PEPEL   That's a lie! It's hard for her to live here. I can see that.

KLESHCH   You just wait until Vasilisa catches you talking to her!

BUBNOV   Vasilisa? She's not one to give away things for nothing. She's a ferocious dame!

PEPEL (*lying on the bed*)   To hell with the two of you! A couple of prophets!

KLESHCH   You'll see. Just wait.

LUKA (*singing in the kitchen*)   Midnight glo-o-om . . . the road is lost in da-a-rkness. . . .

KLESHCH (*going into the passage*)   What's he howling about? Another one!

PEPEL   What a bore life is! Funny, how I get like this at times. A bloke lives along day after day, without noticing anything, and then all of a sudden he feels as if he had caught a chill. Very tiresome.

BUBNOV   Tiresome? Hm.

PEPEL   Very.

LUKA (*singing*)   Ah-h! No pa-a-th in sight! . . .

PEPEL   Hey! Old man!

LUKA (*peering through the door*)   Is it me you're calling?

PEPEL   Yes, you. Stop singing.

LUKA (*coming out*)   Don't you like it?

PEPEL   I might if it was good.

LUKA   You mean to say it's no good?

PEPEL   Exactly.

LUKA   Fancy that! And here was I thinking I had a good voice. It's always like that: a person thinks to himself—my, don't I do that nice; and then somebody comes along and says it's no good.

PEPEL (*laughing*)   True enough.

BUBNOV   A minute ago you were bored to death, and now you're laughing.

PEPEL   What do you care, you old croaker!

LUKA   What's that? Who's feeling bored?

PEPEL   Me. I'm the one.

(*The* BARON *comes in.*)

LUKA   Fancy that! There's a girl sitting out there in the kitchen reading a book and crying. Really crying. Tears running down her cheeks. I says to her: "What is it, dearie?" And she says, "The poor man!" And I says, "What man?" "Here in the book," she says. Now what would make a person spend time on things like that? She must be bored, like you.

BARON   She's a fool.

PEPEL   Ah, the Baron! Had your tea?

BARON   I have. What next?

PEPEL   Would you like me to stand you a half-pint?

BARON   I would. What next?

PEPEL   Get down on all fours and bark like a dog.

BARON   Blockhead! Do you take yourself for a rich merchant? Or are you just drunk?

PEPEL   Go ahead and bark to amuse me. You're a gentleman, and once upon a time you didn't look on people like us as human beings.

BARON   Well, what next?

PEPEL   Well, so now I'm telling you to get down on all fours and bark like a dog, and you're going to do it, do you hear?

BARON   I do, you fool, and I'm going to do it. But I don't see what pleasure it can give you, once I myself realize I've become almost worse than you are. You wouldn't have tried to make me get down on all fours when I was your superior.

BUBNOV   True enough.

LUKA   Very well put.

BUBNOV   What's past is past and nothing left but chicken feathers. There's none of your fine gentlemen here. All the colours have been washed off. Nothing but naked people.

LUKA   In other words, everybody's equal. But were you really a baron once, my good man?

BARON   What do you call this? Who are you, you hobgoblin?

LUKA (*laughing*)   I've seen a count, I've seen a prince, but never before have I seen a baron, and a mangy one at that.

PEPEL (*laughing*)   A baron! You make me blush!

BARON   It's time you had more sense, Vasya!

LUKA   Dear, dear, dear! When I look at you, brothers, the way you live! Ah, me!

BUBNOV   We wake with a groan, and sleep with a moan—that's the way we live.

BARON   We lived better once upon a time. I remember waking up in the morning and having coffee served to me in bed. Coffee and cream.

LUKA   It's human beings we are, all of us. No matter what airs we put on, no matter how we make believe, it's human beings we were born, and it's human beings we'll die. People are getting wiser, the way I see it, and more interesting. The worse they live, the better they want to live. A stubborn lot, human beings!

BARON   Who are you, old man? Where did you come from?

LUKA   Me?

BARON   Are you a pilgrim?

LUKA   We're all pilgrims on this earth. I've heard it said that this very earth of ours is a pilgrim in the skies.

BARON (*sternly*)   Let that be as it may, but you—have you a passport?

LUKA (*after a pause*)   And who might you be, a nark?

PEPEL (*joyfully*)   Good for you, old man! He took a pretty nip out of you that time, you Baron, you!

BUBNOV   Yes, he put our fine gentleman in his place!

BARON (*embarrassed*)   Well, what of it? I was only joking, old man. I don't own one of those documents myself.

BUBNOV   Liar!

BARON   That is, I have some papers, but they're no good.

LUKA   They're all the same, those papers. None of them's any good.

PEPEL   Let's go and have a drink, Baron.

BARON   I don't object! Well, good-bye, old man. You're a rascal, that's what you are!

LUKA   Takes all kinds of people to make the world.

PEPEL (*at the door to the passage*)   Come on if you're coming! (*Goes out. The* BARON *hurries after him.*)

LUKA   Was he really a baron once?

BUBNOV   Who knows? It's true he's from the gentry. Even now, all of a sudden, he'll do something that shows he's from the gentry. He don't seem to have got out of the habit yet.

LUKA   Belonging to the gentry's like having the smallpox—a person may recover, but the scars remain.

BUBNOV   He's all right on the whole—just gets up on his hind legs once in a while, like about your passport.

ALYOSHKA (*enters slightly drunk, whistling and playing on an accordion*)   Hey, lodgers!

BUBNOV   What are you bawling about?

ALYOSHKA   Excuse me. Forgive me. I'm very polite by nature.

BUBNOV   Been on a spree again?

ALYOSHKA   Haven't I, just! The policeman Medyakin just threw me out of the station and said, "Don't let me catch a sniff of you in the street again! —Not a teeny-weenty!" says he. But I'm a person of character. My boss snarls at me, but what's a boss? Pooh, pooh! A mere misunderstanding! He's a drunk, my boss is, and I'm a person as doesn't care about nothing. I don't want nothing! Here, take me for half a ruble. I don't want nothing! (NASTYA *enters from the kitchen.*) Offer me a million —I won't have it! And do you think I'll let anybody, especially a drunk, tell me what to do? Not on your life!

(*As she stands in the doorway,* NASTYA *watches* ALYOSHKA *and shakes her head.*)

LUKA (*kindly*)   What a muddle you've got yourself into, young man!

BUBNOV   Crazy, that's what he is!

ALYOSHKA (*throwing himself on the floor*)   Here, eat me up! I don't want nothing! I'm a desperate fellow! Try and prove to me who's my betters!

Why am I any worse than the rest? That Medyakin says to me, I'll
smash your mug in if I catch you in the street! But out I'll go! Out I'll
go and lie down in the middle of the street—here, run over me! I don't
want nothing!

NASTYA   Poor fellow! Twisted and knotted at such an early age!

ALYOSHKA (*catching sight of her and getting up on his knees*)   Mademoiselle!
Parlez français! Merci! Bouillon! I've been on a spree!

NASTYA (*in a loud whisper*)   Vasilisa!

VASILISA (*opening the door quickly and speaking to* ALYOSHKA)   You here again?

ALYOSHKA   How d'ye do! Be so kind—

VASILISA   I warned you not to show yourself again, you puppy, and here
you are!

ALYOSHKA   Vasilisa Karpovna! Here, I'll play you a funeral march, want me to?

VASILISA (*taking him by the shoulder*)   Get out!

ALYOSHKA (*making for the door*)   Wait a minute! The funeral march! I just
learned it! A brand-new tune! Wait a minute! You can't do that!

VASILISA   I'll show you whether I can or not! I'll set the whole street against
you, you heathen! You're too young to go around yapping about me!

ALYOSHKA (*running out*)   I'm off!

VASILISA (*to* BUBNOV)   Don't let me catch him here again, hear?

BUBNOV   I'm not a watchdog.

VASILISA   What do I care what you call yourself. Don't forget you're living
on charity. How much do you owe me?

BUBNOV (*undisturbed*)   I haven't counted.

VASILISA   Well, I'll count it for you!

ALYOSHKA (*opening the door and shouting*)   Vasilisa Karpovna! You can't
scare me! You can't scare me-e-e! (*Disappears.*)
          (LUKA *laughs.*)

VASILISA   And who might you be?

LUKA   A wanderer. A pilgrim.

VASILISA   For the night or to stay?

LUKA   I'll have a look around first.

VASILISA   Passport?

LUKA   If you like—

VASILISA   Give it to me!

LUKA   I'll deliver it . . . er . . . to your chambers in person.

VASILISA   A pilgrim? A tramp's more like it!

LUKA (*with a sigh*)   You're not a very gentle soul.
          (VASILISA *goes over to the door of* PEPEL'S *room.*
          ALYOSHKA *pokes his head through the kitchen door and
          whispers,* "Has she gone?")

VASILISA (turning to him)   You still here?
          (ALYOSHKA *gives a piercing whistle and disappears.*
          NASTYA *and* LUKA *laugh.*)

BUBNOV (*to* VASILISA)   He's not here.

VASILISA   Who?

BUBNOV   Vasya.

VASILISA   Did I ask you where he was?

BUBNOV   Well, you were sniffing about.

VASILISA   I'm looking to see that everything's in order, see? Why hasn't the
floor been swept? How many times have I ordered you to keep this
place clean?

BUBNOV   It's the Actor's turn to sweep.

VASILISA   I don't care whose turn it is! If the sanitary inspector comes and
fines me I'll throw you all out!

BUBNOV (*calmly*)   And then what'll you live on?

VASILISA   Don't let me find a speck on the floor! (*Going towards the kitchen
and speaking to* NASTYA.) What are you moping here for with your mug
all swollen? Standing there like a dummy! Sweep up this floor! Have
you seen Natasha? Has she been here?

NASTYA   I don't know. I didn't see her.

VASILISA   Bubnov! Was my sister here?

BUBNOV (*indicating* LUKA)   She brought him in.

VASILISA   And that one—was he home?

BUBNOV   Vasya? He was. But Natasha only spoke to Kleshch.

VASILISA   I'm not asking you who she spoke to! Dirt everywhere! Filth! A
lot of swine! Get this place cleaned up, do you hear?
(*Goes out quickly.*)

BUBNOV   Was there ever a woman as nasty as her?

LUKA   She's not one to fool with!

NASTYA   Anybody'd get nasty from such a life. Tie anybody up to a husband
like hers—

BUBNOV   She's not tied very tight.

LUKA   Does she always go about exploding like that?

BUBNOV   Always. She came to see her lover, and he wasn't here.

LUKA   That *is* annoying, of course. (*Sighs.*) Dear, dear, dear! The number of
people as try to run this earth of ours, all of them threatening fearful
threats. And still there's no order and no cleanliness!

BUBNOV   They want order, but they haven't got the brains to make it. Still,
the floor's got to be swept. Nastya! Why don't you do it?

NASTYA   Why do you suppose? Am I your chambermaid? (*After a moment's
silence.*) I'm going to get drunk today—crazy drunk.

BUBNOV   At least that's something.

LUKA   Why do you want to get drunk, my girl? Just a little while back you
were crying, and now you say you want to get drunk.

NASTYA (*challengingly*)   I'll get drunk and start crying all over again. That's all.

BUBNOV   Not very much.

LUKA   But what's the cause? Even a pimple has its cause.
(NASTYA *shakes her head in silence.*)

LUKA   Dear, dear, dear! Such people! Whatever's going to become of you?
Here, I'll sweep the floor for you. Where's the broom?

BUBNOV   Behind the door in the passage.
(LUKA *goes out into the passage.*)

BUBNOV   Nastya!

NASTYA   What?

BUBNOV   Why did Vasilisa go after Alyoshka like that?

NASTYA   He's been telling everybody that Vasya was sick of her and was going to throw her over for Natasha. I'd better get out of here—move to another place.

BUBNOV   What's that? Where to?

NASTYA   I'm sick of it all. I'm not wanted here.

BUBNOV (*complacently*)   Nor anywhere else. Nobody's wanted on this earth.

> (NASTYA *shakes her head, gets up and quietly goes out into the passage.* MEDVEDEV *enters, followed by* LUKA *with the broom.*)

MEDVEDEV   I don't think I know you.

LUKA   And do you know all the others?

MEDVEDEV   I'm supposed to know all the people on my beat. But I don't know you.

LUKA   That's because not all the earth falls within your beat, uncle. There's a wee little bit left over.

> (*Goes out into the kitchen.*)

MEDVEDEV (*going over to* BUBNOV)   My beat may not be big, but it's worse than a big one. Just now, before knocking off, I had to take Alyoshka the cobbler to the station, and what do you suppose he did? Laid down in the middle of the street, started playing on his accordion and yelling "I don't want nothing!" There was horses going by, and carts and things. He might have got run over or something. He's a noisy youngster. But I've fixed him up, all right. He seems to like making a row.

BUBNOV   Coming over for a game of draughts tonight?

MEDVEDEV   All right. Hm. . . . What about that Vasya?

BUBNOV   Nothing special. Same as ever.

MEDVEDEV   In other words, alive and kicking?

BUBNOV   Why not? No reason why he shouldn't be alive and kicking.

MEDVEDEV (*doubtfully*)   You think so? (LUKA *goes out into the passage carrying a pail.*) There was some gossip going round about Vasya. Haven't you heard it?

BUBNOV   I hear lots of gossip.

MEDVEDEV   About him and Vasilisa. It seems . . . er . . . haven't you noticed anything?

BUBNOV   What, for instance?

MEDVEDEV   Well . . . anything. Maybe you know and won't tell. Everybody knows. (*Sternly.*) No lying, now!

BUBNOV   Why should I lie?

MEDVEDEV   That's it, the dirty dogs! They say Vasya and Vasilisa . . . you know. But what do I care? I'm not her father—only her uncle. Why should folk laugh at me? (KVASHNYA *comes in.*) Whatever's come over people latley—laughing at everybody. Ah, it's you! Back already!

KVASHNYA   My most respected police force! He kept pestering me at the market again, Bubnov. Nothing will do but I must marry him!

BUBNOV   Go ahead. Why not? He's got money, and isn't too rickety yet.

MEDVEDEV   Me? Ho-ho!

KVASHNYA   You, old wolf, you! Don't touch my sore spot. I tried it once, getting married. It's like jumping through a hole in the ice. Once you've done it, you'll never forget it.

MEDVEDEV   Oh, come—husbands are different.

KVASHNYA   But I'm the same. As soon as my darling better half passed out—may he sizzle in hell!—I sat there blissfully for a whole day all by myself: just sat there trying to believe my good luck.

MEDVEDEV   If your husband beat you without good cause, you should have complained to the police.

KVASHNYA   I complained to God for eight years. He didn't help.

MEDVEDEV   It's forbidden to beat your wife nowadays. They're very strict nowadays. Law and order! Mustn't beat anybody without good cause —only to preserve order.

LUKA (*leading in* ANNA)   Now you see, we made it. How can a body like you go walking about all by herself—so shaky on her legs? Where's your place here?

ANNA (*showing him*)   Thank you, grandad.

KVASHNYA   There she is, a married woman. Look at her!

LUKA   She's put together very shaky, poor little thing! I heard her moaning and found her clutching the wall, trying to make her way through the passage. You shouldn't let her walk about by herself.

KVASHNYA   Forgive us such an oversight, good sir. Her chambermaid, it seems, is having a day off.

LUKA   Look at that—turning it into a joke! You can't do that to a person. Everybody's got some worth, however slight.

MEDVEDEV   You'd ought to keep an eye on her. What if she should die all of a sudden? That would be a great nuisance. Don't let her out of your sight.

LUKA   Quite right, Sergeant.

MEDVEDEV   Well, now, I may not quite be a sergeant as yet—

LUKA   Think of that, now! From the looks of you—
(*Noise and confusion in the passage. Stifled cries are heard.*)

MEDVEDEV   A row?

BUBNOV   Sounds like it.

KVASHNYA   I'll go and have a look.

MEDVEDEV   I've got to go too. Oh, these duties! I don't see why we should pull people apart who are fighting. They'd stop of themselves when they got tired. It'd be better to let them slug each other as much as they liked. They'd remember it and wouldn't be so quick to pick a fight the next time.

BUBNOV (*climbing down off his bunk*)   You speak to your chief about that.

KOSTYLYOV (*throwing open the door and shouting*)   Abram! Come quick! Vasilisa's after Natasha. She'll kill her! Hurry up!
(KVASHNYA, MEDVEDEV *and* BUBNOV *rush into the passage.* LUKA *shakes his head and gazes after them.*)

ANNA   Oh, Lord! Poor Natasha!

LUKA   Who's fighting?

ANNA   Our landladies. They're sisters.

LUKA (*going over to* ANNA)   What are they fighting over?

ANNA   Nothing special. They've got too much energy, that's all.

LUKA   What's your name?

ANNA   Anna. I keep looking at you—you remind me of my father, so soft and gentle.

LUKA   I've been pushed around a lot. That's what makes me so soft. (*He gives a crackling laugh.*)

(Curtain)

Act Two

> *The same scene. Evening.* SATIN, KRIVOI ZOB, *the* BARON *and the* TATAR *are playing cards near the stove, while* KLESHCH *and the* ACTOR *look on.* BUBNOV *and* MEDVEDEV *are having a game of draughts on* BUBNOV'S *bunk.* LUKA *is sitting beside* ANNA. *The lodging is lighted by two lamps, one of them on the wall near the cardplayers, the other on* BUBNOV'S *bunk.*

TATAR   Once more I play. That's all I play . . .

BUBNOV   Zob! Sing us a song! (*Sings.*)

> Every morn the sun arises. . . .

KRIVOI ZOB (*joining in*)

> Still my cell is filled with gloom. . . .

TATAR (*to* SATIN)   Shuffle cards. Shuffle good. We know how you play.

BUBNOV and KRIVOI ZOB (*together*)

> Day and night the prison sentries,
> Ah-h!
> Watch the window of my room. . . .

ANNA   Fights . . . insults . . . nothing else. . . . That's all I've seen . . . all I've known.

LUKA   Ah, my poor dearie, don't fret!

MEDVEDEV   Hey, where are you moving! Watch out!

BUBNOV   Hm. Well. . . .

TATAR (*shaking his fist at* SATIN)   Why you hide them cards? I see! You god-damn. . . .

KRIVOI ZOB   Forget it, Asan! They'll cheat us anyway. Bubnov, start up the song again!

ANNA   I never had enough to eat . . . counted every crumb . . . always trembled with fear . . . scared to eat more than the other person . . . never had anything to wear but rags. Why?

LUKA   Poor little thing! Are you tired? Everything will be all right.

ACTOR (*to* KRIVOI ZOB)   Throw on your Jack—your Jack, damn you!

BARON   And we've got the King!

KLESHCH   They always go one higher.

SATIN   It's a habit of ours.

MEDVEDEV   King!

BUBNOV   Me too. Well, now?

ANNA   And now I'm dying. . . .

KLESHCH   See that? See that? Quit the game, Asan! Quit it, I say!

ACTOR   Can't he think for himself?

BARON   You watch out, Andrei, or I'll send you flying straight to hell!

TATAR   Come on. Deal again. The pitcher bring water and broke herself. Me too.

(KLESHCH *shakes his head and goes over to* BUBNOV.)

ANNA   I keep thinking: dear God, will this torture go on in the next world too? There too?

LUKA   No, no. You won't suffer there, my pretty. Sleep in peace. Everything will be all right. You'll have a good rest there. Be patient just a little longer. Everybody has got to be patient—each in his own way.

(*He gets up and goes into the kitchen with quick little steps.*)

BUBNOV (*singing*)

Guard my window at your pleasure—

KRIVOI ZOB

I will never run away!

(*In unison.*)

Though I languish for my freedom,
Ah-h!
Chains are forcing me to stay!

TATAR (*shouting*)   Aha! Put card up sleeve!

BARON (*in some embarrassment*)   Well, where do you expect me to put it—up your nose'?

ACTOR (*convincingly*)   You're mistaken, Asan. No one has ever—

TATAR   I see! Cheat! I no play!

SATIN (*gathering up the cards*)   All right, get out, Asan. You knew we were cheats. Why did you start playing with us?

BARON   Lost twenty kopeks and makes a noise like three rubles! And calls himself a Tatar!

TATAR (*angrily*)   Gotta play fair!

SATIN   What for?

TATAR   What you mean, what for?

SATIN   Just what I said—what for?

TATAR   You don't know?

SATIN   No, I don't know. Do you know?

(*The* TATAR *spits in anger, the others laugh at him.*)

KRIVOI ZOB (*undisturbed*)   You're crazy, Asan. Can't you see that if they tried living honestly, they'd starve to death in three days?

TATAR   I no care. Gotta live honest.

KRIVOI ZOB   Harping on the old string. Come on, let's go and have our tea. Bubnov!

Ah, my chains, my iron halter. . . .

BUBNOV
Unrelenting iron guard. . . .

KRIVOI ZOB   Come along, Asan! (*He goes out singing.*)
I can neither loose nor break them. . . .

(*The* TATAR *shakes his fist at the* BARON, *then follows his friend out.*)

SATIN (*laughing and addressing the* BARON)   Once again, your honourable honour, it seems you have been dumped in a ditch. Hm, an educated gentleman, and don't know how to slip a card up your sleeve!

BARON (*shrugging his shoulders*)   How the devil it ever happened!

ACTOR   No talent. No faith in yourself. Without that—nothing. Failure.

MEDVEDEV   I've got one King, but you've got two.

BUBNOV   You can still win if you're smart. Your move.

KLESHCH   You've lost already, Abram Ivanich!

MEDVEDEV   Keep out of this, hear? Shut up!

SATIN   Winnings—fifty-three kopeks!

ACTOR   Three of them go to me. But what do I want with three kopeks?

LUKA (*entering from the kitchen*)   Well, now you've stripped the Tatar, I suppose you'll be going out for a drink?

BARON   Come with us.

SATIN   I'd like to see what you're like when you're drunk.

LUKA   No better than when I'm sober.

ACTOR   Come on, old man. I'll recite some verses to you.

LUKA   What's that?

ACTOR   Poetry.

LUKA   Poetry? What do I want with poetry?

ACTOR   It can be amusing. But it can also be sad.

SATIN   Well, poet, are you coming?
(*Goes out with the* BARON.)

ACTOR   Coming. I'll catch you up! Listen to this, old man. It's from some poem. Ugh . . . I can't remember the beginning. Can't remember! (*Rubs his forehead.*)

BUBNOV   Here goes your King! Your move!

MEDVEDEV   I shouldn't have moved there, damn it all!

ACTOR   Formerly, when my organism was not yet poisoned with alcohol, I had a good memory, old man. But now—? Everything's over for me now. I always brought down the house with those lines—tremendous applause! And you don't know what applause means, my friend. Applause is like vodka! I used to come out and stand like this. (*Strikes a pose.*) I'd stand like this . . . and . . . (*He is silent.*) Can't remember a word—not a word. And it was my favourite poem. That's pretty bad, isn't it, old man?

LUKA   It is, once it's your favourite. All your soul goes into your favourite.

ACTOR   I've drunk up my soul, old man. I'm ruined. And why? Because I had no faith in myself. I'm done for.

LUKA   That's nothing. All you have to do is take a cure. They cure people of drunkenness nowadays, haven't you heard? Cure them free of charge.

They've opened up a kind of healing centre, so to speak, where they cure them for nothing. That's because they see a drunkard's also a human being, and they're even glad when he wants to be cured. So you just go there. Go and try it, do.

ACTOR (*pensively*)   Where? Where is this place?

LUKA   It's in some city or other. What do they call it? A funny name. Let me see . . . never fear, I'll find out the name. Meantime, you be getting yourself ready. Drop the vodka. Take yourself in hand and hold on, and then you'll go for a cure and begin life all over again. Won't that be fine? All over again. Just make up your mind, once and for all!

ACTOR (*smiling*)   All over again. All from the beginning. Yes, that sounds fine. All over again. (*Laughs.*) Of course! I can do it! Don't you think I can do it?

LUKA   Of course you can. A person can do anything, if he wants to badly enough.

ACTOR (*as though suddenly waking up*)   You're a little cracked, aren't you, old man? Well, good-bye for the present. (*Whistling*) Good-bye, old man. (*Goes out.*)

ANNA   Grandad.

LUKA   What is it, dearie?

ANNA   Talk to me.

LUKA (*going over to her*)   Very well. You and me'll have a nice little chat.
> (KLESHCH *watches them, then silently goes over to his wife, looks at her and makes movements with his hands as if there were something he wanted to say.*)

LUKA   What is it, brother?

KLESHCH (*under his breath*)   Nothing.
> (*Goes slowly towards the door to the passage, stands in front of it in hesitation a second or so, then suddenly goes out.*)

LUKA (*following him with his eyes*)   It's hard for that man of yours.

ANNA   I can't be thinking of him now.

LUKA   Did he often beat you?

ANNA   Something awful. It's because of him I got like this.

BUBNOV   My wife had a lover once. The rascal played a good game of draughts.

MEDVEDEV   Hm.

ANNA   Grandad, please tell me something. . . . I'm feeling so bad. . . .

LUKA   That's nothing. That's just before you die, pigeon. It'll be all right, dearie. You just keep hoping. This is how it'll be—you'll die now, you see, and everything'll be quiet and peaceful. You won't have to be afraid of nothing any more, nothing at all. Just lie there in peace and quiet. Death's kind to us poor mortals. He smooths out all the wrinkles, death does. That's why they say: eternal rest. And that's the truth, lovey, because where can a person hope to get any rest in this world?
> (PEPEL *comes in. He has had a drink, looks dishevelled and is in a sullen mood. He sinks down on a bunk by the door and sits there silent and motionless.*)

ANNA   But there in that other world—will we be tortured there too?

LUKA   There won't be nothing there. Nothing at all. You just believe me.
Peace and quiet and nothing else. They'll summon you before the Lord
God and say: See, Lord, it's your faithful servant Anna who has come.

MEDVEDEV (*sternly*)   How do you know what they'll say there? You're a fine
one, you are!

> (*On hearing* MEDVEDEV'S *voice,* PEPEL *lifts his head
> and listens.*)

LUKA   If I say it, I must be knowing it, Sergeant—

MEDVEDEV (*appeased*)   Hm. Maybe. I suppose that's your business. But I told
you I'm not a sergeant. Not yet.

BUBNOV   Double jump.

MEDVEDEV   You devil. I hope you—

LUKA   And the Lord God will look at you so gentle and tender like, and say:
Of course I know Anna! And He'll say: You just lead our Anna right
into Paradise—that's what He'll say. Let her rest up a bit. I know what
a hard life she's had. I know how tired she is. Let her have peace and
quiet now.

ANNA (*gasping*)   Oh, grandad . . . dearest grandad . . . if it would only be like
that! If only . . . peace and quiet . . . not to feel anything. . . .

LUKA   You won't feel anything, my pretty. Nothing at all. Believe me. You
must die now gladly, without any fear. Death, I'm telling you, is a tender
father to us, his children.

ANNA   But . . . maybe . . . maybe I'll get well?

LUKA (*smiling deprecatingly*)   What for, dearie? To be tortured again?

ANNA   To live . . . just a little . . . just a little longer. Once you say there
won't be any suffering there. . . . I could bear it here . . . I could.

LUKA   There won't be nothing at all there. Just—

PEPEL (*getting up*)   You're right. But maybe—you're wrong.

ANNA (*startled*)   Good heavens!

LUKA   What's that, my handsome fellow?

MEDVEDEV   Who's shouting?

PEPEL (*going over to him*)   Me! What of it?

MEDVEDEV   You oughtn't to shout, that's what. A person should conduct
himself peaceful.

PEPEL   Blockhead! And their uncle! Ho-ho!

LUKA (*to* PEPEL, *under his breath*)   Stop shouting, hear? The woman's dying.
The earth colour has come to her lips already. Leave her alone.

PEPEL   Out of respect for you, grandad. You're a smart feller, grandad. You
lie beautifully. Nice to listen to your fairy-tales. Go ahead and lie.
That's all right. Not many pleasant things to listen to in this world.

BUBNOV   Is it true she's dying?

LUKA   I think so.

BUBNOV   That means the end of her coughing. A nasty cough she had.
Double jump.

MEDVEDEV   Pooh! Devil take you!

PEPEL   Abram!

MEDVEDEV   Who said you could call me by my first name?

PEPEL   Abram! Is Natasha sick?

MEDVEDEV   What business is it of yours?

PEPEL   You'd better tell me. Did Vasilisa beat her bad?

MEDVEDEV   It's none of your business. It's a family affair. Who are you to butt in?

PEPEL   Whoever I am, you'll never get another look at Natasha if I don't want you to.

MEDVEDEV   (*leaving his draughts*)   What? What's that? Who are you talking about? She's my niece, you thief, you!

PEPEL   I may be a thief, but you haven't caught me!

MEDVEDEV   Just wait! I'll catch you, all right. And soon!

PEPEL   If you catch me, it'll be the end of this little nest of yours. Do you think I'll keep my mouth shut in court? The wolf will bare his fangs. They'll ask me: Who taught you to steal and showed you where? Mishka Kostylyov and his wife! Who handled your stolen goods? Mishka Kostylyov and his wife!

MEDVEDEV   You're a liar. Nobody'll believe you!

PEPEL   They'll believe me because it's the truth! And I'll drag you in, too— hah! I'll ruin all of you, you bastards! You'll see!

MEDVEDEV   (*frightened*)   Liar! You liar! What harm have I ever done you? Throwing yourself on me like a mad dog!

PEPEL   What *good* have you ever done me?

LUKA   Hm!

MEDVEDEV   (*to* LUKA)   What are you croaking about? What business is it of yours? This is a family affair.

BUBNOV   (*to Luka*)   Keep out of it. The noose isn't for you and me.

LUKA   (*meekly*)   Yes, I'm just saying if a person hasn't done his neighbour good, he's done him bad

MEDVEDEV   (*missing the point*)   Blah! We here, we all know each other, but you—who are you? (*Gives an angry snort and hurries out.*)

LUKA   The gentleman seems to be angry. Dear me! Your affairs here, brothers, are a bit tangled, as I see it.

PEPEL   He's run off to tell Vasilisa.

BUBNOV   You're a fool, Vasya. Showing off how brave you are! Watch out! It's all right to be brave when you go to the woods for mushrooms, but there's no sense in it here. They'll snap off your head in an instant.

PEPEL   Oh, no, they won't! Nobody's taking a fellow from Yaroslavl with his bare hands! If it's a fight they want, they'll get it!

LUKA   But *really* now, don't you think you'd do well to clear out of here, lad?

PEPEL   Where'll I go? Tell me that.

LUKA   Well now, Siberia for instance.

PEPEL   Not me. No, thank you. I'll wait to be sent to Siberia free of charge.

LUKA   Take my advice and go out there. Out there you'll find the right path to follow. They need people like you out there.

PEPEL   My path has been laid out for me. My father spent most of his life in jail and ordered me to do the same. Ever since I was a kid I've been called a thief, or the son of a thief.

LUKA   It's a fine place, Siberia. A golden land. If a person is strong and has a good head on his shoulders, he'll feel as snug there as a cucumber in a hot-house.

PEPEL   Why do you tell such lies, old man?

LUKA   Eh?

PEPEL   Deaf. What do you tell lies for, I say?

LUKA   What lies have I told?

PEPEL   Everything you say's a lie. Everything's good, according to you: this place, that place. A pack of lies. What makes you tell them?

LUKA   You just believe what I say and go out there to see for yourself. Then you'll say thank you. Why should you stay here? And why should you be so anxious to know the truth? The truth may turn out to be an axe on your neck.

PEPEL   It's all the same to me. If it's an axe, it's an axe.

LUKA   Foolish lad. There's no sense in killing yourself.

BUBNOV   What are you two arguing about? Is it the truth you're after, Vasya? What for? You know it without being told. Everybody knows it.

PEPEL   Quit your croaking. Let him tell me. Listen, old man—is there a God?
          (LUKA *smiles, but says nothing.*)

BUBNOV   People are like chips of wood floating on the river—and chips fly off as houses are built.

PEPEL   Well, is there? Speak up.

LUKA   (*quietly*)   There is if you believe there is; there isn't if you don't. Whatever you believe in, that's what there is.
          (PEPEL *stares at the old man in silent wonder.*)

BUBNOV   I'm going for my tea. Anyone coming along?

LUKA   (*to* PEPEL)   What are you staring at?

PEPEL   Nothing. Listen, you mean—?

BUBNOV   Then I'll go alone.
          (*Goes to the door and is met by* VASILISA.)

PEPEL   In other words, you—

VASILISA   (*to* BUBNOV)   Is Nastya here?

BUBNOV   No. (*Goes out.*)

PEPEL   Ah, here she is.

VASILISA   (*going over to* ANNA)   Still alive?

LUKA   Don't disturb her.

VASILISA   What are you doing here?

LUKA   I can leave if you want me to.

VASILISA   (*going to the door of* PEPEL'S *room*)   Vasya, there's something I want to speak to you about.
          (LUKA *goes to the door into the passage, opens it and slams it shut. Then he cautiously climbs from one of the bunks up on to the stove.*)

VASILISA   (*from* PEPEL'S *room*)   Vasya, come here!

PEPEL   I don't feel like it.

VASILISA   What's the matter? What are you sore about?

PEPEL   I'm fed up. I'm sick of all this business.

VASILISA   Sick of me too?

PEPEL   Yes, you too.

> (VASILISA *pulls her shawl tight, pressing her hands to her
> breast. She goes over to* ANNA's *bed, glances through the
> curtains, and crosses to* PEPEL.)

PEPEL   Well, say what's on your mind.

VASILISA   What's there to say? I can't make you love me, and it's not my
nature to go begging. Thanks for telling me the truth.

PEPEL   What truth?

VASILISA   That you're sick of me. Or maybe it's not the truth?

> (PEPEL *stares at her in silence.*)

VASILISA (*going up to him*)   What are you looking at? Don't you recognize me?

PEPEL (*with a sigh*)   You're too damn good-looking, Vasilisa. (*She puts her
hand on his shoulder, but he shrugs it off.*) But you never won my heart.
I lived with you, and all the rest, but I never liked you.

VASILISA (*under her breath*)   So that's it! Well—

PEPEL   Well, and there's nothing for you and me to talk about! Nothing at all.
Get away from me!

VASILISA   Have you fallen for somebody else?

PEPEL   What business is it of yours? If I had, I wouldn't ask you to help me
get her.

VASILISA (*significantly*)   Too bad. Maybe I *could* help you get her.

PEPEL (*suspiciously*)   Get who?

VASILISA   You know. Why pretend? I'm used to talking straight, Vasya.
(*Lowering her voice*) I won't deny it—you've hurt me. It's as if you'd
given me a lashing for no good reason and to no purpose. You said you
loved me, and then all of a sudden—

PEPEL   Not all of a sudden. It's been like this for a long time. You have no
heart, woman. A woman ought to have a heart. Us men are beasts, and
you've got to . . . you've got to teach us. What did you ever teach me?

VASILISA   Let bygones be bygones. I know a person's not free in himself. If
you don't love me any more, I can take it. That's how it'll be.

PEPEL   So now it's all over between us? And we part peaceable, without any
scenes? That's good.

VASILISA   Oh, no! Wait a minute! Don't forget I always hoped you'd help me
throw this yoke off my neck. I thought you'd help me get away from my
husband, my uncle, from all this life. And maybe it wasn't you I loved
so much as this hope, this idea of mine, see? I was waiting for you to
pull me out.

PEPEL   You're no nail, I'm no pliers. I, too, thought that one as smart as
you—you *are* smart—you're a clever one—

VASILISA (*straining towards him*)   Vasya, let's help each other.

PEPEL   How?

VASILISA (*forcefully, in lowered tones*)   My sister . . . I know you like her.

PEPEL   And so that's why you beat her? You watch out, Vasilisa! Keep your
hands off her!

VASILISA Wait. Don't flare up. We can arrange everything quietly, without getting mad. How would you like to—to marry her? I'd give you some money—three hundred rubles. If I get more, you can have that too.

PEPEL (*moving away*) What? What's behind this?

VASILISA Help me get rid of my husband. Take that noose off my neck.

PEPEL (*whistling softly*) So that's it! Oho! You *are* smart! Your husband in his grave, your lover in jail, and you yourself—

VASILISA Vasya! Why in jail? Don't do it yourself—get somebody else to do it. And even if you did do it yourself, who'd know? Natasha . . . think it over. . . . You'll have money. . . . You can go away. . . . I'll be free forever. . . . As for my sister—it'll be good for her to get away from me. It's hard for me to see her all the time. She makes me sore because of you. I can't stop myself. I torture her. I beat her. I beat her until it makes even me cry to see her. But I beat her just the same, and I'll keep on beating her.

PEPEL You're a brute, and you boast of it.

VASILISA No, I don't. I just tell the truth. Think, Vasya. Twice they threw you in jail on account of that husband of mine—on account of his greediness. He sucks my blood like a leech—been sucking it for four years. What kind of a husband is he? And he keeps squeezing Natasha out, nagging her, calling her a beggar. He's poison for everybody.

PEPEL You're a sly one.

VASILISA It's clear as day. You'd have to be a fool not to understand what I'm after.

(KOSTYLYOV *comes in quietly and steals forward.*)

PEPEL (*to* VASILISA) Get out!

VASILISA Think it over. (*Catches sight of her husband.*) What do you want? Have you come for me?

(PEPEL *starts up and stares wildly at* KOSTYLYOV.)

KOSTYLYOV It's me, just me. You two here—alone? Having a little talk? (*Suddenly he stamps his foot and begins to screech.*) God damn you, Vasilisa! You beggar, you! (*He is frightened by his own shouts and by the frozen silence with which they are received.*) O Lord, forgive me! Leading me into sin again, Vasilisa! Here I am searching for you everywhere. (*Again raising his voice.*) It's high time you were in bed! Forgot to fill the icon lamp again, damn you! You pig! You pauper! (*He shakes a trembling finger at her.* VASILISA *goes slowly to the door of the passage, her eyes fixed on* PEPEL.)

PEPEL (*to* KOSTYLYOV) Get out of here! Get out, I tell you!

KOSTYLYOV (*shouting*) It's me who owns this place. Get out yourself, you thief!

PEPEL (*in a strained voice*) Get out, I say,

KOSTYLYOV Don't you dare! I'll show you! I'll—

(PEPEL *takes him by the collar and starts shaking him. Suddenly someone is heard to move about on top of the stove and to give a loud and long-drawn yawn.* PEPEL *lets go of* KOSTYLYOV, *who runs with a cry into the passage.*)

PEPEL (*jumping up on to the bunk by the stove*)   Who's there? Who's up on the stove?

LUKA (*poking his head up*)   Eh?

PEPEL   You!

LUKA   Me. Me myself. Oh, dear Lord in heaven!

PEPEL (*shuts the door into the passage and looks vainly for the bar which secures it.*)   Damn it all! Climb down, old man!

LUKA   Ri-ight away! I'm coming!

PEPEL (*roughly*)   Why did you crawl up on the stove?

LUKA   Where should I have crawled?

PEPEL   You went out into the passage.

LUKA   That's a cold place for an old man like me.

PEPEL   Did you . . . hear anything?

LUKA   'Deed I did. How could I have helped hearing? Did you think I was deaf? Ah, lad, luck comes your way. You're a lucky one.

PEPEL (*suspiciously*)   What makes you say that?

LUKA   It's lucky for you I crawled up on that stove.

PEPEL   Why did you make all that noise?

LUKA   It was getting too hot for me, that's why. And you can be thankful for that. The lad will be forgetting himself, thinks I. He'll be squeezing the breath out of that old feller.

PEPEL   I would have for sure. Ugh, how I hate—

LUKA   I know. Easy as sitting down. Lots of times people make slips like that.

PEPEL (*smiling*)   Maybe you made such a slip yourself once upon a time?

LUKA   Listen, lad, listen to me. Keep away from that woman. Shoo her away. Shoo! Shoo! She'll get rid of that man of hers without your help, and better than you could do it. Don't listen to her, to that she-devil. Look at me—see how bald I am? And what might be the cause. Women. I've known more women in my time than I had hairs on my head. But this Vasilisa here is worse than any harpy.

PEPEL   I don't know whether I should say thank you or—

LUKA   Don't say nothing. You'll not find better words than those I've spoken. Listen to me—the lady that you're fond of—you just take her arm, right about face, and forward march! Get away from here! As far away as you can go!

PEPEL (*sullenly*)   There's no knowing people—who's good and who's bad. There's no knowing.

LUKA   What's there to know? A person's not always the same. It all depends on how his heart's tuned. Today he's good, tomorrow he's bad. But if that girl has got a real grip on your soul, then be off with her, and that's that. Or else be off alone. You're young yet. You've got plenty of time to get a woman.

PEPEL (*taking him by the shoulders*)   Tell me the truth. Why are you saying this?

LUKA   Here, let me go. I'll just have a look at Anna. She was breathing hard a minute ago. (*He goes over to* ANNA'S *bed, opens the curtains, looks in, touches her.* PEPEL *watches him with a thoughtful, perplexed look on his face.*) Have mercy, O Lord! Mercifully receive the soul of Thy servant Anna.

PEPEL (*under his breath*)   Dead? (*He strains forward to get a better look at the bed, but he does not go over to it.*)

LUKA (*softly*)   It's all over now, her torture. Where's that man of hers?

PEPEL   In the pub, I suppose.

LUKA   He's got to be told.

PEPEL (*shuddering*)   I hate corpses.

LUKA (*going to the door*)   Why should you like them? It's the live ones we ought to like. The live ones.

PEPEL   I'll go with you.

LUKA   Afraid of the corpse?

PEPEL   Hate it.

> (*They hurry out. The stage is empty and silent. Dull incomprehensible sounds come from beyond the door into the passage. At last the* ACTOR *comes in.*)

ACTOR (*he does not close the door, but stands on the threshold leaning agaisnt the jamb, calling out in a loud voice.*)   Old man! Where are you? It's back to me! Listen! (*He takes two uncertain steps forward, strikes a pose, and recites*).

> If no path can be found that leads
> To the realms of sacred truth.
> Then bléssed the crazéd mind
> That brings men soaring dreams.

> (NATASHA *appears in the doorway behind the* ACTOR.)

ACTOR: Old man!

> If tomorrow the sun should cease
> To light the earth with its rays,
> Tomorrow some madman's dream
> Would illuminate the world.

NATASHA (*laughs*)   Pie-eyed. The simpleton!

ACTOR (*turning to her*)   Ah, it's you. Where's the old man? The lovely old man? Nobody here, it seems. Farewell, Natasha! Fare thee well!

NATASHA (*entering*)   Saying farewell before you've said hullo?

ACTOR (*blocking her path*)   I am . . . going away. When spring comes I shall be no more.

NATASHA   Let me pass. Where are you going?

ACTOR   In search of a certain town. To take a cure. You, too, must leave. Ophelia, hie thee to a convent! There exists, it seems, a healing centre for organisms—for drunkards. A marvellous place. Everything marble— even the floors. Very bright. And clean. And lots of food. All for nothing. Marble floors—fancy that! I'll find it and get well and then . . . I am about to be reborn, as the King said . . . King Lear. My stage name is Sverchkov Zavolzhsky, Natasha, but nobody knows it. Nobody. Here I have no name. Can you understand how it hurts to lose one's name? Even dogs have a name. . . .

> (NATASHA *passes the* ACTOR *at a safe distance and goes over to* ANNA's *bed, looking through the curtains.*)

ACTOR   No name, no man.

NATASHA   Look! Oh, dear! She's dead!

ACTOR (*shaking his head*)   It cannot be.

NATASHA (*stepping back*)   She is. Look.

BUBNOV (*in the doorway*)   Look at what?

NATASHA   Anna. She's dead.

BUBNOV   At last she's stopped that coughing of hers. (*Goes over to* ANNA'S
    bed, looks through the curtains, goes to his own bunk.) Kleshch will have
    to be told. That's his business.

ACTOR   I'll go. I'll say—she's lost her name! (*Goes out.*)

NATASHA (*from centre of the room*)   And me too . . . some day . . . like
    that . . . driven down into some basement . . . downtrodden. . . .

BUBNOV (*spreading some old rags out on the planks of his bunk*)   What's that?
    What're you muttering about?

NATASHA   I was just thinking out loud.

BUBNOV   Waiting for Vasya? Watch out! You'll break your neck over that
    Vasya.

NATASHA   Does it make any difference what I break it over? Let it be him.
    He's better than most.

BUBNOV (*lying down*)   That's your business.

NATASHA   It's a good thing, of course, her dying . . . but a pity. What does
    a person live for?

BUBNOV   It's the same for all of us: we get born, live our lives, and die. I'll
    die, and you will too. Why feel sorry for anybody?

    (LUKA, *the* TATAR, KRIVOI ZOB *and* KLESHCH *come in.*
    KLESHCH *is the last. He walks slowly and all hunched
    over.*)

NATASHA   Sh! Anna—

KRIVOI ZOB   We know. May she rest in peace, now she's dead.

TATAR (*to* KLESHCH)   Have to drag her out. Have to drag her into passage.
    Can't have dead people here. Live people sleep here.

KLESHCH (*in quiet tone*)   We'll drag her out.

    (*They all go over to the bed.* KLESHCH *stares at his wife
    over the shoulders of the others.*)

KRIVOI ZOB (*to the* TATAR)   Do you think she'll smell? There's nothing to
    smell. She dried up while she was still alive.

NATASHA   Good Lord, you might at least feel sorry for her! Say one little
    word of pity! But not you!

LUKA   Don't mind them, dearie. How can they—how can any of us be
    expected to pity the dead if we don't pity the living? We don't even pity
    ourselves, let along the dead!

BUBNOV (*yawning*)   You can't scare death off with words. You can sickness,
    but not death.

TATAR (*moving away*)   Call the police.

KRIVOI ZOB   Yes, we've got to do that, Kleshch! Have you notified the police?

KLESHCH   No. They'll make me bury her, and I've only got forty kopeks.

KRIVOI ZOB   In that case, borrow something. We can take up a collection—five
    kopeks—whatever a man's able. But hurry and notify the police or

they'll be thinking you killed her or something.
>   (*Goes over to the bunks and is about to lie down
>   beside the* TATAR.)

NATASHA (*going over to* BUBNOV)   Now I'll dream about her. I always dream about dead people. I'm afraid to go home alone. It's dark out there in the passage.

LUKA (*following her out*)   It's the living ones you have to be afraid of, take my word for it.

NATASHA   See me out, grandad.

LUKA   Come along, come along, I'll take you. (*They go out. Pause.*)

KRIVOI ZOB   O-ho-ho! Asan! It'll soon be spring. At last we'll get warm. The muzhiks in the village have begun to mend their ploughs and their harrows. Getting ready to turn the soil. Hm. And us? Eh, Asan? Snoring away, the damn Mohammedan.

BUBNOV   Tatars are good at sleeping.

KLESHCH (*standing in the middle of the lodging and staring dully in front of him*)   What am I to do now?

KRIVOI ZOB   Go to sleep, that's what.

KLESHCH (*softly*)   And what about her?
>   (*Nobody answers.* SATIN *and the* ACTOR *come in.*)

ACTOR (*shouting*)   Old man! Come here, my loyal Kent!

SATIN   Make way for Miklukho-Maklai!

ACTOR   It's decided, once and for all. Old man! Where's that town? Where are you?

SATIN   Fata Morgana! The old fellow lied to you. There's nothing of the sort. No towns. No people. Nothing.

ACTOR   That's a lie!

TATAR (*jumping off his bed*)   Where's boss? I go for boss. No can't sleep, why for I pay money? Dead people. Drunks.
>   (*Goes out quickly. Satin whistles after him.*)

BUBNOV (*sleepily*)   Go to bed, fellows. Stop your noise. A man's supposed to sleep at night.

ACTOR   Ah! Here lies a corpse! "Our fishing nets have caught a corpse!" Poetry. Béranger!

SATIN (*shouting*)   A corpse hears nothing! A corpse feels nothing! Shout as much as you like! A corpse hears nothing!
>   (*Luka appears in the doorway.*)

>   (*Curtain*)

Act Three

>   *A back yard littered with rubbish and overgrown with
>   weeds. A high brick fire-wall upstage cuts off a view of
>   the sky. Against this wall grow elder bushes. To the
>   right is a dark log wall—perhaps of a shed or a stable.
>   On the left is Kostylyov's house with the lodging in the
>   basement. It is grey and ramshackle, with the stucco*

crumbling off. It stands at an angle, so that the far corner reaches almost to upstage centre, leaving only a narrow passage between the brick wall and the house. There are two windows in the house, one a basement window downstage, the other about six feet higher and upstage. A log some 12 feet long lies near the house; beside it—a dilapidated and overturned wooden sledge. Old boards and beams form a pile of wood near the building on the right. Day is drawing to a close and the rays of the setting sun cast a red glow upon the brick wall. It is early spring; the snow has just melted and the black branches of the elder bushes are as yet without buds. NATASHA *and* NASTYA *are sitting on the log;* LUKA *and the* BARON *on the sledge;* KLESHCH *is lying on the pile of wood to the right.* BUBNOV'S *face is seen at the basement window.*

NASTYA (*closing her eyes and nodding her head in rhythm to the sing-song chanting of her tale*)   So he comes at night to the garden, to the summer-house, like we planned. I've been waiting so long I'm all atremble with fear and sorrow. And he's all atremble, and white as a sheet, and in his hand he holds an involver—

NATASHA (*chewing sunflower seeds*)   See? So it must be true what they say about students being desperate.

NASTYA   And he says to me in a fearful voice: My precious love, he says—

BUBNOV   Ho-ho! Precious, did you say?

BARON   Shut up! If you don't like it, don't listen, but don't interfere with her lying. Next!

NASTYA   My precious, he says, my beloved! My parents, he says, will never consent to my marrying you. They threaten to lay their curse on me forever for loving you. And for that reason, he says, I must take my own life. And there he has that big involver with all those bullets in it. Farewell, he says, beloved of my heart. There's no changing my mind. I can't go on living without you! And I says to him: My adored friend! My Raoul!

BUBNOV (*in amazement*)   What? How's that? Growl?

BARON (*roaring*)   You've forgotten, Nastya! Last time he was Gaston!

NASTYA (*jumping up*)   Shut up, you scum! You homeless pups! As though you could understand love—true love! But me—I've known it, true love! (*To the Baron.*) You're a nobody! You, with your education! You, as used to drink coffee in bed!

LUKA   Ju-u-ust a minute! Don't go stopping her, now! Let her go on. It's not the words that count, but what's behind them—that's the thing. Go on, my girl. Don't mind them.

BUBNOV   A crow in peacock's feathers. Well, let's hear the rest.

BARON   Go on.

NATASHA   Don't listen to them. Who are they? They're only jealous because they've got nothing to tell about themselves.

NASTYA (*sitting down again*)　I don't want to go on. I won't tell you any more. Once they don't believe me and laugh at me—(*Suddenly she stops, is silent a minute, and then, closing her eyes, continues in a loud, impassioned voice, beating time with her hand as if listening to distant music.*) And I say to him: Joy of my life! Sun of my soul! Nor can I go on living in this world without you, because I love you with all my soul and will go on loving you as long as this heart beats in this breast. But don't end your life, which your dear parents need so bad, since you're all the joy they've got. Throw me over! Better my life should wear away with pining for you, my beloved! I'm all alone. I'm—I'm that sort. Let me go to my ruin. It's all the same. I'm not worth anything. There's nothing left for me. . . . Nothing left. . . . Nothing left. . . .

　　(*She covers her face with her hands and weeps silently.*)

NATASHA (*turning away and speaking softly*)　Don't cry. You mustn't.

　　(LUKA *smiles and strokes* NASTYA'S *head.*)

BUBNOV (*laughing*)　She's a fine one!

BARON (*also laughing*)　You think that's the truth grandad? That's all out of that book "Fatal Love." A lot of nonsense. Let her be!

NATASHA　What do you care? Keep your mouth shut, once the Lord saw fit to make you what you are.

NASTYA (*furiously*)　You lost soul! You emptiness! Where's your heart?

LUKA (*taking* NASTYA *by the hand*)　We'll go away from here, dearie. Don't mind them. You're the one that's right, not them. I know. Once you believe you had that true love, you really did. You did indeed. But don't get angry with the fellow you live with. Maybe it's jealousy makes him laugh. Maybe he never knew that true kind. Maybe he never knew any kind at all. Come away.

NASTYA (*pressing her hands to her breast*)　Believe me, grandad! I swear it was like that! Everything I said. . . . He was a student, a Frenchman. They called him Gaston. He had a black beard and wore patent-leather boots. Strike me dead this minute if it's not the truth! And how he loved me! How he loved me!

LUKA　I know. I believe you. Patent-leather boots, you say? Fancy that! And you loved him too? (*They disappear around the corner.*)

BARON　A stupid wench! She's got a good heart, but there never was anyone so stupid.

BUBNOV　Why should a person want to lie like that? And swear it's the truth, like in court.

NATASHA　It's more pleasant to lie than to tell the truth. Me, too—

BARON　You too? Next?

NATASHA　I keep dreaming and dreaming. And waiting.

BARON　What for?

NATASHA (*smiling self-consciously*)　I don't know. I just keep thinking that tomorrow . . . somebody will come . . . somebody special. Or else something will happen. . . . Something unusual. And I keep waiting. Always waiting. But when you come to think of it, what could happen?

　　(*Pause*)

BARON (*with a wry smile*)   There's nothing to wait for. Me, for instance, I'm not waiting for anything. Everything's over. Passed. Finished. Next?

NATASHA   Or else I imagine tomorrow I'll die all of a sudden. And then everything goes cold inside me. Summer's a good time to imagine you'll die, because of the thunderstorms; you could easily get struck by lightning.

BARON   Yours is a poor sort of life, and it's all the fault of that sister of yours—a devilish temper she's got.

NATASHA   Who's got a good sort of life? Everybody has it bad. Don't I see it?

KLESHCH (*until now he had been lying motionless and detached, but at these words, he springs up.*)   Everybody? That's a lie! Not everybody. If it was everybody it wouldn't be so bad. Then you wouldn't mind.

BUBNOV   What devil stuck his fork in you this time? Yelping like that!

(KLESHCH *lies down again, muttering to himself.*)

BARON   I'd better go and make my peace with Nastya. If I don't, she'll hold out on the drink money.

BUBNOV   Hm. How people love to lie! Nastya, now, you can understand her. She's used to painting her mug, so she thinks she can do the same to her soul. Rouge her soul. But what do the others want to lie for? That Luka, for instance. He lies without getting anything out of it, and him an old man. What does he do it for?

BARON (*with a snort, as he goes out*)   They've all got grey little souls. They'd all like to rouge them a bit.

LUKA (*entering from around the corner*)   Why did you go and upset the girl, your lordship? Let her enjoy her cry. If it gives her pleasure to let the tears flow, why should you mind?

BARON   She's a dunce, old man. She gets on your nerves. Today it's Raoul, tomorrow Gaston, but the story's always the same. I'd better go and make my peace with her just the same. (*Goes out.*)

LUKA   That's right. Be nice and gentle with her. It never does any harm to be gentle with a person.

NATASHA   You've got a good heart, grandad. What makes you so kind?

LUKA   Kind, you say? Very well, if that's the way you see it. (*The soft music of an accordion and singing comes from the other side of the brick wall.*) Somebody has to be kind in this world. You've got to have sympathy for people. Christ loved everybody, and told us to do the same. And I can tell you truly that many a time you can save a person by pitying him in time. Like, for instance, that time I was a watchman on a country estate belonging to an engineer near the town of Tomsk. This estate, now, stood in the middle of the woods. It was winter-time—very beautiful— and me all alone on the estate. One day I hear noises—somebody breaking in!

NATASHA   Thieves?

LUKA   Thieves they were. Breaking in. I pick up my gun and go out. There they are, two of them, opening a window, and so busy at it they don't notice me. "Hey, you!" I shout. "Get out of here!" They turn on me with the axe. "If you don't keep back, I'll shoot!" I cry and point my gun first at one, then at the other. Down they go on their knees, begging me

to let them go. But me, I'm mad by then, on account of the axe, and I
says to them: I chased you away, you pixies, but you wouldn't go, so
now, I says, one of you go and cut a good switch off those bushes. They
bring the switch. Now, says I, one of you get down, and the other give
him a thrashing. And that's how, according to my orders, they flogged
each other. And when the flogging was over they say to me: "Grandad,"
they say, "give us something to eat for the love of Christ. We've been
tramping the countryside on empty bellies." There's your thieves for you,
my dear! (*Laughs.*) There's your axe for you! Both of them fine chaps at
heart. I says to them: "Now why couldn't you have come and just asked
me for something to eat at the very start?" "We're sick and tired of
asking," they say. "We asked and asked and nobody gave us anything."
After that they lived with me for the whole winter. One of them, Stepan
by name, used to take the gun and go off to the woods. The other,
Yakov they called him, was sick all the time. Kept coughing. All three of
us kept watch over that estate. And when spring came they said:
"Farewell, grandad." And off they went. Set out for the west.

NATASHA   Were they escaped convicts?

LUKA   That's what they were. Escaped convicts. Escaped from the place where
they were deported. Fine lads they were! If I hadn't taken pity on them,
now, they might have killed me or done something else just as bad, and
that would have meant a trial, and jail, and Siberia. What for? A jail
can't teach a person what's right, and Siberia can't teach a person what's
right, but a man—he can teach a person what's right, and very easy
at that.

> (*Pause.*)

BUBNOV   Hm. Take me, now—I'm no good at lying. Why lie? The way I see
it, go ahead and speak the whole truth. What's there to be afraid of?

KLESHCH (*jumping up again as if stung and crying out*)   The truth? What truth?
(*Tearing at the rags that cover him.*) Here's the truth! No work. No
strength. That's the truth! No shelter! Not even a roof of my own!
Nothing left but to die like a dog! There's your truth for you, you old
devil! What do I want with your truth? All I want's a chance to take a
breath—to take a living breath! What wrong have I ever done? What do
I want with your truth? I want a chance to live, god-damn it! They don't
let you live, and there's your truth!

BUBNOV   Just see how the fellow's touched!

LUKA   Mother of God! But listen, my friend. You—

KLESHCH (*trembling with agitation*)   All of you babbling about the truth! You,
old man, trying to comfort everybody! Well, I hate everybody, and that's
the truth, may it be cursed and damned forever! Do you understand?
It's high time you understood! To hell with your truth! (*Runs around the
corner of the house, looking back and shouting.*)

LUKA   Dear, dear, dear! How upset the fellow is! Where has he gone?

NATASHA   He's gone off his chump.

BUBNOV   Very amusing. As good as play-acting. That happens every once in a
while. He hasn't got used to life yet.

PEPEL (*entering slowly from behind the house*)   Greetings, friends! Well, Luka, you sly old fox, still telling your fairy-tales?

LUKA   You should have heard how that man went off just now!

PEPEL   Who, Kleshch? What's wrong with him? I met him running as if the devil was after him.

LUKA   Anybody'd run if his heart was touched like that.

PEPEL (*sitting down*)   I don't like the fellow. Too proud and vicious. (*Imitating* KLESHCH.) "Me—I'm a working man!" As though that made him better than anybody else! Go ahead and work if you like it, but why be so proud of yourself? If a person's worth depended on how much work he did, a horse would be better than any human—goes on hauling day in and day out without a word. Natasha! Your folks at home?

NATASHA   They've gone to the cemetery. Then they intended to go to vespers.

PEPEL   So that's why you have nothing to do for a change!

LUKA (*turning thoughtfully to* BUBNOV)   The truth, you say? The truth doesn't always cure a person's ailments. You can't always help a soul with the truth. Once, for instance, there was a case like this: a certain man I knew believed in a true-righteous land.

BUBNOV   In a what?

LUKA   In a true-righteous land. "There ought to be," says he, "a true-righteous land in this world. And that land," thinks he, "must be inhabited by special people—good people, people who honour each other, and who in every little thing help each other. Everything," thinks he, "must be wonderfully fine in that land." And so he thought to go in search of the true-righteous land. He was a poor man and had a hard life. Sometimes things got so bad it looked as if there was nothing left for him to do but lie down and die. But he didn't give up. He would just smile to himself and say: "That's all right, I can bear it. I'll wait just a little longer and then I'll quit this life and go to the true-righteous land." That was his only joy in life—his faith in the true-righteous land.

PEPEL   Well, did he ever get there?

BUBNOV   Where? Ho-ho!

LUKA   And then to the village where he lived—this all happened in Siberia—they exiled a very learned man, with books, and charts, and all the things that go with a man of learning. And this poor man says to the man of learning, he says: "Be so kind as to tell me where this true-righteous land lies, and how to get there." Then and there the learned one gets out his books and opens up his charts and looks and looks, but he can't find the true-righteous land anywhere. Everything is in its place, all the lands are on the charts, but the true-righteous land is nowhere to be found!

PEPEL (*in a hushed voice*)   Nowhere to be found?
            (BUBNOV *laughs.*)

NATASHA   Stop laughing. Go on, grandad.

LUKA   The man cant' believe it. "It must be somewhere," says he. "Take a better look, because if there's no true-righteous land, then all your charts and books are of no account." The learned one doesn't like this. "My charts," says he, "are the very best, but there's no such place as your true-righteous land." That makes the poor one furious. "What's that?" says he. "Here I've gone on living and bearing it all these years just because I was sure there was such a place, and now according to the charts it turns out there isn't any such place! A swindle, that's what it is!" And he says to the learned one: "You wretch! It's a rascal you are, and not a man of learning!" And he gives him a whack over the ear—bang! Then another one—bang! (*A moment's pause.*)   And after that he goes home and hangs himself.

>   (*Everyone is silent.* LUKA, *smiling, glances at*
>   PEPEL *and* NATASHA.)

PEPEL (*under his breath*)   The hell you say! A dreary sort of a story!

NATASHA   He couldn't stand being fooled.

BUBNOV (*sullenly*)   Another fairy-tale.

PEPEL   Hm. . . . So it turns out there isn't any true-righteous land!

NATASHA   It's a pity about the man.

BUBNOV   All made up. Ho-ho! A true-righteous land! Spun out of his head. Ho-ho! (*Withdraws from the window.*)

LUKA (*nodding in the direction of* BUBNOV'S *window*)   Laughing. Tck, tck, tck! (*Pause.*) Well, friends, I wish you well. I'll soon be on my way.

PEPEL   Where are you going?

LUKA   To the Ukraine. I heard as how they've opened up a new faith there and I want to look into it. People are always seeking, always wanting something better. May the Lord give them strength.

PEPEL   Do you think they'll ever find what they're looking for?

LUKA   Indeed I do. He who seeks always finds. He who wants a thing bad enough always gets it.

NATASHA   If only they would! If only they would think of a better way of life!

LUKA   They will. But we've got to help them, my dear. We've got to respect them for their seeking.

NATASHA   How can I help them? I need help myself.

PEPEL (*determinedly*)   I'm going to speak to you again, Natasha. I'm going to ask you again. Here, in front of him, who knows everything. Come away with me.

NATASHA   Where shall we go? To jail?

PEPEL   I told you I'd give up stealing. I swear to heaven I'll give it up. And once I've said it, I'll do it. I know how to read and write. I'll work. He says we ought to go to Siberia of our own free will. Shall we? Do you think I don't hate this life? Oh, Natasha, I understand—I see it all. I console myself by saying that people who are called honest steal more than I do. But it doesn't help. That's not what I want. I don't regret anything, and I don't believe in a conscience. But there's one thing I do believe: this is no way to live. A man ought to live better. He ought to live so that he can respect himself.

LUKA   That's the thing, my lad! May the Lord help you! May Christ show you his mercy. That's the thing: a man has to respect himself.

PEPEL   From my earliest years I've been a thief. I've never been called anything but Vasya the thief; Vasya, the son of a thief. So that's what you think of me, is it? Very well, then that's what I'll be: a thief! See? Maybe it was just for spite I became a thief. Maybe I'm a thief just because nobody ever thought of calling me anything else. But you, Natasha? If you—?

NATASHA (*sadly*)   Somehow I don't believe what anybody says. And I'm uneasy today. I have a sinking feeling, as if something was going to happen. You shouldn't have brought this up today, Vasya.

PEPEL   But when? This isn't the first time I've said it.

NATASHA   Why should I go with you? As for loving you—I can't say I love you so much. Sometimes I like you, and then again I just can't stand the sight of you. I don't suppose I love you. When you love a person you can't see the bad in him. But I see it in you.

PEPEL   Don't be afraid. I'll teach you to love me. You just say the word. I've had my eye on you for more than a year now, and I see you're a serious, upright girl, one who can be depended on. I've fallen hard for you, Natasha.

(VASILISA *appears in the window in all her finery and stands listening, half-hidden by the windowframe.*)

NATASHA   You've fallen for me—and what about my sister?

PEPEL (*uneasy*)   Well, what about her? There are lots like her.

LUKA   Don't you think about that, my dear. When there's no bread, a person'll eat grass.

PEPEL (*moodily*)   Take pity on me. This is no life. A dog's life, with no joy in it. It's like living in a bog where everything you snatch at gives way because it's rotten. That sister of yours—I thought she was different. If she hadn't been so greedy for money I'd have done anything for her sake. If she'd been all mine. But she wanted something else—money. And a free rein. A free rein to live a wanton life. She couldn't help me. But you—you're like a young fir-tree that bends but doesn't break.

LUKA   Take my advice and marry him, my girl. He's not a bad chap. You just keep reminding him that he's good—don't let him forget it. He'll believe you. You just say to him over and over again: "You're a good man, Vasya, and don't you forget it." Think, my dear: what other way out is there for you? That sister of yours is a wicked beast. And as for her husband—the old man is worse than any words can say, and so is this whole life here. What other way out is there? And he's a strong lad.

NATASHA   There's no other way out for me. I know. I've thought about it. Only—I don't believe anybody. But still, there's no other way out.

PEPEL   Yes, there is, but I won't let you take that path. I'd rather kill you.

NATASHA (*smiling*)   I'm not your wife yet, but here you are ready to kill me.

PEPEL (*taking her in his arms*)   Forget it, Natasha! That's how it's got to be.

NATASHA (*nestling against him*)   I must tell you one thing, Vasya, and I swear it before God. The first time you lift your hand against me or do me any other wrong I'll not spare myself. I'll either kill myself or—

PEPEL   May my hand wither and drop off if ever I lift it against you!

LUKA   Don't worry, dearie, he needs you worse'n you do him.

VASILISA (*from the window*)   So the match is made! From now on it's love honour and obey!

NATASHA   They've come back! My God! They've seen us! Ah, Vasya!

PEPEL   What are you scared of? Nobody'll dare touch you now!

VASILISA   Don't worry, Natasha, he won't beat you. He can no more beat you than love you. I know!

LUKA (*under his breath*)   That woman! A snake if there ever was one!

VASILISA   He just knows how to make pretty speeches.

KOSTYLYOV (*entering*)   Natasha! What are you doing here, you lazy-bones? Spreading gossip? Complaining about your relatives? And you haven't got the samovar ready? Haven't set the table?

NATASHA (*going out*)   But you intended going to church.

KOSTYLYOV   It's none of your business what we intended doing. See that you do what you're told to, what you're ordered to.

PEPEL   Hold your tongue! She's not a servant to you any more! Natasha, don't go! Don't do anything for them!

NATASHA   Don't tell me what I'm to do. Your time hasn't come yet! (*Goes out.*)

PEPEL (*to* KOSTYLYOV)   Leave her alone! You've had your way with her long enough. She's mine now.

KOSTYLYOV   Yours? When did you buy her? How much did you pay? (VASILISA *laughs.*)

LUKA   Go away, Vasya.

PEPEL   Take care, or you'll be laughing on the other side of your face!

VASILISA   Aren't I scared, just! Frightened to death!

LUKA   Go away, Vasya! Can't you see she's just egging you on, trying to get your dander up?

PEPEL   Ah. . . . Oh yes. She's lying. You're lying! You won't have things the way you want them!

VASILISA   And I won't have them the way I *don't* want them, Vasya!

PEPEL (*shaking his fist at her*)   We'll see! (*He goes out.*)

VASILISA (*disappearing from the window*)   I'll see you have a proper wedding!

KOSTYLYOV (*going over to* LUKA)   What are you doing here, old man?

LUKA   Nothing, old man.

KOSTYLYOV   They say you're going to leave us?

LUKA   High time.

KOSTYLYOV   Where are you going?

LUKA   To follow my nose.

KOSTYLYOV   Like the tramp you are. Makes you uneasy to stay in one place very long, eh?

LUKA   A rolling stone gathers no moss, as the saying goes.

KOSTYLYOV   That's said about a stone, but a person ought to settle in one place. People aren't supposed to live like roaches—scuttling here and there and everywhere. A person ought to make himself at home in some place and not be a stranger everywhere.

LUKA   And what if a person's at home everywhere?

KOSTYLYOV   That means he's a tramp and a useless creature. There has to be some use got out of a person. He ought to work.

LUKA   Think of that, now!

KOSTYLYOV   Yes, he ought. What's a stranger? A stranger's a strange person, one who isn't like others. If he's a pilgrim with knowledge—that is, if he's learned things—things nobody cares to know—not even if it's the truth he's learned, because—well, people don't always want to know the truth—let him keep it to himself. If he's a true pilgrim, he'll hold his tongue, or else talk so that nobody knows what he's talking about. And he shouldn't want to change things, or interfere in anything, or upset people to no good purpose. It's none of his business how people live. It's for him to lead a pious life. He ought to live in a cave in the forest where nobody can see him. He has no right to mix in people's affairs, trying to tell them what's right and what's wrong. But he ought to pray for everybody—for all our worldly sins—for yours and mine and everybody else's. That's why he renounces the vanities of this world—so he can pray. (*Pause.*) But you—what kind of a pilgrim are you? You haven't even got a passport. A respectable person ought to have a passport. All respectable human beings have got passports. . . .

LUKA   Some of us are humans, some are just beings.

KOSTYLYOV   None of your cleverness, now. None of your riddles. I guess I'm as smart as you are. What's that you're saying—humans and beings?

LUKA   There's no riddle here. I'm just saying as there's barren soil, and there's fertile soil, and whatever you sow on fertile soil is bound to bear fruit. That's all.

KOSTYLYOV   Well, what of it?

LUKA   Take you, for example. If the Lord God himself should say to you: "Mikhail! Be a human!" it wouldn't make any difference at all. You'd just keep right on being what you are.

KOSTYLYOV   Hm. Listen, my wife's uncle, he's a policeman. If I—

VASILISA (*coming in*)   Tea's ready Mikhail Ivanovich.

KOSTYLYOV (*to* LUKA)   Get out of here. Don't let me catch you in my house again!

VASILISA   You'd better clear out, old man! You've got a long tongue. Who knows but what you're an escaped convict.

KOSTYLYOV   Get out of here this very day, or I'll—

LUKA   Call your uncle? Go ahead and call him. Tell him you've caught an escaped convict. Maybe the uncle will get a reward—three kopeks or so.

BUBNOV (*at the window*)   Selling something? What's that for three kopeks?

LUKA   They're threatening to sell me.

VASILISA (*to her husband*)   Come along.

BUBNOV   For three kopeks? Watch out, old man. They'll sell you for half a kopek!

KOSTYLYOV (*to* BUBNOV)   So you've crawled out? Like a goblin from under the stove. (*Goes out with his wife.*)

VASILISA   How many thieves and rascals there are in the world!

LUKA   May you enjoy your tea!

VASILISA (*turning around*)   Hold your tongue, you shrivelled mushroom!
(*She and her husband disappear around the corner of
the house.*)

LUKA   I'll be leaving tonight.

BUBNOV   That's good. It's always well to leave in good time.

LUKA   A truer word was never spoke.

BUBNOV   I know what I'm saying. I probably escaped jail by leaving in time.

LUKA   Did you, now?

BUBNOV   Yes, I did. Here's how it was: my wife got mixed up with a furrier,
an able master—good at turning dog pelts into racoon. Cats, too—into
kangaroos, or muskrats or anything else. A smart chap. It was with
him my wife got mixed up, and they clung so tight to each other I had
to look sharp so they didn't poison me or get rid of me in some other
way. Sometimes I'd beat my wife; then the furrier'd beat me. He was
a fierce fighter. Once he pulled half my beard out and broke a rib.
I used to lose my temper, too. One day I lammed my wife over the
head with an iron poker, and a big war was on. But I see nothing will
come of it—they're sure to get me—so I makes up my mind to bump
off the wife before she bumps off me. I had it all thought out, but I
caught myself in time and went away.

LUKA   Good for you—leave them alone to turn cats into muskrats as much
as they like.

BUBNOV   But the shop belonged to the wife, and I got left in the state you
see me in now. Truth to tell, I'd have drunk up the shop. It's the
drink that makes me—

LUKA   The drink, eh?

BUBNOV   I'm a ferocious drinker. Once I go on a jag, I drink up
everything but my own hide. And I'm lazy. You wouldn't believe how
I hate to work!
(SATIN *and the* ACTOR *come in. They are arguing.*)

SATIN   Nonsense! You won't go, you know you won't. You're just fooling
yourself. Old man! What twaddle have you been pouring into this
fellow's ear?

ACTOR   That's a lie! Grandad, tell him he's lying. I *will* go. I worked today—
swept the street. And I haven't had a single drink. Think of that!
Here they are—my thirty kopeks, and I'm sober!

SATIN   Idiotic. Here, give me that money. I'll drink it up, or else lose it in
a card game.

ACTOR   Hands off! That goes towards buying my ticket.

LUKA (*to* SATIN)   Why should you be wanting to set him off the right path?

SATIN   "Tell me, O wizard, beloved of the gods, just what is the fate that the
future conceals?" I've been cleaned out, brother! Lost all I had! But
there's still hope for the world, grandad; there's cleverer sharks than
me left.

LUKA   You're a gay fellow, Konstantin, and a pleasant one.

BUBNOV   Actor! Come here!

> (*The* ACTOR *goes over to the window and stoops down
> to talk to* BUBNOV *in a low voice.*)

SATIN   I was amusing when I was young. Nice to recall those times. A
rakish lad, I was. Danced superbly, acted on the stage, was always
making people laugh. A charming young fellow.

LUKA   And how did you get switched off the track, eh?

SATIN   You're an inquisitive creature, old man. You'd like to know everything
wouldn't you? What for?

LUKA   I'd like to understand this human business. But when I look at you,
I don't understand a thing. You're a good fellow, Konstantin, and a
clever one, and yet—

SATIN   It was jail did it, grandad. I spent four years and seven months in
jail, and nobody will have you after a jail sentence.

LUKA   Oho! And what were you put in jail for?

SATIN   For killing a rascal. I killed him in a burst of wrath and
indignation. It was in jail I learned to play cards—and other things.

LUKA   Did you kill him on account of a woman?

SATIN   On account of my own sister. But don't you go prying. I don't like to
be asked questions. And that all happened long, long ago. My sister
died. Nine years ago. She was a lovely sister.

LUKA   You don't take life so hard. You should have heard that locksmith
howl a while back! Ai-i-i!

SATIN   Kleshch?

LUKA   Him. "No work!" he shouted. "No nothing!"

SATIN   He'll get used to it in time. Well, what am I to do with myself now?

LUKA (*softly*)   Look. Here he comes.

> (KLESHCH *comes in slowly, with hanging head.*)

SATIN   Hey, you widower! What've you got your nose between your knees for?
What're you thinking about?

KLESHCH   I'm thinking about what I'm going to do. No tools. They all went
for the funeral.

SATIN   Take my advice and don't do anything. Just be a burden to the world.

KLESHCH   It's all right for you to talk, but I have shame.

SATIN   Get rid of it. People aren't ashamed to have you lead a dog's life.
Think it over. You stop working, I stop working, hundreds and
thousands of others—everybody does the same. See? We all stop working,
Nobody will raise a finger to do a thing! What will happen then?

KLESHCH   We'll all die of starvation.

LUKA (*to* SATIN)   You should join the Runaways, with such ideas. There's a
kind of people called Runaways.*

SATIN   I know. They're not such fools, grandad.

> (*From the window of the* KOSTYLYOVS' *flat can be heard
> the cries of* NATASHA: "Stop! Oh, stop! What have
> I done?")

---

*A religious sect.—*Tr.*

LUKA (*anxiously*)   Natasha? Is it her screaming like that?
> (*From the* KOSTYLYOVS' *flat comes a crashing of dishes, a
> murmur of voices, and the shrill cries of* KOSTYLYOV:
> "You bitch! You whore!"*)*

VASILISA   Stop! Wait! I'll show her! Take that! And that!

NATASHA   They're killing me! Killing me!

SATIN (*shouting at the window*)   Hey, you in there!

LUKA (*rushing hither and thither*)   Vasya! It's Vasya we want here! O Lord!
Good people! Brothers!

ACTOR (*running off*)   Here, I'll go and get him.

BUBNOV   They beat her all the time now.

SATIN   Come, old man. We'll be witnesses.

LUKA (*following* SATIN)   A poor sort of witness I make. That's not for me.
It's Vasya we need, and need him quick.

NATASHA   Sister! Sister! Ah-h-h!

BUBNOV   They've gagged her. I'll go and have a look.
> (*The commotion in the* KOSTYLYOVS' *flat dies away as
> the people evidently move out into the hall. The old man
> is heard to cry* "Stop!" *A door slams, and this chops
> off the noise like the blow of an axe. Silence on the
> stage. Spring twilight.* KLESHCH *is sitting on the
> overturned sledge with an air of detachment, rubbing
> his hands tensely. He mutters something unintelligible
> which focuses into the following lines:* "But how? A man's
> got to live hasn't he?" [*In a loud voice*]: "A roof! I
> I need a roof over my head! I haven't got a roof! I
> haven't got anything! A man's alone—all alone.
> That's where the trouble lies. No one to help him."* He
> goes off slowly, all bent over. An ominous silence reigns
> for a few seconds. Then from off stage comes a vague
> murmur which grows into chaotic sound as it draws
> nearer. Separate voices can be distinguished.*)

VASILISA   I'm her sister! Let me at her!

KOSTYLYOV   You have no right.

VASILISA   Jail-bird!

SATIN   Call Vasya! Hurry! Beat him, Zob!
> (*A police whistle blows.*)

TATAR (*running on, his right arm in a sling*)   What kind of law—to kill in
day-time.

KRIVOI ZOB (*followed by* MEDVEDEV)   Hah! I gave him a good one!

MEDVEDEV   You—how dare you fight?

TATAR   And you? What duty you have?

MEDVEDEV (*running after the* TATAR)   Stop! Give me back my whistle!

KOSTYLYOV (*running on*)   Abram! Seize him! He killed—
> (*From behind the corner come* KVASHNYA *and* NASTYA
> *supporting the dishevelled* NATASHA *between them.*
> SATIN *walks backward, pushing off* VASILISA *who is trying
> to get at her sister.* ALYOSHKA *leaps about her like an
> imp, whistling in her ear, shouting, howling. They are
> followed by a small and ragged crowd.*)

SATIN (*to* VASILISA)   What's the idea, you damned slut?

VASILISA   Get away, jail-bird! It may cost me my life, but I'll tear her to pieces!

KVASHNYA (*leading* NATASHA *away*)   Enough, Vasilisa! Have some shame!
You're behaving like a brute.

MEDVEDEV (*seizing* SATIN)   Here you are! Caught at last!

SATIN   Lam into them, Zob. Vasya! Vasya!

> (*They gather in a crowd near the passage between the
> brick wall and the house.* NATASHA *is led over and seated
> on the pile of boards to the right.*)

PEPEL (*coming suddenly through the passage and silently pushing everybody
aside with strong vigorous movements*)   Where's Natasha? You—

KOSTYLYOV (*hiding behind the house*)   Abram! Catch Vasya! Brothers, help
catch Vasya! Theif! Robber!

PEPEL   You old fornicator!

> (*With a great sweep of his arm he strikes the old man,
> who falls in such a way that only his head and shoulders
> can be seen from behind the corner of the house.* PEPEL
> *rushes over to* NATASHA.)

VASILISA   Thrash Vasya, fellows! Thrash the thief!

MEDVEDEV (*shouting to* SATIN)   Keep out of this! It's a family affair! They're all
relatives! You don't belong here!

PEPEL   What is it? What has she done, stabbed you?

KVASHNYA   Just look what the brutes have done! Scalded her legs with
boiling water!

NASTYA   Upset the samovar on her!

TATAR   Maybe accident. Have to know for sure. Mustn't make mistake.

NATASHA (*almost fainting*)   Vasya, take me away. Hide me.

VASALISA   My God! Look here! He's dead! Killed!

> (*Everyone rushes to the passage where* KOSTYLYOV *is
> lying.* BUBNOV *separates himself from the crowd and
> goes over to* VASYA PEPEL.)

BUBNOV (*in a low voice*)   Vasya! The old man— he's done for.

PEPEL (*looks at him without comprehending*)   Call an ambulance. We'll have to
take her to the hospital. I'll get even with them for this!

BUBNOV   I'm saying that somebody's finished off the old man.

> (*The noise on the stage goes out like a fire flooded with
> water. Separate remarks are passed in hushed tones:*
> "Really?" "That's bad." "Hm." "Let's get away from
> here." "What the hell!" "Watch out!" "Beat it before
> the police come." *The crowd dwindles.* BUBNOV, *the*
> TATAR, NASTYA *and* KVASHNYA *rush over to the body of*
> KOSTYLYOV.)

VASILISA (*rising from the ground and crying truimphantly*)   Murdered! There's
the one who murdered my husband! Vasya did it! I saw it myself!
I saw it, friends! Well, Vasya? So the police are coming for you?

PEPEL (*leaving* NATASHA'S *side*)   Let me pass. Out of my way! (*Takes a look at
the old man, then turns to* VASILISA.)   Well, are you satisfied? (*Touches
the body with his foot.*)   Done for, the cur. So you got what you wanted.
Humph! Maybe I ought to bump you off too. (*Throws himself at her.*

SATIN *and* KRIVOI ZOB *quickly intercede.* VASILISA *runs into the passage.*)

SATIN   Think what you're doing!

KRIVIO ZOB   Take your time!

VASILISA (*reappearing*)   Well, friend Vasya, there's no escaping your fate. The police! Abram, blow your whistle!

MEDVEDEV   The devils snatched my whistle away.

ALYOSHKA   Here it is! (*He gives a blow.* MEDVEDEV *runs after him.*)

SATIN (*leading* PEPEL *over to* NATASHA)   Don't let it trouble you, Vasya. You killed him in a fight. That's nothing. That won't cost you dear.

VASILISA   Hold Vasya! He killed him! I saw him do it!

SATIN   I had a whack at him three or four times myself. It didn't take much to finish him off. I'll be a witness, Vasya.

PEPEL   I don't want to slip out of it. I want to drag Vasilisa into it. And I will, so help me God! That's what she wanted. She talked me into killing her husband. She talked me into it.

NATASHA (*suddenly in a loud voice*)   Ah! . . . Now I see! So that's how it is, Vasya! Oh, good people, they did it together! They planned it all! Very well, Vasya! So that's why you talked to me tonight? So she could hear? Good people, she lives with him. You all know that. Everybody knows it. They did it together. She—she talked him into killing her husband. He stood in their way. And I stood in their way. That's why they've made a cripple of me.

PEPEL   Natasha! What are you talking about!

SATIN   Hm, devil take it!

VASILISA   Liar! She's lying! I—he's the one! Vasya killed him!

NATASHA   They did it together! Curse you! Both of you!

SATIN   It's a game. Watch out, Vasya! They'll have a rope round your neck before you know it!

KRIVOI ZOB   Can't make head or tail out of it! A fine business!

PEPEL   Natasha! Do you really. . . . Are you serious? . . . How can you think that I . . . with her. . . .

SATIN   Think what you're saying, Natasha!

VASILISA (*from the passage*)   They've murdered my husband sir. Vasya Pepel, the thief—he did it. I saw him, Inspector. Everybody saw him.

NATASHA (*tossing about in a half-conscious state*)   Good people, it was my sister and Vasya Pepel who did it! Listen to me, Inspector. It was my sister—she showed him how. She talked him into it. He's her lover. There he is, damn his soul! They killed him! Take them both. Take them to jail! And take me, too! Put me in jail! For the love of Christ, put me in jail!

(*Curtain*)

Act Four

The scene is the same as in Act I, except that the partition which once formed PEPEL'S *room has been*

taken down and KLESHCH'S *anvil is gone. The* TATAR
tosses and moans on a bunk in the corner which was
PEPEL'S *room.* KLESHCH *sits at the table repairing an*
accordion, occasionally trying the keys. At the other end
of the table SATIN, *the* BARON *and* NASTYA *are sitting.*
There is a bottle of vodka, three bottles of beer and some
black bread in front of them. The ACTOR *is moving about*
and coughing on top of the stove. Night. The stage is
lighted by a lamp standing in the centre of the table.
The wind is blowing outside.

KLESHCH   He disappeared in all the hubbub.

BARON   Separated himself from the police like smoke from fire.

SATIN   Like the sinful from the righteous.

NASTYA   He was a good old man. But you—you're not humans.
    You're dung!

BARON (*drinking*)   To your health, my fine lady!

SATIN   A queer bird. Nastya, here, she fell in love with him.

NASTYA   Yes, I fell in love with him. That's the truth. He saw everything
    and understood everything.

SATIN (*laughing*)   He was like mush for the toothless.

BARON (*laughing*)   Like a plaster for boils.

KLESHCH   He had pity, but you—you don't know what pity is.

SATIN   What good would my pity do you?

KLESHCH   I don't mean you. You do, well, not exactly pity folk, but at least
    spare their feelings.

TATAR (*sitting down on one of the bunks and rocking his sore arm like a baby*)
    He was good old man. He know law of soul. Who know law of soul—
    he good. Who lost law— he lost himself.

BARON   What law, Asan?

TATAR   Different law. You know what.

BARON   Next!

TATAR   Don't hurt people. That's law.

SATIN   That's called: "Penal Code for Criminals and Miscreants."

BARON   And then there's that "Statutes of Penalties Imposed by Justices of
    the Peace."

TATAR   Koran is law. Your Koran also law. Every soul must have Koran, yes!

KLESHCH (*trying out the accordion*)   Wheezes, damn it! What the Tatar says is
    right. People ought to live according to the law. According to the Bible.

SATIN   Why don't you?

BARON   Just try it.

TATAR   Mohammed gave Koran, Mohammed said: here—the law! Do what
    it say here. Then come time—Koran too little. New time, new law.
    Every new time give new law.

SATIN   Right you are. Now the time's come for the "Penal Code." A good
    strong law. It'll take a lot of time to wear out that law.

NASTYA (*banging a glass on the table*)   Why, oh why should I go on living
    here with you all? I'll go away—anywhere—to the ends of the earth!

BARON   Barefoot, my fine lady?

NASTYA   Naked! Crawling on all fours!

BARON   A sight for sore eyes, my fine lady! Fancy that! On all fours!

NASTYA   That's how I'll go. I'll go any way at all, just to get rid of the sight of you. If you only knew how sick I am of everything! Of everybody and everything!

SATIN   Take the Actor with you when you go. He's planning the same trip He just found out that half a mile from the end of the earth there's a hospital for organons.

ACTOR (*thrusting his head over the edge of the bunk on top of the stove*) Organisms, fool!

SATIN   For organons poisoned by alcohol.

ACTOR   Oh, he's going, have no fear. He's going! You'll see!

BARON   Just who is he, my good sir?

ACTOR   Me!

BARON   Merci, votary of the goddess—what's her name? Goddess of the drama, tragedy. What d'you call her?

ACTOR   Muse, you dolt! She's not a goddess, but a muse!

SATIN   Lachesis? Hera? Aphrodite? Atropos? The devil only knows which. It's all the doings of that old man, Baron. He got the Actor all stirred up.

BARON   The old man's crazy.

ACTOR   Ignoramuses! Barbarians! Mel-po-me-ne! Oh, he'll go away, you can be sure of that! Heartless creatures! "Gorge yourselves, benighted minds!..." That's from Béranger. He'll find a place for himself where there is no...no....

BARON   No nothing, my good sir.

ACTOR   That's it. No nothing. "That yawning hole shall be my grave. This waste frame no hand can save." And why should *you* go on living? Why, oh why?

BARON   Hey you—"Edmund Kean, or Genius and Dissipation." Stop shouting!

ACTOR   I'll shout all I want to!

NASTYA (*raising her head from the table and waving her hands*) Go on shouting. Make them listen.

BARON   What's the sense of it, my fine lady?

SATIN   Leave them alone, Baron! To hell with them! Let them yell! They'll split their heads open. The important thing is: don't interfere with people, as the old man said. It was him, like a cake of yeast, put the ferment in our fellow ledgers.

KLESHCH   He lured them to enchanting places, then slipped away without showing them the road.

BARON   The old man was a faker.

NASTYA   You're a faker yourself!

BARON   Shut up, my fine lady!

KLESHCH   As for the truth—the old man had no use for it. He was very set against the truth, and so he should be. When you come to think of it, what talk of truth can there be? Life's hard enough without it. Take the Tatar here—got his arm smashed at work and now he'll have to chop it off. There's your truth for you!

SATIN (*pounding on the table*) Silence! You're a lot of cattle! Blockheads! Shut up about the old man! (*More calmly.*) And you're the worst of them, Baron. You don't understand anything. And you lie. The old man wasn't a faker. What is the truth? Man!—that's the truth. He knew this, but you don't. Your heads are like bricks. I understand him. Of course he lied, but he did it out of pity for you, devil take you! Lots of people lie out of pity for their brothers. I know. I've read books. They lie beautifully, with inspiration, stirring you up. There are lies that console, that reconcile a person to his lot. Lies find an excuse for the weight that smashed the worker's arm; lies blame a man for starving to death. I know your lies! Only those who are faint-hearted or live at other people's expense have need of lies. Some people are supported by lies, others hide behind them. But the person who is his own boss—the person who is independent and doesn't suck other people's blood—what need has he of lies? Lies are the religion of slaves and bosses! Truth is the god of the free man!

BARON Bravo! Well said! I agree with everything you say! You talk like . . . like a respectable gentleman.

SATIN Why shouldn't a cheat sometimes talk like a respectable gentleman, if your respectable gentlemen so often talk like cheats? There are lots of things I've forgotten, but I still remember a thing or two. That old man was a smart fellow. He acted on me like acid on an old, dirty coin. Let's drink to his health! Fill my glass.

(*Nastya fills Satin's glass with beer and hands it to him.*)

SATIN (*with a short laugh*) The old man lives by his own wits. He sees everything with his own eyes. One day I said to him, "Grandad, what do people live for?" (*Imitating the voice and manners of* LUKA.) "They live to make life better, my friend. Now, for instance, let's say we have some carpenters—junk, all of them. And then from among them is born one carpenter—a carpenter the likes of whom the earth has never seen; outshines all the others, he does, and none can even hold a candle to him. On all carpentering he leaves his own mark, so that the craft moves forward twenty years in one jump. The same it is with all the others—tinsmiths, cobblers, all the working folk, and all the peasants too—and even the gentlefolk. All of them live to make life better. Each thinking it's for himself he's living, but really he lives to make life better. For a hundred years they live—maybe even for more, and all to make life better."

(NASTYA *looks intently at* SATIN. KLESHCH, *too, stops working on the accordion and listens. The* BARON *drops his head on his chest and softly drums on the table. The* ACTOR *quietly lets himself down off the stove on to one of the bunks.*)

SATIN "All of them, my good friend, every last one of them, lives to make life better," says the old man. We ought to be considerate of one another. For you see, it's not for us to know who a person is, and why he was born, and what he can do. Maybe he was born for our good fortune,

to be some great help to us. And particular it's the children we must respect—the little ones. It's freedom they need, the little ones. We mustn't interfere with them; we must be considerate of them."
    (*Laughs softly. Pause.*)

BARON (*meditatively*)   Hm. To make life better? That reminds me of my family—an old family, dating back to Catherine the Great. Nobles. Warriors. Came from France. Served the tsar and kept climbing up and up. During the reign of Nikolai I, my grandfather, Gustave Débile, held high office. Wealth, hundreds of serfs, horses, servants—

NASTYA   Liar! That's all bunk!

BARON (*jumping up*)   Wha-at!?

NASTYA   That's all humbug!

BARON (*shouting*)   A mansion in Moscow! A mansion in St. Petersburg! Carriages with our coat of arms on them!
        (KLESHCH *takes up his accordion and walks off to one side, from where he observes the scene.*)

NASTYA   Claptrap!

BARON   Shut up! Dozens of lackeys, I'm telling you!

NASTYA (*enjoying it*)   Poppycock!

BARON   I'll kill you!

NASTYA (*about to run away*)   You never had a carriage!

SATIN   Drop it, Nastya! Don't make him mad.

BARON   Just wait, you scum! My grandfather—

NASTYA   You never had a grandfather! You never had anything!
        (SATIN *laughs.*)

BARON (*sinks down on a bench, weak with fury*)   Satin, tell her—that bitch— or are you laughing too? Don't you believe it either? (*Shouting in despair, banging the table with his fists.*) It's all true, god-damn you!

NASTYA (*triumphantly*)   Aha! Howling! See what it's like when nobody believes you?

KLESHCH (*returning to the table*)   I was sure there'd be a fight.

TATAR   Ah, stupid people! Very bad!

BARON   I . . . I won't have people making fun of me! I have . . . I can prove it. I have papers, you devils!

SATIN   Forget them! And forget about your grandfather's carriages. They won't get you very far, those bygone carriages.

BARON   How dares she!

NASTYA (*mockingly*)   Hear that? How dares she!

SATIN   Well, she does. And why is she any worse than you are? Even if she never had any carriages, or grandfathers, or even a mother and father.

BARON (*more composed*)   Devil take you! You always take things calmly. I'm afraid I have no character.

SATIN   Get one. It'll come in handy. (*Pause.*)   Nastya, do you ever go to the hospital?

NASTYA   What for?

SATIN   To see Natasha.

NASTYA   A little late, aren't you? She left the hospital long ago. Left it and disappeared. Gone without leaving a trace.

SATIN   That means—all gone.

KLESHCH   I wonder who'll give it to the other harder: Vasya to Vasilisa, or the other way round.

NASTYA   Vasilisa will wriggle out of it somehow. She's foxy. But they'll send Vasya to hard labour in Siberia.

SATIN   Oh no, he'll only get jail for killing in a fight.

NASTYA   Too bad. They ought to send him away—to send all of you away. Sweep you out like garbage. Throw you on some dump.

SATIN (*surprised*)   What's that you're saying? Have you gone clean off your chump?

BARON   I'll give her a smack on the ear. What nerve!

NASTYA   Go ahead and try. Just touch me!

BARON   I'll try it, never fear!

SATIN   Stop it! Don't touch her. You mustn't hurt people. I can't get that old man out of my head. (*Laughs.*) You mustn't hurt people! But what if they hurt me—hurt me so bad I'll never get over it? What then? Am I supposed to forgive them? Never! Nobody!

BARON (*to* NASTYA)   Don't forget you're not my equal! You're . . . you're the scum of the earth!

NASTYA   Ugh, you louse! You live on me like a worm on an apple.
(*Burst of laughter from the men.*)

KLESHCH   You little fool! An apple!

BARON   How can anybody get mad at her? She's an idiot.

NASTYA   Laughing, are you? Fooling yourself. You don't really think it's funny.

ACTOR (*sullenly*)   Give it to them!

NASTYA   If only I could! I'd . . . I'd. . . . (*Picks up a cup and smashes it on the floor.*) That's what I'd do to you!

TATAR   Why break dishes? Eh . . . bad woman!

BARON (*getting up*)   Now I'll teach her some manners!

NASTYA (*running toward the door*)   You can go to hell!

SATIN (*calling after her*)   Enough of this! Who are you scaring? What's it all about, anyway?

NASTYA   Wolves! I hope you choke! Wolves!

ACTOR (*sullenly*)   Amen!

TATAR   O-o-o! Bad woman—Russian woman. Nervy. Too free. Tatar woman not like that. Tatar woman knows law.

KLESHCH   She needs a good shaking.

BARON   The slut!

KLESHCH (*trying out the accordion*)   Good. But the lad doesn't come for it. He's going to the dogs fast.

SATIN   Here, have a drink.

KLESHCH   Thanks. Time to turn in.

SATIN   Getting used to us?

KLESHCH (*drinks, then goes over to a bunk in the corner*)   I suppose so. It turns out there are human beings everywhere. At first you don't notice it, then

you have a better look and there they are—human beings.
(*The* TATAR *spreads a cloth of some sort on his bed,
kneels on it and begins to pray.*)

BARON (*pointing to the* TATAR *and speaking to* SATIN) Look at that.

SATIN Leave him alone. He's a good fellow. Don't disturb him. (*Laughs*). Why
should I be feeling so kind-hearted today?

BARON You always get kind-hearted when you've had a drink—and clever, too.

SATIN When I'm drunk everything looks rosy. He's praying? Fine. A person
can be a believer or not, just as he pleases. That's his business. A
person's free to choose. He pays for everything himself: for believing,
for not believing, for loving, for being clever. A person pays for everything himself, and that's why he's free. Man—there's your truth! What's
a man? Not you, nor me, nor him. Oh no! But you and me and him and
the old man, and Napoleon, and Mohammed—all in one! (*Drawing the
figure of a man in the air.*) Comprehend? That's tremendous! It includes
all beginnings and all endings. All things are part of Man; all things are
for Man. Only Man exists; the rest is merely the work of his hands and
his mind. How marvellous is Man! How proud the word rings—MAN!
A man should be respected. Not pitied—pity is degrading. Respected!
Baron, let's drink to Man! (*Stands up.*) How good to feel oneself a Man!
Here am I—ex-convict, murderer, card-sharper—all of that! When I go
down the street people take me for a thief. They step aside and steal
furtive glances at me. Often they call me a rascal, a faker! Work, they
say! Work? What for? To fill my belly? (*Laughs.*) I've always despised
people who think too much about their bellies. The belly isn't the main
thing, Baron. Indeed it isn't. Man is superior to that. Man is superior
to his belly!

BARON (*shaking his head*) Good for you—thinking things out like this. It
must warm your heart. As for me—I can't. I don't know how. (*Glancing
about and speaking under his breath.*) Sometimes I'm afraid. Understand?
Scared. I keep thinking—what'll happen next?

SATIN (*walking up and down*) Nonsense! What should a man fear?

BARON As long as I can remember there's been a sort of fog in my head. I
never could understand anything. I . . . it's strange, but . . . it seems to
me I've just been changing my clothes all my life. What for? Can't make
it out. First I was a student—wore the uniform of the Institute for Sons
of the Nobility. What did they teach me there? Can't remember. Got
married. Put on a dress suit, then a dressing-gown. But the wife I chose
was a bad one. Why did I marry her? Can't remember. I squandered all
my means—wore some kind of a grey jacket and faded pants. How did
I lose everything? Can't remember. Worked in a government office—
uniform again, cap with a badge on it. Embezzled government money.
They put me in convict clothes. After that I donned these rags. And
that's all. Like in a dream, isn't it? It's even funny.

SATIN Not very. More stupid than funny.

BARON It is. I, too, think it's stupid. After all, I must have been born for
something.

SATIN (*with a short laugh*)   You must have. "Man is born to make life better!" (*Nodding his head.*) Good words.

BARON   Drat that Nastya! Where did she run off to? I'll go and have a look. After all, she's—(*Goes out. Pause.*)

ACTOR   Tatar! (*Pause.*) Asan!
            (*The* TATAR *turns his head.*)

ACTOR   Pray for me.

TATAR   What?

ACTOR (*softly*)   Say a prayer for me.

TATAR (*after a pause*)   Say your own prayers.

ACTOR (*quickly climbs down off the stove, goes over to the table, pours himself out a glass of vodka with shaking hands, swallows it down, almost runs out into the passage*)   I'm off!

SATIN   Hey, you! Sicambri! Where are you going?
            (*Whistles,* BUBNOV *and* MEDVEDEV *come in, the latter wearing a woman's quilted jacket. Both are slightly drunk. In one hand* BUBNOV *is carrying a string of pretzels, in the other a couple of smoked fish. One bottle of vodka is thrust under his arm, another sticks out of the pocket of his coat.*)

MEDVEDEV   A camel is something like a donkey, only without ears.

BUBNOV   You're something like a donkey yourself.

MEDVEDEV   A camel doesn't have any ears at all. He hears with his nose.

BUBNOV (*to* SATIN)   So here you are, friend! I searched the pubs for you. Take this bottle. All my hands are busy.

SATIN   Put those pretzels on the table and one of your hands will be free.

BUBNOV   Quite right. Just look at him. He's a smart fellow, ain't he?

MEDVEDEV   All cheats are smart. I know! They couldn't get on if they weren't. A good fellow can be stupid, but a bad fellow has got to be smart. But about that camel, you're all wrong. It's a beast of burden. No horns, no teeth—

BUBNOV   Where's everybody? How is it nobody's here? Hey, crawl out! The treat's on me! Who's that in the corner?

SATIN   How long will it take you to drink up your last kopek, you old scarecrow?

BUBNOV   Not long. This time the capital I saved up wasn't very big. Zob! Where's Zob?

KLESHCH (*coming over to the table*)   He's gone.

BUBNOV   Gr-r-r-r! You bulldog, you! Grrr! Woof! Woof! No barking! No grumbling! Drink, you dunce. Don't stand there hanging your head! I'm treating tonight! And how I love it! If I was rich, I'd open up a pub and serve drinks free of charge! Honest to God! With music and a chorus for sure. Come on in, everybody! Eat, drink, and listen to the songs for your soul's ease! No money? Here you are—a free pub! As for you, Satin, I'd. . . . I'd give you half my money besides! That's what I'd do!

SATIN   Give me all of it—this very minute!

BUBNOV   Everything I have? This very minute? Hah! Here you are—a ruble . . .
  another . . . twenty kopeks . . . chicken feed. . . .

SATIN   That's enough. It'll be safer with me. I'll gamble with it.

MEDVEDEV   I'm a witness that the money was given out for safe keeping.
  How much?

BUBNOV   You? You're a camel. We don't need witnesses.

ALYOSHKA (*enters barefoot*)   Fellows! I got my feet wet!

BUBNOV   Come on and get your throat wet! That's all you need. Your
  singing and playing is all very good, my lad. But your drinking—that's
  no good. That's harmful, brother. Drinking's harmful.

ALYOSHKA   You're a good example. The only time you're at all like a human
  being is when you're drunk. Kleshch! Is my accordion ready? (*Sings
  and dances.*)

> Oh, if I had a mug,
> As ugly as a bug.
> My lady fair
> Would give me the air!

  I'm cold, brothers. I'm fro-o-zen!

MEDVEDEV   Hm. . . . May I ask who your lady fair is?

BUBNOV   Leave him alone. Mind your own business. You're not a policeman
  now—not a policeman and not an uncle.

ALYOSHKA   You're just the aunt's husband.

BUBNOV   One of your nieces is in jail, the other is dying.

MEDVEDEV (*proudly*)   That's a lie. She's not dying. She simply disappeared.
  (SATIN *laughs.*)

BUBNOV   What difference does it make? Once you've lost your nieces, you're
  no longer an uncle.

ALYOSHKA   Your Excellency! Retired drummer-boy to the goat!

> The dame—she's got money,
> And me—I'm dead broke,
> But still I'm a jolly,
> A marvellous bloke!

  It's damned cold in here.

> (KRIVOI ZOB *comes in. Throughout the rest of the act
> other figures of men and women drift in. They take
> their things off and lie down grumbling on the bunks.*)

KRIVOI ZOB   What did you run away for, Bubnov?

BUBNOV   Come here. Sit down and let's have a song. My favourite, eh?

TATAR   Must sleep night-time. Sing songs day-time.

SATIN   That's all right, Asan. Come over here.

TATAR   What you mean, that's all right? Make noise. Make big noise when
  you sing songs.

BUBNOV (*going over to him*)   How's the arm, Asan? Did they cut it off?

TATAR   What for? Wait. Maybe don't cut it off. Arm isn't old iron. Cut it off
  easy when time come.

KRIVOI ZOB   You're done for, Asan. No good for anything with one arm.
  People like us are worth as much as our arms and our backs, brother.

No arm, no man. Done for. Come on, have a drink and forget it!

KVASHNYA (*coming in*) Hullo, dearies! What weather! Cold and slush! Is my policeman here?

MEDVEDEV Here I am!

KVASHNYA There! You've taken my jacket again! And it looks as if you'd had a nip or two, eh? What do you mean by it?

MEDVEDEV On the occasion of Bubnov's birthday . . . and the cold . . . and the slush. . . .

KVASHNYA Watch your step! The slush! None of your monkey business! Come to bed!

MEDVEDEV (*going into the kitchen*) I really could sleep. It's high time.

SATIN Aren't you pretty strict with him?

KVASHNYA That's the only way, friend. You've got to keep a tight hold on a man like him. When I took him in to live with me, I thinks to myself: I may get some good out of him, seeings as he's on the force and you're all such a bunch of rowdies and I'm a poor defenceless woman. But he starts drinking straight off. I can't be having a thing like that!

SATIN You picked a poor helpmate.

KVASHNYA There aren't any better ones. You wouldn't live with me—such a swell you are! And even if you did, it wouldn't last more than a week. And you'd gamble me away in no time—me and all my claptrap.

SATIN (*laughing*) Right you are, woman. I'd gamble you away for sure.

KVASHNYA See? Alyoshka!

ALYOSHKA Here I am.

KVASHNYA What's this gossip you've been spreading about me?

ALYOSHKA Only the truth. There's a woman for you, I says! Simply a marvel! Ten poods of fat, bones, and muscle, and not an ounce of brains!

KVASHNYA That's a lie now. I've got a very lot of brains. But why did you say I beat that policeman of mine?

ALYOSHKA I thought you gave him a beating that time you dragged him off by the hair.

KVASHNYA (*laughing*) Fool! You ought to pretend not to see. Why hang out your dirty clothes for everybody to gape at? And besides, you've hurt his feelings. He's took to drink because of your gossip.

ALYOSHKA Proof of the saying: even a chicken drinks.

(SATIN *and* KLESHCH *laugh*.)

KVASHNYA Ooh, what a tongue you've got! What sort of a person are you anyway, Alyoshka?

ALYOSHKA The best in the world! I try my hand at anything, and follow my nose wherever it goes!

BUBNOV (*beside the* TATAR's *bunk*) Come on! We won't give you a chance to sleep anyway! We're going to sing all night long! Zob!

KRIVOI ZOB Sing? Why not?

ALYOSHKA And I'll accompany you.

SATIN We'll see how.

TATAR (*smiling*) Well, shaitan Bubno, bring some wine. We drink. We have good time. We die, once upon time.

BUBNOV   Fill up his glass, Satin! Sit down, Zob! It's not much a fellow needs, friends. Here am I with a drink in me and happy as a lord! Zob, start up the song—you know, my favourite! I'm going to sing—and bawl my eyes out.

KRIVOI ZOB (*singing*)

> Every morn the sun arises. . . .

BUBNOV (*joining in*)

> Still my cell is filled with gloom. . . .

> (*Suddenly the door bursts open.*)

BARON (*shouting from the doorway*)   Hey, folks! Come here! Come quick! The Actor has hung himself! Out in the vacant lot!

> (*Silence, All look at the* BARON. NASTYA *appears from behind him and walks slowly, wide-eyed, towards the table.*)

SATIN (*softly*)   Tck! Spoiled the song, the fool!

(*Curtain*)

From the Playwright

In his "Observations on the Theatre," **Gorki** *bemoans his own contribution to drama, believing that the theatre should exist for enjoyment's sake and that plays such as his lose "their value as works of art." In an interesting discussion of this philosophy, Gorki allows us to pass judgement on his work.*

From
Observations on the Theatre

I have written altogether, I think, about ten plays. Among these, however, there is not one that really satisfies me.

The reason for this is probably the fact that, before sitting down to write a play, I first construct its ideological framework, and combine beforehand the course and connection of the various comical and tragical events. But, since I am always and chiefly interested in man and not the group, in the personality and not the society, apparently on account of this, and against my will, every play I have written is about a man with reference to whom all the other characters of the play stand in a subordinate relation, playing the part of illustrations, and characterizing and completing the qualities and faults of the chief hero of the play.

In reality, however, a man does not exist in order to subject the qualities and faults of his neighbor to analysis—although many people busy themselves with such a task, probably because they cannot or will not do anything which carries more purpose!

For the reason given above, my plays acquired a didactical spirit, were saturated with a wordy boredom, and lost their value as works of art. By works of art I mean works in which the will of the author is either absent altogether, or else is so cleverly dissimulated as not to be detected by the reader.

In a play all the characters must act independently of the will of the author according to their natural and social inclinations; they must follow the inspirations of their "fate," and not of the author. They must of themselves create the different comical and tragical events, by submitting to the power of their contradictory natures, interest, and passions. The author, on his part, is supposed to act like the host at a party to which he has invited these imaginary guests; and, without preventing them from tormenting or mutilating one another in every manner, morally as well as otherwise, he describes with perfect composure the manner in which they do it.

If an author takes such an attitude, he becomes capable of writing a play that is a pure work of art—a totally impartial play which merely pictures the struggle of differently directed wills, but is devoid of any moral tendencies imposed by the author. Incidentally, in all European literature I know of no drama that is composed according to this principle. Personally, I should not be able to write on such a principle.

But I think I know of people who could create plays penetrated with an inner harmony. The artificiality in such plays is not discernible—it is replaced by art. I consider the comedy of J. M. Synge, the Irishman, entitled *The Playboy of the Western World*, to be such a play. In it the comical side passes quite naturally into the terrible, while the terrible becomes comical just as easily. J. M. Synge, like a truly wise artist, does not inject his own point of view; he just exhibits the people: they are half gods and half beasts, and are possessed of the childish desire to find a "hero" among themselves. (This is, to my mind, an absurd desire, for every one of us is a hero, if he happens to remember all the victories and defeats he has met with in the struggle for life.)

The characters of Synge act in exactly the same way as people usually act and as we shall probably all act for a long time to come; they create heroes in order to ridicule them afterwards. In Synge's play[1] I feel a subtle irony on the cult of the hero. That irony is not very remote from sadness over the stupidity of mankind, but there is in it, I repeat, nothing artificial; it is merely a pure and lawful irony of facts.

Just as perfect as this play is the *Cena delle Beffe* written by the wonderfully gifted Italian author, Sem Benelli. In this play, too, efforts of the author to hypnotize his audience are altogether absent; all the events in it unroll themselves with indisputable logic, the roused will of the hero becomes his fate and leads him unrelentingly to his perdition. I must admit that I watch the development of modern drama altogether with the greatest of hopes, and that I do not believe in the people who cry over the decline of dramatic art. Such playwrights as Sem Benelli, the wonderful Jacinto Benavente, the English Heraclites, Bernard Shaw, and two or three more men in Western Europe, will create, it seems to me, a new theatre, up to the present still rather unfamiliar and incomprehensible to the audience.

Knowing subtly how to handle the methods of the old tragical art, the modern dramatists bring out on the stage all that our tragicomical twentieth century breathes and is tormented with, all that it laughs and cries over. The dramatists I have mentioned fully possess the capacity of true artists: they can stand above reality, they know how to confront facts and characters in such a way that the spectator and the reader can clearly see the nature of the hidden secret powers, the collision of which creates the drama outside the will of the author as well as of his heroes.

Let me recall what I have already said: very often people consider their own stupidity as the ancient *Moira*, by creating insurmountable and fatal obstacles out of the easily surmounted trifles of life. This very strongly propagated error probably arises among the people of the twentieth century, from a somewhat sickly imagination, roused by the rush of events, the mad "tempo" of life, a splendid subject for all dramatists! The modern man reminds me somewhat of a toy maker who has made a mechanical doll, and who is beaten on the head by

[1]*The Playboy of the Western World.*

that same doll; in a sudden terror, the toymaker forgets that the doll is a product of his own labor, and imagines that a mysterious power is hidden in it. But in our life there is nothing more mysterious than man himself and his creative instinct—I find that this suffices us.

I believe that the dramatists I have mentioned can see perfectly well the comical helplessness of man in the face of the richness and greatness of all that he has created and is creating. They peer more deeply into life and see it from more angles than did the dramatists of the nineteenth century—psychologists, students of modes and customs, registrars of the trifles of life.

I exclude from these, of course, Henrik Ibsen, and some of the plays of Gerhart Hauptmann.

I think that in spite of this very natural and always wholesome scepticism as regards the present, the art of the twentieth century is more optimistic, vigorous and active.

The complexity of life increases the number of peculiar collisions and dramatic subjects. The most amusing now is—man, frightened at his own audacity, amazed by the motley entanglements with relationships and events which he himself has created. For this last subject the present political workers are particularly well adapted to play the part of "heroes" . . .

. . . It seems to me that among Anglo-Saxons the theory of purifying the soul through suffering is not so popular as it used to be in Russia. I say "used to be," in the hope that Russia may have gone through enough torture to have acquired an organic revulsion against suffering. However, I have no definite idea concerning the tastes and tendencies of the contemporary theatre. But rarely do I go to see a play, and when I do it is only after I have made sure that the theatrical performance will permit me to rest from the tragedy of reality which is so abundant in our day.

I should like to see the theatre of today as the Pool of Siloam, from which a man may emerge softened and restored physically. I think that the most wholesome theatre is that in which one can gaily and harmlessly laugh over the stupidity of mankind. It is exactly this stupidity that men consider to be their "fate." It is extremely healthful, for an hour or two, to forget this reality which we ourselves create so heedlessly and inconsiderately, and which, in making us collide with one another, easily breaks our hearts and heads.

A man works so much that he fully deserves a gay and wholesome leisure period. The place for such a rest ought, to my mind, to be the theatre. . . .

From the Critic

In his Modern Dramatists, **Ashley Dukes** *believes Gorki's* The Lower Depths *a "masterpiece of naturalism," noting that the play was a personal as well as critical comment of Russian life. Dukes also contends, in the following essay, that none of Gorki's later attempts ever achieved the magnitude of* The Lower Depths.

From
Modern Dramatists

Maxim Gorky's work took, as has aready been pointed out, the different direction of a different temperament. Gorky's plea for the outcasts has little in common with Tolstoy's religious belief in the destiny of the peasantry. His most successful play, "A Night Shelter" (performed in England by the Stage Society in 1903, under the title of "The Lower Depths") is a work of great power. The power is personal rather than dramatic; it is the most vivid expression of Gorky, and the play is Russian through and through. I have seen it performed only in Zurich, before an audience mainly composed of Russian students. It consists simply of four "scenes from the depths," loosely knit together, casual and incoherent. The curtain rises upon the night shelter. To the right lies a dying woman, moaning at intervals; near her is a man dressed only in a shirt, preparing slowly and deliberately to retire for the night. Pulpit-like partitions, odd scraps of furniture and bedsteads stake out the claim of each sleeper along the wall. Around and above the stove other figures are huddled; a thief, a degenerate aristocrat, a prostitute, an actor who has come down in the world and an inebriate who insists upon repeating the doctor's verdict upon him: "Your system is poisoned through and through with alcohol" (Ihr Organismus ist mit Alkohol durch und durch vergiftet). But each tells his own story, warming himself as it were at the fire of the past, and ignoring the others in a dream-monologue of egoism. Everyone wants to talk; no one to listen. The actor declaims his old parts, the aristocrat describes how the world has passed him by, a begger plays popular tunes upon a harmonium—and in the midst of it all the woman dies. The drama, then, is the drama of moments.

The next figure to appear is the old white-bearded Luka, named by the others the "little father." Luka preaches a gospel of cheerfulness. "One must respect everybody," he says. There is a dignity in life, even here in the night shelter. One must never judge by appearances. For the despairing he has a jolly "Keep your pecker up," and for the aggressive a gentle, self-depreciatory disarmament. Luka is something of a raisonneur. He believes in the magical power of faith, no matter whether the faith be true or no. A pragmatist philospher, then, accepting the Tolstoyan gospel of love and rejection of violence purely as a working hypothesis. But Luka helps nobody. The woman is already dead, the thief is arrested, the actor hangs himself, and all goes on as before. Then one Satin begins to preach another gospel. He sees life today, life in the night shelter, only as the soil from which the man of the future will grow. We are all no more than the servants of this future lord. With this touch of Nietzschean morality in the last act the play closes. All that emerges is: "Here are men living like beasts. But they are men and brothers, and they have their personal dignity and their philosophy." There speaks Gorky.

This "Night Shelter" is strangely impressive. Even a single performance of it can never be forgotten. Its gloom never grows monotonous, and its spirit saves it from being merely an aftermath of the old naturalistic period. It dates from 1902. Since then Gorky has written many plays—among them "Children of the Sun," "Barbarians," and "The Last"—but none of them have realised the hopes for his future to which "A Night Shelter" gave rise. Gorky, like Hauptmann, seems to have made the mistake of writing his masterpiece at the beginning of his career. He was never an accomplished craftsman. Most of his stage devices, even in "A Night Shelter," are borrowed and conventional. These weaknesses would not have mattered greatly, however, if only he had continued as he began, with some attempt to free the drama of the depths from sterile naturalism and from the mere representation of the actual in kinematographic pictures. Instead, he has gone back to monotony and passed out of touch with Western Europe. "A Night Shelter" remains a dramatic phenomenon, like Björnson's "Beyond Human Power" and Wedekind's "Frühlings Erwachen," and Gorky's later plays, for all their apparent modernity, belong to a dead age. It matters nothing that twenty years ago this age was alive and strenuous; for us it can no longer have any meaning. The masterpieces of naturalism, such as they were, have long since been written. They were the masterpieces of revolt—correctives of a certain definite condition in the theatre, remedies for a certain definite disease of unreality. As far as the modern theatre is concerned, the condition has been changed and the disease cured. Europe awaits a new synthesis in drama, and the many playwrights who refuse to recognise the change and persist in repeating the old realistic creed must be classed with Dumas and Sardou as props of an outworn tradition.

From the Director

Konstantin Stanislavski, *after his death, remains the theatre's most remembered director. His work at the Moscow Art Theatre and his ideas on acting have served as an inspiration to all who study theatre. In the following, taken from* My Life in Art, *Stanislavski affords us a rare glimpse of the personal and painstaking self-immersion he felt was essential for understanding a play. In it he recalls the trip made to the "lower depths" felt necessary for interpreting the play.*

Journey to Khitrov Market

We received the second play from Gorky, which he called "The Lower Depths of Life," but later changed to "The Lower Depths" on the advice of Nemirovich-Danchenko. There was a difficult problem before us,—a new author, a new style, a new tone and manner of writing on the part of the author and playing on the part of the actors, and a new and peculiar romanticism and pathos that bordered both on theatricality and propaganda.

"I can't bear to see Gorky come out on the pulpit like a clergyman and read his apostolic letters to his congregation in a churchy manner," said Chekhov about Gorky at one time. "Gorky is a destroyer, who must destroy all that deserves destruction. In this lies his whole strength, and it is for this that life has called him."

Our natures were alien to Gorky's wide gestures, to his revelatory thoughts, to his sharp aphorisms, to his destructive flights, and to his peculiar pathos. One must be able to say Gorky's words so that the phrases live and resound. The instructive and propagandistic speeches of Gorky, even those like the one about Man, must be pronounced simply, with sincere enthusiasm, without any false and highfaluting theatricality. Otherwise a serious play will become a mere melodrama. It was necessary to make our own the peculiar style of the tramp, and not to exchange it or mix it up with the accepted type of theatrical vulgarity. In the tramp there must be breadth, freedom, a nobility that is all his own. It was dangerous to assume the usual declamatory tone. All this was important to me not from the viewpoint of social and political movements and tendencies, but from the viewpoint of the innovator, for whom all that was new was important mostly because it was new.

It was necessary to enter into the spiritual springs of Gorky himself, just as we had done in the case of Chekhov, and find the current of the action in the soul of the writer. Having made our own a part of the Gorky soul, we would have the right to speak, to interpret the contents, the thoughts, the plot of the play, to act simply, without any unnecessary strain or effort, without the necessity of persuading some one, of propagating something,—and the spectator would not be bored in looking at us and listening to us; he would find it pleasant to believe us all of the time, for the spiritual content of Gorky and of ourselves would justify and round out the tendential parts of the play and the empty moments of the performance, which, under other circumstances, might become specifically theatrical stuffing and nothing else.

How were we to enter into the soul of the new dramatist and his play?

Again Nemirovich-Danchenko and I approached both author and play, each in our individual manner. Vladimir Ivanovich, as was his wont, gave a masterly analysis of the play. Being a writer, he knows all the secret approaches of literature which serve him as short cuts to creativeness. I, as was my habit at the beginning of all work, was in a helpless muddle, running from the local color to feeling, from feeling to the image, from the image to the production. I even bothered Gorky, looking for creative material. He told me how he wrote the play, where he found his types, how he wandered in the first part of his life, how he met the originals of the characters in his play. From Gorky I ran to those "creatures that once were men," who furnished him with material for his writing.

We arranged an expedition, in which many of the actors in the play, Nemirovich-Danchenko and I, took part. Under the leadership of the writer Giliarevsky, a connoisseur of the life of tramps, who always helped them with money and advice, we went by night to the Khitrov Market. This was a large section of the town which housed tramps exclusively. Their religion was freedom, their sphere—danger, burglary, adventure, theft, murder. All this created around them an atmosphere of romanticism and a peculiar savage beauty which we were seeking at that time. But we were not in luck. It was hard to get permission from the secret organizations of the Khitrov Market. A large theft had taken place that night and the entire Market was in a state of siege. Patrols of armed gunmen were stationed in various places. They would stop us in the endless underground passages, demanding to see our passes. In one place we had to steal by unseen or disaster would have overtaken us. After we had passed the first line of defence our progress became easier. We walked freely along continuous dormitories with numberless board cots on which lay crowds of tired people that resembled corpses, —men and women. In the very centre of the underground labyrinth was the local university and the intelligentsia of the Market. They were people who could read and write, and who at that time were occupied in copying parts for actors. These copyists lived in a small room. They proved themselves kind and hospitable, especially one of them, a well-educated man with fine hands and a delicate profile. He spoke many languages. He was an ex-officer of the guard, who had lost all his property and who had fallen to the depths. For a time he had been able to resume a decent life, to marry, to secure a good position, to wear a uniform.

"I would like to show myself in this uniform in the Khitrov Market," he thought one fine day.

He forgot the idea rapidly. But it returned again and again. Once, when he was commandeered to Moscow, he appeared in the Khitrov Market, astounded all of its inhabitants,—and remained there for the rest of his life, without any hope of ever getting out.

All these people received us like welcome guests whom they had known for a long time. And, in reality, they knew our names and patronymics, for they often worked for us, copying our roles, and trying to please their favorite actors. As soon as we entered, vodka and sausage appeared on the table and a feast began. When we told them that we intended to produce a play about people like them, they were so touched that they began to weep.

"What honor is ours!" cried one of them.

"What is there so interesting in us that they want to show us on the stage?" another wondered naively.

Their talk ran to the theme that when they would stop drinking and become decent people and leave this place, they would—

One of them especially spoke about his past. His only souvenir of it was a little picture cut out of some illustrated magazine which portrayed an old father showing a check to his son, while the mother stood aside and wept. Simov did not like this picture. This was a signal for the breaking out of chaos. The living vessels full of alcohol came to terrible life; they grasped bottles, sticks, tabourets, and attacked Simov. Another moment, and he would have been killed, but Giliarovsky thundered out a quintuple oath, astounding not only us by the complexity of its construction, but even the denizens of the depths. It is impossible to swear in any other language so picturesquely as in Russian. The copyists turned to stone from the unexpectedness of the oath and the enthusiasm and aesthetic satisfaction it brought them. Their mood changed at once. There was mad laughter, applause, ovations, gratefulness and congratulations for the inspired composition of the curse, which perhaps saved us from death.

The excursion to the Khitrov Market, more than any discussion or analysis of the play, awoke my fantasy and my creative mood. There was nature which one could mold to his desire; there was live material for the creation of men, *mise en scène*, images, models and plans. Everything received a real basis and took its proper place. Making the sketches and the *mise en scène*, or showing the actors any of the scenes, I was guided by living memories, and not by invention or guess-work. But the chief result of the excursion was the fact that it forced me to feel the inner meaning of the play.

"Freedom at any cost!" that was its meaning for me. That freedom for the sake of which men descend into the depths of life and become slaves. But they become slaves of their own will, and can remove their yoke at any time, only to put it on again and become slaves once more. It is said that the play is tendentional, that it has social and political notes. Be it so! For me, the actor, the play is —*freedom*—and the spectator is free to draw his own conclusions from our scenic life.

In this condition, "with a wide open soul," as we Russians say, it was easy for us to understand and feel the remarkable direction of the play by Nemirovich-Danchenko.

But alas, all this was true only in part of me in my role of Satin. Within me I understood and felt all this; it traveled from my soul to my tongue, from my soul to the dynamic centers and periphery of my body that truly reflected the unseen inner life of the role. But in the moment of outward appearance there took place a movement towards my habitual theatricality, and I began to play not the role, but its result, the tendency, the idea, the gospel of Gorky. I overacted romanticism and fell into ordinary theatrical pathos and declamation. In my search for the creative mood I moved now along the line of feeling—but did not live it over intuitively—or along the line of the symbol and reached the most commonplace portrayal of tendency, the embraces of the coldest theatrical pathos and falsity. This went on for a very long time, till that memorable moment of my life when before me there opened some of the mysteries of creativeness. But of these later.

Source Material for *The Lower Depths*

BY THE CRITICS

Beerbohm, Max. *Around Theatres*. British Book Center, 1953.
Burns, J. "Voice from the Depths." *Westminster Review* 160 (1903): 148–56.
Jack, A. A. "Maxim Gorki on Stage." *Nation* 77 (1903): 480–481.
Levin, D. *Stormy Petrel: The Life and Work of Maxim Gorki*. New York: Appleton-Century-Crofts, 1965.

Nathan, George. *Theatre Book of the Year*. New York: Knopf, 1948, pp. 255–257.

BY THE DIRECTOR

"*The Lower Depths:* Director's Copy." *Moscow Art Theatre Yearbook*, 1945, pp. 198–209.

BY THE PLAYWRIGHT

Autobiography of Maxim Gorki: My Childhood, In the World, My University Days, translated by I. Schneider. New York: Citadel Press, 1949.

AUDIO-VISUAL SOURCES

The Lower Depths, B&W (French with Englist subtitles), 91 min., Brandon Films, Inc.
Lower Depths, B&W (excerpts—Moscow Art Theatre with English subtitles), 21 min., Indiana University.

Expressionism

Expressionism, the most radical of the dramatic modes, explored man's innermost feelings and desires by utilizing fantastic shapes and sizes, distorted characterization, and stream-of-consciousness speech. Discarding traditional and conventional methods of storytelling and staging, the expressionist strove to heighten the audience's awareness of the protagonist's mental anguish.

The Beginnings

The first rumblings of expressionism began as a revolt against extreme naturalism and realism prevalent on the stage in the period 1875–1910. For naturalism and realism had inhibited the drama—or so the expressionist thought—and now the drama could reveal the sufferings of men by using all the tools of the theatre (in addition to some new ones) in an attempt to display the essence of men. The expressionist was thus seeking a better way of portraying men on the stage, believing the theatre should use its artistic and inventive capacities to the fullest extent. Through special techniques, the stage could exhibit subconscious and conscious thought. Colored lighting, bizarre sounds, fragmented speech, and distorted characterization were the means the playwright would now use in his quest for the revelation of man's soul.

If Darwin and science had provided the primary impetus for naturalism, then Freud and psychology did the same for expressionism. The psychological discovery that much of man's outward behavior was only a superficial expression of his true feelings provided a foundation for a new mode of drama. If the subconscious dreams and fantasies of men revealed more truth about their motivations than their surface behavior, then the drama must exploit these findings. (Strindberg's *Dream Play* is just that—a dream, which he prefaced by saying, "Anything may happen. . . . Time and space do not exist.") For the expressionist, it was unthinkable that man could be accurately represented by showing his cursory behavior. The psychological state of mind could never be photographed by using the techniques of the realists.

The Expressionist's Dramaturgy

While a novelist may present his story in the first person, allowing the character's nagging thoughts and persistent frustrations to receive expression in a narrative form, the playwright is denied these means. We may read the words of the novel's protagonist as he speaks to another, then read his internal dialogue, expressing his "real" self. For the playwright this was virtually impossible. Before the advent of realism in drama, the character, through asides and soliloquies, *could* inform the audience of his actual desires, but these techniques had been virtually abandoned. Thus the expressionist struggled for a revolutionary dramatic technique for revealing all of man's more hidden desires and subliminal characteristics.

Expressionist playwrights were concerned that drama did not portray the inner nature of man—the crude, the primitive, the base—all of the subconscious elements that are the real key to his understanding.

The Expressionist's Techniques

Since men think in flashes, fragments, and images, the expressionists believed the drama must mirror these sometimes illogical, but nevertheless genuine, manifestations of thought. Expressionism sought to "fling open the windows of the mind and allow the spectator to look in upon the private disordered associative process of the character," as Theodore Hatlen states.[1]

Hence, as Strindberg said, "time and space do not exist." The expressionist felt no compulsion to develop his story with rising action culminating in a climax, from which a resolution is achieved. He did not feel bound to present a logical arrangement of actions, sometimes proceeding episodically, sometimes intuitively. Any method which reflected our frequently fragmented and chaotic process of thought was fair game. Any method that faithfully expressed the most profound aspirations or memories of a man's life were utilized. Thus the expressionist's play— *The Adding Machine*, for example—could be a series of fragmented scenes, one piled on the other. If the emotions of the hero were to be portrayed, there was no need to organize them into an integrated whole (for that is not, after all, how they occur). And the play's structure could then proceed in accordance with these thoughts. Perhaps this is why many critics feel that an expressionistic play needs the *expression* of actual performance for full realization and comprehension.

Even the language of the play had to reflect the language of the mind. Usually clipped and fragmented, the speech of the expressionistic character was closer to actual thought. The stacatto-like delivery of Mr. Zero and his guests in Rice's *The Adding Machine*, for example, more closely resembled the conception Zero had of the situation. The telegraphic-like speech of the Cashier in Kaiser's *From Morn to Midnight* expressed his subconscious interpretation of the external events. (In literature, James Joyce's *Ulysses* paralled these same language techniques).

---

[1]Theodore W. Hatlen, *Orientation to the Theatre* (New York: Appleton-Century-Crofts, 1962), p. 170.

More important, though, was the revival of the soliloquy (Ibsen, if he could, would have screamed from his grave at this). This technique, the expressionist argued, was more akin to our process of thinking—at great length, at times, and compressing overt language into shorter symbols. In order for the audience to better perceive the actuality of the character, they would have to be able to "listen in" on his thinking, getting a firmer grasp of his hidden motivations. To more effectively understand the camouflaged reasons for the protagonist's behavior, these reasons had to be revealed in self-speech—thought—and the technique of their revelation to the audience would be the soliloquy.

The expressionist also felt no compulsion to create thorough characterization or to give his characters complete personalities. Since the world was to be seen through the eyes of the hero, most people he saw were rather one-dimensional and displayed little complexity. In *The Adding Machine*, for instance, Mr. Zero was the only character dealt with in any depth, and he was the only one who possessed more than a few personality characteristics. If the others appeared distorted or terribly subjective, it was because they were being presented as Mr. Zero saw them. The other characters were depersonalized nonentities, important only as they reflected the mood and outlook of the character who saw them.

Complementing the shallow characters and fragmented language of the hero was the distorted view of the world about him. The set designer had to make the physical surroundings intensify the hero's orientation to the world. The stage setting had to reflect the hero's state of mind—the distorted shapes, the disfigured patterns, the bizarre colors, and the malformed images of a troubled being. The external physical reality, with which the realists and naturalists had concerned themselves, was no longer important. The stage instead reflected the hero's mental anguish. This is why we see the distorted judge in the courtroom scene of Mr. Zero; this is the reason for a tree turning into a skeleton in *From Morn to Midnight;* this is the explanation for the wierd (there is no better word) montage of landscapes and nightmares of Strindberg's *The Dream Play.*

The Expressionist Playwrights

Basically, the expressionist sought to portray man being swallowed up in the complex world of the twentieth century. Men were becoming depersonalized, mechanized, and strangled by a multitude of unfair systems. They were being exploited by war-mongering and systematizing governments. Personal identity was being shattered, and materialistic and frustrating philosophies were choking the individual. Expression was being stifled.

Echoing this, Frank Wedekind, in his *Spring's Awakening* (and other plays) dealt with the fantastic images that sex and violence conjure up in the human mind. August Strindberg turned from extreme naturalism to expressionism in *The Dream Play*, which set the criteria for future expressionism. Ernst Toller, an exponent of Communism, believed in peaceful revolution, and his *Man and the Masses* expounded this view (though its futility was evident, even to Toller, who ended his play with violence). Gerog Kaiser's *From Morn to Midnight* followed a bank clerk whose struggle for happiness was always denied by the mechanized and thwarting world about him. In *R. U. R.*, Karel Capek dramatized the destructive and debilitating effects of machines on mankind by having the robots of the factory destroy their human inventors.

In America, Eugene O'Neill in his classic, *The Hairy Ape*, criticized our materialistic world and society's repression of individualism. Kaufman and Connelly, in *Beggar on Horseback*, did a worthy job of ridiculing conservative America. And in America's best example of expressionism, *The Adding Machine*, Elmer Rice painted a portrait of one of the multitude of men who go through the drab existence of life, forever subordinated to machines and materials, mercilessly trapped in an impersonal world.

These men, united by a bond of dissatisfaction with the realists and the naturalists, were the exponents of expressionism. They sought to correct the regimentation and impersonalization of society; they believed that man is within, rather than without; they strove to rid the stage of conventional techniques by utilizing theatricalism to its fullest; and they hoped to promote individual dignity in a world that had just seen one global war, and was heading for another.

As a distinct mode of the drama, expressionism was short-lived. Bent on challenging the realist, its method of story development lacked cohesiveness. Its structure was frequently chaotic and disorganized. Characterization was sketchy, and its people, events, and settings were so distorted that at times the audience was taxed to make order out of the chaos the expressionist was struggling to represent. (Strindberg's *The Dream Play* is a most difficult play to perform, let alone to read.)

Expressionism was, however, not without lasting influence. The plays of Pirandello, Thornton Wilder, Tennessee Williams, and Arthur Miller display expressionistic techniques (the hallucinations of Willy Loman in *Death of a Salesman* help display an effective picture of his mental anguish). In addition, expressionism has served as an impetus for propelling modern playwrights and stage designers to discover new, more imaginative techniques of staging a play.

The slanted platforms, titled table, and collection of colors await
Zero in his scene with Daisy. Northern Michigan University.
David Meneghel, director; P. Gibson Ralph, designer; Robert
H. Miller, lighting.

The omnipotent adding machine haunts Zero in death as well
as life. University of Iowa. Greg Foley, director; A. Gillette,
designer.

As if to remind us of an insurmountable communication barrier
between Zero and Daisy, Zero's office desk stands bleakly on
the stage platform. Eastern Illinois University. Theodore
Herstand, director.

After twenty-five years Zero still remains anonymous to his boss, who fires him in this scene. University of Oregon. Horace Robinson, director.

In his own mind Zero has become an exhibit, and the onlookers marvel at this new creature. Carnegie-Mellon University. Lawrence Carra, director; Oren Parker, designer; costumes by Mark Halpin; lighting by Leonard Alexander. 1967.

Zero cowers from the Head in the graveyard scene. Note rear screen projections of expressionistic mood. California State College at Los Angeles. Harry Singleton, director; Barry McGee, designer; costumes by Lolita K. Lejins.

The Greatest task before civilization at present is to make machines what they ought to be, the slaves, instead of the masters, of men.

Havelock Ellis

The Adding Machine

Elmer Rice

The Adding Machine

Characters

Scene One

A small bedroom containing an "installment plan" bed, dresser, and chairs. An ugly electric light fixture over the bed with a single glaring, naked lamp. One small window with the shade drawn. The walls are papered with sheets of foolscap covered with columns of figures.
Mr. Zero *is lying on the bed, facing the audience, his head and shoulders visible. He is thin, sallow, undersized, and partially bald.* Mrs. Zero *is standing before the dresser arranging her hair for the night. She is forty-five, sharp-featured, gray streaks in her hair. She is shapeless in her long-sleeved cotton nightgown. She is wearing her shoes, over which sag her ungartered stockings.*
Mrs. Zero (*as she takes down her hair*)   I'm gettin' sick o' them Westerns. All

them cowboys ridin' around an' foolin' with them ropes. I don't care
nothin' about that. I'm sick of 'em. I don't see why they don't have
more of them stories like *For Love's Sweet Sake*. I like them sweet little
love stories. They're nice an' wholesome. Mrs. Twelve was sayin' to me
only yesterday, "Mrs. Zero," says she, "what I like is one of them
wholesome stories, with just a sweet, simple little love story." "You're
right, Mrs. Twelve," I says. "That's what I like too." They're showin'
too many Westerns at the Rosebud. I'm gettin' sick of them. I think
we'll start goin' to the Peter Stuyvesant. They got a good bill there
Wednesday night. There's a Chubby Delano comedy called *Sea-Sick*.
Mrs. Twelve was tellin' me about it. She says it's a scream. They're
havin' a picnic in the country and they sit Chubby next to an old maid
with a great big mouth. So he gets sore an' when she ain't lookin' he
goes and catches a frog and drops it in her clam chowder. An' when
she goes to eat the chowder the frog jumps out of it an' right into her
mouth. Talk about laugh! Mrs. Twelve was tellin' me she laughed so she
nearly passed out. He sure can pull some funny ones. An' they got that
big Grace Darling feature, *A Mother's Tears*. She's sweet. But I don't
like her clothes. There's no style to them. Mrs. Nine was tellin' me she
read in *Pictureland* that she ain't livin' with her husband. He's her
second too. I don't know whether they're divorced or just separated.
You wouldn't think it to see her on the screen. She looks so sweet and
innocent. Maybe it ain't true. You can't believe all you read. They say
some Pittsburgh millionaire is crazy about her and that's why she ain't
livin' with her husband. Mrs. Seven was tellin' me her brother-in-law
has a friend that used to go to school with Grace Darling. He says her
name ain't Grace Darling at all. Her right name is Elizabeth Dugan,
he says, an' all them stories about her gettin' five thousand a week is the
bunk, he says. She's sweet though. Mrs. Eight was tellin' me that *A
Mother's Tears* is the best picture she ever made. "Don't miss it, Mrs.
Zero," she says. "It's sweet," she says. "Just sweet and wholesome.
Cry!" she says, "I nearly cried my eyes out." There's one part in it
where this big bum of an Englishman—he's a married man too—an'
she's this little simple country girl. An' she nearly falls for him too. But
she's sittin' out in the garden, one day, and she looks up and there's her
mother lookin' at her, right out of the clouds. So that night she locks
the door of her room. An' sure enough, when everybody's in bed, along
comes this big bum of an Englishman an' when she won't let him in
what does he do but go an' kick open the door. "Don't miss it, Mrs.
Zero," Mrs. Eight was tellin' me. It's at the Peter Stuyvesant Wednesday
night, so don't be tellin' me you want to go to the Rosebud. The Eights
seen it downtown at the Strand. They go downtown all the time. Just
like us—nit! I guess by the time it gets to the Peter Stuyvesant all that
part about kickin' in the door will be cut out. Just like they cut out that
big cabaret scene in *The Price of Virtue*. They sure are pullin' some
rough stuff in the pictures nowadays. "It's no place for a young girl,"
I was tellin' Mrs. Eleven, only the other day. An' by the time they get

uptown half of it is cut out. But you wouldn't go downtown—not if
wild horses was to drag you. You can wait till they come uptown! Well,
I don't want to wait, see? I want to see 'em when everybody else is
seein' 'em an' not a month later. Now don't go tellin' me you ain't got
the price. You could dig up the price all right, all right, if you wanted
to. I notice you always got the price to go to the ball game. But when
it comes to me havin' a good time, then it's always: "I ain't got the
price, I gotta start savin'." A fat lot you'll ever save! I got all I can do
now makin' both ends meet, an' you talkin' about savin'. (*She seats
herself on a chair and begins removing her shoes and stockings.*) An' don't
go pullin' that stuff about bein' tired. "I been workin' hard all day.
Twice a day in the subway's enough for me." Tired! Where do you get
that tired stuff, anyhow? What about me? Where do I come in? Scrubbin' floors an' cookin' your meals an' washin' your dirty clothes. An'
you sittin' on a chair all day, just addin' figgers an' waitin' for five-
thirty. There's no five-thirty for me. I don't wait for no whistle. I don't
get no vacations neither. And what's more I don't get no pay envelope
every Saturday night neither. I'd like to know where you'd be without
me. An' what have I got to show for it?—slavin' my life away to give
you a home. What's in it for me, I'd like to know? But it's my own
fault, I guess. I was a fool for marryin' you. If I'd 'a' had any sense,
I'd 'a' known what you were from the start. I wish I had it to do over
again, I hope to tell you. You was goin' to do wonders, you was! You
wasn't goin' to be a bookkeeper long—oh, no, not you. Wait till you got
started—you was goin' to show 'em. There wasn't no job in the store
that was too big for you. Well, I've been waitin'—waitin' for you to get
started—see? It's been a good long wait too. Twenty-five years! An' I
ain't seen nothin' happen. Twenty-five years in the same job. Twenty-five
years tomorrow! You're proud of it, ain't you? Twenty-five years in the
same job an' never missed a day! That's somethin' to be proud of, ain't
it? Sittin' for twenty-five years on the same chair, addin' up figgers.
What about bein' store manager? I guess you forgot about that, didn't
you? An' me at home here lookin' at the same four walls an' workin'
my fingers to the bone to make both ends meet. Seven years since you
got a raise! An' if you don't get one tomorrow, I'll bet a nickel you
won't have the guts to go an' ask for one. I didn't pick much when I
picked you, I'll tell the world. You ain't much to be proud of. (*She rises,
goes to the window, and raises the shade. A few lighted windows are
visible on the other side of the closed court. Looking out for a moment.*)
She ain't walkin' around tonight, you can bet your sweet life on that.
An' she won't be walkin' around any more nights neither. Not in this
house, anyhow. (*She turns away from the window.*) The dirty bum! The
idea of her comin' to live in a house with respectable people. They
should 'a' gave her six years, not six months. If I was the judge I'd of
gave her life. A bum like that. (*She approaches the bed and stands there
a moment.*) I guess you're sorry she's gone. I guess you'd like to sit home
every night an' watch her goin's-on. You're somethin' to be proud of,

you are! (*She stands on the bed and turns out the light. A thin stream of moonlight filters in from the court. The two figures are dimly visible.* MRS. ZERO *gets into bed.*) You'd better not start nothin' with women, if you know what's good for you. I've put up with a lot, but I won't put up with that. I've been slavin' away for twenty-five years, makin' a home for you an' nothin' to show for it. If you was any kind of a man you'd have a decent job by now an' I'd be gettin' some comfort out of life—instead of bein' just a slave, washin' pots an' standin' over the hot stove. I've stood it for twenty-five years an' I guess I'll have to stand it twenty-five more. But don't you go startin' nothin' with women—

(*She goes on talking as the curtain falls.*)
(*Curtain.*)

Scene Two

An office in a department store. Wood and glass partitions. In the middle of the room two tall desks back to back. At one desk on a high stool is ZERO. *Opposite him at the other desk, also on a high stool, is* DAISY DIANA DOROTHEA DEVORE, *a plain, middle-aged woman. Both wear green eyeshades and paper sleeve-protectors. A pendent electric lamp throws light upon both desks.* DAISY *reads aloud figures from a pile of slips which lie before her. As she reads the figures* ZERO *enters them upon a large square sheet of ruled paper which lies before him.*

DAISY (*reading aloud*)   Three ninety-eight. Forty-two cents. A dollar fifty. A dollar fifty. A dollar twenty-five. Two dollars. Thirty-nine cents. Twenty-seven fifty.

ZERO (*petulantly*)   Speed it up a little, cancha?

DAISY   What's the rush? Tomorrer's another day.

ZERO   Aw, you make me sick.

DAISY   An' you make me sicker.

ZERO   Go on. Go on. We're losin' time.

DAISY   Then quit bein' so bossy. (*She reads.*) Three dollars. Two sixty-nine. Eighty-one fifty. Forty dollars. Eight seventy-five. Who do you think you are, anyhow?

ZERO   Never mind who I think I am. You tend to your work.

DAISY   Aw, don't be givin' me so many orders. Sixty cents. Twenty-four cents. Seventy-five cents. A dollar fifty. Two fifty. One fifty, One fifty. Two fifty. I don't have to take it from you and what's more I won't.

ZERO   Aw, quit talkin'.

DAISY   I'll talk all I want. Three dollars. Fifty cents. Fifty cents. Seven dollars. Fifty cents. Two fifty. Three fifty. Fifty cents. One fifty. Fifty cents.

(*She goes on, bending over the slips and transferring them from one pile to another.* ZERO *bends over his desk. busily entering the figures.*)

ZERO (*without looking up*)   You make me sick. Always shootin' off your face about somethin'. Talk, talk, talk. Just like all the other women. Women make me sick.

DAISY (*busily fingering the slips*).   Who do you think you are, anyhow? Bossin'
me around. I don't have to take it from you, and what's more I won't.
(*They both attend closely to their work, neither looking
up. Throughout, each intones figures during the other's
speeches.*)

ZERO   Women make me sick. They're all alike. The judge gave her six months.
I wonder what they do in the workhouse. Peel potatoes. I'll bet she's
sore at me. Maybe she'll try to kill me when she gets out. I better be
careful. Hello Girl Slays Betrayer. Jealous Wife Slays Rival. You can't
tell what a woman's liable to do. I better be careful.

DAISY   I'm gettin' sick of it. Always pickin' on me about somethin'. Never a
decent word out of you. Not even the time o' day.

ZERO   I guess she wouldn't have the nerve at that. Maybe she don't even know
it's me. They didn't even put my name in the paper, the big bums.
Maybe she's been in the workhouse before. A bum like that. She didn't
have nothin' on that one time—nothin' but a shirt. (*He glances up
quickly, then bends over again.*) You make me sick. I'm sick of lookin'
at your face.

DAISY   Gee, ain't that whistle ever goin' to blow? You didn't used to be like
that. Not even good mornin' or good evenin'. I ain't done nothin' to
you. It's the young girls. Goin' around without corsets.

ZERO   Your face is gettin' all yeller. Why don't you put some paint on it?
She was puttin' on paint that time. On her cheeks and on her lips. And
that blue stuff on her eyes. Just sittin' there in a shimmy puttin' on the
paint. An' walkin' around the room with her legs all bare.

DAISY   I wish I was dead.

ZERO   I was a goddam fool to let the wife get on to me. She oughta get six
months at that. The dirty bum. Livin' in a house with respectable people.
She'd be livin' there yet if the wife hadn't o' got on to me. Damn her!

DAISY   I wish I was dead.

ZERO   Maybe another one'll move in. Gee, that would be great. But the
wife's got her eye on me now.

DAISY   I'm scared to do it though.

ZERO   You oughta move into that room. It's cheaper than where you're livin'
now. I better tell you about it. I don't mean to be always pickin' on you.

DAISY   Gas. The smell of it makes me sick. (ZERO *looks up and clears his
throat.* DAISY *looks up, startled.*) Whadja say?

ZERO   I didn't say nothin'.

DAISY   I thought you did.

ZERO   You thought wrong.
(*They bend over their work again.*)

DAISY   A dollar sixty. A dollar fifty. Two ninety. One sixty-two.

ZERO   Why the hell should I tell you? Fat chance of you forgettin' to pull
down the shade!

DAISY   If I asked for carbolic they might get on to me.

ZERO   Your hair's gettin' gray. You don't wear them shirtwaists any more
with the low collars. When you'd bend down to pick somethin' up—

DAISY   I wish I knew what to ask for. Girl Takes Mercury After All-Night Party. Woman In Ten-Story Death Leap.

ZERO   I wonder where'll she go when she gets out. Gee, I'd like to make a date with her. Why didn't I go over there the night my wife went to Brooklyn? She never woulda found out.

DAISY   I seen Pauline Frederick do it once. Where could I get a pistol though?

ZERO   I guess I didn't have the nerve.

DAISY   I'll bet you'd be sorry then that you been so mean to me. How do I know though? Maybe you wouldn't.

ZERO   Nerve! I got as much nerve as anybody. I'm on the level, that's all. I'm a married man and I'm on the level.

DAISY   Anyhow, why ain't I got a right to live? I'm as good as anybody else. I'm too refined, I guess. That's the whole trouble.

ZERO   The time the wife had pneumonia I thought she was goin' to pass out. But she didn't. The doctor's bill was eighty-seven dollars. (*Looking up.*) Hey, wait a minute! Didn't you say eighty-seven dollars?

DAISY (*looking up*)   What?

ZERO   Was the last you said eighty-seven dollars?

DAISY (*consulting the slip*)   Forty-two fifty.

ZERO   Well, I made a mistake. Wait a minute. (*He busies himself with an eraser.*) All right. Shoot.

DAISY   Six dollars. Three fifteen. Two twenty-five. Sixty-five cents. A dollar twenty. You talk to me as if I was dirt.

ZERO   I wonder if I could kill the wife without anybody findin' out. In bed some night. With a pillow.

DAISY   I used to think you was stuck on me.

ZERO   I'd get found out though. They always have ways.

DAISY   We used to be so nice and friendly together when I first came here. You used to talk to me then.

ZERO   Maybe she'll die soon. I noticed she was coughin' this mornin'.

DAISY   You used to tell me all kinds o' things. You were goin' to show them all. Just the same, you're still sittin' here.

ZERO   Then I could do what I damn please. Oh, boy!

DAISY   Maybe it ain't all your fault neither. Maybe if you'd had the right kind o' wife—somebody with a lot of common sense, somebody refined—me!

ZERO   At that, I guess I'd get tired of bummin' around. A feller wants some place to hang his hat.

DAISY   I wish she would die.

ZERO   And when you start goin' with women you're liable to get into trouble. And lose your job maybe.

DAISY   Maybe you'd marry me.

ZERO   Gee, I wish I'd gone over there that night.

DAISY   Then I could quit workin'.

ZERO   Lots o' women would be glad to get me.

DAISY   You could look a long time before you'd find a sensible, refined girl like me.

ZERO   Yes, sir, they could look a long time before they'd find a steady meal-ticket like me.

DAISY   I guess I'd be too old to have any kids. They say it ain't safe after thirty-five.

ZERO   Maybe I'd marry you. You might be all right, at that.

DAISY   I wonder—if you don't want kids—whether—if there's any way—

ZERO (*looking up*)   Hey! Hey! Can't you slow up? What do you think I am —a machine?

DAISY (*looking up*).   Say, what do you want, anyhow? First it's too slow an' then it's too fast. I guess you don't know what you want.

ZERO   Well, never mind about that. Just you slow up.

DAISY   I'm gettin' sick o' this. I'm goin' to ask to be transferred.

ZERO   Go ahead. You can't make me mad.

DAISY   Aw, keep quiet. (*She reads*) Two forty-five. A dollar twenty. A dollar fifty. Ninety cents. Sixty-three cents.

ZERO   Marry you! I guess not! You'd be as bad as the one I got.

DAISY   You wouldn't care if I did ask. I got a good mind to ask.

ZERO   I was a fool to get married.

DAISY   Then I'd never see you at all.

ZERO   What chance has a guy got with a woman tied around his neck?

DAISY   That time at the store picnic—the year your wife couldn't come—you were nice to me then.

ZERO   Twenty-five years holdin' down the same job!

DAISY   We were together all day—just sittin' around under the trees.

ZERO   I wonder if the boss remembers about it bein' twenty-five years.

DAISY   And comin' home that night—you sat next to me in the big delivery wagon.

ZERO   I got a hunch there's a big raise comin' to me.

DAISY   I wonder what it feels like to be really kissed. Men—dirty pigs! They want the bold ones.

ZERO   If he don't come across I'm goin' right up to the front office and tell him where he gets off.

DAISY   I wish I was dead.

ZERO   "Boss," I'll say, "I want to have a talk with you." "Sure," he'll say, "sit down. Have a Corona Corona." "No," I'll say, "I don't smoke." "How's that?" he'll say. "Well, boss," I'll say, "it's this way. Every time I feel like smokin' I just take a nickel and put it in the old sock. A penny saved is a penny earned, that's the way I look at it." "Damn sensible," he'll say. "You got a wise head on you, Zero."

DAISY   I can't stand the smell of gas. It makes me sick. You coulda kissed me if you wanted to.

ZERO   "Boss," I'll say, "I ain't quite satisfied. I been on the job twenty-five years now and if I'm gonna stay I gotta see a future ahead of me." "Zero," he'll say, "I'm glad you came in. I've had my eye on you, Zero, Nothin' gets by me." "Oh, I know that, boss," I'll say. That'll hand him a good laugh, that will. "You're a valuable man, Zero," he'll say, "and I want you right up here with me in the front office. You're done addin' figgers. Monday mornin' you move up here."

DAISY   Them kisses in the movies—them long ones—right on the mouth—

ZERO   I'll keep a-goin' right on up after that. I'll show some of them birds where they get off.

DAISY   That one the other night—*The Devil's Alibi*—he put his arms around her—and her head fell back and her eyes closed—like she was in a daze.

ZERO   Just give me about two years and I'll show them birds where they get off.

DAISY   I guess that's what it's like—a kinda daze—when I see them like that, I just seem to forget everything.

ZERO   Then me for a place in Jersey. And maybe a little Buick. No tin Lizzie for mine. Wait till I get started—I'll show 'em.

DAISY   I can see it now when I kinda half close my eyes. The way her head fell back. And his mouth pressed right up against hers. Oh, Gawd! it must be grand!

> *There is a sudden shrill blast from a steam whistle.*

DAISY *and* ZERO (*together*)   The whistle!

> *With great agility they get off their stools, remove their eyeshades and sleeve-protectors and put them on the desks. Then each produces from behind the desk a hat—* ZERO, *a dusty derby,* DAISY, *a frowsy straw.* DAISY *puts on her hat and turns toward* ZERO *as though she were about to speak to him. But he is busy cleaning his pen and pays no attention to her. She sighs and goes toward the door at the left.*)

ZERO (*looking up*)   G'night, Miss Devore.

> (*But she does not hear him and exits.* ZERO *takes up his hat and goes left. The door at the right opens and the Boss enters—middle-aged, stoutish, bald, well dressed.*)
> (*The Boss calling*) Oh—er—Mister—er——
> (ZERO *turns in surprise, sees who it is, and trembles nervously.*)

ZERO (*obsequiously*)   Yes, sir. Do you want me, sir?

BOSS   Yes. Just come here a moment, will you?

ZERO   Yes, sir. Right away, sir. (*He fumbles his hat, picks it up, stumbles, recovers himself, and approaches the Boss, every fiber quivering.*)

BOSS   Mister—er—er——

ZERO   Zero.

BOSS   Yes, Mr. Zero. I wanted to have a little talk with you.

ZERO (*with a nervous grin*)   Yes, sir, I been kinda expectin' it.

BOSS (*staring at him*)   Oh, have you?

ZERO   Yes, sir.

BOSS   How long have you been with us, Mister—er—Mister——

ZERO   Zero.

BOSS   Yes, Mr. Zero.

ZERO   Twenty-five years today.

BOSS   Twenty-five years! That's a long time.

ZERO   Never missed a day.

BOSS   And you've been doing the same work all the time?

ZERO   Yes, sir. Right here at this desk.

BOSS   Then, in that case, a change probably won't be unwelcome to you.

ZERO   No, sir, it won't. And that's the truth.

BOSS   We've been planning a change in this department for some time.

ZERO   I kinda thought you had your eye on me.

BOSS   You were right. The fact is that my efficiency experts have recommended the installation of adding machines.

ZERO (*staring at him*)   Addin' machines?

BOSS   Yes, you've probably seen them. A mechanical device that adds automatically.

ZERO   Sure. I've seen them. Keys—and a handle that you pull. (*He goes through the motions in the air.*)

BOSS   That's it. They do the work in half the time and a high-school girl can operate them. Now, of course, I'm sorry to lose an old and faithful employee——

ZERO   Excuse me, but would you mind sayin' that again?

BOSS   I say I'm sorry to lose an employee who's been with me for so many years——(*Soft music is heard—the sound of the mechanical player of a distant merry-go-round. The part of the floor upon which the desk and stools are standing begins to revolve very slowly.*) But, of course, in an organization like this, efficiency must be the first consideration——(*The music becomes gradually louder and the revolutions more rapid.*) You will draw your salary for the full month. And I'll direct my secretary to give you a letter of recommendation——

ZERO   Wait a minute, boss. Let me get this right. You mean I'm canned?

BOSS (*barely making himself heard above the increasing volume of sound*)   I'm sorry—no other alternative—greatly regret—old employee—efficiency—economy—business—*business*—BUSINESS——

> (*His voice is drowned by the music. The platform is revolving rapidly now.* ZERO *and the* BOSS *face each other. They are entirely motionless save for the* BOSS'S *jaws, which open and close incessantly. But the words are inaudible. The music swells and swells. To it is added every offstage effect of the theater: the wind, the waves, the galloping horses, the locomotive whistle, the sleigh bells, the automobile siren, the glass-crash. New Year's· Eve, Election Night, Armistice Day, and Mardi Gras. The noise is deafening, maddening, unendurable. Suddenly it culminates in a terrific peal of thunder. For an instant there is a flash of red and then everything is plunged into blackness.*)
> (*Curtain.*)

Scene Three

The ZERO *dining room. Entrance door at right. Doors to kitchen and bedroom at left. The walls, as in the first scene, are papered with foolscap sheets covered with columns of figures. In the middle of the room, upstage, a table set for two.*

Along each side wall seven chairs are ranged in symmetrical rows.
At the rise of the curtain MRS. ZERO *is seen seated at the table looking alternately*
at the entrance door and a clock on the wall. She wears a bungalow apron over
her best dress.
After a few moments the entrance door opens and ZERO *enters. He hangs his*
hat on a rack behind the door and, coming over to the table, seats himself at
the vacant place. His movements throughout are quiet and abstracted.

MRS. ZERO (*breaking the silence*)   Well, it was nice of you to come home.
You're only an hour late and that ain't very much. The supper don't
get very cold in an hour. An' of course the part about our havin' a lot
of company tonight don't matter. (*They begin to eat.*)

Ain't you even got sense enough to come home on time? Didn't
I tell you we're goin' to have a lot o' company tonight? Didn't you
know the Ones are comin'? An the Twos? An' the Threes? An' the
Fours? An' the Fives? And the Sixes? Didn't I tell you to be home on
time? I might as well talk to a stone wall. (*They eat for a few moments*
in silence.)

I guess you musta had some important business to attend to. Like
watchin' the scoreboard. Or was two kids havin' a fight an' you was the
referee? You sure do have a lot of business to attend to. It's a wonder
you have time to come home at all. You gotta tough life, you have.
Walk in, hang up your hat, an' put on the nosebag. An' me in the hot
kitchen all day, cookin' your supper an' waitin' for you to get good an'
ready to come home! (*Again they eat in silence.*)

Maybe the boss kept you late tonight. Tellin' you what a big noise
you are and how the store couldn't 'a' got along if you hadn't been
pushin' a pen for twenty-five years. Where's the gold medal he pinned
on you? Did some blind old lady take it away from you or did you
leave it on the seat of the boss's limousine when he brought you home?
(*Again a few moments of silence.*)

I'll bet he gave you a big raise, didn't he? Promoted you from the
third floor to the fourth, maybe. Raise? A fat chance you got o' gettin'
a raise. All they gotta do is put an ad in the paper. There's ten thousand
like you layin' around the streets. You'll be holdin' down the same job
at the end of another twenty-five years—if you ain't forgot how to add
by that time.

(*A noise is heard offstage, a sharp clicking such as is*
made by the operation of the keys and levers of an
adding machine. ZERO *raises his head for a moment but*
lowers it almost instantly.)

MRS. ZERO   There's the doorbell. The company's here already. And we ain't
hardly finished supper. (*She rises.*) But I'm goin' to clear off the table
whether you're finished or not. If you want your supper, you got a right
to be home on time. Not standin' around lookin' at scoreboards. (*As she*
piles up the dishes ZERO *rises and goes toward the entrance door.*) Wait a
minute! Don't open the door yet. Do you want the company to see all
the mess? An' go an' put on a clean collar. You got red ink all over it.

(ZERO *goes toward bedroom door.*) I should think after pushin' a pen for twenty-five years, you'd learn how to do it without gettin' ink on your collar. (ZERO *exits to bedroom.* MRS. ZERO *takes dishes to kitchen, talking as she goes.*)

I guess I can stay up all night now washin' dishes. You should worry! That's what a man's got a wife for, ain't it? Don't he buy her her clothes an' let her eat with him at the same table? An' all she's gotta do is cook the meals an' do the washin' an' scrub the floor, an' wash the dishes when the company goes. But, believe me, you're goin' to sling a mean dish towel when the company goes tonight!

> (*While she is talking* ZERO *enters from bedroom. He wears a clean collar and is cramming the soiled one furtively into his pocket.* MRS. ZERO *enters from kitchen. She has removed her apron and carries a table cover which she spreads hastily over the table. The clicking noise is heard again.*)

MRS. ZERO   There's the bell again. Open the door, cancha?

> (ZERO *goes to the entrance door and opens it. Six men and six women file into the room in a double column. The men are all shapes and sizes, but their dress is identical with that of* ZERO *in every detail. Each, however, wears a wig of a different color. The women are all dressed alike too, except that the dress of each is of a different color.*)

MRS. ZERO (*taking the first woman's hand*)   How de do, Mrs. One.

MRS. ONE   How de do, Mrs. Zero.

> (MRS. ZERO *repeats this formula with each woman in turn.* ZERO *does the same with the men except that he is silent throughout. The files now separate, each man taking a chair from the right wall and each woman one from the left wall. Each sex forms a circle with the chairs very close together. The men—all except* ZERO—*smoke cigars. The women munch chocolates.*)

SIX   Some rain we're havin'.

FIVE   Never saw the like of it.

FOUR   Worst in fourteen years, paper says.

THREE   Y' can't always go by the papers.

TWO   No, that's right too.

ONE   We're liable to forget from year to year.

SIX   Yeh, come t' think, last year was pretty bad too.

FIVE   An' how about two years ago?

FOUR   Still, this year's pretty bad.

THREE   Yeh, no gettin' away from that.

TWO   Might be a whole lot worse.

ONE   Yeh, it's all the way you look at it. Some rain though.

MRS. SIX   I like them little organdie dresses.

MRS. FIVE   Yeh, with a little lace trimmin' on the sleeves.

MRS. FOUR   Well, I like 'em plain myself.

MRS. THREE   Yeh, what I always say is the plainer the more refined.

MRS. TWO   Well, I don't think a little lace does any harm.

MRS. ONE   No, it kinda dresses it up.

MRS. ZERO   Well, I always say it's all a matter of taste.

MRS. SIX   I saw you at the Rosebud Movie Thursday night, Mr. One.

ONE   Pretty punk show, I'll say.

TWO   They're gettin' worse all the time.

MRS. SIX   But who was the charming lady, Mr. One?

ONE   Now don't you go makin' trouble for me. That was my sister.

MRS. FIVE   Oho! That's what they all say.

MRS. FOUR   Never mind! I'll bet Mrs. One knows what's what, all right.

MRS. ONE   Oh, well, he can do what he likes—'slong as he behaves himself.

THREE   You're in luck at that, One. Fat chance I got of gettin' away from the frau even with my sister.

MRS. THREE   You oughta be glad you got a good wife to look after you.

THE OTHER WOMEN (*in unison*)   That's right, Mrs. Three.

FIVE   I guess I know who wears the pants in your house, Three.

MRS. ZERO   Never mind. I saw them holdin' hands at the movie the other night.

THREE   She musta been tryin' to get some money away from me.

MRS. THREE   Swell chance anybody'd have of gettin' any money away from you.
(*General laughter.*)

FOUR   They sure are a loving couple.

MRS. TWO   Well, I think we oughta change the subject.

MRS. ONE   Yes, let's change the subject.

SIX (*sotto voce*)   Did you hear the one about the travelin' salesman?

FIVE   It seems this guy was in a sleeper.

FOUR   Goin' from Albany to San Diego.

THREE   And in the next berth was an old maid.

TWO   With a wooden leg.

ONE   Well, along about midnight——
(*They all put their heads together and whisper.*)

MRS. SIX (*sotto voce*)   Did you hear about the Sevens?

MRS. FIVE   They're gettin' a divorce.

MRS. FOUR   It's the second time for him.

MRS. THREE   They're two of a kind, if you ask me.

MRS. TWO   One's as bad as the other.

MRS. ONE   Worse.

MRS. ZERO   They say that she——
(*They all put their heads together and whisper.*)

SIX   I think this woman suffrage is the bunk.

FIVE   It sure is! Politics is a man's business.

FOUR   Woman's place is in the home.

THREE   That's it! Lookin' after the kids, 'stead of hangin' around the streets.

TWO   You hit the nail on the head that time.

ONE   The trouble is they don't know what they want.

MRS. SIX   Men sure get me tired.

MRS. FIVE   They sure are a lazy lot.

MRS. FOUR   And dirty.

MRS. THREE   Always grumblin' about somethin'.

MRS. TWO   When they're not lyin'!

MRS. ONE   Or messin' up the house.

MRS. ZERO   Well, believe me, I tell mine where he gets off.

SIX   Business conditions are sure bad.

FIVE   Never been worse.

FOUR   I don't know what we're comin' to.

THREE   I look for a big smash-up in about three months.

TWO   Wouldn't surprise me a bit.

ONE   We're sure headin' for trouble.

MRS. SIX   My aunt has gallstones.

MRS. FIVE   My husband has bunions.

MRS. FOUR   My sister expects next month.

MRS. THREE   My cousin's husband has erysipelas.

MRS. TWO   My niece has St. Vitus's dance.

MRS. ONE   My boy has fits.

MRS. ZERO   I never felt better in my life. Knock wood!

SIX   Too damn much agitation, that's at the bottom of it.

FIVE   That's it! Too damn many strikes.

FOUR   Foreign agitators, that's what it is.

THREE   They oughta be run outa the country.

TWO   What the hell do they want anyhow?

ONE   They don't know what they want, if you ask me.

SIX   America for the Americans is what I say!

ALL (*in unison*)   That's it! Damn foreigners! Damn dagoes! Damn Catholics! Damn sheenies! Damn niggers! Jail 'em! Shoot 'em! Hang 'em! Lynch 'em! Burn 'em!

> (*They all rise. Sing in unison.*)
> My country 'tis of thee,
> Sweet land of liberty!

MRS. FOUR   Why so pensive, Mr. Zero?

ZERO (*speaking for the first time*)   I'm thinkin'.

MRS. FOUR   Well, be careful not to sprain your mind.

> (*Laughter.*)

MRS. ZERO   Look at the poor men all by themselves. We ain't very sociable.

ONE   Looks like we're neglectin' the ladies.

> (*The women cross the room and join the men, all chattering loudly. The doorbell rings.*)

MRS. ZERO   Sh! The doorbell!

> (*The volume of sound slowly diminishes. Again the doorbell.*)

ZERO (*quietly*)   I'll go. It's for me.

> (*They watch curiously as ZERO goes to the door and opens it, admitting a POLICEMAN. There is a murmur of surprise and excitement.*)

POLICEMAN   I'm lookin' for Mr. Zero. (*They all point to ZERO.*)

ZERO   I've been expectin' you.

POLICEMAN   Come along!

ZERO   Just a minute. (*He puts his hand in his pocket.*)

POLICEMAN   What's he tryin' to pull? (*He draws a revolver.*) I got you covered.

ZERO   Sure, that's all right. I just want to give you somethin'. (*He takes the collar from his pocket and gives it to the* POLICEMAN.)

POLICEMAN (*suspiciously*)   What's that?

ZERO   The collar I wore.

POLICEMAN   What do I want it for?

ZERO   It's got bloodstains on it.

POLICEMAN (*pocketing it*)   All right, come along!

ZERO (*turning to* MRS. ZERO)   I gotta go with him. You'll have to dry the dishes yourself.

MRS. ZERO (*rushing forward*)   What are they takin' you for?

ZERO (*calmly*)   I killed the boss this afternoon. (*The* POLICEMAN *takes him off.*) (*Quick Curtain.*)

Scene Four

A court of justice. Three bare white walls without doors or windows except for a single door in the right wall. At the right is a jury box in which are seated MESSRS. ONE, TWO, THREE, FOUR, FIVE, *and* SIX *and their respective wives. On either side of the jury box stands a uniformed officer. Opposite the jury box is a long, bare oak table piled high with law books. Behind the books* ZERO *is seated, his face buried in his hands. There is no other furniture in the room. A moment after the rise of the curtain one of the officers rises and, going around the table, taps* ZERO *on the shoulder.* ZERO *rises and accompanies the officer. The officer escorts him to the great empty space in the middle of the courtroom, facing the jury. He motions to* ZERO *to stop, then points to the jury and resumes his place beside the jury box.* ZERO *stands there looking at the jury, bewildered and half afraid. The jurors give no sign of having seen him. Throughout they sit with folded arms, staring stolidly before them.*

ZERO (*beginning to speak, haltingly*)   Sure I killed him. I ain't sayin' I didn't, am I? Sure I killed him. Them lawyers! They give me a good stiff pain, that's what they give me. Half the time I don't know what the hell they're talkin' about. Objection sustained. Objection overruled. What's the big idea anyhow? You ain't heard me do any objectin', have you? Sure not! What's the idea of objectin'? You got a right to know. What I say is, if one bird kills another bird, why you got a right to call him for it. That's what I say. I know all about that. I been on the jury too. Them lawyers! Don't let 'em fill you full of bunk. All that bull about it bein' red ink on the bill file. Red ink nothin'! It was blood, see? I want you to get that right. I killed him, see? Right through the heart with the bill file, see? I want you to get that right—all of you. One, two, three, four, five, six, seven, eight, nine, ten, eleven, twelve. Twelve of you. Six and six. That makes twelve. I figgered it up often enough. Six and six makes twelve.

And five is seventeen. And eight is twenty-five. And three is twenty-eight. Eight and carry two. Aw, cut it out! Them damn figgers! I can't forget 'em. Twenty-five years, see? Eight hours a day, exceptin' Sundays. And July and August half-day Saturday. One week's vacation with pay. And another week without pay if you want it. Who the hell wants it? Layin' around the house listenin' to the wife tellin' you where you get off. Nix! An' legal holidays. I nearly forgot them. New Year's, Washington's Birthday, Decoration Day, Fourth o' July, Labor Day, Election Day, Thanksgivin', Christmas. Good Friday if you want it. An' if you're a Jew, Young Kipper an' the other one—I forget what they call it. The dirty sheenies—always gettin' two to the other bird's one. An' when a holiday comes on Sunday, you get Monday off. So that's fair enough. But when the Fourth o' July comes on Saturday, why you're out o' luck on account of Saturday bein' a half-day anyhow. Get me? Twenty-five years—I'll tell you somethin' funny. Decoration Day an' the Fourth o' July are always on the same day o' the week. Twenty-five years. Never missed a day, and never more'n five minutes late. Look at my time card if you don't believe me. Eight twenty-seven, eight thirty, eight twenty-nine, eight twenty-seven, eight thirty-two. Eight an' thirty-two's forty an'— Goddam them figgers! I can't forget 'em. They're funny things, them figgers. They look like people sometimes. The eights, see? Two dots for the eyes and a dot for the nose. An' a line. That's the mouth, see? An' there's others remind you of other things—but I can't talk about them, on account of there bein' ladies here. Sure I killed him. Why didn't he shut up? If he'd only shut up! Instead o' talkin' an' talkin' about how sorry he was an' what a good guy I was an' this an' that. I felt like sayin' to him: "For Christ's sake, shut up!" But I didn't have the nerve, see? I didn't have the nerve to say that to the boss. An' he went on talkin', sayin' how sorry he was, see? He was standin' right close to me. An' his coat only had two buttons on it. Two an' two makes four an'— aw, can it! An' there was the bill file on the desk. Right where I could touch it. It ain't right to kill a guy. I know that. When I read all about him in the paper an' about his three kids I felt like a cheapskate, I tell you. They had the kids' pictures in the paper, right next to mine. An' his wife too. Gee, it must be swell to have a wife like that. Some guys sure is lucky. An' he left fifty thousand dollars just for a rest room for the girls in the store. He was a good guy at that. Fifty thousand. That's more'n twice as much as I'd have if I saved every nickel I ever made. Let's see. Twenty-five an' twenty-five an' twenty-five an'—aw, cut it out! An' the ads had a big, black border around 'em; an' all it said was that the store would be closed for three days on account of the boss bein' dead. That nearly handed me a laugh, that did. All them floorwalkers an' buyers an' high-muck-a-mucks havin' me to thank for gettin' three days off. I hadn't oughta killed him. I ain't sayin' nothin' about that. But I thought he was goin' to give me a raise, see? On account of bein' there twenty-five years. He never talked to me before, see? Except one mornin' we happened to come in the store together and I held the door open for him and he said

"Thanks." Just like that, see? "Thanks!" That was the only time he ever
talked to me. An' when I seen him comin' up to my desk, I didn't know
where I got off. A big guy like that comin' up to my desk. I felt like I
was chokin' like and all of a sudden I got a kind o' bad taste in my
mouth like when you get up in the mornin'. I didn't have no right to kill
him. The district attorney is right about that. He read the law to you,
right out o' the book. Killin' a bird—that's wrong. But there was that
girl, see? Six months they gave her. It was a dirty trick tellin' the cops on
her like that. I shouldn't 'a' done that. But what was I gonna do? The
wife wouldn't let up on me. I hadda do it. She used to walk around the
room, just in her undershirt, see? Nothin' else on. Just her undershirt.
An' they gave her six months. That's the last I'll ever see of her. Them
birds—how do they get away with it? Just grabbin' women, the way you
see 'em do in the pictures. I've seen lots I'd like to grab like that, but I
ain't got the nerve—in the subway an' on the street an' in the store buyin'
things. Pretty soft for 'them shoe salesmen, I'll say, lookin' at women's
legs all day. Them lawyers! They give me a pain, I tell you—a pain!
Sayin' the same thing over an' over again. I never said I didn't kill him.
But that ain't the same as bein' a regular murderer. What good did it do
me to kill him? I didn't make nothin' out of it. Answer yes or no! Yes
or no, me elbow! There's some things you can't answer yes or no. Give
me the once-over, you guys. Do I look like a murderer? Do I? I never
did no harm to nobody. Ask the wife. She'll tell you. Ask anybody. I
never got into trouble. You wouldn't count that one time at the Polo
Grounds. That was just fun like. Everybody was yellin', "Kill the empire!
Kill the empire!" An' before I knew what I was doin' I fired the pop
bottle. It was on account of everybody yellin' like that. Just in fun like,
see? The yeller dog! Callin' that one a strike—a mile away from the
plate. Anyhow, the bottle didn't hit him. An' when I seen the cop
comin' up the aisle, I beat it. That didn't hurt nobody. It was just in fun
like, see? An' that time in the subway. I was readin' about a lynchin',
see? Down in Georgia. They took the nigger an' they tied him to a tree.
An' they poured kerosene on him and lit a big fire under him. The dirty
nigger! Boy, I'd of liked to been there, with a gat in each hand, pumpin'
him full of lead. I was readin' about it in the subway, see? Right at
Times Square where the big crowd gets on. An' all of a sudden this big
nigger steps right on my foot. It was lucky for him I didn't have a gun
on me. I'd of killed him sure, I guess. I guess he couldn't help it all right
on account of the crowd, but a nigger's got no right to step on a white
man's foot. I told him where he got off all right. The dirty nigger. But
that didn't hurt nobody either. I'm a pretty steady guy, you gotta admit
that. Twenty-five years in one job an' I never missed a day. Fifty-two
weeks in a year. Fifty-two an' fifty-two an' fifty-two an'—They didn't
have t' look for me, did they? I didn't try to run away, did I? Where was
I goin' to run to! I wasn't thinkin' about it at all, see? I'll tell you what
I was thinkin' about—how I was goin' to break it to the wife about bein'
canned. He canned me after twenty-five years, see? Did the lawyers tell

you about that? I forget. All that talk gives me a headache. Objection sustained. Objection overruled. Answer yes or no. It gives me a headache. And I can't get the figgers outta my head neither. But that's what I was thinkin' about—how I was goin' t' break it to the wife about bein' canned. An' what Miss Devore would think when she heard about me killin' him. I bet she never thought I had the nerve to do it. I'd of married her if the wife had passed out. I'd be holdin' down my job yet if he hadn't o' canned me. But he kept talkin' an' talkin'. An' there was the bill file right where I could reach it. Do you get me? I'm just a regular guy like anybody else. Like you birds, now. (*For the first time the jurors relax, looking indignantly at each other and whispering.*)
Suppose you was me, now. Maybe you'd 'a' done the same thing. That's the way you oughta look at it, see? Suppose you was me——

JURORS (*rising as one and shouting in unison*)   *GUILTY!*
(ZERO *falls back, stunned for a moment by their vociferousness. The* JURORS *right-face in their places and file quickly out of the jury box and toward the door in a double column.*)

ZERO (*recovering speech as the* JURORS *pass out at the door*)   Wait a minute. Jest a minute. You don't get me right. Jest give me a chance an' I'll tell you how it was. I'm all mixed up, see? On account of them lawyers. And the figgers in my head. But I'm goin' to tell you how it was. I was there twenty-five years, see? An' they gave her six months, see?
(*He goes on haranguing the empty jury box as the curtain falls.*)
(*Curtain.*)

SCENE FIVE

In the middle of the stage is a large cage with bars on all four sides. The bars are very far apart and the interior of the cage is clearly visible. The floor of the cage is about six feet above the level of the stage. A flight of wooden steps lead up to it on the side facing the audience. ZERO *is discovered in the middle of the cage seated at a table above which is suspended a single naked electric light. Before him is an enormous platter of ham and eggs which he eats voraciously with a large wooden spoon. He wears a uniform of very broad black and white horizontal stripes. A few moments after the rise of the curtain a man enters at left wearing the blue uniform and peaked cap of a* GUIDE. *He is followed by a miscellaneous crowd of Men, Women, and Children—about a dozen in all.*

GUIDE (*stopping in front of the cage*)   Now ladies and gentlemen, if you'll kindly step right this way! (*The crowd straggles up and forms a loose semicircle around him.*) Step right up, please. A little closer so's everybody can hear. (*They move up closer.* ZERO *pays no attention whatever to them.*) This, ladies and gentlemen, is a very in-ter-est-in' specimen; the North American murderer, Genus homo sapiens, Habitat North America. (*A titter of excitement. They all crowd up around the cage.*) Don't push. There's room enough for everybody.

Note: This scene was part of the original script. It was omitted, however, when the play was produced, and was performed for the first time (in its present revised form) when the play was revived at the Phoenix Theatre in New York in February, 1956.-ELMER RICE

TALL LADY   Oh, how interesting!

STOUT LADY (*excitedly*)   Look, Charley, he's eating!

CHARLEY (*bored*)   Yeh, I see him.

GUIDE (*repeating by rote*)   This specimen, ladies and gentlemen, exhibits the
   characteristics which are typical of his kind——

SMALL BOY (*in a Little Lord Fauntleroy suit, whiningly*)   Mama!

MOTHER   Be quiet, Eustace, or I'll take you right home.

GUIDE   He has the opposable thumbs, the large cranial capacity, and the highly
   developed prefrontal areas which distinguish him from all other species.

YOUTH (*who has been taking notes*)   What areas did you say?

GUIDE (*grumpily*)   Pre-front-al areas. He learns by imitation and has a
   language which is said by some eminent philiologists to bear many
   striking resemblances to English.

BOY OF FOURTEEN   Pop, what's a philiologist?

FATHER   Keep quiet, can't you, and listen to what he's sayin'.

GUIDE   He thrives and breeds freely in captivity. This specimen was taken alive
   in his native haunts shortly after murdering his boss. (*Murmurs of great
   interest.*)

TALL LADY   Oh, how charming!

YOUTH (*again taking notes*)   What was that last? I didn't get it.

SEVERAL (*helpfully*)   Murdering his boss.

YOUTH   Oh—thanks.

GUIDE   He was tried, convicted and sentenced in one hour, thirteen minutes
   and twenty-four seconds, which sets a new record for the territory east
   of the Rockies and north of the Mason and Dixon line

LITTLE LORD FAUNTLEROY (*whiningly*)   Ma-ma!

MOTHER   Be quiet, Eustace, or Mama won't let you ride in the choo-choo.

GUIDE   Now take a good look at him, ladies and gents. It's his last day here.
   He's goin' to be executed at noon. (*Murmurs of interest.*)

TALL LADY   Oh, how lovely!

MAN   What's he eating?

GUIDE   Ham and eggs.

STOUT LADY   He's quite a big eater, ain't he?

GUIDE   Oh, he don't always eat that much. You see we always try to make
   'em feel good on their last day. So about a week in advance we let them
   order what they want to eat on their last day. They can have eight courses
   and they can order anything they want—don't make no difference what
   it costs or how hard it is to get. Well, he couldn't make up his mind till
   last night and then he ordered eight courses of ham and eggs. (*They all
   push and stare.*)

BOY OF FOURTEEN   Look, Pop! He's eatin' with a spoon. Don't he know how to
   use a knife and fork?

GUIDE (*overhearing him*)   We don't dare trust him with a knife and fork,
   sonny. He might try to kill himself.

TALL LADY   Oh, how fascinating!

GUIDE (*resuming his official tone*)   And now, friends, if you'll kindly give me your kind attention for just a moment. (*He takes a bundle of folders from his pocket.*) I have a little souvenir folder, which I'm sure you'll all want to have. It contains twelve beautiful colored views relating to the North American Murderer you have just been looking at. These include a picture of the murderer, a picture of the murderer's wife, the blood-stained weapon, the murderer at the age of six, the spot where the body was found, the little red schoolhouse where he went to school, and his vine-covered boyhood home in southern Illinois, with his sweet-faced, white-haired old mother plainly visible in the foreground. And many other interesting views. I'm now going to distribute these little folders for your examination. (*Sotto voce.*) Just pass them back, will you. (*In louder tones*) Don't be afraid to look at them. You don't have to buy them if you don't want to. It don't cost anything to look at them. (*To the* YOUTH, *who is fumbling with a camera*) Hey, there, young feller, no snapshots allowed. All right now, friends, if you'll just step this way. Keep close together and follow me. A lady lost her little boy here one time and by the time we found him, he was smoking cigarettes and hollering for a razor.

> (*Much laughter as they all follow him off left.* ZERO *finishes eating and pushes away his plate. As the crowd goes at left,* MRS. ZERO *enters at right. She is dressed in mourning garments. She carries a large parcel. She goes up the steps to the cage, opens the door and enters.* ZERO *looks up and sees her.*)

MRS. ZERO   Hello.

ZERO   Hello, I didn't think you were comin' again.

MRS. ZERO   Well, I thought I'd come again. Are you glad to see me?

ZERO   Sure. Sit down. (*She complies.*) You're all dolled up, ain't you?

MRS. ZERO   Yeh, don't you like it? (*She gets up and turns about like a mannequin.*)

ZERO   Gee. Some class.

MRS. ZERO   I always look good in black. There's some weight to this veil though; I'll tell the world. I got a fierce headache.

ZERO   How much did all that set you back?

MRS. ZERO   Sixty-four dollars and twenty cents. And I gotta get a pin yet and some writin' paper—you know, with black around the edges.

ZERO   You'll be scrubbin' floors in about a year, if you go blowin' your coin like that.

MRS. ZERO   Well, I gotta do it right. It don't happen every day. (*She rises and takes up the parcel.*) I brought you somethin'.

ZERO (*interested*)   Yeh, what?

MRS. ZERO (*opening the parcel*)   You gotta guess.

ZERO   Er—er—gee, search me.

MRS. ZERO   Somethin' you like. (*She takes out a covered plate.*)

ZERO (*with increasing interest*)   Looks like somethin' to eat.

MRS. ZERO (*nodding*)   Yeh. (*She takes off the top plate.*) Ham an' eggs!

ZERO (*joyfully*)   Oh, boy! Just what I feel like eatin'. (*He takes up the wooden spoon and begins to eat avidly.*)

MRS. ZERO (*pleased*)   Are they good?

ZERO (*his mouth full*)   Swell.

MRS. ZERO (*a little sadly*)   They're the last ones I'll ever make for you.

ZERO (*busily eating*)   Uh-huh.

MRS. ZERO   I'll tell you somethin'—shall I?

ZERO   Sure.

MRS. ZERO (*hesitantly*)   Well, all the while they were cookin' I was cryin'.

ZERO   Yeh? (*He leans over and pats her hand.*)

MRS. ZERO   I jest couldn't help it. The thought of it jest made me cry.

ZERO   Well—no use cryin' about it.

MRS. ZERO   I jest couldn't help it.

ZERO   Maybe this time next year you'll be fryin' eggs for some other bird.

MRS. ZERO   Not on your life.

ZERO   You never can tell.

MRS. ZERO   Not me. Once is enough for me.

ZERO   I guess you're right at that. Still, I dunno. You might jest happen to meet some guy——

MRS. ZERO   Well, if I do, there'll be time enough to think about it. No use borrowin' trouble.

ZERO   How do you like bein' alone in the house?

MRS. ZERO   Oh, it's all right.

ZERO   You got plenty room in the bed now, ain't you?

MRS. ZERO   Oh yeh. (*A brief pause*) It's kinda lonesome though—you know, wakin' up in the mornin' and nobody around to talk to.

ZERO   Yeh, I know. It's the same with me.

MRS. ZERO   Not that we ever did much talkin'.

ZERO   Well, that ain't it. It's just the idea of havin' somebody there in case you want to talk.

MRS. ZERO   Yeh, that's it. (*Another brief pause*) I guess maybe I use t'bawl you out quite a lot, didn't I?

ZERO   Oh well—no use talkin' about it now.

MRS. ZERO   We were always at it, weren't we?

ZERO   No more than other married folks, I guess.

MRS. ZERO (*dubiously*)   I dunno——

ZERO   I guess I gave you cause, all right.

MRS. ZERO   Well, I got my faults too.

ZERO   None of us are perfect.

MRS. ZERO   We got along all right, at that, didn't we?

ZERO   Sure! Better'n most.

MRS. ZERO   Remember them Sundays at the beach, in the old days!

ZERO   You bet. (*With a laugh*)   Remember that time I ducked you? Gee, you was mad!

MRS. ZERO (*with a laugh*)   I didn't talk to you for a whole week.

ZERO (*chuckling*)   Yeh, I remember.

MRS. ZERO   And the time I had pneumonia and you brought me them roses. Remember?

ZERO   Yeh, I remember. And when the doctor told me maybe you'd pass out, I nearly sat down and cried.

MRS. ZERO   Did you?

ZERO   I sure did.

MRS. ZERO   We had some pretty good times at that, didn't we?

ZERO   I'll say we did!

MRS. ZERO (*with a sudden soberness*)   It's all over now.

ZERO   All over is right. I ain't got much longer.

MRS. ZERO (*rising and going over to him*)   Maybe—maybe—if we had to do it over again, it would be different.

ZERO (*taking her hand*)   Yeh. We live and learn.

MRS. ZERO (*crying*)   If we only had another chance.

ZERO   It's too late now.

MRS. ZERO   It don't seem right, does it?

ZERO   It ain't right. But what can you do about it?

MRS ZERO   Ain't there somethin'—somethin' I can do for you—before——

ZERO   No. Nothin'. Not a thing.

MRS. ZERO   Nothin' at all?

ZERO   No. I can't think of anything. (*Suddenly*) You're takin' good care of that scrapbook, ain't you? With all the clippings in it?

MRS. ZERO   Oh, sure. I got it right on the parlor table. Right where everybody can see it.

ZERO (*pleased*)   It must be pretty near full, ain't it?

MRS. ZERO   All but about three pages.

ZERO   Well, there'll be more tomorrow. Enough to fill it, maybe. Be sure to get them all, will you?

MRS. ZERO   I will. I ordered the papers already.

ZERO   Gee, I never thought I'd have a whole book full of clippings all about myself. (*Suddenly*) Say, that's somethin' I'd like to ask you.

MRS. ZERO   What?

ZERO   Suppose you should get sick or be run over or somthin', what would happen to the book?

MRS. ZERO   Well, I kinda thought I'd leave it to little Beatrice Elizabeth.

ZERO   Who? Your sister's kid?

MRS. ZERO   Yeh.

ZERO   What would she want with it?

MRS. ZERO   Well, it's nice to have, ain't it? And I wouldn't know who else to give it to.

ZERO   Well, I don't want her to have it. That fresh little kid puttin' her dirty fingers all over it.

MRS. ZERO   She ain't fresh and she ain't dirty. She's a sweet little thing.

ZERO   I don't want her to have it.

MRS. ZERO   Who do you want to have it then?

ZERO   Well, I kinda thought I'd like Miss Devore to have it.

MRS. ZERO   Miss Devore?

ZERO Yeh. You know. Down at the store.

MRS. ZERO Why should she have it?

ZERO She'd take good care of it. And anyhow, I'd like her to have it.

MRS. ZERO Oh you would, would you?

ZERO Yes.

MRS ZERO Well, she ain't goin' to have it. Miss Devore! Where does she come in, I'd like to know, when I got two sisters and a niece.

ZERO I don't care nothin' about your sisters and your niece.

MRS. ZERO Well, I do! And Miss Devore ain't goin' to get it. Now put that in your pipe and smoke it.

ZERO What have you got to say about it? It's my book, ain't it?

MRS. ZERO No, it ain't. It's mine now—or it will be tomorrow. And I'm goin' to do what I like with it.

ZERO I should of given it to her in the first place, that's what I should of done.

MRS. ZERO Oh, should you? And what about me? Am I your wife or ain't I?

ZERO Why remind me of my troubles?

MRS. ZERO So it's Miss Devore all of a sudden, is it? What's been goin' on, I'd like to know, between you and Miss Devore?

ZERO Aw, tie a can to that!

MRS. ZERO Why didn't you marry Miss Devore, if you think so much of her?

ZERO I would if I'd met her first.

MRS. ZERO (*shrieking*) Ooh! A fine way to talk to me. After all I've done for you. You bum! You dirty bum! I won't stand for it! I won't stand for it!

> (*In a great rage* MRS. ZERO *takes up the dishes and smashes them on the floor. Then crying hysterically she opens the cage door, bangs it behind her, comes down the steps, and goes off toward left.* ZERO *stands gazing ruefully after her for a moment, and then with a shrug and a sigh begins picking up the pieces of broken crockery.*)

> (*As* MRS. ZERO *exits at left a door in the back of the cage opens and a* MAN *enters. He is dressed in a sky-blue padded silk dressing gown which is fitted with innumerable pockets. Under this he wears a pink silk union suit. His bare feet are in sandals. He wears a jaunty Panama hat with a red feather stuck in the brim. Wings are fastened to his sandals and to the shoulders of his dressing gown.* ZERO, *who is busy picking up the broken crockery, does not notice him at first. The* MAN *takes a gold toothpick and begins carefully picking his teeth, waiting for* ZERO *to notice him.* ZERO *happens to look up and suddenly sees the* MAN. *He utters a cry of terror and shrinks into a corner of the cage, trembling with fear.*)

ZERO (*hoarsely*) Who are you?

MAN (*calmly, as he pockets his toothpick*) I'm the Fixer from the Claim Department.

ZERO Whaddya want?

THE FIXER   It's no use, Zero. There are no miracles.

ZERO   I don't know what you're talkin' about.

THE FIXER   Don't lie, Zero. (*Holding up his hand*) And now that your course is run—now that the end is already in sight, you still believe that some thunderbolt, some fiery bush, some celestial apparition will intervene between you and extinction. But it's no use, Zero. You're done for.

ZERO (*vehemently*)   It ain't right! It ain't fair! I ain't gettin' a square deal!

THE FIXER (*wearily*)   They all say that, Zero. (*Mildly*) Now just tell me why you're not getting a square deal.

ZERO   Well, that addin' machine. Was that a square deal—after twenty-five years?

THE FIXER   Certainly—from any point of view, except a sentimental one. (*Looking at his wrist watch*) The machine is quicker, it never makes a mistake, it's always on time. It presents no problems of housing, traffic congestion, water supply, sanitation.

ZERO   It costs somethin' to buy them machines, I'll tell you that!

THE FIXER   Yes, you're right there. In one respect you have the advantage over the machine—the cost of manufacture. But we've learned from many years' experience, Zero, that the original cost is an inconsequential item compared to upkeep. Take the dinosaurs, for example. They literally ate themselves out of existence. I held out for them to the last. They were damned picturesque—but when it came to a question of the nitrate supply, I simply had to yield. (*He begins to empty and clean his pipe.*) And so with you. Zero. It costs a lot to keep up all that delicate mechanism of eye and ear and hand and brain which you've never put to any use. We can't afford to maintain it in idleness—and so you've got to go. (*He puts the pipe in one of his pockets.*)

ZERO (*falling to his knees, supplicatingly*)   Gimme a chance, gimme another chance!

THE FIXER   What would you do if I gave you another chance?

ZERO   Well—first thing I'd go out and look for a job.

THE FIXER   Adding figures?

ZERO   Well, I ain't young enough to take up somethin' new.

> (THE FIXER *takes out a police whistle and blows shrilly. Instantly two guards enter.*)

THE FIXER   Put the skids under him, boys, and make it snappy. (*He strolls away to the other side of the cage, and taking a nail clipper from a pocket, begins to clip his nails as the* GUARDS *seize* ZERO.)

ZERO (*struggling and shrieking*)   No! No! Don't take me away! Don't kill me! Gimme a chance! Gimme another chance!

GUARD (*soothingly*)   Ah, come on! Be a good fellow! It'll all be over in a minute!

ZERO   I don't want to die! I don't want to die! I want to live!

> (THE GUARDS *look at each other dubiously. Then one of them walks rather timidly over to* THE FIXER, *who is busy with his nails.*)

GUARD (*clearing his throat*)   H'm!

THE FIXER (*looking up*)   Well?

GUARD (*timidly*)   He says he wants to live.

THE FIXER   No. He's no good.

GUARD (*touching his cap, deferentially*)   Yes sir! (*He goes back to his companion and the two of them drag* ZERO *out at the back of the cage, still struggling and screaming.*)

> (THE FIXER *puts away his nail clippers, yawns, then goes to the table and sits on the edge of it. From a pocket he takes an enormous pair of horn-rimmed spectacles. Then from another pocket he takes a folded newspaper, which he unfolds carefully. It is colored comic supplement. He holds it up in front of him and becomes absorbed in it.*)
> (*A moment later the door at the back of the cage opens and a tall, brawny, bearded* MAN *enters. He wears a red flannel undershirt and carries a huge blood-stained axe.* THE FIXER, *absorbed in the comic supplement, does not look up.*)

MAN (*hoarsely*)   O.K.

THE FIXER (*looking up*)   What?

MAN   O.K.

THE FIXER (*nodding*)   Oh, all right. (*The* MAN *bows deferentially and goes out at the back.* THE FIXER *puts away his spectacles and folds the comic supplement carefully. As he folds the paper.*) That makes a total of 2,137 black eyes for Jeff.

> (*He puts away the paper, turns out the electric light over his head, and leaves the cage by the front door. Then he takes a padlock from a pocket, attaches it to the door, and saunters off.*)
> (*Curtain.*)

Scene Six

*A graveyard in full moonlight. It is a second-rate graveyard—no elaborate tombstones or monuments, just simple headstones and here and there a cross. At the back is an iron fence with a gate in the middle. At first no one is visible, but there are occasional sounds throughout: the hooting of an owl, the whistle of a distant whippoorwill, the croaking of a bullfrog, and the yowling of a serenading cat. After a few moments two figures appear outside the gate—a man and a woman. She pushes the gate and it opens with a rusty creak. The couple enter. They are now fully visible in the moonlight—*JUDY O'GRADY *and a* YOUNG MAN.

JUDY (*advancing*)   Come on, this is the place.

YOUNG MAN (*hanging back*)   This! Why this here is a cemetery.

JUDY   Aw, quit yer kiddin'!

YOUNG MAN   You don't mean to say——

JUDY   What's the matter with this place?

YOUNG MAN   A cemetery?

JUDY   Sure. What of it?

YOUNG MAN   You must be crazy.

JUDY   This place is all right, I tell you. I been here lots o' times.

YOUNG MAN   Nix on this place for me!

JUDY   Ain't this place as good as another? Whaddya afraid of? They're all dead ones here! They don't bother you. (*With sudden interest*) Oh, look, here's a new one.

YOUNG MAN   Come on out of here.

JUDY   Wait a minute. Let's see what it says. (*She kneels on a grave in the foreground and putting her face close to the headstone spells out the inscription.*) Z-E-R-O. Z-e-r-o. Zero! Say, that's the guy——

YOUNG MAN   Zero? He's the guy killed his boss, ain't he?

JUDY   Yeh, that's him, all right. But what I'm thinkin' of is that I went to the hoosegow on account of him.

YOUNG MAN   What for?

JUDY   You know, same old stuff. Tenement House Law. (*Mincingly*) Section blaa-blaa of the Penal Code. Third offense. Six months.

YOUNG MAN   And this bird—

JUDY (*contemptuously*)   Him? He was mama's whitehaired boy. We lived in the same house. Across the airshaft, see? I used to see him lookin' in my window. I guess his wife musta seen him too. Anyhow, they went and turned the bulls on me. And now I'm out and he's in. (*Suddenly.*) Say—say——(*She bursts into a peal of laughter.*)

YOUNG MAN (*nervously*)   What's so funny?

JUDY (*rocking with laughter*)   Say, wouldn't it be funny—if—if——(*She explodes again.*) That would be a good joke on him, all right, He can't do nothin' about it now, can he?

YOUNG MAN   Come on out of here. I don't like this place.

JUDY   Aw, you're a bum sport. What do you want to spoil my joke for?
(*A cat yammers mellifluously.*)

YOUNG MAN (*half hysterically*)   What's that?

JUDY   It's only the cats. They seem to like it here all right. But come on if you're afraid. (*They go toward the gate. As they go out.*) You nervous men sure are the limit.
(*They go out through the gate. As they disappear* ZERO'S *grave opens suddenly and his head appears.*)

ZERO (*looking about*)   That's funny! I thought I heard her talkin' and laughin'. But I don't see nobody. Anyhow, what would she be doin' here? I guess I must 'a' been dreamin'. But how could I be dreamin' when I ain't been asleep? (*He looks about again.*) Well, no use goin' back. I can't sleep anyhow. I might as well walk around a little. (*He rises out of the ground, very rigidly. He wears a full-dress suit of very antiquated cut and his hands are folded stiffly across his breast. Walking woodenly.*) Gee! I'm stiff! (*He slowly walks a few steps, then stops.*) Gee, it's lonesome here! (*He shivers and walks on aimlessly.*) I should 'a' stayed where I was. But I thought I heard her laughin'. (*A loud sneeze is heard.* ZERO *stands motionless, quaking with terror. The sneeze is repeated.* ZERO *says hoarsely.*) What's that?

A MILD VOICE   It's all right. Nothing to be afraid of.

(*From behind a headstone* SHRDLU *appears. He is dressed
in a shabby and ill-fitting cutaway. He wears
silver-rimmed spectacles and is smoking a cigarette.*)

SHRDLU   I hope I didn't frighten you.

ZERO (*still badly shaken*)   No-o. It's all right. You see, I wasn't expectin'
to see anybody.

SHRDLU   You're a newcomer, aren't you?

ZERO   Yeh, this is my first night. I couldn't seem to get to sleep.

SHRDLU   I can't sleep either. Suppose we keep each other company,
shall we?

ZERO (*eagerly*)   Yeh, that would be great. I been feelin' awful lonesome.

SHRDLU (*nodding*)   I know. Let's make ourselves comfortable.
(*He seats himself easily on a grave.* ZERO *tries to follow his
example but he is stiff in every joint and groans with pain.*)

ZERO   I'm kinda stiff.

SHRDLU   You mustn't mind the stiffness. It wears off in a few days. (*He
produces a package of cigarettes.*) Will you have a Camel?

ZERO   No, I don't smoke.

SHRDLU   I find it helps keep the mosquitoes away. (*He lights a cigarette.
Suddenly taking the cigarette out of his mouth.*) Do you mind if I smoke,
Mr.—Mr.—?

ZERO   No, go right ahead.

SHRDLU (*replacing the cigarette*)   Thank you. I didn't catch your name.
(ZERO *does not reply. Mildly.*) I say I didn't catch your name.

ZERO   I heard you the first time. (*Hesistantly*) I'm scared if I tell you who
I am and what I done, you'll be off me.

SHRDLU (*sadly*)   No matter what your sins may be, they are as snow
compared to mine.

ZERO   You got another guess comin'. (*He pauses dramatically.*) My name's
Zero. I'm a murderer.

SHRDLU (*nodding calmly*)   Oh, yes, I remember reading about you, Mr. Zero.

ZERO (*a little piqued*)   And you still think you're worse than me?

SHRDLU (*throwing away his cigarette*)   Oh, a thousand times worse,
Mr. Zero—a million times worse.

ZERO   What did you do?

SHRDLU   I, too, am a murderer.

ZERO (*looking at him in amazement*)   Go on! You're kiddin' me!

SHRDLU   Every word I speak is the truth, Mr. Zero. I am the foulest, the
most sinful of murderers! You only murdered your employer, Mr. Zero.
But I—I murdered my mother. (*He covers his face with his hands
and sobs.*)

ZERO (*horrified*)   The hell yer say!

SHRDLU (*sobbing*)   Yes, my mother! My beloved mother!

ZERO (*suddenly*)   Say, you don't mean to say you're Mr.——

SHRDLU (*nodding*)   Yes. (*He wipes his eyes, still quivering with emotion.*)

ZERO   I remember readin' about you in the papers.

SHRDLU   Yes, my guilt has been proclaimed to all the world. But that would be a trifle if only I could wash the stain of sin from my soul.

ZERO   I never heard of a guy killin' his mother before. What did you do it for?

SHRDLU   Because I have a sinful heart—there is no other reason.

ZERO   Did she always treat you square and all like that?

SHRDLU   She was a saint—a saint, I tell you. She cared for me and watched over me as only a mother can.

ZERO   You mean to say you didn't have a scrap or nothin'?

SHRDLU   Never a harsh or an unkind word. Nothing except loving care and good advice. From my infancy she devoted herself to guiding me on the right path. She taught me to be thrifty, to be devout, to be unselfish, to shun evil companions, and to shut my ears to all the temptations of the flesh—in short, to become a virtuous, respectable, and God-fearing man. (*He groans.*) But it was a hopeless task. At fourteen I began to show evidence of my sinful nature.

ZERO   (*breathlessly*)   You didn't kill anybody else, did you?

SHRDLU   No, thank God, there is only one murder on my soul. But I ran away from home.

ZERO   You did!

SHRDLU   Yes. A companion lent me a profane book—the only profane book I have ever read, I'm thankful to say. It was called *Treasure Island.* Have you ever read it?

ZERO   No, I never was much on readin' books.

SHRDLU   It is a wicked book—a lurid tale of adventure. But it kindled in my sinful heart a desire to go to sea. And so I ran away from home.

ZERO   What did you do—get a job as a sailor?

SHRDLU   I never saw the sea—not to the day of my death. Luckily my mother's loving intuition warned her of my intention and I was sent back home. She welcomed me with open arms. Not an angry word, not a look of reproach. But I could read the mute suffering in her eyes as we prayed together all through the night.

ZERO   (*sympathetically*)   Gee, that must 'a' been tough. Gee, the mosquitoes are bad, ain't they? (*He tries awkwardly to slap at them with his stiff hands.*)

SHRDLU   (*absorbed in his narrative*)   I thought that experience had cured me of evil and I began to think about a career. I wanted to go in foreign missions at first, but we couldn't bear the thought of the separation. So we finally decided that I should become a proofreader.

ZERO   Say, slip me one o' them Camels, will you? I'm gettin' all bit up.

SHRDLU   Certainly. (*He hands* ZERO *cigarettes and matches.*)

ZERO   (*lighting up*)   Go ahead. I'm listenin'.

SHRDLU   By the time I was twenty I had a good job reading proof for a firm that printed catalogues. After a year they promoted me and let me specialize in shoe catalogues.

ZERO   Yeh? That must 'a' been a good job.

SHRDLU   It was a very good job. I was on the shoe catalogues for thirteen years. I'd been on them yet, if I hadn't—— (*He chokes back a sob.*)

ZERO   They oughta put a shot o' citronella in that embalmin' fluid.

SHRDLU (*sighs*)   We were so happy together. I had my steady job. And Sundays we would go to morning, afternoon, and evening service. It was an honest and moral mode of life.

ZERO   It sure was.

SHRDLU   Then came that fatal Sunday. Dr. Amaranth, our minister, was having dinner with us—one of the few pure spirits on earth. When he had finished saying grace, we had our soup. Everything was going along as usual—we were eating our soup and discussing the sermon, just like every other Sunday I could remember. Then came the leg of lamb—— (*He breaks off, then resumes in a choking voice.*) I see the whole scene before me so plainly—it never leaves me—Dr. Amaranth at my right, my mother at my left, the leg of lamb on the table in front of me, and the cuckoo clock on the little shelf between the windows. (*He stops and wipes his eyes.*)

ZERO   Yeh, but what happened?

SHRDLU   Well, as I started to carve the lamb—— Did you ever carve a leg of lamb?

ZERO   No, corned beef was our speed.

SHRDLU   It's very difficult on account of the bone. And when there's gravy in the dish there's danger of spilling it. So Mother always used to hold the dish for me. She leaned forward, just as she always did, and I could see the gold locket around her neck. It had my picture in it and one of my baby curls. Well, I raised my knife to carve the leg of lamb—and instead I cut my mother's throat! (*He sobs.*)

ZERO   You must 'a' been crazy!

SHRDLU (*raising his head, vehemently*)   No! Don't try to justify me. I wasn't crazy. They tried to prove at the trial that I was crazy. But Dr. Amaranth saw the truth! He saw it from the first! He knew that it was my sinful nature—and he told me what was in store for me.

ZERO (*trying to be comforting*)   Well, your troubles are over now.

SHRDLU (*his voice rising*)   Over! Do you think this is the end?

ZERO   Sure. What more can they do to us?

SHRDLU (*his tones growing shriller and shriller*)   Do you think there can ever be any peace for such as we are—murderers, sinners? Don't you know what awaits us—flames, eternal flames!

ZERO (*nervously*)   Keep your shirt on, buddy—they wouldn't do that to us.

SHRDLU   There's no escape—no escape for us, I tell you. We're doomed! We're doomed to suffer unspeakable torments through all eternity. (*His voice rises higher and higher.*)

(*A grave opens suddenly and a head appears.*)

THE HEAD   Hey, you birds! Can't you shut up and let a guy sleep?

(ZERO *scrambles painfully to his feet.*)

ZERO (*to* SHRDLU)   Hey, put on the soft pedal.

SHRDLU (*too wrought up to attend*)   It won't be long now! We'll receive our summons soon.

THE HEAD   Are you goin' to beat it or not? (*He calls into the grave.*) Hey, Bill, lend me your head a minute. (*A moment later his arm appears holding a skull.*)

ZERO (*warningly*)   Look out! (*He seizes* SHRDLU *and drags him away just as* THE HEAD *throws the skull.*)

THE HEAD (*disgustedly*)   Missed 'em. Damn old tabby cats! I'll get 'em next time. (*A prodigious yawn.*) Ho-hum! Me for the worms!
> (THE HEAD *disappears as the curtain falls.*)
> (*Curtain.*)

Scene Seven

A pleasant place. A scene of pastoral loveliness. A meadow dotted with fine old trees and carpeted with rich grass and field flowers. In the background are seen a number of tents fashioned of gay-striped silks, and beyond gleams a meandering river. Clear air and a fleckless sky. Sweet distant music throughout.

At the rise of the curtain SHRDLU *is seen seated under a tree in the foreground in an attitude of deep dejection. His knees are drawn up and his head is buried in his arms. He is dressed as in the preceding scene.*

A few minutes later ZERO *enters at right. He walks slowly and looks about him with an air of half-suspicious curiosity. He too is dressed as in the preceding scene. Suddenly he sees* SHRDLU *seated under the tree. He stands still and looks at him half fearfully. Then, seeing something familiar in him, goes closer.* SHRDLU *is unaware of his presence. At last* ZERO *recognizes him and grins in pleased surprise.*

ZERO   Well, if it ain't——! (*He claps* SHRDLU *on the shoulder.*) Hello, buddy!
> (SHRDLU *looks up slowly, then, recognizing* ZERO, *he rises gravely and extends his hand courteously.*)

SHRDLU   How do you do, Mr. Zero? I'm very glad to see you again.

ZERO   Same here. I wasn't expectin' to see you either. (*Looking about.*) This is a kinda nice place. I wouldn't mind restin' here a while.

SHRDLU   You may if you wish.

ZERO   I'm kinda tired. I ain't used to bein' outdoors. I ain't walked so much in years.

SHRDLU   Sit down here, under the tree.

ZERO   Do they let you sit on the grass?

SHRDLU   Oh, yes.

ZERO (*seating himself*)   Boy, this feels good. I'll tell the world my feet are sore. I ain't used to so much walkin'. Say, I wonder would it be all right if I took my shoes off; my feet are tired.

SHRDLU   Yes. Some of the people here go barefoot.

ZERO   Yeh? They sure must be nuts. But I'm goin' t' leave 'em off for a while. So long as it's all right. The grass feels nice and cool. (*He stretches out comfortably.*) Say, this is the life of Riley all right, all right. This sure is a nice place. What do they call this place, anyhow?

SHRDLU The Elysian Fields.

ZERO The which?

SHRDLU The Elysian Fields.

ZERO (*dubiously*) Oh! Well it's a nice place, all right.

SHRDLU They say that this is the most desirable of all places. Only the most favored remain here.

ZERO Yeh? Well, that lets me out, I guess. (*Suddenly*) But what are you doin' here? I thought you'd be burned by now.

SHRDLU (*sadly*) Mr. Zero, I am the most unhappy of men.

ZERO (*in mild astonishment*) Why, because you ain't bein' roasted alive?

SHRDLU (*nodding*) Nothing is turning out as I expected. I saw everything so clearly—the flames, the tortures, an eternity of suffering as the just punishment for my unspeakable crime. And it has all turned out so differently.

ZERO Well, that's pretty soft for you, ain't it?

SHRDLU (*wailingly*) No, no, no! It's right and just that I should be punished. I could have endured it stoically. All through those endless ages of indescribable torment I should have exulted in the magnificence of divine justice. But this—this is maddening! What becomes of justice? What becomes of morality? What becomes of right and wrong? It's maddening—simply maddening! Oh, if Dr. Amaranth were only here to advise me! (*He buries his face and groans.*)

ZERO (*trying to puzzle it out*) You mean to say they ain't called you for cuttin' your mother's throat?

SHRDLU No! It's terrible—terrible! I was prepared for anything—anything but this.

ZERO Well, what did they say to you?

SHRDLU (*looking up*) Only I was to come here and remain until I understood.

ZERO I don't get it. What do they want you to understand?

SHRDLU (*despairingly*) I don't know—I don't know! If I only had an inkling of what they meant—— (*Interrupting himself.*) Just listen quietly for a moment: do you hear anything? (*They are both silent, straining their ears.*)

ZERO (*at last*) Nope.

SHRDLU You don't hear any music? Do you?

ZERO Music? I don't hear nothin'.

SHRDLU The people here say that the music never stops.

ZERO They're kiddin' you.

SHRDLU Do you think so?

ZERO Sure thing. There ain't a sound.

SHRDLU Perhaps. They're capable of anything. But I haven't told you of the bitterest of my disppointments.

ZERO Well, spill it. I'm gettin' used to hearin' bad news.

SHRDLU When I came to this place my first thought was to find my dear mother. I wanted to ask her forgiveness. And I wanted her to help me to understand.

ZERO An' she couldn't do it?

SHRDLU (*with a deep groan*)   She's not here, Mr. Zero! Here where only the most favored dwell, that wisest and purest of spirits is nowhere to be found. I don't understand it.

A WOMAN'S VOICE (*in the distance*)   Mr. Zero! Oh, Mr. Zero! (ZERO *raises his head and listens attentively.*)

SHRDLU (*going on, unheedingly*)   If you were to see some of the people here— the things they do——

ZERO (*interrupting*)   Wait a minute, will you? I think somebody's callin' me.

VOICE (*somewhat nearer*)   Mr. Ze-ro! Oh! Mr. Ze-ro!

ZERO   Who the hell's that now? I wonder if the wife's on my trail already. That would be swell, wouldn't it? An' I figgered on her bein' good for another twenty years anyhow.

VOICE (*nearer*)   Mr. Ze-ro! Yoo-hoo!

ZERO   No. That ain't her voice. (*Calling savagely.*) Yoo-hoo. (*To* SHRDLU.) Ain't that always the way? Just when a guy is takin' life easy an' havin' a good time! (*He rises and looks off left.*) Here she comes, whoever she is. (*In sudden amazement.*) Well, I'll be—! Well, what do you know about that!

> (*He stands looking in wonderment as* DAISY DIANA DOROTHEA DEVORE *enters. She wears a much-beruffled white muslin dress which is a size too small and fifteen years too youthful for her. She is red-faced and breathless.*)

DAISY (*panting*)   Oh! I thought I'd never catch up to you. I've been followin' you for days—callin' an' callin'. Didn't you hear me?

ZERO   Not till just now. You look kinda winded.

DAISY   I sure am. I can't hardly catch my breath.

ZERO   Well, sit down an' take a load off your feet. (*He leads her to the tree.*)
> (DAISY *sees* SHRDLU *for the first time and shrinks back a little.*)

ZERO   It's all right, he's a friend of mine. (*To* SHRDLU.) Buddy, I want you to meet my friend, Miss Devore.

SHRDLU (*rising and extending his hand courteously*)   How do you do, Miss Devore?

DAISY (*self-consciously*)   How do!

ZERO (*to* DAISY)   He's a friend of mine. (*To* SHRDLU.) I guess you don't mind if she sits here a while an' cools off, do you?

SHRDLU   No, no, certainly not.
> (*They all seat themselves under the tree.* ZERO *and* DAISY *are a little self-conscious.* SHRDLU *gradually becomes absorbed in his own thoughts.*)

ZERO   I was just takin' a rest myself. I took my shoes off on account of my feet bein' so sore.

DAISY   Yeh, I'm kinda tired too. (*Looking about.*) Say, ain't it pretty here though?

ZERO   Yeh, it is at that.

DAISY   What do they call this place?

ZERO   Why—er—let's see. He was tellin' me just a minute ago. The—er—I
don't know. Some kind o' fields. I forget now. (*To* SHRDLU.) Say, buddy,
what do they call this place again? (SHRDLU, *absorbed in his thoughts,
does not hear him. To* DAISY.) He don't hear me. He's thinkin' again.

DAISY (*sotto voce*)   What's the matter with him?

ZERO   Why, he's the guy that murdered his mother—remember?

DAISY (*interested*)   Oh, hey! Is that him?

ZERO   Yeh. An' he had it all figgered out how they was goin' t' roast him or
somethin'. And now they ain't goin' to do nothin' to him an' it's kinda
got his goat.

DAISY (*sympathetically*)   Poor feller!

ZERO   Yeh. He takes it kinda hard.

DAISY   He looks like a nice young feller.

ZERO   Well, you sure are good for sore eyes. I never expected to see you here.

DAISY   I thought maybe you'd be kinda surprised.

ZERO   Surprised is right. I thought you was alive an' kickin'. When did you
pass out?

DAISY   Oh, right after you did—a coupla days.

ZERO (*interested*)   Yeh? What happened? Get hit by a truck or somethin'?

DAISY   No. (*hesitantly*) You see—it's this way. I blew out the gas.

ZERO (*astonished*)   Go on! What was the big idea?

DAISY (*falteringly*)   Oh, I don't know. You see, I lost my job.

ZERO   I'll bet you're sorry you did it now, ain't you?

DAISY (*with conviction*)   No. I ain't sorry. Not a bit. (*Then hesitantly*) Say,
Mr. Zero, I been thinkin'—(*She stops*)

ZERO   What?

DAISY (*plucking up courage*)   I been thinkin' it would be kinda nice—if you an'
me—if we could kinda talk things over.

ZERO   Yeh. Sure. What do you want to talk about?

DAISY   Well—I don't know—but you and me—we ain't really ever talked
things over, have we?

ZERO   No, that's right, we ain't. Well, let's go to it.

DAISY   I was thinkin' if we could be alone—just the two of us, see?

ZERO   Oh, yeh! Yeh, I get you. (*He turns to* SHRDLU *and coughs loudly.* SHRDLU
does not stir.)

ZERO (*to* DAISY)   He's dead to the world. (*He turns to* SHRDLU). Say, buddy!
(*No answer.*) Say, buddy!

SHRDLU (*looking up with a start*)   Were you speaking to me?

ZERO   Yeh. How'd you guess it? I was thinkin' that maybe you'd like to walk
around a little and look for your mother.

SHRDLU (*shaking his head*)   It's no use. I've looked everywhere. (*He relapses
into thought again.*)

ZERO   Maybe over there they might know.

SHRDLU   No, no! I've searched everywhere. She's not here.

(ZERO *and* DAISY *look at each other in despair.*)

ZERO   Listen, old shirt, my friend here and me—see?—we used to work in the
same store. An' we got some things to talk over—business, see?—kinda

confidential. So if it ain't askin' too much—

SHRDLU (*springing to his feet*)   Why, certainly! Excuse me! (*He bows politely to* DAISY *and walks off.* DAISY *and* ZERO *watch him until he has disappeared.*)

ZERO (*with a forced laugh*)   He's a good guy at that.

(*Now that they are alone, both are very self-conscious, and for a time they sit in silence.*)

DAISY (*breaking the silence*)   It sure is pretty here, ain't it?

ZERO   Sure is.

DAISY   Look at the flowers! Ain't they just perfect! Why, you'd think they was artificial, wouldn't you?

ZERO   Yeh, you would.

DAISY   And the smell of them. Like perfume.

ZERO   Yeh.

DAISY   I'm crazy about the country, ain't you?

ZERO   Yeh. It's nice for a change.

DAISY   Them store picnics—remember?

ZERO   You bet. They sure was fun.

DAISY   One time—I guess you don't remember—the two of us—me and you— we sat down on the grass together under a tree— just like we're doin' now.

ZERO   Sure I remember.

DAISY   Go on! I'll bet you don't.

ZERO   I'll bet I do. It was the year the wife didn't go.

DAISY (*her face brightening*)   That's right! I didn't think you'd remember.

ZERO   An' comin' home we sat together in the truck.

DAISY (*eagerly, rather shamefacedly*)   Yeh! There's somethin' I've always wanted to ask you.

ZERO   Well, why didn't you?

DAISY   I don't know. It didn't seem refined. But I'm goin' to ask you now anyhow.

ZERO   Go ahead. Shoot.

DAISY (*falteringly*)   Well—while we was comin' home—you put your arm up on the bench behind me—and I could feel your knee kinda pressin' against mine. (*She stops.*)

ZERO (*becoming more and more interested*)   Yeh—well, what about it?

DAISY   What I wanted to ask you was—was it just kinda accidental?

ZERO (*with a laugh*)   Sure it was accidental. Accidental on purpose.

DAISY (*eagerly*)   Do you mean it?

ZERO   Sure I mean it. You mean to say you didn't know it?

DAISY   No. I've been wantin' to ask you—

ZERO   Then why did you get sore at me?

DAISY   Sore? I wasn't sore! When was I sore?

ZERO   That night. Sure you was sore. If you wasn't sore why did you move away?

DAISY   Just to see if you meant it. I thought if you meant it you'd move up closer. An' then when you took your arm away I was sure you didn't mean it.

ZERO   An' I thought all the time you was sore. That's why I took my arm away. I thought if I moved up you'd holler and then I'd be in a jam, like you read in the paper all the time about guys gettin' pulled in for annoyin' women.

DAISY   An' I was wishin' you'd put your arm around me —just sittin' there wishin' all the way home.

ZERO   What do you know about that? That sure is hard luck, that is. If I'd 'a' only knew! You know what I felt like doin'—only I didn't have the nerve?

DAISY   What?

ZERO   I felt like kissin' you.

DAISY (*fervently*)   I wanted you to.

ZERO (*astonished*)   You would 'a' let me?

DAISY   I wanted you to! I wanted you to! Oh, why didn't you—why didn't you?

ZERO   I didn't have the nerve. I sure was a dumbbell.

DAISY   I would 'a' let you all you wanted to. I wouldn't 'a' cared. I know it would 'a' been wrong but I wouldn't 'a' cared. I wasn't thinkin' about right an' wrong at all. I didn't care—see? I just wanted you to kiss me.

ZERO (*feelingly*)   If I'd only knew. I wanted to do it, I swear I did. But I didn't think you cared nothin' about me.

DAISY (*passionately*)   I never cared nothin' about nobody else.

ZERO   Do you mean it—on the level? You ain't kiddin' me, are you?

DAISY   No, I ain't kiddin'. I mean it. I'm tellin' you the truth. I ain't never had the nerve to tell you before—but now I don't care. It don't make no difference now. I mean it—every word of it.

ZERO (*dejectedly*)   If I'd only knew it.

DAISY   Listen to me. There's somethin' else I want to tell you. I may as well tell you everything now. It don't make no difference now. About my blowin' out the gas—see? Do you know why I done it?

ZERO   Yeh, you told me—on account o' bein' canned.

DAISY   I just told you that. That ain't the real reason. The real reason is on account o' you.

ZERO   You mean to say on account o' me passin' out?

DAISY   Yeh. That's it. I didn't want to go on livin'. What for? What did I want to go on livin' for? I didn't have nothin' to live for with you gone. I often thought of doin' it before. But I never had the nerve. An' anyhow I didn't want to leave you.

ZERO   An' me bawlin' you out, about readin' too fast an' readin' too slow.

DAISY (*reproachfully*)   Why did you do it?

ZERO   I don't know, I swear I don't. I was always stuck on you. An' while I'd be addin' them figgers, I'd be thinkin' how if the wife died, you an' me could get married.

DAISY   I used to think o' that too.

ZERO   An' then before I knew it I was bawlin' you out.

DAISY   Them was the times I'd think o' blowin' out the gas. But I never did till you was gone. There wasn't nothin' to live for then. But it wasn't so easy to do anyhow. I never could stand the smell o' gas. An' all the while I was gettin' ready, you know, stuffin' up all the cracks, the way you read about in the paper—I was thinkin' of you and hopin' that maybe I'd meet you again. An' I made up my mind if I ever did see you, I'd tell you.

ZERO (*taking her hand*)   I'm sure glad you did. I'm sure glad. (*Ruefully.*) But it don't do much good now, does it?

DAISY   No, I guess it don't. (*Summoning courage.*) But there's one thing I'm goin' to ask you.

ZERO   What's that?

DAISY (*in a low voice*)   I want you to kiss me.

ZERO   You bet I will! (*He leans over and kisses her cheek.*)

DAISY   Not like that. I don't mean like that. I mean really kiss me. On the mouth. I ain't never been kissed like that.

> (ZERO *puts his arms about her and presses his lips to*
> *hers. A long embrace. At last they separate and sit side*
> *by side in silence.*)

DAISY (*putting her hands to her cheeks*)   So that's what it's like. I didn't know it could be like that. I didn't know anythin' could be like that.

ZERO (*fondling her hand*)   Your cheeks are red. They're all red. And your eyes are shinin'. I never seen your eyes shinin' like that before.

DAISY (*holding up her hand*)   Listen—do you hear it? Do you hear the music?

ZERO   No, I don't hear nothin'!

DAISY   Yeh—music. Listen an' you'll hear it. (*They are both silent for a moment.*)

ZERO (*excitedly*)   Yeh! I hear it! He said there was music, but I didn't hear it till just now.

DAISY   Ain't it grand?

ZERO   Swell! Say, do you know what?

DAISY   What?

ZERO   It makes me feel like dancin'.

DAISY   Yeh? Me too.

ZERO (*springing to his feet*)   Come on! Let's dance! (*He seizes her hands and tries to pull her up.*)

DAISY (*resisting laughingly*)   I can't dance. I ain't danced in twenty years.

ZERO   That's nothin'. I ain't neither. Come on! I feel just like a kid! (*He pulls her to her feet and seizes her about the waist.*)

DAISY   Wait a minute! Wait till I fix my skirt. (*She turns back her skirts and ins them above the ankles.*)

> (ZERO *seizes her about the waist. They dance clumsily*
> *but with gay abandon.* DAISY's *hair becomes loosened*
> *and tumbles over her shoulders. She lends herself more*
> *and more to the spirit of the dance. But* ZERO *soon begins*
> *to tire and dances with less and less zest.*)

ZERO (*stopping at last, panting for breath*)   Wait a minute! I'm all winded. (*He releases* DAISY, *but before he can turn away, she throws her arms about him and presses her lips to his. Freeing himself.*) Wait a minute!

Let me get my wind! (*He limps to the tree and seats himself under it, gasping for breath.* DAISY *looks after him, her spirits rather dampened.*) Whew! I sure am winded! I ain't used to dancin'. (*He takes off his collar and tie and opens the neckband of his shirt.* DAISY *sits under the tree near him, looking at him longingly. But he is busy catching his breath.*) Gee, my heart's goin' a mile a minute.

DAISY   Why don't you lay down an' rest? You could put your head on my lap.

ZERO   That ain't a bad idea. (*He stretches out, his head in* DAISY'S *lap.*)

DAISY (*fondling his hair*)   It was swell, wasn't it?

ZERO   Yeh. But you gotta be used to it.

DAISY   Just imagine if we could stay here all the time—you an' me together— wouldn't it be swell?

ZERO   Yeh. But there ain't a chance.

DAISY   Won't they let us stay?

ZERO   No. This place is only for the good ones.

DAISY   Well, we ain't so bad, are we?

ZERO   Go on! Me a murderer an' you committin' suicide. Anyway, they wouldn't stand for this—the way we been goin' on.

DAISY   I don't see why.

ZERO   You don't! You know it ain't right. Ain't I got a wife?

DAISY   Not any more you ain't. When you're dead that ends it. Don't they always say "until death do us part"?

ZERO   Well, maybe you're right about that but they wouldn't stand for us here.

DAISY   It would be swell—the two of us together—we could make up for all them years.

ZERO   Yeh, I wish we could.

DAISY   We sure were fools. But I don't care. I've got you now. (*She kisses his forehead and cheeks and mouth.*)

ZERO   I'm sure crazy about you. I never saw you lookin' so pretty before, with your cheeks all red. An' your hair hangin' down. You got swell hair. (*He fondles and kisses her hair.*)

DAISY (*ecstatically*)   We got each other now, ain't we?

ZERO   Yeh. I'm crazy about you. Daisy! That's a pretty name. It's a flower, ain't it? Well—that's what you are—just a flower.

DAISY (*happily*)   We can always be together now, can't we?

ZERO   As long as they'll let us. I sure am crazy about you. (*Suddenly he sits upright.*) Watch your step!

DAISY (*alarmed*)   What's the matter?

ZERO (*nervously*)   He's comin' back.

DAISY   Oh, is that all? Well, what about it?

ZERO   You don't want him to see us layin' around like this, do you?

DAISY   I don't care if he does.

ZERO   Well, you oughta care. You don't want him to think you ain't a refined girl, do you? He's an awful moral bird, he is.

DAISY   I don't care nothin' about him. I don't care nothin' about anybody but you.

ZERO   Sure, I know. But we don't want people talkin' about us. You better fix your hair an' pull down your skirts. (DAISY *complies rather sadly. They are both silent as* SHRDLU *enters. With feigned nonchalance.*)   Well, you got back all right, didn't you?

SHRDLU   I hope I haven't returned too soon.

ZERO   No, that's all right. We were just havin' a little talk. You know—about business an' things.

DAISY (*boldly*)   We were wishin' we could stay here all the time.

SHRDLU   You may if you like.

ZERO and DAISY (*in astonishment*)   What!

SHRDLU   Yes. Anyone who likes may remain——

ZERO   But I thought you were tellin' me——

SHRDLU   Just as I told you, only the most favored do remain. But anyone may.

ZERO   I don't get it. There's a catch in it somewheres.

DAISY   It don't matter as long as we can stay.

ZERO (*to* SHRDLU)   We were thinkin' about gettin' married, see?

SHRDLU   You may or may not, just as you like.

ZERO   You don't mean to say we could stay if we didn't, do you?

SHRDLU   Yes. They don't care.

ZERO   An' there's some here that ain't married?

SHRDLU   Yes.

ZERO (*to* DAISY)   I don't know about this place, at that. They must be kind of a mixed crowd.

DAISY   It don't matter, so long as we got each other.

ZERO   Yeh, I know, but you don't want to mix with people that ain't respectable.

DAISY (*to* SHRDLU)   Can we get married right away? I guess there must be a lot of ministers here, ain't there?

SHRDLU   Not as many as I had hoped to find. The two who seem most beloved are Dean Swift and the Abbé Rabelais. They are both much admired for some indecent tales which they have written.

ZERO (*shocked*)   What! Ministers writin' smutty stories! Say, what kind of a dump is this anyway?

SHRDLU (*despairingly*)   I don't know, Mr. Zero. All these people here are so strange, so unlike the good people I've known. They seem to think of nothing but enjoyment or of wasting their time in profitless occupations. Some paint pictures from morning until night, or carve blocks of stone. Others write songs or put words together, day in and day out. Still others do nothing but lie under the trees and look at the sky. There are men who spend all their time reading books and women who think only of adorning themselves. And forever they are telling stories and laughing and singing and drinking and dancing. There are drunkards, thieves, vagabonds, blasphemers, adulterers. There is one——

ZERO   That's enough. I heard enough. (*He seats himself and begins putting on his shoes.*)

DAISY (*anxiously*)   What are you goin' to do?

ZERO   I'm goin' to beat it, that's what I'm goin' to do.

DAISY   You said you liked it here.

ZERO (*looking at her in amazement*)   Liked it! Say, you don't mean to say you want to stay here, do you, with a lot of rummies an' loafers an' bums?

DAISY   We don't have to bother with them. We can just sit here together an' look at the flowers an' listen to the music.

SHRDLU (*eagerly*)   Music! Did you hear music?

DAISY   Sure. Don't you hear it?

SHRDLU   No, they say it never stops. But I've never heard it.

ZERO (*listening*)   I thought I heard it before but I don't hear nothin' now. I guess I must 'a' been dreamin'. (*Looking about.*) What's the quickest way out of this place?

DAISY (*pleadingly*)   Won't you stay just a little longer?

ZERO   Didn't yer hear me say I'm goin'? Good-by, Miss Devore. I'm goin' to beat it. (*He limps off at the right.* DAISY *follows him slowly.*)

DAISY (*to* SHRDLU)   I won't ever see him again.

SHRDLU   Are you goin' to stay here?

DAISY   It don't make no difference now. Without him I might as well be alive.
> (*She goes off right.* SHRDLU *watches her a moment, then sighs and seating himself under the tree, buries his head on his arm.*)
> (*Curtain.*)

Scene Eight

Before the curtain rises the clicking of an adding machine is heard. The curtain rises upon an office similar in appearance to that in Scene II except that there is a door in the back wall through which can be seen a glimpse of the corridor outside. In the middle of the room ZERO *is seated completely absorbed in the operation of an adding machine. He presses the keys and pulls the lever with mechanical precision. He still wears his full-dress suit but he has added to it sleeve-protectors and a green eyeshade. A strip of white paper-tape flows steadily from the machine as* ZERO *operates. The room is filled with this tape—streamers, festoons, billows of it everywhere. It covers the floor and the furniture, it climbs the walls and chokes the doorways. A few moments later* LIEUTENANT CHARLES *and* JOE *enter at the left.* LIEUTENANT CHARLES *is middle-aged and inclined to corpulence. He has an air of world-weariness. He is barefooted, wears a Panama hat, and is dressed in bright red tights which are a very bad fit—too tight in some places, badly wrinkled in others.* JOE *is a youth with a smutty face dressed in dirty blue overalls.*

CHARLES (*after contemplating* ZERO *for a few moments*)   All right, Zero, cease firing.

ZERO (*looking up, surprised*)   Whaddja say?

CHARLES   I said stop punching that machine.

ZERO (*bewildered*)   Stop? (*He goes on working mechanically.*)

CHARLES (*impatiently*)   Yes. Can't you stop? Here, Joe, give me a hand. He can't stop.
> (JOE *and* CHARLES *each take one of* ZERO's *arms and with enormous effort detach him from the machine. He resists*

*passively—mere inertia. Finally they succeed and swing
him around on his stool.* CHARLES *and* JOE *mop their
foreheads.*)

ZERO (*querulously*)   What's the idea? Can't you lemme alone?

CHARLES (*ignoring the question*)   How long have you been here?

ZERO   Jes' twenty-five years. Three hundred months, ninety-one hundred and
thirty-one days, one hundred thirty-six thousand——

CHARLES (*impatiently*)   That'll do! That'll do!

ZERO (*proudly*)   I ain't missed a day, not an hour, not a minute. Look at all
I got done. (*He points to the maze of paper.*)

CHARLES   It's time to quit.

ZERO   Quit? Whaddya mean quit? I ain't goin' to quit!

CHARLES   You've got to.

ZERO   What for? What do I have to quit for?

CHARLES   It's time for you to go back.

ZERO   Go back where? Whaddya talkin' about?

CHARLES   Back to earth, you dub. Where do you think?

ZERO   Aw, go on, Cap, who are you kiddin'?

CHARLES   I'm not kidding anybody. And don't call me Cap. I'm a lieutenant.

ZERO   All right, Lieutenant, all right. But what's this you're tryin' to tell me
about goin' back?

CHARLES   Your time's up, I'm telling you. You must be pretty thick. How
many times do you want to be told a thing?

ZERO   This is the first time I heard about goin' back. Nobody ever said
nothin' to me about it before.

CHARLES   You didn't think you were going to stay here forever, did you?

ZERO   Sure. Why not? I did my bit, didn't I? Forty-five years of it.
Twenty-five years in the store. Then the boss canned me and I knocked
him cold. I guess you ain't heard about that——

CHARLES (*interrupting*)   I know all about that. But what's that got to do with it?

ZERO   Well, I done my bit, didn't I? That oughta let me out.

CHARLES (*jeeringly*)   So you think you're all through, do you?

ZERO   Sure, I do. I did the best I could while I was there and then I passed
out. And now I'm sittin' pretty here.

CHARLES   You've got a fine idea of the way they run things, you have. Do you
think they're going to all of the trouble of making a soul just to use
it once?

ZERO   Once is often enough, it seems to me.

CHARLES   It seems to you, does it? Well, who are you? And what do you
know about it? Why, man, they use a soul over and over again—over
and over until it's worn out.

ZERO   Nobody ever told me.

CHARLES   So you thought you were all through, did you? Well, that's a hot
one, that is.

ZERO (*sullenly*)   How was I to know?

CHARLES   Use your brains! Where would we put them all! We're crowded
enough as it is. Why, this place is nothing but a kind of repair and
service station—a sort of cosmic laundry, you might say. We get the

souls in here by the bushelful. Then we get busy and clean them up. And you ought to see some of them. The muck and the slime. Phoo! And as full of holes as a flour sifter. But we fix them up. We disinfect them and give them a kerosene rub and mend the holes and back they go—practically as good as new.

ZERO You mean to say I've been here before—before the last time, I mean?

CHARLES Been here before! Why, you poor boob—you've been here thousands of times—fifty thousand at least.

ZERO (*suspiciously*) How is it I don't remember nothin' about it?

CHARLES Well—that's partly because you're stupid. But it's mostly because that's the way they fix it. (*Musingly.*) They're funny that way—every now and then they'll do something white like that—when you'd least expect it. I guess economy's at the bottom of it though. They figure that the souls would get worn out quicker if they remembered.

ZERO And don't any of 'em remember?

CHARLES Oh, some do. You see there's different types: there's the type that gets a little better each time it goes back—we just give them a wash and send them right through. Then there's another type—the type that gets a little worse each time. That's where you belong!

ZERO (*offended*) Me? You mean to say I'm gettin' worse all the time?

CHARLES (*nodding*) Yes. A little worse each time.

ZERO Well—what was I when I started? Somethin' big? A king or somethin'?

CHARLES (*laughing derisively*) A king! That's a good one! I'll tell you what you were the first time—if you want to know so much—a monkey.

ZERO (*shocked and offended*) A monkey!

CHARLES (*nodding*) Yes, sir—just a hairy, chattering, long-tailed monkey.

ZERO That musta been a long time ago.

CHARLES Oh, not so long. A million years or so. Seems like yesterday to me.

ZERO Then look here, whaddya mean by sayin' I'm gettin' worse all the time?

CHARLES Just what I said. You weren't so bad as a monkey. Of course, you did just what all the other monkeys did, but still it kept you out in the open air. And you weren't woman-shy—there was one little red-headed monkey— Well, never mind. Yes, sir, you weren't so bad then. But even in those days there must have been some bigger and brainier monkey that you kowtowed to. The mark of the slave was on you from the start.

ZERO (*sullenly*) You ain't very particular about what you call people, are you?

CHARLES You wanted the truth, didn't you? If there ever was a soul in the world that was labeled slave it's yours. Why, all the bosses and kings that there ever were have left their trademarks on your backside.

ZERO It ain't fair, if you ask me.

CHARLES (*shrugging his shoulders*) Don't tell me about it. I don't make the rules. All I know is, you've been getting worse—worse each time. Why, even six thousand years ago you weren't so bad. That was the time you were hauling stones for one of those big pyramids in a place they call Africa. Ever hear of the pyramids?

ZERO Them big pointy things?

CHARLES (*nodding*) That's it.

ZERO I seen a picture of them in the movies.

CHARLES   Well, you helped build them. It was a long step down from the happy days in the jungle, but it was a good job—even though you didn't know what you were doing and your back was striped by the foreman's whip. But you've been going down, down. Two thousand years ago you were a Roman galley slave. You were on one of the triremes that knocked the Carthaginian fleet for a goal. Again the whip. But you had muscles then—chest muscles, back muscles, biceps. (*He feels* ZERO's *arm gingerly and turns away in disgust.*) Phoo! A bunch of mush! (*He notices that* JOE *has fallen asleep. Walking over, he kicks him in the shin.*) Wake up, you mutt! Where do you think you are! (*He turns to* ZERO *again.*) And then another thousand years and you were a serf—a lump of clay digging up other lumps of clay. You wore an iron collar then—white ones hadn't been invented yet. Another long step down. But where you dug, potatoes grew, and that helped fatten the pigs. Which was something. And now—well, I don't want to rub it in——

ZERO   Rub it in is right! Seems to me I got a pretty healthy kick comin'. I ain't had a square deal! Hard work! That's all I've ever had!

CHARLES   (*callously*)   What else were you ever good for?

ZERO   Well, that ain't the point. The point is I'm through! I had enough! Let 'em find somebody else to do the dirty work. I'm sick of bein' the goat! I quit right here and now! (*He glares about defiantly. There is a thunderclap and a bright flash of lightning. Screaming.*) Ooh! What's that? (*He clings to* CHARLES.)

CHARLES   It's all right. Nobody's going to hurt you. It's just their way of telling you that they don't like you to talk that way. Pull yourself together and calm down. You can't change the rules—nobody can— they've got it all fixed. It's a rotten system—but what are you going to do about it?

ZERO   Why can't they stop pickin' on me? I'm satisfied here—doin' my day's work. I don't want to go back.

CHARLES   You've got to, I tell you. There's no way out of it.

ZERO   What chance have I got—at my age? Who'll give me a job?·

CHARLES   You big boob, you don't think you're going back the way you are, do you?

ZERO   Sure, how then?

CHARLES   Why, you've got to start all over.

ZERO   All over?

CHARLES   (*nodding*)   You'll be a baby again—a bald, red-faced little animal, and then you'll go through it all again. There'll be millions of others like you—all with their mouths open, squalling for food. And then when you get a little older you'll begin to learn things—and you'll learn all the wrong things and learn them all in the wrong way. You'll eat the wrong food and wear the wrong clothes, and you'll live in swarming dens where there's no light and no air! You'll learn to be a liar and a bully and a braggart and a coward and a sneak. You'll learn to fear the sunlight and to hate beauty. By that time you'll be ready for school. There they'll tell you the truth about a great many things that you don't give a damn

about, and they'll tell you lies about all the things you ought to know—
and about all the things you want to know they'll tell you nothing at all.
When you get through you'll be equipped for your life work. You'll be
ready to take a job.

ZERO (*eagerly*)   What'll my job be? Another adding machine?

CHARLES   Yes. But not one of these antiquated adding machines. It will be a
superb, super-hyper-adding machine, as far from this old piece of junk
as you are from God. It will be something to make you sit up and take
notice, that adding machine. It will be an adding machine which will be
installed in a coal mine and which will record the individual output of
each miner. As each miner down in the lower galleries takes up a
shovelful of coal, the impact of his shovel will automatically set in
motion a graphite pencil in your gallery. The pencil will make a mark in
white upon a blackened, sensitized drum. Then your work comes in.
With the great toe of your right foot you release a lever which focuses
a violet ray on the drum. The ray, playing upon and through the white
mark, falls upon a selenium cell which in turn sets the keys of the adding
apparatus in motion. In this way the individual output of each miner is
recorded without any human effort except the slight pressure of the
great toe of your right foot.

ZERO (*in breathless, round-eyed wonder*)   Say, that'll be some machine, won't it?

CHARLES   Some machine is right. It will be the culmination of human effort—
the final triumph of the evolutionary process. For millions of years the
nebulous gases swirled in space. For more millions of years the gases
cooled and then through inconceivable ages they hardened into rocks.
And then came life. Floating green things on the waters that covered the
earth. More millions of years and a step upward—an animate organism
in the ancient slime. And so on—step by step, down through the ages—
a gain here, a gain there—the mollusk, the fish, the reptile, then
mammal, man! And all so that you might sit in the gallery of a coal
mine and operate the super-hyper-adding machine with the great toe of
your right foot!

ZERO   Well, then—I ain't so bad after all.

CHARLES   You're a failure, Zero, a failure. A waste product. A slave to a
contraption of steel and iron. The animal's instincts, but not his strength
and skill. The animal's appetites, but not his unashamed indulgence of
them. True, you move and eat and digest and excrete and reproduce.
But any microscopic organism can do as much. Well—time's up! Back
you go—back to your sunless groove—the raw material of slums and
wars—the ready prey of the first jingo or demagogue or political
adventurer who takes the trouble to play upon your ignorance and
credulity and provincialism. You poor, spineless, brainless boob—I'm
sorry for you!

ZERO (*falling to his knees*)   Then keep me here! Don't send me back! Let me stay!

CHARLES   Get up. Didn't I tell you I can't do anything for you? Come on,
time's up!

ZERO   I can't! I can't! I'm afraid to go through it all again.

CHARLES   You've got to, I tell you. Come on, now!

ZERO   What did you tell me so much for? Couldn't you just let me go, thinkin' everythin' was goin' to be all right?

CHARLES   You wanted to know, didn't you?

ZERO   How did I know what you were goin' to tell me? Now I can't stop thinkin' about it! I can't stop thinkin'! I'll be thinkin' about it all the time.

CHARLES   All right! I'll do the best I can for you. I'll send a girl with you to keep you company.

ZERO   A girl? What for? What good will a girl do me?

CHARLES   She'll help make you forget.

ZERO (*eagerly*)   She will? Where is she?

CHARLES   Wait a minute, I'll call her. (*He calls in a loud voice.*) Oh! Hope! Yoo-hoo! (*He turns his head aside and speaks in the manner of a ventriloquist imitating a distant feminine voice.*) Ye-es. (*Then in his own voice:*) Come here, will you? There's a fellow who wants you to take him back. (*Ventriloquously again.*) All right. I'll be right over, Charlie dear. (*He turns to* ZERO.) Kind of familiar, isn't she? Charlie dear!

ZERO   What did you say her name is?

CHARLES   Hope. H-o-p-e.

ZERO   Is she good-lookin'?

CHARLES   Is she good-looking! Oh, boy, wait until you see her! She's a blonde with big blue eyes and red lips and little white teeth and——

ZERO   Say, that listens good to me. Will she be long?

CHARLES   She'll be here right away. There she is now! Do you see her?

ZERO   No. Where?

CHARLES   Out in the corridor. No, not there. Over farther. To the right. Don't you see her blue dress? And the sunlight on her hair?

ZERO   Oh, sure! Now I see her! What's the matter with me anyhow? Say, she's some jane! Oh, you baby vamp!

CHARLES   She'll make you forget your troubles.

ZERO   What troubles are you talkin' about?

CHARLES   Nothing. Go on. Don't keep her waiting.

ZERO   You bet I won't! Oh, Hope! Wait for me! I'll be right with you! I'm on my way! (*He stumbles out eagerly.* JOE *bursts into uproarious laughter.*)

CHARLES (*eyeing him in surprise and anger*)   What in hell's the matter with you?

JOE (*shaking with laughter*)   Did you get that? He thinks he saw somebody and he's following her! (*He rocks with laughter.*)

CHARLES (*punching him in the jaw*)   Shut your face!

JOE (*nursing his jaw*)   What's the idea? Can't I even laugh when I see something funny?

CHARLES   Funny! You keep your mouth shut or I'll show you something funny. Go on, hustle out of here and get something to clean up this mess with. There's another fellow moving in. Hurry now. (*He makes a threatening gesture.* JOE *exits hastily.* CHARLES *goes to chair and seats himself. He looks weary and dispirited. Shaking his head.*) Hell, I'll tell the world this is a lousy job! (*He takes a flask from his pocket, uncorks it, and slowly drains it.*)

(*Curtain.*)

From the Playwright

In his autobiography, **Rice** *recalls the astounding yet memorable circumstances surrounding his authoring* The Adding Machine—*an instantaneous "flash" that accounted for this noteworthy expressionistic work.*

The Birth of a Play

A few months after we moved to East Hampton, I had an experience which still puzzles and amazes me. One night, long after everyone else had gone to bed, I sat wide awake on the front porch, trying to concentrate on the marriage play. Suddenly, as though a switch had been turned or a curtain raised, a new play flashed into my mind, wholly unrelated to anything I had ever consciously thought about. When I say "flashed into my mind," I mean that quite literally, for in that sudden instant I saw the whole thing complete: characters, plot, incidents, even the title and some of the dialogue. Nothing like it ever happened to me before or since. I was actually possessed, my brain in a whirl, my whole being alive. I sat for a while trembling with excitement, almost gasping for breath. Then, hardly knowing what I was doing, I went to my study and began to write!

I wrote until dawn, spent a few sleepless hours in bed, breakfasted, and immediately went back to work. I kept at it day after day, scarcely speaking, sometimes leaving in the middle of a meal to hurry to my desk. My family must have thought me demented. In a sense I was: moving about in a semitrance, driven by an irresistible compulsion. It was as close to automatic writing as anything I have known. At the end of seventeen days the play was finished— finished, at any rate, as far as I am concerned, for except for cuts and typographical corrections I never changed any of it. I have just been looking at the original manuscript. It was written in pencil, on both sides of sheets of yellow paper of different sizes, some ruled, some unruled, whatever came to hand, I suppose. Obviously I had no very clear idea of what I was about.

I can best convey the effect that this extraordinary experience had upon me by quoting from a letter I wrote to Frank Harris, made available to me by his widow:

> I've just finished a job that has left me rather limp. About a month ago, a hurricane in the form of a new play swept me out to sea, and before I could struggle back to shore I had a first draft completed. Seventeen days and an average of eight or ten hours' work a day. I think I've stated that it left me rather limp. It was grand, though!—the best time I've had in years. I'm hugging myself for coming up here, where my silly nerves have had a chance to iron themselves out and my thoughts to place themselves end to end. Such a work jag would have been utterly impossible in the city. Of course, it is pertinent to inquire

whether the result is worth while. Frankly, I don't know. It's very different from anything I've done. It's new—a radical departure in technique and subject matter (for me, at any rate). And what's more, it's the most spontaneous, the most deeply felt thing I've ever done. Of course, novelty does not connote merit and neither does sincerity (despite the sentimental belief to the contrary). But whether or not it's good, I think it's as good as I'm capable of doing, at this stage of my development. . . . .

For the moment, then, I'm out of the bog in which I've been floundering. The sense of frustration which has been choking me for four years has abated. I actually feel a consciousness of liberation, a relief from a state of psychic congestion which I cannot help believing strangely akin to that physical congestion which the psychologists tell us finds release in a sexual orgasm. That may strike you as farfetched, but it comes nearer to conveying my present condition than anything else that occurs to me.

The play was called *The Adding Machine*. It was the case history of one of the slave souls who are both the raw material and the product of a mechanized society. In eight scenes it told the story of Mr. Zero, a white collar worker tied to a monotonous job and a shrewish wife. Replaced by a machine, he murders his boss in an access of resentment and panic, and he is condemned to die by a jury of his peers. His fears and frustrations make him reject an eternity of happiness and self-expression; he returns to earth to begin another treadmill existence, sustained only by the mirage of hope. The play was written in the stylized, intensified form loosely known as expressionism, though I had hardly heard the term at the time. It was a compound of comedy, melodrama, fantasy, satire and polemics. The dialogue was unlike any I had written before: an attempt to reproduce authentic human speech.

Not the least puzzling part of the cathartic effect that the writing of the play had upon me was the purging of my lingering antagonism toward my father. I had never really hated him, but I had always resented his failure to measure up to my standards of fatherhood. Now my animosity was washed away and replaced, not by love certainly, but by a kind pity. I cannot explain the connection between this abatement and the writing of *The Adding Machine*. It was not as though I had vented my ill-will by portraying my father in an unfavorable light. For, though he had many of Mr. Zero's prejudices and malevolences, he was proud, self-assertive and anything but a conformist. My release is part of the mystery that enshrouds the whole creation of the play. . . .

I tried several times to define expressionism. In an article written for the *New York Times* I said: "The author attempts not so much to depict events faithfully as to convey to the spectator what seems to him to be their inner significance. To achieve this end the dramatist often finds it expedient to depart entirely from objective reality and to employ symbols, condensations and a dozen devices which, to the conservative, must seem arbitrarily fantastic." And in my memorandum to Digges:[1] "What we must convey . . . is a subjective picture of a

---

[1]During rehearsals, Dudley Digges, who portrayed Mr. Zero, asked Rice for an interpretation of the character. The playwright wrote approximately six pages of analysis, including comments on expressionism and interpretations of the other characters as well.

man who is at once an individual and a type. . . . In the realistic play, we look at the character from the outside. We see him in terms of action and of actuality. But in the expressionistic play we subordinate and even discard objective reality and seek to express the character in terms of his own inner life. An x-ray photograph bears no resemblance to the object as it presents itself to our vision, but it reveals the inner mechanism of the object as no mere photographic likeness can. . . ."

From the Critic

The Adding Machine *opened at the Garrick Theatre, New York, on March 18, 1923. Two weeks later,* **Ludwig Lewishon,** *friend of the playwright and critic for* The Nation *wrote an inspiring and glowing review of the play, which is reproduced below.*

Creative Irony:
Mr. Rice's The Adding Machine

Expressionism has two chief aims: to fling the inner life of the dramatic figures immediately upon the stage; to synthesize, instead of describing, their world and their universe into symbolic visions that shall sum up whole histories, moralities, cosmogonies in a brief minute and a fleeting scene. If this form of art is to be effective and beautiful, it must be very sensitive and very severe at once. Beneath it must be fundamental brainwork, thinking as resilient as steel and as clean-cut as agate. The symbolic masses must glow with a clear irradiation from within. Otherwise all is murky and muddled. You can describe fragmentarily and produce fragments of truth. Realism does not commit you to any whole. In expressionism the antecedent intellectual grasp of your entire material must be firm, definite, complete. Everything must be thought out and thought through. This is what, despite moments of the highest brilliancy and glow, Mr. Eugene O'Neill did not do in *The Hairy Ape*. This is what, in a harder, drier, less poetical vein, Mr. Elmer Rice has actually succeeded in doing in *The Adding Machine*.

Mr. Rice's vision of the world may infuriate you. There were people behind me at the Garrick who first grumbled and then cursed politely. You cannot miss it; you cannot withdraw yourself from its coherence and completeness. Examine his play scene by scene, symbol by symbol. The structure stands. There are no holes in its roof. It gives you the pleasure of both poetry and science, the warm beauty of life and love, the icy delight of mathematics. I am aware of the fact— critics should make this confession oftener—that my profound sympathy with Mr. Rice's substance necessarily colored my reaction to his play. Not, however, to its form, not to the heartening fact that here is an American drama with no

loose ends or ragged edges or silly last-act compromises, retractions, reconcilia-
tions. The work, on its own ground, in its own mood, is honest, finished, sound.

What Mr. Rice has to tell us is not new. But creative literature, I hasten to
add, need not have novelty. What Edgar Lee Masters, Sinclair Lewis, Sherwood
Anderson, Zona Gale, what the whole new American literature of moral protest
has told us, is also told here. This particular world of ours deliberately hides or
chokes with dust and ashes the very sources of human life. It has made fetishes
of ugliness and monotony and intolerance. It has given to these fetishes high-
sounding names. It is wedded to denial and has made a pact with death. From
the intolerable repressions of Mr. Zero's life flames one explosion of the nerves.
But it is an explosion of the sickened nerves only. Slavery is in his soul. He is,
in reality, doomed to add figures, doomed to chant in unison the pack-formulæ so
terribly and hauntingly projected in the third scene. He cannot stay in the Elysian
Fields with Swift and Rabelais and the great company of the confessors of life
and light. He cannot hear the music which is the music of life. The place is not
respectable. It is no place for him. He "beats it"—beats it back to an eternal
adding machine, back finally to an earth where slavery is his eternal portion and
hope an ironic delusion. Mr. Rice is terribly bitter, terribly relentless. There is
the other murderer in the Elysian Fields who turned upon the torment of his life
who was so steeped in hell that he thought it heaven, who now thirsts for flames
to burn away the guilt of his one moment of blind protest and dumb liberation.
Only to the shabby office girl a better knowledge is given. In the woman soul
alone Mr. Rice sees a ray of beauty. She wanted Zero to fulfil her womanhood
even on earth; she hears the music of life at once. Hers are courage and insight
and love.

It is not just to speak of the Theatre Guild's production of this play in the
ordinary sense of that word. How much or how little Mr. Rice had in his stage
directions concerning the scenic embodiment of his vision I do not know. It is
clear, however, that there has been here an imaginative collaboration between
dramatist and producer which is not necessary in the case of a realistic play. It is
necessary here. And the results are extraordinarily telling and beautiful. There
is for instance, the place of justice to which poor Zero is brought. The tall windows are crooked; the railing is crooked. But the lines are not crinkled. To the
perverse vision they may seem straight. They lean diagonally. The judge is
petrified. He is literally of stone. The mob cries "guilty"; a dead heart deals out
mercilessness and calls it justice. Not all the scenes are as finely conceived as this.
But all have been designed by an imagination packed with close thinking, profoundly akin to the imagination that shaped the play itself. The acting is in the
same mood of absorption in the author's intention. Here, too, is creative collaboration. Mr. Dudley Digges gives the finest performance since his Henry
Clegg. And here he is more varied, more expressive. He makes shabbiness of
body and soul true to every dusty detail and also a thing of cosmic dread. Miss
Helen Westley has her accustomed edge and veracity, Miss Margaret Wycherly
her pathos and yearning, Mr. Louis Calvert his depth and richness of reality.
Mr. Edgar G. Robinson and Miss Elise Bartlett contribute to the strange eloquence of this play and production which constitute, without question, one of the
major achievements in the entire field of the American arts.

From the Director

Barnard Hewitt *calls* The Adding Machine *"a director's play" and as such allows the potential director more creative expression (and as many possible headaches) as most other plays. From his production at Brooklyn College, Professor Hewitt describes some of his techniques.*

Director's Notes on The Adding Machine

The episodic structure and expressionistic style of Elmer Rice's play present particular problems for director, designer, and actors. As first produced by Theatre Guild in 1923, it consists of seven scenes; as revived by the Phoenix Theatre in 1956, it consists of eight scenes, each with a different setting. These notes apply to the earlier version; they would require modification for the later version.

Scenes one through four present a clear, unbroken line of action which culminates in Mr. Zero's conviction for murdering the Boss. An intermission comes naturally after scene four. In the scenes which follow, the line is not so clear nor so continuous. They all deal with Zero's life after death, but each in its own way. Scene five is ironic and grotesque; scene six is pathetic and lyrical; scene seven is ironic and philosophic. Scene five acts very well—so well, that the play will seem to go downhill, unless a strong actor is cast as Lieutenant Charles and scenes six and seven are performed to the hilt by all.

If the play is to have its full impact, changes of scene should be nearly instantaneous. Therefore, some kind of permanent frame is indicated, within which changes are made as much as possible with projections and the absolute minimum of scenery and furniture shifted by hand. Projections are essential to express the murder of the Boss. They may provide the columns of figures on the walls in scenes one and three. They may suggest an office imprisoning Daisy and Zero in scene two; the judge, his bench, and an American flag in scene four; distorted tree and tomb forms framing set gravestones in scene five; an appropriately idyllic background for scene six; and an oversize version of the earlier office scene for scene seven. I preferred to use for scene seven a cyclorama lighted to give an effect of infinite space, in which stood the giant adding machine.

The Adding Machine is concerned with the life of ordinary Americans in a big city in the 1920s, but everything is distorted in order to express the author's view of the dehumanizing character of that life. The first four scenes present situations and actions from that life, although these are obviously distorted. What happens in the last three scenes is pure fantasy, and yet it involves Zero and two other characters who appeared in the first four scenes. The distortions of the last three scenes should have a different quality and yet should remain congruous with the distortions of the first four scenes.

The playwright suggests that Zero and Messers One through Six be dressed alike, Mrs. Zero and the six other wives also. In addition, I found it effective to put them in identical masks. In scene two, it seemed to me desirable to have Daisy as well as Zero masked, to have them wear their masks when they spoke to each other, and to remove them when they spoke their "thoughts." To permit this, the masks had to be light weight and fitted, not only with an elastic to hold them on the face, but also with a thread or string so that they could sometimes hang from the neck. Daisy's mask was different from those of the other women— thin and pale, as well as middle-aged, to reveal a much younger face when it was removed.

The banal dialogue and actions of the guests in scene three should have a mechanical effect but should not lose touch with the life materials from which they have been selected and arranged. In scene two the dialogue between Daisy and Zero which is necessitated by their work should be extremely mechanical. The few lines in which they attempt to communicate as persons require a tentative quality. Their "thoughts," however, are more important than their "spoken" lines, and therefore should not be uttered on a lower vocal level, but rather should be given prominence by somewhat greater volume and by being delivered front. Mr. Zero's defense in scene four can be very moving—it is the emotional high-point of the play—but it is a speech that no one would be allowed to make in a real court room. It may help the actor to get the right effect, if he thinks of that speech as what went on inside Zero during the examination of witnesses, the speeches by the opposing attorneys, and the judge's summing up.

As the stage directions indicate, music and sound effects are essential to this play, not only within the scenes but also as bridges between scenes. Instead of music, the opening scene might be preceded by sounds of the big city—somewhat muted by walls and distance—the rumble of trucks, automobile horns, the sirens of a fire truck or ambulance, angry voices—which fade out when Mrs. Zero begins to speak, but are heard from time to time throughout the scene. This same tape might take the curtain down on scene one and modulate into office noises— typewriters, telephones, buzzers, and particularly an adding machine—to lead into scene two. The office noises will fade out or to a low level when Zero and Daisy begin to speak, but will be brought in briefly from time to time to punctuate their scene.

The stage directions suggest using music and the whole repertoire of standard sound effects to express the frenzy in which Zero murders the Boss. The clicking of an adding machine mingled with big city traffic noises can be used to bridge between scenes two and three and between scenes three and four. The click of the adding machine might come in as an accompaniment to Zero's desperate last plea to the departing jurors, growing louder to the curtain.

After the intermission, the first curtain might be preceded by desolate exterior night sounds—the hooting of an owl, the distant whistle of a whippoorwill, the croaking of bullfrogs, the yowling of cats—sounds which the playwright suggests be heard occasionally throughout the graveyard scene. At the end of the scene, these lonesome sounds might be heard as the curtain falls, and then fade out to be replaced by the sweet music brought up to prepare for the scene in the Happy Place, which the playwright calls for throughout that scene. At the end of the scene, the music will fade out to be replaced perhaps by the click of an adding machine, considerably amplified.

The Adding Machine is a director's play. This does not mean that it can do without good acting, but that good acting is not enough for this modern morality play. All the resources of the theatre—scenery, light, sound, costume, and makeup or masks—are required, if this ironic fable of the little man with his slave mentality is to receive full expression.

Source Material for *The Adding Machine*

BY THE CRITICS

Block, A. *Changing World in Plays and Theatre.* pp. 216–224.
Broussard, L. *American Stage.* pp. 39–50.
Rabkin, G. *Drama and Commitment: Politics in the American Theatre of the Thirties.* Bloomington: Indiana University Press, 1964, pp. 237–259.
Sievers, W. D. *Freud on Broadway.* pp. 146–149.
Young, Stark. "Review of *The Adding Machine.*" *New Republic* 34 (1923): 164-165.

BY THE DIRECTOR

Eaton, W. P., ed. *The Theatre Guild—The First Ten Years.* New York: Brentano's, 1929, pp. 157–169.
Moeller, Philip (original director). "A Foreword." In *The Adding Machine* by Elmer Rice. New York: Doubleday and Page, 1923, pp. vii–x.

BY THE PLAYWRIGHT

Elwood, W. R. "An Interview with Elmer Rice on Expressionism." *Educational Theatre Journal,* March 1968, pp. 1–7.
Rice, Elmer. "American Theatre and the Human Spirit," *Saturday Review,* December 17, 1955.

Epic Theatre

The epic theatre has a meaning, a message, and a microphone. Its meaning is evident from its inception—a revolt against the dramatist's using the theatre as an end in itself; its message resides in the sociological problems it portrays; and its microphone is used as a method to "alienate" the audience from the action.

Though Bertolt Brecht and epic theatre have become synonymous, Brecht's co-worker, Erwin Piscator, deserves mention as the founder of epic theatre. His play, *The Good Soldier Schweik* (1927), was a satire on German militarism told in a new and revolutionary way. Piscator desired to stir the audience into the realization that certain conditions needed improving, and he believed this could be best accomplished by radical methods of story-telling designed to jolt the audience from intellectual laziness. Being opposed to conventional melodramatic techniques, Piscator thus utilized in the play huge drawings, treadmills, projection, slides, and scenic units and elements in full view of the audience, all for the purpose of halting the spectator's involvement in the play. Piscator was attempting to comment on the frightening rise in Germany's military orientation, and at the same time sought to provoke the audience into exercising their intellects for a solution to the problem.

The Meaning

But the real hero of epic theatre has been Bertolt Brecht, playwright, theorist, and director. Brecht sincerely believed that the "dramatic theatre" had lost its usefulness, since it encouraged emotional involvement and dissuaded intellectual responses, thus requiring nothing more of the spectator than the warming of his seat. He argued that conventional theatre techniques had lost (or lacked) effectiveness as instruments of change. The theatre must be a teacher, Brecht said, and the traditional theatre could only fail in this attempt because it relied too heavily on empathy, or the emotional identification of the audience with the character, for effect. Too often, our intellectual awareness was being sacrificed and our critical senses lulled into passivity.

Epic theatre requires that the audience realize at all times that they are watching a *play* that has something to say about conditions and their results. Traditional theatre's immersion of our senses is, therefore, not the best way to effect this response. Brecht outlines this point by comparing the two methods in an issue of the *Tulane Drama Review* devoted to epic theatre:[1]

dramatic form	epic form
The stage incarnates an event.	It relates it.
Involves the audience in an action, uses up its activity.	Makes the audience an observer, but arouses its activity.
Communicates experiences.	Communicates insights.
The audience is projected into an event.	Is confronted with it.
Suggestion is used.	Argument is used.
The character is a known quantity.	The character is subjected to investigation.
Sensations are preserved.	Impelled to the level of perceptions.
Man unchangeable.	Man who can change and make changes.
His drives.	His motives.
Events in a straight line.	In "irregular" curves.
*Natura non facit saltus.*The world as it is.	*Facit saltus.* The world as it is becoming.

What we have here is the *meaning* of epic theatre derived from a dissatisfaction with traditional methods of story development. Believing the "dramatic form" inhibited thought and intellectual awareness, Brecht thus sought to free the mind from the emotional stranglehold put on it by the extreme sentiment, total empathy, and crass emotionalism characteristic of the conventional stage.

The Message

In all of Brecht's great epic plays—*Galileo, Mother Courage, The Good Woman of Setzuan, The Caucasian Chalk Circule*—a strong indication of Marxist dogma is present. As a Communist sympathizer, Brecht would represent the injustices he felt existed in the world of our making. Whether they be political, economic, or sociological, these inequities deserved expression in play form as a didactic method of improving conditions by revealing their causes. If the traditional drama was meant to be enjoyed, the epic was meant to instruct—to inform the audience of the deep-rooted problems plaguing mankind, their causes and their results—and to argue by communication that these problems needed solving. If the ironies and catastrophes of war were to be realized—if an awareness of the degradation of militarism and warfare were to be taught (*Mother Courage*), the intellect, not the emotions, should be used to bring about such a realization. If an individual was to be shown struggling in an impersonal and self-centered world (*The Good Woman of Setzuan*), the theatre had to make use of techniques designed to bring the audience to an understanding that the situation demands improvement (not the immediate situation, but the universal causes). Interestingly enough, the purpose of epic theatre, in this respect, greatly resembled the purpose of tragedy.

For Brecht and the epic theatre, then, the stage had a higher purpose, and most of Brecht's plays carry this strong message of socialist dogma. They are really social plays, picturing suffering, asking for changes. But many other modes of the drama have grown out of a dissatisfaction with realism, and some, like expressionism, also proclaim a message. What, then, makes epic theatre so radical?

The Microphone

Probably the most often used (and possibly least understood) term associated with epic theare is "alienation." Brecht felt that the best way for the drama to achieve its purpose of teaching was to appeal to the critical faculties, not the emotional needs, of the learners—the audience. Thus the stage should "alienate" (or "make strange"—a closer definition to the actual German) the actor from the audience, the stage from the spectator. No longer would the audience be allowed to get "caught up" in the drama. Emotional involvement, empathy, and identification must be minimal, for the reception and understanding of the play's purpose was paramount. Stage events should comment on reality, not approximate it. Therefore, almost any method of depicting an event that discouraged identification and involvement was incorporated into epic theatre.

Though Brecht advocated minimizing emotion, discouraging involvement, and lessening sensations, he was not opposed to *feeling* per se, but rather was against using emotion or empathy *as ends in themselves*. Brecht believed feelings could be aroused, but should be interrupted when they began to interfere with the play's teachings. Thus it is possible for us to feel sympathy for, say, Mother Courage. But Brecht exploits its occurrence by continually jolting us from our involvement, hoping to make us aware at all times that a play is being performed. Thus emotion and sympathy could be utilized, but only as a conscious technique minimally invoked by the playwright to further underscore the message of the story. Consequently, when sympathy was aroused, it was interrupted rudely. Therefore, when we did become emotionally involved, Brecht jarred us from this entanglement— all for the pre-determined purpose of causing us to critically evaluate the message of the play.

What, then, were the techniques and methods Brecht employed to achieve his purpose? They can be broken down into methods of play-writing and story presentation, methods of acting and techniques of staging.

Methods of Story Presentation

One key to the epic theatre can be found in its name, "epic," coined by Piscator. Since Brecht believed the theatre should teach (particularly social-istic doctrine), then a pattern of development was needed that would *not* progress like a well-oiled machine, having one event logically following another, with smooth transitions. The epic method—similar to the epic poem, with its narrative style of storytelling intermixed with scenes of dialogue and boundaries unrestricted by time and place—was ideally suited for the teaching purpose.

Taking his cue from epic poems such as *Beowulf* and *the Iliad*, Brecht fashioned the unfolding of his story along these lines, interjecting dance and song, narrative and dialogue. In doing this, the epic theatre made use of techniques designed not so much to completely destroy the sense of illusion, but rather to interrupt it. If traditional dramatic development had for too long captured our emotional awareness, Brecht reasoned, then here was a method of storytelling that would allow minimal involvement.

In conjunction with the epic method was the "historification" of the setting and the people. Keeping in mind that alienation was the desired objective, what better way to prevent empathy was there, according to Brecht, than to place the action in the past. It is much more difficult to relate to—hence get involved in—stage events taking place in a period foreign to us. The historical setting of *Mother Courage* or *The Good Woman of Setzuan* (together, of course, with other techniques of alienation) pre-vented, to some degree, identification with the characters. Looking at it another way, if the heroine in *Mother Courage* had been drawn from the Viet Nam war, the possibility for empathy would be greatly expanded.

Methods of Acting

Probably the least successful—but, nevertheless, essential—of the alien-ation techniques was the method of acting Brecht advocated (Brecht's own words to this effect are to be found in the essay by the "Director," following his play). In direct contrast to the Stanislavski method, Brecht believed the actor must not attempt to achieve identification with his character; instead he should remain at a distance, so that he may better "see" the audience and relate to them the play's teaching. Acting should thus take place in the third, rather than the first, person.

Brecht proposed that if the actor was the medium for the message, the idea of the play could very well be destroyed if the actor lost himself in his role. Since objectivity, not stark reality, was to be sought by the production, the actor must stand apart from the character he was creating— hoping at all times not to elicit emotional identification, but critical evaluation. It is interesting to note also that when "method actors" have portrayed Brecht's characters, they have failed miserably, as *Mother Courage* did on Broadway. For the essence of audience objectivity can only be elicited by the actor's "objectifying" the character he is playing, an extremely difficult thing to do. Perhaps this is the reason Brecht's alienation technique has been least successful in the area of acting.

Methods of Staging

The greatest use of alienation technique can be found in the method of staging. Together with the epic method of storytelling, historic placing of the action, and the "objective" method of acting, Brecht coupled revolutionary methods of staging to complete the severing of emotions from the stage. The first of these staging techniques was Brecht's use of the proscenium stage exclusively, to outline the events and reduce the intimacy felt, say, in a theatre-in-the-round. The traditional "picture frame" stage, Brecht believed, was ideally suited for epic theatre. The audience could at all times be made aware it was watching a play since they were being physically alienated from the stage. The proscenium arch, with its restricting influence and artificial enclosure (which was broken purposely, many times, by the actors) could only serve to better alienate the events from the spectators.

Other staging techniques used to minimize identification were moving pictures shown behind the central action to interrupt the audience's visual sense, which up to this time had become conditioned to seeing only actors and scenery (slides might also be used); dancing and singing occurred when least expected, both to point out the play's message and to remind the audience they were watching a play; direct address by actors to the audience better served the epic purpose of telling a story rather than showing it; scenery suggested, rather than re-created, a locale; changes of scenery were made in full view of the audience. All of these production methods served to objectify the play's message. In order for the purpose of the play to be clear in the mind of the spectator, the mind of the *spectator* must be clear—free of the heavy emotional identification that encompasses the critical faculties. Pure theatricalism best served to cut through this heavy emotional identification.

The songs of the epic plays are excellent examples of this alienation technique. Unlike musical comedy (or musical drama), where the music and words embellish the play as an integrated part of the whole, epic songs are usually stinging criticism, revolving around the play's message. In addition, the words often are set to music contradictory to the situation that produced them; they are at odds with the scene. What this causes, in effect, is temporary bewilderment, intended so that the audience will question the relation of the song to the play, and will examine intellectually its content and meaning. In this sense, the song serves as an instrument of instruction, underlying the message and rousing the spectator from any strong degree of involvement he may have allowed himself.

Each play of the epic theatre may include, then, devices and techniques planned to interrupt, disturb, and arouse—all for the purpose of teaching (Brecht's theatre has been called, by some, the Theatre of the Didactic). Besides those techniques mentioned above, all of the hardware of the play's staging may be in full view of the audience, additional mechanical and visual elements may be added, and the acting and the script must be molded in such a way that the spectator is at all times cognizant that a play is being performed. Placing the story in a historical setting, objectifying the acting, and including methods and techniques fashioned to instruct rather than involve are all elements basic to the success of epic theatre.

Brecht does not seem to have succeeded in achieving the audience response he desired. It seems that alienation, particularly in acting, is as difficult for the audience to muster as it is for the cast to master. Also, despite how cleverly Brecht tries to divorce emotion from the stage, it is almost impossible to do since human beings are not machines. In *Mother Courage*, for instance, our sympathies cannot help but be aroused, and even when interrupted, remain to cloud the overall critical estimation Brecht was calling for. Too often, epic audiences have felt a sympathy for the "good woman of Setzuan" that interfered with their ability to gain the "insights" Brecht advocated. For Brecht's characters, though drawn from historical periods and surrounded by theatrical devices, are nevertheless human beings, and he can rarely avoid creating them so. In addition, the fact that epic theatre is "good" theatre implies that some degree of empathy is essential for success, for when identification is no longer possible, drama becomes no more than a lecture.

Thus, for the average theatregoer, despite epic techniques—the songs and the narratives, the motion pictures and the slides—the message of an epic theatre production may still remain quite distant.

Azdak the village scrivener is made a judge by the Ironshirts. University of Colorado.
Daniel S. P. Yang, director; Bernard Tushaus, designer; Thomas Schmunk, costumer.

The Governor's wife and Grusha make ready for the human tug-of-war. Wayne State
University. Leonard Leone, director; settings by Timothy R. Dewart; costumes by Judith
Haugan; lighting by Gary M. Witt.

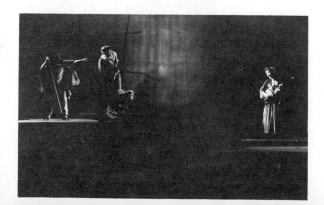

Grusha has made the treacherous
journey across the ròtten bridge.
Carnegie-Mellon University.
Lawrence Carra, director, 1958.

The Chalk Circle waits menacingly in the background as Grusha prepares for the play's high point. The Arena Stage. Alan Schneider, director (first professional U.S.A. production.)

Justice is served as the child is awarded to Grusha. Minnesota Theatre Company. Edward Payson Call, director.

Wrong rules the land, and waiting Justice sleeps.
J. G. Holland

The Caucasian Chalk Circle

Bertolt Brecht

Adapted by Eric Bentley

The Caucasian Chalk Circle

Characters

A Old Man *on the right*
Peasant Woman *on the right*
Young Peasant
A Very Young Worker
Old Man *on the left*
Peasant Woman *on the left*
Agriculturist Kato
Girl Tractorist
Wounded Soldier
The Delegate *from the capital*
The Singer
Georgi Abashwili, *the Governor*
Natella, *the Governor's wife*
Michael, *their son*
Shalva, *an adjutant*
Arsen Kazbeki, *a fat prince*
Messenger *from the capital*
Niko Mikadze *and* Mika Loladze,
    doctors
Simon Shashava, *a soldier*
Grusha Vashnadze, *a kitchen maid*
Old Peasant *with the milk*
Corporal *and* Private
Peasant *and his wife*
Lavrenti Vashnadze, *Grusha's*
    brother

Aniko, *his wife*
Peasant Woman, *for a while*
    Grusha's mother-in-law
Jussup, *her son*
Monk
Azdak, *village recorder*
Shauwa, *a policeman*
Grand Duke
Doctor
Invalid
Limping Man
Blackmailer
Ludovica
Innkeeper, *her father-in-law*
Stableboy
Poor Old Peasant Woman
Irakli, *her brother-in-law, a bandit*
Three Wealthy Farmers
Illo Shuboladze *and* Sandro
    Oboladze, *lawyers*
Old Married Couple
Soldiers, Servants, Peasants,
    Beggars, Musicians,
    Merchants, Nobles, Architects

The time and the place: After a prologue, set in 1945, we move back perhaps 1000 years.

The action of The Caucasian Chalk Circle *centers on Nuka (or Nukha), a town in Azerbaijan. However, the capital referred to in the prologue is not Baku (capital of Soviet Azerbaijan) but Tiflis (or Tbilisi), capital of Georgia. When Azdak, later, refers to "the capital" he means Nuka itself; though whether Nuka was ever capital of Georgia I do not know: in what reading I have done on the subject I have only found Nuka to be the capital of a Nuka Khanate.*

The word "Georgia" has not been used in this English version because of its American associations; instead, the alternative name "Grusinia" (in Russian, Gruziya) has been used.

The reasons for resettling the old Chinese story in Transcaucasia are not far to seek. The play was written when the Soviet chief of state, Joseph Stalin, was a

Georgian, as was his favorite poet, cited in the Prologue, Mayakovsky. And surely there is a point in having this story acted out at the place where Europe and Asia meet, a place incomparably rich in legend and history. Here Jason found the Golden Fleece. Here Noah's Ark touched ground. Here the armies of both Genghis Khan and Tamerlane wrought havoc.—E.B.

Prologue

Summer, 1945.

(*Among the ruins of a war-ravaged Caucasian village the members of two kolkhoz villages, mostly* WOMEN *and* OLDER MEN, *are sitting in a circle, smoking and drinking wine. With them is a* DELEGATE *of the State Reconstruction Commission from Nuka.*)

PEASANT WOMAN (*left*) (*pointing*)   In those hills over there we stopped three Nazi tanks, but the apple orchard was already destroyed.

OLD MAN (*right*)   Our beautiful dairy farm: a ruin.

GIRL TRACTORIST   I laid the fire, Comrade.

(*Pause*)

DELEGATE   Nuka, Azerbaijan S.S.R. Delegation received from the goat-breeding Kolkhoz "Rosa Luxemburg." This is a collective farm which moved eastwards on orders from the authorities at the approach of Hitler's armies. They are now planning to return. Their delegates have looked at the village and the land and found a lot of destruction. (*Delegates on the right nod.*) But the neighboring fruit farm—Kolkhoz (*to the left*) "Galinsk"—proposes to use the former grazing land of Kolkhoz "Rosa Luxemburg" for orchards and vineyards. This land lies in a valley where grass doesn't grow very well. As a delegate of the Reconstruction Commission in Nuka I request that the two Kolkhoz villages decide between themselves whether Kolkhoz "Rosa Luxemburg" shall return or not.

OLD MAN (*right*)   First of all, I want to protest against the time limit on discussion. We of Kolkhoz "Rosa Luxemburg" have spent three days and three nights getting here. And now discussion is limited to half a day.

WOUNDED SOLDIER (*left*)   Comrade, we haven't as many villages as we used to have. We haven't as many hands. We haven't as much time.

GIRL TRACTORIST   All pleasures have to be rationed. Tobacco is rationed, and wine. Discussion should be rationed.

OLD MAN (*right*) (*sighing*)   Death to the fascists! But I will come to the point and explain why we want our valley back. There are a great many reasons, but I'll begin with one of the simplest. Makina Abakidze, unpack the goat cheese. (*A peasant woman from right takes from a basket an enormous cheese wrapped in a cloth. Applause and laughter.*) Help yourselves, Comrades, start in!

OLD MAN (*left*) (*suspiciously*)   Is this a way of influencing us?

OLD MAN (*right*) (*amid laughter*)   How could it be a way of influencing you, Surab, you valley-thief? Everyone knows you'll take the cheese and the valley, too. (*Laughter*) All I expect from you is an honest answer. Do you like the cheese?

OLD MAN (*left*)   The answer is: yes.

OLD MAN (*right*)   Really. (*Bitterly*) I ought to have known you know nothing about cheese.

OLD MAN (*left*)   Why not? When I tell you I like it?

OLD MAN (*right*)   Because you can't like it. Because it's not what it was in the old days. And why not? Because our goats don't like the new grass as they did the old. Cheese is not cheese because grass is not grass, that's the thing. Please put that in your report.

OLD MAN (*left*)   But your cheese is excellent.

OLD MAN (*right*)   It isn't excellent. It's just passable. The new grazing land is no good, whatever the young people may say. One can't live there. It doesn't even smell of morning in the morning. (*Several people laugh.*)

DELEGATE   Don't mind their laughing: they understand you. Comrades, why does one love one's country? Because the bread tastes better there, the air smells better, voices sound stronger, the sky is higher, the ground is easier to walk on. Isn't that so?

OLD MAN (*right*)   The valley has belonged to us from all eternity.

SOLDIER (*left*)   What does *that* mean—from all eternity? Nothing belongs to anyone from all eternity. When you were young you didn't even belong to yourself. You belonged to the Kazbeki princes.

OLD MAN (*right*)   Doesn't it make a difference, though, what kind of trees stand next to the house you are born in? Or what kind of neighbors you have? Doesn't that make a difference? We want to go back just to have you as our neighbors, valley-thieves! Now you can all laugh again.

OLD MAN (*left*) (*laughing*)   Then why don't you listen to what your neighbor, Kato Wachtang, our agriculturist, has to say about the valley?

PEASANT WOMAN (*right*)   We've not said all we have to say about our valley. By no means. Not all the houses are destroyed. As for the dairy farm, at least the foundation wall is still standing.

DELEGATE   You can claim State support—here and there—you know that. I have suggestions here in my pocket.

PEASANT WOMAN (*right*)   Comrade Specialist, we haven't come here to haggle. I can't take your cap and hand you another, and say "This one's better." The other one might *be* better, but you *like* yours better.

GIRL TRACTORIST   A piece of land is not a cap—not in our country, Comrade.

DELEGATE   Don't get mad. It's true we have to consider a piece of land as a tool to produce something useful, but it's also true that we must recognize love for a particular piece of land. As far as I'm concerned, I'd like to find out more exactly what you (*to those on the left*) want to do with the valley.

OTHERS   Yes, let Kato speak.

KATO (*rising; she's in military uniform*)   Comrades, last winter, while we were fighting in these hills here as Partisans, we discussed how, once the Germans were expelled, we could build up our fruit culture to ten times its original size. I've prepared a plan for an irrigation project. By means of a cofferdam on our mountain lake, 300 hectares of unfertile land can be irrigated. Our Kolkhoz could not only cultivate more fruit, but also have vineyards. The project, however, would pay only if the disputed valley of Kolkhoz "Rosa Luxemburg" were also included. Here are the calculations. (*She hands* DELEGATE *a briefcase.*)

OLD MAN (*right*)   Write into the report that our Kolkhoz plans to start a new stud farm.

GIRL TRACTORIST   Comrades, the project was conceived during days and nights when we had to take cover in the mountains. We were often without ammunition for our half-dozen rifles. Even finding a pencil was difficult. (*Applause from both sides*)

OLD MAN (*right*)   Our thanks to the Comrades of Kolkhoz "Galinsk" and all those who've defended our country! (*They shake hands and embrace.*)

PEASANT WOMAN (*left*)   In doing this our thought was that our soldiers—both your men and our men—should return to a still more productive homeland.

GIRL TRACTORIST   As the poet Mayakovsky said: "The home of the Soviet people shall also be the home of Reason!"
(*The delegates excluding the* OLD MAN *have got up, and with the* DELEGATE *specified proceed to study the* AGRICULTURIST'S *drawings. Exclamations such as:*)
"Why is the altitude of fall 22 meters?"—"This rock will have to be blown up"—"Actually, all they need is cement and dynamite"—"They force the water to come down here, that's clever!"

A VERY YOUNG WORKER (*right*) (*to* OLD MAN, *right*)   They're going to irrigate all the fields between the hills, look at that, Aleko!

OLD MAN (*right*)   I'm not going to look. I knew the project would be good. I won't have a pistol pointed at me!

DELEGATE   But they only want to point a pencil at you!
(*Laughter*)

OLD MAN (*right*) (*gets up gloomily, and walks over to look at the drawings*)   These valley-thieves know only too well that we in this country are suckers for machines and projects.

PEASANT WOMAN (*right*)   Aleko Bereshwili, you have a weakness for new projects. That's well known.

DELEGATE   What about my report? May I write that you will all support the cession of your old valley in the interests of this project when you get back to your Kolkhoz?

PEASANT WOMAN (*right*) I will. What about you, Aleko?

OLD MAN (*right*) (*bent over drawings*)   I suggest that you give us copies of the drawings to take along.

PEASANT WOMAN (*right*) Then we can sit down and eat. Once he has the drawings and he's ready to discuss them, the matter is settled. I know him. And it will be the same with the rest of us.
(*Delegates laughingly embrace again.*)

OLD MAN (*left*)   Long live the Kolkhoz "Rosa Luxemburg" and much luck to your horse-breeding project!

PEASANT WOMAN (*left*)   In honor of the visit of the delegates from Kolkhoz "Rosa Luxemburg" and of the Specialist, the plan is that we all hear a presentation of the Singer Arkadi Tscheidse.

> (*Applause.* GIRL TRACTORIST *has gone off to bring the* SINGER.)

PEASANT WOMAN (*right*)   Comrades, your entertainment had better be good. It's going to cost us a valley.

PEASANT WOMAN (*left*)   Arkadi Tscheidse knows about our discussion. He's promised to perform something that has a bearing on the problem.

KATO   We wired Tiflis three times. The whole thing nearly fell through at the last minute because his driver had a cold.

PEASANT WOMAN (*left*)   Arkadi Tscheidse knows 21,000 lines of verse.

OLD MAN (*left*)   He's hard to get. You and the Planning Commission should persuade him to come north more often, Comrade.

DELEGATE   We are more interested in economics, I'm afraid.

OLD MAN (*left*) (*smiling*)   You arrange the redistribution of vines and tractors, why not songs?

> (*Enter the* SINGER *Arkadi Tscheidse, led by* GIRL TRACTORIST. *He is a well-built man of simple manners, accompanied by* FOUR MUSICIANS *with their instruments. The artists are greeted with applause.*)

GIRL TRACTORIST   This is the Comrade Specialist, Arkadi.

> (*The* SINGER *greets them all.*)

DELEGATE   Honored to make your acquaintance. I heard about your songs when I was a boy at school. Will it be one of the old legends?

SINGER   A very old one. It's called "The Chalk Circle" and comes from the Chinese. But we'll do it, of course, in a changed version. Comrades, it's an honor for me to entertain you after a difficult debate. We hope you will find that the voice of the old poet also sounds well in the shadow of Soviet tractors. It may be a mistake to mix different wines, but old and new wisdom mix admirably. Now I hope we'll get something to eat before the performance begins—it would certainly help.

VOICES   Surely. Everyone into the Club House!

> (*While everyone begins to move,* DELEGATE *turns to* GIRL TRACTORIST.)

DELEGATE   I hope it won't take long. I've got to get back tonight.

GIRL TRACTORIST   How long will it last, Arkadi? The Comrade Specialist must get back to Tiflis tonight.

SINGER (*casually*)   It's actually two stories. An hour or two.

GIRL TRACTORIST (*confidentially*)   Couldn't you make it shorter?

SINGER   No.

VOICE   Arkadi Tscheidse's performance will take place here in the square after the meal.

> (*And they all go happily to eat.*)

1 The Noble Child

As the lights go up, the SINGER *is seen sitting on the floor, a black sheepskin cloak round his shoulders, and a little, well-thumbed notebook in his hand. A small group of listeners—the chorus—sits with him. The manner of his recitation makes it clear that he has told his story over and over again. He mechanically fingers the pages, seldom looking at them. With appropriate gestures, he gives the signal for each scene to begin.*

SINGER

In olden times, in a bloody time,
There ruled in a Caucasian city—
Men called it City of the Damned—
A Governor.
His name was Georgi Abashwili.
He was rich as Croesus
He had a beautiful wife
He had a healthy baby.
No other governor in Grusinia
Had so many horses in his stable
So many beggars on his doorstep
So many soldiers in his service
So many petitioners in his courtyard.
Georgi Abashwili—how shall I describe him to you?
He enjoyed his life.
On the morning of Easter Sunday
The Governor and his family went to church.

(*At the left a large doorway, at the right an even larger gateway.* BEGGARS *and* PETITIONERS *pour from the gateway, holding up thin* CHILDREN, *crutches, and petitions. They are followed by* IRONSHIRTS, *and then, expensively dressed, the* GOVERNOR'S FAMILY.)

BEGGARS AND PETITIONERS

—Mercy! Mercy, Your Grace! The taxes are too high.
—I lost my leg in the Persian War, where can I get . . .
—My brother is innocent, Your Grace, a misunderstanding . . .
—The child is starving in my arms!
—Our petition is for our son's discharge from the army, our last remaining son!
—Please, Your Grace, the water inspector takes bribes.

(*One servant collects the petitions. Another distributes coins from a purse. Soldiers push the crowd back, lashing at them with thick leather whips.*)

SOLDIER   Get back! Clear the church door!

(*Behind the* GOVERNOR, *his* WIFE, *and the* ADJUTANT, *the* GOVERNOR'S CHILD *is brought through the gateway in an ornate carriage.*)

CROWD

—The baby!
—I can't see it, don't shove so hard!
—God bless the child, Your Grace!

SINGER (*while the crowd is driven back with whips*)

For the first time on that Easter Sunday, the people saw the Governor's
heir.

Two doctors never moved from the noble child, apple of the Governor's
eye.

Even the mighty Prince Kazbeki bows before him at the church door.

(*The* FAT PRINCE *steps forward and greets the* FAMILY.)

FAT PRINCE   Happy Easter, Natella Abashwili! What a day! When it was
raining last night, I thought to myself, gloomy holidays! But this morning
the sky was gay. I love a gay sky, a simple heart. Natella Abashwili. And
little Michael is a governor from head to foot! Tititi! (*He tickles the*
CHILD.)

GOVERNOR'S WIFE   What do you think, Arsen, at last Georgi has decided to
start building the east wing. All those wretched slums are to be torn
down to make room for the garden.

FAT PRINCE   Good news after so much bad! What's the latest on the war,
Brother Georgi? (*The* GOVERNOR *a lack of interest.*) Strategical retreat, I
hear. Well, minor reverses are to be expected. Sometimes things go well,
sometimes not. Such is war. Doesn't mean a thing, does it?

GOVERNOR'S WIFE   He's coughing. Georgi, did you hear? (*She speaks sharply
to the* DOCTORS, *two dignified men standing close to the little carriage.*) He's
coughing!

FIRST DOCTOR (*to the* SECOND)   May I remind you, Niko Mikadze, that I was
against the lukewarm bath? (*To the* GOVERNOR'S WIFE:) There's been a
little error over warming the bath water, Your Grace.

SECOND DOCTOR (*equally polite*)   Mika Loladze, I'm afraid I can't agree with
you. The temperature of the bath water was exactly what our great,
beloved Mishiko Oboladze prescribed. More likely a slight draft during
the night, Your Grace.

GOVERNOR'S WIFE   But do pay more attention to him. He looks feverish,
Georgi.

FIRST DOCTOR (*bending over the* CHILD)   No cause for alarm, Your Grace. The
bath water will be warmer. It won't occur again.

SECOND DOCTOR (*with a venomous glance at the* FIRST)   I won't forget that, my
dear Mika Loladze. No cause for concern, Your Grace.

FAT PRINCE   Well, well, well! I always say: "A pain in my liver? Then the
doctor gets fifty strokes on the soles of his feet." We live in a decadent
age. In the old days one said: "Off with his head!"

GOVERNOR'S WIFE   Let's go into church. Very likely it's the draft here.

(*The procession of* FAMILY *and* SERVANTS *turns into the
doorway. The* FAT PRINCE *follows, but the* GOVERNOR *is
kept back by the* ADJUTANT, *a handsome young man.
When the crowd of* PETITIONERS *has been driven off, a
young dust-stained* RIDER, *his arm in a sling, remains
behind.*)

ADJUTANT (*pointing at the* RIDER, *who steps forward*)   Won't you hear the
messenger from the capital, Your Excellency? He arrived this morning.
With confidential papers.

GOVERNOR   Not before Service, Shalva. But did you hear Brother Kazbeki
   wish me a happy Easter? Which is all very well, but I don't believe it did
   rain last night.
ADJUTANT (*nodding*)   We must investigate.
GOVERNOR   Yes, at once. Tomorrow.
   (*They pass through the doorway. The* RIDER, *who has
   waited in vain for an audience, turns sharply round and,
   muttering a curse, goes off. Only one of the palace
   guards—*SIMON SHASHAVA*—remains at the door.*)
SINGER
   The city is still.
   Pigeons strut in the church square.
   A soldier of the Palace Guard
   Is joking with a kitchen maid
   As she comes up from the river with a bundle.
   (*A girl—*GRUSHA VASHNADZE*—comes through the gateway
   with a bundle made of large green leaves under her arm.*)
SIMON   What, the young lady is not in church? Shirking?
GRUSHA   I was dressed to go. But they needed another goose for the banquet.
   And they asked me to get it. I know about geese.
SIMON   A goose? (*He feigns suspicion.*) I'd like to see that goose. (GRUSHA *does
   not understand.*) One must be on one's guard with women. "I only went
   for a fish," they tell you, but it turns out to be something else.
GRUSHA (*walking resolutely toward him and showing him the goose*)   There!
   If it isn't a fifteen-pound goose stuffed full of corn, I'll eat the feathers.
SIMON   A queen of a goose! The Governor himself will eat it. So the young
   lady has been down to the river again?
GRUSHA   Yes, at the poultry farm.
SIMON   Really? At the poultry farm, down by the river . . . not higher up
   maybe? Near those willows?
GRUSHA   I only go to the willows to wash the linen.
SIMON (*insinuatingly*)   Exactly.
GRUSHA   Exactly what?
SIMON (*winking*)   Exactly that.
GRUSHA   Why shouldn't I wash the linen by the willows?
SIMON (*with exaggerated laughter*)   "Why shouldn't I wash the linen by the
   willows!" That's good, really good!
GRUSHA   I don't understand the soldier. What's so good about it?
SIMON (*slyly*)   "If something I know someone learns, she'll grow hot and cold
   by turns!"
GRUSHA   I don't know what I could learn about those willows.
SIMON   Not even if there was a bush opposite? That one could see everything
   from? Everything that goes on there when a certain person is—"washing
   linen"?
GRUSHA   What does go on? Won't the soldier say what he means and have
   done?
SIMON   Something goes on. Something can be seen.

GRUSHA   Could the soldier mean I dip my toes in the water when it's hot? There's nothing else.

SIMON   There's more. Your toes. And more.

GRUSHA   More what? At most my foot?

SIMON   Your foot. And a little more. (*He laughs heartily.*)

GRUSHA (*angrily*)   Simon Shashava, you ought to be ashamed of yourself! To sit in a bush on a hot day and wait till a girl comes and dips her legs in the river! And I bet you bring a friend along too! (*She runs off.*)

SIMON (*shouting after her*)   I didn't bring any friend along!

> (*As the* SINGER *resumes his tale, the* SOLDIER *steps into the doorway as though to listen to the service.*)

SINGER

> The city lies still
> But why are there armed men?
> The Governor's palace is at peace
> But why is it a fortress?
> And the Governor returned to his palace
> And the fortress was a trap
> And the goose was plucked and roasted
> But the goose was not eaten this time
> And noon was no longer the hour to eat:
> Noon was the hour to die.

> (*From the doorway at the left the* FAT PRINCE *quickly appears, stands still, looks around. Before the gateway at the right two* IRONSHIRTS *are squatting and playing dice. The* FAT PRINCE *sees them, walks slowly past, making a sign to them. They rise: one goes through the gateway, the other goes off at the right. Muffled voices are heard from various directions in the rear:* "To your posts!" *The palace is surrounded. The* FAT PRINCE *quickly goes off. Church bells in the distance. Enter, through the doorway, the Governor's family and procession, returning from church.*)

GOVERNOR'S WIFE (*passing the* ADJUTANT)   It's impossible to live in such a slum. But Georgi, of course, will only build for his little Michael. Never for me! Michael is all! All for Michael!

> (*The procession turns into the gateway. Again the* ADJUTANT *lingers behind. He waits. Enter the wounded* RIDER *from the doorway. Two* IRONSHIRTS *of the Palace Guard have taken up positions by the gateway.*)

ADJUTANT (*to the* RIDER)   The Governor does not wish to receive military news before dinner—especially if it's depressing, as I assume. In the afternoon His Excellency will confer with prominent architects. They're coming to dinner too. And here they are! (*Enter three gentlemen through the doorway.*) Go to the kitchen and eat, my friend. (*As the* RIDER *goes, the* ADJUTANT *greets the* ARCHITECTS.) Gentlemen, His Excellency expects you at dinner. He will devote all his time to you and your great new plans. Come!

ONE OF THE ARCHITECTS   We marvel that His Excellency intends to build. There are disquieting rumors that the war in Persia has taken a turn for the worse.

ADJUTANT   All the more reason to build! There's nothing to those rumors anyway. Persia is a long way off, and the garrison here would let itself be hacked to bits for its Governor. (*Noise from the palace. The shrill scream of a woman. Someone is shouting orders. Dumbfounded, the* ADJUTANT *moves toward the gateway. An* IRONSHIRT *steps out, points his lance at him.*) What's this? Put down that lance, you dog.

ONE OF THE ARCHITECTS   It's the Princes! Don't you know the Princes met last night in the capital? And they're against the Grand Duke and his Governors? Gentlemen, we'd better make ourselves scarce. (*They rush off The* ADJUTANT *remains helplessly behind.*)

ADJUTANT (*furiously to the Palace Guard*)   Down with those lances! Don't you see the Governor's life is threatened?

> (*The* IRONSHIRTS *of the Palace Guard refuse to obey.
> They stare coldly and indifferently at the* ADJUTANT *and
> follow the next events without interest.*)

SINGER

O blindness of the great!
They go their way like gods,
Great over bent backs,
Sure of hired fists,
Trusting in the power
Which has lasted so long.
But long is not forever.
O change from age to age!
Thou hope of the people!

> (*Enter the* GOVERNOR, *through the gateway, between
> two* SOLDIERS *armed to the teeth. He is in chains. His face is gray.*)

Up, great sir, deign to walk upright!
From your palace the eyes of many foes follow you!
And now you don't need an architect, a carpenter will do.
You won't be moving into a new palace
But into a little hole in the ground.
Look about you once more, blind man!

> (*The arrested man looks round.*)

Does all you had please you?
Between the Easter Mass and the Easter meal
You are walking to a place whence no one returns.

> (*The* GOVERNOR *is led off. A horn sounds an alarm.
> Noise behind the gateway.*)

When the house of a great one collapses
Many little ones are slain.
Those who had no share in the *good* fortunes of the mighty
Often have a share in their *mis*fortunes.
The plunging wagon
Drags the sweating oxen down with it

Into the abyss.

> (*The* SERVANTS *come rushing through the gateway in panic.*)

SERVANTS (*among themselves*)

—The baskets!

—Take them all into the third courtyard! Food for five days!

—The mistress has fainted! Someone must carry her down.

—She must get away.

—What about us? We'll be slaughtered like chickens, as always.

—Goodness, what'll happen? There's bloodshed already in the city, they say.

—Nonsense, the Governor has just been asked to appear at a Princes' meeting. All very correct. Everything'll be ironed out. I heard this on the best authority . . .

> (*The two* DOCTORS *rush into the courtyard.*)

FIRST DOCTOR (*trying to restrain the other*)   Niko Mikadze, it is your duty as a doctor to attend Natella Abashwili.

SECOND DOCTOR   My duty! It's yours!

FIRST DOCTOR   Whose turn is it to look after the child today, Niko Mikadze, yours or mine?

SECOND DOCTOR   Do you really think, Mika Loladze, I'm going to stay a minute longer in this accursed house on that little brat's account? (*They start fighting. All one hears is:* "You neglect your duty!" *and* "Duty, my foot!" *Then the* SECOND DOCTOR *knocks the* FIRST *down.*) Go to hell! (*Exit.*)

> (*Enter the soldier,* SIMON SHASHAVA. *He searches in the crowd for* GRUSHA.)

SIMON   Grusha! There you are at last! What are you going to do?

GRUSHA   Nothing. If worst comes to worst, I've a brother in the mountains. How about you?

SIMON   Forget about me. (*Formally again*) Grusha Vashnadze, your wish to know my plans fills me with satisfaction. I've been ordered to accompany Madam Abashwili as her guard.

GRUSHA   But hasn't the Palace Guard mutinied?

SIMON (*seriously*)   That's a fact.

GRUSHA   Isn't it dangerous to go with her?

SIMON   In Tiflis, they say: Isn't the stabbing dangerous for the knife?

GRUSHA   You're not a knife, you're a man, Simon Shashava, what has that woman to do with you?

SIMON   That woman has nothing to do with me. I have my orders, and I go.

GRUSHA   The soldier is pigheaded: he is running into danger for nothing— nothing at all. I must get into the third courtyard, I'm in a hurry.

SIMON   Since we're both in a hurry we shouldn't quarrel. You need time for a good quarrel. May I ask if the young lady still has parents?

GRUSHA   No, just a brother.

SIMON   As time is short—my second question is this: Is the young lady as healthy as a fish in water?

GRUSHA   I may have a pain in the right shoulder once in a while. Otherwise
I'm strong enough for my job. No one has complained. So far.

SIMON   That's well known. When it's Easter Sunday, and the question arises
who'll run for the goose all the same, she'll be the one. My third question
is this: Is the young lady impatient? Does she want apples in winter?

GRUSHA   Impatient? No. But if a man goes to war without any reason and then
no message comes—that's bad.

SIMON   A message will come. And now my final question . . .

GRUSHA   Simon Shashava, I must get to the third courtyard at once. My
answer is yes.

SIMON   (*very embarrassed*)   Haste, they say, is the wind that blows down the
scaffolding. But they also say: The rich don't know what haste is. I'm
from . . .

GRUSHA   Kutsk . . .

SIMON   The young lady has been inquiring about me? I'm healthy, I have no
dependents, I make ten piasters a month, as paymaster twenty piasters,
and I'm asking—very sincerely—for your hand.

GRUSHA   Simon Shashava, it suits me well.

SIMON   (*taking from his neck a thin chain with a little cross on it*)   My
mother gave me this cross, Grusha Vashnadze. The chain is silver.
Please wear it.

GRUSHA   Many thanks, Simon.

SIMON   (*hangs it round her neck*)   It would be better to go to the third courtyard
now. Or there'll be difficulties. Anyway, I must harness the horses.
The young lady will understand?

GRUSHA   Yes, Simon.

> (*They stand undecided.*)

SIMON   I'll just take the mistress to the troops that have stayed loyal. When
the war's over, I'll be back. In two weeks. Or three. I hope my intended
won't get tired, awaiting my return.

GRUSHA

> Simon Shashava, I shall wait for you.
> Go calmly into battle, soldier
> The bloody battle, the bitter battle
> From which not everyone returns:
> When you return I shall be there.
> I shall be waiting for you under the green elm
> I shall be waiting for you under the bare elm
> I shall wait until the last soldier has returned
> And longer
> When you come back from the battle
> No boots will stand at my door
> The pillow beside mine will be empty
> And my mouth will be unkissed.
> When you return, when you return
> You will be able to say: It is just as it was.

SIMON   I thank you, Grusha Vashnadze. And good-bye!

*(He bows low before her. She does the same before him.
Then she runs quickly off without looking round. Enter
the* ADJUTANT *from the gateway.)*

ADJUTANT (*harshly*)   Harness the horses to the carriage! Don't stand there
doing nothing, scum!

> (SIMON SHASHAVA *stands to attention and goes off. Two*
> SERVANTS *crowd from the gateway, bent low under huge
> trunks. Behind them, supported by her women, stumbles*
> NATELLA ABASHWILI. *She is followed by a* WOMAN
> *carrying the* CHILD.)

GOVERNOR'S WIFE   I hardly know if my head's still on. Where's Michael? Don't
hold him so clumsily. Pile the trunks onto the carriage. No news from
the city, Shalva?

ADJUTANT   None. All's quiet so far, but there's not a minute to lose. No room
for all those trunks in the carriage. Pick out what you need. (*Exit
quickly.*)

GOVERNOR'S WIFE   Only essentials! Quick, open the trunks! I'll tell you what I
need. (*The trunks are lowered and opened. She points at some brocade
dresses.*) The green one! And, of course, the one with the fur trimming.
Where are Niko Mikadze and Mika Loladze? I've suddenly got the most
terrible migraine again. It always starts in the temples. (*Enter* GRUSHA.)
Taking your time, eh? Go and get the hot water bottles this minute!
(GRUSHA *runs off, returns later with hot water bottles; the* GOVERNOR'S
WIFE *orders her about by signs.*) Don't tear the sleeves.

A YOUNG WOMAN   Pardon, madam, no harm has come to the dress.

GOVERNOR'S WIFE   Because I stopped you. I've been watching you for a long
time. Nothing in your head but making eyes at Shalva Tzereteli. I'll kill
you, you bitch! (*She beats the* YOUNG WOMAN.)

ADJUTANT (*appearing in the gateway*)   Please make haste, Natella Abashwili.
Firing has broken out in the city.

> (*Exit.*)

GOVERNOR'S WIFE (*letting go of the* YOUNG WOMAN)   Oh, dear, do you think
they'll lay hands on us? Why should they? Why? (*She herself begins to
rummage in the trunks.*) How's Michael? Asleep?

WOMAN WITH THE CHILD   Yes, madam.

GOVERNOR'S WIFE   Then put him down a moment and get my little saffron-
colored boots from the bedroom. I need them for the green dress. (*The
WOMAN puts down the* CHILD *and goes off.*) Just look how these things
have been packed! No love! No understanding! If you don't give them
every order yourself . . . At such moments you realize what kind of
servants you have! They gorge themselves at your expense, and never a
word of gratitude! I'll remember this.

ADJUTANT (*entering, very excited*)   Natella, you must leave at once!

GOVERNOR'S WIFE   Why? I've got to take this silver dress—it cost a thousand
piasters. And that one there, and where's the wine-colored one?

ADJUTANT (*trying to pull her away*)   Riots have broken out! We must leave
at once. Where's the baby?

GOVERNOR'S WIFE (*calling to the* YOUNG WOMAN *who was holding the baby*)
Maro, get the baby ready! Where on earth are you?

ADJUTANT (*leaving*) We'll probably have to leave the carriage behind and go ahead on horseback.

> (*The* GOVERNOR'S WIFE *rummages again among her dresses, throws some onto the heap of chosen clothes, then takes them off again. Noises, drums are heard. The* YOUNG WOMAN *who was beaten creeps away. The sky begins to grow red.*)

GOVERNOR'S WIFE (*rummaging desperately*) I simply cannot find the wine-colored dress. Take the whole pile to the carriage. Where's Asja? And why hasn't Maro come back? Have you all gone crazy?

ADJUTANT (*returning*) Quick! Quick!

GOVERNOR'S WIFE (*to the* FIRST WOMAN) Run! Just throw them into the carriage!

ADJUTANT We're not taking the carriage. And if you don't come now, I'll ride off on my own.

GOVERNOR'S WIFE (*as the* FIRST WOMAN *can't carry everything*) Where's that bitch Asja? (*The* ADJUTANT *pulls her away.*) Maro, bring the baby! (*To the* FIRST WOMAN) Go and look for Masha. No, first take the dresses to the carriage. Such nonsense! I wouldn't dream of going on horseback!

> (*Turning round, she sees the red sky, and starts back rigid. The fire burns. She is pulled out by the* ADJUTANT. *Shaking, the* FIRST WOMAN *follows with the dresses.*)

MARO (*from the doorway with the boots*) Madam! (*She sees the trunks and dresses and runs toward the* CHILD, *picks it up, and holds it a moment.*) They left it behind, the beasts. (*She hands it to* GRUSHA.) Hold it a moment. (*She runs off, following the* GOVERNOR'S WIFE.)

> (*Enter* SERVANTS *from the gateway.*)

COOK Well, so they've actually gone. Without the food wagons, and not a minute too early. It's time for us to clear out.

GROOM This'll be an unhealthy neighborhood for quite a while. (*To one of the* WOMEN:) Suliko, take a few blankets and wait for me in the foal stables.

GRUSHA What have they done with the Governor?

GROOM (*gesturing throat cutting*) Ffffft.

A FAT WOMAN (*seeing the gesture and becoming hysterical*) Oh, dear, oh dear, oh dear, oh dear! Our master Georgi Abashwili! A picture of health he was, at the morning Mass—and now! Oh, take me away, we've all lost, we must die in sin like our master, Georgi Abashwili!

OTHER WOMAN (*soothing her*) Calm down, Nina! You'll be taken to safety. You've never hurt a fly.

FAT WOMAN (*being led out*) Oh dear, oh dear, oh dear! Quick! Let's all get out before they come, before they come!

A YOUNG WOMAN Nina takes it more to heart than the mistress, that's a fact. They even have to have their weeping done for them.

COOK We'd better get out, all of us.

ANOTHER WOMAN (*glancing back*) That must be the East Gate burning.

YOUNG WOMAN (*seeing the* CHILD *in* GRUSHA'S *arms*) The baby! What are you doing with it?

GRUSHA It got left behind.

YOUNG WOMAN She simply left it there. Michael, who was kept out of all the drafts!

(*The* SERVANTS *gather round the* CHILD.)

GRUSHA   He's waking up.

GROOM   Better put him down, I tell you. I'd rather not think what'd happen to anybody who was found with that baby.

COOK   That's right. Once they get started, they'll kill each other off, whole families at a time. Let's go.

(*Exeunt all but* GRUSHA, *with the* CHILD *on her arm, and* TWO WOMEN.)

TWO WOMEN   Didn't you hear? Better put him down.

GRUSHA   The nurse asked me to hold him a moment.

OLDER WOMAN   She's not coming back, you simpleton.

YOUNGER WOMAN   Keep your hands off it.

OLDER WOMAN (*amiably*)   Grusha, you're a good soul, but you're not very bright, and you know it. I tell you, if he had the plague he couldn't be more dangerous.

GRUSHA (*stubbornly*)   He hasn't got the plague. He looks at me! He's human!

OLDER WOMAN   Don't look at *him*. You're a fool—the kind that always gets put upon. A person need only say, "Run for the salad, you have the longest legs," and you run. My husband has an ox cart—you can come with us if you hurry! Lord, by now the whole neighborhood must be in flames.

(*Both women leave, sighing. After some hesitation,* GRUSHA *puts the sleeping* CHILD *down, looks at it for a moment, then takes a brocade blanket from the heap of clothes and covers it. Then both women return, dragging bundles.* GRUSHA *starts guiltily away from the* CHILD *and walks a few steps to one side.*)

YOUNGER WOMAN   Haven't you packed anything yet? There isn't much time, you know. The Ironshirts will be here from the barracks.

GRUSHA   Coming!

(*She runs through the doorway. Both women go to the gateway and wait. The sound of horses is heard. They flee screaming. Enter the* FAT PRINCE *with drunken* IRONSHIRTS. *One of them carries the Governor's head on a lance.*)

FAT PRINCE   Here! In the middle! (*One soldier climbs onto the other's back, takes the head, holds it tentatively over the door.*) That's not the middle. Farther to the right. That's it. What I do, my friends, I do well. (*While with hammer and nail, the soldier fastens the head to the wall by its hair:*) This morning at the church door I said to Georgi Abashwili: "I love a gay sky." Actually, I prefer the lightning that comes out of a gay sky. Yes, indeed. It's a pity they took the brat along, though, I need him, urgently.

(*Exit with* IRONSHIRTS *through the gateway. Trampling of horses again. Enter* GRUSHA *through the doorway looking cautiously about her. Clearly she has waited for the* IRONSHIRTS *to go. Carrying a bundle, she walks toward the gateway. At the last moment, she turns to see if the* CHILD *is still there. Catching sight of the head over the*

*doorway, she screams. Horrified, she picks up her bundle
again, and is about to leave when the* SINGER *starts to
speak. She stands rooted to the spot.*)

SINGER

As she was standing between courtyard and gate,
She heard or she thought she heard a low voice calling.
The child called to her,
Not whining, but calling quite sensibly,
Or so it seemed to her.
"Woman," it said, "help me."
And it went on, not whining, but saying quite sensibly:
"Know, woman, he who hears not a cry for help
But passes by with troubled ears will never hear
The gentle call of a lover nor the blackbird at dawn
Nor the happy sigh of the tired grape-picker as the Angelus rings."
(*She walks a few steps toward the* CHILD *and bends
over it.*)
Hearing this she went back for one more look at the child:
Only to sit with him for a moment or two,
Only till someone should come,
His mother, or anyone.
(*Leaning on a trunk, she sits facing the* CHILD.)
Only till she would have to leave, for the danger was too great,
The city was full of flame and crying.
(*The light grows dimmer, as though evening and night
were coming on.*)
Fearful is the seductive power of goodness!
(GRUSHA *now settles down to watch over the* CHILD
*through the night. Once, she lights a small lamp to look
at it. Once, she tucks it in with a coat. From time to time
she listens and looks to see whether someone is coming.*)
And she sat with the child a long time,
Till evening came, till night came, till dawn came.
She sat too long, too long she saw
The soft breathing, the small clenched fists,
Till toward morning the seduction was complete
And she rose, and bent down and, sighing, took the child
And carried it away.
(*She does what the* SINGER *says as he describes it.*)
As if it was stolen goods she picked it up.
As if she was a thief she crept away.

2   The Flight into the Northern Mountains

SINGER

When Grusha Vashnadze left the city
On the Grusinian highway

On the way to the Northern Mountains
She sang a song, she bought some milk.

CHORUS

How will this human child escape
The bloodhounds, the trap-setters?
Into the deserted mountains she journeyed
Along the Grusinian highway she journeyed
She sang a song, she bought some milk.

(GRUSHA VASHNADZE *walks on. On her back she carries the* CHILD *in a sack, in one hand is a large stick, in the other a bundle. She sings.*)

THE SONG OF THE FOUR GENERALS

Four generals
Set out for Iran.
With the first one, war did not agree.
The second never won a victory.
For the third the weather never was right.
For the fourth the men would never fight.
Four generals
And not a single man!
Sosso Robakidse
Went marching to Iran
With him the war did so agree
He soon had won a victory.
For him the weather was always right.
For him the men would always fight.
Sosso Robakidse,
He is our man!

(*A peasant's cottage appears.*)

GRUSHA (*to the* CHILD)   Noontime is meal time. Now we'll sit hopefully in the grass, while the good Grusha goes and buys a little pitcher of milk. (*She lays the* CHILD *down and knocks at the cottage door. An* OLD MAN *opens it.*) Grandfather, could I have a little pitcher of milk? And a corn cake, maybe?

OLD MAN   Milk? We have no milk. The soldiers from the city have our goats. Go to the soldiers if you want milk.

GRUSHA   But grandfather, you must have a little pitcher of milk for a baby?

OLD MAN   And for a God-bless-you, eh?

GRUSHA   Who said anything about a God-bless-you? (*She shows her purse.*) We'll pay like princes. "Head in the clouds, backside in the water." (*The peasant goes off, grumbling, for milk*) How much for the milk?

OLD MAN   Three piasters. Milk has gone up.

GRUSHA   Three piasters for this little drop? (*Without a word the* OLD MAN *shuts the door in her face.*) Michael, did you hear that? Three piasters! We can't afford it! (*She goes back, sits down again, and gives the* CHILD *her breast.*) Suck. Think of the three piasters. There's nothing there, but you *think* you're drinking, and that's something. (*Shaking her head, she sees that the* CHILD *isn't sucking any more. She gets up, walks back to the door, and knocks again.*) Open, grandfather, we'll pay. (*Softly*) May lightning strike you! (*When the* OLD MAN *appears:*) I thought it would be half a piaster. But the baby must be fed. How about one piaster for that little drop?

OLD MAN   Two.

GRUSHA   Don't shut the door again. (*She fishes a long time in her bag.*) Here are two piasters. The milk better be good. I still have two days' journey ahead of me. It's a murderous business you have here—and sinful, too!

OLD MAN   Kill the soldiers if you want milk.

GRUSHA (*giving the* CHILD *some milk*)   This is an expensive joke. Take a sip, Michael, it's a week's pay. Around here they think we earned our money just sitting on our behinds. Oh, Michael, Michael, you're a nice little load for a girl to take on! (*Uneasy, she gets up, puts the* CHILD *on her back, and walks on. The* OLD MAN, *grumbling, picks up the pitcher and looks after her unmoved.*)

SINGER
> As Grusha Vashnadze went northward
> The Princes' Ironshirts went after her.

CHORUS
> How will the barefoot girl escape the Ironshirts,
> The bloodhounds, the trap-setters?
> They hunt even by night.
> Pursuers never tire.
> Butchers sleep little.

> (*Two* IRONSHIRTS *are trudging along the highway.*)

CORPORAL   You'll never amount to anything, blockhead, your heart's not in it. Your senior officer sees this in little things. Yesterday, when I made the fat gal, yes, you grabbed her husband as I commanded, and you did kick him in the belly, at my request, but did you *enjoy* it, like a loyal Private, or were you just doing your duty? I've kept an eye on you, blockhead, you're a hollow reed and a tinkling cymbal, you won't get promoted. (*They walk a while in silence.*) Don't think I've forgotten how insubordinate you are, either. Stop limping! I forbid you to limp! You limp because I sold the horses, and I sold the horses because I'd never have got that price again. You limp to show me you don't like marching. I know you. It won't help. You wait. Sing!

TWO IRONSHIRTS (*singing*)
> Sadly to war I went my way
> Leaving my loved one at her door.
> My friends will keep her honor safe
> Till from the war I'm back once more.

CORPORAL   Louder!

TWO IRONSHIRTS (*singing*)
> When 'neath a headstone I shall be
> My love a little earth will bring:
> "Here rest the feet that oft would run to me

And here the arms that oft to me would cling."
> (*They begin to walk again in silence.*)

CORPORAL   A good soldier has his heart and soul in it. When he receives an
order, he gets a hard-on, and when he drives his lance into the enemy's
guts, he comes. (*He shouts for joy.*) He lets himself be torn to bits for his
superior officer, and as he lies dying he takes note that his corporal is
nodding approval, and that is reward enough, it's his dearest wish. *You*
won't get any nod of approval, but you'll croak all right. Christ, how'm
I to get my hands on the Governor's bastard with the help of a fool like
you! (*They stay on stage behind.*)

SINGER
> When Grusha Vashnadze came to the River Sirra
> Flight grew too much for her, the helpless child too heavy.
> In the cornfields the rosy dawn
> Is cold to the sleepless one, only cold.
> The gay clatter of the milk cans in the farmyard where the smoke rises
> Is only a threat to the fugitive.
> She who carries the child feels its weight and little more.

> (GRUSHA *stops in front of a farm. A fat* PEASANT WOMAN
> *is carrying a milk can through the door.* GRUSHA *waits
> until she has gone in, then approaches the house
> cautiously.*)

GRUSHA (*to the* CHILD)   Now you've wet yourself again, and you know I've no
linen. Michael, this is where we part company. It's far enough from the
city. They wouldn't want you *so* much that they'd follow you all *this* way,
little good-for-nothing. The peasant woman is kind, and can't you just
smell the milk? (*She bends down to lay the* CHILD *on the threshold.*) So
farewell, Michael, I'll forget how you kicked me in the back all night to
make me walk faster. And you can forget the meager fare—it was meant
well. I'd like to have kept you—your nose is so tiny—but it can't be. I'd
have shown you your first rabbit, I'd have trained you to keep dry, but
now I must turn around. My sweetheart the soldier might be back soon,
and suppose he didn't find me? You can't ask that, can you? (*She creeps
up to the door and lays the* CHILD *on the threshold. Then, hiding behind a
tree, she waits until the* PEASANT WOMAN *opens the door and sees the
bundle.*)

PEASANT WOMAN   Good heavens, what's this? Husband!

PEASANT   What is it? Let me finish my soup.

PEASANT WOMAN (*to the* CHILD)   Where's your mother then? Haven't you got
one? It's a boy. Fine linen. He's from a good family, you can see that.
And they just leave him on our doorstep. Oh, these are times!

PEASANT   If they think we're going to feed it, they're wrong. You can take it
to the priest in the village. That's the best we can do.

PEASANT WOMAN   What'll the priest do with him? He needs a mother. There,
he waking up. Don't you think we could keep him, though?

PEASANT (*shouting*)   No!

PEASANT WOMAN   I could lay him in the corner by the armchair. All I need is a
crib. I can take him into the fields with me. See him laughing? Husband,

we have a roof over our heads. We can do it. Not another word out of
you!

> (*She carries the* CHILD *into the house. The* PEASANT
> *follows protesting.* GRUSHA *steps out from behind the
> tree, laughs, and hurries off in the opposite direction.*)

SINGER

Why so cheerful, making for home?

CHORUS

Because the child has won new parents with a laugh,
Because I'm rid of the little one. I'm cheerful.

SINGER

And why so sad?

CHORUS

Because I'm single and free, I'm sad
Like someone who's been robbed
Someone who's newly poor.

> (*She walks for a short while, then meets the two*
> IRONSHIRTS *who point their lances at her.*)

CORPORAL   Lady, you are running straight into the arms of the Armed Forces.
Where are you coming from? And when? Are you having illicit relations
with the enemy? Where is he hiding? What movements is he making in
your rear? How about the hills? How about the valleys? How are your
stockings held in position? (GRUSHA *stands there frightened.*) Don't be
scared, we always withdraw, if necessary . . . what, blockhead? I always
withdraw. In that respect at least, I can be relied on. Why are you staring
like that at my lance? In the field no soldier drops his lance, that's a rule.
Learn it by heart, blockhead. Now, lady, where are you headed?

GRUSHA   To meet my intended, one Simon Shashava, of the Palace Guard in
Nuka.

CORPORAL   Simon Shashava? Sure, I know him. He gave me the key so I could
look you up once in a while. Blockhead, we are getting to be unpopular.
We must make her realize we have honorable intentions. Lady, behind
apparent frivolity I conceal a serious nature, so let me tell you officially:
I want a child from you. (GRUSHA *utters a little scream.*) Blockhead, she
understands me. Uh-huh, isn't it a sweet shock? "Then first I must take
the noodles out of the oven, Officer. Then first I must change my torn
shirt, Colonel." But away with jokes, away with my lance! We are
looking for a baby. A baby from a good family. Have you heard of such
a baby, from the city, dressed in fine linen, and suddenly turning up here?

GRUSHA   No, I haven't heard a thing. (*Suddenly she turns round and runs back,
panic-stricken. The* IRONSHIRTS *glance at each other, then follow her,
cursing.*)

SINGER

Run, kind girl! The killers are coming!
Help the helpless babe, helpless girl!
And so she runs!

CHORUS

In the bloodiest times

There are kind people.

(*As* GRUSHA *rushes into the cottage, the* PEASANT WOMAN *is bending over the* CHILD'S *crib.*)

GRUSHA   Hide him. Quick! The Ironshirts are coming! I laid him on your doorstep. But he isn't mine. He's from a good family.

PEASANT WOMAN   Who's coming? What Ironshirts?

GRUSHA   Don't ask questions. The Ironshirts that are looking for it.

PEASANT WOMAN   They've no business in my house. But I must have a little talk with you, it seems.

GRUSHA   Take off the fine linen. It'll give us away.

PEASANT WOMAN   Linen, my foot! In this house I make the decisions! "*You* can't vomit in *my* room!" Why did you abandon it? It's a sin.

GRUSHA (*looking out of the window*)   Look, they're coming out from behind those trees! I shouldn't have run away, it made them angry. Oh, what shall I do?

PEASANT WOMAN (*looking out of the window and suddenly starting with fear*) Gracious! Ironshirts!

GRUSHA   They're after the baby.

PEASANT WOMAN   Suppose they come in!

GRUSHA   You mustn't give him to them. Say he's yours.

PEASANT WOMAN   Yes.

GRUSHA   They'll run him through if you hand him over.

PEASANT WOMAN   But suppose they ask for it? The silver for the harvest is in the house.

GRUSHA   If you let them have him, they'll run him through, right here in this room! You've got to say he's yours!

PEASANT WOMAN   Yes. But what if they don't believe me?

GRUSHA   You must be firm.

PEASANT WOMAN   They'll burn the roof over our heads.

GRUSHA   That's why you must say he's yours. His name's Michael. But I shouldn't have told you. (*The* PEASANT WOMAN *nods.*) Don't nod like that. And don't tremble—they'll notice.

PEASANT WOMAN   Yes.

GRUSHA   And stop saying yes, I can't stand it. (*She shakes the* WOMAN.) Don't you have any children?

PEASANT WOMAN (*muttering*)   He's in the war.

GRUSHA   Then maybe *he's* an Ironshirt? Do you want *him* to run children through with a lance? You'd bawl him out. "No fooling with lances in my house!" you'd shout, "is that what I've reared you for? Wash your neck before you speak to your mother!"

PEASANT WOMAN   That's true, he couldn't get away with anything around here!

GRUSHA   So you'll say he's yours?

PEASANT WOMAN   Yes.

GRUSHA   Look! They're coming!

(*There is a knocking at the door. The women don't answer. Enter* IRONSHIRTS. *The* PEASANT WOMAN *bows low.*)

CORPORAL   Well, here she is. What did I tell you? What a nose I have! I *smelt* her. Lady, I have a question for you. Why did you run away? What did you think I would do to you? I'll bet it was something unchaste. Confess!

GRUSHA (*while the* PEASANT WOMAN *bows again and again.*) I'd left some milk on the stove, and I suddenly remembered it.

CORPORAL Or maybe you imagined I looked at you unchastely? Like there could be something between us? A carnal glance, know what I mean?

GRUSHA I didn't see it.

CORPORAL But it's possible, huh? You admit that much. After all, I might be a pig. I'll be frank with you: I could think of all sorts of things if we were alone. (*To the* PEASANT WOMAN:) Shouldn't you be busy in the yard? Feeding the hens?

PEASANT WOMAN (*falling suddenly to her knees*): Soldier, I didn't know a thing about it. Please don't burn the roof over our heads.

CORPORAL What are you talking about?

PEASANT WOMAN I had nothing to do with it. She left it on my doorstep, I swear it!

CORPORAL (*suddenly seeing the* CHILD *and whistling*): Ah, so there's a little something in the crib! Blockhead, I smell a thousand piasters. Take the old girl outside and hold on to her. It looks like I have a little cross-examining to do. (*The* PEASANT WOMAN *lets herself be led out by the* PRIVATE, *without a word.*) So, you've got the child I wanted from you! (*He walks toward the crib.*)

GRUSHA Officer, he's mine. He's not the one you're after.

CORPORAL I'll just take a look. (*He bends over the crib.*)
　　　　　(GRUSHA *looks round in despair.*)

GRUSHA He's mine! He's mine!

CORPORAL Fine linen!
　　　　　(GRUSHA *dashes at him to pull him away. He throws her off and again bends over the crib. Again looking round in despair, she sees a log of wood, seizes it, and hits the* CORPORAL *over the head from behind. The* CORPORAL *collapses. She quickly picks up the* CHILD *and rushes off.*)

SINGER

And in her flight from the Ironshirts
After twenty-two days of journeying
At the foot of the Janga-Tau Glacier
Grusha Vashnadze decided to adopt the child.

CHORUS

The helpless girl adopted the helpless child.
　　　　　(GRUSHA *squats over a half-frozen stream to get the* CHILD *water in the hollow of her hand.*)

GRUSHA

Since no one else will take you, son,
I must take you.
Since no one else will take you, son,
You must take me.

O black day in a lean, lean year,
The trip was long, the milk was dear,
My legs are tired, my feet are sore:
But I wouldn't be without you any more.
I'll throw your silken shirt away
And wrap you in rags and tatters.
I'll wash you, son, and christen you in glacier water.
We'll see it through together.

> (*She has taken off the child's fine linen and wrapped it
> in a rag.*)

SINGER

When Grusha Vashnadze
Pursued by the Ironshirts
Came to the bridge on the glacier
Leading to the villages of the Eastern Slope
She sang the Song of the Rotten Bridge
And risked two lives.

> (*A wind has risen. The bridge on the glacier is visible in
> the dark. One rope is broke and half the bridge is
> hanging down the abyss.* MERCHANTS, *two men and a
> woman, stand undecided before the bridge as* GRUSHA *and
> the* CHILD *arrive. One man is trying to catch the hanging
> rope with a stick.*)

FIRST MAN   Take your time, young woman. You won't get across here anyway.

GRUSHA   But I *have* to get the baby to the east side. To my brother's place.

MERCHANT WOMAN   Have to? How d'you mean, "have to"? I have to get there, too—because I have to buy carpets in Atum—carpets a woman had to sell because her husband had to die. But can *I* do what I have to? Can she? Andrei's been fishing for that rope for hours. And I ask you, how are we going to fasten it, even if he gets it up?

FIRST MAN (*listening*)   Hush, I think I hear something.

GRUSHA   The bridge isn't quite rotted through. I think I'll try it.

MERCHANT WOMAN   *I* wouldn't—if the devil himself were after me. It's suicide.

FIRST MAN (*shouting*)   Hi!

GRUSHA   Don't shout! (*To the* MERCHANT WOMAN) Tell him not to shout.

FIRST MAN   But there's someone down there calling. Maybe they've lost their way.

MERCHANT WOMAN   Why shouldn't he shout? Is there something funny about you? Are they after you?

GRUSHA   All right, I'll tell. The Ironshirts are after me. I knocked one down.

SECOND MAN   Hide our merchandise!

> (*The* WOMAN *hides a sack behind a rock.*)

FIRST MAN   Why didn't you say so right away? (*To the others:*) If they catch her they'll make mincemeat out of her!

GRUSHA   Get out of my way. I've got to cross that bridge.

SECOND MAN   You can't. The precipice is two thousand feet deep.

FIRST MAN   Even with the rope it'd be no use. We could hold it up with our hands. But then we'd have to do the same for the Ironshirts.

GRUSHA   Go away.

> (*There are calls from the distance*) "Hi, up there!"

MERCHANT WOMAN   They're getting near. But you can't take the child on that bridge. It's sure to break. And look!

> (GRUSHA *looks down into the abyss. The* IRONSHIRTS *are heard calling again from below.*)

SECOND MAN   Two thousand feet!

GRUSHA   But those men are worse.

FIRST MAN   You can't do it. Think of the baby. Risk your life but not a child's.

SECOND MAN   With the child she's that much heavier!

MERCHANT WOMAN   Maybe she's *really* got to get across. Give *me* the baby. I'll hide it. Cross the bridge alone!

GRUSHA   I won't. We belong together. (*To the* CHILD) "Live together, die together." (*She sings.*)

> THE SONG OF THE ROTTEN BRIDGE
> Deep is the abyss, son,
> I see the weak bridge sway
> But it's not for us, son,
> To choose the way.
>
> The way I know
> Is the one you must tread,
> And all you will eat
> Is my bit of bread.
>
> Of every four pieces
> You shall have three.
> Would that I knew
> How big they will be!

Get out of my way, I'll try it without the rope.

MERCHANT WOMAN   You are tempting God!

> (*There are shouts from below.*)

GRUSHA   Please, throw that stick away, or they'll get the rope and follow me.

> (*Pressing the* CHILD *to her, she steps onto the swaying bridge. The* MERCHANT WOMAN *screams when it looks as though the bridge is about to collapse. But* GRUSHA *walks on and reaches the far side.*)

FIRST MAN   She made it!

MERCHANT WOMAN (*who has fallen on her knees and begun to pray, angrily*)   I still think it was a sin.

> (*The* IRONSHIRTS *appear; the* CORPORAL'S *head is bandaged.*)

CORPORAL   Seen a woman with a child?

FIRST MAN (*while the* SECOND MAN *throws the stick into the abyss*)   Yes, there! But the bridge won't carry you!

CORPORAL   You'll pay for this, blockhead!

> (GRUSHA, *from the far bank, laughs and shows the* CHILD *to the* IRONSHIRTS. *She walks on. The wind blows.*)

GRUSHA (*turning to the* CHILD)   You mustn't be afraid of the wind. He's a poor thing too. He has to push the clouds along and he gets quite cold doing it. (*Snow starts falling.*) And the snow isn't so bad, either, Michael. It covers the little fir trees so they won't die in winter. Let me sing you a little song.

(*She sings.*)

THE SONG OF THE CHILD

Your father is a bandit
A harlot the mother who bore you.
Yet honorable men
Shall kneel down before you.

Food to the baby horses
The tiger's son will take.
The mothers will get milk
From the son of the snake.

3 In the Northern Mountains

SINGER

Seven days the sister, Grusha Vashnadze,
Journeyed across the glacier
And down the slopes she journeyed.
"When I enter my brother's house," she thought,
"He will rise and embrace me."
"Is that you, sister?" he will say,
"I have long expected you.
This is my dear wife,
And this is my farm, come to me by marriage,
With eleven horses and thirty-one cows. Sit down.
Sit down with your child at our table and eat."
The brother's house was in a lovely valley.
When the sister came to the brother,
She was ill from walking.
The brother rose from the table.

> (*A fat peasant couple rise from the table.* LAVRENTI
> VASHNADZE *still has a napkin round his neck, as* GRUSHA,
> *pale and supported by a* SERVANT, *enters with the* CHILD.)

LAVRENTI   Where've *you* come from, Grusha?

GRUSHA (*feebly*)   Across the Janga-Tu Pass, Lavrenti.

SERVANT   I found her in front of the hay barn. She has a baby with her.

SISTER-IN-LAW   Go and groom the mare.

> (*Exit the* SERVANT.)

LAVRENTI   This is my wife Aniko.

SISTER-IN-LAW   I thought you were in service in Nuka.

GRUSHA (*barely able to stand*)   Yes, I was.

SISTER-IN-LAW   Wasn't it a good job? We were told it was.

GRUSHA   The Governor got killed.

LAVRENTI   Yes, we heard there were riots. Your aunt told us. Remember, Aniko?

SISTER-IN-LAW   Here with us, it's very quiet. City people always want something going on. (*She walks toward the door, calling:*) Sosso, Sosso, don't take the cake out of the oven yet, d'you hear? Where on earth are you? (*Exit, calling.*)

LAVRENTI (*quietly, quickly*)   Is there a father? (*As she shakes her head*) I thought not. We must think up something. She's religious.

SISTER-IN-LAW (*returning*)   Those servants! (*To* GRUSHA) You have a child.

GRUSHA   It's mine. (*She collapses.* LAVRENTI *rushes to her assistance.*)

SISTER-IN-LAW   Heavens, she's ill—what are we going to do?

LAVRENTI (*escorting her to a bench near the stove*)   Sit down, sit. I think it's just weakness. Aniko.

SISTER-IN-LAW   As long as it's not scarlet fever!

LAVRENTI   She'd have spots if it was. It's only weakness. Don't worry, Aniko (*To* GRUSHA:) Better, sitting down?

SISTER-IN-LAW   Is the child hers?

GRUSHA   Yes, mine.

LAVRENTI   She's on her way to her husband.

SISTER-IN-LAW   I see. Your meat's getting cold. (LAVRENTI *sits down and begins to eat.*) Cold food's not good for you, the fat mustn't get cold, you know your stomach's your weak spot. (*To* GRUSHA) If your husband's not in the city, where is he?

LAVRENTI   She got married on the other side of the mountain, she says.

SISTER-IN-LAW   On the other side of the mountain. I see. (*She also sits down to eat.*)

GRUSHA   I think I should lie down somewhere, Lavrenti.

SISTER-IN-LAW   If it's consumption we'll all get it. (*She goes on cross-examining her.*) Has your husband got a farm?

GRUSHA   He's a soldier.

LAVRENTI   But he's coming into a farm—a small one—from his father.

SISTER-IN-LAW   Isn't he in the war? Why not?

GRUSHA (*with effort*)   Yes, he's in the war.

SISTER-IN-LAW   Then why d'you want to go to the farm?

LAVRENTI   When he comes back from the war, he'll return to his farm.

SISTER-IN-LAW   But you're going there now?

LAVRENTI   Yes, to wait for him.

SISTER-IN-LAW (*calling shrilly*)   Sosso, the cake!

GRUSHA (*murmuring feverishly*)   A farm—a soldier—waiting—sit down, eat.

SISTER-IN-LAW   It's scarlet fever.

GRUSHA (*starting up*)   Yes, he's got a farm!

LAVRENTI   I think it's just weakness, Aniko. Would you look after the cake yourself, dear?

SISTER-IN-LAW   But when will he come back if war's broken out again as people say? (*She waddles off, shouting:*) Sosso! Where on earth are you? Sosso!

LAVRENTI (*getting up quickly and going to* GRUSHA)   You'll get a bed in a minute. She has a good heart. But wait till after supper.

GRUSHA (*holding out the* CHILD *to him*)   Take him.

LAVRENTI (*taking it and looking around*)   But you can't stay here long with the child. She's religious, you see.

(GRUSHA *collapses.* LAVRENTI *catches her.*)

SINGER

    The sister was so ill,
    The cowardly brother had to give her shelter.
    Summer departed, winter came.
    The winter was long, the winter was short.
    People mustn't know anything.
    Rats mustn't bite.
    Spring mustn't come.

        (GRUSHA *sits over the weaving loom in a workroom. She
        and the* CHILD, *who is squatting on the floor, are wrapped
        in blankets. She sings.*)
        (*Enter* LAVRENTI. *He sits down beside his sister.*)

          THE SONG OF THE CENTER
    And the lover started to leave
    And his betrothed ran pleading after him
    Pleading and weeping, weeping and teaching:
    "Dearest mine, dearest mine
    When you go to war as now you do
    When you fight the foe as soon you will
    Don't lead with the front line
    And don't push with the rear line
    At the front is red fire
    In the rear is red smoke
    Stay in the war's center
    Stay near the standard bearer
    The first always die
    The last are also hit
    Those in the center come home."

Michael, we must be clever. If we make ourselves as small as cockroaches, the sister-in-law will forget we're in the house, and then we can stay till the snow melts.

    (*Enter* LAVRENTI. *He sits down beside his sister.*)

LAVRENTI   Why are you sitting there muffled up like coachmen, you two? Is it too cold in the room?

GRUSHA (*hastily removing one shawl*)   It's not too cold, Lavrenti.

LAVRENTI   If it's too cold, you shouldn't be sitting here with the child. Aniko would never forgive herself! (*Pause*) I hope our priest didn't question you about the child?

GRUSHA   He did, but I didn't tell him anything.

LAVRENTI   That's good. I wanted to speak to you about Aniko. She has a good heart but she's very, very sensitive. People need only mention our farm and she's worried. She takes everything hard, you see. One time our milk-maid went to church with a hole in her stocking. Ever since, Aniko has worn two pairs of stockings in church. It's old family in her. (*He listens.*) Are you sure there are no rats around? If there are rats, you couldn't live here. (*There are sounds as of dripping from the roof.*) What's that, dripping?

GRUSHA   It must be a barrel leaking.

LAVRENTI   Yes, it must be a barrel. You've been here six months, haven't you? Was I talking about Aniko? (*They listen again to the snow melting.*) You can't imagine how worried she gets about your soldier-husband. "Suppose he comes back and can't find her!" she says and lies awake. "He can't come before the spring," I tell her. The dear woman! (*The drops begin to fall faster.*) When d'you think he'll come? What do *you* think? (GRUSHA *is silent.*) Not before the spring, you agree? (GRUSHA *is silent.*) You don't believe he'll come at all? (GRUSHA *is silent.*) But when the spring comes and the snow melts here and on the passes, you can't stay on. They may come and look for you. There's already talk of an illegitimate child. (*The "glockenspiel" of the falling drops has grown faster and steadier.*) Grusha, the snow is melting on the roof. Spring is here.

GRUSHA   Yes.

LAVRENTI (*eagerly*)   I'll tell you what we'll do. You need a place to go, and, because of the child (*he sighs*), you have to have a husband, so people won't talk. Now I've made cautious inquiries to see if we can find you a husband. Grusha, I *have* one. I talked to a peasant woman who has a son. Just the other side of the mountain. A small farm. And she's willing.

GRUSHA   But I *can't* marry! I must wait for Simon Shashava.

LAVRENTI   Of course. That's all been taken care of. You don't need a man in bed—you need a man on paper. And I've found you one. The son of this peasant woman is going to die. Isn't that wonderful? He's at his last gasp. And all in line with our story—a husband from the other side of the mountain! And when you met him he was at the last gasp. So you're a widow. What do you say?

GRUSHA   It's true I could use a document with stamps on it for Michael.

LAVRENTI   Stamps make all the difference. Without something in writing the Shah couldn't prove he's a Shah. And you'll have a place to live.

GRUSHA   How much does the peasant woman want?

LAVRENTI   Four hundred piasters.

GRUSHA   Where will you find it?

LAVRENTI (*guiltily*)   Aniko's milk money.

GRUSHA   No one would know us there. I'll do it.

LAVRENTI (*getting up*)   I'll let the peasant woman know.
          (*Quick exit.*)

GRUSHA   Michael, you make a lot of work. I came by you as the pear tree comes by sparrows. And because a Christian bends down and picks up a crust of bread so nothing will go to waste. Michael, it would have been better had I walked quickly away on that Easter Sunday in Nuka in the second courtyard. Now I *am* a fool.

SINGER
          The bridegroom was on his deathbed when the bride arrived.
          The bridegroom's mother was waiting at the door, telling her to hurry.
          The bride brought a child along.
          The witness hid it during the wedding.
          (*On one side the bed. Under the mosquito net lies a very sick man.* GRUSHA *is pulled in at a run by her future*

mother-in-law. They are followed by LAVRENTI *and the* CHILD.)

MOTHER-IN-LAW   Quick! Quick! Or he'll die on us before the wedding. (*To* LAVRENTI) I was never told she had a child already.

LAVRENTI   What difference does it make? (*Pointing toward the dying man.*) It can't matter to him—in his condition.

MOTHER-IN-LAW   To him? But I'll never survive the shame! We are honest people. (*She begins to weep.*) My Jussup doesn't have to marry a girl with a child!

LAVRENTI   All right, make it another two hundred piasters. You'll have it in writing that the farm will go to you: but she'll have the right to live here for two years.

MOTHER-IN-LAW   (*drying her tears*)   It'll hardly cover the funeral expenses. I hope she'll really lend a hand with the work. And what's happened to the monk? He must have slipped out through the kitchen window. We'll have the whole village on our necks when they hear Jussup's end is come! Oh dear! I'll go get the monk. But he mustn't see the child!

LAVRENTI   I'll take care he doesn't. But why only a monk? Why not a priest?

MOTHER-IN-LAW   Oh, he's just as good. I only made one mistake: I paid half his fee in advance. Enough to send him to the tavern. I only hope . . .
       (*She runs off.*)

LAVRENTI   She saved on the priest, the wretch! Hired a cheap monk.

GRUSHA   You *will* send Simon Shashava to see me if he turns up after all?

LAVRENTI   Yes. (*Pointing at the* SICK PEASANT.) Won't you take a look at him?
       (GRUSHA, *taking* MICHAEL *to her, shakes her head.*) He's not moving an eyelid. I hope we aren't too late.
           (*They listen. On the opposite side enter neighbors who look around and take up positions against the walls, thus forming another wall near the bed, yet leaving an opening so that the bed can be seen. They start murmuring prayers. Enter the* MOTHER-IN-LAW *with a* MONK. *Showing some annoyance and surprise, she bows to the guests.*)

MOTHER-IN-LAW   I hope you won't mind waiting a few moments? My son's bride has just arrived from the city. An emergency wedding is about to be celebrated. (*To the* MONK *in the bedroom*) I might have known you couldn't keep your trap shut. (*To* GRUSHA) The wedding can take place at once. Here's the license. Me and the bride's brother (LAVRENTI *tries to hide in the background, after having quietly taken* MICHAEL *back from* GRUSHA. *The* MOTHER-IN-LAW *waves him away.*) are the witnesses.
           (GRUSHA *has bowed to the* MONK. *They go to the bed. The* MOTHER-IN-LAW *lifts the mosquito net. The* MONK *starts reeling off the marriage ceremony in Latin. Meanwhile the* MOTHER-IN-LAW *beckons to* LAVRENTI *to get rid of the* CHILD, *but fearing that it will cry he draws its attention to the ceremony.* GRUSHA *glances once at the* CHILD, *and* LAVRENTI *waves the* CHILD'S *hand in a greeting.*)

MONK   Are you prepared to be a faithful, obedient, and good wife to this man, and to cleave to him until death you do part?

GRUSHA (*looking at the* CHILD)   I am.

MONK (*to the* SICK PEASANT)   Are you prepared to be a good and loving husband to your wife until death you do part? (*As the* SICK PEASANT *does not answer, the* MONK *looks inquiringly around.*)

MOTHER-IN-LAW   Of course he is! Didn't you hear him say yes?

MONK   All right. We declare the marriage contracted! How about extreme unction?

MOTHER-IN-LAW   Nothing doing! The wedding cost quite enough. Now I must take care of the mourners. (*To* LAVRENTI) Did we say seven hundred?

LAVRENTI   Six hundred. (*He pays.*) Now I don't want to sit with the guests and get to know people. So farewell, Grusha, and if my widowed sister comes to visit me, she'll get a welcome from my wife, or I'll show my teeth.

> (*Nods, gives the* CHILD *to* GRUSHA, *and leaves. The mourners glance after him without interest.*)

MONK   May one ask where this child comes from?

MOTHER-IN-LAW   Is there a child? I don't see a child. And you don't see a child either—you understand? Or it may turn out I saw all sorts of things in the tavern! Now come on.

> (*After* GRUSHA *has put the* CHILD *down and told him to be quiet, they move over left;* GRUSHA *is introduced to the neighbors.*)

This is my daughter-in-law. She arrived just in time to find dear Jussup still alive.

ONE WOMAN   He's been ill now a whole year, hasn't he? When our Vassili was drafted he was there to say good-bye.

ANOTHER WOMAN   Such things are terrible for a farm. The corn all ripe and the farmer in bed! It'll really be a blessing if he doesn't suffer too long, I say.

FIRST WOMAN (*confidentially*)   You know why we thought he'd taken to his bed? Because of the draft! And now his end is come!

MOTHER-IN-LAW   Sit yourselves down, please! And have some cakes!

> (*She beckons to* GRUSHA *and both women go into the bedroom, where they pick up the cake pans off the floor. The guests, among them the* MONK, *sit on the floor and begin conversing in subdued voices.*)

ONE PEASANT (*to whom the* MONK *has handed the bottle which he has taken from his soutane*)   There's a child, you say! How can that have happened to Jussup?

A WOMAN   She was certainly lucky to get herself married, with him so sick!

MOTHER-IN-LAW   They're gossiping already. And wolfing down the funeral cakes at the same time! If he doesn't die today, I'll have to bake some more tomorrow!

GRUSHA   I'll bake them for you.

MOTHER-IN-LAW   Yesterday some horsemen rode by, and I went out to see who it was. When I came in again he was lying there like a corpse! So I sent for you. It can't take much longer. (*She listens.*)

MONK   Dear wedding and funeral guests! Deeply touched, we stand before a bed of death and marriage. The bride gets a veil; the groom, a shroud:

how varied, my children, are the fates of men! Alas! One man dies and has a roof over his head, and the other is married and the flesh turns to dust from which it was made. Amen.

MOTHER-IN-LAW   He's getting his own back. I shouldn't have hired such a cheap one. It's what you'd expect. A more expensive monk would behave himself. In Sura there's one with a real air of sanctity about him, but of course he charges a fortune. A fifty piaster monk like that has no dignity, and as for piety, just fifty piasters' worth and no more! When I came to get him in the tavern he'd just made a speech, and he was shouting: "The war is over, beware of the peace!" We must go in.

GRUSHA (*giving* MICHAEL *a cake*)   Eat this cake, and keep nice and still, Michael.

> (*The two women offer cakes to the guests. The dying man sits up in bed. He puts his head out from under the mosquito net, stares at the two women, then sinks back again. The* MONK *takes two bottles from his soutane and offers them to the peasant beside him. Enter three* MUSICIANS *who are greeted with a sly wink by the* MONK.)

MOTHER-IN-LAW (*to the* MUSICIANS)   What are you doing here? With instruments?

ONE MUSICIAN   Brother Anastasius here (*pointing at the* MONK) told us there was a wedding on.

MOTHER-IN-LAW   What? You brought them? Three more on my neck! Don't you know there's a dying man in the next room?

MONK   A very tempting assignment for a musician: something that could be either a subdued Wedding March or a spirited Funeral Dance.

MOTHER-IN-LAW   Well, you might as well play. Nobody can stop you eating in any case.

> (*The musicians play a potpourri. The women serve cakes.*)

MONK   The trumpet sounds like a whining baby. And you, little drum, what have you got to tell the world?

DRUNKEN PEASANT (*beside the* MONK, *sings*)
There was a young woman who said:
I thought I'd be happier, wed.
But my husband is old
And remarkably cold
So I sleep with a candle instead.

> (*The* MOTHER-IN-LAW *throws the* DRUNKEN PEASANT *out.*
> *The music stops. The guests are embarrassed.*)

GUESTS (*loudly*)
—Have you heard? The Grand Duke is back! But the Princes are against him.
—They say the Shah of Persia has lent him a great army to restore order in Grusinia.
—But how is that possible? The Shah of Persia is the enemy . . .
—The enemy of Grusinia, you donkey, not the enemy of the Grand Duke!
—In any case, the war's over, so our soldiers are coming back.

> (GRUSHA *drops a cake pan.* GUESTS *help her pick up the cake.*)

AN OLD WOMAN (*to* GRUSHA)   Are you feeling bad? It's just excitement about dear Jussup. Sit down and rest a while, my dear. (GRUSHA *staggers.*)

GUESTS   Now everything'll be the way it was. Only the taxes'll go up because now we'll have to pay for the war.

GRUSHA (*weakly*)   Did someone say the soldiers are back?

A MAN   I did.

GRUSHA   It can't be true.

FIRST MAN (*to a woman*)   Show her the shawl. We bought it from a soldier. It's from Persia.

GRUSHA (*looking at the shawl*)   They are here. (*She gets up, takes a step, kneels down in prayer, takes the silver cross and chain out of her blouse, and kisses it.*)

MOTHER-IN-LAW (*while the guests silently watch* GRUSHA)   What's the matter with you? Aren't you going to look after our guests? What's all this city nonsense got to do with us?

GUESTS (*resuming conversation while* GRUSHA *remains in prayer*)

—You can buy Persian saddles from the soldiers too. Though many want crutches in exchange for them.

—The leaders on one side can win a war, the soldiers on both sides lose it.

—Anyway, the war's over. It's something they can't draft you any more.

(*The dying man sits bolt upright in bed. He listens.*)

—What we need is two weeks of good weather.

—Our pear trees are hardly bearing a thing this year.

MOTHER-IN-LAW (*offering cakes*)   Have some more cakes and welcome! There are more!

(*The* MOTHER-IN-LAW *goes to the bedroom with the empty cake pans. Unaware of the dying man, she is bending down to pick up another tray when he begins to talk in a hoarse voice.*)

PEASANT   How many more cakes are you going to stuff down their throats? D'you think I can shit money?

(*The* MOTHER-IN-LAW *starts, stares at him aghast, while he climbs out from behind the mosquito net.*)

FIRST WOMAN (*talking kindly to* GRUSHA *in the next room*)   Has the young wife got someone at the front?

A MAN   It's good news that they're on their way home, huh?

PEASANT   Don't stare at me like that! Where's this wife you've saddled me with?

(*Receiving no answer, he climbs out of bed and in his nightshirt staggers into the other room. Trembling, she follows him with the cake pan.*)

GUESTS (*seeing him and shrieking*)   Good God! Jussup!

(*Everyone leaps up in alarm. The women rush to the door.* GRUSHA, *still on her knees, turns round and stares at the man.*)

PEASANT   A funeral supper! You'd enjoy that, wouldn't you? Get out before I throw you out! (*As the guests stampede from the house, gloomily to* GRUSHA) I've upset the apple cart, huh? (*Receiving no answer, he turns round and takes a cake from the pan which his mother is holding.*)

SINGER

> O confusion! The wife discovers she has a husband.
> By day there's the child, by night there's the husband.
> The lover is on his way both day and night.
> Husband and wife look at each other.
> The bedroom is small.

> > (*Near the bed the* PEASANT *is sitting in a high wooden
> > bathtub, naked, the* MOTHER-IN-LAW *is pouring water
> > from a pitcher. Opposite,* GRUSHA *cowers with* MICHAEL,
> > *who is playing at mending straw mats.*)

PEASANT (*to his mother*) That's her work, not yours. Where's she hiding out now?

MOTHER-IN-LAW (*calling*) Grusha! The peasant wants you!

GRUSHA (*to* MICHAEL) There are still two holes to mend.

PEASANT (*when* GRUSHA *approaches*) Scrub my back!

GRUSHA Can't the peasant do it himself?

PEASANT "Can't the peasant do it himself?" Get the brush! To hell with you! Are you the wife here? Or are you a visitor? (*To the* MOTHER-IN-LAW) It's too cold!

MOTHER-IN-LAW I'll run for hot water.

GRUSHA Let me go.

PEASANT You stay here. (*The* MOTHER-IN-LAW *exits.*) Rub harder. And no shirking. You've seen a naked fellow before. That child didn't come out of thin air.

GRUSHA The child was not conceived in joy, if that's what the peasant means.

PEASANT (*turning and grinning*) You don't look the type. (GRUSHA *stops scrubbing him, starts back. Enter the* MOTHER-IN-LAW.)

PEASANT A nice thing you've saddled me with! A simpleton for a wife!

MOTHER-IN-LAW She just isn't cooperative.

PEASANT Pour—but go easy! Ow! Go easy, I said. (*To* GRUSHA) Maybe you did something wrong in the city . . . I wouldn't be surprised. Why else should you be here? But I won't talk about that. I've not said a word about the illegitimate objects you brought into my house either. But my patience has limits! It's against nature. (*To the* MOTHER-IN-LAW) More! (*To* GRUSHA) And even if your soldier does come back, you're married.

GRUSHA Yes.

PEASANT But your soldier won't come back. Don't you believe it.

GRUSHA No.

PEASANT You're cheating me. You're my wife and you're not my wife. Where you lie, nothing lies, and yet no other woman can lie there. When I go to work in the morning I'm tired—when I lie down at night I'm awake as the devil. God has given you sex—and what d'you do? I don't have ten piasters to buy myself a woman in the city. Besides, it's a long way. Woman weeds the fields and opens up her legs, that's what our calendar says. D'you hear?

GRUSHA (*quietly*) Yes. I didn't mean to cheat you out of it.

PEASANT   She didn't mean to cheat me out of it! Pour some more water!
(*The* MOTHER-IN-LAW *pours.*) Ow!

SINGER

As she sat by the stream to wash the linen
She saw his image in the water
And his face grew dimmer with the passing moons.
As she raised herself to wring the linen
She heard his voice from the murmuring maple
And his voice grew fainter with the passing moons.
Evasions and sighs grew more numerous,
Tears and sweat flowed.
With the passing moons the child grew up.
(GRUSHA *sits by a stream, dipping linen into the water.*
In the rear, a few children are standing.)

GRUSHA (*to* MICHAEL)   You can play with them, Michael, but don't let them
boss you around just because you're the littlest. (MICHAEL *nods and joins*
the children. They start playing.)

BIGGEST BOY   Today it's the Heads-Off Game. (*To a* FAT BOY) You're the
Prince and you laugh. (*To* MICHAEL) You're the Governor. (*To a* GIRL)
You're the Governor's wife and you cry when his head's cut off. And I do
the cutting. (*He shows his wooden sword.*) With this. First, they lead the
Governor into the yard. The Prince walks in front. The Governor's wife
comes last.
(*They form a procession. The* FAT BOY *is first and laughs.*
Then comes MICHAEL, *then the* BIGGEST BOY, *and then the*
GIRL, *who weeps.*)

MICHAEL (*standing still*)   Me cut off head!

BIGGEST BOY   That's my job. You're the littlest. The Governor's the easy part.
All you do is kneel down and get your head cut off—simple.

MICHAEL   Me want sword!

BIGGEST BOY   It's mine! (*He gives* MICHAEL *a kick.*)

GIRL (*shouting to* GRUSHA)   He won't play his part!

GRUSHA (*laughing*)   Even the little duck is a swimmer, they say.

BIGGEST BOY   You can be the Prince if you can laugh. (MICHAEL *shakes*
his head.)

FAT BOY   I laugh best. Let him cut off the head just once. Then you do it,
then me.
(*Reluctantly, the* BIGGEST BOY *hands* MICHAEL *the wooden*
sword and kneels down. The FAT BOY *sits down, slaps his*
thigh, and laughs with all his might. The GIRL *weeps*
loudly. MICHAEL *swings the big sword and "cuts off" the*
head. In doing so, he topples over.)

BIGGEST BOY   Hey! I'll show you how to cut heads off!
(MICHAEL *runs away. The children run after him.* GRUSHA
laughs, following them with her eyes. On looking back,
she sees SIMON SHASHAVA *standing on the opposite bank.*
He wears a shabby uniform.)

GRUSHA   Simon!

SIMON   Is that Grusha Vashnadze?

GRUSHA   Simon!

SIMON (*formally*)   A good morning to the young lady. I hope she is well.

GRUSHA (*getting up gaily and bowing low*)   A good morning to the soldier. God be thanked he has returned in good health.

SIMON   They found better fish, so they didn't eat me, said the haddock.

GRUSHA   Courage, said the kitchen boy. Good luck, said the hero.

SIMON   How are things here? Was the winter bearable? The neighbor considerate?

GRUSHA   The winter was a trifle rough, the neighbor as usual, Simon.

SIMON   May one ask if a certain person still dips her toes in the water when rinsing the linen?

GRUSHA   The answer is no. Because of the eyes in the bushes.

SIMON   The young lady is speaking of soldiers. Here stands a paymaster.

GRUSHA   A job worth twenty piasters?

SIMON   And lodgings.

GRUSHA (*with tears in her eyes*)   Behind the barracks under the date trees.

SIMON   Yes, there. A certain person has kept her eyes open.

GRUSHA   She has, Simon.

SIMON   And has not forgotten? (GRUSHA *shakes her head.*)   So the door is still on its hinges as they say? (GRUSHA *looks at him in silence and shakes her head again.*) What's this? Is anything not as it should be?

GRUSHA   Simon Shashava, I can never return to Nuka. Something has happened.

SIMON   What can have happened?

GRUSHA   For one thing, I knocked an Ironshirt down.

SIMON   Grusha Vashnadze must have had her reasons for that.

GRUSHA   Simon Shashava, I am no longer called what I used to be called.

SIMON (*after a pause*)   I do not understand.

GRUSHA   When do women change their names, Simon? Let me explain. Nothing stands between us. Everything is just as it was. You must believe that.

SIMON   Nothing stands between us and yet there's something?

GRUSHA   How can I explain it so fast with the stream between us? Couldn't you cross the bridge there?

SIMON   Maybe it's no longer necessary.

GRUSHA   It is very necessary. Come over on this side, Simon, Quick!

SIMON   Does the young lady wish to say someone has come too late?

> (GRUSHA *looks up at him in despair, her face streaming with tears.* SIMON *stares before him. He picks up a piece of wood and starts cutting it.*)

SINGER

> So many words are said, so many left unsaid.
> The soldier has come.
> Where he comes from, he does not say.
> Hear what he thought and did not say:
> "The battle began, gray at dawn, grew bloody at noon.

The first man fell in front of me, the second behind me, the third at my side.

I trod on the first, left the second behind, the third was run through by the captain.

One of my brothers died by steel, the other by smoke.

My neck caught fire, my hands froze in my gloves, my toes in my socks.

I fed on aspen buds, I drank maple juice, I slept on stone, in water."

SIMON   I see a cap in the grass. Is there a little one already?

GRUSHA   There is, Simon. There's no keeping *that* from you. But please don't worry, it is not mine.

SIMON   When the wind once starts to blow, they say, it blows through every cranny. The wife need say no more. (GRUSHA *looks into her lap and is silent.*)

SINGER

There was yearning but there was no waiting.

The oath is broken. Neither could say why.

Hear what she thought but did not say:

"While you fought in the battle, soldier,

The bloody battle, the bitter battle

I found a helpless infant

I had not the heart to destroy him

I had to care for a creature that was lost

I had to stoop for breadcrumbs on the floor

I had to break myself for that which was not mine

That which was other people's.

Someone must help!

For the little tree needs water

The lamb loses its way when the shepherd is asleep

And its cry is unheard!"

SIMON   Give me back the cross I gave you. Better still, throw it in the stream.
    (*He turns to go.*)

GRUSHA (*getting up*)   Simon Shashava, don't go away! He isn't mine! He isn't mine! (*She hears the children calling.*) What's the matter, children?

VOICES   Soldiers! And they're taking Michael away!

    (GRUSHA *stands aghast as two* IRONSHIRTS, *with* MICHAEL *between them, come toward her.*)

ONE OF THE IRONSHIRTS   Are you Grusha? (*She nods.*) Is this your child?

GRUSHA   Yes. (SIMON *goes.*) Simon!

IRONSHIRT   We have orders, in the name of the law, to take this child, found in your custody, back to the city. It is suspected that the child is Michael Abashwili, son and heir of the late Governor Georgi Abashwili, and his wife, Natella Abashwili. Here is the document and the seal. (*They lead the* CHILD *away.*)

GRUSHA (*running after them, shouting*)   Leave him here. Please! He's mine!

SINGER

The Ironshirts took the child, the beloved child.

The unhappy girl followed them to the city, the dreaded city.

She who had borne him demanded the child.
She who had raised him faced trial.
Who will decide the case?
To whom will the child be assigned?
Who will the judge be? A good judge? A bad?
The city was in flames.
In the judge's seat sat Azdak.[1]

4 The Story of the Judge

SINGER
Hear the story of the judge
How he turned judge, how he passed judgment, what kind of judge
he was.
On that Easter Sunday of the great revolt, when the Grand Duke was
overthrown
And his Governor Abashwili, father of our child, lost his head
The Village Scrivener Azdak found a fugitive in the woods and hid
him in his hut.
(AZDAK, *in rags and slightly drunk, is helping an old
beggar into his cottage.*)
AZDAK Stop snorting, you're not a horse. And it won't do you any good with
the police to run like a snotty nose in April. Stand still, I say. (*He
catches the* OLD MAN, *who has marched into the cottage as if he'd like
to go through the walls.*) Sit down. Feed. Here's a hunk of cheese.
(*From under some rags, in a chest, he fishes out some cheese, and the
OLD MAN greedily begins to eat.*) Haven't eaten in a long time, huh?
(*The* OLD MAN *growls.*) Why were you running like that, asshole? The
cop wouldn't even have seen you.
OLD MAN Had to! Had to!
AZDAK Blue funk? (*The* OLD MAN *stares, uncomprehending.*) Cold feet? Panic?
Don't lick your chops like a Grand Duke. Or an old sow. I can't stand
it. We have to accept respectable stinkers as God made them, but not
you! I once heard of a senior judge who farted at a public dinner to show an
independent spirit! Watching you eat like that gives me the most awful
ideas. Why don't you say something? (*Sharply.*) Show me your hand.
Can't you hear? (*The* OLD MAN *slowly puts out his hand.*) White! So
you're not a beggar at all! A fraud, a walking swindle! And I'm
hiding you from the cops like you were an honest man! Why were
you running like that if you're a landowner? For that's what you are.
Don't deny it! I see it in your guilty face! (*He gets up.*) Get out! (*The
OLD MAN looks at him uncertainly.*) What are you waiting for,
peasant-flogger?
OLD MAN Pursued. Need undivided attention. Make proposition . . .
AZDAK Make what? A proposition? Well, if that isn't the height of insolence.

---

[1]The name Azdak should be accented on the second syllable.—E. B.

He's making me a proposition! The bitten man scratches his fingers bloody, and the leech that's biting him makes him a proposition! Get out, I tell you!

OLD MAN   Understand point of view! Persuasion! Pay hundred thousand piasters one night! Yes?

AZDAK   What, you think you can buy me? For a hundred thousand piasters? Let's say a hundred and fifty thousand. Where are they?

OLD MAN   Have not them here. Of course. Will be sent. Hope do not doubt.

AZDAK   Doubt very much. Get out!

>   (*The* OLD MAN *gets up, waddles to the door. A* VOICE *is
>   heard offstage.*)

VOICE   Azdak!

>   (*The* OLD MAN *turns, waddles to the opposite corner,
>   stands still.*)

AZDAK (*calling out*)   I'm not in! (*He walks to door.*) So *you're* sniffing around here again, Shauwa?

SHAUWA (*reproachfully*)   You caught another rabbit, Azdak. And you'd promised me it wouldn't happen again!

AZDAK (*severely*)   Shauwa, don't talk about things you don't understand. The rabbit is a dangerous and destructive beast. It feeds on plants, especially on the species of plants known as weeds. It must therefore be exterminated.

SHAUWA   Azdak, don't be so hard on me. I'll lose my job if I don't arrest you. I know you have a good heart.

AZDAK   I do not have a good heart! How often must I tell you I'm a man of intellect?

SHAUWA (*slyly*)   I know, Azdak. You're a superior person. You say so yourself. I'm just a Christian and an ignoramus. So I ask you: When one of the Prince's rabbits is stolen, and I'm a policeman, what should I do with the offending party?

AZDAK   Shauwa, Shauwa, shame on you, You stand and ask me a question, than which nothing could be more seductive. It's like you were a woman—let's say that bad girl Nunowna, and you showed me your thigh—Nunowna's thigh, that would be—and asked me: "What shall I do with my thigh, it itches?" Is she as innocent as she pretends? Of course not. I catch a rabbit, but you catch a man. Man is made in God's image. Not so a rabbit, you know that. I'm a rabbit-eater, but you're a man-eater, Shauwa. And God will pass judgment on you. Shauwa, go home and repent. No, stop, there's something . . . (*He looks at the* OLD MAN *who stands trembling in the corner.*) No, it's nothing. Go home and repent. (*He slams the door behind* SHAUWA.) Now you're surprised, huh? Surprised I didn't hand you over? I couldn't hand over a bedbug to that animal. It goes against the grain. Now don't tremble because of a cop! So old and still so scared? Finish your cheese, but eat it like a poor man, or else they'll still catch you. Must I even explain how a poor man behaves? (*He pushes him down, and then gives him back the cheese.*) That box is the table. Lay your elbows on the table. Now, encircle the cheese on the plate like it might be snatched from you at any moment—what right have you to be safe, huh?—now, hold your knife like an undersized sickle, and give your cheese a troubled look because, like all beautiful things, it's already fading away. (AZDAK *watches him.*) They're after you, which speaks in your favor, but how can we be sure they're not mistaken about you? In Tiflis one time they hanged a landowner, a Turk, who could prove he quartered his peasants instead of merely cutting them in half, as is the custom, and he squeezed twice the usual amount of taxes out of them, his zeal was above suspicion. And yet they hanged him like a common criminal—because he was a Turk—a thing he couldn't do much about. What injustice! He got onto the gallows by a sheer fluke. In short, I don't trust you.

SINGER
   Thus Azdak gave the old beggar a bed,
   And learned that old beggar was the old butcher, the Grand Duke himself,
   And was ashamed.
   He denounced himself and ordered the policeman to take him to Nuka,
      to court, to be judged.
      (*In the court of justice three* IRONSHIRTS *sit drinking.*
      From a beam hangs a man in judge's robes. Enter
      AZDAK, *in chains, dragging* SHAUWA *behind him.*)

AZDAK (*shouting*)   I've helped the Grand Duke, the Grand Thief, the Grand Butcher, to escape! In the name of justice I ask to be severely judged in public trial!

FIRST IRONSHIRT   Who's this queer bird?

SHAUWA   That's our Village Scrivener, Azdak.

AZDAK   I am contemptible! I am a traitor! A branded criminal! Tell them, flatfoot, how I insisted on being tied up and brought to the capital. Because I sheltered the Grand Duke, the Grand Swindler, by mistake. And how I found out afterwards. See the marked man denounce himself! Tell them how I forced you to walk half the night with me to clear the whole thing up.

SHAUWA   And all by threats. That wasn't nice of you, Azdak.

AZDAK   Shut your mouth, Shauwa. You don't understand. A new age is upon us! It'll go thundering over you. You're finished. The police will be wiped out—poof! Everything will be gone into, everything will be brought into the open. The guilty will give themselves up. Why? They couldn't escape the people in any case. (*To* SHAUWA:) Tell them how I shouted all along Shoemaker Street (*with big gestures, looking at the* IRONSHIRTS) "In my ignorance I let the Grand Swindler escape! So tear me to pieces, brothers!" I wanted to get it in first.

FIRST IRONSHIRT   And what did your brothers answer?

SHAUWA   They comforted him in Butcher Street, and they laughed themselves sick in Shoemaker Street. That's all.

AZDAK   But with you it's different. I can see you're men of iron. Brothers, where's the judge? I must be tried.

FIRST IRONSHIRT (*pointing at the hanged man*) There's the judge. And please stop "brothering" us. It's rather a sore spot this evening.

AZDAK "There's the judge." An answer never heard in Grusinia before. Townsman, where's His Excellency the Governor? (*Pointing to the ground.*) There's His Excellency, stranger. Where's the Chief Tax Collector? Where's the official Recruiting Officer? The Patriarch? The Chief of Police? There, there, there—all there. Brothers, I expected no less of you.

SECOND IRONSHIRT What? *What* was it you expected, funny man?

AZDAK What happened in Persia, brother, what happened in Persia?

SECOND IRONSHIRT What did happen in Persia?

AZDAK Everybody was hanged. Viziers, tax collectors. Everybody. Forty years ago now. My grandfather, a remarkable man by the way, saw it all. For three whole days. Everywhere.

SECOND IRONSHIRT And who ruled when the Vizier was hanged?

AZDAK A peasant ruled when the Vizier was hanged.

SECOND IRONSHIRT And who commanded the army?

AZDAK A soldier, a soldier.

SECOND IRONSHIRT And who paid the wages?

AZDAK A dyer. A dyer paid the wages.

SECOND IRONSHIRT Wasn't it a weaver, maybe?

FIRST IRONSHIRT And why did all this happen, Persian?

AZDAK Why did all this happen? Must there be a special reason? Why do you scratch yourself, brother? War! Too long a war! And no justice! My grandfather brought back a song that tells how it was. I will sing it for you. With my friend the policeman. (*To* SHAUWA) And hold the rope tight. It's very suitable. (*He sings, with* SHAUWA *holding the rope tight around him.*

THE SONG OF INJUSTICE IN PERSIA

Why don't our sons bleed any more? Why don't our daughters weep?
Why do only the slaughterhouse cattle have blood in their veins?
Why do only the willows shed tears on Lake Urmia?
The king must have a new province, the peasant must give up his savings.
That the roof of the world might be conquered, the roof of the cottage is
torn down.
Our men are carried to the ends of the earth, so that great ones can eat
at home.
The soldiers kill each other, the marshals salute each other.
They bite the widow's tax money to see if it's good, their swords break.
The battle was lost, the helmets were paid for.
Refrain: Is it so? Is it so?

SHAUWA (*refrain*) Yes, yes, yes, yes, yes it's so.

AZDAK Want to hear the rest of it? (*The* FIRST IRONSHIRT *nods.*)

SECOND IRONSHIRT (*to* SHAUWA) Did he teach you that song?

SHAUWA Yes, only my voice isn't very good.

SECOND IRONSHIRT No. (*To* AZDAK) Go on singing.

AZDAK The second verse is about the peace. (*He sings.*)

The offices are packed, the streets overflow with officials.
The rivers jump their banks and ravage the fields.
Those who cannot let down their own trousers rule countries.
They can't count up to four, but they devour eight courses.
The corn farmers, looking round for buyers, see only the starving.
The weavers go home from their looms in rags.
Refrain: Is it so? Is it so?

SHAUWA (*refrain*)   Yes, yes, yes, yes, yes it's so.
AZDAK

That's why our sons don't bleed any more, that's why our daughters
    don't weep.
That's why only the slaughterhouse cattle have blood in their veins,
And only the willows shed tears by Lake Urmia toward morning.

FIRST IRONSHIRT   Are you going to sing that song here in town?
AZDAK   Sure. What's wrong with it?
FIRST IRONSHIRT   Have you noticed that the sky's getting red? (*Turning round,*
    AZDAK *sees the sky red with fire.*) It's the people's quarters on the
    outskirts of town. The carpet weavers have caught the "Persian Sickness,"
    too. And they've been asking if Prince Kazbeki isn't eating too many
    courses. This morning they strung up the city judge. As for us we beat
    them to pulp. We were paid one hundred piasters per man, you
    understand?
AZDAK (*after a pause*)   I understand. (*He glances shyly round and, creeping
    away, sits down in a corner, his head in his hands.*)
IRONSHIRTS (*to each other*)   If there ever was a troublemaker it's him. —He
    must've come to the capital to fish in the troubled waters.
SHAUWA   Oh, I don't think he's a really bad character, gentlemen. Steals a few
    chickens here and there. And maybe a rabbit.
SECOND IRONSHIRT (*approaching* AZDAK)   Came to fish in the troubled waters,
    huh?
AZDAK (*looking up*)   I don't know why I came.
SECOND IRONSHIRT   Are you in with the carpet weavers maybe? (AZDAK *shakes
    his head.*) How about that song?
AZDAK   From my grandfather. A silly and ignorant man.
SECOND IRONSHIRT   Right. And how about the dyer who paid the wages?
AZDAK (*muttering*)   That was in Persia.
FIRST IRONSHIRT   And this denouncing of yourself? Because you didn't hang
    the Grand Duke with your own hands?
AZDAK   Didn't I tell you I let him run? (*He creeps farther away and sits on the
    floor.*)
SHAUWA   I can swear to that: he let him run.

        (*The* IRONSHIRTS *burst out laughing and slap* SHAUWA *on
        the back.* AZDAK *laughs loudest. They slap* AZDAK *too,
        and unchain him. They all start drinking as the* FAT
        PRINCE *enters with a young man.*)
FIRST IRONSHIRT (*to* AZDAK, *pointing at the* FAT PRINCE)   There's your "new
    age" for you! (*More laughter.*)

FAT PRINCE   Well, my friends, what is there to laugh about? Permit me a serious word. Yesterday morning the Princes of Grusinia overthrew the warmongering government of the Grand Duke and did away with his Governors. Unfortunately the Grand Duke himself escaped. In this fateful hour our carpet weavers, those eternal troublemakers, had the effrontery to stir up a rebellion and hang the universally loved city judge, our dear Illo Orbeliani. Ts—ts—ts. My friends, we need peace, peace, peace in Grusinia! And justice! So I've brought along my dear nephew Bizergan Kazbeki. He'll be the new judge, hm? A very gifted fellow. What do you say? I want your opinion. Let the people decide!

SECOND IRONSHIRT   Does this mean *we* elect the judge?

FAT PRINCE   Precisely. Let the people propose some very gifted fellow! Confer among yourselves, my friends. (*The* IRONSHIRTS *confer.*) Don't worry, my little fox. The job's yours. And when we catch the Grand Duke we won't have to kiss this rabble's ass any longer.

IRONSHIRTS (*among themselves*)

—Very funny: they're wetting their pants because they haven't caught the Grand Duke.

When the outlook isn't so bright, they say: "My friends!" and "Let the people decide!"

—Now he even wants justice for Grusinia! But fun is fun as long as it lasts! (*Pointing at* AZDAK.) *He* knows all about justice. Hey, rascal, would you like this nephew fellow to be the judge?

AZDAK   Are you asking me? You're not asking *me?!*

FIRST IRONSHIRT   Why not? Anything for a laugh!

AZDAK   You'd like to test him to the marrow, correct? Have you a criminal on hand? An experienced one? So the candidate can show what he knows?

SECOND IRONSHIRT   Let's see. We do have a couple of doctors downstairs. Let's use them.

AZDAK   Oh, no, that's no good, we can't take real criminals till we're sure the judge will be appointed. He may be dumb, but he must be appointed, or the law is violated. And the law is a sensitive organ. It's like the spleen, you mustn't hit it—that would be fatal. Of course you can hang those two without violating the law, because there was no judge in the vicinity. But judgment, when pronounced, must be pronounced with absolute gravity—it's all such nonsense. Suppose, for instance, a judge jails a woman—let's say she's stolen a corn cake to feed her child—and this judge isn't wearing his robes—or maybe he's scratching himself while passing sentence and half his body is uncovered—a man's thigh *will* itch once in a while—the sentence this judge passes is a disgrace and the law is violated. In short it would be easier for a judge's robe and a judge's hat to pass judgment than for a man with no robe and no hat. If you don't treat it with respect, the law just disappears on you. Now you don't try out a bottle of wine by offering it to a dog; you'd only lose your wine.

FIRST IRONSHIRT   Then what do you suggest, hairsplitter?

AZDAK   I'll be the defendant.

FIRST IRONSHIRT   You? (*He bursts out laughing.*)

FAT PRINCE   What have you decided?

FIRST IRONSHIRT   We've decided to stage a rehearsal. Our friend here will be the defendant. Let the candidate be the judge and sit there.

FAT PRINCE   It isn't customary, but why not? (*To the* NEPHEW) A mere formality, my little fox. What have I taught you? Who got there first— the slow runner or the fast?

NEPHEW   The silent runner, Uncle Arsen.

> (*The* NEPHEW *takes the chair. The* IRONSHIRTS *and the*
> FAT PRINCE *sit on the steps. Enter* AZDAK, *mimicking the*
> *gait of the Grand Duke.*)

AZDAK (*in the Grand Duke's accent*)   Is any here knows me? Am Grand Duke.

IRONSHIRTS

> —*What* is he?
> —The Grand Duke. He knows him, too.
> —Fine. So get on with the trial.

AZDAK   Listen! Am accused instigating war? Ridiculous! Am saying ridiculous! That enough? If not, have brought lawyers. Believe five hundred. (*He points behind him, pretending to be surrounded by lawyers.*) Requisition all available seats for lawyers! (*The* IRONSHIRTS *laugh; the* FAT PRINCE *joins in.*)

NEPHEW (*to the* IRONSHIRTS)   You really wish me to try this case? I find it rather unusual. From the taste angle, I mean.

FIRST IRONSHIRT   Let's go!

FAT PRINCE (*smiling*)   Let him have it, my little fox!

NEPHEW   All right. People of Grusinia versus Grand Duke. Defendant, what have you got to say for yourself?

AZDAK   Plenty. Naturally, have read war lost. Only started on the advice of patriots. Like Uncle Arsen Kazbeki. Call Uncle Arsen as witness.

FAT PRINCE (*to the* IRONSHIRTS, *delightedly*)   What a madcap!

NEPHEW   Motion rejected. One cannot be arraigned for declaring a war, which every ruler has to do once in a while, but only for running a war badly.

AZDAK   Rubbish! Did not run it at all! Had it run! Had it run by Princes! Naturally, they messed it up.

NEPHEW   Do you by any chance deny having been commander-in-chief?

AZDAK   Not at all! Always *was* commander-in-chief. At birth shouted at wet nurse. Was trained drop turds in toilet, grew accustomed to command. Always commanded officials rob my cash box. Officers flog soldiers only on command. Landowners sleep with peasants' wives only on strictest command. Uncle Arsen here grew his belly at *my* command!

IRONSHIRTS (*clapping*)   He's good! Long live the Grand Duke!

FAT PRINCE   Answer him, my little fox: I'm with you.

NEPHEW   I shall answer him according to the dignity of the law. Defendant, preserve the dignity of the law!

AZDAK   Agreed. Command you proceed with trial!

NEPHEW   It is not your place to command me. You claim that the Princes forced you to declare war. How can you claim, then, that they—er— "messed it up"?

AZDAK   Did not send enough people. Embezzled funds. Sent sick horses. During attack, drinking in whorehouse. Call Uncle Arsen as witness.

NEPHEW   Are you making the outrageous suggestion that the Princes of this country did not fight?

AZDAK   No. Princes fought. Fought for war contracts.

FAT PRINCE (*jumping up*)   That's too much! This man talks like a carpet weaver!

AZDAK   Really? Told nothing but truth.

FAT PRINCE   Hang him! Hang him!

FIRST IRONSHIRT (*pulling the* PRINCE *down*)   Keep quiet! Go on, Excellency!

NEPHEW   Quiet! I now render a verdict: You must be hanged! By the neck! Having lost war!

AZDAK   Young man, seriously advise not fall publicly into jerky clipped speech. Cannot be watchdog if howl like wolf. Got it? If people realize Princes speak same language as Grand Duke, may hang Grand Duke *and Princes*, huh? By the way, must overrule verdict. Reason? War lost, but not for Princes. Princes won their war. Got 3,863,000 piasters for horses not delivered, 8,240,000 piasters for food supplies not produced. Are therefore victors. War lost only for Grusinia, which is not present in this court.

FAT PRINCE   I think that will do, my friends. (*To* AZDAK) You can withdraw, funny man. (*To the* IRONSHIRTS) You may now ratify the new judge's appointment, my friends.

FIRST IRONSHIRT   Yes, we can. Take down the judge's gown. (*One* IRONSHIRT *climbs on the back of the other, pulls the gown off the hanged man.*) (*To the* NEPHEW) Now you run away so the right ass can get on the right chair. (*To* AZDAK) Step forward! Go to the judge's seat! Now sit in it! (AZDAK *steps up, bows, and sits down.*) The judge was always a rascal! Now the rascal shall be a judge! (*The judge's gown is placed round his shoulders, the hat on his head.*) And what a judge!

SINGER

> And there was civil war in the land.
> The mighty were not safe.
> And Azdak was made a judge by the Ironshirts.
> And Azdak remained a judge for two years.

SINGER AND CHORUS

> When the towns were set afire
> And rivers of blood rose higher and higher,
> Cockroaches crawled out of every crack.
> And the court was full of schemers
> And the church of foul blasphemers.
> In the judge's cassock sat Azdak.

> (AZDAK *sits in the judge's chair, peeling an apple.*
> SHAUWA *is sweeping out the hall. On one side an* INVALID
> *in a wheelchair. Opposite, a young man accused of
> blackmail. An* IRONSHIRT *stands guard, holding the
> Ironshirts' banner.*)

AZDAK   In consideration of the large number of cases, the Court today will hear two cases at a time. Before I open the proceedings, a short announcement—I accept. (*He stretches out his hand. The* BLACKMAILER *is the only one to produce any money. He hands it to* AZDAK.) I reserve the right to punish one of the parties for contempt of court. (*He glances at the* INVALID.) You (*to the* DOCTOR) are a doctor, and you (*to the* INVALID) are bringing a complaint against him. Is the doctor responsible for your condition?

INVALID   Yes. I had a stroke on his account.

AZDAK   That would be professional negligence.

INVALID   Worse than negligence. I gave this man money for his studies. So far, he hasn't paid me back a cent. It was when I heard he was treating a patient free that I had my stroke.

AZDAK   Rightly. (*To a* LIMPING MAN) And what are *you* doing here?

LIMPING MAN   I'm the patient, Your Honor.

AZDAK   He treated your leg for nothing?

LIMPING MAN   The wrong leg! My rheumatism was in the left leg, he operated on the right. That's why I limp.

AZDAK   And you were treated free?

INVALID   A five-hundred-piaster operation free! For nothing! For a God-bless-you! And I paid for this man's studies! (*To the* DOCTOR) Did they teach you to operate free?

DOCTOR   Your Honor, it is the custom to demand the fee before the operation, as the patient is more willing to pay before an operation than after. Which is only human. In the case in question I was convinced, when I started the operation, that my servant had already received the fee. In this I was mistaken.

INVALID   He was mistaken! A good doctor doesn't make mistakes! He examines before he operates!

AZDAK   That's right: (*To* SHAUWA) Public Prosecutor, what's the other case about?

SHAUWA (*busily sweeping*)   Blackmail.

BLACKMAILER   High Court of Justice, I'm innocent. I only wanted to find out from the landowner concerned if he really *had* raped his niece. He informed me very politely that this was not the case, and gave me the money only so I could pay for my uncle's studies.

AZDAK   Hm. (*To the* DOCTOR) You, on the other hand, can cite no extenuating circumstances for your offense, huh?

DOCTOR   Except that to err is human.

AZDAK   And you are aware that in money matters a good doctor is a highly responsible person? I once heard of a doctor who got a thousand piasters for a sprained finger by remarking that sprains have something to do with blood circulation, which after all a less good doctor might have overlooked, and who, on another occasion made a real gold mine out of a somewhat disordered gall bladder. He treated it with such loving care. You have no excuse, Doctor. The corn merchant Uxu had his son study medicine to get some knowledge of trade, our medical schools are so good. (*To the* BLACKMAILER) What's the landowner's name?

SHAUWA   He doesn't want it mentioned.

AZDAK   In that case I will pass judgment. The Court considers the blackmail proved. And you (*to the* INVALID) are sentenced to a fine of one thousand piasters. If you have a second stroke, the doctor will have to treat you free. Even if he has to amputate. (*To the* LIMPING MAN) As compensation, you will receive a bottle of rubbing alcohol. (*To the* BLACKMAILER) You are sentenced to hand over half the proceeds of your deal to the Public Prosecutor to keep the landowners' man secret. You are advised, moreover, to study medicine—you seem will suited to that calling. (*To the* DOCTOR) You have perpetrated an unpardonable error in the practice of your profession: you are acquitted. Next cases!

SINGER AND CHORUS

Men won't do much for a shilling.

For a pound they may be willing.

For twenty pounds the verdict's in the sack.

As for the many, all too many,

Those who've only got a penny—

They've one single, sole recourse: Azdak.

> (*Enter* AZDAK *from the caravansary on the highroad, followed by an old bearded* INNKEEPER. *The judge's chair is carried by a* STABLEMAN *and* SHAUWA. *An* IRONSHIRT, *with a banner, takes up his position.*)

AZDAK   Put me down. Then we'll get some air, maybe even a good stiff breeze from the lemon grove there. It does justice good to be done in the open: the wind blows her skirts up and you can see what she's got. Shauwa, we've been eating too much. These official journeys are exhausting. (*To the* INNKEEPER) It's a question of your daughter-in-law?

INNKEEPER   Your Worship, it's a question of the family honor. I wish to bring an action on behalf of my son, who's away on business on the other side the mountain. This is the offending stableman, and here's my daughter-in-law.

> (*Enter the* DAUGHTER-IN-LAW, *a voluptuous wench. She is veiled.*)

AZDAK (*sitting down*)   I accept. (*Sighing, the* INNKEEPER *hands him some money.*) Good. Now the formalities are disposed of. This is a case of rape?

INNKEEPER   Your Honor, I caught the fellow in the act. Ludovica was in the straw on the stable floor.

AZDAK   Quite right, the stable. Lovely horses! I specially liked the little roan.

INNKEEPER   The first thing I did, of course, was to question Ludovica. On my son's behalf.

AZDAK (*seriously*)   I said I specially liked the little roan.

INNKEEPER (*coldly*)   Really? Ludovica confessed the stableman took her against her will.

AZDAK   Take your veil off, Ludovica. (*She does so.*) Ludovica, you please the Court. Tell us how it happened.

LUDOVICA (*well schooled*)   When I entered the stable to see the new foal the stableman said to me on his own accord: "It's hot today!" and laid his hand on my left breast. I said to him: "Don't do that!" But he continued to handle me indecently, which provoked my anger. Before I realized his sinful intentions, he got much closer. It was all over when my father-in-law entered and accidentally trod on me.

INNKEEPER (*explaining*)   On my son's behalf.

AZDAK (*to the* STABLEMAN)   You admit you started it?

STABLEMAN   Yes.

AZDAK   Ludovica, you like to eat sweet things?

LUDOVICA   Yes, sunflower seeds!

AZDAK   You like to lie a long time in the bathtub?

LUDOVICA   Half an hour or so.

AZDAK   Public Prosecutor, drop your knife—there on the ground. (SHAUWA *does so.*) Ludovica, pick up that knife. (LUDOVICA, *swaying her hips, does so.*) See that? (*He points at her.*) The way it moves? The rape is now proven. By eating too much—sweet things, especially—by lying too long in warm water, by laziness and too soft a skin, you have raped that unfortunate man. Think you can run around with a behind like that and get away with it in court? This is a case of intentional assault with a dangerous weapon! You are sentenced to hand over to the Court the little roan which your father liked to ride "on his son's behalf." And now, come with me to the stables, so the Court can inspect the scene of the crime, Ludovica.

SINGER AND CHORUS
    When the sharks the sharks devour
    Little fishes have their hour.
    For a while the load is off their back.
    On Grusinia's highways faring
    Fixed-up scales of justice bearing
    Strode the poor man's magistrate: Azdak.

    And he gave to the forsaken
    All that from the rich he'd taken.
    And a bodyguard of roughnecks was Azdak's.
    And our good and evil man, he
    Smiled upon Grusinia's Granny.
    His emblem was a tear in sealing wax.

    All mankind should love each other
    But when visiting your brother
    Take an ax along and hold it fast.
    Not in theory but in practice
    Miracles are wrought with axes
    And the age of miracles is not past.

        (AZDAK's *judge's chair is in a tavern. Three rich*
        FARMERS *stand before* AZDAK. SHAUWA *brings him*
        wine. In a corner stands an OLD PEASANT WOMAN. *In the*

open doorway, and outside, stand villagers looking on.
An IRONSHIRT *stands guard with a banner.*)

AZDAK The Public Prosecutor has the floor.

SHAUWA It concerns a cow. For five weeks, the defendant has had a cow in her stable, the property of the farmer Suru. She was also found to be in possession of a stolen ham, and a number of cows belonging to Shutoff were killed after he asked the defendant to pay the rent of a piece of land.

FARMERS
    —It's a matter of my ham, Your Honor.
    —It's a matter of my cow, Your Honor.
    —It's a matter of my land, Your Honor.

AZDAK Well, Granny, what have *you* got to say to all this?

OLD WOMAN Your Honor, one night toward morning, five weeks ago, there was a knock at my door, and outside stood a bearded man with a cow. "My dear woman," he said "I am the miracle-working Saint Banditus and because your son has been killed in the war, I bring you this cow as a souvenir. Take good care of it."

FARMERS
    —The robber, Irakli, Your Honor!
    —Her brother-in-law, Your Honor!
    —The cow-thief!
    —The incendiary!
    —He must be beheaded!
        (*Outside, a woman screams. The crowd grows restless,*
        retreats. Enter the BANDIT *Irakli with a huge ax.*)

BANDIT A very good evening, dear friends! A glass of vodka!

FARMERS (*crossing themselves*) Irakli!

AZDAK Public Prosecutor, a glass of vodka for our guest. And who are you?

BANDIT I'm a wandering hermit, Your Honor. Thanks for the gracious gift.
    (*He empties the glass which* SHAUWA *has brought.*) Another!

AZDAK I am Azdak. (*He gets up and bows. The* BANDIT *also bows.*) The Court welcomes the foreign hermit. Go on with your story, Granny.

OLD WOMAN Your Honor, that first night I didn't yet know Saint Banditus could work miracles, it was only the cow. But one night, a few days later, the farmer's servants came to take the cow away again. Then they turned round in front of my door and went off without the cow. And bumps as big as a fist sprouted on their heads. So I knew that Saint Banditus had changed their hearts and turned them into friendly people.
    (*The* BANDIT *roars with laughter.*)

FIRST FARMER I know what changed them.

AZDAK That's fine. You can tell us later. Continue.

OLD WOMAN Your Honor, the next one to become a good man was the farmer Shutoff—a devil, as everyone knows. But Saint Banditus arranged it so he let me off the rent on the little piece of land.

SECOND FARMER Because my cows were killed in the field.
    (*The* BANDIT *laughs.*)

OLD WOMAN (*answering* AZDAK'S *sign to continue*)   Then one morning the
ham came flying in at my window. It hit me in the small of the back. I'm
still lame, Your Honor, look. (*She limps a few steps. The* BANDIT
laughs.) Your Honor, was there ever a time when a poor old woman
could get a ham *without* a miracle?
      (*The* BANDIT *starts sobbing.*)
AZDAK (*rising from his chair*)   Granny, that's a question that strikes straight
at the Court's heart. Be so kind as to sit here. (*The* OLD WOMAN,
hesitating, sits in the judge's chair.)
AZDAK (*sits on the floor, glass in hand, reciting*)
      Granny
      We could almost call you Granny Grusinia
      The Woebegone
      The Bereaved Mother
      Whose sons have gone to war.
      Receiving the present of a cow
      She bursts out crying.
      When she is beaten
      She remains hopeful.
      When she's not beaten
      She's surprised.
      On us
      Who are already damned
      May you render a merciful verdict
      Granny Grusinia!
      (*Bellowing at the* FARMERS)   Admit you don't believe in miracles, you
      atheists! Each of you is sentenced to pay five hundred piasters! For
      godlessness! Get out! (*The* FARMERS *slink out.*) And you, Granny, and
      you (to the BANDIT) pious man, empty a pitcher of wine with the Public
      Prosecutor and Azdak!
SINGER AND CHORUS
      And he broke the rules to save them.
      Broken law like bread he gave them,
      Brought them to shore upon his crooked back.
      At long last the poor and lowly
      Had someone who was not too holy
      To be bribed by empty hands: Azdak.

      For two years it was his pleasure
      To give the beasts of prey short measure:
      He became a wolf to fight the pack.
      From All Hallows to All Hallows
      On his chair beside the gallows
      Dispensing justice in his fashion sat Azdak.
SINGER
      But the era of disorder came to an end.
      The Grand Duke returned.
      The Governor's wife returned.
      A trial was held.

Many died.
The people's quarters burned anew.
And fear seized Azdak.

(AZDAK'S *judge's chair stands again in the court of
justice.* AZDAK *sits on the floor, shaving and talking to*
SHAUWA. *Noises outside. In the rear the* FAT PRINCE'S
head is carried by on a lance.)

AZDAK   Shauwa, the days of your slavery are numbered, maybe even the
minutes. For a long time now I have held you in the iron curb of reason,
and it has torn your mouth till it bleeds. I have lashed you with
reasonable arguments, I have manhandled you with logic. You are by
nature a weak man, and if one slyly throws an argument in your path,
you *have* to snap it up, you can't resist. It is your nature to lick the
hand of some superior being. But superior beings can be of very
different kinds. And now, with your liberation, you will soon be able
to follow your natural inclinations, which are low. You will be able to
follow your infallible instinct, which teaches you to plant your fat heel
on the faces of men. Gone is the era of confusion and disorder, which
I find described in the Song of Chaos. Let us now sing that song together
in memory of those terrible days. Sit down and don't do violence to the
music. Don't be afraid. It sounds all right. And it a has fine refrain. (*He sings*)

THE SONG OF CHAOS

Sister, hide your face! Brother, take your knife!
The times are out of joint!
Big men are full of complaint
And small men full of joy.
The city says:
"Let us drive the mighty from our midst!"
Offices are raided. Lists of serfs are destroyed.
They have set Master's nose to the grindstone.
They who lived in the dark have seen the light.
The ebony poor box is broken.
Sesnem[2] wood is sawed up for beds.

Who had no bread have full barns.
Who begged for alms of corn now mete it out.

SHAUWA (*refrain*)   Oh, oh, oh, oh.
AZDAK (*refrain*)

Where are you, General, where are you?
Please, please, please, restore order!

The nobleman's son can no longer be recognized;
The lady's child becomes the son of her slave-girl

---

[2]I do not know what kind of wood this is, so I have left the word exactly as it stands in
the German original. The song is based on an Egyptian papyrus which Brecht cites as
such in his essay, "Five Difficulties in the Writing of the Truth." I should think he must
have come across it in Adolf Erman's *Die Literatur der Aegypter*, 1923, p. 130 ff. Erman
too gives the word as Sesnem. The same papyrus is quoted in Karl Jaspers' *Man in the
Modern Age* (Anchor edition, pp. 18–19) but without the sentence about the Sesnem
wood.—E. B.

The councilors meet in a shed.
Once, this man was barely allowed to sleep on the wall;
Now, he stretches his limbs in a bed.
Once, this man rowed a boat; now, he owns ships.
Their owner looks for them, but they're his no longer.
Five men are sent on a journey by their master.
"Go yourself," they say, "we have arrived."

SHAUWA (*refrain*)   Oh, oh, oh, oh.

AZDAK (*refrain*)

Where are you, General, where are you?
Please, please, please, restore order!

Yes, so it might have been, had order been neglected much longer. But now the Grand Duke has returned to the capital, and the Persians have lent him an army to restore order with. The people's quarters are already aflame. Go and get me the big book I always sit on. (SHAUWA *brings the big book from the judge's chair.* AZDAK *opens it.*) This is the Statute Book and I've always used it, as you can testify. Now I'd better look in this book and see what they can do to me. I've let the down-and-outs get away with murder, and I'll have to pay for it. I helped poverty onto its skinny legs, so they'll hang me for drunkenness. I peeped into the rich man's pocket, which is bad taste. And I can't hide anywhere—everybody knows me because I've helped everybody.

SHAUWA   Someone's coming!

AZDAK (*in panic, he walks trembling to the chair*)   It's the end. And now they'd enjoy seeing what a Great Man I am. I'll deprive them of that pleasure. I'll beg on my knees for mercy. Spittle will slobber down my chin. The fear of death is in me.

(*Enter Natella Abashwili, the* GOVERNOR'S WIFE, *followed by the* ADJUTANT *and an* IRONSHIRT.)

GOVERNOR'S WIFE   What sort of a creature is that, Shalva?

AZDAK   A willing one, Your Highness, a man ready to oblige.

ADJUTANT   Natella Abashwili, wife of the late Governor, has just returned. She is looking for her two-year-old son, Michael. She has been informed that the child was carried off to the mountains by a former servant.

AZDAK   The child wil be brought back, Your Highness, at your service.

ADJUTANT   They say that the person in question is passing it off as her own.

AZDAK   She will be beheaded, Your Highness, at your service.

ADJUTANT   That is all.

GOVERNOR'S WIFE (*leaving*)   I don't like that man.

AZDAK (*following her to door, bowing*)   At your service, Your Highness, it will all be arranged.

5 The Chalk Circle

SINGER

Hear now the story of the trial
Concerning Governor Abashwili's child.

And the determination of the true mother
By the famous test of the Chalk Circle.

> (*Law court in Nuka.* IRONSHIRTS *lead* MICHAEL *across stage and out at the back.* IRONSHIRTS *hold* GRUSHA *back with their lances under the gateway until the child has been led through. Then she is admitted. She is accompanied by the former Governor's* COOK. *Distant noises and a fire-red sky.*)

GRUSHA (*trying to hide*)   He's brave, he can wash himself now.

COOK   You're lucky. It's not a real judge. It's Azdak, a drunk who doesn't know what he's doing. The biggest thieves have got by through him. Because he gets everything mixed up and the rich never offer him big enough bribes, the like of us sometimes do pretty well.

GRUSHA   I *need* luck right now.

COOK   Touch wood. (*She crosses herself.*) I'd better offer up another prayer that the judge may be drunk. (*She prays with motionless lips, while* GRUSHA *looks around, in vain, for the child.*) Why must you hold on to it at any price if it isn't yours? In days like these?

GRUSHA   He's mine. I brought him up.

COOK   Have you never thought what'd happen when she came back?

GRUSHA   At first I thought I'd give him to her. Then I thought she wouldn't come back.

COOK   And even a borrowed coat keeps a man warm, hm? (GRUSHA *nods.*) I'll swear to anything for you. You're a decent girl. (*She sees the soldier* SIMON SHASHAVA *approaching.*) You've done wrong by Simon, though. I've been talking with him. He just can't understand.

GRUSHA (*unaware of* SIMON's *presence*)   Right now I can't be bothered whether he understands or not!

COOK   He knows the child isn't yours, but you married and not free "till death you do part"—he can't understand *that.*

> (GRUSHA *sees* SIMON *and greets him.*)

SIMON (*gloomily*)   I wish the lady to know I will swear I am the father of the child.

GRUSHA (*low*)   Thank you, Simon.

SIMON   At the same time I wish the lady to know my hands are not tied—nor are hers.

COOK   You needn't have said that. You know she's married.

SIMON   And it needs no rubbing in.

> (*Enter an* IRONSHIRT.)

IRONSHIRT   Where's the judge? Has anyone seen the judge?

ANOTHER IRONSHIRT (*stepping forward*)   The judge isn't here yet. Nothing but a bed and a pitcher in the whole house!

> (*Exeunt* IRONSHIRTS.)

COOK   I hope nothing has happened to him. With any other judge you'd have as much chance as a chicken has teeth.

GRUSHA (*who has turned away and covered her face*)   Stand in front of me. I shouldn't have come to Nuka. If I run into the Ironshirt, the one I hit over the head . . .

(*She screams. An* IRONSHIRT *had stopped and, turning
his back, had been listening to her. He now wheels
around. It is the* CORPORAL, *and he has a huge scar
across his face.*)

IRONSHIRT (*in the gateway*)   What's the matter, Shotta? Do you know her?

CORPORAL (*after staring for some time*)   No.

IRONSHIRT   She's the one who stole the Abashwili child, or so they say. If you
know anything about it you can make some money, Shotta.

(*Exit the* CORPORAL, *cursing.*)

COOK   Was it him? (GRUSHA *nods.*) I think he'll keep his mouth shut, or he'd
be admitting he was after the child.

GRUSHA   I'd almost forgotten him.

(*Enter the* GOVERNOR'S WIFE, *followed by the* ADJUTANT
and two LAWYERS.)

GOVERNOR'S WIFE   At least there are no common people here, thank God. I
can't stand their smell. It always gives me migraine.

FIRST LAWYER   Madam, I must ask you to be careful what you say until we
have another judge.

GOVERNOR'S WIFE   But I didn't say anything, Illo Shuboladze. I love the people
with their simple straightforward minds. It's only that their smell brings
on my migraine.

SECOND LAWYER   There won't be many spectators. The whole population is
sitting at home behind locked doors because of the riots in the people's
quarters.

GOVERNOR'S WIFE (*looking at* GRUSHA)   Is that the creature?

FIRST LAWYER   Please, most gracious Natella Abashwili, abstain from invective
until it is certain the Grand Duke has appointed a new judge and we're
rid of the present one, who's about the lowest fellow ever seen in judge's
gown. Things are all set to move, you see.

(*Enter* IRONSHIRTS *from the courtyard.*)

COOK   Her Grace would pull your hair out on the spot if she didn't know
Azdak is for the poor. He does by the face.

(IRONSHIRTS *begin fastening a rope to a beam.* AZDAK, *in
chains, is led in, followed by* SHAUWA, *also in chains. The
three* FARMERS *bring up the rear.*)

AN IRONSHIRT   Trying to run away, were you? (*He strikes* AZDAK.)

ONE FARMER   Off with his judge's gown before we string him up!

(IRONSHIRTS *and* FARMERS *tear off Azdak's gown. His
torn underwear is visible. Then someone kicks him.*)

AN IRONSHIRT (*pushing him into someone else*)   Want a load of justice? Here
it is!

(*Accompanied by shouts of* "You take it!" *and* "Let me
have him, Brother!" *they throw* AZDAK *back and forth
until he collapses. Then he is lifted up and dragged under
the noose.*)

GOVERNOR'S WIFE (*who, during this "ballgame," has clapped her hands hysterically*)   I disliked that man from the moment I first saw him.

AZDAK (*covered with blood, panting*)   I can't see. Give me a rag.

AN IRONSHIRT   What is it you want to see?

AZDAK   You, you dogs! (*He wipes the blood out of his eyes with his shirt.*) Good morning, dogs! How goes it, dogs! How's the dog world? Does it smell good? Got another boot for me to lick? Are you back at each other's throats, dogs?

(*Accompanied by a* CORPORAL, *a dust-covered* RIDER *enters. He takes some documents from a leather case, looks at them, then interrupts.*)

RIDER   Stop! I bring a dispatch from the Grand Duke, containing the latest appointments.

CORPORAL (*bellowing*)   Atten—shun!

RIDER   Of the new judge it says: "We appoint a man whom we have to thank for saving a life indispensable to the country's welfare—a certain Azdak of Nuka." Which is he?

SHAUWA (*pointing*)   That's him, Your Excellency.

CORPORAL (*bellowing*)   What's going on here?

AN IRONSHIRT   I beg to report that His Honor Azdak was already His Honor Azdak, but on these farmers' denunciation was pronounced the Grand Duke's enemy.

CORPORAL (*pointing at the* FARMERS)   March them off! (*They are marched off. They bow all the time.*) See to it that His Honor Azdak is exposed to no more violence.

(*Exeunt* RIDER *and* CORPORAL.)

COOK (*to* SHAUWA)   She clapped her hands! I hope he saw it!

FIRST LAWYER   It's a catastrophe.

(AZDAK *has fainted. Coming to, he is dressed again in judge's robes. He walks, swaying, toward the* IRONSHIRTS.)

AN IRONSHIRT   What does Your Honor desire?

AZDAK   Nothing, fellow dogs, or just an occasional boot to lick. (*To* SHAUWA) I pardon you. (*He is unchained.*) Get me some red wine, the sweet kind. (SHAUWA *stumbles off.*) Get out of here, I've got to judge a case. (*Exeunt* IRONSHIRTS. SHAUWA *returns with a pitcher of wine.* AZDAK *gulps it down.*) Something for my backside. (SHAUWA *brings the Statute Book, puts it on the judge's chair.* AZDAK *sits on it.*) I accept.

(*The Prosecutors, among whom a worried council has been held, smile with relief. They whisper.*)

COOK   Oh dear!

SIMON   A well can't be filled with dew, they say.

LAWYERS (*approaching* AZDAK, *who stands up, expectantly*)   A quite ridiculous case, Your Honor. The accused has abducted a child and refuses to hand it over.

AZDAK (*stretching out his hand, glancing at* GRUSHA)   A most attractive person. (*He fingers the money, then sits down, satisfied.*) I declare the proceedings open and demand the whole truth. (*To* GRUSHA) Especially from you.

FIRST LAWYER   High Court of Justice! Blood, as the popular saying goes, is thicker than water. This old adage . . .

AZDAK (*interrupting*) The Court wants to know the lawyers' fee.

FIRST LAWYER (*surprised*) I beg your pardon? (AZDAK, *smiling, rubs his thumb and index finger*.) Oh, I see. Five hundred piasters, Your Honor, to answer the Court's somewhat unusual question.

AZDAK Did you hear? The question is unusual. I ask it because I listen in quite a different way when I know you're good.

FIRST LAWYER (*bowing*) Thank you, Your Honor. High Court of Justice, of all ties the ties of blood are strongest. Mother and child—is there a more intimate relationship? Can one tear a child from its mother? High Court of Justice, she has conceived it in the holy ecstasies of love. She has carried it in her womb. She has fed it with her blood. She has borne it with pain. High Court of Justice, it has been observed that the wild tigress, robbed of her young, roams restless through the mountains, shrunk to a shadow. Nature herself . . .

AZDAK (*interrupting, to* GRUSHA) What's your answer to all this and anything else that lawyer might have to say?

GRUSHA He's mine.

AZDAK Is that all? I hope you can prove it. Why should I assign the child to you in any case?

GRUSHA I brought him up like the priest says "according to my best knowledge and conscience." I always found him something to eat. Most of the time he had a roof over his head. And I went to such trouble for him. I had expenses too. I didn't look out for my own comfort. I brought the child up to be friendly with everyone, and from the beginning taught him to work. As well as he could, that is. He's still very little.

FIRST LAWYER Your Honor, it is significant that the girl herself doesn't claim any tie of blood between her and the child.

AZDAK The Court takes note of that.

FIRST LAWYER Thank you, Your Honor, And now permit a woman bowed in sorrow—who has already lost her husband and now has also to fear the loss of her child—to address a few words to you. The gracious Natella Abashwili is . . .

GOVERNOR'S WIFE (*quietly*) A most cruel fate, sir, forces me to describe to you the tortures of a bereaved mother's soul, the anxiety, the sleepless nights, the . . .

SECOND LAWYER (*bursting out*) It's outrageous the way this woman is being treated! Her husband's palace is closed to her! The revenue of her estates is blocked, and she is cold-bloodedly told that it's tied to the heir. She can't do a thing without that child. She can't even pay her lawyer!! (*To the* FIRST LAWYER, *who, desperate about this outburst, makes frantic gestures to keep him from speaking:*) Dear Illo Shuboladze, surely it can be divulged now that the Abashwili estates are at stake?

FIRST LAWYER Please, Honored Sandro Oboladze! We agreed . . . (*To* AZDAK:) Of course it is correct that the trial will also decide if our noble client can take over the Abashwili estates, which are rather extensive. I say "also" advisedly, for in the foreground stands the human tragedy of a mother, as Natella Abashwili very properly explained in the first words of her moving statement. Even if Michael Abashwili were not heir to the estates, he would still be the dearly beloved child of my client.

AZDAK Stop! The Court is touched by the mention of estates. It's a proof of human feeling.

SECOND LAWYER Thanks, Your Honor. Dear Illo Shuboladze, we can prove in any case that the woman who took the child is not the child's mother. Permit me to lay before the Court the bare facts. High Court of Justice, by an unfortunate chain of circumstances, Michael Abashwili was left behind on that Easter Sunday while his mother was making her escape. Grusha, a palace kitchen maid, was seen with the baby . . .

COOK All her mistress was thinking of was what dresses she'd take along!

SECOND LAWYER (*unmoved*) Nearly a year later Grusha turned up in a mountain village with a baby and there entered into the state of matrimony with . . .

AZDAK How'd you get to that mountain village?

GRUSHA On foot, Your Honor. And he was mine.

SIMON I'm the father, Your Honor.

COOK I used to look after it for them, Your Honor. For five piasters.

SECOND LAWYER This man is engaged to Grusha, High Court of Justice: his testimony is suspect.

AZDAK Are you the man she married in the mountain village?

SIMON No, Your Honor, she married a peasant.

AZDAK (*to* GRUSHA) Why? (*Pointing at* SIMON.) Is he no good in bed? Tell the truth.

GRUSHA We didn't get that far. I married because of the baby. So he'd have a roof over his head. (*Pointing at* SIMON.) He was in the war, Your Honor.

AZDAK And now he wants you back again, huh?

SIMON I wish to state in evidence . . .

GRUSHA (*angrily*) I am no longer free, Your Honor.

AZDAK And the child, you claim, comes from whoring? (GRUSHA *doesn't answer.*) I'm going to ask you a question: What kind of child is he? A ragged little bastard? Or from a good family?

GRUSHA (*angrily*) He's an ordinary child.

AZDAK I mean—did he have refined features from the beginning?

GRUSHA He had a nose on his face.

AZDAK A very significant comment! It has been said of me that I went out one time and sniffed at a rosebush before rendering a verdict—tricks like that are needed nowadays. Well, I'll make it short, and not listen to any more lies. (*To* GRUSHA:) Especially not yours. (*To all the accused*) I can imagine what you've cooked up to cheat me! I know you people. You're swindlers.

GRUSHA (*suddenly*) I can understand your wanting to cut it short, now I've seen what you accepted!

AZDAK Shut up! Did I accept anything from you?

GRUSHA (*while the* COOK *tries to restrain her*) I haven't got anything.

AZDAK   True. Quite true. From starvelings I never get a thing. I might just as well starve, myself. You want justice, but do you want to pay for it, hm? When you go to a butcher you know you have to pay, but you people go to a judge as if you were off to a funeral supper.

SIMON (*loudly*)   When the horse was shod, the horsefly held out its leg, as the saying is.

AZDAK (*eagerly accepting the challenge*)   Better a treasure in manure than a stone in a mountain stream.

SIMON   A fine day. Let's go fishing, said the angler to the worm.

AZDAK   I'm my own master, said the servant, and cut off his foot.

SIMON   I love you as a father, said the Czar to the peasants, and had the Czarevitch's head chopped off.

AZDAK   A fool's worst enemy is himself.

SIMON   However, a fart has no nose.

AZDAK   Fined ten piasters for indecent language in court! That'll teach you what justice is.

GRUSHA (*furiously*)   A fine kind of justice! You play fast and loose with us because we don't talk as refined as that crowd with their lawyers.

AZDAK   That's true. You people are too dumb. It's only right you should get it in the neck.

GRUSHA   You want to hand the child over to her, and she wouldn't even know how to keep it dry, she's so "refined"! You know about as much about justice as I do!

AZDAK   There's something in that. I'm an ignorant man. Haven't even a decent pair of pants on under this gown. Look! With me, everything goes on food and drink—I was educated in a convent. Incidentally, I'll fine you ten piasters for contempt of court. And you're a very silly girl, to turn me against you, instead of making eyes at me and wiggling your backside a little to keep me in a good temper. Twenty piasters!

GRUSHA   Even if it was thirty, I'd tell you what I think of your justice, you drunken onion! (*Incoherently.*) How dare you talk to me like the cracked Isaiah on the church window? As if you were somebody? For you weren't born to this. You weren't born to rap your own mother on the knuckles if she swipes a little bowl of salt someplace. Aren't you ashamed of yourself when you see how I tremble before you? You've made yourself their servant so no one will take their houses from them— houses they had stolen! Since when have houses belonged to the bedbugs? But you're on the watch, or they couldn't drag our men into their wars! You bribetaker!

> (AZDAK *half gets up, starts beaming. With his little hammer he halfheartedly knocks on the table as if to get silence. As* GRUSHA's *scolding continues, he only beats time with his hammer.*)

I've no respect for you. No more than for a thief or a bandit with a knife! You can do what you want. You can take the child away from me, a hundred against one, but I tell you one thing: only extortioners should be chosen for a profession like yours, and men who rape children!

As punishment! Yes, let *them* sit in judgment on their fellow creatures. It is worse than to hang from the gallows.

AZDAK (*sitting down*) Now it'll be thirty! And I won't go on squabbling with you—we're not in a tavern. What'd happen to my dignity as a judge? Anyway, I've lost interest in your case. Where's the couple who wanted a divorce? (*To* SHAUWA) Bring 'em in. This case is adjourned for fifteen minutes.

FIRST LAWYER (*to the* GOVERNOR'S WIFE) Even without using the rest of the evidence, Madam, we have the verdict in the bag.

COOK (*to* GRUSHA) You've gone and spoiled your chances with him. You won't get the child now.

GOVERNOR'S WIFE Shalva, my smelling salts!

(*Enter a very old couple.*)

AZDAK I accept. (*The old couple don't understand.*) I hear you want to be divorced. How long have you been together?

OLD WOMAN Forty years, Your Honor.

AZDAK And why do you want a divorce?

OLD MAN We don't like each other, Your Honor.

AZDAK Since when?

OLD WOMAN Oh, from the very beginning, Your Honor.

AZDAK I'll think about your request and render my verdict when I'm through with the other case. (SHAUWA *leads them back.*) I need the child. (*He beckons* GRUSHA *to him and bends not unkindly toward her.*) I've noticed you have a soft spot for justice. I don't believe he's your child, but if he *were* yours, woman, wouldn't you want him to be rich? You'd only have to say he wasn't yours, and he'd have a palace and many horses in his stable and many beggars on his doorstep and many soldiers in his service and many petitioners in his courtyard, wouldn't he? What do you say— don't you want him to be rich?

(GRUSHA *is silent.*)

SINGER

Hear now what the angry girl thought but did not say:
Had he golden shoes to wear
He'd be cruel as a bear.
Evil would his life disgrace.
He'd laugh in my face.
Carrying a heart of flint
Is too troublesome a stint.
Being powerful and bad
Is hard on a lad.
Then let hunger be his foe!
Hungry men and women, no.
Let him fear the darksome night
But not daylight!

AZDAK I think I understand you, woman.

GRUSHA (*suddenly and loudly*) I won't give him up. I've raised him, and he knows me.

(*Enter* SHAUWA *with the* CHILD.)

GOVERNOR'S WIFE   He's in rags!

GRUSHA   That's not true. But I wasn't given time to put his good shirt on.

GOVERNOR'S WIFE   He must have been in a pigsty.

GRUSHA (*furiously*)   I'm not a pig, but there are some who are! Where did you leave your baby?

GOVERNOR'S WIFE   I'll show you, you vulgar creature! (*She is about to throw herself on* GRUSHA, *but is restrained by her lawyers.*) She's a criminal, she must be whipped. Immediately!

SECOND LAWYER (*holding his hand over her mouth*)   Natella Abashwili, you promised . . . Your Honor, the plaintiff's nerves . . .

AZDAK   Plaintiff and defendant! The Court has listened to your case, and has come to no decision as to who the real mother is; therefore, I, the judge, am obliged to *choose* a mother for the child. I'll make a test. Shauwa, get a piece of chalk and draw a circle on the floor. (SHAUWA *does so.*) Now place the child in the center. (SHAUWA *puts* MICHAEL, *who smiles at* GRUSHA, *in the center of the circle.*) Stand near the circle, both of you. (*The* GOVERNOR'S WIFE *and* GRUSHA *step up to the circle.*) Now each of you take the child by one hand. (*They do so.*) The true mother is she who can pull the child out of the circle.

SECOND LAWYER (*quickly*)   High Court of Justice, I object! The fate of the great Abashwili estates, which are tied to the child, as the heir, should not be made dependent on such a doubtful duel. In addition, my client does not command the strength of this person, who is accustomed to physical work.

AZDAK   She looks pretty well fed to me. Pull! (*The* GOVERNOR'S WIFE *pulls the* CHILD *out of the circle on her side;* GRUSHA *has let go and stands aghast.*) What's the matter with you? You didn't pull.

GRUSHA   I didn't hold on to him.

FIRST LAWYER (*congratulating the* GOVERNOR'S WIFE)   What did I say! The ties of blood!

GRUSHA (*running to* AZDAK)   Your Honor, I take back everything I said against you. I ask your forgiveness. But could I keep him till he can speak all the words? He knows a few.

AZDAK   Don't influence the Court. I bet you only know about twenty words yourself. All right. I'll make the test once more, just to be certain. (*The two women take up their positions again.*) Pull! (*Again* GRUSHA *lets go of the* CHILD.)

GRUSHA (*in despair*)   I brought him up! Shall I also tear him to bits? I can't!

AZDAK (*rising*)   And in this manner the Court has determined the true mother. (*To* GRUSHA:) Take your child and be off. I advise you not to stay in the city with him. (*To the* GOVERNOR'S WIFE:) And you disappear before I fine you for fraud. Your estates fall to the city. They'll be converted into a playground for the children. They need one, and I've decided it'll be called after me: Azdak's Garden.

> (*The* GOVERNOR'S WIFE *has fainted and is carried out by the* LAWYERS *and the* ADJUTANT. GRUSHA *stands motionless.* SHAUWA *leads the* CHILD *toward her.*)

Now I'll take off this judge's gown—it's got too hot for me. I'm not cut out for a hero. In token of farewell I invite you all to a little dance in the meadow outside. Oh, I'd almost forgotten something in my excitement . . . to sign the divorce decree.

> (*Using the judge's chair as a table, he writes something on a piece of paper, and prepares to leave. Dance music has started.*)

SHAUWA (*having read what is on the paper*)   But that's not right. You've not divorced the old people. You've divorced Grusha!

AZDAK   Divorced the wrong couple? What a pity! And I never retract! If I did, how could we keep order in the land? (*To the old couple:*) I'll invite you to my party instead. You don't mind dancing with each other, do you? (*To* GRUSHA *and* SIMON:) I've got forty piasters coming from you.

SIMON (*pulling out his purse*)   Cheap at the price, Your Honor. And many thanks.

AZDAK (*pocketing the cash*)   I'll be needing this.

GRUSHA (*to* MICHAEL)   So we'd better leave the city tonight, Michael? (*To* SIMON) You like him?

SIMON   With my respects, I like him.

GRUSHA   Now I can tell you: I took him because on that Easter Sunday I got engaged to you. So he's a child of love. Michael, let's dance.

> (*She dances with* MICHAEL, SIMON *dances with the* COOK, *the old couple with each other.* AZDAK *stands lost in thought. The dancers soon hide him from view. Occasionally he is seen, but less and less as more couples join the dance.*)

SINGER

And after that evening Azdak vanished and was never seen again.
The people of Grusinia did not forget him but long remembered
The period of his judging as a brief golden age,
Almost an age of justice.

> (*All the couples dance off.* AZDAK *has disappeared.*)

But you, you who have listened to the Story of the Chalk Circle,
Take note what men of old concluded:
That what there is shall go to those who are good for it,
Children to the motherly, that they prosper,
Carts to good drivers, that they be driven well,
The valley to the waterers, that it yield fruit.

From the Playwright

Possibly no more of a definitive essay on the function of epic theatre can be found than **Brecht's** *"Theatre for Pleasure or Theatre for Instruction," Ways in which* The Caucasian Chalk Circle, *as well as other epic dramas, can be analyzed and justified are presented by Brecht in this often quoted composition. The Epic theatre's principal playwright has always been its chief spokesman.*

Theatre for Pleasure or Theatre for Instruction

THE EPIC THEATRE

Many people imagine that the term 'epic theatre' is self-contradictory, as the epic and dramatic ways of narrating a story are held, following Aristotle, to be basically distinct. The difference between the two forms was never thought simply to lie in the fact that the one is performed by living beings while the other operates via the written word; epic works such as those of Homer and the medieval singers were at the same time theatrical performances, while dramas like Goethe's *Faust* and Byron's *Manfred* are agreed to have been more effective as books. Thus even by Aristotle's definition the difference between the dramatic and epic forms was attributed to their different methods of construction, whose laws were dealt with by two different branches of aesthetics. The method of construction depended on the different way of presenting the work to the public, sometimes via the stage, sometimes through a book; and independently of that there was the 'dramatic element' in epic works and the 'epic element' in dramatic. The bourgeois novel in the last century developed much that was 'dramatic,' by which was meant the strong centralization of the story, a momentum that drew the separate parts into a common relationship. A particular passion of utterance, a certain emphasis on the clash of forces are hallmarks of the 'dramatic.' The epic writer Döblin provided an excellent criterion when he said that with an epic work, as opposed to a dramatic, one can as it were take a pair of scissors and cut it into individual pieces, which remain fully capable of life.

This is no place to explain how the opposition of epic and dramatic lost its rigidity after having long been held to be irreconcilable. Let us just point out that the technical advances alone were enough to permit the stage to incorporate an element of narrative in its dramatic productions. The possibility of projections, the greater adaptability of the stage due to mechanization, the film, all completed the theatre's equipment, and did so at a point where the most important transactions between people could no longer be shown simply by personifying the motive forces or subjecting the characters to invisible metaphysical powers.

To make these transactions intelligible the environment in which the people lived had to be brought to bear in a big and 'significant' way.

This environment had of course been shown in the existing drama, but only as seen from the central figure's point of view, and not as an independent element. It was defined by the hero's reactions to it. It was seen as a storm can be seen when one sees the ships on a sheet of water unfolding their sails, and the sails filling out. In the epic theatre it was to appear standing on its own.

The stage began to tell a story. The narrator was no longer missing, along with the fourth wall. Not only did the background adopt an attitude to the events on the stage—by big screens recalling other simultaneous events elsewhere, by projecting documents which confirmed or contradicted what the characters said, by concrete and intelligible figures to accompany abstract conversations, by figures and sentences to support mimed transactions whose sense was unclear— but the actors too refrained from going over wholly into their role, remaining detached from the character they were playing and clearly inviting criticism of him.

The spectator was no longer in any way allowed to submit to an experience uncritically (and without practical consequences) by means of simple empathy with the characters in a play. The production took the subject-matter and the incidents shown and put them through a process of alienation: the alienation that is necessary to all understanding. When something seems 'the most obvious thing in the world' it means that any attempt to understand the world has been given up.

What is 'natural' must have the force of what is startling. This is the only way to expose the laws of cause and effect. People's activity must simultaneously be so and be capable of being different.

It was all a great change.

The dramatic theatre's spectator says: Yes, I have felt like that too—Just like me—It's only natural—It'll never change—The sufferings of this man appal me, because they are inescapable—That's great art; it all seems the most obvious thing in the world—I weep when they weep, I laugh when they laugh.

The epic theatre's spectator says: I'd never have thought it—That's not the way—That's extraordinary, hardly believable—It's got to stop—The sufferings of this man appal me, because they are unnecessary—That's great art: nothing obvious in it—I laugh when they weep, I weep when they laugh.

THE INSTRUCTIVE THEATRE

The stage began to be instructive.

Oil, inflation, war, social struggles, the family, religion, wheat, the meat market, all became subjects for theatrical representation. Choruses enlightened the spectator about facts unknown to him. Films showed a montage of events from all over the world. Projections added statistical material. And as the 'background' came to the front of the stage so people's activity was subjected to criticism. Right and wrong courses of action were shown. People were shown who knew what they were doing, and others who did not. The theatre became an affair for philosophers, but only for such philosophers as wished not just to explain the world but also to change it. So we had philosophy, and we had instruction. And where was the amusement in all that? Were they sending us back to school, teaching us to read and write? Were we supposed to pass exams, work for diplomas?

Generally there is felt to be a very sharp distinction between learning and amusing oneself. The first may be useful, but only the second is pleasant. So we have to defend the epic theatre against the suspicion that it is a highly disagreeable, humourless, indeed strenuous affair.

Well: all that can be said is that the contrast between learning and amusing oneself is not laid down by divine rule; it is not one that has always been and must continue to be.

Undoubtedly there is much that is tedious about the kind of learning familiar to us from school, from our professional training, etc. But it must be remembered under what conditions and to what end that takes place.

It is really a commercial transaction. Knowledge is just a commodity. It is acquired in order to be resold. All those who have grown out of going to school have to do their learning virtually in secret, for anyone who admits that he still has something to learn devalues himself as a man whose knowledge is inadequate. Moreover the usefulness of learning is very much limited by factors outside the learner's control. There is unemployment, for instance, against which no knowledge can protect one. There is the division of labour, which makes generalized knowledge unnecessary and impossible. Learning is often among the concerns of those whom no amount of concern will get any forwarder. There is not much knowledge that leads to power, but plenty of knowledge to which only power can lead.

Learning has a very different function for different social strata. There are strata who cannot imagine any improvement in conditions: they find the conditions good enough for them. Whatever happens to oil they will benefit from it. And: they feel the years beginning to tell. There can't be all that many years more. What is the point of learning a lot now? They have said their final word: a grunt. But there are also strata 'waiting their turn' who are discontented with conditions, have a vast interest in the practical side of learning, want at all costs to find out where they stand, and know that they are lost without learning; these are the best and keenest learners. Similar differences apply to countries and peoples. Thus the pleasure of learning depends on all sorts of things; but none the less there is such a thing as pleasurable learning, cheerful and militant learning.

If there were not such amusement to be had from learning, the theatre's whole structure would unfit it for teaching.

Theatre remains theatre even when it is instructive theatre, and in so far as it is good theatre it will amuse.

THEATRE AND KNOWLEDGE

But what has knowledge got to do with art? We know that knowledge can be amusing, but not everything that is amusing belongs in the theatre.

I have often been told, when pointing out the invaluable services that modern knowledge and science, if properly applied, can perform for art and specially for the theatre, that art and knowledge are two estimable but wholly distinct fields of human activity. This is a fearful truism, of course, and it is as well to agree quickly that, like most truisms, it is perfectly true. Art and science work in quite different ways: agreed. But, bad as it may sound, I have to admit that I cannot get along as an artist without the use of one or two sciences. This may well arouse serious doubts as to my artistic capacities. People are used to seeing poets as unique and slightly unnatural beings who reveal with a truly godlike assurance things that other people can only recognize after much sweat and toil. It is naturally distasteful to have to admit that one does not belong to this select band. All the same, it must be admitted. It must at the same time be made clear that the scientific occupations just confessed to are not pardonable side interests, pursued on days off after a good week's work. We all know how Goethe was interested in natural history, Schiller in history: as a kind of hobby, it is charitable to assume. I have no wish promptly to accuse these two of having needed these sciences for poetic activity; I am not trying to shelter behind them; but I must say that I do need the sciences. I have to admit, however, that I look askance at all sorts of people who I know do not operate on the level of scientific understanding: that is to say, who sing as the birds sing, or as people imagine the birds to sing. I don't mean by that I would reject a charming poem about the taste of fried fish or the delights of a boating party just because the writer had not studied gastronomy or navigation. But in my view the great and complicated things that go on in the world cannot be adequately recognized by people who do not use every possible aid to understanding.

Let us suppose that great passions or great events have to be shown which influence the fate of nations. The lust for power is nowadays held to be such a passion. Given that a poet 'feels' this lust and wants to have someone strive for power, how is he to show the exceedingly complicated machinery within which the struggle for power nowadays takes place? If his hero is a politician, how do politics work? If he is a business man, how does business work? And yet there are writers who find business and politics nothing like so passionately interesting as the individual's lust for power. How are they to acquire the necessary knowledge? They are scarcely likely to learn enough by going round and keeping their eyes open, though even then it is more than they would get by just rolling their eyes in an exalted frenzy. The foundation of a paper like the *Völkischer Beobachter* or a business like Standard Oil is a pretty complicated affair, and such things cannot be conveyed just like that. One important field for the playwright is psychology. It is taken for granted that a poet, if not an ordinary man, must be able without further instruction to discover the motives that lead a man to commit murder; he must be able to give a picture of a murderer's mental state 'from within himself.' It is taken for granted that one only has to look inside oneself in such a case; and then there's always one's imagination. . . . There are various reasons why I can no longer surrender to this agreeable hope of getting a result quite so simply. I can no longer find in myself all those motives which the press or scientific reports show to have been observed in people. Like the average judge when pronouncing sentence, I cannot without further ado conjure up an adequate picture of a murderer's mental state. Modern psychology, from psychoanalysis to behaviourism, acquaints me with facts that lead me to judge the case quite differently, especially if I bear in mind the findings of sociology and do not overlook economics and history. You will say: but that's getting complicated. I have to answer that it *is* complicated. Even if you let yourself be convinced, and agree with me that a large slice of literature is exceedingly primitive, you may still ask with profound concern: won't an evening in such a theatre be a most alarming affair? The answer to that is: no.

Whatever knowledge is embodied in a piece of poetic writing has to be wholly transmuted into poetry. Its utilization fulfils the very pleasure that the poetic element provokes. If it does not at the same time fulfil that which is fulfilled by the scientific element, none the less in an age of great discoveries and inventions one must have a certain inclination to penetrate deeper into things— a desire to make the world controllable—if one is to be sure of enjoying its poetry.

IS THE EPIC THEATRE SOME KIND OF 'MORAL INSTITUTION'?

According to Friedrich Schiller the theatre is supposed to be a moral institution. In making this demand it hardly occurred to Schiller that by moralizing from the stage he might drive the audience out of the theatre. Audiences had no objection to moralizing in his day. It was only later that Friedrich Nietzsche attacked him for blowing a moral trumpet. To Nietzsche any concern with morality was a depressing affair; to Schiller it seemed thoroughly enjoyable. He knew of nothing that could give greater amusement and satisfaction than the propagation of ideas. The bourgeoisie was setting about forming the ideas of the nation.

Putting one's house in order, patting oneself on the back, submitting one's account, is something highly agreeable. But describing the collapse of one's house, having pains in the back, paying one's account, is indeed a depressing affair, and that was how Friedrich Nietzsche saw things a century later. He was poorly disposed towards morality, and thus towards the previous Friedrich too.

The epic theatre was likewise often objected to as moralizing too much. Yet in the epic theatre moral arguments only took second place. Its aim was less to moralize than to observe. That is to say it observed, and then the thick end of the wedge followed: the story's moral. Of course we cannot pretend that we started our observations out of a pure passion for observing and without any more practical motive, only to be completely staggered by their results. Undoubtedly there were some painful discrepancies in our environment, circumstances that were barely tolerable, and this not merely on account of moral considerations. It is not only moral considerations that make hunger, cold and oppression hard to bear. Similarly the object of our inquiries was not just to arouse moral objections to such circumstances (even though they could easily be felt—though not by all the audience alike; such objections were seldom for instance felt by those who profited by the circumstances in question) but to discover means for their elimination. We were not in fact speaking in the name of morality but in that of the victims. These truly are two distinct matters, for the victims are often told that they ought to be contented with their lot, for moral reasons. Moralists of this sort see man as existing for morality, not morality for man. At least it should be possible to gather from the above to what degree and in what sense the epic theatre is a moral institution.

CAN EPIC THEATRE BE PLAYED ANYWHERE?

Stylistically speaking, there is nothing all that new about the epic theatre. Its expository character and its emphasis on virtuosity bring it close to the old

Asiatic theatre. Didactic tendencies are to be found in the medieval mystery plays and the classical Spanish theatre, and also in the theatre of the Jesuits.

These theatrical forms corresponded to particular trends of their time, and vanished with them. Similarly the modern epic theatre is linked with certain trends. It cannot be any means be practised universally. Most of the great nations today are not disposed to use the theatre for ventilating their problems. London, Paris, Tokyo and Rome maintain their theatres for quite different purposes. Up to now favourable circumstances for an epic and didactic theatre have only been found in a few places and for a short period of time. In Berlin Fascism put a very definite stop to the development of such a theatre.

It demands not only a certain technological level but a powerful movement in society which is interested to see vital questions freely aired with a view to their solution, and can defend this interest against every contrary trend.

The epic theatre is the broadest and most far-reaching attempt at large-scale modern theatre, and it has all those immense difficulties to overcome that always confront the vital forces in the sphere of politics, philosophy, science and art.

From the Critic

The method of rousing an audience from identification with the play and its characters —called alienation—remains at the heart of epic theatre. In the following essay, Professor **Maria Alter** *examines the ways in which Brecht employed this technique in* The Caucasian Chalk Circle.

The Technique of Alienation in Bertolt Brecht's The Caucasian Chalk Circle

The Caucasian Chalk Circle is generally admitted to be one of Brecht's most successful plays. In addition to its dramatic value, it presents also a more theoretical interest as one of the most obvious illustrations of Brecht's technique of "alienation." While it is true that toward the end of his life, when he actually had the opportunity of applying his theories to stage managing, Brecht drew away to a certain extent from his theory of "epic theater," and hence also from the technique of alienation,[1] this evolution postdates clearly the writing of *The*

---

[1]John Willett, *The Theatre of Bertolt Brecht* (New Directions, 1959), p. 183. Willett reports that after 1948, when staging his plays for the Berliner Ensemble, Brecht refused to discuss his theory; stated that he was misunderstood, etc.

Caucasian Chalk Circle. A close structural analysis of that play reveals indeed the tight relationship between the playwright's theoretical views and both the content and form of the fictional work.

The concept of alienation may be broken down into a purpose, which affects mainly the general impact of the play and a certain number of technical devices used to achieve this purpose. The purpose, which connects alienation to the general theory of the "epic theater," is to develop the political awareness of the audience, to teach while entertaining, and to force the spectators to draw concrete (and preferably revolutionary) conclusions from the issues presented on the stage.[2] The alienation thus establishes a special relation between the audience and the play, whereby the former views the latter as an object lesson.

The overall design of *The Caucasian Chalk Circle* fits this role perfectly. In the first place, it obviously presents the main characteristics of a parable in the form of a drama; *i.e.*, it appears as a fictitious story from which a moral or spiritual truth is to be drawn. Brecht extends the definition to include political truth as well, but keeps the usual features of the parable. The action of the play takes place in a half-imaginary, exotic setting (for the Western audience, the Russian province of Georgia is indeed a legendary land); it is supernatural in some aspects; and it tells a tale specifically designed to yield a lesson. In fact, the final and key scene refers directly to one of Solomon's sentences (as well as to a similar conclusion in an old Chinese play). Besides, as if to prevent any misunderstanding of his intentions, Brecht prefaced the play proper by a prologue set in modern society— a meeting between the delegates of two Soviet collective farms arguing about their respective rights to a piece of land—and introduced the main story as an illustration of a correct decision to be reached by the parties.

The same purpose may be traced in the structural reinforcement of the main argument. The moral of the play is carried forward on four different levels. There is first the fable itself, *i.e.*, the succession of scenes that make up the plot and present an implicit lesson. Then, perhaps fearing that the lesson might not be forceful enough, or prove too subtle for the popular audience at which he was aiming, Brecht adds a second medium in the form of songs which express more clearly the same political or moral attitude. On the third level, a running commentary of the story-teller interprets those actions or events which may still seem obscure. Finally, as mentioned before, a prologue anticipates the entire development by stating the problem at issue in a different context. It is interesting to note that the play does not have a symmetrical epilogue, but ends with a summary by the story-teller, so that the dramatic impact is preserved, without a return to the everyday situation.

The technical devices of alienation serve the main purpose by establishing a distance between the audience and the play, so that the spectators may be con-

---

[2]The general purpose of Brecht's theater is to contribute to the development of workers' self-conscience as a revolutionary class in the Marxist sense. However, the theory of "epic theater" and more specifically the concept of "alienation," may be considered on their own as dramatic techniques. Furthermore, in his "Kleines Organon für das Theater," completed in 1948, Brecht himself shifted his theories to a new ground, viewing the purpose of his plays as entertainment rather than as instruction. See Bertolt Brecht, *Schriften zum Theater* (Suhrkamp Verlag, 1962), pp. 128–174.

stantly reminded that they are viewing a play (hence an object lesson) and not a real event. In that sense, alienation is the very opposite of the technique of illusion which has been traditionally employed on the Western stage, where the main aim of the playwright was always to draw the spectator into the world created in the play, cause him to identify with the heroes, and live emotionally the theatrical experience for the sake of catharsis. Brecht, on the contrary, tries to break the magic of the theater and to startle periodically the spectator into realization that he is attending only a performance, looking at actors, witnessing parables from which he should draw dispassionate conclusions.

Viewed in this perspective, *The Caucasian Chalk Circle* shows clearly that Brecht does not make any attempt at realism or any illusion of reality. The feeling of unreality is first created not only by the prologue, discussed above, but especially by the way in which that prologue introduces *The Caucasian Chalk Circle* proper as merely a play within a play.[3] Indeed, the characters in the prologue discuss the origin of the play, comment on the reputation and the skill of the story-teller, and are shown in advance the masks to be used—all devices which serve to remind the audience that it is going to witness a theatrical performance and not to participate in a real experience. The same effect is obtained through the presence of musicians on the stage, and the use of some characters from the prologue as the chorus in the body of the play. In addition, Brecht indicates that the story-teller must appear with a book, which he is supposed to consult from time to time. Obviously, each time the spectators see him turning a page, they remember the literary and artificial character of the spectacle, and realize anew that they attend a parable.

Alienation devices abound also in the text of the play. Its construction testifies to a search for discontinuous impressions, throwing the spectator in and out of the main stream of action. This sensation is achieved especially by the songs, which interrupt the flow of scenes and often have no relation whatever to the story. The *Song of the Child*, for example, is both very shocking and completely irrelevant in the context in which it occurs. The same jarring effect is obtained by the frequent and unexpected transition from prose to verse, and by the insertion of proverbs and maxims expressed in a poetic form. Each time the dramatic movement of the play is sharply interrupted. This disruption of movement is also brought about by the succession of different moods, as *The Caucasion Chalk Circle* moves back and forth between comedy, violence, fantasy, terror, irony, pity, poetic love, with a rapidity that leaves no time for adjustment. The versatile function of the chorus contributes to the same end. As in the Greek drama, it comments on the action, summarizes the problems, and underscores the ideas of the play. In addition, however, it substitutes occasionally for the characters of the play and tells what they are thinking while they remain silent on the stage. As a result, the audience is forced to shift its perspective, and suddenly finds itself on the sidelines, after having been immersed in the action: the distance between the

---

[3]There is obviously a reminiscence of Pirandello in this device, just as there was a certain influence of Piscator in the introduction of foreign (non-theatrical) elements in the play. However, we are not dealing here with the influences to which Brecht was submitted, and which range from the Greek drama to the Japanese "No" plays (for example, the use of masks).

spectators and the actors becomes more pronounced through this interposition of the chorus. The same impression is created, though less strikingly perhaps, in scenes where Grusha and Simon speak of themselves in the third person.

Other alienation effects stem from the impact of Brecht's ironical paradoxes and belong to the content rather than the structure of the play. They bring about the kind of surprise which breaks the emotional spell of the action. For instance, an ironshirt corporal berates his subordinate, not as one would expect for acts of brutality that he committed, but for not having enjoyed them! Obviously such a remark comes as a jolt, awakens the spectator, and makes him suddenly aware that he is witnessing the display of the wit of the playwright and not a real incident. It also makes him reflect on the implications of the military mind. Similarly, when Azdak demonstrates quite logically that justice, like meat, should be bought at a price, the spectator is shocked, stops identifying with the advocate of such subversive ideas, but nonetheless is encouraged to re-examine the nature of justice. In fact, all of Azdak's paradoxical pronouncements disturb the average spectator's worldview.

The very character of Azdak provides another illustration of the alienation effect. On the one hand, he represents the most "positive hero" in *The Caucasian Chalk Circle*: he expounds Brecht's ideas on justice, defends the underdog against the powerful, redistributes the wealth by taking from the rich and giving to the poor, makes it clear that in his, and Brecht's opinion, all wealth is dishonestly acquired. Yet he can hardly be proposed as a model, and his "positive" traits are incidental to his general portrait which, far from corresponding to the image of the socialist hero, displays many features suitable for the traditional villain. He is swayed by fear and despair; he likes the pleasures of the flesh as well as specious intellectual arguments; and he is not above lying and stealing when it suits his fancy. When in danger, he forgets his idealistic principles and is ready for any compromise in order to survive. The average spectator does not know very well what to think of Azdak, and this very incertitude constitutes an incentive for reflection and judgment. It is because of the alienation from Azdak that the audience submits his character to a critical analysis.

Part of the alienation extends thus beyond the purely technical devices and concerns the psychology and action of the characters, *i.e.*, the plot. Humanistic as it may appear in that respect, especially because of the stress on the power of natural love,[4] *The Caucasian Chalk Circle* evokes an alien universe where the rules of action such as we know them do not apply. In part this impression derives from simple exaggerations which flaunt credibility, as is the case for the Governor's wife who flees with her dresses but forgets her child, or for the inanity of doctors or lawyers. This may be good comedy or acceptable satire, but it is certainly unrealistic. In part the same effect is compounded by a more radical departure from realism through a certain number of frankly improbable, and indeed absurd, actions. The best known is Azdak's self-denunciation as the savior of the Great Duke. It stresses the surprising and irrational aspect of man's personality, for

---

[4] The entire sequence of Grusha and the child, running parallel to the Azdak story, stresses the power and virtue of real love. This aspect of *The Caucasian Chalk Circle* is less marked by "alienation," as it presents a rather straightforward action and simple, perhaps oversimplified, characters. Of course, it is possible that this humanistic side of the play accounts for the popular success of *The Caucasian Chalk Circle*.

nothing in Azadak's psychology, even within the framework of the duality hero-villain, has prepared for this gratuitous and short-lived thirst for martyrdom. It is just an additional shock, and one more surprise. Similarly, there are no reasons to expect the ironshirts' whim to make a judge out of Azdak. Obviously the plot requires this development, but, although it may be justified in terms of the classical *deux ex machina*, the fact remains that it is eminently arbitrary and stresses the irrational character of life. In that sense, *The Caucasian Chalk Circle* portrays a world where anything is possible, nothing is certain, and where the acquired habits of thinking, interpreting, and reaching conclusions must be revised. Which is exactly the aim of alienation.

From the Director

Besides the actual authoring of his plays, Brecht's extensive comments on their staging has made his name synonomous with epic theatre. Expounding on the philosophy, method and rationale, Brecht attempted to make his epic theatre the "theatre of the future." In order to accomplish this, he feels, the director and actor must have complete comprehension of the epic theatre's basic tenet—alienation. In the following, **Brecht** *attempts to explain this new method for acting.*

A New Technique of Acting

What follows represents an attempt to describe a technique of acting which was applied in certain theatres with a view to taking the incidents portrayed and alienating them from the spectator. The aim of this technique, known as the alienation effect, was to make the spectator adopt an attitude of inquiry and criticism in his approach to the incident. The means were artistic.

The first condition for the A-effect's application to this end is that stage and auditorium must be purged of everything 'magical' and that no 'hypnotic tensions' should be set up. This ruled out any attempt to make the stage convey the flavour of a particular place (a room at evening, a road in the autumn), or to create atmosphere by relaxing the tempo of the conversation. The audience was not 'worked up' by a display of temperament or 'swept away' by acting with tautened muscles; in short, no attempt was made to put it in a trance and give it the illusion of watching an ordinary unrehearsed event. As will be seen presently, the audience's tendency to plunge into such illusions has to be checked by specific artistic means.

The first condition for the achievement of the A-effect is that the actor must invest what he has to show with a definite gest of showing. It is of course necessary to drop the assumption that there is a fourth wall cutting the audience off from the stage and the consequent illusion that the stage action is taking place in reality and without an audience. That being so, it is possible for the actor in principle to address the audience direct.

It is well known that contact between audience and stage is normally made on the basis of empathy. Conventional actors devote their efforts so exclusively to bringing about this psychological operation that they may be said to see it as the principal aim of their art. Our introductory remarks will already have made it clear that the technique which produces an A-effect is the exact opposite of that which aims at empathy. The actor applying it is bound not to try to bring about the empathy operation.

Yet in his efforts to reproduce particular characters and show their behaviour he need not renounce the means of empathy entirely. He uses these means just as any normal person with no particular acting talent would use them if he wanted to portray someone else, i.e. show how he behaves. This showing of other people's behaviour happens time and again in ordinary life (witnesses of an accident demonstrating to newcomers how the victim behaved, a facetious person imitating a friend's walk, etc.), without those involved making the least effort to subject their spectators to an illusion. At the same time they do feel their way into their characters' skins with a view to acquiring their characteristics.

As has already been said, the actor too will make use of this psychological operation. But whereas the usual practice in acting is to execute it during the actual performance, in the hope of stimulating the spectator into a similar operation, he will achieve it only at an earlier stage, at some time during rehearsals.

To safeguard against an unduly 'impulsive', frictionless and uncritical creation of characters and incidents, more reading rehearsals can be held than usual. The actor should refrain from living himself into the part prematurely in any way, and should go on functioning as long as possible as a reader (which does not mean a reader-aloud). An important step is memorizing one's first impressions.

When reading his part the actor's attitude should be one of a man who is astounded and contradicts. Not only the occurrence of the incidents, as he reads about them, but the conduct of the man he is playing, as he experiences it, must be weighed up by him and their peculiarities understood; none can be taken as given, as something that 'was bound to turn out that way', that was 'only to be expected from a character like that'. Before memorizing the words he must memorize what he felt astounded at and where he felt impelled to contradict. For these are dynamic forces that he must preserve in creating his performance.

When he appears on the stage, besides what he actually is doing he will at all essential points discover, specify, imply what he is not doing; that is to say he will act in such a way that the alternative emerges as clearly as possible, that his acting allows the other possibilities to be inferred and only represents one out of the possible variants. He will say for instance 'You'll pay for that', and not say 'I forgive you'. He detests his children; it is not the case that he loves them. He moves down stage left and not up stage right. Whatever he doesn't do must be contained and conserved in what he does. In this way every sentence and every gesture signifies a decision; the character remains under observation and is tested.

The technical term for this procedure is 'fixing the "not . . . but" '.

The actor does not allow himself to become completely transformed on the stage into the character he is portraying. He is not Lear, Harpagon, Schweik; he shows them. He reproduces their remarks as authentically as he can; he puts forward their way of behaving to the best of his abilities and knowledge of men; but he never tries to persuade himself (and thereby others) that this amounts to a complete transformation. Actors will know what it means if I say that a typical kind of acting without this complete transformation takes place when a producer or colleague shows one how to play a particular passage. It is not his own part, so he is not completely transformed; he underlines the technical aspect and retains the attitude of someone just making suggestions.

Once the idea of total transformation is abandoned the actor speaks his part not as if he were improvising it himself but like a quotation. At the same time he obviously has to render all the quotation's overtones, the remark's full human and concrete shape; similarly the gesture he makes must have the full substance of a human gesture even though it now represents a copy.

Given this absence of total transformation in the acting there are three aids which may help to alienate the actions and remarks of the characters being portrayed:

1. Transposition into the third person.
2. Transposition into the past.
3. Speaking the stage directions out loud.

Using the third person and the past tense allows the actor to adopt the right attitude of detachment. In addition he will look for stage directions and remarks that comment on his lines, and speak them aloud at rehearsal ('He stood up and exclaimed angrily, not having eaten: . . .', or 'He had never been told so before, and didn't know if it was true or not', or 'He smiled, and said with forced nonchalance: . . .'). Speaking the stage directions out loud in the third person results in a clash between two tones of voice, alienating the second of them, the text proper. This style of acting is further alienated by taking place on the stage after having already been outlined and announced in words. Transposing it into the past gives the speaker a standpoint from which he can look back at his sentence. The sentence too is thereby alienated without the speaker adopting an unreal point of view; unlike the spectator, he has read the play right through and is better placed to judge the sentence in accordance with the ending, with its consequences, than the former, who knows less and is more of a stranger to the sentence.

This composite process leads to an alienation of the text in the rehearsals which generally persists in the performance too. The directness of the relationship with the audience allows and indeed forces the actual speech delivery to be varied in accordance with the greater or smaller significance attaching to the sentences. Take the case of witnesses addressing a court. The underlinings, the characters' insistence on their remarks, must be developed as a piece of effective virtuosity. If the actor turns to the audience it must be a whole-hearted turn rather than the asides and soliloquizing technique of the old-fashioned theatre. To get the full A-effect from the poetic medium the actor should start at rehearsal by paraphrasing the verse's content in vulgar prose, possibly accompanying this by the gestures designed for the verse. A daring and beautiful handling of verbal media will alienate the text. (Prose can be alienated by translation into the actor's native dialect.)

Gesture will be dealt with below, but it can at once be said that everything to do with the emotions has to be externalized; that is to say, it must be developed into a gesture. The actor has to find a sensibly perceptible outward expression for his character's emotions, preferably some action that gives away what is going on inside him. The emotion in question must be brought out, must lose all its restrictions so that it can be treated on a big scale. Special elegance, power and grace of gesture bring about the A-effect.

A masterly use of gesture can be seen in Chinese acting. The Chinese actor achieves the A-effect by being seen to observe his own movements.

Whatever the actor offers in the way of gesture, verse structure, etc., must be finished and bear the hallmarks of something rehearsed and rounded-off. The impression to be given is one of ease, which is at the same time one of difficulties overcome. The actor must make it possible for the audience to take his own art, his mastery of technique, lightly too. He puts an incident before the spectator with perfection and as he thinks it really happened or might have happened. He does not conceal the fact that he has rehearsed it, any more than an acrobat conceals his training, and he emphasizes that it is his own (actor's) account, view, version of the incident.

Because he doesn't identify himself with him he can pick a definite attitude to adopt towards the character whom he portrays, can show what he thinks of him and invite the spectator, who is likewise not asked to identify himself, to criticize the character portrayed.

The attitude which he adopts is a socially critical one. In his exposition of the incidents and in his characterization of the person he tries to bring out those features which come within society's sphere. In this way his performance becomes a discussion (about social conditions) with the audience he is addressing. He prompts the spectator to justify or abolish these conditions according to what class he belongs to.

The object of the A-effect is to alienate the social gest underlying every incident. By social gest is meant the mimetic and gestural expression of the social relationships prevailing between people of a given period.

It helps to formulate the incident for society, and to put it across in such a way that society is given the key, if titles are thought up for the scenes. These titles must have a historical quality.

This brings us to a crucial technical device: historicization.

The actor must play the incidents as historical ones. Historical incidents are unique, transitory incidents associated with particular periods. The conduct of the person involved in them is not fixed and 'universally human'; it includes elements that have been or may be overtaken by the course of history, and is subject to criticism from the immediately following period's point of view. The conduct of of those born before us is alienated from us by an incessant evolution.

It is up to the actor to treat present-day events and modes of behaviour with the same detachment as the historian adopts with regard to those of the past. He must alienate these characters and incidents from us.

Characters and incidents from ordinary life, from our immediate surroundings, being familiar, strike us as more or less natural. Alienating them helps to make them seem remarkable to us. Science has carefully developed a technique of getting irritated with the everyday, 'self-evident', universally accepted occurrence, and there is no reason why this infinitely useful attitude should not be taken over by art. It is an attitude which arose in science as a result of the growth in human productive powers. In art the same motive applies.

As for the emotions, the experimental use of the A-effect in the epic theatre's German productions indicated that this way of acting too can stimulate them, though possibly a different class of emotion is involved from those of the orthodox theatre. A critical attitude on the audience's part is a thoroughly artistic one. Nor does the actual practice of the A-effect seem anything like so unnatural as its description. Of course it is a way of acting that has nothing to do with stylization as commonly practised. The main advantage of the epic theatre with its A-effect, intended purely to show the world in such a way that it becomes manageable, is precisely its quality of being natural and earthly, its humour and its renunciation of all the mystical elements that have stuck to the orthodox theatre from the old days.

THE SET

It's more important nowadays for the set to tell the spectator he's in a theatre than to tell him he's in, say, Aulis. The theatre must acquire *qua* theatre the same fascinating reality as a sporting arena during a boxing match. The best thing is to show the machinery, the ropes and the flies.

If the set represents a town it must look like a town that has been built to last precisely two hours. One must conjure up the reality of time.

Everything must be provisional yet polite. A place need only have the creditability of a place glimpsed in a dream.

The set needs to spring from the rehearsal of groupings, so in effect it must be a fellow-actor.

Space needs to be brought to life in the vertical plane. This can be achieved by stairs, though not by covering the stairs with people.

On the time-scale the set must plainly become intensified; it must have its own climax and special round of applause.

The materials of the set must be visible. A play can be performed in pasteboard only, or in pasteboard and wood, or in canvas, and so on; but there mustn't by any faking.

Source Material for *The Caucasian Chalk Circle*

BY THE CRITICS

Bunge, Hans-Joachim. "The Dispute Over the Valley: An Essay on Bertolt Brecht's Play, *The Caucasian Chalk Circle*." *The Tulane Drama Review* 4 (1959): 50–66.

Esslin, Martin. *Brecht, The Man and His Work*. New York: Doubleday, 1960, pp. 309–311.

Gray, R. *Brecht*. pp. 105–113.

Weideli, W. *Art of Bertolt Brecht*. New York: New York University Press, 1963, pp. 95–101.

Willett, John. *The Theatre of Bertolt Brecht*. New York: New Directions, 1968.

BY THE PLAYWRIGHT

Brecht, Bertolt. "A Short Organum for the Theatre." In *Playwrights on Playwriting*, pp. 72–105, edited by T. Cole. New York: Hill and Wang.

Willet, John, ed. *Brecht on Theatre*. New York: Hill and Wang.

AUDIO-VISUAL SOURCES

Bentley on Brecht. Folkways Recording Co.

Work of Bertolt Brecht, 16mm, B&W Division of Educational Communications, State Department of Education, Albany, New York.

Theatre of the Absurd

The theatre of the absurd is the most perplexing of the dramatic modes. Perhaps this is because it is also the most abstract; that is, the events on stage rarely try to approximate reality but are instead poetic images, representing micro-seconds in the void of time. Each absurdist playwright strives to present his perception of his relationship with a paradoxical world. Since our world is anything but satisfying, absurd plays appear to be gloomy and are heavily laden with symbols for the paradoxical world they represent. In what appears a confused blend of poetry and prose, the absurdist presents his picture of humanity.

In the history of the arts, drama has usually lagged behind other art forms in presenting new ways of looking at the world, but the theatre of the absurd constitutes a unique creation, born from the marriage of calamity and confusion that best characterizes our world. Absurd theatre is a vanguard movement partly responsible for crystalizing and communicating this mood (our human condition) in its infancy—while it is happening—setting the pace for other artistic modes.

Background to Absurdism

Although certain earlier dramatic movements had some similarities to the theatre of the absurd—dadaism (1916–1924), surrealism (1924–1935), and the plays of Luigi Pirandello (during 1918–1930 Pirandello interestingly argued that "truth" was entirely a subjective matter)—the existential philosophy and playwrights gave immediate rise to the absurd, both the term and the theatre. The atomic bomb and the destruction wrought by both world wars seemed to be the final sentence on the paragraph of mankind Time had shown that conventional methods, means, and morality had failed, and that all of man's inventiveness, liberalism, and values had led him nowhere—indeed, perhaps backwards.

Since exterior values were now questionable, some thinkers were convinced that they had to turn inward; that any "truth" was to be found in the "self." I exist, and "my existence precedes essence" became the existentialist credo, which is to say, each man is the designer of his own meaning, each individual the architect of his own being. Furthermore, every individual should be free, free to choose his own values, for his can be no worse (or better) than those superficially imposed on him. These imposed values have produced a condition that is grave, to say the least; and in an existence where such values have given rise to chaotic conditions, it would be illogical to go on accepting them, be they ideological, social, or religious.

Since men create values, it is also men who assign meaning to them. If this is true, the existentialist says, then there can be no *ultimate* meaning, no *ultimate* truths or values. As Oscar Brockett comments: "Each man can only seek a set of values by which he can live, but he must be willing to recognize that his values are as absurd as any others."[1] His life becomes its own yardstick and the conditions that surround his life—transient and imposed values, ill-defined truths, inanities, illogic, baselessness, anxiety, chaos and contradiction—these conditions are the closest to any ultimate truths that might exist. They are the results of our existence. Any well-made values, like any well-made plays, are arbitrary and expedient. Speaking of the way these values have been created, Brockett adds: "Man, adrift in a chaotic universe, constructs whatever fictions he can to help him survive."[2] Hence, each man must ponder his own existence, and the sense of this existence may be represented in play form.

But there is yet another anguish for the existentialist. Although a man has the freedom to choose and select his own values, he remains a virtual "nothing." He will die, be forgotten, and life will slide on just as easily without him. His single instance is paradoxical, for while no one else will ever "be" him (his existence is unique), his total existence has meant very little. He is both replaceable and erasable, with little effect or alteration on the course of life. This is the existential "awareness of nothingness." The resulting anxiety, or sense of alienation—that man is a stranger in his own world—exists as a tenet basic to the existential and absurdist theme. The individual can never be at home in his world: he knows at all times while he may mean everything, he also means nothing, that the world would remain unruffled by his departure.

Most important for the codification of these views were the two apostles of existentialism, Albert Camus and Jean-Paul Sartre. Camus' plays (it was Camus who first used the term "absurd") exemplify man's struggle to find meaning and explanation in a world seemingly devoid of both. As Camus himself says in his inquisitive *The Myth of Sisyphus:*

> A world that can be explained by reasoning, however faulty, is a familiar world. But in a universe that is suddenly deprived of illusions and of light, man feels a stranger. His is an irremediable exile, because he is deprived of memories of a lost homeland as much as he lacks the hope of a promised land to come. This divorce between man and his life, the actor and his setting, truely constitutes the feeling of Absurdity.

Of Camus' plays, *Caligula* and *The Just Assassins* best picture the absurdity that stems from the impossible reconciliation between man's hopes and the world in which those hopes beg to be fulfilled.

Jean-Paul Sartre has best stated the existential philosophy, winning

---

[1]Oscar Brockett, *The Theatre: An Introduction* (New York: Holt, Rinehart and Winston, Inc., 1969), p. 362.
[2]Ibid.

(and refusing) the Nobel Prize for Literature in 1964 (Sartre's refusal is the final tribute to his intense individualism). His plays, *The Flies*, *No Exit*, and *The Condemned of Altona* all tend to underscore the philosophy that each man must create his own set of values, since there are certainly no universal ones worth using, and that each man is responsible only to himself. The individual must search for and substitute his own values—he must be able to choose between his and others—so he may help to reconcile his *self* in a world of estrangement. As Sartre writes:

> Man can count on no one but himself: he is alone, abandoned on earth in the midst of his infinite responsibilities, without help, with no other aim than the one he sets himself, with no other destiny than the one he forges for himself on this earth.[3]

Jean Anouilh, has written what is probably the most often performed existential play, *Antigone*, based on Sophocles' *Antigone*. Antigone, who has chosen to bury her brother in defiance of the king's order, has chosen to die for what she believed right, a commendable notion indeed. But informed by Creon that her brother was a liar and a cheat, "a cheap idiotic bounder," Antigone no longer has external justification for death. The glorified image of her brother shattered, she still chooses to die, creating a value for herself in death. Her choice may seem stubborn to Creon, but to him she does not have to justify it. Antigone's choice might be compared to that of a single man picketing the steps of the state capital against the death penalty. An official peers out the window shouting, "What are you doing there? No one knows you're here!" The inevitable reply of the existentialist would be, "You're wrong—*I* know."

The Absurdist Dramaturgy

All the threads of existentialism are fully woven into absurdism, with two differences. First, the form and structure of the plays may differ radically. That is, the illogical world absurdist plays represent may appear in an equally illogical form—a mirror of disharmony. The structure of the play becomes a representation of its subject matter. But more important, the absurdist, like the naturalist, is a *reporter* of the human condition (*his* particular image of the human condition), and he is content with merely reflecting that seemingly hopeless situation instead of trying to bring hope to it. While the existentialist would offer man a choice, confident he would at least find a value in that choice, the absurdist delights in picturing the futility of our situation and the absurdity of our existence. Eugene Ionesco, first of the well-known absurdists, puts it well: "There are no solutions

---

[3]"What is Existentialism?" *Life Educational Reprint* 68, p. 3.

right now for the human condition. Socialism as well as liberalism has failed. Life is unlivable."[4] Of the two differences, let us examine the second, first.

The absurd subject matter deals with the simple, the basic: living and dying, waiting and seeking, isolation and communication. True, these conditions are not simple *per se;* that is, they certainly involve a great deal of the complexity of life and form the essence of our being, but that is the very point: the subject matter of the absurdist deals with the "guts" of mankind, the fundamentals upon which everything we do is predicated. And it is precisely these fundamentals which suffer from the sickness of baselessness (no foundation for existence). Their representation becomes justifiable in itself. In farce, man is reduced to his basics for purposes of laughter; in absurdism, the playwright presents his *image* of this basic man for purposes of exposure, even, perhaps, of satirizing. Thus his is an inward vision of the world reflected in the subject of his play. The orientation of this subject matter is treated by William Packard:

> And the fact that so many of our leading playwrights feel compelled to confront the so-called darker side of life—the anguish of their own estrangement, the disintegration of their own psyche, the breakdown of communication in personal relationships—this is also something which cannot be accounted for. It is simply something that has to be done in our own time, because it is a large part of the world we live in . . . the only honest exercise in faith when all other faiths have failed.
>
> Realistically we know that everything in the outside world is in an ethical shambles—over one hundred million human beings have been killed in military action alone in this century—and the killing is still going on . . . and now our leading theologians are telling us that "God is dead," which is to say, we must face the chaos we have made, without the assurance of our traditional convictions.[5]

Thus the absurdist choice of material is the condition mankind has made for itself—a montage of bleakness and breakdown, a world where conventional values and proposed solutions have failed. The gulf between what a man wants and what he has—his dreams and their reality, his hopes and their fulfillment—this constitutes the feeling of absurdity. As Camus put it, the absurd is "that divorce between the mind that desires and the world that disappoints." The theatre of the absurd, then, is not concerned with preaching a doctrine (though an implied one may be present) or advocating a solution, but with a *theatrical presentation*, a poet's picture of the human condition transplanted to the stage.

According to the absurdists, our futile attempts at communication are also a part of this human condition. Observe what mankind embraces: the

[4]T. Bishop, "Ionesco on Olympus," *Saturday Review* 52 (May 16, 1970), p. 91.
[5]William Packard, "The Theatre: Stress on Soul Searching in Plays Reflects the Eras," *The Wall Street Journal*, p. 2.

bomb, instant annihilation, poverty, apathy, disorder, impersonalization, complacency, prejudice, cruelty—the list is endless. All of this, the absurdist says, despite our shotgun ventures at communicating. All our attempts to ameliorate these conditions have failed. Our useless words and hollow phrases echo in an empty room, and the human condition persists as a tribute to this failure.

While most other forms of drama we have studied attempt to convey an idea or message (epic theatre being the clearest exponent), much of absurdist drama questions the possibility of communication. Ionesco calls *The Bald Soprano* a "tragedy of language"; Beckett's characters admit to the anguish of each attempt at communication. Communication between persons (much less nations) seems virtually impossible (or at least totally ineffective, which makes the attempt absurd). This breakdown in communication coupled with the disintegration of values has helped to generate this feeling of absurdity. As Jacobsen and Mueller say in *Ionesco and Genet, Playwrights of Silence*, the attempt to communicate "strikes immediately an unnerving truth for humanity, the truth that communication through language and feelings, the most basic necessity for human joy, simply does not exist—that persons impart nothing to each other because they no longer have anything to impart." For instance, the absurdist might say the lack of any genuine expectance of a factual answer to the perfunctory question, "How are you?" is a prime example of the useless trivia and empty language we indulge in. Listen to Ionesco's characters in *The Bald Soprano:*

MR. SMITH   Hm (Silence)
MRS. SMITH   Hm, hm. (Silence)
MRS. MARTIN   Hm, hm, hm. (Silence)
MR. MARTIN   Hm, hm, hm, hm. (Silence)
MRS. MARTIN   Oh, but definitely. (Silence)
MR. MARTIN   We all have colds. (Silence)
MR. SMITH   Nevertheless, it's not chilly. (Silence)
MRS. SMITH   There's no draft. (Silence)
MR. MARTIN   Oh no, fortunately. (Silence)
MR. SMITH   Oh dear, oh dear, oh dear. (Silence)
MR. MARTIN   Don't you feel well? (Silence)
MRS. SMITH   No, he's wet his pants. (Silence)
MRS. MARTIN   Oh, sir, at your age, you shouldn't. (Silence)
MR. SMITH   The heart is ageless. (Silence)

The banalities and inanities of human conversation have joined hands to point a finger at the meaninglessness of ordinary conversing.

At this point, we have seen that the subject matter and philosophy of the absurdist is founded on five basic principles:

   1. That God is dead (or dying), which is to say he has done very little, if anything, to help the human condition. We must then realize that

any attempt at improvement (if that is at all possible) must come from ourselves.

2. That man will die eventually, his existence having meant very little, and the knowledge of this helps create a feeling of contradiction (absurdity).

3. That part of the human condition can be attributed to a loss of values and the imposition of ready-made ones resulting in a bitter disappointment for the individual. The hopelessness couched in the disparity between the human desire and its ultimate attainment helps flame this feeling of absurdity.

4. That a world devoid of any purpose is an alien world, and man is a stranger in his own backyard.

5. That communication is a fruitless task—witness the plight of mankind.

Jacobsen and Mueller summarize this absurdist position:

> To come to believe that time is his destroyer, that the natural world observes him not, and he is a brother to the machine—such is the way by which man arrives at a knowledge of the absurdity of his world, an absurdity born of the juxtaposition of all that he would wish life to be, and the way life actually seems to be. Man yearns to defy time, to feel at home in his world, to rest confident in his humanity, but he has come to know his mortality, his loneliness, his machine-like rigidity.[6]

The Absurdist Form

An inherent danger in understanding and evaluating an absurd play lies in the way we approach its form (structure and design), which in the case of most absurdist playwrights (particularly Beckett, Ionesco, and Genet) is anything but traditional. If we endeavor to view the play in the perspective of conventional drama we, and the play, are bound to become confused. It is as though we were attempting to fix an American automobile with foreign metric wrenches—while one set of tools will work in its proper place, any attempt at application elsewhere leads to frustration. Perhaps this is why Samuel Beckett feels an absurd play has to be seen and experienced, as well as discussed.

An understanding of the term "absurd" is basic to comprehending the structure of absurdism. The term "absurd" does not mean "ridiculous" or "stupid," but "out of harmony, illogical, unreasonable, inconsistent or incongruous," and these words also describe the state of the human condition. Realizing this, it would be illogical to present this human condition in the "well-made" play form prevalent in previous play-going generations (One of Beckett's most recent plays is a thirty-five second "experience," minus actors, action, and dialogue, that opens with a baby's cry and closes

---

[6]Jacobsen and Mueller, *Ionesco and Genet: Playwrights of Silence* (New York: Hill and Wang, 1968), p. 5.

with what sounds like a dying gasp, probably the most radical play "form" yet devised!). It naturally follows that if the absurdist rejects the logic of the world about him, then he will also reject the traditional dramatic techniques of development. Hence, absurd plays may not build to a climax, present a discernible protagonist or antagonist, be divided into three acts, present well-rounded, full dimensional characters, or create traditional dramatic plots. Indeed, the absurd plot is usually anything but dramatic in the customary sense.

The events of an absurd play present the playwright's conception of reality—*the truth as he sees it*. For example, it is highly doubtful that the tramps of Beckett's *Waiting for Godot* could themselves exist. Instead, they provide us with a glimpse of the playwright's intuitive vision of the human condition. As Martin Esslin says in *The Theatre of the Absurd*, perhaps the most definitive work on the subject, the absurdist is concerned with the "presentation of one individual's basic situation . . . ," the presentation of "a sense of being." The playwright is not concerned with representing events *per se*, that is, a sequence of actual physical happenings that lead to a conclusion and resolution. In fact, the absurdists admit to being hampered by the tools of conventional drama—actors, dialogue, spectacle—for absurdism is not a mirror of life, as naturalism was, but an *expression*, both poetic and lyrical. Though the absurdist *is* trying to present the human condition, it is the image and not the picture he strives to create. To quote Esslin again:

> While former attempts at confronting man with the ultimate realities of his condition projected a coherent and generally recognized version of the truth, the Theatre of the Absurd merely communicates one poet's most intimate and personal intuition of the human situation, his own *sense of being*, his individual vision of the world. This is the *subject matter* of the Theatre of the Absurd, and it determines its *form*, which must, of necessity, represent a convention of the stage basically different from the "realistic" theatre of our own time . . . . The action of the play is intended to convey a pattern of poetic images.[7]

The absurd play is thus a reflection of mood, a communication of perception. No real attempt to mirror life is made as in realism or naturalism. Nor is there an effort at proclaiming a panacea for mankind as in epic theatre. It is possible, however, to see some similarities between absurdism and expressionism; in that, one, the world is being represented through the eyes of one person (though in this case the author's rather than the hero's); and two, there is a quality to both modes which enables the spectator to sense that what is happening is not "reality." Yet absurdist drama, though expressing a personal image of the author's world, is nevertheless demonstrating the playwright's conception of the world of *all* men. Presented in play form the absurdist image of the mind represents the soul of humanity,

[7]Martin Esslin, *The Theatre of the Absurd* (New York: Doubleday and Co., 1961), p. 293.

not the struggles of a single misguided protagonist. In addition, the expressionist extends hope for his hero, implying at least that some betterment can be achieved. On the other hand many critics feel, and I tend to agree, that the theatre of the absurd reflects the ingrained despair that is an innate part of the total human situation (how could it not, the absurdist would argue, if it is but an image of an already present situation; mankind's condition, it seems, precludes the hope of salvation).

The observance of absurdist drama produces a unique effect. The reason for this uniqueness lies in the author's strange blend of the bittersweet. Our responses border on the edge of confusion (isn't that part of our condition?). Should we experience a chuckle or a tear as the two old people of Ionesco's *The Chairs* greet imaginary visitors? Does Beckett ask that we laugh or cry at his two fumbling tramps in *Waiting for Godot?* Does Jonathan command our sympathy or our contempt in Kopit's *Oh Dad, Poor Dad . . . ?* Absurd plays many times evoke a juxtaposition of responses; and as we begin to wade through the meaning of the stage happenings, we may still remain unsure if the catharsis (if any) is to be achieved through laughter or tears. This dilemma is made even more apparent when we look at the labels the absurdist have given their plays. Beckett called *Waiting for Godot* a "tragi-comedy"; Ionesco called *The Chairs* a "tragic-farce"; and Kopit called *Oh Dad, Poor Dad . . .* a "pseudoclassical tragi-farce . . . ."

These labels probably capture the total mood of the theatre of the absurd—each play stopping short of evoking either laughter or tears; each play precariously straddling the fence of emotion—for each play is only an indication of the contradictory nature of man. Each of us should expect to be uncertain whether to laugh or weep over that nature, since the play itself expresses that same confusion.

The Absurdist Playwrights

The most important of these inventive dramatists is Samuel Beckett, a dramatic recluse. Beckett views the world in terms of waiting, of passing time, and probably the most well-known absurdist piece is his *Waiting for Godot*. In the course of the play nothing of substance actually happens. Two tramps (clowns?) wait for an unseen visitor, Godot, punctuated by a visit from three characters—Pozzo and his servant Lucky, plus the elusive Boy who brings news that Godot is sorry he can't make it but most assuredly will "tomorrow."

The play can be viewed positively; there is hope and salvation in waiting, and optimism should remain the key to life. But most critics view it negatively; that life is an endless waiting game and the absurdity of vain hopes is part of the chaotic human condition. (Do we not live in hopes of a better tomorrow, secretly wondering if it is at all possible?) The absurdist would probably deny this possibility, believing his condition results from the realization that it is not likely. Remembering again Camus, the recognition of "the divorce between man and his life . . . truly constitutes the feeling of Absurdity."

Religious critics state the answer to the play's meaning may be found by dropping the last two letters to "Godot"; that perhaps Beckett is either denying or affirming the existence of God. The play is alternately seen as a study in companionship, communication, aggression, and faith. On a grander scale, what happens is an exercise in psychology, philosophy, and sociology. This is the beautiful thing about *Waiting for Godot*: it is open to a multitude of interpretations, each equally valid.[8] As Esslin says, "*Waiting for Godot* does not tell a story, it explores a static situation." It remains as a testament to the futility of the total human predicament, and trying to pinpoint a *single* meaning is self-defeating. Asked many times about the meaning of *Godot*, Beckett answers curtly: "If I knew, I would have said so in the play." Other marks of absurdism are found in Beckett's *End-Game*, *Krapp's Last Tape*, and *Happy Days*.

Jean Genet, the only native Frenchman among the popular absurdists (Beckett, an Irishman, and Ionesco, a Rumanian, write in French, the language of their adopted country), is perhaps the most turbulent of these playwrights. In Genet's plays, *The Balcony*, *The Screens*, *The Blacks*, and *The Maids*, murder is glorified, chaos is worshipped, confusion celebrated, and perversion sanctified. Identities are scrambled and life is a hall of reflections that forever disguises the real, for as each person removes his facade there is only another in its place. For our irrelevant and useless values, Genet has substituted the perverted ("perverted," of course, regarded in the conventional meaning men have assigned to it).

In order for the human being to believe in the goodness of life, death must be a horror, the lowest rung on the ladder of existence. Genet simply reverses this ladder for his characters—the protagonist's ideals are the opposite of our own. Genet's dramatic vehicle is the continual juxtaposition of reality and pretension. For example, in *The Balcony* members of a town frequent a brothel, but not for ordinary purposes, as we soon learn. Each customer may act out his innermost desire, the role in life he longs to play—he may exchange his identity for another. For instance, as the play opens a Bishop listens to the provocative confessions of a young woman. We soon that this "Bishop," as well as all the other patrons of the brothel, are involved in the assumption of a role, and that each is not what he pretends to be. Then, abruptly, the "real" Chief of Police arrives and persuades the Madam to assume the role of Queen in order to stifle a revolution

---

[8]For the most complete compilation of essays on *Waiting for Godot* see Cohn, Ruby *Casebook on Waiting for Godot* (New York: Grove Press).

occurring in town. All of the other patrons supplement this action by acting as the "real" Bishop, General, or Judge, and the revolution is quieted. Reality becomes a mirage, and the unreal becomes just as imaginary as the real.

Eugene Ionesco is concerned with the absurdity of man's attempts to communicate and his need to possess things. His best known works include *The Bald Soprano, Rhinocerous* and *The Chairs.* As if to accentuate his desire to display the absurdity of the communicative condition, Ionesco called his first play (*The Bald Soprano*) an "anti-play." Getting the idea from a handbook for tourists containing translations of everyday sayings, Ionesco fashioned a play built on meaningless language, senseless repetition, lack of action, and shallow characters whose language is replete with clichés (We may wonder how a play that includes all of this is successful, but there is an unusual enjoyment in viewing a strangely brilliant image of the distorted human condition. As in a hall of misshapen mirrors the reflections, though imperfect, are still our reflections, and we appreciate, for a moment, their strange attraction.) Speaking of the play's meaning, Ionesco adds, "In actual fact, if it is criticism of anything, it must be of all societies, of language, of clichés—a parody of human behavior. . . ."[9]

In *The Chairs* two old people occupy a sterile room virtually void, then filled with chairs in which they greet imaginary visitors and later commit suicide. They eagerly await the arrival of the Orator who is to deliver the "meaning of life" (which, in typical Ionesco fashion, the Old Man could not do himself). But when the Orator turns out to be a deaf mute and the sense of existence cannot be realized, the suicide of the old couple becomes tragi-comic.

Ionesco deftly weaves the absurdist theme into *The Chairs* in many ways. The chairs represent our obsession with possessions and how it may crowd out our very existence. They also stand for the uselessness of things in a world where we have yet to establish a meaning for values. The conversations of the two old people, infused with triteness and clichés, illustrate the illusion of man's belief that he has successfully communicated, and the physical impairment of the Orator is a testament to the futility of ever finding an ultimate meaning to life. The entire play is a portrait of the false hopes and absurd monotony of life. Ionesco himself says, "In *The Chairs* I have tried to deal more directly with the themes that obsess me; with emptiness, with frustration, with this world, at once fleeting and crushing, with despair and death."[10]

America's chief absurdist is Edward Albee, whose popular fame stems from the conventionally structured, *Who's Afraid of Virginia Woolf?* In his absurdist drama Albee questions the validity of present values in a contra-

[9]"The World of Eugene Ionesco," *The New York Times*, June 1, 1958.
[10]Ibid.

dictory world, and he does it in almost allegorical fashion. In *The American Dream*, Albee examines our impotent values, and leads us to conclude that the "American dream" is a life of uninvolvement, stagnation, and pseudo-aspiration. In *The Sandbox*, and *The Zoo Story*, middle-class America and feminine dominance are effectively treated in an absurd manner.

Harold Pinter is England's main absurdist, although most of his plays follow traditional dramatic development. In *The Room*, *The Dumb Waiter*, *The Birthday Party*, and *The Caretaker*, Pinter's characters are contradictory, banal, depressing, and sometimes vicious. His themes deal with the wicked and contradictory nature of man. Pinter's more important work, *The Homecoming*, stops short of true absurdism by use of conventional development, discernible plot, and well-rounded characters. Beneath the surface, however, the characters of the play are a mixture of the tragicomic—depressing and confusing, sardonic and humorous. (Some similarities can be seen between *The Homecoming* and the early English avant-garde play, John Osborne's *Look Back in Anger*.)

Most of the theatre of the absurd is a left-handed portrait of man. Man is adrift in an unfriendly world, and his evidently futile attempts at happiness represent the condition of absurdity. In a world deprived of any ultimate meanings, of any ultimate truths, man is forced to invent his own. The representation of this absurd condition through the structure of a play constitutes an effort by its author to picture the plight of humanity—an image sometimes distorted, a mirror sometimes cracked, a reflection sometimes out of focus—and in most cases the plight of that humanity seems a sorry one indeed.

The coffin drops suddenly foreshadowing a similar occurrence to its contents later in the play. University of North Carolina. (Courtesy photo lab.)

One of Jonathan's rare coins is about to be used as a tip. American Conservatory Theatre.

The Commodore's evening starts merrily. Not for long. Aurora Community Theatre.

The sweet but determined Rosalie plans for later with the cowering Jonathan. Notice the coffin standing watch. Asolo State Theatre.

"Dad's anticipated appearance is about to be made. McNeese State College.

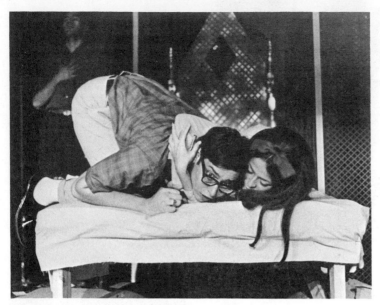

Finally getting him into bed, Rosalie struggles with the desperate Jonathan. Miami-Dade Junior College.

The provocative Rosalie pursues her seduction of Jonathan. California State College at Los Angeles. Jonathon Hauser, director.

Happy be with such a mother!
Faith in Womankind. . . .

Alfred, Lord Tennyson

Oh Dad, Poor Dad,
Mamma's Hung You in the Closet
and I'm Feelin' So Sad

A Pseudoclassical Tragifarce in a Bastard French Tradition

Arthur L. Kopit

Oh Dad, Poor Dad, Mamma's Hung You in the Closet and I'm Feelin' So Sad

Characters   MADAME ROSEPETTLE
JONATHAN ROSEPETTLE
ROSALIE
COMMODORE ROSEABOVE
ROSALINDA THE FISH
TWO VENUS'-FLYTRAPS
A CUCKOO CLOCK
VARIOUS BELLBOYS

Scene   *A hotel in Havana, Cuba*
The play is in three scenes, without intermission.

Scene One

A lavish hotel room in Havana, Cuba. Downstage center French windows open onto a large balcony that juts out over the audience. Upstage center are the doors to the master bedroom. At stage left is the door to another bedroom, while at stage right is the door to the suite itself. On one of the walls is hung a glass case with a red fire axe inside it and a sign over it that reads, "In Case of Emergency, Break."
      The door to the suite opens and BELLBOYS NUMBER ONE *and* TWO *enter carrying a coffin.*
WOMAN'S VOICE (*From off stage*)   Put it in the bedroom!
BELLBOYS NUMBER ONE *and* TWO (*Together*)   The bedroom.
      (BELLBOY NUMBER ONE *starts toward the bedroom at*
      stage left. BELLBOY NUMBER TWO *starts toward the*
      bedroom at upstage center. The handles come off the
      coffin. It falls to the floor. The BELLBOYS *freeze with*
      horror.)
WOMAN'S VOICE (*Still off stage*)   Fools!
      (*Enter* MADAME ROSEPETTLE, *dressed in black, a veil*
      hiding her face. JONATHAN, *a boy seventeen years old*
      but dressed like a child of ten, enters directly behind her.
      He follows her about the room like a small helpless
      puppy trailing his master.)
MADAME ROSEPETTLE   Morons! Imbeciles!
BELLBOY NUMBER ONE   Uh . . . *which* bedroom, madame?
BELLBOY NUMBER TWO   Yes. *Which* bedroom?

MADAME ROSEPETTLE   *Which bedroom!?* They have the nerve to ask, which bedroom? The *master* bedroom, of course. Which bedroom did you think? (*The* BELLBOYS *smile ashamedly, bow, pick up the coffin and carry it toward the master bedroom.*) Gently! (*They open the bedroom doors.* MADAME ROSEPETTLE *lowers her face as blindingly bright sunlight pours from the room.*) People have no respect for coffins nowadays. They think nothing of the dead. (*Short pause.*) I wonder what the dead think of them? Agh! The world is growing dismal.

> (*The* BELLBOYS *reappear in the doorway, the coffin in their hands.*)

BELLBOY NUMBER ONE   Uh . . . begging your pardon, madame, but . . . but . . .

MADAME ROSEPETTLE   Speak up! Speak up!

BELLBOY NUMBER ONE   Well, you see . . .

BELLBOY NUMBER TWO   You see . . . we were curious.

BELLBOY NUMBER ONE   Yes. Curious. That is . . .

BELLBOY NUMBER TWO   What we mean to say is . . .

BELLBOY NUMBER ONE   Just *where* in your bedroom would you like us to put it?

MADAME ROSEPETTLE   Next to the *bed,* of course!

BELLBOYS NUMBER ONE *and* TWO   *Of course.*

> (*Exit,* BELLBOYS NUMBER ONE *and* TWO.)

MADAME ROSEPETTLE   *Fools.*

> (*There is a rap on the door to the suite.*)

BELLBOY NUMBER THREE (*Off stage*)   The dictaphone, madame.

MADAME ROSEPETTLE   Ah, splendid.

> (BELLBOY NUMBER THREE *enters carrying a dictaphone on a silver tray and black drapes under his arm.* BELLBOYS NUMBER ONE *and* TWO *leave the bedroom and exit from the suite, bowing fearfully to Madame Rosepettle as they leave.*)

BELLBOY NUMBER THREE   Where would you like it placed?

MADAME ROSEPETTLE   Great gods! Are you all the same? The center table, naturally! One never dictates one's memoirs from *anywhere* but the middle of a room. Any nincompoop knows that.

BELLBOY NUMBER THREE   It must have slipped my mind.

MADAME ROSEPETTLE   You flatter yourself. (*He puts the dictaphone and drapes down on the table.*)

BELLBOY NUMBER THREE   Will there be anything else?

MADAME ROSEPETTLE   *Will there be anything else,* he asks!? Will there be anything else? Of course there'll be something else. There's *always* something else. That's one of the troubles with Life.

BELLBOY NUMBER THREE   Sorry, madame.

MADAME ROSEPETTLE   So am I. (*Pause.*) Oh, this talk is getting us nowhere. Words are precious. On bellboys they're a waste. And so far you have thoroughly wasted my time.

BELLBOY NUMBER THREE   Madame, this must end. I can take no more. I will have you know I am not a *common* bellboy. I am a lieutenant. Notice, if you will, the finely embroidered stripes on my hand-tailored sleeve. I am a lieutenant, madame, and being a lieutenant am in charge of other bellboys and thereby entitled to a little more respect from you.

MADAME ROSEPETTLE   Well, *you* may consider yourself a lieutenant, lieutenant, but *I* consider you a *bore!* If you're going to insist upon pulling rank, however, I'll have you know that I am a tourist. Notice, if you will, the money. And being a tourist I am in charge of you. Remember that and I'll mail you another stripe when I leave. As for "respect," we'll have none of that around here. We've got too many important things to do. Right, Albert? (JONATHAN *tries to speak but cannot.*) Rrrright, Albert?

JONATHAN   Ra . . . ra . . . ra . . . ra-right.

MADAME ROSEPETTLE   You may begin by picking up the drapes you so ingeniously dropped in a lump on my table, carrying them to the master bedroom and tacking them over the windowpanes. I don't wear black in the tropics for my health, my boy. I'm in mourning. And since the problems confronting civilization are ultimately moral ones, while I'm here in Havana no single speck of sunlight shall enter and brighten the mournful gloom of my heart. (*Short pause.*) At least, not while I'm in my bedroom. Well, go on, lieutenant, go on. Forward to the field of battle, head high. Tack the drapes across my windows, and when my room is black, call me in.

BELLBOY NUMBER THREE   Yes, madame.
    (*He picks up the drapes and walks into the master bedroom.*)

MADAME ROSEPETTLE   In Buenos Aires the lieutenant clicked his heels when leaving. That's the trouble with these revolutionaries. No regard for the duties of rank. Remind me, Edward, to decrease my usual tip. (JONATHAN *takes a pad out of his pocket and writes with a pencil he has tied on a cord about his neck. To the hallway.*) Well, come in, come in. Don't just stand there with your mouths hanging open.
    (BELLBOYS NUMBER ONE *and* TWO *and* FOUR *enter pushing heavy trunks before them.*)

BELLBOY NUMBER ONE   Where would you like the stamp collection, madame?

MADAME ROSEPETTLE   Ah, your fantastic stamp collection, Robinson. Where should it be put?

JONATHAN   Uh . . . uh . . . uh . . .

MADAME ROSEPETTLE   Oh, stop stammering and speak up! They're only bellboys.

JONATHAN   Uh . . . um . . . um . . . ma . . . ma . . . ma-ma-ma-ma-ma . . . ma—maybe . . . in . . . in . . . in . . .

MADAME ROSEPETTLE   Will you stop this infernal stammering? You know what I think about it! I said, where would you like your fantastic stamp collection put? God knows it's a simple enough question. If you can't muster the nerve to answer, at least point. (*He points to a bureau in the room.*) The bottom drawer of the bureau. And be careful not to get your fingers on them. They stick. (*The* BELLBOYS *go to the bureau, open the drawer, and dump hundreds of loose stamps that had been in the trunk into the drawer.* MADAME ROSEPETTLE *dips her hand into the drawer and plucks out three stamps. She offers one to each of the* BELLBOYS.) Here, for your trouble: 1903 Borneo, limited edition. Very rare. Almost priceless.

> (*The* BELLBOYS *look disappointedly at their tips.*
> BELLBOY NUMBER THREE *returns from the master
> bedroom.*)

BELLBOY NUMBER THREE   I'm terribly sorry, madame, but I find that—

MADAME ROSEPETTLE   I wondered when you'd ask. (*She takes a huge hammer
from her purse and hands it to him.*)

BELLBOY NUMBER THREE   Thank you, madame. Thank you. (*He turns
nervously and starts to leave.*)

MADAME ROSEPETTLE   Bellboy? (*He stops.*) The nails.

BELLBOY NUMBER THREE (*Flustered by his forgetfulness*)   Yes, of course. How
foolish of me. (*She reaches into her purse again and takes out a fistful of
nails which she promptly dumps into his hands.*)

MADAME ROSEPETTLE   Keep the extras. (*He exits into the master bedroom.
To* JONATHAN.) In Buenos Aires the lieutenant came equipped with a
pneumatic drill. Remind me, Albert dearest, to cut this man's tip entirely.
(JONATHAN *scribbles on his pad. To the other* BELLBOYS.) Well?

BELLBOY NUMBER TWO   The . . . uh . . . coin collection, madame. Where
would you like it put?

MADAME ROSEPETTLE   Your fabulous coin collection, Edward. Where should
they put it?

JONATHAN   Uh . . . uh . . . I . . . I . . . I tha . . . tha . . . tha-think—

MADAME ROSEPETTLE   What is wrong with your tongue? Can't you talk like a
normal human being without showering this room with your inarticulate
spit!?

JONATHAN (*Completely flustered*)   I-I-I-I-I . . . I . . . da . . . da . . .
don't . . .

MADAME ROSEPETTLE   Oh, all right, stick out your paw and point. (*He thrusts
out his trembling hand and points again to the bureau.*)

JONATHAN   If . . . if . . . if . . . if they . . . if they would . . . be so
. . . kind.

MADAME ROSEPETTLE   Of course they would! They're bellboys. Remember that.
It's your first lesson in Life for the day. (*To the* BELLBOYS.) Next to the
bottom drawer, bellboys. And make sure none of them gets in with his
fantastic collection of stamps. (*From the master bedroom can be heard
the sound of* BELLBOY NUMBER THREE *smashing nails into the wall. While
the other* BELLBOYS *are busy dumping hundreds of loose coins into the
bureau,* MADAME ROSEPETTLE *walks to the bedroom door and opens it,
shielding her eyes from the blinding light.*) Don't bang, my boy. Don't
bang. That's not the way. Just tap. It takes longer, I will admit, but the
effect is far more satisfactory on one's auditory nerves—and my ears, you
see, are extremely sensitive. (*To* JONATHAN.) The lieutenant in Buenos
Aires had a muffler on his drill. Remind me, Robinson darling, to have this
man fired first thing in the morning. He'll never do. (JONATHAN *scratches
a large "X" on his pad. The* BELLBOYS, *having finished dumping the coins,
stand awaiting a tip.* MADAME ROSEPETTLE *goes to the drawer and takes
out three coins. To* BELLBOY NUMBER ONE.) Here, for your trouble: a little
something. It's a Turkish piaster . . . 1876. Good year for piasters. (*To*

BELLBOY NUMBER TWO.) And for you . . . an 1889 Danzig gulden. Worth a fortune, my boy. A *small* fortune, I will admit, but nevertheless, a fortune. (*To* BELLBOY NUMBER FOUR.) And for you we have a . . . a . . . a 1959 DIME!! *Edward* . . . what is a dime doing in here? Fegh! (*She flings the dime to the ground as if it had been handled by lepers. The* BELLBOYS *leap to get it.*)

JONATHAN (*Sadly*)   Some . . . some . . . someday it will be . . . as rare as the others.

MADAME ROSEPETTLE   Someday! *Someday!* That's the trouble with you, Edward. Always an optimist. I trust you have no more such currency contaminating your fabulous collection. H'm, Albert? Do I assume correctly? H'm? Do I? H'm? Do I? H'm? Do I?

JONATHAN   Ya . . . yes.

MADAME ROSEPETTLE   Splendid. Then I'll give you your surprise for the day.

JONATHAN   Na . . . now?

MADAME ROSEPETTLE   Yes, now.

JONATHAN   In . . . in . . . front of . . . *them?*

MADAME ROSEPETTLE   Turn your backs, bellboys. (*She digs into her handbag and picks out a coin in a velvet box.*) Here, Edward, my sweet. The rarest of all coins for your rarest of all collections. A 1372 Javanese Yen-Sen.

JONATHAN (*Excitedly*)   How . . . how . . . how ma-many were . . . ma-minted?

MADAME ROSEPETTLE   None.

JONATHAN   Na-none?

MADAME ROSEPETTLE   I made it myself. (*She squeezes his hand.*) So glad you like it. (*She turns to the* BELLBOYS.) You may turn around now. (*They turn around as a unit.*) Well, who has the—? (*She stares in horror at the door to the master bedroom. The tapping can clearly be heard. She goes to the door, shielding her eyes from the now less powerful glare.*) You are tapping and not banging, which is good, but when you tap please tap with some sort of rhythm, which is, you see, much better. (*She smiles acidly and closes the door.*) The lieutenant in Buenos Aires, Robinson. The lieutenant in Buenos Aires. Do you remember him? Do you remember the rhythm he had? Oh, the way he shook when he drilled. I fairly danced that day. (*Reminiscent pause.*) Make note, Robinson. This man must be barred from all hotels, everywhere. *Everywhere!* (JONATHAN *retraces his "X" with a hard, firm stroke as if he were carving a figure on stone.*) Now where was I? Oh, yes. Forgive me, but my mind, of late, has been wandering. The books, bellboys. The books! (*The* BELLBOYS *push a large trunk forward.*)

JONATHAN   Ca . . . ca . . . could they . . . open it . . . I . . . I-I wonder?

MADAME ROSEPETTLE   You want to see them, eh Albert? You really want to see them again? That badly? You really want to see them again, that badly?

JONATHAN (*Trying very hard not to stutter*)   Yyyyesssssss.

MADAME ROSEPETTLE (*Very dramatically*)   Then let the trunk be opened! (*They open the trunk. Hundreds of books fall onto the floor in a cloud of dust.* JONATHAN *falls on top of them like a starved man upon food.*)

JONATHAN (*Emotionally*)   Tra-Tra . . . Trollope . . . Ha-Haggard . . .

Dau-Dau-Daudet . . . Gautier . . . Tur-Tur-Tur-genev . . . ma-ma-my old fra-fra . . . friends. (*He collapses over them like a lover over his loved one.*)

MADAME ROSEPETTLE   Enough, Albert. Come. Off your knees. Rise from your books and sing of love.

JONATHAN   But I . . . I ca-can't . . . sing.

MADAME ROSEPETTLE   Well, stand up anyway. (*He rises sadly.*) Now, where are my plants?

BELLBOY NUMBER TWO   Plants?

MADAME ROSEPETTLE   Yes. My plants. Where are they? (BELLBOY NUMBER FOUR *whispers something in* BELLBOY NUMBER TWO's *ear.*)

BELLBOY NUMBER TWO (*Laughing nervously*)   Oh. I . . . I . . . (*He laughs again, more nervously.*) I didn't realize . . . they were . . . plants.

MADAME ROSEPETTLE   What did you *think* they were?

BELLBOY NUMBER FOUR   We have them, madame. Outside.

BELLBOY NUMBER TWO   Yes. Outside.

BELLBOY NUMBER FOUR   Should we . . . bring them in?

MADAME ROSEPETTLE   Of course you should bring them in! Do you think they *enjoy* waiting out there in the hall? *Fools.*

BELLBOYS NUMBER TWO *and* FOUR (*Together, weakly*)   Yes . . . madame.
(*They exit and return immediately carrying two large black-draped "things" before them at arm's length.*)

MADAME ROSEPETTLE   Ah, splendid. Splendid. Set them on the porch, if you will. (*They go out to the porch and set them down.*) Uh . . . not so close together. They fight. (*The* BELLBOYS *move the* PLANTS *apart.*)

BELLBOY NUMBER FOUR (*Weakly*)   Should we . . . uncover them?

MADAME ROSEPETTLE   No. That will be fine. Let the poor things rest awhile.

BELLBOYS NUMBER TWO *and* FOUR (*Together, weakly*)   Yes . . . madame.

MADAME ROSEPETTLE   Now . . . who has my fish? (*All* BELLBOYS *look toward the door.*)

A VOICE (*From outside the door*)   I have it, madame.
(*Enter* BELLBOY NUMBER FIVE *carrying, at arm's length, an object covered by a black cloth. He wears large, thick, well-padded glaves—the sort a snake trainer might wear when handling a newly caught cobra.*)

MADAME ROSEPETTLE (*With love in her voice*)   Ah, bring it here. Put it here, by the dictaphone. Near my memoirs. Bring it here, bellboy. Set it gently, then lift the shawl.

JONATHAN (*Staring sadly at his books*)   Sho-Sho-Sholo-Sholokhov . . . Alain-Fournier . . . Alighieri . . . ma-my ffffriends. (*The* BELLBOY *sets the object down.*)

MADAME ROSEPETTLE   The black shawl of mourning, bellboy. Remove it, if you will. Lift it off and drape it near its side. But gently. Gently. Gently as she goes. (*The* BELLBOY *lifts off the shawl. Revealed is a fish bowl with a* FISH *and a cat's skeleton inside.*) Ah, I see you fed it today. (*She reaches into her handbag and extracts a pair of long tongs. She plucks the skeleton from the fish bowl.*) Siamese, I presume.

BELLBOY NUMBER FOUR   No, madame. Alley.

MADAME ROSEPETTLE   WHAT!? A *common alley cat?* Just who do you think I am? What kind of fish do you think I have? *Alley cat! Alley cat!* The idea! In Buenos Aires, I'll have you know, Rosalinda was fed nothing but Siamese *kittens,* which are even more tender than Siamese cats. *That's* what I call consideration! Edward, make note: we will dismiss this creature from the bellboy squad *first thing in the morning!* (JONATHAN *scribbles on his pad.*)

BELLBOY NUMBER FOUR   Madame, please, there were no Siamese cats.

MADAME ROSEPETTLE   There are *always* Siamese cats!

BELLBOY NUMBER FOUR   Not in Havana.

MADAME ROSEPETTLE   Then you should have flown to Buenos Aires. I would have paid the way. Give me back your 1903 Borneo, limited. (I'll bet you've made it sticky.) (*He hands back the stamp.*) You can keep your Danzig gulden. It's not worth a thing except in Danzig, and hardly a soul uses anything but traveler's checks there anyhow! Shows you should never trust me.

BELLBOY NUMBER FOUR   Madame, *please.* I have a wife.

MADAME ROSEPETTLE   And *I* have a fish. I dare say there are half a million men in Cuba with wives. But show me another woman in Cuba with a silver piranha fish and then you'll be showing me something. Your marital status does not impress me, sir. You are common, do you hear? Common! While my piranha fish is *rare.* Now green piranhas can eat alley cats if they like; and red piranhas, I've been told, will often eat alley cats, tomcats, and even dogs; but my silver piranha has been weaned on Siamese, and Siamese it will be, sir. Siamese it will be. Now get out. All of you. There is much to do. Right, Albert?

JONATHAN   Ra . . . ra . . . ra . . . ra . . .

MADAME ROSEPETTLE   *Right,* Albert!?

JONATHAN   Ra-right.

ROSALINDA THE FISH (*Sadly*)   Glump.

MADAME ROSEPETTLE   Oh, dear thing. You can just tell she's not feeling up to snuff. *Someone will pay for this!*
        (*Enter* LIEUTENANT *of the bellboys from the bedroom.*)

BELLBOY NUMBER THREE   Well, I'm finished.

MADAME ROSEPETTLE   You certainly are, *monsieur lieutenant.* You certainly are.

BELLBOY NUMBER THREE   I beg your pardon?

MADAME ROSEPETTLE.   Make note, Edward. First thing in the morning we speak to the chef. Subject: Siamese cats—kittens if possible, though I seriously doubt it here. And make a further note, Albert, my darling. Let's see if we can't get our cats on the American Plan, while we're at it. (JONATHAN *scribbles on his pad of paper.*)

BELLBOY NUMBER THREE   Madame, is there something I can—?

MADAME ROSEPETTLE   QUIET! And put that hammer down. (*He puts it down. She puts it back in her purse.*) You have all behaved rudely. If the sunset over Guanabacoa Bay were not so full of magenta and wisteria blue I'd leave this place tonight. But the sunset *is* full of magenta and wisteria blue, to say nothing of cadmium orange and cerise, and so I think I'll stay.

Therefore beware, bellboys. Madame Rosepettle will have much to do. Right, Robinson? (JONATHAN *opens his mouth to speak but no words come out*.) I said, *right Robinson?* (*Again he tries to speak, and again no words come out*.) RIGHT, ROBINSON!? (*He nods*.) There's your answer. Now get out and leave us alone. (*They start to exit*.) No. Wait. (*They stop*.) A question before you go. The yacht in the harbor. The pink one with the lilacs draped about the railing. One hundred and eighty-seven feet long, I'd judge. Who owns it?

BELLBOY NUMBER ONE Commodore Roseabove, madame. It's a pretty sloop.

MADAME ROSEPETTLE (*Distantly*) Roseabove. I like that name.

BELLBOY NUMBER ONE He's a strange man, madame. A man who knows no master but the sea.

MADAME ROSEPETTLE (*With a slight smile*) Roseabove . . .

BELLBOY NUMBER ONE A wealthy man but a gentleman, too. Why I've seen him with my own eyes toss *real silver dollars* to the native boats as he sailed into port. And when some poor diver came to the surface without a coin glimmering in his hand, Commodore Roseabove, without the slightest hesitation, dropped a dollar bill instead. Oh he's a well-loved man, madame. A true, true gentleman with a big, big heart. A man who knows no master but the sea. And even the sea, they say, is no match for the commodore and his yacht, which, as you know, is the largest yacht in Cuba.

MADAME ROSEPETTLE And also the largest yacht in Haiti, Puerto Rico, Bermuda, the Dominican Republic, and West Palm Beach. I haven't checked the Virgin Islands yet. I thought I'd leave them till last. But I doubt if I'll find a larger one there. (*She laughs to herself*.) I take great pleasure, you see, in measuring yachts. My hobby, you might say.

BELLBOY NUMBER ONE Your hubby, did you say?

MADAME ROSEPETTLE (*Viciously*) Get out! Get out before I lose my temper! *Imbeciles!* FOOLS! (*They exit, running*.) Edward, make note. First thing in the morning, we restaff this hotel. (JONATHAN *scribbles on his pad of paper*. MADAME ROSEPETTLE *walks over to the French windows and stares wistfully out. There is a short silence before she speaks. Dreamily, with a slight smile*.) Roseabove. I like that name.

ROSALINDA THE FISH (*Gleefully*) Gleep.

MADAME ROSEPETTLE (*Fondly*) Ah, listen. My lovely little fish. She, too, is feeling better already.

(*Curtain.*)

Scene Two

The place is the same. The time, two weeks later. JONATHAN *is in the room with* ROSALIE, *a girl some two years older than he and dressed in sweet girlish pink.*

ROSALIE But if you've been here two weeks, why haven't I seen you?

JONATHAN I've . . . I've been in my room.

ROSALIE All the time?

JONATHAN   Yes. . . . All the time.

ROSALIE   Well, you must get out sometimes. I mean, sometimes you simply must get out. You just couldn't stay inside all the time . . . could you?

JONATHAN   Yyyyyes.

ROSALIE   You never get out at all? I mean, never at all?

JONATHAN   Some-sometimes I do go out on the porch. M-Ma-Mother has some . . . Venus'-flytraps which she bra-brought back from the rain forests of Va-Va-Va-Venezuela. They're va-very rrrrrare and need a . . . a lot of sunshine. Well sir, she ka-keeps them on the porch and I . . . I feed them. Twice a day, too.

ROSALIE   Oh.

JONATHAN   Ma-Ma-Mother says everyone must have a vocation in life. (*With a slight nervous laugh.*) I ga-guess that's . . . my job.

ROSALIE   I don't think I've ever met anyone before who's fed . . . uh . . . Venus'-flytraps.

JONATHAN   Ma-Ma-Mother says I'm va-very good at it. That's what she . . . says. I'm va-very good at it. I . . . don't know . . . if . . . I am, but . . . that's . . . what she says so I . . . guess I am.

ROSALIE   Well, uh, what . . . what do you . . . feed them? You see, I never met anyone before who's fed Venus'-flytraps so . . . that's why I don't know what . . . you're supposed to feed them.

JONATHAN   (*Happy that she asked*)   Oh, I fa-feed them . . . l-l-lots of things. Ga-ga-green peas, chicken feathers, rubber bands. They're . . . not very fussy. They're . . . nice, that way. Ma-Ma-Mother says it it it ga-gives me a feeling of a-co-co-complishment. Iffffff you would . . . like to see them I . . . could show them to you. It's . . . almost fa-feeding time. It is, and . . . and I could show them to you.

ROSALIE   No. That's all right. (JONATHAN *looks away, hurt.*) Well, how about later?

JONATHAN   Do-do-do you ra-really wwwwwwant to see them?

ROSALIE   Yes. Yes I really think I would like to see them . . . later. If you'll show them to me then, I'd really like that. (JONATHAN *looks at her and smiles. There is an awkward silence while he stares at her thankfully.*) I still don't understand why you never go out. How can you just sit in——?

JONATHAN   Sometimes, when I'm on the porch . . . I do other things.

ROSALIE   *What?*

JONATHAN   Sa-sa-sometimes, when I'm . . . on the porch, you know, when I'm on the porch? Ssssssssome-times I . . . do *other things,* too.

ROSALIE   What sort of things? (JONATHAN *giggles.*) What sort of things do you do?

JONATHAN   Other things.

ROSALIE   (*Coyly*)   What do you mean, "Other things"?

JONATHAN   Other things besides feeding my mother's plants. Other things besides that. That's what I mean. Other things besides that.

ROSALIE   What kind of things . . . *in particular?*

JONATHAN   Oh, watching.

ROSALIE   Watching?

JONATHAN   Yes. Like . . . watching.

ROSALIE   Watching what? (*He giggles.*) *Watching what!?*

JONATHAN   You. (*Short pause. She inches closer to him on the couch.*)

ROSALIE   What do you mean . . . watching me?

JONATHAN   I . . . watch you from the porch. That's what I mean. I watch you from the porch. I watch you a lot, too. Every day. It's . . . it's the truth. I . . . I swear it . . . is. I watch you ev-ry day. Do you believe me?

ROSALIE   Of course I believe you, Albert. Why—

JONATHAN   Jonathan!

ROSALIE   What?

JONATHAN   Jonathan. Ca-ca-call me Ja-Jonathan. That's my na-na-na——

ROSALIE   But your mother said your name was—

JONATHAN   Nooooo! Call . . . me Jonathan. Pa-pa-please?

ROSALIE   All right . . . Jonathan.

JONATHAN (*Excitedly*)   You *do* believe me! You rrrrreally do believe me. I-I-I can tell!

ROSALIE   Of course I believe you. Why shouldn't—?

JONATHAN   You want me to tell you how I watch you? You want me to tell you? I'll bet you'll na-never guess.

ROSALIE   How?

JONATHAN   *Guess.*

ROSALIE (*Ponders*)   Through a telescope?

JONATHAN   How did you guess?

ROSALIE   I . . . I don't know. I was just joking. I didn't really think that was—

JONATHAN   I'll bet everyone watches you through a telescope. I'll bet everyone you go out with watches you through a telescope. That's what I'll bet.

ROSALIE   No. Not at all.

JONATHAN   Well, that's how I watch you. Through a telescope.

ROSALIE   I never would have guessed that—

JONATHAN   I thought you were . . . ga-going to say I . . . I watch you with . . . with love in my eyes or some . . . thing like that. I didn't think you were going to guess that I . . . watch you through a telescope. I didn't think you were going to guess that I wa-watch you through a telescope on the fa-first guess, anyway. Not on the *first guess*.

ROSALIE   Well, it was just a guess.

JONATHAN (*Hopefully*)   Do you watch *me* through a telescope?

ROSALIE   I never knew where your room was.

JONATHAN   Now you know. Now will you watch me?

ROSALIE   Well I . . . don't have a telescope.

JONATHAN (*Getting more elated and excited*)   You can make one. That's how I got mine. I made it. Out of lenses and tubing. That's all you need. Lenses and tubing. Do you have any lenses?

ROSALIE   No.

JONATHAN   Do you have any tubing?

ROSALIE   No.

JONATHAN   Oh. (*Pause.*) Well, would you like me to tell you how I made mine in case you find some lenses and tubing? Would you like that?

ROSALIE (*Disinterestedly*)   Sure, Jonathan. I think that would be nice.

JONATHAN   Well, I made it out of lenses and tubing. The lenses I had because

Ma-Ma-Mother gave me a set of lenses so I could see my stamps better.
I have a fabulous collection of stamps, as well as a fantastic collection of
coins and a simply unbelievable collection of books. Well sir, Ma-Ma-
Mother gave me these lenses so I could see my stamps better. She suspected
that some were fake so she gave me the lenses so I might be . . . able to
see. You see? Well sir, I happen to have nearly a billion sta-stamps. So far
I've looked closely at 1,352,769. I've discovered three actual fakes!
Number 1,352,767 was a fake. Number 1,352,768 was a fake, and number
1,352,769 was a fake. They were stuck together. Ma-Mother made me
feed them im-mediately to her flytraps. Well . . . (*He whispers.*) one
day, when Mother wasn't looking . . . that is, when she was out, I heard
an airplane flying. An airplane . . . somewhere . . . far away. It wasn't
very loud, but still I heard it. An airplane. Flying . . . somewhere, far
away. And I ran outside to the porch so that I might see what it looked
like. The airplane. With hundreds of people inside it. Hundreds and
hundreds and hundreds of people. And I thought to myself, if I could just
see . . . if I could just see what they looked like, the people, sitting at
their windows looking out . . . and flying. If I could see . . . *just* once
. . . if I could see *just once* what they looked like . . . then I might . . .
know what I . . . what I . . . (*Slight pause.*) So I . . . built a telescope in case the plane ever . . . came back again. The tubing came from
an old blowgun (*He reaches behind the bureau and produces a huge
blowgun, easily a foot larger than he.*) Mother brought back from her last
hunting trip to Zanzibar. The lenses were the lenses she had given me for
my stamps. So I built it. My telescope. A telescope so I might be able to
see. And . . . (*He walks out to the porch.*) and . . . and I *could* see!
I could! I COULD! I really could. For miles and miles I could see. For
miles and miles and *miles!* (*He begins to lift it up to look through but
stops, for some reason, before he's brought it up to his eye.*) Only . . .
(*He hands it to* ROSALIE. *She takes it eagerly and scans the horizon and the
sky. She hands it back to him.*)

ROSALIE (*With annoyance*)   There's nothing out there to see.

JONATHAN (*Sadly*)   I know. That's the trouble. You take the time to build a
telescope that can sa-see for miles, then there's nothing out there to see.
Ma-Mother says it's a lesson in Life. (*Pause.*) But I'm not sorry I built my
telescope. And you know why? Because I saw you. Even if I didn't see
anything else, I did see you. And . . . and I'm . . . very glad. (ROSALIE
moves slightly closer to him on the couch. She moistens her lips.) I . . .
I remember, you were standing across the way in your penthouse garden
playing blind man's buff with ten little children. (*After a short pause,
fearfully.*) Are . . . are they by any chance . . . *yours?*

ROSALIE (*Sweetly*)   Oh, I'm not married.

JONATHAN   Oh!

ROSALIE   I'm a baby sitter.

JONATHAN (*With obvious relief*)   Oh.

ROSALIE   I work for the people who own the penthouse.

JONATHAN   I've never seen them around.

ROSALIE   I've never seen them either. They're never home. They just mail me a check every week and tell me to make sure I keep the children's names straight.

JONATHAN   If you could tell me which way they went I could find them with my telescope. It can see for miles.

ROSALIE   They must love children very much. I'll bet she's a marvelous woman. (*Pause.*) There's going to be another one, too! Another child is coming! I got a night letter last night.

JONATHAN   By airplane?

ROSALIE   I don't know.

JONATHAN   I bet it was. I can't see at night. Ma-Mother can but I can't. I'll bet that's when the planes fly.

ROSALIE (*Coyly*)   If you like, I'll read you the letter. I have it with me. (*She unbuttons the top of her blouse and turns around in a coquettish manner to take the letter from her brassiere. Reading.*) "Have had another child. Sent it yesterday. Will arrive tomorrow. Call it Cynthia."

JONATHAN   That will make eleven. That's an awful lot of children to take care of. I'll bet it must be wonderful.

ROSALIE   They do pay very well.

JONATHAN   They pay you?

ROSALIE   Of course . . . What did you think? (*Pause. Softly, seductively.*) Jonathan? (*He does not answer but seems lost in thought. With a feline purr.*) Jonathan?

JONATHAN   Yyyyyes?

ROSALIE   It gets very lonesome over there. The children go to sleep early and the parents are never home so I'm always alone. Perhaps . . . well Jonathan, I thought that perhaps you might . . . visit me.

JONATHAN   Well . . . well . . . well, you . . . you see . . . I . . . I . . .

ROSALIE   We could spend the evenings together . . . at my place. It gets so lonesome there, you know what I mean? I mean, I don't know what to do. I get so lonesome there.

JONATHAN   Ma-ma-ma-maybe you . . . you can . . . come over . . . here? Maybe you you can do . . . that.

ROSALIE   Why are you trembling so?

JONATHAN   I'm . . . I'm . . . I'm . . . I'm . . .

ROSALIE   Are you afraid?

JONATHAN   Nnnnnnnnnnnnnnnnnnnnno. Whaaaaaaaaaa-why . . . should I . . . be . . . afraid?

ROSALIE   Then why won't you come visit me?

JONATHAN   I . . . I . . . I . . . I . . .

ROSALIE   I don't think you're allowed to go out. That's what I think.

JONATHAN   Nnnn-o. I . . . I can . . . can . . . can . . .

ROSALIE   Why can't you go out, Jonathan? I want to know.

JONATHAN   Nnnnnnnnn-

ROSALIE   Tell me, Jonathan!

JONATHAN   I . . . I . . .

ROSALIE   I said I want to know! *Tell me.*

JONATHAN   I . . . I don't . . . know. I don't know why. I mean, I've . . . nnnnnnnever really thought . . . about going out. I . . . guess it's . . .

just natural for me to . . . stay inside. (*He laughs nervously as if that explained everything.*) You see . . . I've got so much to do. I mean, all my sssssstamps and . . . ca-coins and books. The pa-pa-plane might fffffffly overhead while I was was going downstairs. And then thhhhere are . . . the plants ta-to feeeeeeed. And I enjoy vvvery much wa . . . watching you and all yyyyyyour chil-dren. I've . . . really got so ma-many things . . . to . . . do. Like . . . like my future, for instance. Ma-Mother says I'm going to be great. That's . . . that's . . . that's what she . . . says. I'm going to be great. I sssswear. Of course, she doesn't know ex-actly what I'm . . . going to be great *in* . . . so she sits every afternoon for . . . for two hours and thinks about it. Na-na-naturally I've . . . got to be here when she's thinking in case she . . . thinks of the answer. Otherwise she might forget and I'd never know . . . what I'm ga-going to be great in. You . . . see what I mean? I mean, I've . . . I've gggggggot so many things to do I . . . just couldn't possibly get *anything* done if I ever . . . went . . . out-side. (*There is a silence.* JONATHAN *stares at* ROSALIE *as if he were hoping that might answer her question sufficiently. She stares back at him as if she knows there is more.*) Besides, Mother locks the front door.

ROSALIE   I thought so.

JONATHAN   No! You-you don't understand. It's not what you think. She doesn't lock the door to kaka-keep me in, which would be malicious. She . . . locks the door so I can't get out, which is for my own good and therefore . . . beneficent.

CUCKOO CLOCK (*From the master bedroom*)   Cuckoo! Cuckoo! Cuckoo!

ROSALIE   What's that?

JONATHAN (*Fearfully*)   A warning.

ROSALIE   What do you mean, a warning?

JONATHAN   A warning that you have to go. Your time is up.

ROSALIE   My time is what?

JONATHAN   Your time is up. You have to go. Now. At once. Right away. You can't stay any longer. You've got to go!

ROSALIE   Why?

JONATHAN (*Puzzled: as if this were the first time the question had ever occurred to him*)   I don't really know.

CUCKOO CLOCK (*Louder*)   Cuckoo! Cuckoo! Cuckoo! (JONATHAN *freezes in terror.* ROSALIE *looks at him calmly.*)

ROSALIE   Why did your mother ask me to come up here?

JONATHAN   What?

ROSALIE   Why did your mother ask me—?

JONATHAN   So I . . . I could meet you.

ROSALIE   Then why didn't you ask me yourself? Something's wrong around here, Jonathan. I don't understand why you didn't ask me yourself.

JONATHAN   Ma-Mother's so much better at those things.

CUCKOO CLOCK (*Very loudly*)   CUCKOO! CUCKOO! CUCKOO!

JONATHAN   You've got to get out of here! That's the third warning. (*He starts to push her toward the door.*)

ROSALIE   Will you call me on the phone?

JONATHAN   Please, you've got to go!

ROSALIE   Instead of your mother telling me to come, will you come and get me yourself? Will you at least call me? Wave to me?

JONATHAN   Yes-yes—I'll do that. Now get out of here!

ROSALIE   I want you to promise to come and see me again.

JONATHAN   Get out!

ROSALIE (*Coyly*)   Promise me.

JONATHAN   GET OUT! (*He pushes her toward the door.*)

ROSALIE   Why do you keep looking at that door?

JONATHAN (*Almost in tears*)   Please.

ROSALIE   Why do you keep looking at that door?

JONATHAN   *Please!* You've got to go before it's too late!

ROSALIE   There's something very wrong here. I want to see what's behind that door. (*She starts toward the master bedroom.* JONATHAN *throws his arms about her legs and collapses at her feet, his face buried against her thighs.*)

JONATHAN (*Sobbing uncontrollably*)   I love you. (ROSALIE *stops dead in her tracks and stares down at* JONATHAN.)

ROSALIE   What did you say?

JONATHAN   I-I-I llllllove you. I love you, I love you, I love you I—
(*The* CUCKOO CLOCK *screams, cackles, and goes out of its mind, its call ending in a crazed, strident rasp as if it had broken all its springs, screws, and innards. The door to the master bedroom opens.* MADAME ROSEPETTLE *appears.*)

JONATHAN (*Weakly*)   *Too late.*

MADAME ROSEPETTLE   Two warnings are enough for any man. Three are enough for any woman. The cuckoo struck three times and then a fourth and still she's here. May I ask why?

ROSALIE   You've been listening at the keyhole, haven't you!

MADAME ROSEPETTLE   I'm talking to my son, harlot!

ROSALIE   What did you say!

MADAME ROSEPETTLE   Harlot, I called you! Slut, scum, sleazy prostitute catching and caressing children and men. Stroking their hearts, I've seen you.

ROSALIE   What are you talking about?

MADAME ROSEPETTLE   Blind man's buff with children in the garden. The redheaded one—fifteen, I think. Behind the bush while the others cover their eyes. Up with the skirt, one-two-three and it's done. Don't try to deny it. I've seen you in action. I know your kind.

ROSALIE   That's a lie!

MADAME ROSEPETTLE   Life is a lie, my sweet. Not words but Life itself. Life in all its ugliness. It builds green trees that tease your eyes and draw you under them. Then when you're there in the shade and you breathe in and say, "Oh God, how beautiful," that's when the bird on the branch lets go his droppings and hits you on the head. Life, my sweet, beware. It isn't what it seems. I've seen what it can do. I've watched you dance.

ROSALIE   What do you mean by that?

MADAME ROSEPETTLE   Don't try to deny it. I've watched you closely and I know what I see. You danced too near him and you let him do too much. I saw you rub your hand across the back of his neck. I saw you laugh and look closely in his eyes. I'll bet you even told him he was the only one. How many, I wonder, have you told that to? I saw you let him stroke you with his hairy paw and saw you smile. I fancy your thighs must have fairly trembled. It was, my dear, obscene, lewd, disgusting, and quite disgraceful. Everyone was staring at you and yet you went right on. Don't try to deny it. Words will only make it worse. It would be best for all concerned if you left at once and never came again. I will keep the story of your dancing quiet. Good day. (MADAME ROSEPETTLE *turns to leave.* ROSALIE *does not move.*)

ROSALIE   Why don't you let Jonathan out of his room?

MADAME ROSEPETTLE (*Sharply*)   Who!?

ROSALIE   Jonathan.

MADAME ROSEPETTLE   Who!?

ROSALIE   Your son.

MADAME ROSEPETTLE   You mean Albert? Is that who you mean? Albert?

JONATHAN   Pa-pa-please do-don't.

MADAME ROSEPETTLE   Is that who you mean, slut! H'm? Speak up? Is that who you mean?

ROSALIE   I mean your son.

MADAME ROSEPETTLE   *I don't let him out because he is my son.* I don't let him out because his skin is as white as fresh snow and he would burn if the sun struck him. I don't let him out because outside there are trees with birds sitting on their branches waiting for him to walk beneath. I don't let him out because he is *susceptible.* That's why. Because he is *susceptible.* Susceptible to trees and to sluts and to sunstroke.

ROSALIE   Then why did you come and get me?

MADAME ROSEPETTLE   Because, my dear, my stupid son has been watching you through that stupid telescope he made. Because, in short, he wanted to meet you and I, in short, wanted him to know what you were really like. Now that he's seen, you may go.

ROSALIE   And if I choose to stay? (*Pause.*)

MADAME ROSEPETTLE (*Softly: slyly*)   Can you cook?

ROSALIE   Yes.

MADAME ROSEPETTLE   How well?

ROSALIE   Fairly well.

MADAME ROSEPETTLE   Not good enough! My son is a connoisseur. A connoisseur, do you hear? I cook him the finest foods in the world. Recipes no one knows exist. Food, my sweet, is the finest of arts. And since you can't cook you are artless. You nauseate my son's aesthetic taste. Do you like cats?

ROSALIE   Yes.

MADAME ROSEPETTLE   What kind of cats?

ROSALIE   Any kind of cats.

MADAME ROSEPETTLE   Alley cats?

ROSALIE   Especially alley cats.

MADAME ROSEPETTLE   I thought so. Go, my dear. Find yourself some weeping willow and set yourself beneath it. Cry of your lust for my son and wait, for a mocking bird waits above to deposit his verdict on your whorish head. My son is as white as fresh snow and you are tainted with sin. You are garnished with garlic and turn our tender stomachs in disgust.

ROSALIE   What did you come to Havana for?

MADAME ROSEPETTLE   To find *you!*

ROSALIE   And now that you've found me . . . ?

MADAME ROSEPETTLE   I throw you out! I toss you into the garbage can! If you'd have left on time I'd have told the sordid details of your dance when you were gone instead of to your face. But it makes no difference. I heard everything, you know. So don't try to call. The phone is in my room . . . and *no one goes into my room but me.*

> (*She stares at* ROSALIE *for a moment, then exits with a flourish.* ROSALIE *and* JONATHAN *move slowly toward each other. When they are almost together* MADAME ROSEPETTLE *reappears.*)

One more thing. If, by some chance, the eleventh child named Cynthia turns out to be a Siamese cat, give it to me. I too pay well. (MADAME ROSEPETTLE *turns toward her room.* ROSALIE *starts toward the door.* JONATHAN *grabs her hand in desperation.*)

JONATHAN   (*In a whisper*)   Come back again. Pa-please . . . come back again.

> (*For a moment* ROSALIE *stops and looks at* JONATHAN. *But* MADAME ROSEPETTLE *stops too, and turning, looks back at both of them, a slight smile on her lips.* ROSALIE, *sensing her glance, walks toward the door, slipping from* JONATHAN'S *outstretched hands as she does. The lights fade about* JONATHAN, *alone in the center of the room.*)

(*Curtain.*)

Scene Three

The hotel room at night, one week later. JONATHAN *is alone in the living room. He is sitting in a chair near the fish bowl, staring at nothing in particular with a particularly blank expression on his face. A clock is heard ticking softly in the distance. For an interminably long time it continues to tick while* JONATHAN *sits in his chair, motionless. After a while the ticking speeds up almost imperceptibly and soon after, laughter is heard. At first it is a giggle from the rear of the theater, then a cough from the side, then a self-conscious laugh from the other side, then a full gusty belly-roar from all corners of the theater. Soon the entire world is hysterical. Cuban drums begin to beat. Fireworks explode. Orgiastic music is heard.*

JONATHAN continues to sit, motionless. Only his eyes have begun to move. The clock continues to tick. The laughter grows louder: the laughter of the insane. Suddenly JONATHAN *leaps up and rushes to the French windows, his fingers pressed against his ears. He slams the French windows shut. The noises stop.* JONATHAN *closes his eyes and sighs with relief. The French windows sway unsteadily on their hinges. They tip forward. They fall to the floor. They shatter. The laughter returns.*

JONATHAN *stares down at them in horror. The* VENUS'-FLYTRAPS *grow larger and growl.*

VENUS'-FLYTRAPS (*Viciously*)   Grrrrrrr. (*The* PIRANHA FISH *stares hungrily from its bowl.*)

ROSALINDA THE FISH (*More viciously*)   Grarrgh!

> (*The* FLYTRAPS *lunge at* JONATHAN *but he walks dazedly past, unaware of their snapping petals, and goes out to the edge of the balcony. He stares out in complete bewilderment. The laughter and music of a carnival, the sounds of people dancing in the streets fill the air. He looks down at them sadly. Meekly he waves. The sounds immediately grow softer and the people begin to drift away. He watches as they leave. Behind him the* FLY-TRAPS *keep growing and reaching out for him, but of this he is unaware. He only stands at the railing, looking down. A last lingering laugh is heard somewhere in the distance, echoing.*)

> (*The door to the suite opens.*)

FIRST VOICE (*From outside the door*)   Are you sure this is the room?

SECOND VOICE (*Also outside*)   This is the room, all right. (JONATHAN *hides behind one of the* FLYTRAPS *and watches.*)

THIRD VOICE   And she wants all this stuff in here?

FOURTH VOICE   That's what she said.

FIFTH VOICE   Seems strange to me.

SECOND VOICE   Well don't worry about it. Just do it. After all . . . she tips very well.

THIRD VOICE   If you do what she wants.

FOURTH VOICE   Yes. If you do what she wants.

ALL TOGETHER   Well . . . shall we?

> (*They enter. The voices, we discover, belong to the* BELLBOYS, *now dressed as waiters. They enter in order.*)

BELLBOY NUMBER ONE (*Carrying a small, round table*)   She said to put it here, I think. (*He sets the table down in the center of the room. The lights slowly begin to fade as an overhead spot begins to illuminate the table.*)

BELLBOYS NUMBER TWO *and* THREE (*Carrying chairs in their arms*)   And these here. (*They set one chair on either side of the table.*)

BELLBOY NUMBER FOUR (*Carrying an ice bucket with a huge bottle of champagne in it*)   And the champagne here. (*He sets the ice bucket on the floor between the two chairs at the rear of the table.*)

BELLBOY NUMBER TWO   But what about the candles?

BELLBOY NUMBER THREE   And the glasses?

BELLBOY NUMBER FOUR   And the one wilting rose?

> (*Enter* BELLBOY NUMBER FIVE *carrying a tray with two champagne glasses on it, two flickering candles, and a flower vase with one wilting rose protruding.*)

BELLBOY NUMBER FIVE   I've got them here.

BELLBOY NUMBER ONE (*Placing a tablecloth on the table*)   Then everything is set.

BELLBOY NUMBER TWO   Just the way she wanted it.

BELLBOY NUMBER THREE   *Exactly* the way she wanted it.

BELLBOY NUMBER FIVE   *Specifically* wanted it. (*He finishes setting the glasses, candles, and flower vase.*)

BELLBOY NUMBER ONE   Yes. Everything is set.

BELLBOY NUMBER FOUR   No. Something is missing.

OTHERS   What!

BELLBOY NUMBER FOUR   We have forgotten something.

OTHERS   Forgotten *what?*

BELLBOY NUMBER FOUR   Well, it seems that we have forgotten the— (*He is interrupted by the sound of a Viennese waltz playing softly, romantically in the background.*)

BELLBOY NUMBER ONE   Oh, I'm sorry. I guess I didn't tell you. She said she'd take care of the music herself.

> (*The lights fade in the room and only the table is lit.
> The* BELLBOYS *disappear into the shadows. The music
> grows in brilliance.* THE COMMODORE *and* MADAME
> ROSEPETTLE *waltz into the room. A spot of light follows
> them about the floor.*)

THE COMMODORE   How lovely it was this evening, madame, don't you think? (*She laughs softly and demurely and discretely lowers her eyes. They waltz about the floor.*) How gentle the wind was, madame. And the stars, how clear and bright they were, don't you think? (*She blushes with innocence. They dance on.*) And the moon, madame, shining across the water, lighting the yachts, anchored, so silent and white and clean, waiting for the wind to come and fill their great, clean, white sails again. How poetic it was. How pure, madame. How innocent . . . don't you think? (*She turns her face away and smiles softly. They begin to whirl about the floor.*) Ah, the waltz. How exquisite it is, madame, don't you think? *One*-two-three, *one*-two-three, *one*-two-three. Ahhhhh, madame, how classically simple. How mathematically simple. How stark; how strong . . . how romantic . . . how sublime. (*She giggles girlishly. They whirl madly about the floor.*) Oh, if only Madame knew how I've waited for this moment. If only Madame knew how long. How this week, these nights, the nights we shared together on my yacht; the warm, wonderful nights, the almost-perfect nights, the would-have been-perfect nights had it not been for the crew peeking through the portholes. Ah, those nights, madame, those nights; almost alone but never quite; but now, tonight, at last, we *are* alone. And now, madame, now we are ready for romance. For the night was made for Love. And tonight, madame . . . we will love.

MADAME ROSEPETTLE (*With the blush of innocence*)   Oh, Commodore, how you do talk. (*They whirl about the room as the lilting rhythm of the waltz grows and sweeps on and on.*)

THE COMMODORE (*Suavely*)   Madame, may I kiss you?

MADAME ROSEPETTLE   Why?

THE COMMODORE (*After recovering from the abruptness of the question; with forced suaveness*)   Your lips . . . are a thing of beauty.

MADAME ROSEPETTLE   My lips, Commodore, are the color of blood. (*She smiles at him. He stares blankly ahead. They dance on.*) I must say, you dance exceptionally well . . . for a man your age.

THE COMMODORE (*Bristling*)   I dance with *you*, madame. That is why I dance well. For to dance with you, madame—is to hold you.

MADAME ROSEPETTLE   Well, I don't mind your holding me, Commodore, but at the moment you happen to be holding me too tight.

THE COMMODORE   I hold you too dear to hold you too tight, madame. I hold you close, that is all. And I hold you close in the hope that my heart may feel your heart beating.

MADAME ROSEPETTLE   *One*-two-three, *one*-two-three. You're not paying enough attention to the music, Commodore. I'm afraid you've fallen out of step.

THE COMMODORE   Then lead me, madame. Take my hand and lead me wherever you wish. For I would much rather think of my words than my feet.

MADAME ROSEPETTLE (*With great sweetness*)   Why certainly, Commodore. Certainly. If that is what you want . . . it will be my pleasure to oblige. (*They switch hands and she begins to lead him about the floor. They whirl wildly about, spinning faster than they had when* THE COMMODORE *led.*)

MADAME ROSEPETTLE   Beautiful, isn't it, Commodore? The waltz. The Dance of Lovers. I'm so glad you enjoy it so much. (*With a gay laugh she whirls him around the floor. Suddenly he puts his arms about her shoulders and leans close to kiss her. She pulls back.*) Commodore! You were supposed to spin just then. When I squeeze you in the side it means *spin!*

THE COMMODORE (*Flustered*)   I . . . I thought it was a sign of affection. (*She laughs.*)

MADAME ROSEPETTLE   You'll learn. (*She squeezes him in the side. He spins about under her arm.*) Ah, you're learning. (*He continues to spin around and around, faster and faster like a runaway top while* MADAME ROSE-PETTLE, *not spinning at all, leads him about the floor, a wild smile of ecstasy spreading over her face.*)

THE COMMODORE   Ho-ho, ho-ho. Stop. I'm dizzy. Dizzy. Stop, please. Stop. Ho-ho. Stop. Dizzy. Ho-ho. Stop. Too fast. Slow. Slower. Stop. Ho-ho. Dizzy. Too dizzy. Weeeeeee! (*And then, without any warning at all, she grabs him in the middle of a spin and kisses him. Her back is to the audience, so* THE COMMODORE'S *face is visible. At first he is too dizzy to realize that his motion has been stopped. But shortly he does, and his first expression is that of shock. But the kiss is long and the shock turns into perplexity and then, finally, into panic; into fear. He struggles desperately and breaks free from her arms, gasping wildly for air. He points weakly to his chest.*)

THE COMMODORE (*Gasping*)   Asthma. (*His chest heaves as he gulps in air.*) Couldn't breathe. Lungs bad. Asthmatic. Nose stuffed, too. Sinus condition. Couldn't get any air. (*He gasps for air. She starts to walk toward him, slowly.*) Couldn't get any . . . air. (*She nears him. Instinctively he backs away.*) You . . . you surprised me . . . you know. Out . . . of breath. Wasn't . . . ready for that. Didn't . . . expect you to kiss me.

MADAME ROSEPETTLE   I know. That's why I did it. (*She laughs and puts her arm tenderly about his waist.*) Perhaps you'd prefer to sit down for a while, Commodore. Catch your breath, so to speak. Dancing can be so terribly tiring . . . when you're growing old. Well, if you like, Commodore, we could just sit and talk. And perhaps . . . sip some pink champagne, eh? Champagne?

THE COMMODORE   Ah, champagne. (*She begins to walk with him toward the table.*)

MADAME ROSEPETTLE   And just for the two of us.

THE COMMODORE   Yes. The two of us. Alone.

MADAME ROSEPETTLE (*With a laugh*)   Yes. All alone.

THE COMMODORE   At last.

MADAME ROSEPETTLE   With music in the distance.

THE COMMODORE   A waltz.

MADAME ROSEPETTLE   A *Viennese* waltz.

THE COMMODORE   The Dance of Lovers. (*She takes his hand, tenderly.*)

MADAME ROSEPETTLE   Yes, Commodore. The Dance of Lovers. (*They look at each other in silence.*)

THE COMMODORE   Madame, you have won my heart. And easily.

MADAME ROSEPETTLE   No, Commodore. You have lost it. *Easily.* (*She smiles seductively. The room darkens till only a single spot of light falls upon the table set in the middle of the room. The waltz plays on.* MADAME ROSE-PETTLE *nods to* THE COMMODORE *and he goes to sit. But before he can pull his chair out, it slides out under its own power. He places himself and the chair slides back in, as if some invisible waiter had been holding it in his invisible hands.* MADAME ROSEPETTLE *smiles sweetly and, pulling out her chair herself, sits. They stare at each other in silence. The waltz plays softly.* THE COMMODORE *reaches across the table and touches her hand. A thin smile spreads across her lips. When finally they speak, their words are soft: the whispered thoughts of lovers.*)

MADAME ROSEPETTLE   Champagne?

THE COMMODORE   Champagne.

MADAME ROSEPETTLE   Pour?

THE COMMODORE   Please. (*She lifts the bottle out of the ice bucket and pours with her right hand, her left being clasped firmly in* THE COMMODORE'S *passionate hands. They smile serenely at each other. She lifts her glass. He lifts his. The music swells.*)

MADAME ROSEPETTLE.   A toast?

THE COMMODORE   To you.

MADAME ROSEPETTLE   No, Commodore, to you.

THE COMMODORE   No, madame. To us.

MADAME ROSEPETTLE⎫
THE COMMODORE   ⎰ (*Together*)   To us. (*They raise their glasses. They gaze wistfully into each other's eyes. The music builds to brilliance.* THE COMMODORE *clinks his glass against* MADAME ROSEPETTLE'S *glass. The glasses break.*)

THE COMMODORE (*Furiously mopping up the mess*)   Pardon, madame! Pardon!

MADAME ROSEPETTLE (*Flicking some glass off her bodice*)   Pas de quoi, monsieur.

THE COMMODORE   J'étais emporté par l'enthousiasme du moment.

MADAME ROSEPETTLE (*Extracting pieces of glass from her lap*)   Pas de quoi.
(THE COMMODORE *suddenly stretches across the table in order to stop the puddle of champagne from spilling over onto* MADAME ROSEPETTLE'S *glass-spattered lap. His elbow knocks over the flower vase. The table is inundated with water.*)

THE COMMODORE (*Gasping*)   Mon dieu!

MADAME ROSEPETTLE (*Watching with a serenely inane grin, as the water pours over the edge of the table and onto her dress*)   Pas de quoi, monsieur. Pas de quoi.
(*She snaps her fingers gaily. Immediately a* WAITER *appears from the shadow with a table in his hands. It is already covered with a tablecloth, two champagne glasses, two candelabra (the candles already flickering in them), and a vase with one wilting rose protruding. Another* WAITER *whisks the wet table away. The new table is placed. The* WAITERS *disappear into the shadows.*)

MADAME ROSEPETTLE (*Lifting the bottle of champagne out of the ice bucket*)   Encore?

THE COMMODORE   S'il vous plaît. (*She pours. They lift their glasses in a toast. The music swells again.*) To us.

MADAME ROSEPETTLE   To us, monsieur . . . Commodore. (*They clink their glasses lightly.* THE COMMODORE *closes his eyes and sips.* MADAME ROSE-PETTLE *holds her glass before her lips, poised but not touching, waiting. She watches him. Then she speaks softly.*) Tell me about yourself.

THE COMMODORE   My heart is speaking, madame. Doesn't it tell you enough?

MADAME ROSEPETTLE   Your heart, monsieur, is growing old. It speaks with a murmur. Its words are too weak to understand.

THE COMMODORE   But the feeling, madame, is still strong.

MADAME ROSEPETTLE   Feelings are for animals, monsieur. Words are the specialty of Man. Tell me what your heart has to say.

THE COMMODORE   My heart says it loves you.

MADAME ROSEPETTLE   And how many others, monsieur, has your heart said this to?

THE COMMODORE   None but you, madame. None but you.

MADAME ROSEPETTLE   And you, monsieur, with all your money and your worldly ways, how many have loved you?

THE COMMODORE   Many, madame.

MADAME ROSEPETTLE   How many, monsieur?

THE COMMODORE   Too many, madame.

MADAME ROSEPETTLE   So I, alone, am different?

THE COMMODORE   You alone . . . do I love.

MADAME ROSEPETTLE   And pray, monsieur, just what is it that I've done to make you love me so?

THE COMMODORE   Nothing, madame. And that is why. You are a strange woman, you see. You go out with me and you know how I feel. Yet, I know nothing of you. You disregard me, madame, but never discourage. You treat my love with indifference . . . but never disdain. You've led me on, madame. That is what I mean to say.

MADAME ROSEPETTLE   I've led you to my room, monsieur. That is all.

THE COMMODORE   To me, that is enough.

MADAME ROSEPETTLE   I know. That's why I did it. (*The music swells. She smiles distantly. There is a momentary silence.*)

THE COMMODORE (*With desperation*)   Madame, I must ask you something. Now. Because in all the days I've been with you there's been something I've wanted to know, but you've never told me so now, right now, I must ask. Madame, why are you here?

MADAME ROSEPETTLE (*She pauses before answering*)   I have to be somewhere, don't I?

THE COMMODORE   But why here, where I am? Why in Havana?

MADAME ROSEPETTLE   You flatter yourself, monsieur. I am in Havana only because Havana was in my way. . . . I think I'll move on tomorrow.

THE COMMODORE   For . . . home?

MADAME ROSEPETTLE (*Laughing slightly*)   Only the very young and the very old have homes. I am neither. And I have none.

THE COMMODORE   But . . . surely you must come from somewhere.

MADAME ROSEPETTLE   Nowhere you've ever been.

THE COMMODORE   I've been many places.

MADAME ROSEPETTLE (*Softly*)   But not many enough. (*She picks up her glass of champagne and sips, a distant smile on her lips.*)

THE COMMODORE (*With sudden, overwhelming, and soul-rendering passion*)   Madame, don't go tomorrow. Stay. My heart is yours.

MADAME ROSEPETTLE   How much is it worth?

THE COMMODORE   A fortune, madame.

MADAME ROSEPETTLE   Good. I'll take it in cash.

THE COMMODORE   But the heart goes with it; madame.

MADAME ROSEPETTLE   And you with the heart, I suppose?

THE COMMODORE   Forever.

MADAME ROSEPETTLE   Sorry, monsieur. The money's enticing and the heart would have been nice, but you, I'm afraid, are a bit too bulky to make it all worth while.

THE COMMODORE   You jest, madame.

MADAME ROSEPETTLE   I never jest, monsieur. There isn't enough time.

THE COMMODORE   Then you make fun of my passion, madame, which is just as bad.

MADAME ROSEPETTLE   But monsieur, I've never taken your passion seriously enough to make fun of it. (*There is a short pause.* THE COMMODORE *sinks slowly back in his seat.*)

THE COMMODORE (*Weakly, sadly*)   Then why have you gone out with me?

MADAME ROSEPETTLE   So that I might drink champagne with you tonight.

THE COMMODORE   That makes no sense.

MADAME ROSEPETTLE   It makes *perfect* sense.

THE COMMODORE   Not to me.

MADAME ROSEPETTLE   It does to me.

THE COMMODORE   But *I* don't understand. And I *want* to understand.

MADAME ROSEPETTLE   Don't worry, Commodore. You will.

THE COMMODORE   When?

MADAME ROSEPETTLE   Soon.

THE COMMODORE   How soon?

MADAME ROSEPETTLE   Very soon. (*He stares at her in submissive confusion. Suddenly, with final desperation, he grabs her hands in his and, leaning across the table, kisses them passionately, sobbingly. Then in a scarcely audible whisper she says.*) Now.

THE COMMODORE   Madame . . . I love you. Forever. Don't you understand? (*He kisses her hand again. A smile of triumph spreads across his face.*) Oh, your husband . . . He must have been . . . a wonderful man . . . to deserve a woman such as you. (*He sobs and kisses her hands again.*)

MADAME ROSEPETTLE (*Nonchalantly*)   Would you like to see him?

THE COMMODORE   A snapshot?

MADAME ROSEPETTLE   No. My husband. He's inside in the closet. I had him stuffed. Wonderful taxidermist I know. H'm? What do you say, Commodore? Wanna peek? He's my very favorite trophy. I take him with me wherever I go.

THE COMMODORE (*Shaken; not knowing what to make of it*)   Hah-hah, hah-hah. Yes. Very good. Very funny. Sort of a . . . um . . . *white elephant,* you might say.

MADAME ROSEPETTLE   *You* might say.

THE COMMODORE   Well, it's . . . certainly very . . . courageous of you, a . . . a woman still in mourning, to . . . to be able to laugh at what most other women wouldn't find . . . well, shall we say . . . funny.

MADAME ROSEPETTLE   Life, my dear Commodore, is *never* funny. It's grim! It's there every morning breathing in your face the moment you open your red baggy eyes. Worst of all, it follows you wherever you go. Life, Mr. Roseabove, is a husband hanging from a hook in the closet. Open the door without your customary cup of coffee and your whole day's shot to hell. But open the door just a little ways, sneak your hand in, pull out your dress, and your day is made. Yet he's still there, and waiting—your husband, hanging by his collar from a hook, and sooner or later the moth balls are gone and you've got to clean house. It's a bad day, Commodore, when you have to stare Life in the face, and you find he doesn't smile at all; just hangs there . . . with his tongue sticking out.

THE COMMODORE   I . . . don't find this . . . very funny.

MADAME ROSEPETTLE   Sorry. I was hoping it would give you a laugh.

THE COMMODORE   I don't think it's funny at all. And the reason that I don't think it's funny at all is that it's not my kind of joke. One must respect the dead.

MADAME ROSEPETTLE   Then tell me, Commodore . . . why not the living, too? (*Pause. She lifts out the bottle of champagne and pours herself some more.*)

THE COMMODORE (*Weakly, with a trace of fear*)   How . . . how did he die?

MADAME ROSEPETTLE   Why, I killed him of course. Champagne? (*She smiles sweetly and fills his glass. She raises hers in a toast.*) To your continued good health. (*He stares at her blankly. The music swells in the background.*) Ah, the waltz, monsieur. Listen. The waltz. The Dance of Lovers. Beautiful . . . *don't you think?* (*She laughs and sips some more champagne. The music grows to brilliance.* THE COMMODORE *starts to rise from his chair.*)

THE COMMODORE   Forgive me, madame. But . . . I find I must leave. Urgent business calls. Good evening. (*He tries to push his chair back, but for some reason it will not move. He looks about in panic. He pushes frantically. It does not move. It is as if the invisible waiter who had come and slid the chair out when he went to sit down now stood behind the chair and held it in so he could not get up. And as there are arms on the chair,* THE COMMODORE *cannot slide out the side.* MADAME ROSEPETTLE *smiles.*)

MADAME ROSEPETTLE   Now you don't *really* want to leave . . . do you, Commodore? After all, the night is still so young . . . and you haven't even seen my husband yet. We shared such love for so many years, Commodore, I would so regret if you had to leave without seeing him. And believe me, Commodore, the expression on his face is easily worth the price of admission. So please, Commodore, won't you reconsider? Won't you stay? . . . *just for a little while?* (*He stares at her in horror. He tries once more to push his chair back. But the chair does not move. He sinks down into it weakly. She leans across the table and tenderly touches his hand.*) Good. I knew you'd see it my way. It would have been such a shame if you'd have had to leave. For you see, Commodore, we are in a way united. We share something in common . . . you and I. . . . We share desire. For you desire me, with love in your heart. While I, my dear Commodore . . . desire your heart. (*She smiles sweetly and sips some more champagne.*) How simple it all is, in the end. (*She rises slowly from her chair and walks over to him. She runs her hands lovingly through his hair and down the back of his neck.*) Tell me, Commodore, how would you like to hear a little story? A bedtime story? A fairy tale of handsome princes and enchanted maidens; full of love and joy and music; tenderness and charm? Would you like to hear it, Commodore? Eh? It's my very favorite story, you see . . . and since you're my very favorite commodore, it seems only appropriate that I tell it to you . . . *don't you think?*

THE COMMODORE   No. I . . . I don't think so.

MADAME ROSEPETTLE   Good. Then I'll tell it. I never leave a place without telling it to at least one person. How very lucky you are. How very lucky. (*The light on the table dims slightly.* MADAME ROSEPETTLE *walks slowly away. A spot of light follows her as she goes. The light on the table fades more.* THE COMMODORE *sits, motionless.*)

His name was Albert Edward Robinson Rosepettle III. How strange and sad he was. All the others who had come to see me had been tall, but he was short. They had been rich, while he was poor. The others had been handsome, but Albert, poor Albert, he was as ugly as a humid day . . . (*She laughs sadly, distantly.*) and just about as wet, too. Oh, he was a fat bundle of sweat, Mr. Roseabove. He was nothing but one great torrent of perspiration. Winter and summer, spring and fall, Albert was dripping wet. And he wasn't very good-looking either. He had a large green wart on the very tip of his nose and he talked with a lisp and walked with a limp and his left ear, which was slightly larger than his right, was as red as a bright red beet. He was round and wet and hideous and I never could figure out how he ever got such a name as Albert Edward Robinson Rosepettle III.

Oh, I must have been very susceptible indeed to have married Albert. I *was* twenty-eight and that *is* a susceptible year in a woman's life. And of course I *was* a virgin, but still I— Oh, stop blushing, Mr. Roseabove. I'm not lying. It's all true. Part of the cause of my condition, I will admit, was due to the fact that I still hadn't gone out with a man. But I am certain, Mr. Roseabove, I am certain that despite your naughty glances my virtue would have remained unsoiled, no matter what. Oh, I had spoken to men. (Their voices are gruff.) And in crowded streets I had often brushed against them. (Their bodies, I found, are tough and bony.) I had observed their ways and habits, Mr. Roseabove. Even at that tender age I had the foresight to realize I must know what I was up against. So I watched them huddled in hallways, talking in nervous whispers and laughing when little girls passed by. I watched their hands in crowded buses and even felt their feeling elbows on crowded streets. And then, one night, when I was walking home I saw a man standing in a window. I saw him take his contact lenses out and his hearing aid out of his ear. I saw him take his teeth out of his thin-lipped mouth and drop them into a smiling glass of water. I saw him lift his snow-white hair off of his wrinkled white head and place it on a gnarled wooden hat tree. And then I saw him take his clothes off. And when he was done and didn't move but stood and stared at a full-length mirror whose glass he had covered with towels, then I went home and wept.

And so one day I bolted the door to my room. I locked myself inside, bought a small revolver just in case, then sat at my window and watched what went on below. It was not a pretty sight. Some men came up to see me. I don't know how they got my name. But I have heard that once a woman reaches womanhood her fragrance wanders out into the world and her name becomes common property of Men. Just as a single drop of blood will attract a distant school of sharks, so Man, without any introduction, can catch the scent of any woman anywhere and find her home. That is what I've heard. No place then is safe from them. You cannot hide. Your name is known and there is nothing left that can be done. I suppose if you like you can lock your door. It doesn't keep them away; just keeps them out. I locked my door. They came and knocked. I did not let them in.

"Hello in there," they said.
"Hello in there,
My name is Steven.
Steven S. (for Steven) Steven.
One is odd

But two is even.
I know you're hot
So I'm not leavin'."
   . . . or something like that.
(*Short pause.*) But they all soon left anyway. I think they caught the
scent of a younger woman down the hall. And so I stayed inside my room
and listened to the constant sound of feet disappearing down the stairs. I
watched a world walk by my window; a world of lechery and lies and
greed. I watched a world walk by and I decided not to leave my room until
this world came to me, *exactly* as I wanted it.

One day Albert came toddling up the stairs. He waddled over to my
room, scratched on the door and said, in a frail and very frightened voice,
"Will you please marry me?" And so I did. It was as simple as that. (*Pause.
Then distantly.*) I still wonder why I did it though. I still wonder why.
(*Short pause. Then with a laugh of resignation.*) I don't really know why.
I guess it just seemed like the right thing to do. Maybe it's because he was
the first one who ever asked me. No, that's not right. . . . Perhaps it's
because he was so ugly and fat; so unlike everything I'd ever heard a
husband should be. No, that doesn't make much sense either. . . .
Perhaps it's . . . yes, perhaps it's because one look at Albert's round, sad
face and I knew he could be mine . . . that no matter where he went, or
whom he saw, or what he did, Albert would be mine, all mine—mine to
love, mine to live with, mine to kill; my husband, my lover, my own . . .
my very own.

And so we were wed. That night I went to bed with a man for the
first time in my life. The next morning I picked up my mattress and
moved myself into another room. Not that there was something wrong
with Albert. Oh, no! He was *quite* the picture of health. His pudgy, pink
flesh bouncing with glee. Oh, how easily is Man satisfied. How easily is
his porous body saturated with "fun." All he asks is a little sex and a little
food and there he is, asleep with a smile and snoring. Never the slightest
regard for you, lying in bed next to him, your eyes wide open. No, he
stretches his legs and kicks you in the shins; stretches his arms and smacks
you in the eye. Lean over to kiss him good night and he'll belch in your
face till all your romantic dreams are dissolved in an image of onions,
garlic, and baked Boston beans. Oh, how considerate is Man when he's
had his fill of sex. How noble, how magical, how marvelous is Love.

And so, I picked up my mattress and left his room. For as long as I
stayed in his room I was not safe. After all, he was a total stranger to me.
We'd only met the day before and I knew far too little. But now that we
were married I had time to find out more. His life was a mystery and his
mind contained too many secrets. In short, I was in danger. So I decided to
find out certain things. A few of these were: what had he done before we'd
ever met, what had he wanted to do, what did he still want to do, what
was he doing about it? What did he dream about while he slept? What did
he think about when he stared out the window? What did he think about
when I wasn't near?

These were the things that concerned me most. And so I began to
watch him closely.

My plan worked best at night, for that was when he slept. . . . I would listen at my door until I heard his door close. Then I'd tiptoe out and watch him through his keyhole. When his lights went out I'd open up his door and creep across the floor to his bed. And that, Mr. Roseabove, is where I stayed, every night—next to him; my husband, my "Love." I never left his side, never took my eyes from his sleeping face. I dare you to find me a wife who's as devoted as that. (*She laughs.*) And so I watched. I listened to him breathe. My ear was a stethoscope that recorded the fluctuations of his dream life. I put my ear next to his mouth so I might hear the slightest word that he might say, the slightest word that would betray his sleeping, secret thoughts. I listened for my name upon his lips. I listened for a word of "love." I listened for anything, but he only snored, and smiled, and slept on and on. So every night I waited and listened, and every morning when the dawn came I left, knowing no more than when I'd come.

A month later I found that I was pregnant. It had happened that first horrible night. How like Albert to do something like that. I fancy he knew it was going to happen all the time, too. I do believe he planned it that way. One night, one shot, one chance in a lifetime and bham! you've had it. It takes an imaginative man to miss. It takes someone like Albert to do something like that. But yet, I never let on. Oh, no. Let him think I'm simply getting fat, I said. And that's the way I did it, too. I, nonchalantly putting on weight; Albert nonchalantly watching my belly grow. If he knew what was happening to me he never let me know it. He was as silent as before. It was only at night that he changed. Only at night while he slept that something strange suddenly occurred. I found that the smile on his face had become a grin. (*Pause.*)

Twelve months later my son was born. He was so overdue that when he came out he was already teething. He bit the index finger off the poor doctor's hand and snapped at the nurse till she fainted. I took him home and put him in a cage in the darkest corner of my room. But still I—

THE COMMODORE   Was it a large cage?

MADAME ROSEPETTLE   What?

THE COMMODORE   Was his cage large? I hope it was. Otherwise it wouldn't be very comfortable.

MADAME ROSEPETTLE   I'm sorry. Did I say cage? I meant crib. I put him in a crib and set the crib in a corner of my room where my husband would not see him. For until I found out exactly why he'd married me, until I understood his dreams, until that time I was not safe, and until that time I would not tell him that his son had been born. And so I went on as if nothing had happened. At night I'd slip into his room and watch him while he slept. He still refused to say a word. And yet, somehow, his grin seemed broader. And then, one night, he made that noise. At first I thought it just some . . . sort of snore. But then I listened closely. I was wrong. I know it sounds peculiar, Mr. Roseabove, but I swear it's true. While I looked on, Albert slept . . . and giggled. (*Pause.*)

Shortly after that, Rosalinda came. She was one of Albert's many secretaries. Since I'd married him, you see, he'd become a multibillionaire. My influence, of course. We'd moved from a four-room flat to a four-acre mansion. Albert had taken the north wing, my son and I the south. But when Rosalinda came, things changed. I've always felt there was something star-crossed about those two, for she was the only person I ever met who was equally as ugly as he. It seems her mother had once owned a laundromat and, at the tender age of five, Rosalinda, a curious child, had taken an exploratory trip through the mangler. The result of the trip being that her figure took on an uncanny resemblance to nothing less than a question mark.

Well, naturally I never let on that I knew she had come. When she walked in front of me I looked straight through her. When she spoke I looked away. I flatly refused to recognize her presence. I simply set an extra place at the table and cooked a little bit more. Though Albert watched me like a naughty boy anxious to see his mother's reaction to a mischievous deed, I disregarded his indiscretions and continued my life as if nothing had changed. If he were searching for some sign of annoyance, I never showed it. If he were waiting to be scolded *I* was waiting for him to give up. So at night, instead of preparing one, I prepared two beds. Instead of fluffing one pillow I fluffed up two and straightened an extra pair of sheets. I said good night as politely as I could and left them alone —the hunchback and my husband, two soulmates expressing their souls through sin. And while they lay in bed I listened at the keyhole. And when they slept I crept in and listened more. Albert had begun to speak!

After months of listening for some meager clue he suddenly began to talk in torrents. Words poured forth and I, like some listening sponge, soaked them up and stayed for more. At last he was talking in his sleep and I was there, sinking farther and farther into his brain, gaining more and more control. He told her things he never told to me. Words of passion and love. He told her how he worshiped the way she cooked; how he worshiped the way she talked; how he'd worshiped the way she'd looked when he'd first met her; even the way she looked now. And this to a hunchback. A hunchback! To a hideous, twisted slut sleeping in sin with him! Words he never told to me. I ask you, Mr. Roseabove, how much is a woman supposed to take?

But the signs of regret were beginning to show. And oh, how I laughed when I found out: when I saw how tired he'd begun to look, when I noticed how little he ate; how little he spoke; how slowly he seemed to move. It's funny, but he never slept any more. I could tell by his breathing. And through the keyhole at night I could see his large, round, empty eyes shining sadly in the dark. (*Pause.*)

Then one night he died. One year after she had come he passed on. The doctors don't know why. His heart, they said, seemed fine. It was as large a heart as they'd ever seen. And yet he died. At one o'clock in the morning his heart stopped beating. (*She laughs softly.*) But it wasn't till dawn that she discovered he was dead. (*She starts to laugh louder.*)

Well, don't you get it? Don't you catch the irony, the joke? What's wrong with you!? He died at one. At ONE O'CLOCK IN THE MORNING!! DEAD!!! Yet she didn't know he was dead till dawn. (*She laughs again, loudly.*)

Well don't you get the point? The point of this whole story? What is wrong with you? He was lying with her in bed for nearly six hours, *dead,* and she never knew it! What a lover he must have been! WHAT A LOVER! (*She laughs uproariously but stops when she realizes he's not laughing with her.*)

Well don't you see? Their affair, their sinfulness—it never even existed! He tried to make me jealous but there was nothing to be jealous of. His love was sterile! He was a child. He was weak. He was impotent. He was *mine!* Mine all the time, even when he was in bed with another, even in death . . . *he was mine!* (THE COMMODORE *climbs up in his chair and crawls over his arm rest. He begins to walk weakly toward the door.*) Don't tell me you're leaving, Commodore. Is there something wrong? (THE COMMODORE *walks weakly toward the door, then runs the last part of the way. In panic he twists the doorknob. The doorknob comes off. He falls to the ground.*) Why Commodore, you're on your knees! *How romantic.* Don't tell me you're going to ask me to marry you again? Commodore, you're trembling. What's wrong? Don't tell me you're afraid that I'll accept?

THE COMMODORE (*Weakly*)   I . . . I-I . . . feel . . . sa-sorry for your . . . sssssson . . . that's . . . all I can . . . sssssay.

MADAME ROSEPETTLE   And I feel sorrier for you! For you are *nothing!* While my son is mine. His skin is the color of fresh snow, his voice is like the music of angels, and his mind is pure. For he is safe, Mr. Roseabove, and it is *I* who have saved him. Saved him from the world beyond that door. The world of you. The world of his father. A world waiting to devour those who trust in it; those who love. A world vicious under the hypocrisy of kindness, ruthless under the falseness of a smile. Well, go on, Mr. Roseabove. Leave my room and enter your world again—your sex-driven, dirt-washed waste of cannibals eating each other up while they pretend they're kissing. Go, Mr. Roseabove, enter your blind world of darkness. My son shall have only one light!

> (*She turns with a flourish and enters her bedroom.* THE COMMODORE *stares helplessly at the doorknob in his hand. Suddenly the door swings open, under its own power.* THE COMMODORE *crawls out. The door closes behind him, under its own power. From outside can be heard the sound of a church bell chiming. The bedroom door reopens and* MADAME ROSEPETTLE *emerges wearing an immense straw hat, sunglasses, tight toreador pants, and a short beach robe. She carries a huge flashlight. She is barefoot. She tiptoes across the floor and exits through the main door. The church bell chimes thirteen times.*)
>
> (JONATHAN *emerges from behind the* VENUS'-FLY-TRAPS. *He runs to the door, puts his ear to it, then races back to the balcony and stares down at the street below. Carnival lights flash weirdly against the night sky and laughter drifts up. The* VENUS'-FLYTRAPS *reach out to*

*grab him but somehow he senses their presence and
leaps away in time.)*

VENUS'-FLYTRAPS (*Gruffly*)   Grrrrrr! (*He walks dazedly into the living room.*)

ROSALINDA THE FISH (*Snarlingly*)   Snarrrrrrl!

(The VENUS'-FLYTRAPS *have grown enormous. Their
monstrous petals wave hungrily in the air while they
growl.* JONATHAN *stares at them fearfully, the laughter
below growing stronger all the while. Suddenly he runs
to the wall and smashes the glass case that covers the
fire axe. He takes out the axe. He advances cautiously
toward the* FLYTRAPS. *He feints an attack, they follow
his movements. He bobs, they weave. It is a cat-and-
mouse game of death. Suddenly* JONATHAN *leaps upon
them and hacks them apart till they fall to the floor,
writhing, then dead.* JONATHAN *stands above them,
victorious, panting, but somehow seeming to breathe
easier. Slowly he turns and looks at the fish bowl. His
eyes seem glazed, his expression insanely determined. He
walks slowly toward the fish bowl. . . . There are
three knocks on the door. He does not hear them. He
raises his axe.)*

(The door opens. ROSALIE *enters. She is dressed
in an absurdly childish pink dress with crinolines and
frills—the picture of innocence, the picture of a girl ten
years old. Her shoes are black leather pumps and she
wears girlish-pink socks. Her cheeks have round circles
of rouge on them—like a young girl might have who
had never put on make-up before.)*

ROSALIE   Jonathan! Jonathan! What *have* you done? (JONATHAN *stops. He does
not look at her but stares at the fish bowl.*) Jonathan! Put down that
silly axe. You might hurt yourself. (*He still does not answer but stares at
the bowl. He does not lower the axe.*) Jonathan! (*Slowly he turns and
faces her.*)

JONATHAN   I killed it.

ROSALIE   Ssh. Not so loudly. Where'd you put her body?

JONATHAN (*Pointing to the* PLANTS)   There.

ROSALIE   Where? I don't see a body. Where is she?

JONATHAN   Who?

ROSALIE   Your mother.

JONATHAN   I haven't killed my mother. I've killed her plants. The ones I used
to feed. I've chopped their hearts out.

ROSALIE (*With an apologetic laugh*)   I thought you'd . . . killed your mother.
(*The* PIRANHA FISH *giggles.* JONATHAN *turns and stares at it again. He
starts to move toward it, slowly.*)

ROSALIE   Jonathan, stop. (*He hesitates, as if he is uncertain what to do. Slowly
he raises the axe.*) Jonathan! (*He smashes the axe against the fish bowl. It
breaks. The fish screams.*)

ROSALINDA THE FISH (*Fearfully*)   AAIEEEEEEEEEEEEEEE!

ROSALIE   Now look at the mess you've made.

JONATHAN   Do you think it can live without water?

ROSALIE   What will your mother say when she gets back?

JONATHAN   Maybe I should hit it again. Just in case. (*He strikes it again.*)

ROSALINDA THE FISH (*Mournfully*)   UGHHHHHHH! (JONATHAN *stares in horror at the dead* FISH. *He drops the axe and turns away, sickened and weak.* ROSALIE *walks over and touches him gently, consolingly, on the arm.*)

ROSALIE   There's something bothering you, isn't there? (*Pause—coyly.*) What's-a matter, Jonathan? (JONATHAN *does not answer at first but stares off into space frightened, bewildered.*)

JONATHAN (*Weakly*)   I never thought I'd see you again. I never thought I'd talk to you again. I never thought you'd come.

ROSALIE   Did you really think that?

JONATHAN   She told me she'd never let you visit me again. She said no one would *ever* visit me again. She told me I had seen enough.

ROSALIE   But I had a key made.

JONATHAN   She . . . she hates me.

ROSALIE   What?

JONATHAN   She doesn't let me do anything. She doesn't let me listen to the radio. She took the tube out of the television set. She doesn't let me use her phone. She makes me show her all my letters before I seal them. She doesn't—

ROSALIE   Letters? What letters are you talking about?

JONATHAN   Just . . . letters I write.

ROSALIE   To *whom?*

JONATHAN   To people.

ROSALIE   *What* people?

JONATHAN   Oh . . . various people.

ROSALIE   Other girls? Could they be to other girls, by any chance?

JONATHAN   No. They're just to people. No people in particular. Just people in the phone book. Just names. I do it alphabetically. That way, someday, I'll be able to cover everyone. So far I've covered all the "A's" and "B's" up to Barrera.

ROSALIE   What is it you say to them? Can you tell me what you say to them . . . or is it private? Jonathan, just what do you say to them!?

JONATHAN   Mostly I just ask them what they look like. (*Pause. Suddenly he starts to sob in a curious combination of laughter and tears.*) But I don't think she ever mails them. She reads them, then takes them out to mail. But I don't think she ever does. I'll bet she just throws them away. Well if she's not going to mail them, why does she say she will? I . . . I could save the stamps. Why must she lie to me? Why doesn't she just say she's not going to mail them? Then I wouldn't have to wait for letters every day.

ROSALIE   Guess why I had this key made.

JONATHAN   I'll bet she's never even mailed one. From Abandono to Barrera, not one.

ROSALIE   Do you know why I had this key made? Do you know why I'm wearing this new dress?

JONATHAN   She doesn't let me stand in the window at noon because the sun is too strong. She doesn't let me stand in the window at night when the wind is blowing because the air is too cold. And today she told me she's going to nail shutters over the windows so I'll never have to worry about being bothered by the sun or the wind again.

ROSALIE Try and guess why I'm all dressed up.

JONATHAN She tells me I'm brilliant. She makes me read and reread books no one's ever read. She smothers me with blankets at night in case of a storm. She tucks me in so tight I can't even get out till she comes and takes my blankets off.

ROSALIE Stop talking about that and pay attention to me!

JONATHAN She says she loves me. Every morning, before I even have a chance to open my eyes, there she is, leaning over my bed, breathing in my face and saying, "I love you, I love you."

ROSALIE Jonathan, isn't my dress pretty?

JONATHAN But I heard everything tonight. I heard it all when she didn't know I was here. (*He stares off into space, bewildered.*)

ROSALIE What's the matter? (*He does not answer.*) Jonathan, what's the matter?

JONATHAN But she must have known I was here. She must have known! I mean . . . where could I have gone? (*Pause.*) But . . . if that's the case . . . *why did she let me hear?*

ROSALIE Jonathan, I do wish you'd pay more attention to me. Here, look at my dress. You can even touch it if you like. Guess how many crinolines I have on. Guess why I'm wearing such a pretty, new dress. *Jonathan!*

JONATHAN (*Distantly*) Maybe . . . it didn't make any difference to her . . . whether I heard or not. (*He turns suddenly to her and hugs her closely. She lets him hold her, then she steps back and away from him. Her face looks strangely old and determined under her girlish powder and pinkness.*)

ROSALIE Come with me.

JONATHAN What?

ROSALIE Leave and come with me.

JONATHAN (*Fearfully*) Where?

ROSALIE Anywhere.

JONATHAN What . . . wha . . . what do you mean?

ROSALIE I mean, let's leave. Let's run away. Far away. Tonight. Both of us, together. Let's run and run. Far, far away.

JONATHAN You . . . mean, leave?

ROSALIE Yes. *Leave.*

JONATHAN Just like that?

ROSALIE *Just like that.*

JONATHAN But . . . but . . . but . . .

ROSALIE You want to leave, don't you?

JONATHAN I . . . I don't . . . don't know. I . . . I . . .

ROSALIE What about the time you told me how much you'd like to go outside, how you'd love to walk by yourself, anywhere you wanted?

JONATHAN I . . . I don't . . . know.

ROSALIE Yes you do. Come. Give me your hand. Stop trembling so. Everything will be all right. Give me your hand and come with me. Just through the door. Then we're safe. Then we can run far away, somewhere where she'll never find us. Come, Jonathan. It's time to go. I've put on a new dress just for the occasion. I even had a key made so I could come and get you.

JONATHAN   There are others you could take.

ROSALIE   But I don't love them. (*Pause.*)

JONATHAN   You . . . you *love* me?

ROSALIE   Yes, Jonathan. I love you.

JONATHAN   Wha-wha-why?

ROSALIE (*Softly*)   Because you watch me every night.

JONATHAN   Well . . . can't we stay here?

ROSALIE   *No.*

JONATHAN   Wha-wha-whhhy?

ROSALIE   Because I want you *alone.* (JONATHAN *turns from her and begins to walk about the room in confusion.*) I want you, Jonathan. Do you understand what I said? *I want you for my husband.*

JONATHAN   I . . . I . . . can't, I mean, I . . . I want to . . . go with you very much but I . . . I don't think . . . I can. I'm . . . sorry. (*He sits down and holds his head in his hands, sobbing quietly.*)

ROSALIE   What time will your mother be back?

JONATHAN   Na—not for a while.

ROSALIE   Are you sure?

JONATHAN   Ya-yes.

ROSALIE   Where is she?

JONATHAN   The usual place.

ROSALIE   What do you mean, "The usual place"?

JONATHAN (*With a sad laugh*)   The beach. (ROSALIE *looks at* JONATHAN *quizzically.*) She likes to look for people making love. Every night at midnight she walks down to the beach searching for people lying on blankets and making love. When she finds them she kicks sand in their faces and walks on. Sometimes it takes her as much as three hours to chase everyone away. (ROSALIE *smiles slightly and walks toward the master bedroom.* JONATHAN *freezes in fear. She puts her hand on the doorknob.*)

JONATHAN   WHAT ARE YOU DOING!? (*She smiles at him over her shoulder. She opens the door.*) STOP! You can't go in there! STOP! (*She opens the door completely and beckons to him.*)

ROSALIE   Come.

JONATHAN   Close it. Quickly!

ROSALIE   Come, Jonathan. Let's go inside.

JONATHAN   Close the door!

ROSALIE (*With a laugh*)   You've never been in here, have you?

JONATHAN   No. And you can't go in, either. No one can go in there but Mother. It's her room. Now close the door! (*She flicks on the light switch. No lights go on.*)

ROSALIE   What's wrong with the lights?

JONATHAN   There are none. . . . Mother's in mourning. (ROSALIE *walks into the room and pulls the drapes off the windows. Weird colored lights stream in and illuminate the bedroom in wild, distorted, nightmarish shadows and lights. They blink on and off, on and off. It's all like some strange, macabre fun house in an insane amusement park. Even the furniture in the room seems grotesque and distorted. The closet next to the bed seems peculiarly prominent. It almost seems to tilt over the bed.)*

JONATHAN (*Still in the main room*)   What have you done!? (ROSALIE *walks back to the door and smiles to him from within the master bedroom.*) *What have you done?*

ROSALIE   Come in, Jonathan.

JONATHAN   GET OUT OF THERE!

ROSALIE   Will you leave with me?

JONATHAN   I can't!

ROSALIE   But you want to, don't you?

JONATHAN   Yes, yes, I want to, but I told you . . . I . . . I . . . I can't! I can't! Do you understand? I can't! Now come out of there.

ROSALIE   Come in and get me.

JONATHAN   Rosalie, *please.*

ROSALIE (*Bouncing on the bed*)   My, what a comfortable bed.

JONATHAN (*Horrified*)   GET OFF THE BED!

ROSALIE   What soft, fluffy pillows. I think I'll take a nap.

JONATHAN   Rosalie, *please listen to me.* Come out of there. You're not supposed to be in that room. Please come out. Rosalie, *please.*

ROSALIE   Will you leave with me if I do?

JONATHAN   Rosalie . . . ? I'll . . . I'll show you my stamp collection if you'll promise to come out.

ROSALIE   Bring it in here.

JONATHAN   Will you come out then?

ROSALIE   Only if you bring it in here.

JONATHAN   But I'm not allowed to go in there.

ROSALIE (*Poutingly*)   Then I shan't come out!

JONATHAN   You've got to!

ROSALIE   Why?

JONATHAN   Mother will be back.

ROSALIE   She can sleep out there. (ROSALIE *yawns.*) I think I'll take a little nap. This bed is so comfortable. Really, Jonathan, you should come in and try it.

JONATHAN   MOTHER WILL BE BACK SOON!

ROSALIE   Give her your room, then, if you don't want her to sleep on the couch. I find it very nice in here. Good night. (*Pause.*)

JONATHAN   If I come in, will you come out?

ROSALIE   If you don't come in I'll never come out.

JONATHAN   And if I do?

ROSALIE   Then I may.

JONATHAN   What if I bring my stamps in?

ROSALIE   Bring them and find out. (*He goes to the dresser and takes out the drawer of stamps. Then he takes out the drawer of coins.*)

JONATHAN   I'm bringing the coins, too.

ROSALIE   How good you are, Jonathan. (*He takes a shelf full of books.*)

JONATHAN   My books, too. How's that? I'll show you my books and my coins and my stamps. I'll show you them all. Then will you leave?

ROSALIE   Perhaps. (*He carries them all into the bedroom and sets them down next to the bed. He looks about fearfully.*)

ROSALIE   What's wrong?

JONATHAN   I've never been in here before.

ROSALIE   It's nothing but a room. There's nothing to be afraid of. (*He looks about doubtfully.*)

JONATHAN   Well, let me show you my stamps. I have one billion, five—

ROSALIE   Later, Jonathan. We'll have time. Let me show you something first.

JONATHAN   What's that?

ROSALIE   You're trembling.

JONATHAN   What do you want to show me?

ROSALIE   There's nothing to be nervous about. Come. Sit down.

JONATHAN   What do you want to show me?

ROSALIE   I can't show you if you won't sit down.

JONATHAN   I don't want to sit down! (*She takes hold of his hand. He pulls it away.*)

ROSALIE   Jonathan!

JONATHAN   You're sitting on Mother's bed.

ROSALIE   Then let's pretend it's my bed.

JONATHAN   It's not your bed!

ROSALIE   Come, Jonathan. Sit down here next to me.

JONATHAN   We've got to get out of here. Mother might come.

ROSALIE   Don't worry. We've got plenty of time. The beach is full of lovers.

JONATHAN   How do you know?

ROSALIE   I checked before I came. (*Pause.*)

JONATHAN   Let . . . let me show you my coins.

ROSALIE   Why are you trembling so?

JONATHAN   Look, we've got to get out! Something terrible will happen if we don't.

ROSALIE   Then leave with me.

JONATHAN   The bedroom?

ROSALIE   The hotel. The island. Your mother. Leave with me, Jonathan. Leave with me now, before it's too late.

JONATHAN   I . . . I . . . I . . .

ROSALIE   I love you, Jonathan, and I won't give you up. I want you . . . all for myself. Not to share with your mother, but for me, alone . . . to love, to live with, to have children by. I want you, Jonathan. You, whose skin is softer and whiter than anyone's I've ever known; whose voice is quiet and whose love is in every look of his eye. I want you, Jonathan, and I won't give you up. (*Short pause.*)

JONATHAN   (*Softly, weakly*)   What do you want me to do?

ROSALIE   Forget about your mother. Pretend she never existed and look at me. Look at my eyes, Jonathan; my mouth, my hands, my skirt, my legs. Look at me, Jonathan. Are you still afraid?

JONATHAN   I'm not afraid. (*She smiles and starts to unbutton her dress.*) What are you doing!? No! (*She continues to unbutton her dress.*)

ROSALIE   Your mother is strong, but I am stronger. (*She rises and her skirt falls about her feet. She stands in a slip and crinolines.*) I don't look so pink and girlish any more, do I? (*She laughs.*) But you want me anyhow. You're ashamed but you want me anyhow. It's written on your face. And I'm glad. Because I want you. (*She takes off a crinoline.*)

JONATHAN   PUT IT ON! *Please,* put it back on!

ROSALIE   Come, Jonathan. (*She takes off another crinoline.*) Lie down. Let me loosen your shirt.

JONATHAN   *No . . . NO . . . NO!* STOP! *Please,* stop! (*She takes her last crinoline off and reaches down to take off her socks. The lights outside blink weirdly. Wild, jagged music with a drum beating in the background is heard.*)

ROSALIE   Don't be afraid, Jonathan. Come. Lie down. Everything will be wonderful. (*She takes her socks off and lies down in her slip. She drops a strap over one shoulder and smiles.*)

JONATHAN   Get off my mother's bed!

ROSALIE   I want you, Jonathan, all for my own. Come. The bed is soft. Lie here by my side.

> (*She reaches up and takes his hand. Meekly he sits down on the edge of the bed. The closet door swings open suddenly and the corpse of Albert Edward Robinson Rosepettle III tumbles forward stiffly and onto the bed, his stone-stiff arms falling across* ROSALIE'S *legs, his head against her side.* JONATHAN, *too terrified to scream, puts his hand across his mouth and sinks down onto the bed, almost in a state of collapse. Outside the music screams.*)

ROSALIE   Who the hell is this!?

JONATHAN   It-it-it-it . . . it . . . it's . . .

ROSALIE   What a stupid place to keep a corpse. (*She pushes him back in the closet and shuts the door.*) Forget it, Jonathan. I put him back in the closet. Everything's fine again.

JONATHAN   It's . . . it's . . . it's my . . . my . . . my . . .

ROSALIE   (*Kneeling next to him on the bed and starting to unbutton his shirt*) It's all right, Jonathan. It's all right. Sshh. Come. Let me take off your clothes.

JONATHAN   (*Still staring dumbly into space*)   It's . . . it's my . . . ffffather. (*The closet door swings open again and the corpse falls out, this time his arms falling about* ROSALIE'S *neck.* JONATHAN *almost swoons.*)

ROSALIE   Oh, for God's sake. (*She pushes the corpse off the bed and onto the floor.*) Jonathan . . . ? LISTEN TO ME, JONATHAN! STOP LOOKING AT HIM AND LOOK AT ME! (*He looks away from his father, fearfully, his mouth open in terror.*) I love you, Jonathan, and I want you *now.* Not later and not as partner with your mother but now and by myself. I want you, Jonathan, as my husband. I want you to lie with me, to sleep with me, to be with me, to kiss me and touch me, to live with me, *forever.* Stop looking at him! He's dead! Listen to me. I'm alive. I want you for my husband! Now help me take my slip off. Then you can look at my body and touch me. Come, Jonathan. Lie down. I want you forever.

JONATHAN   Ma-Mother was right! You *do* let men do anything they want to you.

ROSALIE   Of course she was right! Did you really think I was that sweet and pure? Everything she said was right. (*She laughs.*) Behind the bushes and it's done. One-two-three and it's done. Here's the money. Thanks. Come again. Hah-hah! Come again! (*Short pause.*) So what!? It's only you I love. They make no difference.

JONATHAN   You're dirty! (*He tries to get up but can't, for his father is lying in front of his feet.*)

ROSALIE   No, I'm not dirty. I'm full of love and womanly feelings. I want children. Tons of them. I want a husband. Is that dirty?

JONATHAN   You're dirty!

ROSALIE   No. I'm pure. I want no one but you. I renounce all past lovers. They were mistakes. I confess my indiscretions. Now you know all so I'm pure again. Take off your clothes.

JONATHAN   NO!

ROSALIE   Forget about your father. Drop your pants on top of him, then you won't see his face. Forget about your mother. She's gone. Forget them both and look at me. Love is so beautiful, Jonathan. Come and let me love you; tonight and forever. Come and let me keep you mine. Mine to love when I want, mine to kiss when I want, mine to have when I want. Mine. All mine. So come, Jonathan. Come and close your eyes. It's better that way. Close your eyes so you can't see. Close your eyes and let me lie with you. Let me show you how beautiful it is . . . love.

(*She lies back in bed and slowly starts to raise her slip. JONATHAN stares at her legs in horror. Then, suddenly, he seizes her crumpled skirt and throws it over her face. He smothers her to death. . . . At last he rises and, picking up his box of stamps, dumps the stamps over her limp body. He does the same with his coins and finally his books, until at last she is buried. Then, done, he throws his hands over his eyes and turns to run. But as he staggers past the corpse of his father, his father's lifeless arms somehow come to life for an instant and, reaching out, grab JONATHAN by the feet. JONATHAN falls to the floor. For a moment he lies there, stretched across his father's body, too terrified to move. But a soft, ethereal-green light begins to suffuse the room and heavenly harp music is heard in the air. As if his body had suddenly become immortal and weightless, JONATHAN rises up from the floor and with long, slow, dreamlike steps (like someone walking under water), he floats through the bedroom door and drifts across the living room, picking up his telescope on the way. He floats out to the balcony and begins to scan the sky. The*)

harp music grows louder and more paradisiacal:
Debussy in Heaven. While under the harp music, soft,
muffled laughter can be heard; within the bedroom,
within the living room, from the rear of the theater,
laughter all about.)

(*His mother tiptoes into the living room. Her hair is*
awry, her hat is on crooked, her blouse hangs wrinkled
and out of her pants. Her legs are covered with sand.)

MADAME ROSEPETTLE   Twenty-three couples. I annoyed twenty-three couples, all of them coupled in various positions, all equally distasteful. It's a record, that's what it is. It's a record! (*Breathing heavily from excitement she begins to tuck in her blouse and straighten her hair. She notices the chaotic state of the room. She shrieks slightly.*) What has happened!? (*She notices the* PLANTS.) My plants! (*She notices the* FISH.) Rosalinda! Great gods, my fish has lost her water! ALBERT! ALBERT! (*She searches about the room for her* SON. *She sees him standing on the porch.*) Ah, there you are. Edward, what has been going on during my brief absence? What are you doing out here when Rosalinda is lying in there dead? DEAD!? Oh God, dead. Robinson, answer me. What are you looking for? I've told you there's nothing out there. This place is a madhouse. That's what it is. A madhouse. (*She turns and walks into her bedroom. An airplane is heard flying in the distance.* JONATHAN *scans the horizon frantically. The plane grows nearer. Jonathan follows it with his telescope. It flies overhead. It begins to circle about. Wildly, desperately, Jonathan waves his arms to the plane. . . . It flies away.*)

(MADAME ROSEPETTLE *re-enters the room.*)

Robinson! I went to lie down and I stepped on your father! I lay down and I lay on some girl. Robinson, there is a woman in my bed and I do believe she's stopped breathing. What is more, you've buried her under your fabulous collection of stamps, coins, and books. I ask you, Robinson. As a mother to a son I ask you. *What is the meaning of this?*

(*Blackout and Curtain.*)

From the Playwright

Most playwrights scorn being labled or categorized; **Arthur Kopit** *is no exception. In the brief interview below, Kopit discusses his dramatic techniques and the background to the writing of* Oh Dad, Poor Dad .... *Kopit denies being an absurdist, yet many of his comments could have been made by any existentialist-absurdist* ("*I have no more authority than anyone else to say what they* [*symbols of the play*] *represent; the situation the world is now in is so serious that it's almost funny*"). *Playwrights, like their characters, can be complex souls.*

Interviewer: Do you consider yourself part of the Theatre of the Absurd?

Kopit: Well, supposedly the Theatre of the Absurd deals with an absurd point of view in relation to the universe. A lot of earlier writers have done this—for instance, *Measure for Measure* or *Heartbreak House.* But I think the critics are labeling "absurd" plays written in a certain form which often have nothing in common philosophically. Such plays either dispense with plot or use certain expressionistic techniques. I think the term is a misappellation, and the danger is that it becomes a term of dismissal. I don't think there is such a thing as the Theatre of the Absurd, but if there were, my play would have nothing to do with it. It's not *about* that. Critics are often afraid to judge a work on its own terms, and just because I'm roughly contemporary with Edward Albee and Jack Gebler and Jack Richardson, they put us together. None of us has written a play at all resembling the others. It's just that we're supposed to be avant-garde, whatever that means.

Interviewer: How do you feel about Broadway?

Kopit: Who's adverse to getting three thousand dollars a week?

Interviewer: Do you feel that the future of the theatre is not on Broadway?

Kopit: It isn't on Broadway or off. It is in the theatre, and it happens where it does. There is as much bad produced off Broadway as on. When you write a play you just try to get it produced, it doesn't matter where.

Interviewer: How long have you been writing plays?

Kopit: I started in college, more or less by chance. The Ford Foundation gave grants to all the houses at Harvard, and our house used the grant for a drama workshop, and we studied plays in a nonacademic way—studied Broadway plays and saw why they could never be studied academically. The person in charge asked us if we wanted to write short plays over the Easter holiday, so I wrote this play and there was a contest and I submitted it and I won. And then I took a course in playwriting, and another, and there I was writing plays.

Interviewer: I notice a sort of rhythmic pattern in your play in the use of symbols. How conscious is all this?

Kopit: If I'm being honest and writing well, I am *not* conscious of symbols. The flytraps and the fish aren't symbols; they were just there. Things are what they are basically. And if you are writing well they are also something more—

a symbol of something. But I have no more authority than anyone else to say what they represent.

Interviewer: Your own attitude to the world doesn't seem disenchanted or flea-bitten. Do you identify with your characters at all?

Kopit: Of course, or I couldn't have written them. But I relate to them only as any author relates to his characters if he's being honest. Flaubert said, "I am Madame Bovary," and it's true. If you gave me a dramatic situation, say Adolf Eichmann, well, I'm not Eichmann. Even in my most sadistic moments I wouldn't dream of doing what he did. But I could project myself into him. You just sort of self-narcotize in a way, you try to hallucinate. You become something you are not. But you make use of what you are to become that. I suppose it's you, but there are many yous in each person. The better I'm writing, the more fully each character is some aspect of me. But it doesn't mean that I am any one of them. I can become them, but they are not me. I could take the opposite view in my next play. That's the trouble with judging a writer by one thing.

Interviewer: You called this play a pseudoclassical tragifarce. That seems to encompass every dramatic form.

Kopit: Well, it's a joke, but in a way comedy is a very powerful tool. This is the influence of Shaw, I'd say. You take the most serious thing you can think of and treat it as comically as you can. The situation the world is in now is so serious that it's almost funny. Man finds himself getting smaller and smaller. You can take a tragic situation just so seriously. You have to establish a distance from it—which comedy can do—in order to consider it at all.

From the Critic

Critic **Stephen Foreman** *says Kopit's success is due in part to his successful blending of reality and fantasy. Through the real we are engulfed; through the fantastic we are taught a lasting lesson. The play's form becomes the necessary vehicle for its content. To be sure, the human condition has been viewed in a unique perspective.*

Oh Dad, Poor Dad: *Atmosphere and Fantasy*

Commanding the bellboys like dancing dogs, Madame Rosepettle bans sunlight from her bedroom. By matriarchal decree, the room is off-limits to anything alive, except Madame Rosepettle. The ground rules, well established in Scene 1, are violated by a sirenic babysitter in Scene 3. Rosalie, in the process of baiting Jonathan into his mother's bed, rips the drapes from the windows.

Mad light streaks the darkness, and the stage directions claim, ". . . it's all like some strange, macabre fun house in an insane amusement park." The entire play takes place within this psychotic carnival—a gingerbread arcade with no concessions. They can be quite intimidating, these fantasy worlds, these gaudy assaults of light, sound and unended motion. No place to hide; no place to be found—imagine a child lost here! Imagine Jonathan!

Artaud may not be the barker in our amusement park, but Theatre of Cruelty/ Absurd (the natural result of giving form and purpose to our daily bedlam) is somewhere on the circuit. The real and the fantastic intermingle into believability, i.e., not a suspension of belief, but an involuntary awareness of other levels of reality working together simultaneously. One enjoys wandering through the chamber of horrors because one knows there is an end, another reality; otherwise no ticket would have been bought. On the other hand, Jonathan's total reality is that he wakes and sleeps within a nightmare. He may not be autistic, but he certainly has the symptoms to qualify as seriously disturbed in any casebook. This twenty-five year old child is the central character of a unique play which blends the tempo and nonsense of farce with tragic pain and gothic horror, the surreal and supernatural. However, it is not a spoof of these forms, for the response evoked by much of its action is anxiety rather than laughter. Any production must deal with the fact that *Oh Dad* is not the caper implied in its title, yet it would be foolish to ignore elements which can only be classified as comedic—the Mack Sennet bellboys, Madame Rosepettle's flamboyant scorn and the extravagant conception of each character are examples. Its grotesqueness may jar the audience's sense of propriety, but relief is offered because the situation is so absurd. In Scene 1, the up-tempo of exits and entrances seems standard farce as does the quick dialogue. Start off with a few laughs? We've seen weird ladies before? Enter coffin? So, she's weirder than most! The sad and stuttering Jonathan, however, cannot be dismissed so easily. A farce should be great fun, yet it is harmful to be on that stage. *Oh Dad* may be lunatic, but never zany; it ridicules more than it amuses.

Kopit does not take petulant potshots at some vague concept of "momism," but zeros in on an evil and pathetic situation. Jonathan, as the focal point, is never off stage. All the action affects him—either he is directly involved or watching. We begin to see the other characters through him, so there is a better understanding of who and why he is, psychologically and theatrically. The playwright has conceived a pitiful human story within a phantasmagoric structure.

Jonathan's world is a relentlessly chaotic room—a bizarre collage of movement, sound and light. Like an uneven tower of blocks, it stays on the verge of toppling. Externally, there is no peace or safety for Jonathan. It's open season, and there is a bounty on his head. He is stalked by carnivores—maternal, sexual, floral and finned—and has absolutely no privacy. (Even the dresser drawers are transparent.) If Madame Rosepettle is not guarding him, her zoo is. Each possession has a life of its own, even the corpse, and the room takes its life from them all. No one is safe outside the room, either: Jonathan spies on Rosalie, Rosalie molests children, Madame Rosepettle interrupts lovers on the beach and the commodore's crew peeps through portholes. Each living thing needs another on which to feed. This world is a jungle where a theatrical search and destroy is being waged. Jonathan is lucky to have avoided catatonia.

Ironically, insanity runs the risk of becoming the normal state of affairs—mere eccentricity, simple pandemonium. If an audience becomes complacent about the lunacy, the world on stage ceases to be lunatic. People are comforted by their ability to rationalize or soften an intense situation. In the contemporary United States, for example, there exist drive-in funeral parlors, acceptable kill quotas, poisoned lakes and silicone injections. What could be more insane? But, what the public accepts could never be insane. Insanity is redefined to render our own unrecognizable. Otherwise, we are forced to admit our own sickness and face a world which is suddenly uncertain. Here the audience is not allowed the luxury of relaxation, for predators may strike at anytime. Like the farce, we must wonder who enters now and what happens next? Things move quickly, so we anticipate change. We feel the absurdity until we see its effect on Jonathan. Someone is being threatened, and the eccentricity has shifted to danger. In other words, our recognition keeps increasing beyond the "acceptable" level of insanity, just as the Pentagon recognizes the threat to species survival if an attack goes beyond its acceptable level of destruction. It is hoped the audience will begin to recognize insanity outside the theatre as they have been forced to do on stage.

Because Jonathan is the focal point, if the audience believes in him, they will believe in the play. All its elements, which include Jonathan, function as an integral system—the components of a systemania. The boy is gradually revealed to be so severely disturbed, an audience can accept nearly anything from him. It is difficult to tell where reasons for his disturbance stop and results of it begin. The audience is watching Jonathan respond to his environment, however the environment must soon be perceived by them as it is by Jonathan. The surreal theatrics help them to see with his eyes; for, within this vision, nothing is illogical. Either the audience reacts viscerally, or the play is a silly failure.

It is difficult to avoid considering this play a confessional. However, rather than self-indulgence, the intermingling of real conflicts with fantasy material keeps the author at a distance (unlike Strindberg's *Dream Play*, for instance). It also holds an audience as pure fantasy will not, for it is the human condition—a recognition of ourselves in others—that sustains an audience's interest. Kopit provides identifiable conflicts between human beings. Action moves quickly through the play because the characters are involved in real situations which never obscure the pain of Jonathan's existence. Kopit's fantasy provides the distance necessary to recognize the "humor" of an absurd condition, while his characters enable us to recognize the truth of this condition. Satire, caricature—any exaggeration of significant characteristics— these enable an artist to capture the essential nature of a man, a society or an environment. It is a technique which allows a man to condemn his enemies with relative safety. Laughter and anguish are inextricable allies. One alleviates our existence, the other reminds us of it. *Oh Dad*, however, becomes progressively more painful in very human terms as "comic" action decreases; although, as in *Portnoy's Complaint*, the final line returns us to the atmosphere of a sick joke. That incredible atmosphere and profusion of forms has been consistently orchestrated to maintain the play's balance.

A fantasy like this is uniquely devastating because, to a great extent, it makes its own rules. Everything is contrived to mold the theatrical experience around the spectator, push it pore by pore under his skin, through his bloodstream, into his vital organs. Fantasy assaults more intensively than naturalism because it doesn't have to pretend. Realism is "selected" and, therefore, a facsimile—fantasy attempting to be "real." But, fantasy is itself—a more truthful representation of the images in a man's mind (a basic thread of absurdism). Of course, self-indulgence runs a risk of having interest only for the self. Fantasy will "work," however, when it develops out of a basic realism, i.e., a situation grasped by the director, played by the actor, identified and followed by the audience.

When we view *Oh Dad*, the fantastic and the real have played together. Jonathan's (and Gulliver's and Alice's and Yossarian's) situation is Jonathan's reality. His problems cannot be related to in any other way, either by Jonathan or the actor. Kopit has created a proper fantasia, intimidating and fascinating, but selected and refined. Jonathan's story, not the special effects, is followed through the play (nothing could be more distracting than looking for him in a directorial Disneyland). *Oh Dad* may be a mockery, but it is not frivolous. It has developed a vision in which fantasy is truthful and the human condition pitiful.

From the Director

As an example of the theatre of the absurd, Oh Dad . . . *is indisputably tragi-comic. Yet the potential exists for the play to be viewed as an example of "black comedy" or, perhaps, as a farce done in bad taste. But Kopit's work is a representation of part of the human condition and, as* **Norman DeMarco** *of the University of Arkansas says, that thought must become the key to the director's door.*

Thoughts on Directing Oh Dad, Poor Dad

The eminent French actor-director, Louis Jouvet, described theatre as a dialogue; Artaud expressed his idea of the stage as "a place where language must speak to our senses rather than primarily to the mind"; Ionesco believes that the comic and the tragic are not discrete and separate elements, but rather, "aspects of the same situation"; the inscrutable Spaniard, Arrabal, speaks of his "theatre of panic" as "a composite of stone, music, and the erect shaft to enrich the text"—and a leading clue toward the directorial approach to *Oh Dad, Poor Dad* is Arthur Kopit's own description of his play: "A pseudo-classical tragifarce in a bastard French tradition."

Within the framework of all these ideas lies the challenge of *Oh Dad, Poor Dad* to any director who hopes to project this play to an audience—an audience which must be guided to suspend its traditional theatre concept toward an acceptance of what the Theatre of the Absurd can contribute as an exaltation of a theatrical experience that derives from an impression of man and the perplexities that confound him. For here, indeed, is an assault on the senses provided by numerous aural and visual stimuli inherent in the mood of the play intended to provoke audience response, both covert and overt—the macabre humor of a falling body during a crucial moment of an attempted seduction; mechanical effects such as the cat-eating piranha slithering with murderous intent inside a fish bowl; carnivorous Venus Fly-Traps snatching wildly at any passerby; a screaming cuckoo-clock that suggests a Tinguely self-destroying piece of sculpture.

The quasi-"absurd" style of the play demands an imaginative director who can coordinate, almost to the point of choreography, pantomime and vocal expertise of his actors, and create an astute alignment of interrelationship between the comic and the serious to evoke an atmosphere of satanic humor. "Magnification," "dislocation," "disarticulation"—these words enunciated by Ionesco as essential to his theatre, if applied judiciously for the production of *Oh Dad, Poor Dad*, can do much to supply the aural and visual excitement that must be engendered by this play.

Rather than attempting to communicate symbols and meanings for each movement and speech, it would seem more pertinent for the director to evolve the sense of humanity inherent in the play and thus permit the audience to relate not only to the characters and the words they speak but also to the total structure with laughter, affection, and anguish. Any inner meanings must be those which each individual member of the audience discovers for himself. When Federico Fellini was asked about the meaning of his film, "8½," he answered to the effect that a person must find his own. It was his hope, apparently, that the total concept of the film would ultimately resolve into a pattern of specific personal meaning for each individual viewing the film. This would seem to be a reasonable expectation to be realized from a production of *Oh Dad, Poor Dad*.

In addition to the mechanical externalities offered by the playwright, the style and mood of the play make it incumbent upon the director to integrate harmoniously all elements toward a unified and total dramatic impact of near surrealistic proportions. It must be a madhouse of voracious humans, mischievous, devouring fish, and grasping, slashing plant life. There should be an attempt to suggest a kind of antiphonal, albeit sinister interplay between the speech and actions of the actors, the savage, punctuating antics of fish and plants, weird, flickering lights, and the intermittent, ominous off stage sounds as projected by a hammer, a cuckoo clock, and music. Every detail of rhythm, tempo, timing, movement and speech must be developed with knife-like precision.

The initial scene of the play immediately establishes hints of mood, atmosphere, and style that must dominate the performance. Here is a prime example of Harold Clurman's dictum that the first moments of a play should generate an aura of "trouble in the town" as an attention device. Playwright Kopit provides the ingredients most admirably—an extravagantly furnished hotel suite on an exotic island in the Caribbean; a company of bellboys, some scurrying swiftly about depositing luggage; others giving a quick, last-minute cleaning before the new occupants arrive; a final group of two entering furtively, carrying a coffin. As these two gaze around the room for a likely spot to relieve themselves of their burden, the authoritative voice of Madame Rosepettle comes cascading through with the command, "Put it in the bedroom!". The sudden violence of the command propels the bellboys into momentary consternation, and the coffin falls with an ominous thud just as Madame Rosepettle enters followed by Jonathan who moves with some uncertainty and trepidation. All the bellboys stop in frozen-faced terror as Madame castigates them with biting haughtiness. With this sequence, then, the play starts off on a journey calculated to entwine misery with laughter, innocence juxtaposed with the sensuous, madness and terror overlayed with gay affectation. This scene, as with many others, offers the director a splended opportunity to apply Commedia del'Arte techniques as another facet of Theatre of the Absurd.

Though the play is parodistic and farcical, the characters should strive, not for the obvious as a means of motivating audience response, but rather they can best augment the comic-tragic currents of the play by assuming an honest, straight-faced seriousness. Of course, the characters do smile, and even laugh occasionally, but any smile is a special one. For example, consider that most pungent "love" scene between Madame Rosepettle and the Commodore. The scene is introduced by off-stage sound effects of people, laughter, and carnival music as a background for the gross irony to follow. Madame and the Commodore enter dancing. From this moment on to the completion of the scene, the playwright makes note of the varieties of smiles and laughter, designed to emphasize the perniciousness of Madame Rosepettle, and the gradual disintegration of the Commodore, as she begins to unfold her macabre tale. Smiles and laughter are parenthetisized as follows: "soft and demure," "girlish giggles," "a wild smile of ecstacy," "smiling sweetly," "serene smile," "a laugh of resignation," "laughing sadly," "an uproarious laugh." A dramatic dichotomy of character delineation permeates the scene. While Madame Rosepettle must reveal a viciously false grandeur that grows with each terrifying detail, the Commodore first exudes an external quality of urbanity and pleasant sophistication which slowly dissolves into weakness, fear, and panic as the awful truth of her machinations is ineluctably unraveled.

Rosalie's dual personality, deftly handled, can enhance the bizarre atmosphere surrounding the environment. Her moments of sweet innocence constitute a bitter counterpoint to the devastating reverberations of Madame Rosepettle. Rosalie's bold tiger-thrusts of sexuality during the seduction scene result in pulsating counterblows to the fumbling, erratic, stuttering Jonathan whose whole being has been subjugated to his dominating, sex-hating mother. Here the audience should experience an aesthetic fusion of pity, horror, and sympathy topped by a comic sting induced by the dead body falling across the bed.

Like the "absurd" plays of Beckett, Ionesco, and Pinter with their interplay of verbal, non-verbal, and ritualistic elements mixed with kaleidoscopic emanations of sounds, *Oh Dad, Poor Dad* provides the director with many basic ingredients as a challenge to his inventiveness. A careful orchestration of sight and sound, pantomime and dialogue, action and reaction can graphically reinforce, clarify, and illuminate every dramatic progression of the play. A thoughtful analysis of the script will clearly indicate that no spurious external devices or ornamentations are needed to support the playwright's intentions. As a case in point, consider the opening sequence of scene three. Jonathan is sitting expressionless and motionless. After a momentary silence, a host of sounds start to seep through, slowly at first, and then with increasing, frenetic intensity . . . the ticking of a clock, laughter, drums, fireworks, music. Suddenly, at the height of this nerve shattering cacophony, Jonathan, hands covering his ears, dashes to the windows and violently closes them to drown out the noise. Silence. Soon the windows start slowly toppling, and then they fall shatteringly while resounding laughter fills the air accompanied by expanding growls from the flytraps which also make ferocious thrusts toward a dazed Jonathan who seems unaware of their maniacal intent. As he moves to the balcony, the madness diminishes. The bright music of a waltz begins to increase in volume as a transition for the ironically romantic scene between Madame Rosepettle and the Commodore.

Finally, the director should not overlook the significance apparent between Madame Rosepettle's reprimand of the bellboys in the first scene when she says: "Oh, this talk is getting us nowhere," with her final forceful query at the end of the play when she demands to know "What is the meaning of this?" Here is a key example of what Martin Esslin refers to as the "circular structure," a prime characteristic of the Theatre of the Absurd. Assuredly, then, it seems mandatory for the director to suggest, through every technique at his command, a never-ending merry-go-round world of the tragic-comic—a continuum filled with the complex idiosyncracies that assail all humans.

Source Materials for the Theatre of the Absurd

FROM THE CRITICS

Edward Albee

Harris, Wendel V. "Morality, Absurdity and Albee." *Southwest Review* 49 (1964):249–256.

Lewis, Allan. "The Fun and Games of Edward Albee." *American Plays and Playwrights of the Contemporary Theatre*. New York: Crown, 1965, pp. 81–98.

Wellwarth, George. "The New American Drama." *Theatre of Protest and Paradox*. New York: New York University Press, 1964, pp. 275–284.

Samuel Beckett

Jacobsen, J., and Mueller, W. *The Testament of Samuel Beckett*. New York: Hill and Wang, 1964.

Metman, Eva. "Reflections of Samuel Beckett's Plays." London: *The Journal of Analytical Psychology*, January, 1960.

Jean Genet

Abel, Lionel. "Meta Theatre." *Partisan Review*, Spring, 1960.

Brustein, R. "Antonin Artaud and Jean Genet: The Theatre of Cruelty." *Theatre of Revolt*. Boston: Little, Brown, 1964, pp. 363–411.

Cismarv, A. "The Antitheism of Jean Genet." *Antioch Review* 24 (1964):387.401.

Grossvogel, D. I. "Jean Genet: The Difficulty of Defining." *Four Playwrights and a Postscript*. New York: Cornell University Press, 1962, 135–174.

Markus, T. B. "Jean Genet: The Theatre of the Perverse." *Educational Theatre Journal* 14 (1962):209–214.

Eugene Ionesco

Bentley, Eric. "Ionesco, Playwright of the Fifties." *Columbia Daily Spectator*, March 11, 1958.

Doubrovsky, Serge. "Ionesco and the Comedy of the Absurd." *Yale French Studies*, No. 23, Summer 1959.

Round, Richard. "The Opposite of Sameness." London: *Encoure*, June–July 1957.

Arthur Kopit

Kostelanetz, Richard, ed. "Oh Dad, Poor Dad . . ." *The New American Arts*. New York: Horizon Press, 1965, pp. 71–72.

Wellwarth, George. "Hope Deferred: Reflections on Edward Albee, Jack Richardson, Jack Gelber and Arthur Kopit." *Literary Review* 7 (1963):7–26.

Harold Pinter

Bernhard, F. J. "Beyond Realism: The Plays of Harold Pinter." *Modern Drama* 8 (1965):181–191.

Cohn, Ruby. "The World of Harold Pinter." *Tulane Drama Review* 6 (1962): 55–68.

Esslin, Martin. *Theatre of the Absurd*. New York: Doubleday, 1969, pp. 198–217.

BY THE PLAYWRIGHTS

Genet, Jean. "A Note on the Theatre." *Tulane Drama Review* 7 (1963):37–41.

Albee, Edward. "Which Theatre Is the Absurd One?" *New York Times Magazine*, February 25, 1962.

Ionesco, Eugene. "The Avant-Garde Theatre." *Tulane Drama Review* 5 (1960): 44–53.

————"Notes on My Theatre." *Tulane Drama Review* 7 (1963):127–159.

————*Notes and Counter Notes*. Translated by Donald Watson. New York: Grove Press, 1964.

AUDIO-VISUAL SOURCES

Waiting for Godot, Columbia, 011-238 (recording).

The Chairs, Caedmon, 323-m (recording).

Eh Joe (Beckett) Grove Press Films.

Film (Beckett) Grove Press Films.

The Goad (Beckett) Grove Press Films.

The Lesson (Ionesco) Grove Press Films.

Appendix:
Melodrama

Melodrama is the most dishonest form of serious drama. Endings are contrived and plots are manipulated. Its characters are shallow and its situations unreal. The hero in melodrama often wears a white hat, and the heroine is a pillar of virtue. Evil lurks in the shadows always ready to prey on the innocent, but justice in the end prevails. The hero may get beaten, battered, or bounced, but he usually quickly rebounds to defeat his dastardly opponent. Though character, story, and device in melodrama usually are unreal, we, as an audience, adore it.

What *makes* melodrama, then, and what makes melodrama so popular, are the two topics that will be considered below. In spite of the rather negative description given above, melodrama still can be a worthy form of drama; first because the techniques and refinements recently made have increased its credibility and appeal. Secondly, to the surprise of many, the reader has watched, been exposed to, and enjoyed more melodrama in his lifetime than all other forms of the drama combined. How?—through the media of television and motion pictures.

Theodore Hatlen, in *Orientation to the Theatre*, compares tragedy and melodrama in these ways:

> Tragedy examines values; melodrama exploits action. Tragedy confronts good and evil with unblinking honesty; melodrama escapes from life. Tragedy considers the eternal spiritual problems; melodrama deals with the transitory, the material, the physical. Tragedy evokes pity and fear; melodrama arouses suspense, pathos, terror and sometimes hate.[1]

In order to answer our two original questions and also to trace the development and rationale of melodrama, let us examine these characteristics as they have been stated.

Melodrama Exploits Action

Melodrama perhaps can be said to combine an element of tragedy in the seriousness of its subject, and an element of comedy in the happiness of its conclusion. All tragedies, after all, are concerned with serious subject matter, and most comedies end happily. But in combining these two elements, melodrama goes a step further by including a third—the plot devices and physical action of farce. This reliance on action (together with the other elements to be discussed), marks one of the chief distinguishing characteristics and reasons for the success of melodrama. Most melodramas, from beginning to end, are episodic developments designed to bring about

---

[1]Theodore W. Hatlen, *Orientation to the Theatre* (New York: Appleton-Century-Crofts, 1962), p. 86.

a preconceived ending with its accompanying reactions, almost always predictable. The chases, the fights, the struggles, and the rescues are manipulations of the plot determined to extract the optimal amount of emotion from the audience. Each successive occurrence seems to outdo the former, and since movement holds attention, any potential thought is usually sacrificed for the scene of action.

The authors of the past, who often turned out these plays by the hundreds, were not ignorant men oblivious to the characteristics of good drama. They were, rather, skilled practitioners geared to turning out a product the public wanted. They knew their audiences (as the television writers of today do), and they knew how to manipulate plots and characters to produce the maximum amount of excitement. In order to achieve this effect, each melodrama was designed to elicit strong emotional identification by having in it at least one of the following devices: murders, fistfights, explosions, escapes, reprieves, duels, or executions (some of the more adventurous had most all of these).

All these events are highly physical, and thus attempt to increase our sensual participation. What better way is there to increase our terror than to point a gun at the hero's head while he sits helplessly tied to a chair? What more effective way is there to heighten suspense than to tie the heroine to the railway tracks while the thunder of the train can be heard in the distance? Since melodrama aims at maximum participation, this action, then, serves as a vehicle for achieving that purpose so that we may vicariously feel fear along with that hero. In one evening of prime time television, for instance, one researcher has recorded 23 murders, 44 fistfights, 3 rapings, 6 stolen cars, 27 chases, and one wounded dog. Physical action as a basis for interest appears rampant. It then becomes a basic tenet of melodrama.

As an example of this reliance on action, we can examine the play, *Uncle Tom's Cabin* by George Aiken (which has been, incidentally, America's most often performed play). Included in the play are: (one) chase across the ice; (three) escapes; (many) deaths; (numerous) beatings; and (one) child ascending into heaven. As if this were not enough to capture the audience, *Uncle Tom's Cabin* has thirty scenes of visual splendor to the present unequalled on the stage. Besides full orchestration, the play includes scenes at the slave market, a snowy mountain, the Ohio river filled with ice, a rocky pass in the hills, two plantations, a garden, four rooms, and a heavenly scene of celestial sunlight. This emphasis on the visual, then, really becomes complementary to the action and further serves to immerse the audience in the story.

In examining why television and the motion picture industry have taken over the assembly-line production of melodrama, we have to realize that this reliance on the visual (both action and spectacle) has long been a basic appeal of melodrama. And who other than the movies is better equipped to offer more of the above? When the insatiable appetite of the paying public could no longer be satisfied by the stage's visual splendors, the movies were a natural choice to replace this function of the stage. The raging rivers, awesome train wrecks, and towering explosions not only could be simulated, they could now be fully realized. The spectacle no longer had to look real, it could now *be* real. In effect, this predominant reliance on action and spectacle caused the demise of old-fashioned staged melodrama. It was forced to change; hence today's "psychological thrillers."

So far we have considered only action and spectacle to satisfy our first point, that melodrama exploits action. But a word or two is necessary about the more refined melodrama that adorns our stage, television, and movie screen today. Together with the increasing sophistication of our tastes, and the increasing complexity of our culture, the ever-appealing melodrama has been forced to keep pace. Dealing more with the psychological, and concentrating less on the visual, our stage no longer displays a tendency to bombard our sense of sight (though some could argue this is not true of musical comedy). No longer are stage gadgetry and visual gimmickry essential to play production (though they may be to the movies). Yet even though this visual splendor has been reduced, the basic criterion of action remains. This century's "whodunits" are little more than "well-made plays," each designed to produce thrills and suspense while founded on some rather ingenious (and sometimes ridiculous) plot devices. The point is that the actions and situations rigged to produce maximum identification are still the heart of melodrama.

It is interesting to note that when the stage produces an effective melodrama (*Dial M for Murder, The Children's Hour, Five Finger Exercise, The Little Foxes*) the movies are quick to secure the rights and exploit its action and spectacle even more. Their producers have long recognized that the addition of not just realistic scenery, but *real* scenery together with the inclusion of mood music is more effective in producing the spine-tingling, edge-of-the-seat reaction melodrama calls for. So while the plots of modern melodrama have become more subtle and credible, the reliance on action and its accompanying responses still remains.

Melodrama Escapes from Life

Since real life is filled with many problems, what better way to escape is there than to journey into the romantic world of scenery and spectacle where virtue is rewarded and evil punished? The period in which melodrama was born was not considered the age of enlightenment for Europe or America. The industrial revolution, laissez-faire and manifest destiny all had left their impact, and Americans were busy fighting Indians, each other, and Darwin. The middle class was now comfortably ready to embrace the ideas of conservatism, and the turn of the century was creeping upon them. Life as it should be, with goodness rewarded and wickedness punished, was the answer to the wish-fulfilment and escapist dreams of many. For most of the viewers of melodrama, everyday living was a series of inglorious struggles and much mediocrity. Here, now, was a chance to escape life's worries and imagine the world "as it ought to be." If crime did sometimes pay, the stage would not allow it. If success could not be had in life, it could be on the stage.

Four men deserve mention in connection with these melodramatic beginnings and achievements. August Ferdinand von Kotzebue, Guilbert de Pixérécourt, Dion Boucicault, and Eugene Scribe were men astute enough to gauge the feeling of their age, and among them they produced over 800 melodramas. On the continent, de Pixérécourt and von Kotzebue capitalized on the romantic leanings of the European public to grind out over 300 plays designed to thrill, chill, and captivate the escape-seeking masses. And in America, their counterpart, Boucicault, was not far behind.

But, by far, the most well-known playwright to entertain the masses was Eugene Scribe, inventor of the "well-made play," a formula of dramatic development designed to make playwriting a prosperous business. It was an assembly-line technique of organization comparable to our automotive industry, where, while the color of the exterior and choice of options may change, the body style and engine specifications of a particular model remain the same. Each play was characterized by orderly exposition, "stock" characters, mounting suspense, and a believable ending, all formulated more for heightening emotion than for increasing concern for mankind. Once the mind of the audience was off the structure and on the story, thought was at a minimum and participation at its maximum.

The stock-type characters melodrama uses helps aid in this escape. These characters are easily identifiable, and easy to identify with. They are clear-cut, shallow, and usually one-dimensional. They also may be vicious, profane, or brutal. The virtuous heroine, noble hero, heartless villain, and comforting best friend are all vehicles for advancing the story value. There is usually an easy-to-find dividing line between those we feel sympathy for and those we do not. Stock characters may be used also for variety or for comic relief. These may include the well-meaning neighbor, the stumbling partner, or the heroine's confidant. While the story usually concerns deceit or trickery by the forces of vice, the characters it involves are normally clean-cut and easily discernible. As contrasted with characters in tragedy, they never change; they remain constant and crystal clear. Only their names are changed to protect the author.

The melodrama that appears on today's stage and screen, while taking a more sophisticated form, nevertheless allows escapism to remain as a basic function. Our present television series, soap operas, and many stage plays still rely heavily on the visual, but have subordinated this even further to story value. The heart-rending, tear-jerking plot situations are employed to achieve maximum identification. Illicit romances, adultery, adolescent problems, family squabbles, and more than a few murder mysteries still are designed to allow the housewife an afternoon of sentimental fantasy. The psychological thriller and complex whodunits are meant to allow the tired businessman an evening of escape from his everyday family troubles and business concerns. Melodrama has been said to exist for two primary reasons: entertainment and escape. And while each may be the complement of the other, they are still realized by the excitement of our senses.

Melodrama Deals with the Transitory, the Material, the Physical

The plots, subject matter, and even occasional messages of melodrama are generally inconsequential. Usually, they are of no real significance for anyone but the characters in the play. There is, most often, no underlying theme or message. Unlike tragedy, melodrama serves as an end in itself, desiring not to elicit concern for mankind, but instead for the plight of the hero; no universality exists. Some critics believe that melodrama exists on a game level, with the audience guessing what new predicaments the hero is going to be involved in, or who the real villain is, while all the time knowing the story will end happily. (Television, in the 1960's, had a code which forbade the success of evil forces.) There is usually a clear-cut division of these forces (as well as the characters), and the audience is never in doubt as to who will be victorious. Instead, what commands our attention is the means to that end, or the new story line or plot.

Although the above approach may seem divorced from reality, it nevertheless must prevail if we are to escape into this world of almost make-believe. While the plots are manipulated, the characters standard, and the ending contrived, the *story* must seem plausible. In order to do this, melodrama must be founded on incidents associated with real life and theoretical occurrences. To say that the stage, screen, or television has "jazzed up" or altered a real-life situation is to say the story must be made a melodrama if it is to achieve its success—and it often is. Illicit romances, conquering heroes, financial problems, success stories—these transitory problems besetting contemporary man—become the crux of *our* drama then transformed to the context of the stage. In melodrama, "the scale of thought and feeling is in proportion to daily life, never transcending the scale of the play." Perhaps this is why, Goldstone adds, "the play can therefore rarely survive the times which produced it."[2]

---

[2]Richard Goldstone, *Contexts of the Drama* (New York: McGraw-Hill, 1968), p. 11.

In dealing with murders, thefts, romances and vice, this materialistic story value becomes most important. The plot is manipulated or rigged and the outcome is rarely in doubt. Already guessing the ending, we become more interested in the physical events. We become totally immersed in the skillful and plausible story line, suspensefully unfolding, which so many times is founded on raw courage, phenomenal luck, and the amazing ability to be in the right place at the right time. We are excited during the action; but once it is completed, we are relieved and walk away as unthinking as when we entered. The effects, and not the causes, concern us in melodrama. The transitory and physical material allows no catharsis and permits us to exercise primarily our senses, rarely our intellect.

Melodrama Arouses Suspense, Pathos, Terror, and Sometimes Hate

Fear and pity may be aroused by melodrama, but not the fear and pity of tragedy. They are the mutated forms of fear and pity—suspense, terror, and hate. Designed almost solely to elicit an emotional reaction, they are melodrama's baser effects. Going a step further, most melodramas will attempt to arouse sentimentality, an additional element necessary if melodrama is to accomplish its purpose. In *A Primer for Playgoers*, Wright and Downs say that this sentimentality:

> . . . is said to exist when we are so anxious to experience an emotion vicariously that, as long as we get the thrill we do not pause to discriminate. We sympathize with a child because she is a child, or with a troubled pretty girl because she is pretty and in distress, without analyzing the causes. Sentimentality is said to exist . . . when we are permitted to experience an emotion without paying for it; for the sentimentalist lives on wish-fulfilment, on emotion rather than reason. He sees just what he wants to see. To him, life is a conflict between good and bad—with no in-between. He refuses to apply intelligence or fact to a situation or reason it through. Instead he relies solely on human feeling. . . .[3]

Thus, perhaps, fear is designed primarily to elicit the sentiment necessary for identification with the character. Unlike in tragedy, we are asked and are able to place ourselves in the *actual* situation and experience emotion because of *it*, rather than because of its characters. After all, in tragedy the hero has it within *himself* to find the answer. Melodrama relies completely on the external and its necessary emotions. As a result, any "melodramatic catharsis" of our weeping audience is short-lived.

---

[3]Lentheir H. Downs and Edward H. Wright, *A Primer for Playgoers* (Englewood Cliffs: Prentice-Hall, 1969), p. 143.

Modern Melodrama

Within the past fifty years there have been plays written that lack the stature of tragedy and yet exclude most aspects of melodrama—Arthur Miller's *Death of a Salesman*, Tennessee William's *The Glass Menagerie*, Eugene O'Neill's *Mourning Becomes Electra*—but a great many of the plays written today, including some written by those just mentioned, are just a more sophisticated form of melodrama—worthy, commendable and brilliant, but melodrama just the same. These plays perhaps have lost some of the negative aspects of the melodrama of 100 years ago, but they retain as much as they have lost.

In differing from melodrama of the nineteenth century, today's play's characterization may be more subtle, sometimes more ambiguous; themes are more daring (as are the times they reflect); action decreases while language becomes even stronger; and plots are less involved. Contrast *Cat On A Hot Tin Roof* with a nineteenth century melodrama to prove this point—while both are melodrama they will differ markedly, but that is to be expected. Our melodrama must be drawn from *our* consciousness, our temper, and the technique and treatment of this mood must keep pace with us, the people it reflects. This changing treatment requires increasing refinement and artistry of the playwright who produces modern melodrama. Plays such as *The Little Foxes*, *Desire under the Elms*, and *A Streetcar named Desire* are all melodrama and are all notable; their dramatic obituaries are bound to be longer in coming then were those of earlier, less-refined melodramas.

Melodramas do, then, play an important part in contemporary drama. They may serve as an answer to the world of things "as they should be," as a release and escape from our troubles, as a concentrated emotional experience, or as a simple form of entertainment designed to appeal to the greatest number of people. In any case, this principal form of entertainment remains one of our most popular.

BACK COVER:
Effective use of mask in *Oedipus*. Note how eyes stand out.
McCarter Theatre, Princeton University. Photo by Jim
MacDonald.